The Energetics of Western Herbs

Vol. 2

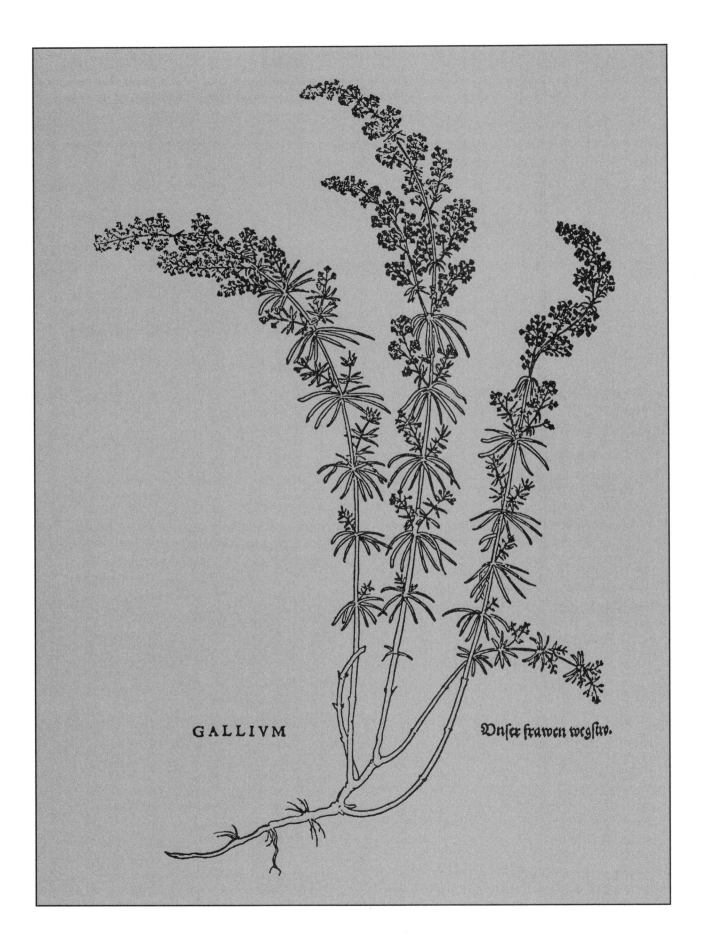

GALLIVM   Vnſer frawen wegſtro.

THE ENERGETICS OF WESTERN HERBS

A Materia Medica
Integrating Western and Chinese
Herbal Therapeutics

PETER HOLMES

Revised & Enlarged Fourth Edition

Vol. 2

Snow Lotus Press ❧ Boulder

Important Notice

The information contained in this book is for educational purposes only. It is not intended to diagnose, treat or prescribe, and does not purport to replace the services of a duly trained physician or practitioner. The information presented herein is correct and accurate to the author's knowledge up to the time of printing. As herbal medicine (like everything else) is in constant development, however, it is possible that new information may cause future modifications to become neccessary.

The only Chinese medical terms that have been retained in their original form is the word Qi, pronouced "chee" and meaning breath(s) or vital force(s), and the terms Yin and Yang.

Acknowledgement is made for permission to reprint the following:

From Henri Leclerc, *Précis de phytothérapie,* © 1983 Masson; reprinted by permission of Masson et Cie., Paris, France.

From Virgil Vogel, *American Indian Medicine,* © 1970 Virgil Vogel; reprinted by permission of the University of Oklahoma Press, Norman.

From Georg Harig, *Bestimmung der Intensität im Medizinischen System Galens,* © 1974 Georg Harig; reprinted by permission of the author, Berlin, Germany.

From Merlin Stone, *Ancient Mirrors of Womanhood,* © 1979 Merlin Stone; reprinted by permission of Beacon Press, Boston.

Herb illustrations by Hazel Thornley
Cover art by Ken Bernstein
Cover design by Peter Holmes
Woodcut herb illustrations from Leonhardt Fuchs' *Kreuterbuch,* 1542

ISBN 978-1-890029-43-2
Library of Congress Number 89-080816
10 9 8 7 6 5 4 3 2 1

Published by Snow Lotus Press, Inc.
P.O. Box 3812
Boulder, Colorado, 80307, U.S.A.
www.snowlotus.org
Manufactured in the United States of America

Contents

The Materia Medica (ctd.)

AMARACVS Diofcor: lib: 7 cap 38   Maioran.
plin: lib: 2. rep Xi. vocah ab gsdam
grecis, Sam piuzeis, item a Theophrasto

Herbs for Draining

Herbal remedies that drain are classed as follows:

Class 11   *Relaxants:* Regulate the Qi and relax constraint
Class 12   *Refrigerants:* Clear heat and reduce fever and infection

The Nature and Dynamics of Draining

Botanical remedies in these two classes are able to cause an active draining or discharging effect on an energetic level. They are called *drainers* or *draining remedies. Drainers* discharge and reduce an excess of energetic processes, which results from endogenous or exogenous stressors to internal homeostasis. In so doing, they oppose the natural reflexes of the organism's vital force *(physis* or *zhen qi)* in its striving for balance. For example, when natural, normally useful responses such as fever, inflammation and nervous tension become too intense or turn from acute to chronic, they become counter-productive to the healing process. At this point, *drainers* specifically slow down and eventually terminate such overspent reactions. In this way, *drainers* ultimately support the overall healing process initiated by the individual's vital responses.

Draining as a Principle of Treatment

The treatment principle of draining is well recognized in Chinese medicine and is called *xiao.* In the West, although it is not explicitly mentioned in the earliest Greek medical texts, draining has been well defined by practitioners since Renaissance times. Around that time Western physicians increasingly made the distinction between the Draining and Eliminating principles of treatment. It became clear to them, for example, that causing sweating was primarily an eliminant, not a draining method of treatment, because sweating does not invariably

clear heat or reduce tension. *Diaphoretics* may increase or decrease heat, depending on their type, and some can also be used for reducing tension (see Class 1). Likewise, promoting urination with *diuretics* was understood to be mainly a treatment strategy for eliminating water congestion rather than for clearing heat.

Today we can summarize the difference between the principles of eliminating and draining as follows. Eliminating primarily involves a physical elimination and secondarily an energetic discharge. Conversely, draining mainly involves an energetic discharge and secondarily physiological changes (such as relief from pain, tension, cramps, etc.). Equally fundamental is the fact that elimination essentially works in conjunction with the body's vital responses, the *zhen qi,* whereas draining works in opposition to them.

Clearly, draining herbs should not be confused with eliminating herbs. It is true that both types directly treat pathogens that cause excess conditions, rather than supporting the vital force itself. Draining and Eliminating herbs also primarily address acute, rather than chronic, symptoms. However, *drainers* generally remove an excess caused by a response to *external* conditions, whereas *eliminants* remove an excess caused by an *internal* obstruction of waste elimination. Moreover, internal excess conditions are by nature more qualitative and energetic (e.g., nervous tension and fever), whereas external excess conditions involve substantial obstruction by one of the fluid eliminations (e.g., fluids, feces, sputum and menstrual blood).

Draining remedies address conditions of **excess** entailing either **tension** or **heat.** The first condition is usually known in Chinese medicine as **constrained Qi.** Class 12 *refrigerants* that clear heat and reduce infection, for example, consist of *antipyretic, anti-inflammatory* and *anti-infective* remedies. These remedies gently limit excessive febrile and inflammatory responses to pathogens (toxins). In so doing, they allow the body's immune and detoxification functions to proceed at a more safe, even and controlled rate.

Because certain constitutional types naturally tend to present excess conditions, *draining* herbs, like *restoratives,* can also be used for preventive constitutional therapy. This is evident when we consider that Draining is one of three constitution-altering treatment strategies, like its complementary methods, Restoring and Altering and Regulating.

Because they treat conditions of energetic excess, the two draining treatment methods should not be used for conditions presenting deficiency of any kind. The exception is when deficiency presents with some aspects of excess. Here again, as with the eliminating treatment strategies, it is important to carefully weigh the relative strengths of the pathogenic factors and the person's own vitality to achieve best results.

Drainers also have little in common with *sedatives* or *tranquilizers,* which act on the nervous system selectively. *Drainers* are no more toxic or selective than *restoratives* and are routinely included in many formulas that address chronic and constitutional disorders. Because the effect of botanical remedies is largely determined by the individual ground, a bitter remedy such as Gentian root, for example, can be used either as a general *draining* remedy in heat conditions with fever, or as a *restorative* ground remedy to balance the Hematogenic/Tai Yang type of individual.

Herbs to Regulate the Qi and Relax Constraint

Regulating the Qi and relaxing constraint is a treatment strategy that addresses conditions characterized by tension and pain. These conditions are known in Chinese medicine as constrained Qi. When the Qi's normal configurating, organizing activity in the body diminishes from endogenous or exogenous stressors, it causes stagnation of physiological functions. The Qi is then said to be "constrained" or "compressed," which is a tense type of condition. Because a person's Qi is an expression of their psyche or soul, Qi constraint in essence describes an energetic tension or overload of the psyche. Until very recently this condition was covered by Western concepts such as neurosis and hysteria. Today it usually falls into the category of stress-related disorders, while anxiety and somatoform disorders, for instance, may also be diagnosed in this context.

Remedies in this class, called *relaxants,* are used to limit this normal Qi response to stress when it becomes too intense or prolonged and therefore counterproductive to the healing process.

The Nature and Dynamics of Qi Constraint

The main factor that leads to constrained Qi is mental and emotional stress, and specifically chronic unproductive stress. Positive stress is one thing and a normal part of life, but chronic stress with little or no possibility of release through direct expression is now known to cause a wide variety of mental, emotional and physical complaints. The main symptoms reported are general nervous tension, feeling stressed out, anxiety and emotional distress. These are a routine part of today's hectic and general overload city lifestyle.

The constraining effect on the Qi caused by chronic stress physiologically involves the autonomic nervous system, and tends to generate symptom patterns typified by **tension, pain, spasm** and **dryness.** The physiological mechanisms can vary depending on whether sympathetic or parasympa-

thetic nervous system functions are increased, which in turn are dependent on the weaknesses of the individual constitution. In general they are known to include a rise in blood pressure, gastric acid release and blood glucose, in lipid and cholesterol levels, as well as a sharp increase or decrease of digestive and urinary activity. Adrenal cortisol levels are usually high from adrenocortical hyperfunctioning (stress). Nervous behavior may develop, along with feelings of tension and irritability, inexplicable pains (neuralgias), including lower back pain, intestinal IBS, dysmenorrhea); cramps, sudden spasmodic movements, palpitations, hyperventilation, insomnia, irregular cycles, frequent and scanty urination and premature ejaculation.

The organ fundamentally involved with Qi constraint is the kidney-adrenal-nervous system. This organ system is the physical substratum for the feeling life in terms of response to the environment.[1] Any emotional overload on this sensitive system will produce symptoms such as tension, restlessness, agitated depression, nausea, indigestion with flatus and colic, internal vibrating or trembling sensations and a wiry pulse. This typifies the preclinical syndrome **kidney/adrenal Qi constraint,** often accompanied by thyroid or adrenal hyperfunctioning and sympathetic nervous system hyperfunctioning.[2]

However, constrained Qi can also affect certain organ systems in particular and cause a variety of symptoms. These are grouped into particular syndromes such as **lung Qi constraint, heart Qi constraint, intestines Qi constraint,** and so on. Each of these has its own distinct sign and symptom pattern (see below).

Constrained Qi may also lead to the condition known as **internal wind,** so called because it produces wind-like symptoms of tremors, twitches, spasms and convulsions (see Class 21). These symptoms incidentally confirm the kidney as an organ of the element Air. Many *relaxant* remedies that regulate the Qi address the basic syndrome kidney/adrenal Qi constraint.

The Diagnosis of Qi Constraint

Constrained Qi is recognized and diagnosed in Chinese medicine mainly by the pulse as much as by its other symptoms. Tension will generally produce a tight pulse (*jin mai*), while pain and spasms will produce a wiry pulse (*xuan mai*). Chronic suppressed anxiety may produce a hidden pulse (*fu mai*). In the West, Eclectic physicians such as JOHN SCUDDER assessed chronic tense conditions by the presence of a thin, elongated tongue.

As in all Draining types of treatment methods, it is important to differentiate between the benign expression of Qi constraint and its pathological manifestation. Strongly felt and expressed emotions such as joy, anger, fear and grief, if appropriate in every way to their context, are considered entirely normal and beneficial. They are non-pathological, adaptive responses to stressors. They usually resolve spontaneously back into the positive synergic feelings from which they arose.

However, when normal responsive emotions tend to either persist or become repressed, and fail to resolve into synergic feelings, this is a maladaptive, pathological reaction to stress. The responsive emotions then completely change in quality and become distressed feelings. It is the large variety of possible distressed feelings that are responsible for causing signs and symptoms in the physical body. They can be considered pathological expressions of constrained Qi. At this point it is necessary to treat the energetic imbalance and relieve symptoms of tension, spasm and pain. This is achieved physiologically by reducing nervous responses that work on automatic, thereby allowing physiological processes to once again run smoothly, without damage to the whole individual.

Treatment Considerations

• Disorders caused by **tension** or **Qi constraint** are treated at their root by reducing excessively intense Qi responses to stressors. Typical of a treatment method designed to drain excessive energy, it is always important to assess the relative strength of the individual's righteous energies (the Air body) and the intensity of the constrained Qi, as well as the degree of physiological and psychological injury involved. This is particularly true when Qi constraint is caused by a deficiency condition.

Once the Qi begins to freely circulate throughout the body/mind, constraint and tension are relieved on every level and systemic relaxation can occur. Physiologically speaking, local spasms and pain are relieved, while psychological clarity and sensitivity to internal and external information is increased. Both these factors assist in reducing the maladaptive distressed feeling response and, conversely, encourage the adaptive resolution of primary emotions.

• Constrained Qi is often treated with the other conditions from which it arises or that result from it. This includes chronic deficiency conditions such as Qi, Blood or Yin deficiency, and acute excess conditions such as internal heat and Liver Yang rising. As a result, *relaxants* should often be combined with *restoratives* of various types (Classes 7-10) and *refrigerants* (Class 12) as needed.

• Chronic Qi constraint causes deficiency specifically by depleting nerve tone and creating physical weakness, depression, anxiety and so on. As a result, *trophic (nutritive) nervous restoratives* such as Milky oat berry, Sage leaf, Skullcap herb, St. John's wort and Schisandra berry are often used together with *relaxants* in the treatment of chronic tense/Qi constraint conditions.

• *Relaxant* remedies are significant in the health care of children, along with a good diet and proper hygiene. By regulating and relaxing autonomic and neuromuscular functions, they ease volatile emotional tension that underlies seemingly unrelated conditions such as bedwetting, asthma, relentless crying (especially at night), recurring infections (especially respiratory infections), a strong tendency to create fever or inflammation (e.g., in sinusitis, otitis and tonsilitis), earache and catarrhal (mucousy) conditions in general.

• Herbal medicines in this class can go quite some way in reducing constrained Qi. However, for a more long-term treatment of this condition (which to some extent affects almost everyone in the West), it is clear that the soul (psyche) itself needs to breathe and, like the Qi itself, to freely respond.[3] Systemic lifestyle changes must be initiated and more "astral" remedies such as essential oils, high-potency homeopathic remedies and flower essences should be considered later during the course of treatment. Significant changes can also be achieved, e.g., by creating a regular schedule of daily activities, with physical movement or dance exercises, deep breathing exercises (including various forms of breath therapy), with aromatherapy, color therapy, music therapy and counseling.

These will all assist in the letting go of repressed or, conversely, exaggerated primary emotions, thereby producing an increased connection with normal, synergic feelings. This in turn will promote a better expression of normal responsive emotions. This whole process results in a smoother, more free-flowing exchange between the individual and his/her environment.

The Herbs that Regulate the Qi

Herbal remedies that regulate the Qi and relax constraint are generally known as *relaxants*. Promoting smooth Qi circulation results in autonomic nervous regulation, neuromuscular relaxation and relief of tension, stress and pain. Physiologically, *relaxants* exhibit *nervous sedative, spasmolytic* and *analgesic* actions on a more general or localized scale.

There are two main kinds of *relaxants*.

1. *Relaxants with a pungent taste and penetrating nature.* These herbs also promote sweating and are mostly *vasodilatory diaphoretics*. Rich in essential oils, they include the frequently used Camomile flower, Linden flower, Lavender flower, Marjoram herb, Melissa leaf, Spearmint leaf, Chrysanthemum flower, Tansy herb and Meadowsweet herb. Because they relax both smooth and striated muscles, *diaphoretic relaxants* work best on Qi constraint patterns involving both visceral and skeletal muscle spasms. See Class 1 as well as this class.

2. *Relaxants with sweet, moist qualities* and a high mucilage content, called *demulcents*. These work mainly locally to reduce tension, irritation and pain. They affect not only the gastrointestinal tract but also other tissues and organs by reflex action. Plantain leaf, Comfrey leaf, Marshmallow root, Licorice root, Chickweed herb and Iceland moss are much used *demulcent relaxants* (see Class 10).

Demulcent relaxants also tend to clear heat and inflammation, moisten dryness, slow down hyperactivity and restore deficiency. They are ideal for nourishing the Yin in Yin and fluids deficiency conditions involving Qi constraint and dryness.

Like other main categories of herbal remedies, *relaxants* have a variety of physiological functions and tropisms, and are used in many different disorders and conditions. Dividing them into the following seven subcategories is clinically very useful as they correspond to the main patterns that constrain-

ed Qi tends to follow. Combination syndromes are of course very commonly seen, especially those involving one of the first two general Qi constraint syndromes (the first deficient, the second excess).

Relax Constraint, Relieve Pain, Restore the Nerves and Lift the Mind
General relaxants, nervous/cerebral restoratives

These *relaxants* treat general **Qi constraint** arising from deficiency, typically from **neurasthenia.** Symptoms include fatigue, nervous tension, nervous depression, vague feelings of anxiety, poor sleep, aches and pains that come and go, as well as an overall feeling of being stressed-out—even when no actual stressors are present.

Cerebral/nervous restorative relaxants are usually sweet, bitter, cool by nature. The most commonly used include St. John's wort herb, Skullcap herb, Melissa leaf, Ladies' slipper root and Vervain herb. In the case of pronounced cerebral or neuroendocrine deficiency, they should be combined with more tonifying *cerebral restoratives* such as American ginseng root, Sage leaf, Milky oat berry, Flowery knotweed root and Rhodiola root—all in Class 8.

Relax Constraint, Relieve Pain and Calm the Mind
General relaxants, nervous/cerebral sedatives

These *relaxants* treat **Qi constraint** arising from excess/hyperfunctioning. Symptoms include irritability, insomnia, nervous tension and anxiety. They encourage mental and emotional relaxation when the mind is tense and grasping and when feelings are tense and distressed.

Important *nervous sedative relaxants* are often sweet, bitter, pungent, cool, and include Camomile flower, Lavender flower, Melissa leaf, Cramp bark (relatively mild), Marjoram herb, Hops flower, Passionflower herb, Wild lettuce leaf, Valerian root and Kava root (all moderate).

Descend Lung Qi, Open the Chest and Relieve Wheezing
Bronchial relaxants (bronchodilators, antiasthmatics)

When constrained Qi affects the lower respiratory tract, the result is **lung Qi constraint.** This syndrome displays recurrent attacks of apnea, wheezing, a tight chest, a dry rasping cough, sometimes repetitive thoughts, expectoration of hard sputum, a dry tongue (especially at the front) and a tight, wiry pulse. This is typically seen in atopic asthma.

Similar to this syndrome is the Chinese symptom picture "Kidney fails to grasp the Qi," or **Lung and Kidney Yang deficiency,** in which the tongue is pale and the pulse tight, slow and deep, or thin and weak. This is asthma that involves kidney/adrenocortical deficiency at its root, e.g., intrinsic asthma.

Bronchodilators are the specific type of *relaxant* used for diffusing and descending constrained lung Qi. They are pungent, warm on the whole and often contain active essential oils, alkaloids, saponins and glycosides. Wild cherry bark, Cramp bark, Thyme herb, Hyssop herb, Black cohosh root, Aniseed, Gumweed flower, Elecampane root and Lobelia herb are among the most important *bronchodilators* used in Western herbal medicine. They correspond to Chinese medicinals such as Ephedra Ma Huang and Prunus Xing Ren.

Adrenocortical restorative antiasthmatics are the type of remedy used for treating Lung and Kidney Yang deficiency. They include Scots pine needle (and essential oil) and Rosemary herb (and essential oil). Chinese medicine here uses Juglans Hu Tao Ren (Walnut meat) and Gecko Ge Jie, among others.

Class 10 *demulcents* such as Plantain leaf, Chickweed herb, Borage leaf, Marshmallow leaf and so on, are also useful in these conditions for their additional *relaxant* action, as well as their moistening effect when lung dryness is also present.

Regulate Heart Qi, Balance Circulation and Relieve Palpitations
Neurocardiac relaxants (vasodilators, hypotensives)

Chronic emotional and nervous stress can erode the heart's ability to maintain a balance between the nervous intensity generated by constrained Qi and blood-based metabolic functions. The result is **heart Qi constraint (stagnation).** This syndrome correlates with neurocardiac syndrome, or cardiac neurosis, as it is sometimes called, and may include hypertension, atherosclerosis and arterial spasms. It is often marked with a minimal symptomatology such as occasional palpitations, chest pains and oppression, nervous tension, sadness, as well as possible headache, irritability, ringing ears,

rapid heart beat, a red-tipped tongue and a wiry, rapid pulse. This condition only becomes urgent during an acute anginal or heart attack presenting sharp chest pains running down the left arm to the little finger, as well as shortness of breath, anguish and fear of death.

Cardiovascular relaxants are the type of remedy used for regulating the Qi throughout the cardiovascular system. These remedies specifically involve *vasodilatory* and *hypotensive* actions. Frequently used are Hawthorn berry, Cramp bark, Lavender flower, Melissa leaf, Bugleweed herb, Selfheal spike, Melilot herb, Motherwort herb, Marjoram herb, Valerian root, Mistletoe herb and Black cohosh root. These herbs correspond to Chinese *cardiovascular relaxants* such as Ilex Mao Dong Qing, Clerodendron Chou Wu Tong, Chrysanthemum Ye Ju Hua and Cassia Jue Ming Zi.

Regulate Intestines Qi, Harmonize Digestion and Relieve Pain
Intestinal relaxants (gastrointestinal spasmolytics)

Remedies in this section address the syndrome **intestines Qi constraint.** This stems from emotional upset, worry or anxiety involving the enteritic nervous system, as well as from physiological causes such as intestinal dysbiosis and hypersensitivity reactions (type I through IV). Typical presenting symptoms are indigestion, abdominal bloating and pain, flatulence, nausea, appetite loss, slight sweating, irregular bowel movement and variable stool, and a wiry, tight pulse. All symptoms are worsened with moods and emotions. Western medical conditions seen here include spastic-type irritable bowel syndrome (IBS) (mucous colitis), spastic colon (intestinal colic), diverticulitis, ulcerative colitis and dysentery.

Intestinal relaxants for this condition possess bitter, pungent qualities and have *spasmolytic* and *analgesic* actions on the gut's smooth muscles. Frequently used are Hops flower, Wild yam root, Camomile flower, Cramp bark, Melissa herb, Lavender flower, Tansy herb, Silverweed root and Celandine herb. In Chinese medicine, Citrus Qing Pi, Saussurea Mu Xiang and Magnolia Hou Po are important equivalent herbs.

In the case where vagal nerve hypofunctioning affects the stomach, symptoms typical of **stomach dryness (stomach Yin deficiency)** may appear, such as heartburn, distressing lumpy sensations in the epigastrium, dry vomiting and hunger without a true appetite. This condition may change into **stomach fire** as the increase in hydrochloric acid begins to ulcerate the stomach lining. This condition presents as intense thirst with desire for iced drinks, ravenous hunger, constipation and swollen, painful and possibly bleeding gums. Sweet, cool *demulcents* (Class 10) that moisten dryness should then be used in conjunction with *intestinal relaxants*.

Regulate Bladder Qi, Harmonize Urination and Relieve Strangury
Urinary relaxants (urinary spasmolytics)

Given the right predisposition, emotional distress and nervous tension can also lead to **bladder Qi constraint.** This symptom picture includes frequent, scanty and dripping (incontinent) urination without a feeling of fullness, some urinary irritation or pain, bedwetting, sometimes even supressed urination (anuria), and a tight or wiry pulse. Frequently, the disorders neurogenic bladder (all types), acute renal colic, acute pyelonephritis and Reiter's syndrome are involved.

The *urinary relaxants* that regulate bladder Qi are mainly *spasmolytic.* They include Wild carrot seed, Parsley seed, St. John's wort herb, Marjoram herb, Kava root, Cleavers herb, Hops flower, Red clover flower, Cramp bark, Stone root, Arborvitae tip, Henbane herb, Parsley piert and Heather herb. In Chinese medicine, Coix Yi Yi Ren, Malva Dong Kui Zi and Pyrrosia Shi Wei figure here prominently.

In the case of urinary irritation, pain or irregularity from urinary stones, *antilithic* herbs should be added. These include Hydrangea root, Cleavers herb, Nettle herb, Madder root, Birch leaf and Pellitory of the wall.

Regulate Uterus Qi, Harmonize Menstruation and Relieve Pain
Uterine relaxants (uterine spasmolytics)

These herbs address the syndrome **uterus Qi constraint,** presenting difficult, painful, copious or irregular periods, and to some extent premenstrual syndrome (PMS) with its long retinue of symptoms; and a tight or wiry pulse. Often linked to an imbalance between the hormones estrogen or progesterone, this syndrome invariably involves tense uterus tone giving rise to sthenic or asthenic spasms—called spasmodic dysmenorrhea for short.

Uterine spasmolytics are the specific *relaxants* used. They include Motherwort herb, Wild yam root, Cramp bark, Blackhaw bark, Marjoram herb, Tansy herb, Feverfew herb, Black cohosh root, Pasque flower root/herb, White peony root, Dong quai root, Lavender flower (and essential oil), Pennyroyal herb, Melissa herb, Camomile flower (both types) and Clary sage essential oil. Many of these not only relieve menstrual cramps, but also tend to promote general relaxation and rest. They can also be used to relieve symptoms of PMS such as irritability, anger, anxiety and depression; some of them have a hormonal action that plays into their *relaxant* effect. Chinese remedies here include Cyperus Xiang Fu and Ligusticum Chuan Xiong.

During labor, many of these herbs act as *relaxant parturients.* They can play an important role in promoting overall relaxation and reducing hypertonic contractions (see Class 17).

A summary list of remedies in this section may be found in the end Repertory under the conditions mentioned in each subcategory.

NOTES
1. Apart from older writings throughout the Galenic, Hermetic and Neoplatonic lineages, good studies of the mental and psychic functions of the organs can be found in the works of RUDOLF TREICHLER. This author summarizes information from the Western wisdom traditions and relates it to the findings of modern psychiatry. The medical lectures of RUDOLF STEINER also contain many references and presentations of this knowledge.
2. The concept of Kidney wind is not as unfamiliar to Chinese medicine as it sounds. The Kidney Yin, after all, is the basis for the Liver Yin. When Kidney or Liver Yin is deficient, Liver Yang and Liver wind arise. Although incompatible with the mnemonic shorthand system of the Chinese five-element theory, the concept of Kidney wind is not essentially in disharmony with Chinese internal physiopathology.
3. For a lovely early text on the nature and functions of the Qi, or breath, and its relation to the heart and emotions, see O.C. GRUNER's translation (1930) of *De viribus cordis.* The translator inserts this text at the end of his translation of IBN SINA's *Al Quanun,* or *Canon of Medicine* (pp. 534-552 in the 1970 edition published by Augustus M. Kelley).

Relax Constraint, Relieve Pain, Restore the Nerves and Lift the Mind

General relaxants, cerebral/nervous restoratives, spasmolytics

St. John's Wort Herb

Botanical source: *Hypericum perforatum* L.
(Hypericaceae)
Pharmaceutical name: Herba Hyperici
Ancient names: Yperiko(n) (Gr)
Herba perforata, Herba S. Johannis,
Fugae daemonum, Corona regia (Lat)
Other names: Touch and heal, Amber, Rosin rose,
Witches' herb, St. John's grass, Terrestrial
sun, Goatweed (Eng)
St. Joan's wort, Klamath weed, Tipton weed
(Am)
Millepertuis, Herbe de St-Jean, Chasse-diable,
Herbe aux piqures (Fr)
Johanniskraut, Tüpfelhartheu, Waldhopff,
Wundkraut, Blutkraut, Tausendlöcherkraut,
Liebfrauenbettstroh, Frauenkraut, Konradskraut, Donnerkraut, Teufelsflucht, Hexenkraut (Ge)
Part used: the herb

NATURE

Therapeutic category: mild remedy with minimal chronic toxicity
Constituents: essential oil (incl. germacrene, sesquiterpenes), tannins, flavonoids (incl. rutin, phloba-phene), polyphenolic flavonoid derivative (hyperoside), rhodan, red dianthrones (hypericin, pseudohy-pericin), resins, carotenoids, pectin, xanthones, stearic/myric/palmic acid, alkaloid, phloroglucinol derivatives, hypeforin
Effective qualities: somewhat bitter, sweet and astringent, cool, dry
relaxing, restoring, astringing, stimulating
Tropism: lungs, intestines, kidneys, bladder, nerves, blood
Liver, Lung, Bladder meridians
Air, Warmth bodies
Ground: Sanguine krasis Tough/Shao Yang biotypes; all three constitutions

FUNCTIONS AND INDICATIONS

1 **RELAXES CONSTRAINT AND RELIEVES PAIN;**
RESTORES THE NERVES, LIFTS THE MIND AND RELIEVES DEPRESSION AND ANXIETY

kidney / adrenal & intestines Qi constraint with *deficiency:* mental/nervous tension (esp. from chronic
nervous exhaustion, frustration or depression, stress, pain, menopause), abdominal, kidney or
sacrum pain; agitated depression
STRESS-RELATED CONDITIONS in general
DIGESTIVE COLIC, irritable bowel syndrome
NEURALGIA, NEURITIS (incl. sciatica), arthralgia, fibromyalgia

SPINAL PAIN, soreness or burning sensation, deep coccyx pain

HEADACHE, migraine

MUSCLE TENSION / SPASMS, pain, soreness

nerve and brain deficiency (Kidney Essence deficiency): chronic depression, stress, sleep problems

NEURASTHENIA, DEPRESSION, ANXIETY, insomnia, hypersomnia, chronic psychosis

2   **REGULATES BLADDER AND UTERUS QI, HARMONIZES URINATION AND RELIEVES IRRITATION AND PAIN; PROMOTES URINATION AND DISSOLVES STONES**

bladder Qi constraint: suppressed or scanty dripping urination, irritation, bedwetting, painful sacrum

NEUROGENIC BLADDER, STRANGURY, ENURESIS

uterus Qi constraint: difficult, painful periods, cramps, irritability

SPASMODIC DYSMENORRHEA

kidney Qi stagnation with *metabolic toxicosis:* headaches, painful urination, nervousness, malaise

URINARY IRRITATION or PAIN (incl. from stones)

URINARY STONES

3   **PROMOTES EXPECTORATION, RESOLVES PHLEGM AND RELIEVES WHEEZING**

lung phlegm with *Qi accumulation:* wheezing, shortness of breath, coughing up thin white sputum

BRONCHITIS (chronic)

4   **CLEARS DAMP-HEAT, REDUCES INFLAMMATION AND INFECTION, ASTRINGES AND STOPS DISCHARGE AND BLEEDING**

DERMATITIS with *skin damp-heat:* painful wet skin sores, wet rashes, redness

VIRAL CONDITIONS (incl. cold sores [herpes], shingles, chickenpox; esp. with burning, tingling; all viral disorders in general)

CYSTITIS with *damp-heat;* ENTERITIS (esp. dysentery, esp. chronic) with *damp-heat*

BURNS, INFLAMMATIONS, neuritis, sunstroke

REMITTENT FEVER (*shao yang* stage)

URINARY INCONTINENCE, leucorrhea, albuminuria

HEMORRHAGE from all internal organs (incl. blood in urine or stool, coughing up blood, nosebleed, uterine bleeding)

CHILDREN'S INFECTIONS (bacterial and viral)

ANIMAL BITES and stings

INTESTINAL PARASITES (esp. in children)

5   **REDUCES CONTUSION, SWELLING AND PAIN, AND PROMOTES TISSUE REPAIR**

INJURY with swelling and pain (incl. NERVE INJURY, bruises, sprains, strains, concussions, punctures, shaking trauma [e.g. from travel])

BREAST ENGORGEMENT, TUMORS, lumps

ULCERS, SORES, (internal and external), varicose veins, skin blemishes

PREPARATION

Use: St. John's wort herb is prepared by expressed **juice, infusion** and **tincture.** For good rather than poor results, the flowering *fresh* herb must be used. Topical and first aid preparations using this herb include **ointments, compresses, washes** and **infused oils.** Applications include muscle tension and cramps, headache, burns and scalds, insect stings and neuralgias.

Ointments and **compresses** are better for treating viral skin conditions such as herpes, cold sores and shingles. Note that for best results, external application should always be supported by internal use.

When taken for its *antidepressant* action, St. John's wort herb only becomes fully effective after several weeks of use. For more permanent results, two or three months of continuous intake may be needed. Combining with other *nervine antidepressant* herbs like Melissa, Skullcap or Milky oats through synergy will produce an enhanced effect.

Dosage: Infusion: 8-14 g

Tincture: 2-4 ml at 1:3 strength in 50% ethanol

Caution: Use with caution during pregnancy because of a mild *uterine stimulant* action. There is some risk of increased skin photosensitivity by its hypericin content, and should be monitored if high or concentrated doses of St. John's wort are taken. In general, avoid exposure to natural or artificial sunlight. Extended use is also generally cautioned, as a link with cataract formation has been established.

NOTES

Like many plants that traditionally were used by a large variety of healers, especially wise women, the uses of St. John's wort are lost in the mists of unrecorded history. Because of this, the plant brings with it a legacy of magical and talismanic uses—witness names such as "Touch and heal," "Devil router" and "Witch's herb." Herbal practitioners have always had a definite preference for a particular therapeutic style. Some preferred more rational uses, such as those that Galenic theory offered during the last two millenniums. Others, however—and these were by far the largest group —chose the way of magical, ritualistic and imagistic usage. These were the wise woman healers. Many hybrid practices also came and went, such as medieval Monastic medicine and fifteenth/sixteenth century Iatromathematics (today known as medical astrology). Curiously, the latter was influenced by both the Neoplatonic and Wiccan traditions—not unlikely bedfellows, by any means.

It comes as no surprise, therefore, to learn that as late as 1673 a university-trained medic such as BARTOLOMEUS CARRICHTER felt confident in stating that "if a person be possessed of an evil mind, St. John's wort leaves should be given," judiciously adding that "the best time to pick the entire herb is when the sun enters the sixth degree of Leo." The recorded use of plants such as St. John's wort in the context of a holistic view of the human, plant and cosmos offers some proof that wise women healers generally did not rely on toxic plants for their daily practice. Not all wise women were active practi-tioners of the Wiccan craft, after all. Toxic plants such as Henbane, Deadly nightshade and other sub-stances like toad's skin were only used at certain times for specific psychotropic purposes in the context of Wiccan trance practices. Still, the *Flying ointment* used in these rituals certainly set people's imagination alight.

St. John's wort herb is a gentle remedy especially suited to children and the elderly. It combines easily and well. Like Horsetail herb, its use is polarized between treating very acute conditions and very chronic ones. As a first-aid remedy that combines *anti-inflammatory, analgesic* and *tissue-repairing* actions, this Woundwort is one of the best *vulneraries* for treating **burns, ulcers** and **wounds** presenting **inflammation** and **pain.** Pain from nerve injury or neuritis is especially well relieved. The exquisite *Compound oil of Hypericum* given in RYFF's *Reformierte Deutsche Apotheck* of 1573 is a silent witness from the past of its status as a premier topical remedy. The long formula for this medicated oil includes balsamic resins such as Myrrh, various gums and Aloe vera.

St. John's wort's *antiviral* action treats viral skin disorders as well as all **viral conditions** in general. "The herb seems to interfere with the virus capsule as well as inhibiting reverse transcriptase, which stops the virus from using our cells as virus factories" (DANIELA TURLEY 2005).

In chronic conditions St. John's wort scores with **empty tense** conditions involving the whole nervous system. Beyond the symptomatic use of St. John's wort as a Prozac substitute, this *nervous relaxant* and *nervous (tropho)restorative* remedy is especially helpful for those presenting **constrained Qi** with **nervous tension, spasms** and, especially, **depression** and **inner frustration.** The concept of **neurasthenia** fits the bill here perfectly. Here the herb's *nervous trophorestorative* effect promotes relaxation, reduction of **anxiety** and in the long-term a gradual recouperation of energies and spirits. Its cerebral activity has today been shown *anti-depressant* and *sleep-regulating*. In these conditions, St. John's wort is well complemented with the likes of Melissa, Skullcap, Wood betony, Rhodiola and Vervain.

As a *relaxant* that releases tension and spasms in both smooth and striated muscles, St. John's wort is *spasmolytic, analgesic* and *neuromuscular relaxant*. The herb works on conditions as diverse as spasmodic dysmenorrhea, neuralgia, tight muscles and headaches. However, empirically the remedy's action on the bladder stands out. Individuals with **difficult, painful urination** with leakage, especially when arising from **neurogenic bladder,** are comprehensively treated. Nice complementary herbs here would be Wild carrot seed, Parsley seed

Melissa leaf and Marjoram herb.

Because of its particular tropism for the urinary tract, St. John's wort addresses not only incontinence and bedwetting, but also albuminuria and mucous in the urine. In energetic terms it tonifies **Kidney Qi** and clears **damp-cold** in the urogenital system. Combining St. John's wort with Buchu leaf or Poplar bark would be excellent here.

The herb's *astringency* extends to the capillaries in a *hemostatic* action that again works particularly well for bleeding from the lower orifices.

Skullcap Herb

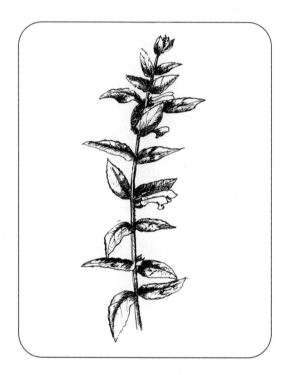

Botanical source: *Scutellaria lateriflora,*
    S. galericulata L. (Lamiaceae/Labiatae)
Pharmaceutical name: Herba Scutellariae lateriflorae
Other names: Helmet flower, Blue pimpernel,
    Madweed, Hooded willow herb (Am)
    Scutellaire, Toque (Fr)
    Helmkraut, Sumpf/Virginisches Helmkraut,
    Fieberkraut, Schildkraut (Ge)
Part used: the herb

NATURE
Therapeutic category: mild remedy with minimal chronic toxicity
Constituents: essential oil, fixed oil, flavonoids (incl. baicalin, scutellarin), albumen, tannin, bitter scutellarein, lignin, iron, silicon, zinc, calcium/potassium/magnesium phosphate, chlorophyll, potassium and magnesium sulphate, resin, fat, sugar
Effective qualities: bitter, somewhat sweet and astringent, cool, dry
    relaxing, restoring, stabilizing, stimulating
Tropism: heart, kidneys, urogenital organs, autonomic and central nervous system, brain and spine
    Heart, Kidney, Liver meridians
    Air body
Ground: all krases, biotypes and constitutions; Neurogenic Iris subtype

FUNCTIONS AND INDICATIONS

1 **RELAXES CONSTRAINT AND RELIEVES PAIN;**
   RESTORES THE NERVES, LIFTS THE MIND AND RELIEVES DEPRESSION

   kidney / adrenal Qi constraint: mental/nervous tension (esp. from chronic stress, pain, illness,
      mental/physical exhaustion), unrest, agitated depression, kidney or sacrum pain
   STRESS-RELATED CONDITIONS in general
   PAIN (incl. NEURALGIA, NEURITIS, tension headache, uterine pain, teething pains)
   nerve and brain deficiency: chronic weakness, fatigue or exhaustion, depression, paresis or paralysis
   NEURASTHENIA, DEPRESSION from chronic stress or disease, drug addictions, etc.

2 **REGULATES HEART QI AND BALANCES CIRCULATION;**
   CLEARS INTERNAL WIND AND STOPS SPASMS

   heart Qi constraint: chest pains, palpitations, intermittent pulse, shortness of breath, insomnia
   HYPERTENSION, spasmodic angina
   internal wind: tremors, twitches, hysteria, convulsions, facial paralysis, aphasia
   EPILEPSY, RABIES, tetanus, delirium tremens, rheumatic chorea, multiple sclerosis
   SPINAL DISEASES (incl. spinal meningitis)

3 **CALMS THE MIND AND PROMOTES REST;**
   TONIFIES THE YIN, CLEARS EMPTY HEAT AND REDUCES FEVER & SEXUAL OVERSTIMULATION

   Heart and Kidney Yin deficiency: insomnia, palpitations, nervous restlessness, intense dreams,
      wet dreams
   INSOMNIA in deficiency conditions
   SEXUAL OVERSTIMULATION in all conditions
   Kidney Yin deficiency: afternoon hot spells, night sweats, ringing ears, anxiety
   LOW-GRADE TIDAL FEVERS with empty heat (*shao yin* stage)

4 **STIMULATES DIGESTION, PROMOTES URINATION AND ANTIDOTES POISON**

   stomach Qi stagnation: indigestion, appetite loss, stress, nervous tension
   GASTRIC DYSPEPSIA
   kidney Qi stagnation: nervousness, malaise, dry skin, urinary irritation
   POISONOUS INSECT and SNAKE BITES

PREPARATION

Use: Skullcap herb is prepared fresh or dried by **long infusion** or **tincture.** The infusion makes a relaxing tea for nervous tension or indigestion from stress, and combines well with Camomile flower, Melissa leaf, Spearmint leaf, Linden flower or Orange flower, for instance.
Dosage: Long infusion: 8-14 g
         Tincture: 2-4 ml at 1:3 strength in 45% ethanol
Caution: None. **Skullcap root,** if ever used, should be avoided during pregnancy because of its content in steroid precursors.
Note: Skullcap herb deteriorates quite rapidly with age and should be used within six months of being collected. Beware of fraudulent substitutions for Skullcap—which posesses a typical bitter-sweet taste.

NOTES

Although it actually contains very little essential oil, the North American Skullcap is no exception to the rule that the essential oil-laden mint family has a general affinity for the nervous system. Skullcap herb excels as a *nerve restorative* remedy with *relaxant* properties. Its main area of application is **nervous/cerebral deficiency** presenting neurological symptoms such as chronic depression, fatigue, anxiety, restlessness, sleep loss, pain and spasms. Traditional Western medicine defines this syndrome as **neurasthenia.**

In vitalistic terms, Skullcap is best applied in patterns of **constrained Qi** arising from deficiency, not from excess—**empty tense** conditions, for short. This herb is clearly one for the *chronic* phase of disasaptation to stressors, not the acute phase. It is as appropriate today for chronic urban stress and its derivative conditions as it was two-hundred years ago for chronic pioneering stress.

In addition, Skullcap's content in essential oil, minerals and glycosides makes for a more comprehensive *trophorestorative* effect on actual nerve cells. This is an essential requirement for individuals suffering from the debilitating effects on the nerves of **longstanding unproductive stress,** whether caused by disease or excessive lifestyle. Skullcap's *restorative* action is seen in its taste energetics, which is mainly bitter and sweet. These effective qualities ensure tonification of the whole system through digestive and hormonal stimulation. The bitter taste is also said to strengthen the heart. True to form, Skullcap has shown *cardiac stimulant* activity.

As a *systemic relaxant* Skullcap herb exhibits mild *sedative* and good *spasmolytic, analgesic* and *hypotensive* actions that in concert are very effective for those presenting internal spasms and pains, tremors of the extremities, neuralgic pain and tension headache, among others. The syndrome **heart Qi constraint** is a particularly good application of this herb. In these individuals the remedy will help lower blood pressure and relieve such related

symptoms as irritability, anxiety and insomnia. Where constrained Qi or Yin deficiency generates trembling limbs, convulsions or local paralysis, Skullcap is still the right remedy. Tetanus, rabies, meningitis and epilepsy figure prominently among its many traditional uses in both town and country.

The energetic quality of bitter taste, however, also indicates a general cooling effect on the body that goes hand-in-hand with the *relaxant* action. Skullcap herb's function here is to clear the **empty heat** of **Yin deficiency,** especially of **Heart and Kidney Yin deficiency** presenting hot spells, insomnia, panic attacks and night sweats. In this respect, Skullcap herb, Marjoram herb, Black cohosh root, Hops flower and Scrophularia Xuan Shen are completely interchangeable.

Despite the fact that Skullcap herb is a cousin to the **Baikal skullcap root** (Scutellaria Huang Qin) used in Chinese medicine, these two plants share little in common, in both therapeutic and biochemical respects. Baikal skullcap has very bitter, dry and cold qualities whose *draining* effect is used for clearing full, not empty, heat. Its main application is infectious damp-heat conditions. This once again highlights the dangers of making therapeutic equations and inferences across continents between plants of the same genus.

The related native Californian species, *Scutellaria californica,* is more bitter in taste and cooling in effect. This **California skullcap herb** seems to act similarly to the standard Skullcap except that it is a stronger *digestive stimulant* (function 4) and may have a mild *liver decongestant* and damp-heat clearing effect like the Class 8 *liver decongestants.*

Ladies' Slipper Root

Botanical source: *Cypripedium calceolus* L. and var.,
　　　C. pubescens Willdenow, *C acaule* L. and spp.
　　　(Orchidaceae)
Pharmaceutical name: Rhizoma Cypripedii
Other names: Moccasin flower, Yellows, Nerve root,
　　　American valerian, Noah's ark,
　　　Virgins' sleeve, Umbel (Am)
　　　Sabot de Vénus, Soulier de Notre Dame (Fr)
　　　Frauenschuh, Venusschuh, Nervenwurzel (Ge)
Part used: the rhizome

NATURE

Therapeutic category: mild remedy with minimal chronic toxicity
Constituents: essential oil, bitter glycoside, volatile acid, oleoresin cypripedin, resins, tannins, gallic and tannic acids, gums, starch, calcium oxalate, potassium, trace minerals (incl. magnesium)
Effective qualities: somewhat pungent, sweet and bitter, cool, dry
　　　relaxing, restoring, stimulating
Tropism: nervous, reproductive systems
　　　Liver, Kidney, Heart meridians
　　　Air, Warmth bodies
Ground: all krases, biotypes and constitutions

FUNCTIONS AND INDICATIONS

1 **RELAXES CONSTRAINT AND RELIEVES PAIN;**
　RESTORES THE NERVES, LIFTS THE MIND AND RELIEVES DEPRESSION

kidney / adrenal Qi constraint: mental/emotional tension, nervous restlessness, agitated depression,
　　pain (esp. from chronic stress, pain, illness)
STRESS-RELATED CONDITIONS in general
TENSION HEADACHE, NEURITIS, NEURALGIA
nerve and brain deficiency: weakness, listlessness, poor concentration and memory
NEURASTHENIA, NERVOUS DEPRESSION in all deficiency conditions (incl. from sexual abuse)

2 **REGULATES UTERUS QI, CLEARS INTERNAL WIND AND STOPS SPASMS**

uterus Qi constraint: difficult periods, cramps, irritability, fatigue
SPASMODIC DYSMENORRHEA, PMS
internal wind: agitated depression, spasms, tremors, hyperaesthesia, convulsions
MUSCLE SPASMS
SEIZURES (incl. of epilepsy, hysteria, chorea, infants)

**3 TONIFIES THE YIN, CLEARS EMPTY HEAT AND REDUCES FEVER;
PROMOTES REST AND REDUCES SEXUAL OVERSTIMULATION**

Heart and Kidney Yin deficiency: exhaustion, anxiety, sleep loss, hot spells, palpitations, wet dreams
TIDAL FEVERS with empty heat (*shao yin* stage)
INSOMNIA, IRRITABILITY, MENOPAUSAL SYNDROME
SEXUAL OVERSTIMULATION from *Kidney fire*

4 PROMOTES SWEATING, DISPELS WIND-HEAT AND REDUCES FEVER

external wind-heat: fever, irritability, aches and pains
COLD and FLU ONSET with FEVER

PREPARATION

Use: Ladies' slipper root is prepared by **cold infusion** (at least 12 hours) or **tincture.**
Dosage: Cold infusion: 4-8 g
        Tincture: 1-3 ml at 1:2 strength in 45% ethanol
Caution: Ladies' slipper is a somewhat endangered and protected plant and should be used with circumspection in this regard. Its extensive and shortsighted exploitative use throughout the twentieth century explains its relative scarcity at the present day. Do not pick if ever seen in the wild: the plant needs to freely grow and reproduce. Today, cultivated and etically-harvested sources are fortunately available.

NOTES

The names "Ladies' slipper" and "Moccasin flower" evoke the colorful baroque appearance of this now officially protected genus of North American orchid. It was CARL LINNAEUS, founder of today's system of botanical nomenclature, who in the late eighteenth century chose the name *kupris podeion,* literally meaning "Aphrodite's boot." After all, he lived in a time still immersed in the ideals of classical Greece. *Kupris* was one of the goddess Aphrodite's ancient names in the Mediterranean island of Crete. The mere presence of this plant today links us to ancient, pre-Hellennic Crete where flourished the last of the West's great matris-tic civilizations.

There are several *relaxant* remedies in this class that are better at treating tense conditions arising from deficiency rather than from excess. With its combined *nervous trophorestorative* and *spasmolytic* actions, Ladies' slipper root is one of them, alongside the likes of Skullcap and St. John's wort. It should specifically be used for **chronic nervous deficiency/neurasthenia** with **tension,** typically in those presenting the symptom picture of chronic depression, irritability, exhaustion and tension headaches or other neuralgias. Ladies' slipper is a good *nervous restorative* that possesses *spasmolytic* and *analgesic* actions as well.

In terms of Chinese medical syndromes, this herb addresses **Yin deficiency** and **Qi constraint** combined. Ladies' slipper root will also clear any heat resulting from this deficiency. **Kidney and Heart Yin deficiency,** presenting hot spells, insomnia and restlessness, could here become a classic indication. Because it also clears **internal wind** (often arising from Yin deficiency and heat), Ladies' slipper will also reduce internal and external spasms, including the sensation of internal trembling and the accompanying overall tension, mental and muscular

Like Black cohosh root, Marjoram herb and Skullcap herb (all in this class), this herb addresses **empty tense** and **empty heat** conditions, for which they all make excellent combinations.

Ladies' slipper's reputation as a domestic medicine for painful menstrual cramps among the early American pioneers was only surpassed by that of Boneset herb for fevers. The plant was freely used as an all-purpose woman's *relaxant,* especially for "hysteria," or PMS, spasmodic dysmenorrhea and labor pains. The pioneers' Tylenol, no doubt. Today with differential diagnosis we can say that the remedy is more specifically for **uterus Qi constraint** with underlying kidney-adrenal deficiency or Yin deficiency.

Wood Betony Herb

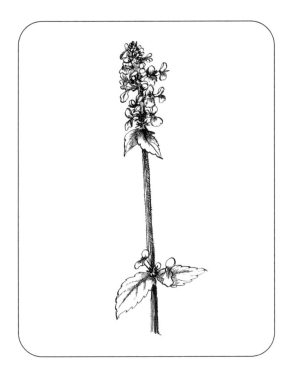

Botanical source: *Betonica officinalis* L.
    (syn. *Stachys betonica* Bentham) (Lamiaceae)
Pharmaceutical name: Herba Betonicae
Ancient names: Kesgon, Psychotrophon (Gr)
    Betonica, Sideritis, Serratula, Cestron (Lat)
Other names: Betony, Bishopswort, Bidney,
    Wild hop, Betayne (Eng)
    Bétoine, Épiaire (Fr)
    Ziestkraut, Heilziest, Zehrkraut, Betonie,
    Pfaffenblume, Katzenwedel, Fleishblume
    (Ge)
Part used: the herb; also the root, Radix Betonicae

NATURE

Dosage: mild remedy with minimal chronic toxicity
Constituents: alkaloids (incl. betaine, betonicin, stachydrin, trigonellin, turicin), glycosides, tannins 15%, bitter compound, caffeeic acid, cholin, essential oil traces, minerals (incl. magnesium, manganese, phosphorus)
Effective qualities: somewhat bitter and astringent, cool, dry
    relaxing, restoring, stimulating, astringing, calming, dissolving
Tropism: lung, liver, bladder, uterus, nerves and brain
    Lung, Liver, Heart meridians; Air body
Ground: Sanguine and Choleric krases
    Expressive/Jue Yin and Tough/Shao Yang biotypes
    Biliary/Phosphoric and Hematogenic/Sulphuric constitutions

FUNCTIONS AND INDICATIONS

1 **RELAXES CONSTRAINT AND RELIEVES PAIN;**
   RESTORES THE NERVES, LIFTS THE MIND AND RELIEVES DEPRESSION

   kidney / adrenal Qi constraint: mental/nervous tension, unrest, pains
   STRESS-RELATED CONDITIONS in general
   PAIN (incl. NEURALGIA, NEURITIS, esp. facial and cranial, e.g. trigeminal)
   nerve and brain deficiency: chronic weakness, mental dullness, depression,
   NEURASTHENIA, DEPRESSION from chronic stress or disease
   PARALYSIS, PARESTHESIA

2 **REGULATES HEART QI AND BALANCES CIRCULATION**

   heart Qi constraint and Liver Yang rising: palpitations, dizziness, headache, vision disturbances
   HYPERTENSION
   TENSION HEADACHE, migraine

3 **DESCENDS LUNG QI, OPENS THE CHEST, PROMOTES EXPECTORATION, RESOLVES PHLEGM AND RELIEVES COUGHING AND WHEEZING**

lung Qi constraint: wheezing, chest soreness and tightness
SPASMODIC ASTHMA (esp.chronic)
lung phlegm-damp/heat: copious white or yellow sputum, wheezing, blood in sputum
BRONCHITIS acute or chronic

4 **REGULATES UROGENITAL QI, PROMOTES AND REGULATES MENSTRUATION, AND RELIEVES PAIN; PROMOTES LABOR**

uterus Qi constraint with *stagnation:* delayed, difficult periods, menstrual cramps
DYSMENORRHEA (spasmodic)
bladder Qi constraint: difficult painful urination, dripping urination
DYSURIA
DIFFICULT, PAINFUL LABOR
FAILURE to PROGRESS during LABOR

5 **REDUCES LIVER CONGESTION, PROMOTES URINATION AND ENHANCES VISION**

liver Qi stagnation: painful swollen flank, epigastric distension, constipation, water retention
LIVER CONGESTION, jaundice
kidney Qi stagnation with *metabolic toxicosis:* skin rashes, poor appetite, aches and pains
GOUT, RHEUMATISM (chronic)
IMPAIRED VISION

6 **ASTRINGES AND STOPS DISCHARGE AND BLEEDING; REDUCES INFECTION, ELIMINATES PARASITES AND ANTIDOTES POISON**

HEMORRHAGE (esp. from mouth, nose, in urine, sputum); coughing up blood, uterine bleeding
LEUCORRHEA, DIARRHEA, copious sweating
MOUTH, GUM and THROAT INFECTIONS
CHRONIC WOUNDS, ULCERS (incl. infected ones, leg ulcers), sores
INTESTINAL PARASITES

PREPARATION

Use: Wood betony herb is taken by **infusion** or **tincture**. **Washes, compresses, mouthwashes** and **gargles** make good use of its *astringent* and *hemostatic* actions for topical use. This includes wounds and ulcers, especially with bleeding or putrefaction present. **Douches** and **pessaries** should be used for vaginal discharges and uterine bleeding. The leaves were also **smoked** in the past.

WILLIAM COLE (1657) recommends a nice **medicinal wine** of Wood betony herb, Vervain herb, White horehound herb and Hyssop herb for treating headaches.

Wood betony root is more effective than the herb for stimulating and decongesting the liver (e.g., in jaundice), and for promoting bowel movement. In large doses it can be used as an *emetic*.

Dosage: Infusion: 8-12 g
Tincture: 2-4 ml at 1:3 strength in 60% ethanol

Smaller doses are *astringent* (diarrhea, etc.), while larger doses are *laxative;* above this an *emetic* effect appears.

Half the doses of the herb apply to Wood betony root.

Caution: Contraindicated during pregnancy because of its *uterine stimulant* action.

Note: Wood betony herb should not be confused with or exchanged for **Betony herb**, *Pedicularis* spp. from the figwort family (Scrophulariaceae). The two plants have essentially different uses.

Another plant in the mint family, **Hedge nettle herb,** *Stachys palustris* (a.k.a. Marsh woundwort,

Clown's all-heal, Roughweed), is used in a similar way to Wood betony herb. It is found in the Pacific Northwest and throughout Europe.

NOTES

Wood betony herb is one of those special plant remedies steeped in a thick patina of historical uses. Its glowing reputation was already established when the Roman chronicler PLINIUS wrote his *Natural Histories.* Greek medics named this remedy *psychetrophon,* meaning *soul-nourisher.* ANTONIUS MUSA, physician to CAESAR AUGUSTUS, devoted a whole book to this remedy, listing no less than forty-seven specific conditions that could be treated with it. Centuries later the brilliant and normally sober German pharmacist JOHANN SCHROEDER in his milestone dispensatory of 1611 gleely heaps paeans on Wood betony. He concludes his entry by stating "there is almost no bodily ailment for which it does not fail to prove of especial benefit." He fancifully suggests that the remedy "could therefore rightly be entitled to the name *Omnimorbia.*" Perhaps it is precisely because of this kind of literary hyperbole that modern researchers have shied away from it.

What is clearly needed now is a more level-headed assessment of this plant from the lipflower/ mint family. With its array of alkaloids (some of which are also found in Motherwort herb), it does have the potential for being widely-acting. Distilling all available empirical evidence we can say that Wood betony is mainly a *nervine* remedy. Like Skullcap herb, Sage leaf and St. John's wort, the remedy acts as a deep *restorative* and *relaxant* to the nervous system, including cerebral functions. This is the foundation for its Greek name *psychetrophon.* **Chronic depression, fatigue** and other signs of **cerebral deficiency** and **neurasthenia** are the prominent conditions that it treats. In practice, Wood betony should primarily be taken by those presenting chronic disorders with neurological involvement, especially when typified by **restlessness, insomnia** and **pain.** In vitalistic terms, the remedy relaxes **constrained Qi** arising from **empty tense** conditions. Facial neuralgias especially are relieved in this connection. Wood betony is the traditional Feverfew of Western herbal medicine before the latter tested out as a specific for tension and migraine headaches.

Other key therapeutic uses should be singled out. Wood betony herb is an excellent *uterine stimulant/relaxant* for women with spasmodic dysmenorrhea, or difficult labor with painful hypertonic contractions. Its *astringent* quality helps resolve catarrhal discharges arising from damp-cold, such as diarrhea and leucorrhea.

As its many past folk names attest, Wood betony traditionally was also an esteemed *vulnerary* for tissue trauma, especially with bleeding and chronic non-healing sores present.

Relax Constraint, Relieve Pain and Calm the Mind

General relaxants, cerebral/nervous sedatives, spasmolytics, analgesics

Camomile Flower

Botanical source: a) *Matricaria recucita* (L.)
    Rauschert (syn. *Matricaria chamomilla* L.)
    b) *Anthemis nobilis* L. (Asteraceae/
    Compositae)
Pharmaceutical name: Flos Anthemis seu
    Matricariae
Ancient names: Chrysokome, Eranthemon,
    Chamaimelon, Melanthemon (Gr)
    Chamaemilla, Parthenium nobile (Lat)
Other names: a) German camomile, Motherwort,
    Feverfew, Whitewort (Eng)
    Camomille allemande/vraie/commune,
    Matricaire, Espargoutte (Fr)
    Echte Kamille, Mutterkraut, Mettram,
    Fieberkraut (Ge)
    b) Roman camomile, Mayweed,
    Common/Double camomile (Eng)
    Camomille romaine/noble (Fr)
    Römische Kamille, Römische Hundskamille,
    Magdblume, Hermelein, Langenblume (Ge)
Part used: the flower

NATURE

Therapeutic category: mild remedy with minimal chronic toxicity
Constituents: a) *Matricaria r.:* essential oil (incl. hydrocarbons [incl. blue chamazulene], hydrocarbon esters, caprylic and monylic acid ethers, alcohols, pinocarvone, anthemol, polyphenol, sesquiterpenes, paraffine, furfole, umbellife-ronemethylether, spiroether), flavonoids (incl. anthemidin, luteolin), coumarin, bitter glycoside (anthemic acid) tannins, malic acid
b) *Anthemis n.:* essential oil 0.4-1% (incl. butyl/amyl/hexyl esters of tiglic, isobutyric and angelic acids c. 85%, sesquiterpenes [incl. azulene, artemol], sesquiterpene lactone (nobilin), hydrocarbons chamazulene and proazulenes, terpenes [incl. pinene], farnasene, bisabolol), flavonoids (incl. quercetin, luteolin, apigenin, patuletin), bitter glycoside (anthemic acid), cyanogenic glycoside, tannins and pseudotannins, camphor, valerianic acid, acetylenic and salycilic acid derivative, valerianic acid, polysaccharides, phytosterol, coumarins (incl. scopolin), resin, gum, minerals and trace minerals (incl. calcium, potassium, sulfur, iodine)
Effective qualities: somewhat bitter and sweet, cool, neutral
    relaxing, calming, stimulating, restoring, decongesting, dissolving
Tropism: lungs, stomach, intestines, liver, uterus, nerves, ear, nose and throat
    Liver, Pericardium, Lung, *chong, ren* meridians
    Air, Warmth bodies
Ground: Sanguine and Choleric krasis
    Expressive/Jue Yin, Tough/Shao Yang and Industrious/Tai Yang biotypes
    Hematogenic/Sulphuric constitution

FUNCTIONS AND INDICATIONS

1 **RELAXES CONSTRAINT, RELIEVES PAIN AND CALMS THE MIND**

kidney / adrenal Qi constraint: mental/nervous tension, sensory and emotional oversensitivity (esp. from stress, emotional trauma, pain), unrest, agitated depression

STRESS-RELATED CONDITIONS in general

INSOMNIA, irritability

NEURITIS, NEURALGIA (esp. facial), FIBROMYALGIA, earache, toothache, shingles

Liver Yang rising: intense frontal or occipital headaches, dizziness, tinnitus

HEADACHES, MIGRAINE or TENSION type

2 **REGULATES THE QI AND RELIEVS PAIN;**
   REDUCES STAGNATION AND HARMONIZES DIGESTION AND MENSTRUATION;
   CLEARS INTERNAL WIND AND STOPS SPASMS

intestines Qi constraint (Liver/Spleen disharmony): indigestion, flatulence, abdominal pain, irregular bowel movement, symptoms worse when upset

IBS, COLIC, PEPTIC ULCER (esp. from stress), ulcerative colitis

gallbladder and stomach Qi stagnation: appetite loss, epigastric distension and pain, nausea, flatulence, moodiness

DYSPEPSIA (biliary, gastric)

GASTRITIS, heartburn

uterus Qi constraint: difficult periods, cramps during onset, irritability

SPASMODIC DYSMENORRHEA

PMS with irritability, depression,weepiness, sleep loss, headache

internal wind: tremors, twitches, convulsions

INFANTILE SEIZURES

3 **DESCENDS LUNG QI AND RELIEVES WHEEZING AND COUGHING;**
   PROMOTES EXPECTORATION AND RESOLVES PHLEGM; RELIEVES ALLERGY

lung Qi constraint: difficult breathing, wheezing, dry nervous cough

BRONCHIAL ASTHMA (incl. allergic)

lung phlegm-heat: full cough, expectoration of green or yellow pussy sputum

ACUTE BRONCHITIS, allergic rhinitis

ATOPIC DERMATITIS

4 **PROMOTES SWEATING, DISPELS WIND-HEAT AND REDUCES FEVER;**
   STIMULATES IMMUNITY AND REDUCES INFLAMMATION

lung wind-heat: cough, fever, aches and pains, unrest, irritability, insomnia

COLD and FLU ONSET with FEVER

REMITTENT and INTERMITTENT FEVERS (*shao yang* and *shao yin* stage)

LEUKOPENIA

EYE, MOUTH, GUM and THROAT INFLAMMATIONS (incl. conjunctivitis, otitis, sinusitis, pharyngitis)

5 **CLEARS DAMP-HEAT AND REDUCES INFLAMMATION AND SWELLING;**
   PROMOTES TISSUE REPAIR AND BENEFITS THE SKIN

intestines damp-heat: urgent painful passing of loose stools

ACUTE ENTERITIS

INTESTINAL PARASITES (round and pinworm)

skin wind-damp-heat: skin eruptions and lesions with redness, swelling, itching

ECZEMA, SHINGLES, vulvar pruritis, nettle rash, scurf; boils, abscesses

BURNS, scalds

TUMORS, cancer, scirrhus, etc.

INFECTED WOUNDS (new or chronic), open leg sores or ulcers

PREPARATION

Use: Camomile flower is generally prepared by **infusion** or **tincture.** The fresh flowers are reputedly more effective than the dried ones. The infusion is one of the best symptom-relief and first aid remedies, including digestive upsets, unrest, anxiety or sleep loss, painful periods, colds, teething and other aches and pains.

The tincture is considered somewhat stronger, while the extracted **essential oil** perhaps wins out over the others for practicality and efficiency combined.

For systemic conditions such as chronic gastrointestinal hyperacidity and peptic ulcer, any of these three preparations should be taken every day for up to three months. A little should be drunk throughout the day on an empty stomach—contact with the stomach mucosa is important.

For women's problems, using Camomile in **sitzbaths, vaginal steams** and **sponges** is a perfect complement to internal use. For acute respiratory conditions with sinus and bronchial congestion and pain, **inhalations** come nicely into their own. **Gargling** and **mouthwashes** are best for mouth, gum and throat inflammations with redness, swelling and soreness, while similar lower intestinal conditions benefit from **enemas. Swabs, compresses, ointments** and **liniments** are appropriate in skin conditions and first aid situations manifesting irritation, inflammation and infection. The **eyebath** from the infusion is superb for eye inflammations (e.g., conjunctivitis).

Camomile flowers tied in a nodulus, or cloth bag, make a soothing, relaxing **bath.**

Camomilla is the homeopathic preparation in low potency of the German camomile (Matricaria), and is used for all the symptom pictures above.

Dosage: Infusion: 6-14 g

       Tincture: 2-4 ml at 1:3 strength in 60% ethanol

       Essential oil: 1-2 drops in a gel cap topped with some olive oil

The **infusion** should be kept covered while steeping to retain the essential oils—one hour according to HENRI LECLERC (1935), although 20 minutes is standard.

Caution: Camomile flower should be used cautiously if used on its own internally during pregancy, as it is a *uterine stimulant.* The essential oil is contraindicated during this time.

NOTES

Whether we are partisan of the Roman Camomile (*Anthemis*) or the German camomile (*Matricaria*), one thing is clear: from the therapeutic aspect there is very little to differentiate them. Both varieties have clinically always been used in a similar way. Their chemical make up is also very similar—the differences reflecting research emphasis more than intrinsic difference (MILLS 1984). If any qualification were needed, it is possible that *Anthemis* has a *nervous sedative* edge over *Matricaria,* and that the latter is more strongly *anti-inflammatory.* DIOS-KURIDES in his classic Greek text discusses three kinds of Camomiles, and even today it is difficult to pinpoint which ones he is referring to. GALEN, on the other hand, specifically mentions *Anthemis* but not *Matricaria.*

To understand the essence of Camomile, we could compare the herb to *Diana* by the baroque artist Boucher or to Raphael's *Madonna.* Emblematically, Camomile is a goddess of harmonious light and warmth, the compassionate lady of the composites, as Lavender is the compassionate lady of the lipflowers/mints. Camomile's highly complex biochemical composition offers the body's Qi a bundle of potential avenues for healing. For instance, with combined topical and internal use it enbles it to treat almost any minor ailment and accident situation.

We can see Camomile's harmonizing nature in its complementary effective qualities. Although sweet to the taste, the flower also contains some bitterness. At first gently warming in effect, it then goes on to cool inflammation and calm hyperactivity. In harmonizing, moderating and softening whatever it touches, Camomile is a remedy of the Chinese element Earth. The medieval physician IBN SINA clearly recognized this when, in his *Treatise on Chicory,* he wrote of this herb: "By its coldness it assists in clearing excess heat from the organs, and by its warmth it helps resolve gross substances." How can we disagree with the Persian master of dialectic subtelty?

Camomile flower is essentially a systemic *relaxant* remedy with secondary *sedative* and *stimulant* effects. Fundamentally therefore it addresses **tense** conditions involving aspects of **heat, damp** and **mucus congestion.** These involve **oversensitivity, weakness** and **pain** on the nerve/sensory level, **tension, restlessness** and **agitation** on the emotional level, and **inflammation, irritation** and **discharge** on the skin and mucous membrane level. Camomile's good *spasmolytic, analgesic, anti-inflammatory* and *nervous sedative* actions totally come together for individuals suffering from tense conditions of the digestive organs, such as notably irritable bowel syndrome (most types), colic and ulcers. The Chinese syndrome **Liver-Spleen disharmony** in its broadest sense covers these conditions.

Spasmodic conditions of the striated muscles are also addressed by the remedy's use for tremors and infantile seizures. The keynote symptom here is **neuralgic pain** of any type. Fibromyalgic pain will benefit from Camomile plus Feverfew or Meadowsweet, plus Prickly ash bark, for example. In Chinese medical terms, Camomile spreads Liver Qi and clears internal wind.

Because of its affinity for the respiratory mucosa and skin, Camomile flower acts as a *relaxant expectorant* in **hot, tense, damp respiratory** and **surface** conditions such as acute rhinitis, asthma, bronchitis and dermatitis. Here the remedy's specific *mucostatic, antiallergic, antipruritic* and *anti-inflammatory* actions all engage. The additional *vasodilatory diaphoretic* action reinforces surface relaxation in those at the acute onset of a flu or cold with a climbing temperature, and should be used whenever aches and pains and irritability are a prominent. In other words, because the herb disperses wind, damp and heat from the Lung and skin, it finds application in such traditional syndromes as **lung wind-heat, lung phlegm-heat** and **skin wind-damp-heat.** In red, itchy forms of dermatitis (including atopic dermatitis), Camomile's *antiallergic* action comes especially to the fore—for which again internal usage should be accompanied by topical applications like washes and compresses.

Melissa Leaf

Botanical source: *Melissa officinalis* L.
    (Labiatae/Lamiaceae)
Pharmaceutical name: Folium Melissae
Ancient names: Meliosophyllon (Gr)
    Apiastrum, Citraria, Turego, Herba muscata,
      Pigmentaria (Lat)
Other names: Balm, Lemon balm, Sweet balm (Eng)
    Mélisse, Herbe au citron, Céline, Citronne (Fr)
    Melisse, Mutterkraut, Zitronenkraut, Königs-
      blume, Bienenkraut, Herzkraut (Ge)
Part used: the leaf

NATURE

Therapeutic category: mild remedy with minimal chronic toxicity

Constituents: essential oil (incl. citronellal 40%, citral 30%, linalool, geraniol, aldehydes, pinene, limonene, acids), glycoside (?), crystalline bitter compounds, catechin tannins 3-5%, organic acids, stachyose, minerals

Effective qualities: somewhat bitter, sour and astringent, cool, dry

> relaxing, calming, stimulating, restoring, astringing

Tropism: heart, uterus, brain, stomach, intestines, nerve

> Heart, Pericardium, Triple Heater, Lung, Liver, Kidney, Bladder, *chong, ren* meridians

> Warmth, Air bodies

Ground: Choleric and Sanguine krases

> All biotypes and constitutions

FUNCTIONS AND INDICATIONS

1 **RELAXES CONSTRAINT, CALMS THE MIND AND RELIEVES ANXIETY;**
   SINKS THE YANG, CLEARS HEAT AND REDUCES FEVER AND ALLERGY

kidney / adrenal Qi constraint: kidney or sacral pain, abdominal pain and swelling, agitated depression

STRESS-RELATED CONDITIONS in general (esp. with allergies present)

INSOMNIA, ANXIETY STATES, phobias, paranoias

heart Yin deficiency with *nerve excess:* nervous unrest, anxiety, palpitations, stress

floating Yang with *Heart fire:* restlessness, agitation, sleep loss, irritability, dizziness, palpitations

PMS from fluid/electrolyte imbalance with headache, ringing ears, irritability, anxiety, sleep loss

SYMPATHETIC NERVOUS HYPERFUNCTIONING

IMMEDIATE ALLERGIES (incl. atopic dermatitis, asthma, rhinitis)

yang ming / Qi-stage heat with HIGH FEVER

2 **REGULATES THE QI AND RELIEVES PAIN;**
   BALANCES CIRCULATION AND HARMONIZES DIGESTION, MENSTRUATION AND URINATION

heart Qi constraint (Liver Yang rising): headache in temples and vertex, hot flashes, burning eyes, blurred vision, ringing ears, dizziness, irritability, fast pulse

HYPERTENSION, NEUROCARDIAC SYNDROME, tachycardia

THYROID HYPERFUNCTIONING

lung Qi constraint: wheezing, irritating dry cough, chest pain

ASTHMA (spasmodic, allergic)

stomach Qi constraint: difficult digestion with colic, flatulence, vomiting

uterus Qi constraint: irritability, irregular and painful menstruation

SPASMODIC DYSMENORRHEA

bladder Qi constraint: suppressed or scanty, frequent, painful urination

DYSURIA, STRANGURY

3 **RESTORES THE NERVES, LIFTS THE MIND AND RELIEVES DEPRESSION**

nerve and brain deficiency (Liver and Kidney Essence deficiency): poor memory, absentmindedness, depression, fainting, loss of hearing and vision

NEURASTHENIA, MENTAL DEPRESSION in deficiency and excess conditions

heart Blood and Spleen Qi deficiency: stress, fatigue, dream-disturbed sleep, appetite loss

4 **PROMOTES SWEATING, DISPELS WIND-HEAT AND REDUCES FEVER; PROMOTES EXPECTORATION AND RESOLVES PHLEGM**

external wind-heat: onset of infections with feverishness, aches and pains, unrest, delirium
COLD and FLU ONSET with FEVER
lung phlegm-heat: full cough, coughing up white or greenish sputum, wheezing
ACUTE BRONCHITIS

5 **TONIFIES REPRODUCTIVE QI, HARMONIZES LABOR AND ENHANCES DELIVERY**

INFERTILITY, sterility
PROPHYLACTIC and REMEDIAL in the LAST THREE WEEKS of PREGNANCY and DURING LABOR
DIFFICULT, PAINFUL LABOR

6 **REDUCES CONTUSION AND SWELLING, AND STOPS BLEEDING; REDUCES INFECTION AND ELIMINATES PARASITES; REDUCES TUMORS**

ECCHYMOSIS from injury; engorged breasts
NOSEBLEED, blood in spittle, urine or stool
EYE INFLAMMATIONS, mouth ulcers
HEAD and NECK SWELLINGS, LYMPHADENITIS (scrofula)
VIRAL INFECTIONS (incl. herpes, mumps); TUMORS
CANDIDIASIS (chronic), INTESTINAL PARASITES
INSECT STINGS

PREPARATION

Uses: Melissa leaf is used in **infusion** and **tincture** form. The infusion is a gentle, yet effective nervous *relaxant* and *sedative*—a good unwinder for the evening, before exams or for any stress causing anxiety. Melissa leaf tea is also a pleasant *relaxant digestive/carminative* before, with or after meals. Prepared strong and drunk hot, it causes sweating and reduces fever in wind-heat infections.

The fresh **plant juice, tincture** and **essential oil** bring out Melissa's *relaxing, restoring* and *sedating* properties (see Note below). The costly, precious Melissa essential oil should be diluted no more than 1% in a carrier oil when used topically. These preparations are used to prepare topical **washes, compresses,** etc.

Starting two to three weeks before the due date, Melissa infusion and tincture may also be used in moderate doses for preparing labor.

In the past, Melissa was considered *the* cordial remedy, being the main ingredient in countless cordials—calming, heart and nerve-stabilizing medicinal drinks.

Dosage: Infusion: 8-16 g
      Tincture: 2-5 ml at 1:3 strength in 45% ethanol
      Essential oil: 1 drop in a gel cap topped with some olive oil

To prime the uterus in preparation for labor starting two to three weeks before the due date: take three cups of Melissa infusion or 15-30 drops of the tincture daily.

Caution: Use with caution during pregnancy bacause of its mild *uterine stimulant* effect.

Note: German research indicates that smaller doses of Melissa essential oil might be the most effective (WEISS 1986). Note that true Melissa oil is scarce and expensive because of the low yield. Beware of the cheaper reconstituted "Melissa oil," an analog that is created using lemongrass, citronella and lemon oils as main ingredients.

NOTES

The lovely, fragrant lemon-scented balm was called *melissa* by Ancient Greeks—the same name given to the honeybee. Like the bee's various prod-ucts (honey, royal jelly and propolis), Melissa is an amazing healing plant whose deep therapeutic iden-tity has remained an undisclosed secret to this day.

Melissa leaf received no lack of praise by the ancients. Throughout history Western practitioners used this remedy as a major *restorative*. For PARACELSUS it was the ultimate aging-retardant remedy. Unfortunately, no record explaining his belief has survived from his pen, nor do any indications remain for the preparation of his Melissa elixir of longevity. As so often the case, we have to make do with the often meager recompense of current pharmacological rationalizations to supplement the clinical experience of countless traditional healers. Experimentally the remedy has shown *spasmolytic, sedative* and *restorative* activity.

GALEN maintained that Melissa leaf acted like White horehound herb, but was weaker in effect. Although this perspective is incomplete, it does reveal the fact that (like its botanical cousins White horehound, Motherwort and Bugleweed) Melissa's functions unfold mainly in the rhythmic system of heart, circulation and lungs. Melissa was rightly known as a *cordial* herb in the past, a remedy that treats the heart. Specifically, Melissa operates where nerves and heart, nerve and blood, intersect—where the one affects the other. It is a *neurocardiac* remedy that operates in two modes, restoring and relaxing.

In restoring mode, Melissa leaf is an important *nervous/cerebral restorative*, like Skullcap, St. John's wort anf others in the previous subsection. German research has shown that it influences the brain's limbic system, which explains its effect on the autonomic nervous system and on emotions in general (like Camomile). In Chinese medicine terms this neuroendocrine action translates as a tonification of **Kidney essence** (*jing*). This is surely the basis for the plant's fabled reputation. EUCHARIUS ROESZLIN's statement that it "makes for a quick wit, good understanding and memory" becomes clearer in this respect. **Chronic depression** is another key neurological symptom addressed here.

Because Melissa has *neurocardiac restorative* and *relaxant* actions that essentially stabilize neurocardiac functions, it is appropriate for weak and tense conditions in those presenting physical and mental fatigue, anxiety, depression and palpitations. Melissa is a remedy for intense emotional states of both the depressive *and* manic kinds.

In *relaxing* mode, Melissa leaf affects all inner organs. PITTON DE TOURNEFORT (1716) for example, wrote that it is "prized as an incomparable secret in kidney and bladder pain with anuria when not caused by the presence of stones, and when there is inflammation of the parts that filter and drain urine." Better known generally is Melissa as a *gastrointestinal relaxant,* similar to Camomile flower, releasing constrained Qi from digestive functions. Like Prunella Xia Ku Cao, also called Selfheal spike, the remedy also sinks rising Liver Yang presenting neurological symptoms in the head, and hot flashes. This is useful in **menopause** and with **PMS** arising from **fluid/electrolyte imbalance. Pain relief** from whatever cause is another recurring theme throughout past medical literature on Melissa.

However, because of the plant's paramount content in essential oil, Melissa leaf also excells as a *cardiovascular relaxant.* Like many other remedies in this section, it treats functional cardiovascular conditions that arise from constrained Qi. The main conditions relieved through the plant's *sedative, vasodilatant* and *hypotensive* actions are **anxiety, migraine** and **hypertension**. These are found in the traditional syndromes **heart Qi constraint** and **heart Yin deficiency**. Although the Chinese remedy Polygala Yuan Zhi like Melissa leaf is also a *neurocardiac restorative/relaxant,* there is really nothing exactly like it in the Oriental materia medica. Its sour and somewhat bitter-sweet qualities are energetically unique and distinctive.

Although warmth is the main element in which this plant thrives, allowing it to develop its prec-ious essential oil, Melissa leaf's overall warmth quality is cooling. In a sea of warming, stimulating mints, Melissa is one of the few that actually clear heat. The testimony of early writers makes this clear. The seventh century medical translator AL ISRAILI recommends its use in "atrabilious palpitations caused by burning phlegm," while the contemporary *Book of Experiences* discusses its cold nature at length. The Galenic concept of burning phlegm is equivalent to the Chinese syndromes **Heart fire** and **Heart phlegm-fire.** Both conditions include manic agitation presenting symptoms of heat. Moreover, unlike most other heat-clearing remedies, Melissa also supports and stabilizes the heart in hot conditions such as these.

Marjoram Herb

Botanical source: *Origanum majorana* L.
    (syn. *Majorana hortensis* Moench)
    (Lamiaceae/Labiatae)
Pharmaceutical name: Herba Origani majoranae
Ancient names: Amarakon, Sampsychon (Gr)
Other names: Sweet marjoram, Knotted marjoram
    (Eng)
    Marjolaine, Marjolaine des jardins, Marjolaine
      à coquilles, Marone, Grand origan (Fr)
    Majoran, Meyran, Wurstkraut (Ge)
Part used: the herb

NATURE

Therapeutic category: mild remedy wih minimal chronic toxicity
Constituents: essential oil (incl. terpenes 40%, terpineol, origanol, sabinene, pinene, carvacrol, borneol, camphor), alkaloids, cardioactive glycosides, saponins, tannins 10%, proteins 14%, pentosane, bitters, rosmarinic acid, trace minerals
Effective qualities: somewhat bitter, pungent, sweet and astringent, neutral with warming & cooling potential
    relaxing, restoring, stimulating, astringing, stabilizing
Tropism: reproductive organs, circulation, heart, intestines, bladder, kidneys
    Liver, Heart, Lung, Spleen, Kidney, Bladder, *chong, ren* meridians
    Air, Wamth bodies
Ground: Sanguine krasis; Expressive/Jue Yin and Charming/Yang Ming Earth biotypes
    Lymphatic/Carbonic and Biliary/Phosphoric Iris constitutions

FUNCTIONS AND INDICATIONS

1   **RELAXES CONSTRAINT, CALMS THE MIND AND RELIEVES ANXIETY;**
    SINKS THE YANG, CLEARS HEAT AND REDUCES SEXUAL OVERSTIMULATION

    kidney / adrenal Qi constraint: mental/nervous tension, anxiety, internal trembling sensations
    STRESS-RELATED CONDITIONS in general
    INSOMNIA, ANXIETY STATES, phobias, paranoias
    floating Yang with *mind agitation:* restlessness, anxiety, irritability, agitation
    heart Yin deficiency: anxiety, worry, insomnia, palpitations, hot spells
    SYMPATHETIC NERVOUS HYPERFUNCTIONING
    Kidney fire with Yin deficiency: anxiety, sleeping problems, wet dreams
    SEXUAL OVERSTIMULATION (neurosis)

2   **REGULATES THE QI, RELIEVES PAIN, CLEARS INTERNAL WIND AND STOPS SPASMS**

    heart Qi constraint (Liver Yang rising): dizziness, ringing ears, insomnia, palpitations
    NEUROCARDIAC SYNDROME, menopausal syndrome
    MIGRAINE

intestines Qi constraint (Liver-Spleen disharmony): epigastric/abdominal pains, colic, distension
DYSPEPSIA, COLITIS, IBS
lung Qi constraint: irritable cough, wheezing
ASTHMA, whooping cough
uterus Qi constraint: delayed periods, cramps
SPASMODIC DYSMENORRHEA
nerve excess with *internal wind* and *wind-phlegm obstruction:* nausea, agitation, muscle twitches or
    spasms, facial paralysis, hemiplegia, convulsions
SEIZURES, hysteria, paralysis

3   TONIFIES REPRODUCTIVE QI, REDUCES STAGNATION AND PROMOTES MENSTRUATION; HARMONIZES AND PROMOTES URINATION, RELIEVES IRRITATION AND DISSOLVES STONES

uterus Qi deficiency with Qi/blood stagnation: delayed, scanty or stopped periods, painful flow
AMENORRHEA
INFERTILITY(?)
kidney and bladder damp: scanty or copious urination, lower back pain, white vaginal discharges
URINARY IRRITATION with urgent, difficult, scanty urination, bedwetting
URINARY STONES

PREPARATION

Use: Marjoram leaf is taken in **infusion, tincture** and **essential oil** form, in ascending order of strength. The tincture is the best all-round preparation, because it reproduces most important constituents. The essential oil is taken by inhalation, internally or applied topically with a carrier oil.

As a gynecological remedy, Marjoram herb is used in **sitzbaths, sponges** and **pessaries.** Excellent **liniments** can be made to relax and stimulate painful, tight or cold muscles, using a **sun oil** or the **essential oil** as base. "The oyl is very warming, and comfortable to the joints which are stiffe, and the sinews which are hard, to mollifie, supple and stretch them forth" (WILLIAM COLE 1657).

Marjoram is used in **gargles** and **mouthwashes** for mouth and throat inflammation and pain, and **compresses** can be applied to infected wounds or cuts.

A **medicated snuff** for various conditions in the head was traditionally made from powdered Marjoram herb (singly or in combination with other herbs, including spicy *stimulants* such as Carda-mom pod, Clove bud and Cubeb berry). Marjoram snuff was successfully used for conditions ranging from nasal catarrh (rhinitis) and headache to failing vision, vertigo, coma and facial paralysis

Dosage: Infusion: 6-10 g
      Tincture: 1-4 ml at 1:3 strength in 45% ethanol
      Essential oil: 1-2 drops in a gel cap topped with some olive oil

Caution: Because of its *uterine stimulant* action, contraindicated during pregnancy.

NOTES

Originally a Mediterranean remedy, Marjoram herb was much esteemed in traditional Greek medicine. Historical medical texts since early Greece are full of comments like "strengthens the heart and quickens the bodily spirits and natural strength" (RYFF 1573). "Bodily spirits" here is the equivalent of the vital mind, or Righteous Qi (*zheng qi*). Interestingly, modern research has found the herb to contain cardioactive glycosides and rosmarinic acid (also found in Rosemary herb). Rosmarinic acid has shown *interferon-inducing* and *antioxidant* activity

in the body.

Marjoram has a history of consistent empirical use both as a *restorative* and *relaxant* medicinal. Pharmacological research has revealed an effective *sedative* action on the nervous system. The herb has *parasympathetic nervous stimulant* and *sympathetic nervous antagonist* effects, which explains both its *central nervous* and *neuromuscular sedative/relaxant* actions that affect smooth and striated muscles equally. Like Valerian root, Marjoram is not just *spasmolytic* but somewhat *anticonvulsant,* helping to reduce muscle spasms and seizures. Its reputation among certain practitioners for treating migraine headaches is noteworthy, in this connection. **Anxiety, insomnia, pain, nervous indigestion** and **sexual overstimulation** are key symptoms for the use of Marjoram as a systemic *sedative*. The combination with Melissa, Lavender or Hops for these **constrained Qi** types of conditions will prove adequate for most individuals that tend to heat, while the combination with Valerian root will conversely cover those that tend to cold.

From the perspective of clinical differential diagnosis, Marjoram herb essentially treats conditions of **tension** with aspects of **weakness** and **damp,** and especially with reproductive, cardiovascular and neuromuscular functions involved. Like its fellow *relaxant* mints Skullcap herb and Melissa leaf, this remedy's *nervous relaxant* effect may be reinforced by a possible *cerebral restorative* aspect. Marjoram should find primary long-term use for individuals presenting **constrained Qi** with the typical tense symptoms resulting from stress, overwork or illness. The herb may well also address the resultant long-term cerebral deficiency that typically causes poor concentration, weakening memory and spells of dizziness.

We can also think of Marjoram as a trusted woman's ally with similarities to Motherwort herb. It will relieve spasmodic dysmenorrhea, or **uterus Qi constraint,** in women prone to constrained Qi, and in particular **heart and uterus Qi constraint** presenting tension, anxiety, and difficult, painful periods—a common form of PMS. Here, like Motherwort herb and Cyperus Xiang Fu in Chinese medicine, the herb also acts as both a *neurocardiac* and *neurouterine relaxant*. **Infertility** is another empirical indication for Marjoram which—if it is a true indication—may work because of increased pituitary-gonadotropic secretions.

Lavender Flower

Botanical source: *Lavandula angustifolia* Miller
     (syn. *Lavandula officinalis* Chaix)
     (Lamiaceae/Labiatae)
Pharmaceutical name: Flos Lavandulae
Ancient names: Nardos, Nardostachus (Gr)
     Pseudonardus foemina/masculinum (Lat)
Other names: Lavande, Lavande fine (Fr)
     Lavendel, Kopfwehblume, Tabakblumen (Ge)
Part used: the flower spike

NATURE
Therapeutic category: mild remedy with minimal chronic toxicity
Constituents: essential oil, incl. esters (40-55%) (incl. linalylacetate 30-60%, lavandulyle acetate up to 6%, geranyl acetate), monoterpenols (incl. linalool and its acetic esters 26-50%, geraniol, terpineol, borneol, lavandulol), sesquiterpenes 2-8% (incl. caryophyllene 2-8%, farnesene), monoterpenes 4-5% (incl. limonene, pinene, ocimene, camphene, allo-ocimene), oxides 2% (incl. 1.8 cineole 0.5-2.5%, linalool oxide), ketones 4% (incl. camphor up to 1%, octanone up to 3%); tannins up to 12%, coumaric acid, umbelliferonemethylether, cedrene, luteolin

Effective qualities: somewhat bitter and pungent, cool with some warming potential, dry
    calming, relaxing, sinking, stimulating, dispersing, restoring, astringing
Tropism: brain, nerve, heart, lungs, liver, gallbladder, uterus, bladder, skin
    Heart, Pericardium, Liver, Lung, Spleen, Kidney, *chong, ren*
    Warmth, Air, Fluid
Ground: all krases and constitutions

FUNCTIONS AND INDICATIONS

1 **RELAXES CONSTRAINT, CALMS THE MIND AND RELIEVES ANXIETY;**
  SINKS THE YANG, CLEARS HEAT AND REDUCES FEVER

kidney / adrenal Qi constraint: agitated depression, lower back pain, abdominal cramp, nausea
STRESS-RELATED CONDITIONS in general
INSOMNIA, ANXIETY, incl. with depression and neurasthenia
floating Yang with *mind agitation:* restlessness, anxiety, irritability, agitation
Heart fire / Heart Yin deficiency: insomnia, agitation, dizziness, palpitations
FEVERS in general
TACHYCARDIA, sympathetic nervous hyperfunctioning

2 **REGULATES THE QI AND RELIEVES PAIN;**
  BALANCES CIRCULATION, SETTLES THE STOMACH AND STOPS VOMITING

heart Qi constraint with *nerve excess:* emotional or mental unrest, anxiety, palpitations, sleep loss
NEUROCARDIAC SYNDROME
HYPERTENSION, MIGRAINE
PAIN CONDITIONS
lung Qi constraint: dry nervous cough, wheezing, obsessive thoughts
ASTHMA (spasmodic), whooping cough, bronchitis
intestines Qi constraint: abdominal pain, flatulence, worse with emotions
COLIC, IBS
NAUSEA or VOMITING from *stomach Qi reflux* (incl. morning sickness)

3 **PROMOTES SWEATING, DISPELS WIND-HEAT, REDUCES FEVER AND PROMOTES ERUPTIONS;**
  PROMOTES BILE FLOW, REDUCES LIVER CONGESTION AND PROMOTES URINATION

external wind-heat: aches and pains, fever, headache, unrest, irritability, sore throat
COLD and FLU ONSET with FEVER
head damp-heat and *lung wind-heat:* thin nasal discharge, painful congested sinuses, cough
ERUPTIVE FEVERS with ANURIA (incl. measles, chickenpox)
liver / gallbladder Qi stagnation (with *damp-heat):* sore swollen right flank, nausea, constipation,
    irritability, vomiting, headache
LIVER CONGESTION

4 **STIMULATES CIRCULATION, DISPELS COLD, RESOLVES MUCOUS-DAMP & STOPS DISCHARGE;**
  TONIFIES UROGENITAL QI, PROMOTES MENSTRUATION AND TREATS INFERTILITY

heart Yang deficiency: shortness of breath, palpitations, cyanosed lips and tongue, cold limbs
CIRCULATORY DEFICIENCY, hypothermia
wind-damp-cold obstruction: muscle and joint aches and pains
MYALGIA, NEURALGIA
intestines (Spleen) damp: chilliness, appetite loss, abdominal distension and pain, loose stool
ENTERITIS, COLITIS

kidney and bladder damp: scanty, frequent, clear urination, lumbar pain, clear vaginal discharges,
 delayed, scanty menstruation with cramps
INFERTILITY, LEUCORRHEA, urinary incontinence

5 **RESTORES THE UTERUS AND HARMONIZES LABOR; EXPELS THE AFTERBIRTH**
PROPHYLACTIC and REMEDIAL in the LAST THREE WEEKS of PREGNANCY and during LABOR
DIFFICULT, PAINFUL LABOR
RETAINED PLACENTA

6 **REDUCES INFECTION AND INFLAMMATION, STIMULATES IMMUNITY, ANTIDOTES POISON
AND ELIMINATES PARASITES;
PROMOTES TISSUE REPAIR AND BENEFITS THE SKIN AND HAIR**
INFECTIONS and INFLAMMATIONS (incl. colds, bronchitis, TB, vaginitis, gonorrhea, cystitis, urethritis,
 conjunctivitis, otitis media, gastroenteritis)
INTESTINAL and SKIN PARASITES
ANIMAL and INSECT BITES (incl. black widow spider)
BURNS, scalds, skin inflammations, itching
WOUNDS (simple or atonic), ulcers, gangrene, lice, scabies
SKIN CONDITIONS (incl. eczema, psoriasis, dermatitis, acne, urticaria)
HAIR LOSS

PREPARATION

Use: Lavender flower is used in **infusion, tincture** and **essential oil** form for internal and topical use. The hot infusion is excellent for bouts of wind-heat with feverishness, irritability, aches and sore throat, and for children's eruptive fevers. The tincture is a good general preparation, especially where astriction is required, as in intestinal, genitourinary or sinus damp-cold conditions with catarrhal mucus discharges.

Lavender essential oil is the most effective and comprehensive preparation because it constitutes the greatest part of its various components. Soothing **nebulizer** or **steam inhalations** are excellent for painful congested sinuses and bronchial wheezing. Repeated undiluted applications of the oil on burns, cuts or wounds (including severe ones) will reduce pain and prevents scarring.

Both tincture and essential oil are used topically in **washes, creams, liniments, sitzbaths** and **enemas.** The essential oil is especially effective in **pessaries, vaginal sponges** and **douches.** .

Lavender is an important remedy for preparing for **childbirth** and can make every aspect of the birth easier and smoother. During the first stage of labor, the **essential oil** can be used in **massage** with a carrier oil or taken internally. The oil's *relaxant parturient* action is especially appropriate when contractions are hypertonic. Because of its *relaxant* nature, Lavender oil is generally one of the best fragrances for the delivery room, used in a diffusor or atomiser.

Dosage: Infusion: 8-12 g
 Tincture: 2-4 ml at 1:3 strength in 60% ethanol
 Essential oil: 1-3 drops in a gel cap topped with some olive oil
• *To prime the uterus starting two to three weeks before the due date:* take 15-30 drops of the tincture once daily.
• *To promote or restart labor:* take 1/2-1 teaspoon of the tincture every half hour until contractions resume.
Caution: Lavender is contraindicated during the main part of pregnancy as it is a *uterine stimulant.*

NOTES

The word "lavender" conjures up a kaleidoscope of images. Euphorically fragrant fields of purple lavender swaying in the warm billows of the *mistral* in the French Haute Provence mountains. Sybaritic early Romans luxuriating in lavender water baths. HILDEGARD VON BINGEN in her cloister herb garden in St. Gallen, Switzerland, meditating over her lavender plants. Early European apothecaries preparing *eau de Cologne* with freshly distilled lavender and bergamot essential oils. The street cries for lavender posies in bustling 19th century London. French chemist RENE GATTEFOSSE plunging a badly burnt arm into a vat of lavender essential oil at the beginning of this century, thereby fatalistically discovering its amazing *analgesic, anti-inflammatory* and *tissue-healing* properties.

Lavender is one of the few plants that has seen both consistent and widespread use from earliest to modern times. Although its evocative herbaceous-floral scent currently enjoys popularity with the ongoing increase in herbal and aromatherapy treatments, lavender has long been loved for its fine scent, soothing effect and—for household linen—its freshening and antiseptic properties. RYFF's *Deutsche Apotheck* of 1573, for example, describes a 33-ingredient Lavender Water among the six folio pages devoted to the remedy. With the widespread availability of Lavender essential oil, we now see increased exploration of its versatile therapeutic effects, its emotionally soothing and blancing fragrance, and its usefulness for household first-aid situations and minor complaints. More importantly, we are beginning to explore the fascinating vibrational and energetic applications of this remedy. As substance, fragrance and energy, Lavender flower holds secrets for us yet, as we continue to explore its uses for bodily, emotional and mental well-being.

Lavender flower essentially harmonizes opposites. Its deepest identity, among its many functions, is that of a systemic *relaxant* that regulates the Qi. Working through the nervous and cardiovascular system, Lavender is an excellent example of a remedy possessing the potential to both cool/sedate because of its bitter taste, and warm/stimulate because of its pungent taste—somewhat like Valerian root, in fact. This bivalency is also reflected in its essential oil composition, which is basically a balance of relaxing esters (c. 45%) and more resoring alcohols (c. 36%). Lavender's actual effect will therefore depend on factors such as the person's condition and the type and quantity of preparation being used. For instance, in a person with a hot, acute condition such as **floating Yang**—typified by congestion, inflammation or fever, the remedy will have a *refrigerant, anti-inflammatory* or *antipyretic* effect. On the other hand, when given to someone with a cold and more chronic condition—characterised by chills, fatigue, cold

extremities, etc.—a more generous use of lavender will generate warmth and activity, both local and systemic. In these conditions Lavender also resolves **mucous-damp** pervading the digestive and reproductive organs. The celebrated and erudite physician IBN BAITAR (1225) from the Al-Andalus period in Spain states in this connec tion that "it warms the uterus, arrests chronic discharges, restores its health and helps nubile women to conceive; this is a fact of experience."

This bivalent effect is particularly evident in the cardiovascular system. In excess conditions such as **heart fire** entailing palpitations, rapid heart beat, fever, anxiety or agitation, Lavender has a *sedating* action—at once slowing down the heart rate, calming the mind and soothing the emotions. In deficiency conditions such as **heart Yang deficiency** presenting heart weakness, shortness of breath, fatigue on exertion, cold extremities, depression, etc., it has a *stimulating* action—equally increasing cardiac action, body energy and mood. As a herb that regulates and supports heart Qi, Lavender acts somewhat like acupuncture points Ht 7, P 6, Bl 15 and CV 14.

Likewise, at the onset of an infection with **wind-heat** presenting symptoms such as fever, sore throat, headache, aches and pains and unrest, Lavender's predominantly calming action—*anti-inflammatory, analgesic, antipyretic* and *nervous sedative*—will relieve those symptoms resulting from the individual's response to infection. However, this essential oil's mainly *stimulating* actions —*diaphoretic, anti-infective* (including *immunostimulant*) and *antiseptic*—will simultaneously also directly address the source of the symptoms—the infection itself.

Lavender is well-known for its *sedative* action on the nervous system, especially the brain and autonomic functions. The remedy seems to selectively inhibit either sympathetic or parasympathetic activity (DURAFFOURD 1982). It therefore assists responses to unproductive stress of any kind, adaptively moderating its impact and lessening any resultant symptoms. Lavender can exert either a *sedative* or *stimulant* action, depending on need. It will act as a *nerve sedative* in those presenting mental and emotional agitation, calming the mind, comforting feelings and alleviating fears. However, in those with mental and emotional depletion and depression present, or with literal fainting, lavender has a mild *stimulating* effect: the remedy will ease depression and tend to revive the spirits.

Compassion and gentleness are the keynotes for Lavender as an important, versatile remedy for accidents, injuries and crises. Burns, inflammations, animal and insect bites, wounds, ulcers, lice, and pain and infection in general, all respond very well to lavender applications. The calming, relaxing action of Lavender for insomnia, anxiety, anger, manic depression, asthma, menstrual cramps and digestive colic are further examples of its compassionate nature. In particular, Lavender excells at **acute crisis managment,** e.g., a family crisis, the crisis of stopping an addiction (whether nicotine, caffeine, alcohol, sugar or recreational drugs), as well as emotional crises of all kinds.

Melilot Herb

Botanical source: *Melilotus officinalis* Pallas,
      M. altissimus Pallas (Leguminosae)
Pharmaceutical name: Herba Meliloti
Ancient names: Meliloton (Gr)
      Corona regia, Trifolium melilotus (Lat)
Other names: Sweet clover, Yellow sweet clover,
      Hart's clover, King's clover, Heartwort (Eng
      and Am)
      Mélilot, Trèfle de cheval/des mouches,
      Mirlirot (Fr)
      Steinklee, Honigklee, Ziegenkraut,
      Schabenklee, Mottenklee (Ge)
Part used: the herb

NATURE
Therapeutic category: mild remedy with minimal chronic toxicity
Constituents: flavonoids (incl. melilotoside, coumarin), hydro and orthocoumaric acid, mucilage, tannins, essential oil (incl. melilotic lactone), trace minerals
Effective qualities: somewhat bitter and sweet, cold, dry
      relaxing, calming, decongesting, diluting
Tropism: liver, heart, intestines, nervous system, veins
      Liver, Heart, Lung, Large Intestine, *du* meridians
      Warmth, Air, Fluid bodiess
Ground: Sanguine and Choleric krases
      Hematogenic/Sulphuric constitution

FUNCTIONS AND INDICATIONS
1   **RELAXES CONSTRAINT, CALMS THE MIND AND RELIEVES ANXIETY;
      SINKS THE YANG AND CLEARS HEAT**

      kidney / adrenal Qi constraint: mental/nervous tension, unrest, pains
      STRESS-RELATED CONDITIONS in general
      floating Yang (Yang excess): head congestion, headache, muscle tension, sleep loss, irritability
      INSOMNIA, ANXIETY, restlessness (esp. in children, elderly, convalescents)

SYMPATHETIC NERVOUS HYPERFUNCTIONING

heart fire: palpitations, agitation, irritability, anxiety, hot spells, poor sleep

CHRONIC STRESS, menopausal syndrome

2 **REGULATES THE QI AND RELIEVES PAIN AND WHEEZING;**
BALANCES CIRCULATION AND HARMONIZES DIGESTION

heart Qi constraint (Liver Yang rising): irritability, pounding headache, ringing ears, dizziness

HYPERTENSION, neurocardiac syndrome

PAIN CONDITIONS, incl:

NEURALGIA, neuritis (incl. sciatica)

TENSION HEADACHE, OVARIAN PAIN

PAIN in ears (e.g. in otitis), stomach, uterus, ovaries, rectum, bladder

lung Qi constraint: wheezing, tight painful chest

ASTHMA (spamodic)

intestines Qi constraint: abdominal pains and flatulence, stress, worry, irregular stool

DIGESTIVE COLIC, IBS

3 **VITALIZES THE BLOOD AND LYMPH, REMOVES CONGESTION AND MODERATES MENSES;**
RESTORES THE VEINS AND THINS THE BLOOD

venous blood stagnation: varicosities, heavy or aching legs, leg cramps at night, fatigue

VENOUS DEFICIENCY, phlebitis, hemorrhoids

BLOOD HYPERVISCOSITY, thrombosis

uterus blood congestion: early, copious menstruation, dull pelvic pressure or pain before onset

CONGESTIVE DYSMENORRHEA

LYMPHADENITIS

4 **CLEARS DAMP-HEAT AND REDUCES INFLAMMATION, SWELLING AND CONTUSION;**
SOFTENS BOILS AND DRAWS PUS

intestines damp-heat: burning, loose stool, unrest

ENTERITIS, colitis, dysentery

EYE INFLAMMATIONS of all types

SURFACE SWELLING and INFLAMMATIONS (incl. injuries, erysipelas, hard or sore breasts during
 nursing, mastitis)

heat toxin: boils, furuncles, abscesses, fever

ULCERS, CONTUSIONS, injuries, skin ulcers and tumors

PREPARATION

Use: Melilot herb is taken in **infusion** and **tincture** form. **Compresses, washes,** and so on, make good use of this remedy for topical and first aid conditions, especially in those involving pain and swelling (e.g., conjunctivitis, boils, abdominal pain and rheumatic pain). For these, the compound Melilot **plaster** was an official remedy in traditional European pharmacies.

 Steam inhalations with the herb are said to relieve sinus and middle ear pain.

Dosage: Infusion: 4-10 g

 Tincture: 0.5-3 ml (average is 1.5 ml) at 1:3 strength in 50% ethanol

Caution: Because Melilot herb's coumarin content impairs blood clotting, do not use before surgery or childbirth.

NOTES

Although incorrect by modern botanical classification, melilot in the Greek medical tradition has always been considered one of the various types of clovers. Because of its warm, aromatic, hay-like scent, its leaf formation and bright yellow, sweet pea-like flowers, melilot herb was—and still is—called a "Yellow clover."

Therapeutically, Melilot herb belies the warm, dry and stony conditions favorable to its growth. On the contrary, like the other "clovers" Marsh clover *(Menyanthes)* and Clover broom *(Baptisia)*, Yellow clover is a reliable *relaxant, refrigerant* and *sedative* remedy. This includes *sympathetic nervous inhibition* and *spasmolytic* and *analgesic* actions. Melilot is ideal for treating tense conditions with constrained Qi and heat. The herb should be selected for those presenting **floating Yang** or **heart Qi constraint** with restlessness, insomnia, irritability and throbbing headaches. No question that Melilot is a contemporary remedy for stress-induced hyperactivity: it moves congested blood and heat down from the head and, in tandem with a *nervous sedative* action, promotes relaxation and rest. As a *neurocardiac relaxant* with *hypotensive* action Melilot is also appropriate in formulas for conditions as varied as **menopausal syndrome, hypertension** and **sleep disorders.**

Melilot herb's predilection as a plant for heavy, "sucking" limestone terrain has resulted in a remedy that has challenged gravity's pull and developed the energy to oppose it. Through its flavonoids and coumarins, Melilot has created the ability to stimulate the venous circulation that rises against gravity. The result is a good herb for vitalizing the blood and reducing blood stasis, including conditions of **uterus blood congestion** or **congestive dysmenorrhea** with heavy flow. Melilot's *blood-decongestant* action involves increased venous tone and capillary permeability. Disorders caused by hyperviscous blood, such as the tendency to **thrombosis,** are also helped with the remedy's *anticoagulant* action.

In Greek medicine Melilot was highly regarded as a *demulcent* with *anti-inflammatory* and *detoxicant* actions. It was used both internally and externally for **fire toxin** conditions presenting swelling, redness and pain, such as intestines damp-heat (acute enteritis), conjunctivitis and pyoderma (hot boils and the like). The Melilot plaster was one of the mainstays of Greek external treatment and was available in pharmacies up to the nineteenth century. Its *emollient, softening* and *pus-drawing* properties helped reduce hard, painful swellings, including those from injury, boils, swollen lymph glands and breast lumps.

Black Cohosh Root

Botanical source: *Cimicifuga racemosa* Nuttall
    (syn. *Actaea racemosa*) (Ranunculaceae)
Pharmaceutical name: Rhizoma Cimicifugae
Other names: Black snakeroot, Bugbane, Rattletop,
    Richweed, Squawroot, Macrotys (Am)
    Actée à grappe, Herbe au punaises (Fr)
    Schwarze Schlangenwurzel, Silberkerze,
    Wanzenkraut, Schwindsuchtwurzel (Ge)
Part used: the rhizome

NATURE

Therapeutic category: mild remedy with minimal chronic toxicity

Constituents: resin 15-20% (cimicifugin), aromatic acids (incl. isoferulic and salicylic acids), essential oil, bitter glycoside (racemosin), alkaloid anemonin, triterpenoids (incl. xylosides actein, cimicifugoside, acerylacreol, desoxyacrein, cimigenol, desoxyacetylacteol), estrogenic phytosterol, palmitic/oleic-butyric/gallic acid, salicylic acid, isoflavonoid (formononetin) saponin, tannin, mucilage, fatty oil, sulphur, potassium, magnesium and potassium phosphate

Effective qualities: somewhat pungent, bitter and sweet, cool, dry
  relaxing, calming, stimulating, restoring

Tropism: lungs, heart, circulation, stomach, kidneys, reproductive organs
  Liver, Lung, Heart, Kidney, *chong, ren* meridians
  Air, Warmth bodies

Ground: Sanguine, Choleric krases; Expressive/Jue Yin, Charming/Yang Ming earth biotypes

FUNCTIONS AND INDICATIONS

1 **RELAXES CONSTRAINT AND CALMS THE MIND;**
  CLEARS EMPTY HEAT AND REDUCES FEVER AND INFLAMMATION

  kidney / adrenal Qi constraint: mental/nervous tension, agitation (esp. from pain, chronic stress, mental or physical exhaustion)

  Heart and Kidney Yin deficiency: hot spells, sleep loss, irritability, unrest, anxiety, rapid weak pulse
  INSOMNIA, TACHYCARDIA
  INTERMITTENT and REMITTENT FEVERS (*shao yin* and *shao yang* stages)

  lung Yin deficiency and *lung heat-dryness:* dry painful cough, fever, irritability
  ACUTE BRONCHITIS, whooping cough, croup, lung TB, pleurisy

2 **REGULATES THE QI AND RELIEVES PAIN;**
  OPENS THE CHEST AND RELIEVES COUGHING AND WHEEZING;
  BALANCES CIRCULATION, CLEARS INTERNAL WIND AND STOPS SPASMS

  MUSCLE TENSION with soreness, pain (incl. from strains)
  PAIN, esp. MYALGIA (esp. congestive, dull, aching, sore, intermittent, irregular pain; with fever, inflammation; esp. uterine, ovarian, prostate, seminal vesicle, rheumatic [fibromyalgia], arthritic, thorassic, abdominal, sacral, spinal, sciatic)

  lung Qi constraint: nervous dry cough, wheezing, sore chest, constricted sternum
  SPASMODIC ASTHMA (esp. with Yin deficiency or heat)
  BRONCHITIS (acute and chronic)

  heart Qi constraint (Liver Yang rising): palpitations, anxiety, stress, headaches, ringing ears, dizziness
  NEUROCARDIAC SYNDROME (incl. menopausal),
  TINNITUS, HYPERTENSION, tachycardia

  uterus Qi constraint: delayed, irregular or difficult menstruation, severe cramps with onset of flow, varying flow, irritability, stress
  SPASMODIC DYSMENORRHEA, IRREGULAR CYCLES

  nerve excess with *internal wind:* unrest, tremors, twitches, convulsions
  SEIZURES (incl. of infants, chorea, epilepsy)

3 **TONIFIES REPRODUCTIVE QI, PROMOTES MENSTRUATION & STOPS DISCHARGE & BLEEDING;**
  INCREASES ESTROGEN

  uterus blood and Qi deficiency: short, delayed or stopped painful periods, dry skin and hair, fatigue
  AMENORRHEA, vaginal dryness

ESTROGEN DEFICIENCY conditions, incl.:

PMS with irritability, headache, sleep loss, hot flashes, joint and muscle pains, sore or painful breasts

MENOPAUSAL SYNDROME with HOT FLASHES, dizziness, ringing ears, palpitations, headaches, irritability, depression

kidney and bladder Qi deficiency with damp: fatigue, lumbar pain, clear vaginal discharges, premature ejaculation, female infertility

GENITAL DISCHARGES (incl. leucorrhea, spermatorrhea, gonorrhea)

UTERINE HEMORRHAGE, intermenstrual and postpartum bleeding

4   HARMONIZES AND PROMOTES LABOR, AND ENHANCES DELIVERY

PROPHYLACTIC and REMEDIAL in the LAST THREE WEEKS of PREGNANCY and during LABOR

DIFFICULT, PAINFUL LABOR with irregular, hypertonic contractions

FAILURE to PROGRESS during LABOR

RETAINED PLACENTA, POSTPARTUM PAIN and BLEEDING

UTERINE SUBINVOLUTION

5   PROMOTES SWEATING, DISPELS WIND-HEAT, REDUCES FEVER AND PROMOTES ERUPTIONS; PROMOTES URINATION, RESOLVES TOXICOSIS AND ANTIDOTES POISON

lung wind-heat: aching muscles or "bones", headache, earache, fever, sore throat, dry cough, irritability

COLD or FLU ONSET with FEVER

ERUPTIVE FEVERS (incl. measles, smallpox, scarlet fever)

wind-damp-heat obstruction: muscle or joint pains, back pain, fever, irritability

URIC ACID DIATHESIS, arthritis

FIBROMYALGIA (acute and chronic), rheumatic fever

SNAKE and INSECT BITES

6   STIMULATES DIGESTION

stomach Qi stagnation: dull epigastric or abdominal pain, appetite loss, indigestion

CHRONIC GASTRITIS, acute gastric dyspepsia

PREPARATION

Use: Black cohosh root is used in **decoction** or **tincture** form. A tincture prepared from the dried root less than a year old is needed to obtain the full effect and spectrum of the above actions and indications.

In gynecology, Black cohosh is an excellent *childbirth preparer,* especially for women prone to some of the above syndromes. Its gentle *uterine relaxant* action helps prepare for labor when taken starting about three weeks before the due date. As the due date approaches, this remedy is also said to be a "diagnostic agent to differentiate between spurious and true labor pains, the latter being increased, while the former are dissipated under its use" (JOHN KING 1852).

During the first stage of labor, Black cohosh is a *relaxant oxytocic parturient,* like Lobelia root and herb. It encourages regular, strong contractions while reducing pain and calming the mother.

After delivery, Black cohosh may be successfully used to assist uterine involution and lessen postpartum bleeding and pain through its action of relaxing postpartum uterine spasms.

Dosage: Decoction: 6-12 g

      Tincture: 1-3 ml at 1:2 strength in 60% ethanol (max. 40 ml per week)

• *To prime the uterus for labor starting two or three weeks before the due date:* take 20-40 drops of the tincture once a day.

• *To promote or restart labor:* take 1/2-1 teaspoon of the tincture every half hour until contractions resume.

Caution: Contraindicated during the first trimester of pregnancy, except for uterine or breast pain, because of its *uterine relaxant* action.

In some individuals high doses may cause frontal headaches (MILLS and BONE 2000).

NOTES

Black cohosh was one of several "squaw roots" handed down from American Indian practices from the seventeenth century onwards. The name refers to the plant's traditional use by Native women during pregnancy and childbirth, as well as around menstruation. After JOHN KING began publicising its properties in 1844, and right up to the early twentieth century, Black cohosh was routinely used as an obstetrical remedy by many thousands of midwives and doctors throughout the U.S. The remedy established a solid reputation as fully the equal of Blackhaw bark both as a childbirth preparer before the due date and an oxytocic parturient during labor. See the Preparation section above for further discussion.

To fully understand this complex *relaxant* remedy as a whole, however, it is neccessary to assess its secondary *sedative, stimulant* and *restorative* actions. Black cohosh root essentially addresses tense conditions (both hyper and hypo tense) accompanied by aspects of heat and damp. With its slew of *spasmolytic, analgesic* and mild *nervous depressant* actions, the remedy treats both localised and systemic conditions of **constrained Qi**. It excells in particular in relaxing female reproductive functions, targeting two levels simultaneously: symptom relief of **menstrual cramps** and systemic regulation of **uterus Qi constraint.** The latter involves an *estrogenic* action that addresses deficient estrogen and/or excessive progesterone levels, thereby benefitting the woman with irregular cycles, spasmodic dysmenorrhea and PMS with irritability, oversensitivity, anxiety, depression, headache and insomnia, and menopausal syndrome in general. White peony root, Dong quai root, Cramp bark and Motherwort herb are examples of nice complementary herbs here.

Black cohosh's secondary *uterine restorative* and *mucostatic* actions are useful in **amenorrhea** and chronic clear leucorrhea. Here, combining it with its namesake, Blue cohosh root, as well as with a more *restorative* herb like Helonias root or Red clover flower, would be very appropriate.

Black cohosh root is also deservedly well known for its *relaxant* effect on the bronchial tract, said to be due to the steroidal nature of its saponins. Its *anti-inflammatory* and *bronchodilatory* actions will help relieve various tense respiratory conditions arising from **constrained lung Qi**— typified by an irritating, painful dry cough and chest pain. Most types of asthma, whooping cough, and so on, are relieved in this connection. For those presenting **lung Yin deficiency** with dry heat, this remedy should also be considered—if we can rely on the reports of nineteenth century Eclectic medics—and we surely can. Class 10 *demulcents* that nourish lung Yin should be included in formulations here.

Black cohosh is less understood but still significant as a *neurocardiac relaxant, parasympathetic relaxant, peripheral vasorelaxant* and *cerebral depressant* that addresses conditions of **tension with empty heat.** These are found during perimenopause, in the aftermath of chronic disease with low-grade tidal fever or simply as a result of an extreme lifestyle with chronic stress. Here Black cohosh addresses the syndromes **heart Qi cons-traint** and its follow-up, **Heart and Kidney Yin deficiency.** Keynote symptoms in the latter are palpitations, hot spells, anxiety and watery genital discharges. In tachycardia and hypertension the remedy specifically strengthens and slows down heart functions—like Bugleweed and Motherwort herb. Black Cohosh shares with Scrophularia Xuan Shen (Black figwort) from North China the ability to address both these syndromes. A good Western synergy for these conditions might be Black cohosh, Bugleweed and Hawthorn berry.

Because of its particular tropism for muscle tissues, Black cohosh root also plays out a *neuromuscular relaxant* effect. **Rheumatic, myalgic** and **arthritic** disorders of the **wind-damp-heat obstruction** type also benefit here from Black cohosh's concerted *analgesic, anti-inflammatory* and *diaphoretic* actions. We are looking at a specific remedy for local or generalized congestive, dull muscular aching and soreness—whether involving acute or chronic forms of rheumatism, fibromyalgia, onset of flu, or that arising during labor.

The *relaxant diaphoretic* effect works particularly well in **lung wind-heat** syndromes displaying low fever, aching muscles, sore throat, headache and dry cough. It will be nicely complemented in this condition with such herbs as Feverfew, Vervain, Melissa and Lavender.

Valerian Root

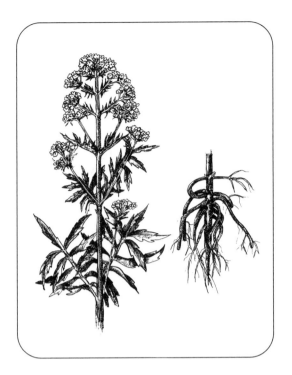

Botanical source: *Valeriana officinalis* L. and spp.
(Valerianaceae)
Pharmaceutical name: Rhizoma Valerianae
Ancient names: Phu (Gr)
Amantilla, Dacia, Genicularis, Marcinella (Lat)
Other names: All-heal, Capon's tail, Setwell, Cut-
heal, Treacle (Eng)
Fragrant valerian, Dysentery root, Tobacco root
(Am)
Valériane, Herbe aux chats (Fr)
Baldrian, Speerkraut, Denmark, Augenwurz,
Balderbracken (Ge)
Part used: the rhizome

NATURE

Therapeutic category: medium-strength remedy with moderate chronic toxicity
Constituents: essential oil (incl. valerianic acid, borneol, bornyl acetate/formate/isovalerianate, isovaler-
oxydidrovaltrate, camphene, pinene, sesquiterpenes, terpenoid alcohols/acids/aldehydes/esters/ketones up
to 1.4%, eugenol, terpenes [incl. monoterpene iridin]), volatile alkaloids (incl. valerianine, chatarine,
chatinine), iridoid valepotriates (incl. valtrate, didrovaltrate, acevaltrate, valechlorine, isovalerocyhydrin),
sesquiterpene alcohol valerianol, GABA, choline, glycosides, ferments, caffeic/tannic acid, glucose, resin,
minerals (incl. magnesium, potassium, copper, zinc)
Effective qualities: somewhat sweet, bitter and pungent, warm with cooling potential, dry
relaxing, restoring, stimulating, decongesting
Tropism: heart, arterial circulation, brain, spine and nerves, lungs, uterus, kidney, bladder, pancreas
Heart, Pericardium, Lung, Spleen, Kidney meridians; Air, Fluid bodies
Ground: Sanguine krasis; Charming/Yang Ming Earth and Expressive/Jue Yin biotypes
Lymphatic/Carbonic/Blue Iris constitution

FUNCTIONS AND INDICATIONS

1 **RELAXES CONSTRAINT, CALMS THE MIND AND RELIEVES ANXIETY;**
CLEARS EMPTY HEAT AND REDUCES FEVER

kidney / adrenal Qi constraint: agitated depression, kidney or sacral pain
SEVERE or ACUTE STRESS-RELATED CONDITIONS
Heart and Kidney Yin deficiency: mental/nervous unrest, anxiety, irritability, hot spells, sleep loss
INSOMNIA, ANXIETY STATES, phobias, neuroses, paranoias
LOW-GRADE TIDAL FEVERS with empty heat (*shao yin* stage)
MENOPAUSAL SYNDROME, PMS

2 **REGULATES THE QI AND RELIEVES PAIN;**
CLEARS INTERNAL WIND AND STOPS SPASMS

heart Qi constraint with *nerve excess:* palpitations, sleep loss, emotional distress, worry
NEUROCARDIAC SYNDROME, spasmodic angina
TENSION HEADACHE, MIGRAINE, PAIN in general

lung Qi constraint: wheezing, dry nervous cough
ASTHMA (incl. cardiac asthma)
genitourinary Qi constaint: irregular, painful menstruation, difficult, painful scanty urination
nerve excess with *internal wind:* agitation, tremors, muscle spasms, convulsions
SEIZURES, CHOREA, EPILEPSY, hysteria

3 **STIMULATES THE HEART, CIRCULATION AND BRAIN, AND RELIEVES DEPRESSION**

heart Qi and Yang deficiency: palpitations, shortness of breath, cold limbs, mental depression
CARDIOVASCULAR DEFICIENCY
nerve and brain deficiency (Heart phlegm obstruction): mental stupor, headache, dizziness, depression
CEREBRAL DEFICIENCY/ISCHEMIA, concussion, cerebral contusion
CHRONIC NERVOUS DEPRESSION from stress, chronic or severe disease; catatonia, hypochondria
SPINAL WEAKNESS
Heart Blood and Spleen Qi deficiency: fatigue, insomnia, poor memory, appetite loss

4 **STIMULATES DIGESTION, PROMOTES URINATION, STRENGTHENS THE EYES AND ENHANCES VISION**

liver and stomach Qi stagnation: poor appetite, indigestion, epigastric pain, constipation
DYSPEPSIA
DIABETES (supportive)
VISION IMPAIRMENT

5 **STIMULATES IMMUNITY, REDUCES INFECTION AND ANTIDOTES POISON; ELIMINATES PARASITES AND PROMOTES TISSUE REPAIR**

PROPHYLACTIC in EPIDEMICS
FOOD or HERB POISONING
INTESTINAL PARASITES
BITES and STINGS
INJURIES, fractures, chronic ulcers (all internal or external)
SPLINTERS (drawing action)

PREPARATION

Use: Valerian root is prepared by **cold infusion** or **tincture**. The fresh root will make better preparations, partly or even entirely because it is simpler to use and poses less chance of unpredictable results (see also below) (Swiss folk tradition and MOORE 1993). Valerian **wine** is another stimulating and warming traditional preparation.

Enemas and **suppositories** have proved useful in the above menstrual and kidney conditions. Valerian is an effective topical *vulnerary* in **washes, fomentations** and the like for injuries, fractures and for drawing splinters.

Homeopathic preparations are also used for the same indications as above, with an emphasis on the empty heat and Qi constraint symptomatology.

Dosage: The dosage varies with the effect needed as well as with the person taking it. Some people respond to Valerian root more quickly or strongly than others.

As a general rule, Valerian root has three dosage levels:
• A **low dosage** for *restoring* (functions 3 and 4);
• A **medium dosage** for *stimulating* and *relaxing* (functions 1, 2 and 5 mainly);
• A **high dosage** for greater *sedating* effects. The problem with the high dosage is that there is a chance that Valerian may produce the opposite effects, namely excess symptoms like excitation, headache and vision disturbances. Valerian root can be variable and unpredictable, partly because of different consitutional responses, and partly because that is the nature of the dried root.

• *Low dose:*

  Cold infusion: 2 tsp of finely–chopped or ground root steeped in two cups of cold water for at least 10-20 hrs. This is a one-day supply. Warm up before drinking.

  Tincture: 0.5-1 ml (5-25 drops) at 1:2 strength in 50% ethanol

• *Medium dose:*

  Cold infusion: 4 tsp prepared as above for a one-day supply

  Tincture: 1-2 ml at 1:2 strength in 50% ethanol

• *High dose:*

  Tincture: 2-5 ml at 1:2 strength in 50% ethanol

Caution: Do not exceed the recommended doses. Because it is a medium–strength remedy with some cumulative toxicity, Valerian root should either be used intermittently or as a 10% maximum component in a formula. The root may produce a mild dependence and eventually create the same symptoms that it initially relieved (an example of spontaneous homeopathic proving?). Extreme excessive or high dosage use can cause paralysis and heart problems.

In **tincture** form (especially when prepared from the dried root), Valerian should be restricted to conditions of Qi constraint and Yin deficiency with empty heat, and never given to those with full heat conditions, sthenic fevers or inflammations. The exception is acute situations like migraine and epileptic or hysteric convulsions.

Valerian should not be taken with sleep medications, as it has a potentizing effect on these.

NOTES

In German–speaking countries valerian has significantly been given well over 500 distinct names. The Romans already graced the plant with a string of feminine names. This reflects its traditional importance and confirms an impression often obtained when the plant is seen in sunny woodland clearings, for instance: tall, upright, crowned with minute pale pink blossoms and exuding a delicate fragrance, somewhat like a princess.

Valerian is a good example not only of versatile naming, but also of polyvalent therapeutic use. As a remedy it has also undergone several changes of fashions—appropriately enough for this herb. Before the arrival of germ theory in the last century, Valerian root was regarded essentially as a *restorative* remedy to the heart, mind and eyes. It was a main ingredient in the thick, dark all-purpose Theriack paste that gave it one of its many names, "Treacle." Chamaeleon that it is, Valerian's image today has changed to the exact opposite. It is now popularly seen as a reliable herbal *sedative* in the pharmaceutical sense.

Clearly it is time to cut through the images that this elusive, paradoxic herb has generated. For a start, Valerian root's *nervous sedative* action, although present, does not go as deep as that of Wild lettuce or Yellow jessamine, for instance (MILLS 1980). Its action is *hypnotic* and *euphoric* rather than *depressant*—which is why it *treats* depression (see below). The remedy excels at relieving anxie-ty states, emotional distress and paranoid conditions due to a *neurocardiac sedative* action. It does not interfere with activity and coordination like numerous other herbs.

We can gain a more secure basis for understanding this plant by reviewing it in the light of vitalistic pharmacology. This can provide us with a therapeutic basis that is anything but speculative or ephemeral. Valerian root's mild sweet and bitter taste qualities clearly reveal its *restoring* potential. Fundamentally, this remedy is a *nervous* and *cardiovascular restorative* with a particular tropism for the brain. The famous physician CHRISTOPH HUFE-LAND in the early 1800s, for example, used this remedy for "chronic weakness of the nerves." Eclectic practitioners like HARVEY FELTER IN THE 1900S above all stressed application for "enfeebled cerebral circulation."

It has been suggested (SIMONIS, PELIKAN) that Valerian's real identity is the result of phosphorus bioenergies. This element that in Greek means "light-bearer" is intimately connected with the substance of the nervous system that brings us the light of sensation and consciousness. There is something to be said for the traditional use of Valerian for those presenting **cerebral/nervous deficiency** (e.g., ischemia) accompanied by memory loss, long-term mental depression and poor vision. For two-thousand years, Valerian was in fact considered the main herb for promoting clear thinking and maintaining good eyesight. Valerian is a perfect remedy for deficiencies caused by chronic stress or disease.

Like the energy of phosphorus itself, Valerian root also possesses cool, dry, contracting qualities that clear symptoms of empty heat. By impressing the cool, calm and hidden sphere of brain and nerves, this remedy proves useful in such syndromes as **Kidney and Heart Yin deficiency**—like the companion *neurocardiac restoratives* Hawthorn berry and Lily of the valley herb. Hot spells, low-grade fever and restlessness are resolved in this connection.

Closely connected with the above actions is Valerian's systemic *relaxant* effect. This is evident in its pungent taste, arising from the content in essential oil, valepotriates and (iso)valerianic acids. A *spasmolytic* action is evident on the smooth muscles, addressing various **Qi Constraint** syndromes. Traditionally this action was also successfully applied to the treatment of conditions involving seizures. This *anticonvulsant* effect Chinese medicine describes as a clearing of **internal wind.**

The root's pungent taste also carries stimulating and warming dynamics, however, which come to the fore in the *dried root* tincture preparation. Here the paradoxical plant goes for the rhythmic region of the chest. Like Rosemary, the unlikely Valerian stimulates **Heart** and **Lung Yang,** thereby turning around apathy and depression. Coronary deficiency is improved (Qi moves blood), and asthmatic conditions from Lung and Kidney Yang deficiency are relieved. Far from throwing a monkey wrench in its pharmacological works, therefore, Valerian's mild pungency through hormonal feedback creates a link between the nervous system and the heart, and between the heart/lungs and kidneys. Small wonder that the German physician WEISENBERG in 1853 elegantly summed up Valerian as a "*stimulating nervine.*" As such, a comparison with Pasqueflower is inevitable. Both herbs combine *restoring, stimulating* and *relaxing* actions on virtually the same organs.

The final outcome of Valerian's paradoxic actions is this. In terms of the six conditions, it addresses tense and weak conditions with empty cold or empty heat. Therefore the remedy will successfully treat insomnia, fatigue, depression, anxiety, hot spells and cold extremities only in those individuals in whom these arise from deficiency, not hyperfunctioning. Valerian only promotes rest and sleep with exhaustion, not overstimulation present—when the person needs to recuperate. Anything else is liable to fail.

Lobelia Root and Herb

Botanical source: *Lobelia inflata* L. (Lobeliaceae)
Pharmaceutical name: Radix et herba Lobeliae inflatae
Other names: Indian tobacco, Bladderpod, Emetic/Puke weed, Asthma root, Gag root (Am)
Lobélie enflée (Fr)
Aufgeblasene Lobelie (Ge)
Part used: the root, herb or fruit

NATURE

Therapeutic category: medium-strength remedy with moderate chronic toxicity

Constituents: 14 pyridine alkaloids 0.3-0.48% (incl. lobeline [highest in seeds], lobelanidine, isolobinine, lobinaline), essential oil, resin, lipids, bitter glycoside lobelacrin, resin, lobelic and chelidonic acid, chlorophyll, lignin, potassium, lime, ferric oxide

Effective qualities: pungent, somewhat bitter, warm with cooling potential, neutral
relaxing, stimulating, restoring

Tropism: heart and circulation, intestines, lungs, kidneys, bladder, nerves, uterus, skin
Lung, Liver, Heart, Kidney, Bladder meridians
Air, Warmth, Fluid bodies

Ground: all krases, biotypes and constitutions

FUNCTIONS AND INDICATIONS

1 **REGULATES THE QI, RELAXES CONSTRAINT AND RELIEVES PAIN;
CLEARS INTERNAL WIND AND STOPS SPASMS**

kidney / adrenal Qi constraint: nervous tension, pain, internal vibrating sensations, forceful pulse
SEVERE, ACUTE STRESS-RELATED CONDITIONS

heart Qi constraint: anxiety, precordial chest oppression and pain, labored breathing, panic
ANGINA PECTORIS (incl. acute)

intestines Qi constraint: abdominal pains, constipation, nausea
INTESTINAL COLIC, IBS, strangulated hernia

bladder Qi constraint: difficult, painful urination; neurogenic bladder

nerve excess with *internal wind:* tremors, spasms, hysteria, convulsions (incl. infantile)
SEIZURES from tetanus, chorea, epilepsy, puerperal eclampsia

2 **DESCENDS LUNG QI, OPENS THE CHEST AND RELIEVES WHEEZING AND COUGHING;
PROMOTES EXPECTORATION AND RESOLVES PHLEGM**

lung Qi constraint: chest oppression and constriction, heavy sore chest pain, wheezing
ASTHMA (spasmodic), croup, whooping cough, pleurisy, cardiac asthma, asthmatic seizure
PNEUMONIA (acute)

lung phlegm-damp: cough, expectoration of copious sputum, fatigue, chest pain and heaviness, wheezing
BRONCHITIS, DRY HARD COUGH

3 **STIMULATES THE HEART AND CIRCULATION, DISPELS COLD AND RELIEVES DEBILITY;
REGULATES BLOOD PRESSURE, RESCUES COLLAPSE AND REVIVES CONSCIOUSNESS**

Heart and Kidney Yang deficiency: exhaustion, mental stupor, chilliness with cold extremities, nausea,
chest pain and constriction, palpitations, difficult breathing, slow/deep/knotted pulse
HYPOTENSION, arrhythmia
CHRONIC EXHAUSTION or DEBILITY from stress, overwork, illness

nerve and brain deficiency (Heart phlegm obstruction): stupor, slurred speech, confusion, fainting
SHOCK, COLLAPSE, COMA, CEREBRAL CONTUSION, concussion

devastated Yang: fainting, coma, collapse, shock, moving pulse
CIRCULATORY DEFICIENCY or COLLAPSE, congestive heart failure, heatstroke

4 **STIMULATES DIGESTION, HARMONIZES THE MIDDLE AND RELIEVES CONSTIPATION**

liver and stomach Qi stagnation: epigastric pain and distension, appetite loss, bilious headache, nausea
DYSPEPSIA (biliary, gastrointestinal; esp. chronic)

intestines Qi stagnation: chronic hard dry stool, abdominal fullness, sick headache, poor appetite
CONSTIPATION (esp. chronic), NAUSEA, vomiting

5   **PROMOTES MENSTRUATION AND CLEARS STAGNATION;**
    HARMONIZES AND PROMOTES LABOR, AND ENHANCES DELIVERY; PREVENTS MISCARRIAGE
    uterus Qi stagnation: delayed, clotted periods, cramps, fatigue
    DYSMENORRHEA
    DIFFICULT, PAINFUL LABOR; perineal, vaginal or cervical rigidity
    FAILURE to PROGRESS DURING LABOR

6   **PROMOTES SWEATING AND URINATION, AND DISPELS WIND-HEAT;**
    REDUCES FEVER, PROMOTES ERUPTIONS, EASES THE THROAT AND BENEFITS THE SKIN
    external wind-heat: fever, unrest, aches and pains, sore throat
    COLD and FLU ONSET with FEVER, SORE THROAT (esp. chronic), LARYNGITIS, pharyngitis
    REMITTENT and ERUPTIVE FEVERS (e.g. measles, scarlet fever, chickenpox)
    ANURIA
    skin wind-damp-heat: skin eruptions with redness, itching, pain
    ECZEMA, dermatitis

7   **REDUCES INFECTION, STIMULATES IMMUNITY AND ANTIDOTES POISON;**
    REDUCES PAIN, INFLAMMATION AND CONTUSION, AND BENEFITS THE SKIN
    PREVENTIVE and REMEDIAL in epidemics and infections
    DIPHTHERIA, tetanus, meningitis, malaria
    ANIMAL and INSECT BITES, FOOD or HERB POISONING
    INJURIES (incl. sprains, strains, bruises)
    PAINFUL CONDITIONS in general (incl. myalgia, neuralgia, muscle spasms)
    SKIN CONDITIONS (incl. eczema, herpes, hives, erysipelas, tines, poison ivy/oak rash)

PREPARATION

Use: Lobelia root should be **decocted** or **tinctured**, the **herb infused** or **tinctured.** The crushed **seed** is made into a long **infusion.** Lobelia **vinegar** (tincture) used internally and topically is excellent for skin disorders. External preparations include **poultices, compresses, ointments** and **enemas** for tissue trauma, pain and skin conditions. **Gargles** benefit chronic sore throat.

Lobelia herb was also called "Indian tobacco" and may be **smoked** for constrained/asthmatic lung Qi.

Lobelia root or herb is given during the first stage of labor when contractions are hypertonic and ineffective, and with failure to progress. It is used especially when the woman has lost the will to continue. Lobelia will space out the contraction waves and make them more effective, allowing her to regain a balanced state and therefore the willingness to continue on her own.

Dosage: Smaller doses are generally more *stimulant* (functions 3-6 mainly), whereas larger ones are more *relaxant.* For Lobelia *seed,* reduce the dosage by 20%.

Decoction and **long infusion** (root, herb or seed): 3-8 g (an average dose is 5 g).

Tincture: 0.5-2 ml (c.10-50 drops) at 1:5 or 1:10 strength in 60% ethanol (the average dose is 1 ml)
• *In acute anginal attacks:* take 20-60 drops (up to half a teaspoonful) of the tincture immediately.
• *To prevent threatening miscarriage:* take up to 2 ml of the tincture every half hour.
• *In failure to progress with hypertonic contractions:* take 1-2 ml of the tincture every half hour.
• *As an emetic to cause therapeutic vomiting:* take 4-5 ml of the tincture (see also Class 6)

Caution: Lobelia root and herb belongs to the medium-strength category and should be taken occasionally or short-term, or as minor component in a formula. Signs of overdosing include nausea, diarrhea, salivation, vision and hearing disturbances, mental confusion and general weakness. In addition, the plant may cause mild idiosyncratic reactions at any dosage level.

However, Lobelia is essentially a safe remedy. It has a built-in safety mechanism whereby overdosing will produce vomiting. The alkaloid isolobinine effectively causes emesis if an overdose of the alkaloid lobeline should occur (although this mechanism may occasionally fail). Also, there are records of herbalists using as much as 15 ml (3 fluid oz) per day for up to a week without negative side effects.

Lobelia root and herb is contraindicated in dyspnea from enlarged or fatty heart, weak heart with valvular incompetence, sinus arrhythmia, bundle branch block, hydropericardium, hypertension, pneumonia, hydrothorax, asthma of cardiac decompensation, pregnancy and tobacco sensitivity.

NOTES

Lobelia has had a checkered history, partly due to the alleged misuse by SAMUEL THOMSON in the early nineteenth century and partly due to the unusual nature of the plant remedy itself. It is unclear whether through the use of Lobelia someone actually died at the hands of this Popular Health Movement practitioner. However, the whole incident was used politically by opportunistic regular physicians to attack Thomsonian herbal therapy as such. A familiar tale. The rampant popularity of the "steam and vegetable practitioners" (PORCHER) then posed a serious threat to the "regulars"— although not nearly as serious as the homeopaths did later in the century.

Lobelia root and herb was the Thomsonians' most popular medication, especially for emetic therapy. While they were following Native American footsteps in this respect (*Pukeweed* and *Indian tobacco* were Lobelia's more common names at the time), it was only later that the Physiomedical and Eclectic physicians properly assessed the remedy's systemic *relaxant* and *stimulant* effect.

FINLEY ELLINGWOOD himself, writing in 1919, has this to say about Lobelia:

> I would say that Lobelia seems at once to supply a subtle but wholly sufficient force, power, or renewed vital influence, by which the nervous system and the essential vital force within the system again reassert themselves and obtain complete control of the functional action of every organ. From this influence, in a natural and sufficient manner, a complete harmonious operation of the whole combined forces is at once resumed, in some cases in an almost startling manner. Other agents stimulate, prop up, whip up and temporarily increase the force and power of one or another function, while this remedy with this peculiar power at once assumes control of the whole, and succeeds against all the opposing influences.

This passage is interesting beyond just throwing light on the nature of this medicinal. Here we see ELLINGWOOD unwittingly reformulating the hoary Hippokratic doctrine of the vital spirits (*spiritus vitalis*) that had officially finally been laid to rest only fifty years before! The Persian dialectitian IBN SINA himself could not have described the

restoring, protecting and regulating effects of the vital spirit housed in the heart more accurately. And as a description of the righteous Qi, the *zheng qi*, it is passing fair. Even if we reduce this Greek medical concept to immune functions, this statement still stands intact: Lobelia in fact does in fact possess an *immunostimulant* action. Only an exceptional remedy such as this one could have induced ELLINGWOOD to spend seven and a half pages describing its clinical actions.

Certainly, Lobelia's net *regulating* effect through its "increase of vital force" makes it as unique as the efficacy and safety of its action makes it desirable. This herb is a Qi regulator that balances both **excess Yang** and **deficient Yang** conditions. Likewise, being amphoteric it normalizes both an excess or deficiency of arterial blood pressure. Lobelia can both *relax* sympathetic autonomic nerve functions (function 1) or *stimulate* them (function 2), as well as balance sympathetic with parasympathetic functions—all depending on the condition presenting, the dosage used and the other remedies it is combined with. Small wonder that Lobelia has been dubbed the "thinking herb."

Lobelia's action splays over the whole organism, but especially the thorassic area. Its use for respiratory and cardiovascular conditions involving constrained Qi should be singled out. Here Lobelia is again both *relaxant* (*spasmolytic, vasodilatant*), causing bronchial and coronary dilation, and *stimulant* (*expectorant, coronary stimulant*) for expectoration and coronary stimulation. Like Cereus stem and flower, Lobelia is for those with serious chest constriction, wheezing, coughing and expectoration of hard sputum caused by **lung Qi constraint** —like Pleurisy root, too.

We should not underestimate Lobelia root as a remedy during **labor.** It is one of the most efficient botanical *cervical dilators* that ensures smooth progress during the first phase. This remedy is also a good *relaxant parturient* for women who tend to hypertonic contractions from general tension. Here again Lobelia allows the woman to assume (self-) control over the process by making the contractions less frequent, yet stronger.

Descend Lung Qi, Open the Chest and Relieve Wheezing

Bronchial relaxants (bronchodilators, antiasthmatics), antitussives

Aniseed

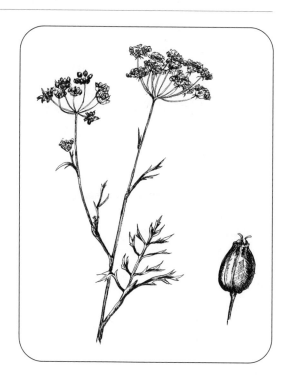

Botanical source: *Pimpinella anisum* L.
     (Apiaceae/Umbelliferae)
Pharmaceutical name: Fructus Anisi
Ancient names: Anison (Gr)
     Anisum (Lat)
Other names: Anis vert, Pimprenelle, Boucage (Fr)
     Anis, Süsser Kümmel (Ge)
Part used: the fruit

NATURE

Therapeutic category: mild remedy with minimal chronic toxicity
Constituents: essential oil 2-6% (incl. anethol and estragol 90%, methylchavicol, terpenes, creosol, acetylaldehyde, isoamyaline, umbelliferone, bergaptene, sphondin, isopimpinellin), cholin, malic acid, resins, fatty oil 30%, flavonoid quercetin, minerals (incl. calcium, iron, zinc)
Effective qualities: pungent, sweet, warm, dry
     relaxing, stimulating, restoring
Tropism: cardiovascular system, intestines, lungs, uterus
     Lung, Heart, Spleen meridians
     Air body
Ground: all krases, biotypes and constitutions

FUNCTIONS AND INDICATIONS

1 **DESCENDS LUNG QI, OPENS THE CHEST AND RELIEVES WHEEZING; PROMOTES EXPECTORATION AND RESOLVES PHLEGM**

    lung Qi constraint: dry irritating cough, wheezing, sore chest
    SPASMODIC ASTHMA (esp. chronic)
    lung phlegm-cold: expectoration of copious white sputum, coughing, tight chest
    BRONCHITIS (chronic)

2 **REGULATES THE QI, RELAXES CONSTRAINT AND RELIEVES PAIN**

    heart Qi constraint: palpitations, nervousness, stress
    NEUROCARDIAC SYNDROME
    intestines Qi constraint: abdominal pains, indigestion, flatulence
    COLIC, IBS

541

uterus Qi constraint: menstrual cramps, difficult menstruation

SPASMODIC DYSMENORRHEA

PAIN from gout, rheumatism, neuralgia, childbirth

2 TONIFIES HEART AND LUNG QI, AND GENERATES STRENGTH; GENERATES FLUIDS, PROMOTES LACTATION AND BENEFITS VISION

heart and lung Qi deficiency: fatigue, shortness of breath, palpitations

DEBILITY from overwork, stress, chronic illness (esp. bronchitis), constitution, nicotine detox

INSUFFICIENT BREAST MILK, congealed breast milk

INSUFFICIENT SPERM

VISION IMPAIRMENT

3 STIMULATES DIGESTION, RESOLVES MUCOUS-DAMP AND STOPS VOMITING AND HICCUPS

intestines (Spleen) mucous-damp: nausea, indigestion, flatulence, gurgling distended abdomen

GASTROENTERITIS, COLITIS

NAUSEA, VOMITING

HICCUPS (esp. severe, chronic)

4 ANTIDOTES POISON AND KILLS PARASITES

ANIMAL BITES

INSECT REPELLENT

SCABIES, lice

PREPARATION

Use: Aniseed is prepared by **long infusion** or **tincture.** The latter carries the full therapeutic range. The infusion of the crushed seeds is a mild warming relaxant, stimulant *(carminative)* for the digestive system, and is often used in formulas addressing respiratory and digestive disorders.

Aniseed **essential oil** is applied topically diluted 3-10% in a carrier oil, inhaled in nebulizer sessions or taken orally (see below), especially for bronchial conditions.

Dosage: Long infusion: 6-12 g

Tincture: 2-4 ml at 1:2 strength in 45% ethanol

Essential oil: 1-3 drops in a gel cap topped with some olive oil

Caution: Avoid Aniseed in those with immediate allergies; occasional reactions may occur.

NOTES

Although Aniseed is closely related to other spicy seeds of the carrot family, such as fennel, caraway, cumin, carrot and parsley, this should not prevent us from seeing what is unique about it from a therapeutic standpoint. Nor should the usual view of Aniseed as a simple *carminative* deter us from viewing this remedy essen-tially as a *relaxant* one.

Granted, for symptom relief, Aniseed is a good remedy for relieving flatulence. The twelfth century Italian dithyramb on Aniseed from the Salerno medical college opens with the words *solamen intestinorum,* "the intestines' solace"—not a gratuitous remark. However, with Aniseed tincture and essential oil now available to us, the indications for this traditional remedy deepen considerably. It was

Renaissance herbalists and pagyrists like PIERANDREA MATTIOLI who began preparing tinctures and distillations of common kitchen spices such as Aniseed and opened wide the field of their indications. They found Aniseed excellent for internal **spasms** and **pain** in general, including painful colic and distension. As a *stimulant* they also considered it to transform **mucous-damp** in the digestive tract.

Pungent, sweet, warming and dispersing by nature, Aniseed regulates constrained Qi in the middle and upper warmer, resulting in *spasmolytic* and *analgesic* actions. Perhaps its strongest tropism is for the organs of the chest. Here, with its combined *bronchodilatant* and *expectorant* actions, Aniseed in particular treats acute and chronic bronchial disorders involving **constrained lung Qi** and **lung phlegm-cold,** as in chronic asthma. Neurogenic cardiovascular disorders with palpitations and chest pains will also benefit greatly. The similarity with the Chinese herbs Magnolia Hou Po (Magnolia bark) and Aquilaria Chen Xiang (Aloeswood) is striking.

Aniseed also distinguishes itself from others in the carrot family by an underlying *restorative* effect that again mainly affects the chest organs and indicates application for long-term as well as acute conditions. In addressing the syndrome **lung and heart Qi deficiency,** Aniseed actually tonifies the Ancestral Qi, the *zong qi* of Chinese medicine, which supports cardiac and respiratory functions. A comparable acupuncture point formula would be P 6, Lu 3 and CV 12 and 17. This tonifying action can support the whole individual in many types of chronic deficiency conditions signaled by low energy, shallow breathing, chronic cough, chronic chest infections, smoking detox programs and such like.

Wild Cherry Bark

Botanical source: *Prunus serotina* Ehrhart
      (syn. *Prunus virginiana* Miller) (Rosaceae)
Pharmaceutical name: Cortex Pruni
Other names: Choke cherry, Black cherry, Virginian
      prune (Am)
      Cerisier de Virginie (Fr)
      Virginianische Traubenkirsche (Ge)
Part used: the bark

NATURE
Therapeutic category: mild remedy with minimal chronic toxicity
Constituents: cyanogenic glycosides (incl. prunasin hydrolysed to HCN), coumarins (incl. scopoletin), tannin, gallic/azulic/endosminic/benzoic acid, essential oil, starch, lignin, gallitannins, resin, minerals (incl. calcium, potassium, iron)
Effective qualities: bitter, astringent, somewhat pungent, cool, dry
      relaxing, restoring
Tropism: lungs, heart, stomach, intestines, nerves
      Lung, Heart, Large Intestine meridians
      Air, Warmth bodies
Ground: Melancholic krasis
      Sensitive/Tai Yin Metal biotype
      all constitutions for symptomatic use

FUNCTIONS AND INDICATIONS
1   **DESCENDS LUNG QI, OPENS THE CHEST AND RELIEVES WHEEZING AND COUGHING;**
     REGULATES HEART AND INTESTINES QI, AND RELIEVES CHEST OPPRESSION
     lung Qi constraint: asthmatic breathing, dry harsh cough, irritability, fatigue
     SPASMODIC ASTHMA, whooping cough, croup
     COUGH of any type (esp. irritating, relentless, spasmodic)

heart Qi constraint: palpitations, chest oppression, stress

PALPITATIONS

intestines Qi constraint: indigestion, abdominal pain, loose stool, stress

STRESS-INDUCED chronic respiratory, cardiac and digestive disorders

2   **CLEARS EMPTY HEAT, REDUCES FEVER AND GENERATES STRENGTH**

Yin deficiency with heat: exhaustion, weakness, hot spells, low-grade fever, weak-rapid pulse

REMITTENT FEVER (*shao yin* stage)

CONVALESCENT DEBILITY after acute inflammatory disorders (esp. pneumonia, pleurisy, acute hepatitis, gastroenteritis)

lung Yin deficiency: night sweats, feverishness, dry irritating cough

LUNG TB, whooping cough

3   **ASTRINGES, REDUCES INFLAMMATION AND STOPS DIARRHEA**

intestines damp-cold: chronic loose stool, fatigue

CHRONIC DIARRHEA

EYE INFLAMMATIONS (acute)

CHRONIC ULCERS

PREPARATION

Use: Wild cherry bark is prepared by **cold water infusion** or **tincture.** The completely dried bark only should only used; the fresh bark takes about a year to completely dry.

Cooling, astringing **washes** or **swabs** are prepared for ulcers and eye inflammations.

The dried **Wild cherry fruit** is sour, cool in quality. It is used to clear empty heat in low-grade fever (*shao yin* stage), and to relieve mild diarrhea.

Dosage: Cold infusion: 6-10 g

            Tincture: 2-4 ml at 1:2 strength in 25% ethanol

Caution: Contraindicated in stomach/intestines cold disorders. Contraindicated during pregnancy because of the *teratogenic* cyanogenic glycoside.

NOTES

The outer bark of the lovely wild cherry tree is best thought of as a *relaxant* remedy for the Upper Warmer, the thorassic area, with a secondary systemic *restorative* effect. **Constrained lung Qi** that tightens the chest, dries the throat and causes uncontrollable coughing is the primary syndrome of application for this *respiratory relaxant*. Cyanogenic glycosides, essential oil and benzoic acid work together here for *bronchodilatant, antiinflammatory* and downright *antitussive* actions.

Like the similar Chinese herb Morus Sang Bai Pi (Mulberry root bark), Wild cherry is usually combined with other *pectoral* remedies. Because of its somewhat drying nature, more moist, remedies such as Licorice root, Fennel seed, Slippery elm bark and other *demulcents* in Class 10 will generally go well with it. Unless the condition is one of damp-phlegm in the lung, causing copious sputum, where Thyme herb or White horehound herb would be good choices.

As a general *restorative,* Wild cherry treats those presenting **Yin deficiency** with **empty heat** resulting from chronic stress, perimenopause or actual illness, i.e. with autonomic imbalance or fever. In these individuals, Wild cherry can speed recovery by recouping lost forces, strengthening the heart, kindling the appetite and clearing any remaining heat in the skin. In **lung Yin deficiency** conditions the remedy acts like Mullein leaf and Lycium Di Gu Pi (Wolfberry root bark) in particular. Its *nervous restorative* action strengthens respiratory, cardiac and digestive functions in the same way as Poplar bark restores urogenital ones. Here it indicates usage for chronic conditions in particular, conditions where deficiency has lead to empty heat or lung or heart Qi constraint.

Gumweed Flower

Botanical source: *Grindelia robusta* Wildenow et
     Nuttall, *G. squarrosa* Dunal and spp.
     (Asteraceae/Compositae)
Pharmaceutical name: Flos Grindeliae
Other names: Grindelia, Wild sunflower, Gumplant,
     Rosinweed, Hardy/Scaly grindelia,
     Tarweed (Am)
     Yerba del buey (Sp)
     Goldkörbchen (Ge)
Part used: the flower (or stem and flower)

NATURE

Therapeutic category: medium-strength remedy with moderate chronic toxicity
Constituents: saponins 2% (incl. grindelin), bitter alkaloid grindeline, essential oil (incl. alpha-pinene, camphene, limonene, borneol, borneol acetate, methyleugenol), resin 20% (incl. diterpenes), phytosterin, matricianol, matricarianol-acetate, tannins, laevoglucose
Effective qualities: bitter, somewhat pungent, cool, moist
     stimulating, relaxing, decongesting
Tropism: lungs, heart, arterial circulation, skin
     Lung, Heart meridians
     Air, Fluid bodies
Ground: all krases, biotypes and constitutions for symptomatic use

FUNCTIONS AND INDICATIONS

1   **DESCENDS LUNG QI, OPENS THE CHEST AND RELIEVES WHEEZING AND COUGHING;
    PROMOTES EXPECTORATION AND RESOLVES VISCOUS PHLEGM**

    lung Qi constraint: asthmatic breathing, tight sore chest, dry hacking cough
    ASTHMA (spasmodic, allergic)
    lung phlegm-dryness: coughing with scanty viscous sputum, difficult dry cough
    BRONCHITIS, whooping cough
    heart Qi constraint: nervous rapid heartbeat, palpitations, stress
    NEUROCARDIAC SYNDROME

2   **PROMOTES URINATION, DRAINS WATER AND RELIEVES EDEMA;
    REDUCES KIDNEY STAGNATION**

    heart / lung water congestion: wheezing, labored breathing, general edema, palpitations
    LUNG EDEMA (acute)
    kidney Qi stagnation: skin rashes, malaise, fatigue, bladder irritation
    URINARY TRACT INFECTIONS with DYSURIA

3   PROMOTES TISSUE REPAIR, REDUCES INFLAMMATION AND BENEFITS THE SKIN

CHRONIC SKIN CONDITIONS (dermatoses) in deficiency conditions

SKIN ULCERS (indolent or malignant), running sores

skin wind-heat: skin eruptions with redness, irritation, itching

DERMATITIS, ECZEMA (acute and chronic, allergic)

BURNS, blisters, poison ivy/oak rash or inflammation

INSECT BITES and stings

PREPARATION

Use: Gumweed flower is prepared in **short decoction** or **tincture.** For decocting, the leaves or the whole flowering tops are used by preference. Healing, soothing and cooling **washes** and **compresses** are prepared for skin sores, ulcers, rashes, poison oak/ivy rashes and insect bites.

Dosage: Short decoction: 3-8 g

         Tincture: 0.5-2 ml at 1:3 strength in 60% ethanol

Caution: Because Gumweed flower can be somewhat irritating to the kidneys, do not exceed the above doses or use with acute kidney infection (e.g., nephritis) present. Gumweed is best used in a formula or in occasional small doses as it is a medium-strength remedy with mild cumulative toxicity.

Note: The *Grindelia squarrosa* species of Gumweed was in the past much used to treat intermittent fevers arising from infections such as malaria. It was also effectively used to reduce spleen enlargement (splenomegaly), especially when associated with liver congestion. The main symptoms picture relived is indigestion, fullness and dull pain in left hypochondrium; a pallid, sallow complexion, weakness and lethargy.

NOTES

Gumweed flower is an effective respiratory remedy from North America's Mountain West. It has a narrow, specific range of uses. The bitter-pungent remedy is basically a *respiratory relaxant* and *circulatory stimulant* in one, similar in this respect to Inmortal herb, Celandine herb and Hyssop herb. Gumweed is a choice herb for individuals with **constrained lung Qi** causing wheezing, harsh, dry spasmodic coughing and difficult expectoration of thick, sticky sputum. In this syndrome, saponins and essential oils together ensure *bronchodilatant* and *expectorant* effects on the bronchi.

If necessary, Gumweed flower could easily replace Aster Zi Wan or Perilla Zi Su Zi commonly used in Chinese formulas. In acupuncture terms, Lu 7 and 5, Ki 7, CV 17 and Bl 13 would be a comparable point selection. In the treatment of chronic bronchitis or asthma, this remedy's very high resin content ensures a moistening, softening effect on the bronchi that contributes to its excellent *mucolytic* action. In addition, the remedy is a

heart relaxant, like the Chinese herb Lilium Bai He.

Because Gumweed combines good *kidney* and *arterial stimulant* actions, it acts as a good *draining diruretic* in **heart/lung water congestion** or lung edema. Here it should be supported with *cardiac stimulants* like Lily of the valley herb because of left-sided heart failure.

Gumweed flower has also enjoyed a reputation in treating **eczema** when secretions are at a standstill. The main pattern it treats is **wind-heat** skin rashes and itching.

Because of its consistent use for both skin eruptions and asthma, Gumweed should be seriously considered for individuals with **atopic terrain,** e.g., asthma alternating or presenting with eczema. There is a good possibility (again awaiting research) that the remedy is actually *antiallergic*. Regardless, topical use has demonstrated excellent results in acute irritated, inflammatory skin conditions ranging from acute dermatitis to poison oak and other similar plant irritations.

Skunk Cabbage Root

Botanical source: *Symplocarpus foetidus* (L.) Nuttall
(syn. *Pothos foetida* Michaux, *Dracontium foetidum* L). (Araceae)
Pharmaceutical name: Radix Symplocarpi
Other names: Skunk weed, Swamp cabbage, Meadow
cabbage, Collard, Polecat weed
Pothos fétide (Fr)
Stinkende Drachenwurzel (Ge)
Part used: the root

NATURE

Therapeutic category: medium-strength remedy with moderate chronic toxicity
Constituents: essential oil, lipids, resin, starch, saccharides, gum
Effective qualities: pungent, somewhat bitter, cool, dry
relaxing, stimulating
Tropism: lungs, kidneys, bladder, nerves, muscles
Lung, Liver meridians; Air, Fluid bodies
Ground: all krases, biotypes and constitutions for symptomatic use

FUNCTIONS AND INDICATIONS

1   **DESCENDS LUNG QI, OPENS THE CHEST AND RELIEVES WHEEZING AND COUGHING;
    PROMOTES EXPECTORATION AND RESOLVES PHLEGM**

   lung Qi constraint: asthmatic breathing, tight sore chest, dry hacking cough
   SPASMODIC ASTHMA, whooping cough, pleurisy, lung TB
   COUGH (esp. spasmodic, irritable)
   NASAL CONGESTION with discharge, pain (sinusitis)
   lung phlegm-damp: coughing, expectoration of white sputum, tight chest
   BRONCHITIS

2   **RELAXES CONSTRAINT, CLEARS INTERNAL WIND AND STOPS SPASMS**

   kidney / adrenal Qi constraint: tension, stress, irritability, pains, cramps
   internal wind: tremors, spasms, hysteria
   SEIZURES (incl. children's convulsions)

3   **PROMOTES URINATION, DRAINS WATER AND RELIEVES EDEMA**

   liver and kidney water congestion: general bloating, fatigue
   EDEMA
   kidney Qi stagnation: malaise, muscle aches and pains
   RHEUMATISM

4   **REDUCES PAIN, IRRITATION AND HARDNESS**

   WOUNDS, skin irritation, toothache
   CAKED BREASTS

PREPARATION

Use: Skunk cabbage root is prepared by **short decoction** or the more effective **tincture.** Never use the fresh root to prepare these because of its intense acridity and slight toxicity that can cause vomiting when ingested. Only use the thoroughly dried root. However, after two months Skunk cabbage root already begins to loose its effectiveness. Discard after six months.

Soothing topical preparations are made for skin irritations, etc. (function 4).

Skunk cabbage root hairs were used topically by one Native American tribe to stop bleeding.

Dosage: Short decoction: 4-8 g

Tincture: 1-4 ml at 1:2 strength in 50% ethanol

Honey powder: Mix 1/2 oz of the powdered dried root in 3-4 oz of honey. Take 1/2-1 teaspoon three times a day for respiratory disorders.

Caution: Skunk cabbage root *may* possess moderate cumulative toxicity and at full dose should therefore not be taken continuously on its own. It is usually combined with others for long-term use.

NOTES

The skunk cabbage is a true North American native and, peculiarly, the only species of its genus. Growing in boggy, swampy terrain, it develops a penetratingly fetid, skunk-like offensive odor. The root of this plant was extensively used by Eclectic practitioners during the nineteenth century, among whom it enjoyed an "enviable reputation" (H. DIERS RAU). Curiously, with the demise of the Eclectic Medical colleges in the early twentieth century, Skunk cabbage root fell into general disuse.

Although the systemic action of Skunk cabbage root is *relaxation* (extending to the treatment of tremors and seizures), the main area for its exhibition is the respiratory tract. The remedy primarily treats **constrained Qi** affecting breathing and causing a dry, hacking, irritable cough. Its secondary *stimulant* effect promotes a drying, *expectorant* effect tha tis useful in bronchial conditions presenting the syndrome **lung phlegm-damp.** We should think of Skunk cabbage as a stronger version of Coltsfoot herb, Hyssop herb or Perilla Zi Su Zi from Chinese medicine.

Pungent and bitter, Skunk cabbage root operates mainly because of its essential oil content that also opens up painful congested sinuses. Several important formulas used in the past typically combined the root with Lobelia herb or Pleurisy root for asthmatic conditions, and with Cramp bark for painful internal spasms, or **internal wind.**

Sundew Herb

Botanical source: *Drosera rotundifolia* L.
    (Droseraceae)
Pharmaceutical name: Herba Droserae
Ancient names: Ros solis, Rorella (Lat)
Other names: Round-leaf sundew, Moorgrass, Dew-
    plant, Lustplant, Youthroot (Eng)
    Drosère (à feuilles rondes), Rosée du soleil
    (Fr)
    Sonnentau, Rundblättriger Sonnentau (Ge)
Part used: the herb

NATURE
Therapeutic category: medium-strength remedy with moderate chronic toxicity
Constituents: flavonoids (incl. droserone, droserin), carboxyoxynaphthaquinones (incl. plumbagin), tannins, citric and malic acids, resin, glucose, red pigment (dioxyanthraquinone alizarin), enzymes, trace minerals
Effective qualities: bitter, pungent, cool, dry
    relaxing, stimulating
Tropism: lungs, throat, circulation, reproductive organs
    Lung, Liver meridians; Air body;
Ground: all krases, biotypes and constitutions for symptomatic use

FUNCTIONS AND INDICATIONS

1 **DESCENDS LUNG QI, OPENS THE CHEST AND RELIEVES WHEEZING AND COUGHING; BENEFITS THE THROAT AND RELIEVES IRRITATION**

    lung Qi constraint: wheezing, constricted, raw or painful chest, dry explosive cough, dry throat, irritating dry throat tickle

    SPASMODIC ASTHMA, WHOOPING COUGH

    COUGH (all types, esp. nervous, spasmodic, irritating, dry, with dry retching; of measles, whooping cough, chronic bronchitis)

    HOARSENESS, voice loss

    LUNG TB (early stage), lung ulcers

    SYMPATHETIC NERVOUS HYPERFUNTIONING

    PERIPHERAL CRAMPS, arteriosclerosis

2 **SETTLES THE STOMACH AND STOPS VOMITING; RELIEVES DIARRHEA**

    stomach Qi stagnation: nausea, stomach upset, vomiting

    VOMITING

    DIARRHEA (esp. of whooping cough and measles)

3 **TONIFIES REPRODUCTIVE QI, FORTIFIES THE YANG AND RELIEVES IMPOTENCE; PROMOTES MENSTRUATION AND DELIVERY**

    Kidney Yang deficiency: sexual disinterest, impotence, delayed, scanty periods

    IMPOTENCE, AMENORRHEA

    STALLED LABOR (uterine dystocia)

4 **CLEARS HEAT AND REDUCES FEVER; REDUCES LYMPH CONGESTION**

    INTERMITTENT FEVERS (*shao yang* stage)

    LYMPHADENITIS (incl. scrofula)

5 **BENEFITS THE SKIN**

    WARTS, corns, freckles, skin blemishes, sunburn

PREPARATION
Use: Sundew herb is used in **infusion** or **tincture** form. The remedy is usually used in small doses added to formulas.

    Sundew juice (from the whole plant) was formerly used (straight or diluted in water) for swabbing skin blemishes, especially warts.
Dosage: Infusion: 3-6 g
    Tincture: 0.5-1 ml at 1:3 strength in 60% ethanol

Caution: Because of its medium-strength status, do not use this remedy continuously or exceed the above dosages. Contraindicated during pregnancy because of its *uterine stimulant* action.

NOTES

Found throughout the northern hemisphere, the little-known sundew is an insectivorous plant with a yen for damp, dank environments such as sandy swamps and the muddy shores of rivers and ponds. Needing animal protein to survive, it uses gland-bearing, secreting hairs that glisten dew-like in the sunlight to ensnare, dissolve and assimilate passing insects.

Many of this remedy's uses have been lost in time, and those that have survived present intriguing possibilities for future clinical exploration and lab research. Alone the presence of naphthaquinones (of Brazilian Pau d'arco bark fame) is provocative. Sundew's many names, which include "Lustplant" and "Youthroot," also witness uses currently almost forgotten. The remedy was taken for functional **reproductive deficiencies** such as impotence, frigidity and amenorrhea—essentially **Kidney Yang deficiency** conditions—among others.

By far the most common area of application for Sundew herb in the last two-hundred years has been tense, or constrained, conditions of the bronchi and throat. Through its inhibiting action on the sympathetic nerves, the remedy's *bronchodilatant* effect moves **constrained Qi** in the **lung,** relieving the keynote symptoms wheezing, tight, painful chest, irritating throat tickle and uncontrollable, explosive dry cough. Sundew is one of those remedies applicable on a symptom relief basis to anyone with a **cough**—but should be used especially for the individual coughing from stress, overwork or simply an irritating scratchy throat. Like Wild lettuce leaf and Wild cherry bark but stronger, Sundew is a true *antitussive*. Unless used on its own, it should be added to formulas only in small amounts.

In the European past, Sundew was given as a preventive for **whooping cough** in crude, tincture and homeopathic preparation form. Today the glycoside plumbagin has shown activity against *Streptococcus, Staphylococcus* and *Pneumococcus* bacteria. Mental disorders (of which kind is not known) were also formerly treated with this intriguing remedy.

Oregano Herb

Botanical source: *Origanum vulgare* L.
      (Lamiaceae/Labiatae)
Pharmaceutical name: Herba Origani vulgari
Ancient names: Oreiganon (Gr)
      Golena, Cunila, Glitonum (Lat)
Other names: Wild marjoram, European oregano,
      Argan, Organy (Eng)
      Origan, Marjolaine sauvage/batarde, Grande
      marjolaine, Thym de berger (Fr)
      Dosten, Wilder Majoran, Kostenz, Dorant
      (Ge)
Part used: the herb

NATURE

Therapeutic category: mild remedy with minimal chronic toxicity

Constituents: essential oil c. 2% (incl. phenols up to 63% [incl. carvacrol, thymol, borneol], mono-terpenes 7-10% [incl. paracymene, terpinenes, cymene, caryophyllene, pinene], linalyle/geranyl acetate, 1.8 cineol), bitters, tannins, coffeic/ursolic/rosmarinic acids, resins, gum

Effective qualities: pungent, bitter, warm, dry
      relaxing, stimulating, dispersin

Tropism: lungs, intestines, circulation, reproductive organs, skin
      Lung, Liver, Spleen meridians; Air body

Ground: all krases, biotypes and constitutions for symptomatic use

FUNCTIONS AND INDICATIONS

1 **DESCENDS LUNG QI, OPENS THE CHEST AND RELIEVES WHEEZING; PROMOTES EXPECTORATION, RESOLVES PHLEGM AND RELIEVES COUGHING**

lung Qi constraint: irritable cough, wheezing, chest pain

ASTHMA, whooping cough

lung phlegm-cold / -damp: cough, expectoration of copious or viscous sputum, fatigue, wheezing

BRONCHITIS, pharyngitis, laryngitis, tonsilitis

2 **PROMOTES SWEATING, DISPELS WIND-COLD AND PROMOTES ERUPTIONS**

lung wind-cold: body aches and pains, headache, cough with sputum

COLD and FLU ONSET

MEASLES, chickenpox

3 **STIMULATES DIGESTION, RESOLVES MUCOUS-DAMP AND RELIEVES FULLNESS; STIMULATES THE APPETITE AND RELIEVES FATIGUE**

intestines mucous-damp: indigestion, epigastric and abdominal pain, distension, flatulence, diarrhea

GASTROENTERITIS, colic

ANOREXIA

4 **PROMOTES MENSTRUATION, REDUCES STAGNATION AND RELIEVES AMENORRHEA**

uterus cold: delayed periods, cramps before flow

AMENORRHEA, spasmodic dysmenorrhea

5 **REDUCES INFECTION AND PAIN; PROMOTES TISSUE REPAIR**

VIRAL / BACTERIAL / FUNGAL INFECTIONS (esp. chronic; respiratory, gastrointestinal, dermal,
    incl. bronchitis, gastroenteritis, food poisoning, dermatitis)

ANIMAL / INSECT BITES, herb poisoning

PARASITIC SKIN CONDITIONS (esp. with pruritus)

RHEUMATIC / MYALGIC / ARTHRITIC PAIN

SORES, ULCERS

CELLULITE

PREPARATION

Use: Oregano herb is prepared by **tincture** or **infusion.** The latter is primarily a *diaphoretic* and *emmenagogue* (functions 2 and 4). Compresses are prepared for infectious eczema, skin parasites and sores.

 Liniments, ointments and **compresses** are prepared for muscle and joint pain, parasitic and other skin infections, and for cellulite.

Dosage: Infusion: 6-8 g

      Tincture: 1-3 ml at 1:3 strength in 45% ethanol

      Essential oil: 2-4 drops in a gel cap topped with some olive oil (but see caution below)

Caution: Being a *uterine stimulant*, Oregano herb is contraindicated during pregnancy. The above doses should not be exceeded.

Oregano **essential oil** is one of the strongest *skin* and *mucosal irritants*. When used in topical applications of no more than 0.5% dilution, this should be for occasional use only.

When taken internally, Oregano oil should only be administered in a gel cap. When this is used to treat infections, continuous use is also contraindicated, as the microbes will eventually build up a resistance to the oil. Oregano oil should be discontinued once the infection has cleared, or different, gentler oils such as Niaouli, Tea tree and Palmarosa should be selected once the acute phase of infection is under control.

Note: Do not confuse the various oregano species (*Origanum* spp.) with "Spanish oregano," *Thymus capitata* and *T. mastichina*. These species of thyme should properly be called Cretan thyme or conehead thyme. Their functions and uses resemble both Thyme herb and Oregano herb.

The species *Origanum compactum* Bentham (usually used in essential oil form) is the strongest *anti-infective* of all Oreganos. It has the strongest *immunostimulant, antibacterial, antifungal, antiviral* and *antiparasitic* actions, as well as *nervous restorative* properties in neurasthenic conditions.

NOTES

Also known as Wild marjoram, Oregano herb was once an important remedy in ancient Greece. The fragrant herb was praised for its *stimulating, warming* and *relaxing* effects, especially on the respiratory, digestive and reproductive organs. In obstructed or painful menstruation caused by **Qi stasis,** it often worked wonders, effectively preventing the local wise woman or herbal practitioner from resorting to stronger Mediterranean *stimulant/relaxant emmenagogues*. These included Aloe from the island Sokotra, Water and Poison hemlock which grew wild everywhere, and Spurge laurel berry from the island Knidos. (Interestingly, Knidos was the stronghold of the disease and local pathology-oriented school of early Greek medicine, in contrast to the prevention and systemic diathesis-oriented school on the island of Kos.)

Many centuries later, the Italian physician PIERANDREA MATTIOLI (1610) recommended combining Oregano with Mugwort, Camomile and Fieldmint for women presenting delayed, difficult menstruation with cramps brought on by the energy of cold. Can we improve on this formula today for *stimulant, spasmolytic* and *relaxant* actions?

We hardly think so, when we are using only European herbs.

With its stimulating, dispersing, pungent-warm qualities, Oregano herb also has a strong affinity for the respiratory tract and the body's exterior. Acting simultaneously as a *stimulant* and *relaxant,* the herb addresses tense and damp bronchial conditions such as chronic bronchitis and chronic asthma. Oregano will treat **lung Qi constraint** and **lung phlegm-cold** primarily, especially in those presenting low energy and cough.

However, if the pure essential oil is used (compress, gel cap), Oregano's *broad-spectrum anti-infective (anti-viral, antibacterial, antifungal)* action engages and is also superb in acute respiratory conditions of the **lung phlegm-heat** and **lung wind-heat** type. Here we see the combined actions of monoterpenes and phenols at work.

Oregano is also an important topical *antiseptic* and *analgesic* remedy in whatever form and preparation it is used, notably for conditions involving pain and infection (including parasitic), and whenever topical stimulation is required.

Common Ivy Leaf

Notes On Its Functions and Indications

Common ivy leaf, from the evergreen climber *Hedera helix* L. (Araliaceae) is similar to Oregano herb in that it is a *cool bronchial relaxant* and *expectorant* that both diffuses Lung Qi and resolves phlegm. However, it is a medium-strength remedy with moderate chronic toxicity. The plant contains saponins, glycosides, the bitter alkaloid hederine, hedera-tannic acid, an emetin alkaloid and a phytoestrogen, among others.

Ivy leaf is astringent, bitter, cool by nature. Its *bronchial spasmolytic* action is given for uncontrollable coughs, especially in **whooping cough.** As a *stimulant* and *mucolytic expectorant* it treats chronic bronchitis.

Secondary uses for this remedy include throat inflammations (especially tracheitis), rheumatic and gouty conditions, bile stones, hypertension and scanty/delayed/absent periods from estrogen deficiency.

Topical uses for ivy leaf in **compresses, ointments,** etc., include treatment of neuralgia and myalgia, lymphadenitis, cellulite, burns, wounds, ulcers, eczema, corns, calluses and phlebitic edema. *Analgesic, softening, anti-inflammatory* and *vasoconstrictant* actions are here evident. Nasal polyps may be treated with **insufflations** of the powder. Scalp applications are *antivermin* and hair-darkening.

Dose: Short decoction: 0.5-1.5 g. Tincture: 4-8 drops at 1:3 strength in 50% ethanol

Pillbearing Spurge Herb

Notes On Its Functions and Indications

Pillbearing spurge herb, from the (sub)tropical herbaceous *Euphorbia pilulifera* (Euphorbiaceae), is an important *bronchial relaxant* remedy. Also known as Cat's hair, Queensland asthma weed and Snakeweed, the plant is widely found in Australia and to some extent in the American South. Among other constituents, it contains essential oil, glycosidal resins, tannins and minerals.

Bitter, pungent and cool in effective qualities, Pillbearing spurge strongly descends Lung Qi to relieve wheezing. Its excellent *bronchodilatant* action has prime applications in spasmodic asthma and cough. Wheezing seen in the context of congestion, as in emphysema, bronchitis and heart disease is also relieved by it.

Secondary uses include chronic bronchitis, sinusitis, allergic rhinitis (hayfever) and asthma from combined *anti-inflammatory, expectorant, nasal decongestant* and possibly *antiallergic* actions. **Lung Qi constraint** and **lung phlegm-damp** are the main traditional syndromes addressed here.

Dose: Short decoction: 5-10 g. Tincture: 0.5-2 ml at 1:3 strength in 50% ethanol. The leaves of Pillbearing spurge may be smoked to relieve asthma attacks.

Regulate Heart Qi, Balance Circulation and Relieve Palpitations

Neurocardiac relaxants (vasodilators, hypotensives, neurocardiac sedatives)

Bugleweed Herb

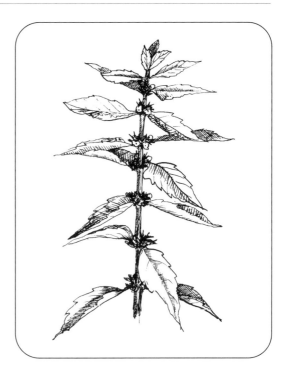

Botanical source: *Lycopus virginicus* L.,
  L. americanus Muhl., *L. europaeus* L.
  and spp. (Lamiaceae/Labiatae)
Pharmaceutical name: Herba Lycopi
Ancient names: Marrubium palustre/aquaticum,
  Sideritis prima, Lancea Christi (Lat)
Other names: Water/Sweet bugle, Water/Marsh hore-
  hound, Gypsywort (Eng and Am)
  Pied de loup, Chanvre d'eau (Fr)
  Wolfstrapp, Wolfsfuss, Chinakraut,
  Zigeunerkraut, Wasser Andorn (Ge)
Part used: the herb

NATURE
Therapeutic category: mild remedy with minimal chronic toxicity
Constituents: essential oil, bitter glycoside (lycopine), tannin, gallic acid, calcium chloride, magnesium, resin
Effective qualities: bitter, somewhat astringent, cool, dry
  relaxing, restoring, astringing, stabilizing, sinking
Tropism: heart, lung, intestines, nerves
  Heart, Liver, Lung meridians; Air body
Ground: Sanguine and Choleric krases
  Expressive/Jue Yin and Tough/Shao Yang biotypes
  Hematogenic/Sulphuric constitution

FUNCTIONS AND INDICATIONS
  1 **REGULATES HEART QI AND RELIEVES PALPITATIONS AND CHEST OPPRESSION;**
    REGULATES THE QI AND RELIEVES PAIN;
    INHIBITS THE THYROID

    heart Qi constraint (Liver Yang rising): palpitations, rapid heartbeat, chest oppression, ringing ears,
      anxiety
    TACHYCARDIA, PALPITATIONS, hypertension, spasmodic angina, PMS
    THYROID HYPERFUNCTIONING (hyperthyroid conditions)
    MENOPAUSAL HOT FLASHES
    ENDO/PERICARDITIS, cardiac hypertrophy/dilatation
    lung Qi constraint: dry nervous coughing, wheezing, sore chest
    ASTHMA (spasmodic)
    intestines Qi constraint: abdominal pains, colic, stress
    DIGESTIVE COLIC, IBS

**2 RELAXES CONSTRAINT, CALMS THE MIND AND RELIEVES ANXIETY;
CLEARS EMPTY HEAT, REDUCES FEVER AND RELIEVES COUGHING**

kidney / adrenal Qi constraint: mental/nervous tension (esp. from chronic stress, illness, etc.)

heart Yin deficiency with *nerve excess:* restlessness, anxiety, insomnia, night sweats

INSOMNIA, sleep disorders

ANXIETY STATES, phobias

lung Yin deficiency: dry cough, cough with blood in sputum, fatigue, low-grade fever

LUNG TB, consumption

COUGH (esp. irritating) in chronic TB, acute and chronic pneumonia, bronchitis

LOW-GRADE TIDAL FEVERS with empty heat (*shao yin* stage), exhaustion, weak fast pulse

3 ASTRINGES AND STOPS DISCHARGE AND BLEEDING

HEMORRHAGING from internal organs (esp. lung hemorrhage); blood in saliva, spittle, stool, urine (esp. with frequent and little bleeding); uterine bleeding

DIARRHEA (all forms), GASTROENTERITIS

ALBUMINURIA

4 STIMULATES DIGESTION AND APPETITE

liver and stomach Qi stagnation: appetite loss, epigastric pain and distress, indigestion

DYSPEPSIA

PREPARATION

Use: Bugleweed herb is best **infused** or **tinctured.** The tincture of the fresh herb is the most effective. **Washes, compresses** and **mouthwashes** can be prepared for various types of bleeding and injuries.

Dosage: Infusion: 8-16 g

Tincture: 2-5 ml at 1:3 strength in 40% ethanol

Caution: Contraindicated in low thyroid function or nontoxic goiter because of its *thyroid inhibitant* action. Avoid during pregnancy and lactation for the same reason and for its *antiprolactin* and *antigonadotropic* actions.

Note: The medium-strength European remedy **Adonis flower,** from *Adonis vernalis* L. (Ranunculaceae), also known as Pheasant's eye, is similar to Bugleweed in slowing down and strengthening heart functions. As a *heart relaxant* Adonis addresses the syndrome constrained heart Qi presenting tachycardia, palpitations and precordial pains. As a gentle *cardiovascular restorative,* it treats arrythmia, asystole and hypotension with feeble intermittent or irregular pulse. Its gentle *renal diuretic* action treats cardiac edema and chronic nephritis, and can prevent uremia. **Dose:** Decoction: 2-3 g. Tincture: 5-20 drops at 1:3 strength in 35% ethanol.

NOTES

The diminutive Bugleweed is found in wet, shady places such as woods and swamps throughout North America. The remedy has two important main aspects: a *cardiovascular* and a *relaxant* aspect. Eclectic herbal medics stressed using Bugleweed as a safe, gentle, nonaccumulative *heart relaxant* that does not cause the gastric irritation of the more spectacular remedy, Digitalis.

The key condition calling for Bugleweed's use is an "excited circulation and fast beats with deficient heart force" (FELTER 1922). In other words, the remedy addresses empty tense conditions of the cardiovascular system—in syndrome terms, **heart Qi constraint** and **heart Yin deficiency.** Bugleweed's *neurocardiac sedative* action, like that of Motherwort herb and Skullcap herb (fellow mints both) includes relief from anxiety, tension, irritability and insomnia. Whether unproductive stress, prolonged sickness or hyperthyroid functioning originally caused these conditions, Bugleweed will always work well.

Being one of the precious few *thyroid inhibitors,* the remedy can be helpful in those with thyroid hyperfunctioning. The typical symptoms seen correspond to the Chinese syndrome **Liver Yang rising,** presenting neurological disturbances in the head, such as blurred vision and ringing ears.

Where constrained Qi or Liver Yang rising is caused by **Yin deficiency,** Bugleweed herb acts as a Yin tonic. It is particularly good at relieving symptoms of **empty heat** such as hot spells and fever, along with any irritability and insomnia present. Here it acts in essentially the same way as Skullcap herb and Wood betony herb.

For individuals presenting **lung Yin deficiency,** Bugleweed is again superb not only in clearing the empty heat, but also in relieving the resultant dry cough and blood-streaked sputum. Lung TB and acute bronchitis of this type can be successfully treated, in this connection. It is Bugleweed's additional mild but effective *astringent* and

hemostatic actions that specifically address the hemoptysis, which are also effective for blood found in *any* of the body's fluid eliminations.

Bugleweed herb is also *relaxant* to respiratory and digestive functions, addressing constrained Qi syndromes such as **lung Qi constraint.** Its *bronchodilatant* action in particular relieves asthmatic breathing with anxiety and palpitations, like the acupuncture points Lu 7, P 6, Ht 7 and Bl 13 and 15. Because of the herb's calcium and magnesium content, Bugleweed has an excellent *spasmolytic* action that also applies to children's convulsions.

There is little overlap here in the way the Chinese species of Bugleweed, *Lycopus lucidus,* also known as Ze Lan, is used—despite the latter's proven *cardiotonic* action.

Selfheal Spike

Botanical source: *Prunella vulgaris* L.
    (Lamiaceae/Labiatae)
Pharmaceutical name: Spica Prunellae
Ancient names: Consolida minor, Brunella,
    Symphytum petraeum (Lat)
Other names: Woundwort, Healall, Carpenter's herb,
    Hookheal, Bumble bees, Pimpernel, Heart of
    the earth (Eng)
    Brunelle, Herbe au charpentier, Brunette, Petite
    consoude, Herbe St.-Quentin (Fr)
    Kleine Braunelle, Gaucheil, Mundfäulkraut,
    Halskraut (Ge)
    Xia Ku Cao (Mand)
    Ha Fu Chou (Cant)
Part used: the flower spike

NATURE

Therapeutic category: mild remedy with minimal chronic toxicity
Constituents: essential oil (incl. camphor, pinene, cineol, linalool, myrcene, phellandrene), bitter, tannins 5%, resins, triterpenoid saponins with triterpene acids, ursol, oleanolic/caffeic/ursolic acids, rutin, hyperoside, fenchone, delphinidin, cyanidin, alkaloids, soluble salts (incl. potassium chloride 68%), vitamins A, B^1, K, trace minerals
Effective qualities: somewhat sweet, bitter, astringent and pungent, cold, dry
    relaxing, calming, sinking, astringing, dissolving
Tropism: liver, stomach, blood
    Liver, Heart, Stomach meridians
    Warmth body
Ground: all krases, biotypes and constitutions

FUNCTIONS AND INDICATIONS

1 REGULATES HEART QI AND BALANCES CIRCULATION

heart Qi constraint (Liver Yang rising): headache, irritability, dizziness, ringing ears, eyeball pain
HYPERTENSION, neurocardiac syndrome

2 PROMOTES URINATION, RESOLVES TOXICOSIS, REDUCES LYMPH AND WATER CONGESTION, AND RELIEVES EDEMA

metabolic / heavy metal toxicosis: joint pains, malaise, fatigue, frequent headaches, swollen glands
RHEUMATISM, gout, arthritis, lymphadenitis
LYMPHADENITIS
EDEMA

3 CLEARS TOXIC HEAT AND REDUCES INFLAMMATION AND INFECTION; STIMULATES IMMUNITY

FEVER, heat cramps, heat exhaustion with *Qi-level heat*
MOUTH, GUM, THROAT, EAR and BREAST INFLAMMATIONS (incl. laryngitis, gingivitis, mastitis)
EYE INFLAMMATIONS (e.g. acute conjunctivitis, keratitis)
HOT, TIRED, PAINFUL EYES
BACTERIAL and VIRAL INFECTIONS (incl. herpes simplex, HIV)
LEUKOPENIA

4 ASTRINGES AND STOPS DISCHARGE AND BLEEDING; PROMOTES TISSUE REPAIR AND REDUCES CONTUSION AND SWELLING; LOWERS BLOOD SUGAR

HEMORRHAGE in general from any part
MENORRHAGIA in all hot and congestive conditions
DIARRHEA
HIYPERGLYCEMIA
FRESH WOUNDS, sores, ulcers (esp. of mouth and genitals), bites, sore nipples
CONTUSIONS
INJURIES (external and internal): fractures, ruptures, wounds, bruises (incl. lung injuries)

PREPARATION

Use: Selfheal spike is taken in **long infusion** and **tincture** form. **Ointments, plasters, compresses, washes, gargles, douches** and so on, are used topically for inflammatory conditions and tissue injury. These and many other Selfheal preparations were staples of the Greek medical pharmacy.
Dosage: Infusion: 8-18 g
             Tincture: 2-5 ml at 1:3 strength in 30% ethanol
Caution: Avoid using with digestive deficiency present.

NOTES

Selfheal herb joins the list of candidates contending for the prize of the most forgotten wound remedy—a title that might also go to Tansy mustard, Sanicle, Plantain and Woundwort. Only four hundred years ago Selfheal was among the top of this class, at a time when *vulneraries* were in high demand and used with extreme skill. Selfheal possesses strong *anti-inflammatory, antiecchy-* *motic, tissue-repairing* and *astringent* actions, and so is appropriate for a variety of external tissue traumas. Like Fleabane, Shepherd's purse and Geranium, it is also a true *hemostatic* with active or passive bleeding present.

When we consider the hot/cold dialectic in regard to its symptomatology, however, Selfheal herb assumes another dimension—as a good agent for clearing heat, a *refrigerant* for fevers, inflammation and simple functional hot conditions in general. Chinese medicine considers the herb particularly effective in conditions of **toxic heat** and **Qi-level heat.**

This comprehensive heat-clearing effect is reinforced by a good *resolvent detoxicant* action that addresses the two main forms of endogenous toxicosis, **metabolic** and **heavy metal toxicosis** —with their retinue of often vague and mysterious symptoms. When these toxicoses turn into an actual infection, Selfheal is still the right remedy, displaying a *broad-spectrum anti-infective* effect that's *antiviral, antibacterial* and *phagocyte stimulant.*

With so much to offer, Selfheal herb still stands out as a *cardiovascular relaxant* remedy with an excellent *hypotensive* action. We have modern Chinese research to thank for this usage, which corresponds to the traditional syndrome **heart Qi constraint.** From a holistic perspective, the remedy will always yield best results in individuals presenting **hypertension** along with underlying **toxicosis** and **heat.**

Cowslip flower

Botanical source: *Primula veris* L. (syn. *Primula officinalis* Hill), *P. elatior* L. (Primulaceae)
Pharmaceutical name: Flos Primulae
Ancient names: Paralysio, Palladium, Sanamunda, Verbascum odoratum, Herba arthritica, Tradella, Clavis S. Petri (Lat)
Other names: White betony, Palsywort, Bear's ears, Fairy cups, Horse buckles, Galligaskins, Mayflower, Herb Peter, Our Lady's keys, Culverkeys (Eng)
Primevère, Coucou, Oreille d'ours, Herbe à la paralysie (Fr)
Schlüsselblume, Himmelsschlüssel, Weisse Betonie, Frühlingsprimel, Lerchenblume (Ge)
Part used: the flower

NATURE
Category: mild remedy with minimal chronic toxicity
Constituents: essential oil, primulic camphor, glycoside, cyclamine, bitter compounds, yellow pigment
Effective qualities: somewhat sweet and pungent, neutral, dry
relaxing, restoring, calming
Tropism: heart, pericardium, vascular system, nerves, lungs
Heart, Pericardium, Liver, Lung meridians
Air, Warmth bodies
Ground: all for symptom use

FUNCTIONS AND INDICATIONS
1 **REGULATES HEART QI, CLEARS INTERNAL WIND AND STOPS SPASMS;**
 RELIEVES PAIN AND PROMOTES REST

heart Qi constraint: stress, tight chest, palpitations, unrest, irritability
NEUROCARDIAC SYNDROME

heart Yin deficiency with *nerve excess (Liver Yang Rising):* palpitations, headache, dizziness,
  irritability, sleep loss

TENSION and MIGRAINE HEADACHE

internal wind with *nerve excess:* tremors, spasms (esp. in extremities), convulsions

INFANTILE SEIZURES

NEURALGIA, NEURITIS

WHOOPING COUGH, bronchitis, asthma

INSOMNIA, unrest

2 PROMOTES SWEATING, DISPELS WIND-HEAT AND REDUCES FEVER; OPENS THE SINUSES AND REDUCES INFLAMMATION

lung wind-heat: fever, headache, aches and pains, coughing worse with stress

COLD and FLU ONSET

head damp-heat: nasal discharge, sinus congestion, frontal headache

SINUSITIS, RHINITIS

PERICARDITIS, cardiac edema

3 TONIFIES HEART QI, RESTORES THE NERVES AND RELIEVES DIZZINESS

heart Qi deficiency: chest oppression, palpitations, fatigue

nerve and brain deficiency: weakness, fatigue, local paralysis, numbness, dizziness, fainting

VERTIGO, CONCUSSION

PREPARATION

Use: Cowslip flower is prepared by **infusion** or **tincture.** The whole flowerheads should be used, including the calyx, which is high in vitamin C and saponins. Fresh Cowslip flowers should be immediately dried to ensure they don't lose their color. They require the same care in preparing as Marigold flowers do, for example.

To cause sweating with an oncoming cold or flu, Cowslip flower **infusion** should be sipped hot. External preparations include **liniments, compresses** and **ointments** for headaches, neuralgias, numbness, paralysis and so on. In European pharmacies, Cowslip flower preparations were standard items until the eighteenth century for nervous and cerebral disorders.

Being one of Cowslip flower's main ingredients, it may be possible to distill the **essential oil** from the flowering tops.

Dosage: Infusion: 8-12 g

　　　　　 Tincture: 2-4 ml at 1:3 strength in 35% ethanol

Caution: None

Note: The related *Primula vulgaris* L., or Primrose, is not used in herbal medicine.

NOTES

Cowslip flower is an important remedy for the nervous system, a *nervine*—in contrast to Cowslip root, which mainly stimulates the circulation and dispels wind-damp-cold. Called "White betony" in the past, Cowslip flower was considered second only to the alkaloidal Wood betony herb in treating disorders of the head and of the brain and consciousness in particular.

Cowslip flower seems to be simultaneously *relaxant, stimulant* and *sedative* to the nervous system, addressing both autonomic and voluntary nerve branches. Its dominant *neurocardiac relaxant* action treats tense neurocardiac conditions encapsulated in the syndrome **heart Qi constraint,** with its retinue of subclinical, often vague pre-anginal symtoms. In the next progressive syndrome, **heart Yin deficiency,** the symptoms become more prominent, and include recurring palpitations, anxiety, restlessness and irritability. However, Cowslip flower will always succeed best in subjects also presenting **chronic cardiac weakness,** as it exhibits a *cardiac restorative* effect. Here it is the equivalent of the acupuncture point selection Ht 5 and 9, P 4 and 7, and Bl 15.

In the past, Cowslip preparations were much used for treating **dizziness, vertigo** and **fainting spellls,** and often included the synergistic remedy Lily of the valley. Presumably a *cerebral stimulant* effect is operative, one that also recalls Arnica flower. Clearly, it seems that remedies prepared from *flowers* were considered particularly appropriate for treating conditions of the head.

Cowslip flower also acts as a *neuromuscular relaxant,* and its *spasmolytic* action can clear **internal wind** causing limb spasms and tremors. It was formerly esteemed for treating children's

seizures. **Wind-damp** is also released from the meridians and collaterals as the remedy relieves neuralgias, numbness and paralysis, including those in the head region, of course.

Cowslip flower's *relaxant* effect extends to the peripheral circulation and bronchi as a *vasodilatant diaphoretic* and *antipyretic.* This implies usage for **lung wind-heat** onsets of upper respiratory infections with spasmodic coughing. The essential oil and glycoside are probably "responsible" for these actions. The key symptoms that indicate its use here are restlessness, headache, nasal congestion and dry cough.

Mistletoe Herb

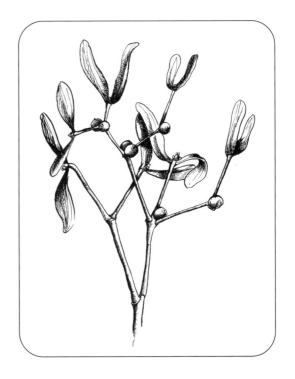

Botanical source: a) *Viscum album* L.
      b) *Phoradendron flavescens* Nuttall and spp.
      (Loranthaceae)
Pharmaceutical name: Herba Visci
Ancient names: Ixos (Gr)
    Lignum visci quercini, Lignum sanctae crucis
      (Lat)
    Auffolter, Kenster (Old Ge)
Other names: a) Birdlime, Masslinn, Allheal,
      European mistletoe (Eng)
    b) American mistletoe, Birdglue, Birdlime
    a) Gui, Herbe de la Croix (Fr)
    a) Mistel, Donarbeere, Heil aller Schäden,
      Affalter, Hexenbesen, Vogelmistel (Ge)
Part used: the twig and leaf, i.e. herb

NATURE

Therapeutic category: mild remedy with minimal chronic toxicity
Constituents: a) cardioactive polypeptide protein (viscotoxin), triterpenoid saponins (sapogenin oleanolic acid), resin (viscin), choline, tyramine, hystamine, pyridine, acetylcholine derivative, glycoside (viscalbin), histamine, ursone, tannin, volatile alkaloids, sterols (incl. beta-sitosterol, stigmasterol), mucilage, fixed oil, acetic, palmitic and phosphoric acids, caffeic acid, GABA, lignans, carotenoid, amines, amyrin, syringin, eleutherosides, polysaccharides, vitamin C, trace elements
Effective qualities: somewhat bitter and sweet, cold, moist
    relaxing, decongesting, softening, calming
Tropism: heart, uterus, kidneys, lungs, stomach, intestines, blood, nervous and muscular system
    Heart, Liver, Lung meridians
    Warmth, Air, Fluid bodies
Ground: all krases, biotypes and constitutions

FUNCTIONS AND INDICATIONS

1 REGULATES HEART QI, BALANCES CIRCULATION AND RELIEVES PALPITATIONS;
STIMULATES THE HEART, DRAINS WATER AND RELIEVES EDEMA

heart Qi constraint (Liver Yang rising): throbbing headache, flushed face, dizziness, ringing ears, palpitations, anxiety

ANGINA, TACHYCARDIA, neurocardiac syndrome

HYPERTENSION, peripheral arterial deficiency

MIGRAINE

MENOPAUSAL SYNDROME with palpitations, wheezing, irritability

PARASYMPATHETIC DEFICIENCY, hyperthyroid

heart water congestion: peripheral or central edema, shortness of breath, nausea, irregular heartbeats

CARDIAC EDEMA, VALVULAR DEFICIENCY, cardiac hypertrophy

CONGESTIVE HEART FAILURE

NEPHRITIS

2 REGULATES THE QI AND RELIEVES PAIN;
CLEARS INTERNAL WIND AND STOPS SPASMS

uterus Qi constraint: irritability, painful, delayed periods

DYSMENORRHEA (spasmodic)

lung Qi constraint: nervous dry cough, wheezing

SPASMODIC ASTHMA, pleurisy, whooping cough

nerve excess with *internal wind (wind-phlegm obstruction):* agitation, kidney, lumbar or abdominal pains, hyperaesthesia, trembling, twitches, convulsions, paralysis

SEIZURES (incl. of epilepsy, hysteria, chorea, infants), stroke, paralysis, hemiplegia

PAIN (arthritic, neuralgic, esp. tearing, paroxysmal)

3 PROMOTES DETOXIFICATION, DISSOLVES DEPOSITS, REDUCES INFLAMMATION AND
RELIEVES ECZEMA;
STIMULATES IMMUNITY AND REDUCES TUMORS

metabolic toxicosis with *wind-damp obstruction:* skin rashes, headaches, malaise, aches and pains

ECZEMA, GOUT, ARTHRITIS, arteriosclerosis

ALBUMINURIA, HYPERURICEMIA

TUMORS (incl. gynecological;. fibroids); cysts

4 VITALIZES THE BLOOD, REDUCES CONGESTION AND STOPS BLEEDING

uterus blood congestion: heavy periods, clots in flow, cramps

DYSMENORRHEA (congestive)

PROSTATE CONGESTION, prostatitis

MENORRHAGIA, HEMORRHAGE from blood congestion (esp. in head and pelvis, incl. hemoptysis, epistaxis, fibroidal bleeding, metrorrhagia, postpartum bleeding)

5 RELIEVES PAIN; SOFTENS BOILS AND DRAWS PUS

ARTHRITIS, spondylitis, neuritis, neuralgia (incl. sciatica), gout, rheumatism, frost bite

BOILS, furuncles

PREPARATION

Use: Mistletoe herb is prepared by **short decoction** (5-10 minutes of simmering followed by 15 minutes of steeping) and by **tincture.** A **cold infusion** of the remedy (overnight) is said to be best for heart Qi constraint or anginal conditions, but requires injection for best results (WEISS 1982).

To be fully effective, Mistletoe preparations should be made from the fresh, green or freshly-dried plant. Old, discolored herb material will reduce or inactivate the remedy's properties. Ignorance of this simple fact has been the basis for the dispute over Mistletoe's effectiveness for over a century.

A mucilagenous drawing **poultice** is made for boils, ulcers and chilblains, while Mistletoe **compresses** and **liniments** address neuralgias and myalgias. **Vaginal sponges** and **douches** are excellent for treating white vaginal discharges from vaginitis.

Dosage: Short decoction and **cold infusion:** 4-8 g

> **Tincture**: 1-3 ml at 1:3 strength in 45% ethanol

In acute cases (e.g., onset of seizure, migraine, asthma, cardiac edema, stroke, hemorrhage): take 3 ml (75 drops) of the standard tincture a few times only.

Usage guidelines: Severe **acute** conditions such as seizures, angina pectoris and asthma attacks generally require repeated intake over a short period of time. ELLINGWOOD (1919): "the dose must be sufficiently large and frequently repeated. In some cases it may be necessary to repeat the dose every fifteen minutes." In essential hypertension, Mistletoe herb is appropriate for cases of mild and medium severity.

Chronic cardiovascular and neurological disorders require regular and long-term use. For these, Eclectic practitioners began with the standard dose and over a few days increased this to 12 g of the herb or more, or over 4 ml of the tincture (three to four times daily). If this caused an excessive *nervous sedative* effect, they would lower the dose again and keep it there.

Caution: Mistletoe herb is a remedy in the mild category, is well tolerated and may be taken continuously for years. Still, it is recommended not to exceed the above doses simply because the remedy is a mild *gastrointestinal irritant* that in larger doses may cause inflammation.

Mistletoe is contraindicated during pregnancy because of its *uterine stimulant* action.

While **European mistletoe herb** (*Viscum album*) is well tolerated, **American mistletoe herb** (*Phoradendron flavescens* and spp.) has been known to cause minor idiosyncratic reactions such as appetite loss, loose stool and mild dizziness.

European mistletoe *berries* are not poisonous, contrary to popular belief (HOLZNER 1986). Nor are they used medicinally. American mistletoe *berries* are toxic, however, and should never be ingested.

Note: Despite the varying therapeutic descriptions of this remedy that arise because of cultural and linguis-tic differences, **European, American** and **Asian Mistletoe** are fairly interchangeable except for the use for tumors (including cancer). In light of insufficient evidence, it is currently unclear whether American mistletoe carries the same *immunostimulant* and *antitumoral* action as European mistletoe herb. However, all mistletoe species originally belonged to the genus *Viscum*, and their constituents are largely the same. Moreover, the Chinese mistletoe, Sang Ji Sheng, is prepared from either *Viscum* or *Loranthus*, and both are considered cancer-inhibitant in clinical practice. These facts taken together empirically support a common area of therapeutic effects for Mistletoe derived from the genuses *Viscum, Phoradendron* and *Loranthus*.

American mistletoe herb's *uterine stimulant* action is used to treat the syndrome **uterus Qi stagnation** and to promote labor with hypotonic contractions present. The remedy also has a traditional Native American use for infertility.

NOTES

The mistletoe was held in great esteem in the era of shamanic healing of the ancient Hibernian and Nordic European cultures, especially among the Druid elders. In North America, Native tribes, early White settlers and nineteenth century doctors all made extensive use of Mistletoe for various conditions. Today, Mistletoe herb is touted for a number of specific ailments, including cancer, hypertension and arthritis. Here we will delineate an area of therapeutic functions and indications common to both *Viscum* and *Phoradendron* species (see Note above).

There is no doubt that Mistletoe's epiphytic life cycle among certain trees is unique, and that this is what intrigues us about the plant. However, we must guard against making direct, literal comparisons between its growth habits as a parasitic plant and its therapeutic effects when ingested. Mistletoe herb's wide range of potential uses—some of which seem contradictory—results from a twin-pronged pharmacology on the nervous system and circulation. The remedy is essentially a systemic *relaxant* and *cardiac stimulant* in one. Its *relaxant* effect works through adrenergic inhibition to relax **tense** conditions among neurocardiac, respiratory, reproductive and neuromuscular functions. It addresses **painful, spasmodic** disorders such as spasmodic angina, vascular headaches, hypertension, neuralgia, asthma, spasmodic dysmenorrhea and muscle spasms, exhibiting *spasmolytic, muscle-relaxant, analgesic, anti-inflammatory* and *anticonvulsant* actions. Among the compounds known to be active here are GABA and alkaloids.

In energetic terms, Mistletoe regulates disordered Qi circulation, thereby releasing **constrained Qi** and its sequelae **rising Liver Yang** and **wind-phlegm** in the **meridians.** Like Uncaria Gou Teng and Gastrodia Tian Ma in Chinese medicine, the remedy has always had an impeccable reputation in the treatment of epilepsy, chorea, seizures in general and other chronic neurological disorders.

As a cardiovascular remedy, Mistletoe herb is both a *neurocardiac relaxant* and *cardiac stimulant*. Over time, the heart and circulation will receive *vasodilatant, hypotensive* and *capillary stimulant* effects because of the aminobutyric acid, viscotoxin and tyramine combined. These provide cumulative benefits for individuals presenting hypertension, tachycardia and neurogenic anginal conditions—summarized in the syndrome **heart Qi constraint.**

Other components (including the resin viscin)

meanwhile cause potential *heart stimulation* and *diuresis* useful for cardiac edema, congestive heart failure and other conditions arising from **heart Yang deficiency.** Because of the concerted action of these various constituents, it seems likely that Mistletoe herb bivalently *regulates* blood pressure rather than simply increasing or decreasing it—as with Lobelia herb, for example.

Mistletoe herb also exerts a strong tropism for the pelvic organs, where it acts as a broad *blood decongestant*. Individuals in whom **pelvic blood congestion** leads to congestive dysmenorrhea or prostate congestion will be the main benefactors. The remedy's good *vasoconstrictant* and *hemostatic* actions in particular address **menorrhagia** and **uterine bleeding.** The image in the U.S. of Mistletoe as a woman's remedy is further reinforced by the use of American mistletoe (*Phorandendron* spp.) as an *emmenagogue* and *oxytocic parturient* that stimulates uterine contractions during menstruation and labor.

In terms of the fluids as a whole, Mistletoe herb is useful for conditions involving **depositions** and **enlargements** such as benign tumors, arthritis, cycts and prostate hyperplasia. With its *resolvent detoxicant* and *diuretic* action, triterpenoid saponins are effective here as they are for the capillaries. European mistletoe in particular is a traditional remedy for treating **malignant tumors,** and has shown activity in all stages of cancer. The *antitumoral* action is thought to result from three concerted actions: the broad-based, non-specific stimulation of immune functions, the specific *cytotoxic* action of the viscotoxins, and the general *vasoconstrictive* effect. At the very least, Mistletoe preparations should become standard for the after-treatment of chemotherapy and radiation therapy.

Regulate Intestines Qi, Harmonize Digestion and Relieve Pain

Intestinal relaxants (intestinal spasmolytics)

Wild Yam Root

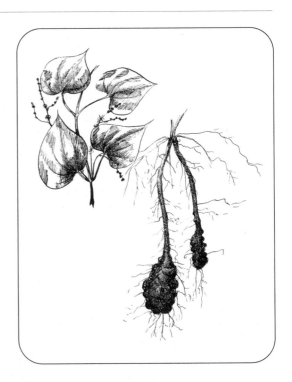

Botanical source: *Dioscorea villosa* L.,
     D. villosa var. *glabra* (Dioscoreaceae)
Pharmaceutical name: Rhizoma Dioscoreae villosae
Other names: Rheumatism root, Colic root, Devil's
     bones, Harry yam, China root, Yuma (Am)
    Igname (Fr)
    Zottige Yamswurzel (Ge)
Part used: the rhizome

NATURE

Therapeutic category: mild remedy with minimal chronic toxicity
Constituents: steroidal saponins (incl. diosgenin, dioscin), phytosterols (incl. pregnenolone), alkaloids, tannins, resin, starch
Effective qualities: bitter, astringent, oily, cool, dry
    relaxing, astringing, stabilizing
Tropism: liver, kidneys, intestines, uterus
    Liver, Gallbladder, Kidney, *chong, ren, dai* meridians
    Air body
Ground: Sanguine and Choleric krases
    Expressive/Jue Yin and Tough/Tai Yang biotypes
    Hematogenic/Sulphuric constitution

FUNCTIONS AND INDICATIONS

1   **REGULATES INTESTINES QI, HARMONIZES DIGESTION AND RELIEVES PAIN;**
     REDUCES LIVER CONGESTION AND REGULATES CIRCULATION

stomach and intestines Qi constraint (Liver/Spleen disharmony): epigastric or abdominal pain,
    indigestion, flatulence, nausea, vomiting, hiccups
GASTROINTESTINAL COLIC, colitis, irritable bowel syndrome, severe hiccups
DIARRHEA
liver and gallbladder Yang excess: acute gastric distress, right rib and right upper back pain, headache
GALLBLADDER COLIC, acute cholecystitis, cholelithiasis
liver Qi stagnation: yellow skin, right flank soreness, nausea, indigestion
LIVER CONGESTION (chronic)
kidney / adrenal Qi constraint: nervous excitability, nausea, spasmodic intestinal colic and griping

PAIN from SPASMS (all kinds, incl. biliary, neuralgic, ovarian, uterine, knee and leg pain)

MIGRAINE, hypertension, arterial spasms, circulatory deficiency

2 REGULATES UTERUS QI AND RELIEVES PAIN

uterus Qi constraint: long cycle, painful or heavy periods, cramps before flow

DYSMENORRHEA (spasmodic), ovulation pains

PAIN during PREGNANCY, LABOR and POSTPARTUM

3 TONIFIES REPRODUCTIVE QI, REGULATES MENSTRUATION, MENOPAUSE AND PREGNANCY, AND STOPS DISCHARGE;
PREVENTS MISCARRIAGE AND STOPS VOMITING;
INCREASES HORMONES

kidney Qi deficiency with damp: vaginal/seminal discharges, irregular periods, long cycles, lumbar pain

LEUCORRHEA, spermatorrhea

ESTROGEN / PROGESTERONE (?) DEFICIENCY conditions, incl.:

PMS with joint pains, oversensitivity, irritability

MENOPAUSAL SYNDROME

THREATENED or HABITUAL MISCARRIAGE

PRE-TERM LABOR PAINS in THIRD TRIMESTER

NAUSEA and VOMITING of pregnancy (not in first trimester)

4 REDUCES INFLAMMATION AND PAIN, AND CLEARS WIND-DAMP-HEAT FROM THE SKIN AND MERIDIANS

wind-damp-heat obstruction: red, swollen, stiff painful joints, muscle aches

FIBROMYALGIA, RHEUMATISM, ARTHRITIS

skin damp-heat: skin rashes with redness, sores

ECZEMA, dermatitis, boils

PREPARATION

Use: Wild yam root is prepared by **decoction** or **tincture.** Two to three months of use is required for the full hormonal action to engage (function 3), which may be *estrogenic* or *progesteronic* (see Notes).

In recent times this remedy has empirically been used as a woman's *contraceptive* that may work by inhibiting ovulation. The average percentage of efficacy, however, has never properly been statistically studied. The *contraceptive* action seems to be free of side effects and completely reverseable at any time.

Dosage: Decoction: 8-16 g

       Tincture: 2-4 ml at 1:2 strength in 60% ethanol

Larger doses than these produce an *emetic* effect.

• *To prevent threatened miscarriage:* take 2.5-5 ml (1/2-1 tsp) of the tincture every hour.

• *For postpartum pain:* take 1-2 ml (25-50 drops) of the tincture in warm water every 30-60 minutes.

Caution: The hormonally-acting Wild yam root is generally considered safe during pregnancy. However, it is best used specifically just to relieve nausea or prevent miscarriage, or used in small amounts in a formula along with other ingredients.

NOTES

The hard, white root of the North American wild yam is one of numerous yams used worldwide in herbal medicine. (At least eight species of *Dioscorea* are used in Oriental medicine alone, for example (see HOLMES 1997). Although they share some uses such as urinary and rheumatic disorders, each yam type has its own specific functions and symptomatologies, or symptom indications.

Wild yam root is an important *relaxant* remedy for **tense** or **constrained Qi** conditions of the **dig-**

estive organs, such as colic, gallstone colic and irritable bowel syndrome. The root exerts good *spasmolytic* and *analgesic* actions that effectively relieve painful spasms throughout the smooth muscle organs. According to Eclectic medical sources, this condition will either dramatically improve within two hours or not change at all—in which case a different *digestive relaxant* should then be chosen. In cases of abdominal pain of this type, Wild yam would certainly be a good complement to an acupuncture point selection like Liv 3, St 36, Liv 13 and 14, P6 and CV 10 and 12, along with other *intestinal relaxants* such as Hops flower, Camomile flower and Cramp bark.

However, Wild yam root actually treats most patterns arising from a stagnation of the Qi. Like Mugwort herb and Cyperus Xiang Fu in Chinese medicine, the root is also excellent for releasing **constrained uterus Qi** in cases of spasmodic dysmenorrhea. Native American Meskwawi women, for example, used Wild yam to ease labor and afterbirth pains—a commendable practice even today. The added hormonal influence also adds weight to its use in PMS and menopause involving low estrogen, or possibly low progesterone.

While most practitioners agree that Wild yam root exerts some kind of hormonal influence, there is no agreement as to exactly what this is. This is partly due to the fact that there are currently new, debated ideas circulating about the nature of progesterone and estrogen hormones, and their functional relationship. What one person may see as an *estrogenic* effect may be defined as a *progesteronic* one by another.

However, the Wild yam debate also revolves around the interpretation of its hormone-like components, the steroidal saponins and the phytosterols. Although recent research has shown *estrogenic* activity for diosgenin, this is currently far from conclusive—especially when transferred to the human lab, the metabolism. Furthermore, nothing is known about the interaction and net hormonal result of these two key players in a woman's body. Alternatively, it may be that in women with progesterone deficiency, the *estrogenic* action in turn causes a secondary increase in *progesterone* levels.

If we look at the Wild yam **hormonal issue** from a purely phenomenological, clinical and historical viewpoint, and interpret this according to JOHN LEE's basic definitions of estrogen and progesterone functions, it is evident that this remedy shows more net *progesteronic* than *estrogenic* effects—or at least shows a greater affinity for treating progesterone insuffficiency conditions. Wild yam was historically prized by Eclectic practitioners for its reliability in treating vomiting during pregnancy, reducing the chances of a miscarriage during the first trimester, stopping acute threatening miscarriage, and reducing the chances of toxemia. These are now thought to be **progesterone deficient** conditions. Today, the remedy's putative *contraceptive* effect may be due to the ovulation-inhibiting action that increased progesterone provides.

Note also, that this discussion of wild yam as a *whole herb remedy* does not apply in any way to the "wild yam" or "progesterone" creams available on the market. Most of these are synthesized from soybean sitosterol, a phytosterol, with an ultimate *progesteronic* effect.

Chronic **inflammatory disorders** such as fibromyalgia, rheumatism, arthritis and eczema are the second main area indicating the use of Wild yam. The remedy's *anti-inflammatory* and *analgesic* actions have shown to involve the activity of its steroidal saponins. Like its Oriental cousin Dioscorea Bi Xie, Wild yam root in energetic terms clears **wind, damp** and **heat** from the **skin** and **meridians.** This function was put to considerable use, for example, among Blacks in the American South—a usage that might well have arisen from the use of similar-looking and acting yams in the African home country. Congenial synergies can be made with the addition of Meadowsweet herb, Heartsease herb, Devil's claw root and Bogbean leaf, for instance.

Hops Flower

Botanical source: *Humulus lupulus* L. (Moraceae)
Pharmaceutical name: Flos Humuli
Ancient names: Bsuon (Gr), Lupulus (Lat)
Other names: Seeder, Bine, Bur (Eng)
    Houblon grimpant (Fr)
    Hopfenzapfen, Zaunhopfen (Ge)
Part used: the strobile (female flower)

NATURE

Therapeutic category: medium-strength remedy with moderate chronic toxicity
Constituents: bitter resin compound (incl. valerianic acid, lupulic acids [lupulone, humulone, cohumulone, lupulene 10%, colupulone, adlupulone]), essential oil up to 2% (incl. monoterpenes 30%, sesquiterpenes [incl. humulene, farnesene, caryophyllene, methylbutene, myrcene, trithiahexane], terpenoid and aliphatic esters), cholin, asparagin, trimethalamine, alkaloids, flavonoids (kaempferol, quercitin), phytoestrogens, gamma-linoleic acid, chalcone (xanthohumol), vitamin C
Effective qualities: bitter, pungent, astringent, cold, dry
    calming, relaxing, restoring, dissolving, sinking
Tropism: reproductive and urinary organs, heart, liver, stomach, intestines, skin, central nervous system
    Heart, Pericardium, Kidney, Liver meridians
    Air, Warmth, Fluid bodies
Ground: Choleric and Sanguine krases
    all biotypes and constitutions

FUNCTIONS AND INDICATIONS

1   **REGULATES INTESTINES QI, HARMONIZES DIGESTION AND RELIEVES PAIN;**
    CLEARS INTERNAL WIND AND STOPS SPASMS

intestines Qi constraint: indigestion worse with stress/emotions, irregular bowel movement,
    abdominal pains
COLITIS (neurogenic), IBS, colic
lung Qi constraint: nervous irritable cough, wheezing, anxiety
ASTHMA
heart Qi constraint (Liver Yang rising): ringing ears, dizziness, palpitations, anxiety, chest pains
NEUROCARDIAC SYNDROME
PAIN (incl. headache, neuralgia, myalgia, toothache, earache)
nerve excess with *internal wind:* nervous unrest, abdominal pains or spasms, tremors, twitches

2   REGULATES UTERUS QI, REGULATES MENSTRUATION AND INCREASES ESTROGEN; PROMOTES LACTATION

uterus Qi constraint: painful periods, cramps esp. with onset, scanty flow, stress
SPASMODIC DYSMENORRHEA, AMENORRHEA
ESTROGEN DEFICIENCY (incl. in dysmenorrhea, PMS)
INSUFFICIENT LACTATION

3   RELAXES CONSTRAINT, CALMS THE MIND AND RELIEVES ANXIETY; CLEARS EMPTY HEAT AND REDUCES FEVER, SEXUAL OVERSTIMULATION AND DISCHARGES

kidney/adrenal Qi constraint: nervous/mental tension (esp. from anxiety, stress, pain), agitation, pains
floating Yang: restlessness, sleep loss, irritability, dizziness, palpitations
INSOMNIA, ANXIETY, AGITATION (esp. with worry, mental overstimulation)
Yin deficiency with empty heat: night sweats, intermittent fever
LOW-GRADE FEVERS (intermittent, remittent, in *shao yin* and *shao yang* stages)
Kidney fire (Heart and Kidney Yin deficiency): hot spells, insomnia, palpitations, sexual
   overstimulation, premature ejaculation, wet dreams
SEXUAL OVERSTIMULATION (neurosis) in all conditions (incl. satyriasis, nymphomania)
GENITAL DISCHARGES (incl. nocturnal emissions, vaginitis, esp. with *damp-heat* or *empty heat*)

4   STIMULATES DIGESTION AND PROMOTES APPETITE

liver-gallbladder-stomach Qi stagnation: appetite loss, fatigue, epigastric bloating and pain, belching
ANOREXIA, ANEMIA, chlorosis
ATONIC ULCERS

5   PROMOTES URINATION AND DETOXIFICATION, AND DISSOLVES STONES

kidney Qi stagnation with *metabolic toxicosis:* dry skin, skin rashes, headaches, painful urination
GOUT, rheumatism
URINARY STONES

6   CLEARS DAMP-HEAT FROM THE SKIN; REDUCES INFECTION, INFLAMMATION AND SWELLING

skin damp-heat: skin eruptions with redness, oozing
ECZEMA, dermatitis, herpes, ringworm, scurvy, lymphadenitis (scrofula), acne, skin tumors
   (incl. malignant ones)
CERVICAL ADENITIS
SKIN BLEMISHES or deformities, bruises
LUNG TUBERCULOSIS, venereal and urinary infections, leprosy

PREPARATION

Use: Hops flower is prepared by **long infusion** or **tincture.** The freshly dried flowers, called strobiles, are best for this. They should steep as long as 30 minutes for the best infusion.

Being a foremost remedy for skin conditions (eruptions, swellings, tumors), Hops flower can be used topically in **ointments, compresses, poultices** and **washes,** alone or combined.

Dosage: Infusion: 6-9 g
   Tincture: 1-2.5 ml at 1:3 strength in 60% ethanol

Caution: Because Hops flower is a mild *nervous depressant,* it should not be used in any condition presenting depression, nor combined with sedative medication like Pentobarbital. For the same reason, and because of its medium-strength status, do not exceed these doses, nor use Hops continuously on its own.

Again, for the same reason and because of its downward-moving energy, Hops flower should be used

with caution during pregnancy, and is then preferably combined with other herbs in a formula.
Note: The older Hops flowers become, the more their lupulin content breaks down and oxidizes, resulting in *stimulating* side effects. For best results, therefore, avoid using flowers over six months old.

NOTES

Because it combines two different main energetic qualities, the bitter and the pungent tastes, Hops flower has very specific therapeutic applications. The herb's many functions can be better understood by examining these two main emblems of vitalistic pharmacology. Hops is thus polarized between the bitter taste quality, which is mainly cooling and downward moving; and the pungent quality, which is mainly relaxing and somewhat stimulating.

As a bitter tasting herb, Hops flower contains bitter resinous compounds and a bitter substance, lupulin, found in the aromatic resinous dust that coats the mature pendulous strobiles, along with some essential oils. Hops in this sense is a classic bitter, cold, downward-moving *digestive stimulant,* like Gentian root in Class 8, for instance. It also includes a nice *cholagogue* action. As such the herb will treat **upper-gastric digestive** disorders presenting stagnation with keynote symptoms of appetite loss and fatigue. **Qi stasis** of the **gallbladder and stomach** is the main syndrome addressed here.

Hops' heat-clearing effect is also evident in its *detoxicant, anti-inflammatory* and *antiseptic* actions. These engage mostly in acute and chronic **skin inflammations, infections** and **suppurations,** including eczema, acne and ringworm. Energetically speaking, the remedy clears **damp-heat** from the **skin.** Its *antiseptic* action has also proven valuable in lung TB, for example—an effect in which the acid lupulone is considered active.

Hops is also a classic Greek bitter medicinal for helping the individual's vital force throw off intermittent fevers, acting in this sense exactly like Wormwood herb or the Chinese herb Artemisia Qing Hao. As a bitter yet somewhat pungent *antipyretic,* the herb was traditionally used both in *shao yang*-stage fevers with intermittent heat and *shao yin*-stage fevers with low-grade, empty heat.

Again as a bitter, sinking remedy, Hops flower is a good cooling *neurocardiac* and *neuroreproductive sedative.* The classic Chinese medicine syndrome it addresses here is **Heart and Kidney Yin deficiency.** In this symptom picture the individual presents anxiety, insomnia and sexual over-stimulation. This is often seen in chronic functional conditions, including perimenopausal syndrome, as well as in organic diseases. Here Hops drains Kidney fire and sinks floating Yang arising from Yin deficiency, while simultaneously supporting the Heart and calming the mind—in a way comparable to the acupuncture points P 8, HT 6 and 8, Kd 3 and 6, and Bl 15. In this context, Hops could easily replace the Chinese remedy Anemarrhena Zhi Mu, if necessary.

As a pungent herb, however, Hops flower contains a generous amount of pungent, aromatic, soporific volatile oil that is sometime extracted and made into an absolute by solvent extraction. This essential oil is high in sesquiterpenes and esters, thereby ensuring reliable general *nervous relaxant* and *sedative* effects. Hops is a well-known remedy for **insomnia** and agitation—but is especially called for in individuals prsenting heat signs because of its cooling effect. Like Passionflower herb and Scruphularia Xuan Shen, Hops is an herb for hot-type insomnia, not the cold type (Valerian root is the opposite).

Likewise, as a *relaxant* the remedy excels in **tense, constrained Qi** conditions that tend towards **heat.** Individuals with conditions that present **nervous tension** and ensuing spasms, pain and irritability will benefit here the most. Even more specifically, Hops is an especially fine *intestinal relaxant* for tense gut conditions that involve not only autonomic/vagal imbalance but also physical digestive stagnation from biliary and gastric insufficiency. Hops is known to systemically inhibit and balance autonomic metabolic and neuromuscular functions in a similar way to Lavender flower.

Given the complexity of the above picture we may think that Hops was now "all wrapped up." Not so. As a *urinary stimulant* this remedy has always enjoyed a good reputation in Europe for its *detoxicant diuretic* action. **Kidney Qi stagnation** and even **metabolic toxicosis** with rheumatic, gouty and urinary stone conditions are true and tried indications here. Note in this respect the synergistic activity of resins, the glycoside asparagin and the monoterpene essential oil fraction.

Bitter Orange Rind
(and Bergamot Essential Oil)

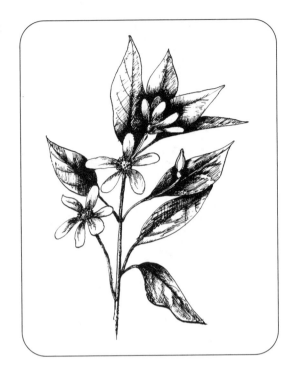

Botanical source: a) *Citrus aurantium* L.;
   b) *C. aurantium* ssp. *bergamia* Risso et
   Poiteau (Rutaceae)

Pharmaceutical name: Pericarpium Citri aurantii
   (bergamotae)

Ancient names: Limonion melon (Gr)
   Malum limonium (Lat)

Other names: a) Bitter orange   b) Bergamot orange
   a) Orange amère   b) Bergamot (Fr)
   a) Bitter Orange   b) Bergamotte (Gr)

Parts used: the rind

NATURE

Therapeutic category: mild remedy with minimal chronic toxicity

Constituents: *Citrus aur.*: essential oil (incl. limonene 90%, geranyl/neryl acetate, nonanal, decanal, garanial, citron-ellal, coumarins and furanocoumarins), flavonoids (incl. hesperidin), coumarins, citric acid, vitamin C

Citrus aur. ssp. *berg.*: essential oil 0.5% (incl. linalylacetate up to 29%, d-limonene, linalool, furano-coumarins bergamotin, bergaptene, citral, dihydrocuminalcohol, camphene, pinene, limonene), flavonoids (incl. hesperidin), coumarins, phytosterols, citric acid, vitamin C

Effective qualities: bitter, sweet, somewhat pungent, neutral with cooling and warming potential
   relaxing, restoring, calming

Tropism: stomach, intestines, liver, lungs, uterus, central nervous system
   Liver, Lung, Stomach meridians
   Air, Warmth bodies

Ground: Sanguine and Choleric krases
   Expressive/Jue Yin and Tough/Shao Yang biotypes
   Hematogenic/Sulphuric constitution

FUNCTIONS AND INDICATIONS

1   **REGULATES INTESTINES QI, STIMULATES AND HARMONIZES DIGESTION,
   RELIEVES PAIN AND STOPS VOMITING**

   intestines Qi constraint (liver/Spleen disharmony): abdominal colic and distension, irregular stool
   COLIC, irritable bowel syndrome

   gallbladder and stomach Qi stagnation: painful digestion, flatus, epigastric distension, appetite loss
   NAUSEA, vomiting, biliary dyspepsia

2   **RELAXES CONSTRAINT, RELIEVES IRRITABILITY AND HARMONIZES THE MIND**

   kidney / adrenal Qi constraint: nervous tension, mood swings, mild insomnia, anxiety
   uterus Qi constraint: painful, difficult periods
   SPASMODIC DYSMENORRHEA

MOOD SWINGS, DEPRESSION with anxiety, irritability, mental fatigue
STRESS-RELATED DISORDERS

3 CLEARS DAMP-HEAT AND REDUCES INFLAMMATION, FEVER AND INFECTION; PROMOTES TISSUE REPAIR AND REDUCES TUMORS (?)

REMITTENT FEVER (*shao yang* stage)

LUNG, UROGENITAL and SKIN, MOUTH and THROAT INFECTIONS (bacterial, with *damp-heat,* acute and chronic, incl. bronchitis, TB, diphtheria, laryngitis, strep throat, tonsillitis); shingles

SKIN conditions (incl. dermatitis, eczema, herpes, acne, psoriasis, seborrhea, scabies)

INTESTINAL PARASITES

WOUNDS, ulcers (esp. chronic, indolent)

REPRODUCTIVE TUMORS (incl. fibroids, cancer) (?)

PREPARATION

Use: Bitter orange rind is prepared by **long infusion** for the first two functions and indications above. It is a common component of traditional formulas to prevent or treat Qi constraint of the digestive organs. For the additional function 3, however, the **tincture** or distilled **essential oil** is required. The easily available essential oil of Bergamot orange is the most effective for this purpose, and is the most effective for function 3. Only the organic essential oil should be used.

Used topically for skin conditions and injuries, Bergamot essential oil should be diluted to 1% (as with all citrus essential oils) with a fatty carrier oil. It should also be considered in **sponges, douches, pessaries** and **sitzbaths** for urogenital infections.

Dosage: Long infusion: 4-10 g

> **Tincture:** 2-4 ml at 1:3 strength in 35% ethanol

> **Essential oil:** 2-4 drops in a gel cap topped with some olive oil

Caution: Use the rinds of organic bitter oranges whenever possible.

Note: The **dried rind** of the **unripe mandarin** (*Citrus reticulata* spp.) is the Chinese remedy Qing Pi. It may be used interchangeably with Bitter orange rind for functions 1 and 2. .

NOTES

Regardless of the type of Bitter orange used, and in what form, two functions have time and again been ascribed to this remedy in all traditional medical systems. First, a *digestive stimulant* and *carminative* effect. This is signaled in the bitter and somewhat pungent taste of its essential oil. Bitter orange rind here exerts a pronounced *stimulating* effect on the gallbladder and stomach, thereby mobilizing upper digestive stagnation through its *cholagogue* and *gastric secretory* actions. The suffering individual finds her epigastric heaviness and distension relieved, and the often-seen despondency or gloom lifted. In essential oil form, Bitter orange or Bergamot oil can act as a specific *antidepressant.*

Bitter orange's second effect is a *relaxant* one, acting both systemically and locally on smooth muscle. The remedy relaxes **constrained Qi** in the abdominal and chest area, eases colicky pain and relieves menstrual cramps. Here the essential oil really scores over the dried orange rind, however green and immature it may be.

We have the perfume industry to thank for the existence of the essential oil of Bitter orange. On a small stretch of the Calabrian coast in Italy, the oil of a local type of bitter orange has been distilled for hundreds of years for its exquisite warm, floral-citrus, refreshing fragrance. Bergamot oil, as it is called today, supersedes the many traditional preparations made from Bitter orange, such as waters (hydrosols), conserves (the original marmalade), ointments and so on. Most of these originated in Italy too, and were made from a variety of bitter oranges and tangerines.

Italian chemist ROVESTI'S work in the 1950s in exploring Bergamot oil's physiological and psychological properties was instrumental in making it more widely known. Modern research has shown Bergamot oil to be a fairly *broad antibacterial* agent for **infections,** enhanced by significant *anti-inflammatory* and possible *antitumoral* actions. In many infective and pruritic **skin problems** Bergamot oil has also been found particularly helpful. Oily, high-sebum skin benefits especially, as do cold sores, ulcers and acne.

In aromatherapy Bergamot oil is often used for its fragrance effect which alone has far-reaching effects on feelings, moods and mind-sets. By working on the hypothalamus as a regulator, the oil promotes relaxation, self-confidence, joy and optimism. States of stress, grief and chronic depression respond particularly well to the nurturing yet bracing quality of this unique essential oil.

Caraway Seed

Botanical source: *Carum carvi* L.
       (Apiaceae/Umbelliferae)
Pharmaceutical name: Fructus Carvii
Ancient names: Kareon (Gr)
       Carum (Lat)
Other names: Carvi, Carvi des prés (Fr)
       Kümmel, Wiesenkümmel (Ge)
Part used: the fruit

NATURE

Therapeutic category: medium-strength remedy with moderate chronic toxicity
Constituents: essential oil 4-7% (incl. monoterpenone carvone 45-50%, monoterpenes 40-45% [incl. carvene 30%, limonene 26-45%], monoterpenols 2-6% [incl. cis-carveol]), tannins, resin, protein

This remedy is virtually identical to **Fennel seed**, Fructus Foeniculi, in its nature, functions and uses. Note the following differences, however:
1. Caraway seed is more effective than Fennel seed for treating gastrointestinal disorders. Its *spasmolytic, cholagogue, choleretic, antifermentative* and *carminative* actions address conditions marked by biliary and gastric dyspepsia, epigastric and abdominal diress, pain and bloating. The main syndromes indicated are **intestines Qi constraint, gallbladder & stomach Qi stagnation** and **intestines damp- cold.**
2. Caraway seed's *stimulant expectorant* and *mucolytic* actions address catarrhal respiratory conditions with cough and abundant sputum, including bronchitis. The syndrome treated is lung **phlegm-damp** and **lung phlegm-cold.**
3. Caraway seed is less effective than Fennel seed in treating the various urinary disorders.
4. The **essential oil** of Caraway is used topically as *antiparasitic* in parasitic skin conditions such as tinea, scabies and pediculosis. Its *analgesic* and *detumescent* actions treat tissue injuries such as sprains, strains and wounds showing swelling and pain.

Preparation, use and dosage: As for Fennel seed.
Caution: Contraindicated in infants, babies and pregnant women. Do not exceed theses doses as higher doses can create cumulative chronic toxicity. In high doses the essential oil is neurotoxic and abortive.

Regulate Bladder Qi, Harmonize Urination and Relieve Strangury

Urinary relaxants (urinary spasmolytics)

Wild Carrot Seed

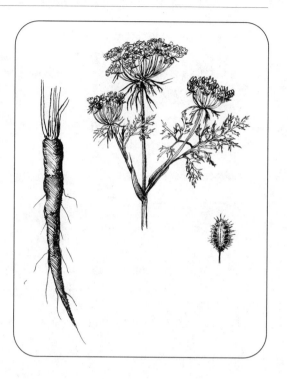

Botanical source: *Daucus carota* L.
     (Apiaceae/Umbelliferae)
Pharmaceutical name: Fructus Dauci
Ancient names: Daukon (Gr)
Other names: Queen Anne's lace, Bird's nest
     (Eng and Am)
     Carotte (Fr)
     Karotte, Möhre, Gelbe Rübe (Ge)
Part used: the fruit; also the root, Radix Dauci

NATURE

Therapeutic category: mild remedy with minimal chronic toxicity
Constituents: essential oil (incl. terpenes [esp. monoterpenes], limonene), alkaloid daucine, asparagin, carotene, glucose, sucrose, pectin, malic acid, xantophyll, pentosane, vitamins C, B^1, B^2, B^6, E, H
Effective qualities: somewhat bitter, sweet and pungent, neutral, moist
     relaxing, stimulating, decongesting, dissolving
Tropism: bladder, kidneys, uterus, intestines, stomach
     Liver, Kidney, Bladder meridians; Air, Fluid bodies
Ground: Sanguine krasis

FUNCTIONS AND INDICATIONS

1   **REGULATES BLADDER QI, HARMONIZES URINATION AND RELIEVES PAIN & INCONTINENCE; REGULATES INTESTINES QI**

    bladder Qi constraint: difficult, painful or obstructed urination; urinary dribbling
    NEUROGENIC BLADDER, incontinence, dysuria
    PROSTATITIS, URINARY INFECTIONS
    intestines Qi constraint: indigestion, flatulence, abdominal pain
    COLIC, hiccup

2   **PROMOTES URINATION, DRAINS WATER AND RELIEVES EDEMA; DECONGESTS THE LIVER, RESOLVES TOXICOSIS, DISSOLVES STONES AND REDUCES ECZEMA**

    kidney water congestion: leg edema, puffy eyes, fatigue
    EDEMA, CHRONIC NEPHRITIS, ANURIA
    liver Qi stagnation: indigestion, right flank soreness
    LIVER CONGESTION

kidney Qi stagnation with *metabolic toxicosis:* malaise, skin rashes, smelly urine, aches and pains

URIC ACID DIATHESIS, GOUT

URINARY STONES

ECZEMA, chronic boils (e.g. furuncles)

3 PROMOTES MENSTRUATION, REDUCES STAGNATION AND EXPELS THE AFTERBIRTH

uterus Qi stagnation/constraint: delayed, painful menstruation

SPASMODIC DYSMENORRHEA, amenorrhea

RETAINED PLACENTA and lochia

4 REDUCES SWELLING AND TUMORS, AND PROMOTES TISSUE REPAIR

SWELLING, sores, abscesses, carbuncles

TUMORS (incl. cancer)

INJURIES, rodent or gangrenous ulcers

SKIN DRYNESS, PRURITUS

PREPARATION

Use: Wild carrot seed is used in **infusion, tincture** or **essential oil** form, in ascending order of strength. **Poultices** and **ointments** are used externally for skin swellings and dry skin. In addition to their use for female contraception, the tincture and essential oil also promote labor contractions and, after the birth, help expel the placenta.

The fresh **juice** of the organically-grown carrot root, drunk regularly, to some extent treats the above conditions if taken over a longer period.

Dosage: Infusion: 6-10 g

Tincture: 1-4 ml at 1:2 strength in 40% ethanol

Essential oil: 1-3 drops in a gel cap with some olive oil

Caution: Carrot seed is forbidden during pregnancy as it is a *uterine stimulant* and potential *abortifacient.*

Note: Wild carrot root and **herb** are used in a similar way to the seed. Wild carrot root is more *stimulating* and *restoring* than the seed; it is a better *draining* and *detoxicant diuretic* for edema with urinary obstruction, and toxicosis with urinary irritation, as well as a *restorative* for urinary incontinence. Wild carrot seed is a better *urinary relaxant* for difficult, painful urination, however. Standard doses are used for Wild carrot root and herb.

NOTES

The Greek physician GALEN classified Wild carrot seed as one of the Minor Warming Seeds. Subsequently the remedy was much used in compound formulas by Persian doctors such as AR-RAZI. Wild carrot seed's double action of relaxing and stimulating unfolds almost entirely on urinary and reproductive functions. As a *urinary relaxant,* it relieves difficult, painful urination arising from **constrained bladder Qi.** And in the words of eighteenth-century Parisian pharmacist PIERRE POMET (1694), Carrot seed "expels Wind and is good against pains of the Wombe and Bowels, vehement Colicks, Vapours and Hysterick Fits ..." ("hysterick" here meaning uterine, from the Greek *hysteros,* womb.)

As a *urinary stimulant,* Wild carrot seed is a good *draining diuretic* for kidney deficiency conditions such as **chronic nephritis.** Note that its edema relieving effect has always been attributed to liver stimulation as much as to kidney stimulation. The remedy's *stone-dissolving* effect was highly praised by the seventeenth-century alchemist VAN HELMONT. This was high praise indeed, coming from a master spagyrist.

The herb's ability to stir sluggish or absent menstruation and relieve attendant cramps, as well as to expel sticking placentas after childbirth, was presumably much used in the past by wise woman practitioners. Today in the U.S., Wild carrot seed has been empirically tested as a woman's *contraceptive,* while in China its essential oil has effectively also shown *contraceptive* activity in a number of clinical trials.

Parsley Seed

Botanical source: *Petroselinum crispum* Hill,
      P. hortense Hoffman (Apiaceae/Umbelliferae)
Pharmaceutical name: Fructus Petroselini
Ancient names: Petroselinon (Gr)
    Apium hortense (Lat)
Other names: Persil (Fr)
    Petersilie, Garteneppich, Bittersilche (Ge)
Part used: the fruit

NATURE

Therapeutic category: mild remedy with minimal chronic toxicity
Constituents: essential oil 2-7% (incl. camphoraceous apiol, myristicin, bergaptene, terpenes), protein 20%, glucoside apiin, volatile alkaloid traces, inositol, sulphur, ß-carotene, vitamins C, K
Effective qualities: bitter and pungent, neutral, dry
    relaxing, stimulating, decongesting
Tropism: bladder, kidneys, liver, intestines, uterus
    Liver, Bladder, Kidney meridians; Air, Fluid bodies
Ground: all krases, biotypes and constitutions

FUNCTIONS AND INDICATIONS

1   **REGULATES BLADDER QI, HARMONIZES URINATION AND RELIEVES PAIN;
    REGULATES QI AND BALANCES CIRCULATION**

bladder Qi constraint: difficult painful urination
NEUROGENIC BLADDER with strangury, dysuria
intestines Qi constraint: abdominal pains, flatulence, indigestion
DIGESTIVE COLIC, COLITIS
uterus Qi constraint: difficult menstruation, cramps
SPASMODIC DYSMENORRHEA
MIGRAINE, HYPERTENSION

2   **PROMOTES URINATION, DRAINS WATER AND RELIEVES EDEMA;
    PROMOTES MENSTRUATION AND BENEFITS THE PROSTATE**

kidney water congestion: general water retention, nausea
EDEMA
uterus Qi stagnation: scanty or delayed periods, stopped periods
AMENORRHEA
kidney Qi stagnation: skin rashes, fetid stool; uric acid retention with arthritis, gout
PROSTATE ENLARGEMENT with painful dripping urination

3   REDUCES INFECTION, KILLS PARASITES AND REDUCES CONTUSION AND SWELLING

CHRONIC INFECTIONS of urinary tract, skin and eyes

HEAD LICE, tinea, scabies

WOUNDS, contusions, swollen breasts, lymphadenitis

PREPARATION

Use: Parsley seed is used in the form of **infusion, tincture** or **essential oil,** in ascending order of strength. The **essential oil** is the most effective as it is the seed's main component. It is massaged into the affected part with a base oil in 2-3% dilution, used as inhalation or taken internally.

Dosage: Infusion: 4-10 g

Tincture: 1-4 ml at 1:2 strength in 40% ethanol

Essential oil: 1-3 drops in a gel cap topped with olive oil

Caution: Parsley seed is forbidden during pregnancy as it is a *uterine stimulant*. Parsley essential oil distilled from *Petroselinum crispum* is safer than the oil from *P. hortense,* which contains the phenol apiol. Never exceed the above doses for the essential oil.

NOTES

The seed of the Parsley plant is very different from the root or leaf. Being high in essential oils, its action is primarily *relaxant* and *stimulant,* with a strong tropism for the urogenital organs. Parsley seed's *spasmolytic* action addresses **difficult** or **painful urination,** whatever the cause, and in the case of **prostate enlargement** will help relieve the congestion. By working on the kidneys and liver as a *draining diuretic,* Parsley also mobilizes stagnant water and relieves **edema.** Although similar in this respect to Carrot seed (another remedy from the parsley family), Parsley seed is far more *antiseptic.* The remedy is a good *antiparasitic* for **topical parasites** like lice, as well as *antibacterial.*

Parsley seed also has a reputation as a *hypotensor,* especially in Jue Yin or Shao Yang biotypes of the Wood element, and also treats bilious migraines.

Hydrangea Root

Botanical source: *Hydrangea arborescens* L.
        (Saxifragaceae)
Pharmaceutical name: Rhizoma Hydrangeae
Other names: Seven barks, Wild hydrangea (Am)
        Hydrangelle de Virginie (Fr)
        Hortensie, Grosser Wasserstrauch, Kehlkopf,
        Baumartige Hydrangie (Ge)
Part used: the rhizome

NATURE

Therapeutic category: mild remedy with minimal chronic toxicity
Constituents: glycosides (hydrangin, parahydrangin), alkaloid, saponins, resins, fixed oils, essential oil,

gum, saccharides, calcium sulphide, trace minerals
Effective qualities: pungent, sweet, cool, neutral
     dissolving, restoring, calming
Tropism: kidney, bladder, liver, lungs, fluids
     Kidney, Bladder, Lung meridians
     Fluid body
Ground: all krases and biotypes for symptomatic use

FUNCTIONS AND INDICATIONS

1 **PROMOTES AND HARMONIZES URINATION, DISSOLVES DEPOSITS AND RELIEVES IRRITATION AND PAIN;**
   PROMOTES URINATION AND DRAINS WATER

genitourinary Qi stagnation: scanty, frequent, irritated urination, sharp urethral pains, cloudy urine

BLADDER and URETHRAL IRRITATION or STRANGURY (acute, from any cause)

PROSTATE ENLARGEMENT, prostatitis

URINARY STONES, sand

liver and kidney water congestion: local or general edema

EDEMA

2 **MOISTENS THE LUNGS AND RELIEVES DRYNESS**

lung dryness: dry hard cough, chest soreness, dry throat

3 **CLEARS DAMP-HEAT AND REDUCES INFECTION AND INFLAMMATION**

bladder and kidney damp-heat: thirst, backache, dark, burning, frequent urination, hematuria, back pain

ACUTE URINARY INFECTIONS (esp. nephritis, cystitis)

PREPARATION

Use: Hydrangea root is prepared in **short decoction** and **tincture** form for all purposes.
Dosage: Short decoction: 8-14 g
       Tincture: 2-4 ml at 1:2 strength in 45% ethanol
Caution: None

NOTES

The root of this beautiful mountain shrub was uniformly praised by nineteenth-century American writers on herbal medicine from COLDEN to FELTER and SHOOK. They ascribed *restorative, lenitive* and somewhat *detoxicant* actions to this remedy whose tropism is almost entirely the urinary organs. In combining these effects, Hydrangea root somewhat resembles Cornsilk and Chinese herb Dianthus Qu Mai in its overall profile.

More specifically, Hydrangea is a gentle, moist-natured *demulcent* and *urinary stimulant*. Its focus is first, as a *demulcent,* the relief of **difficult, irritated, painful urination** (like Couch grass and Cornsilk), regardless of cause.

Today it is still considered one of the best *res-olvent* herbs for the urinary tract, where it can soften and eliminate **urinary stones** (like Cornsilk). In **acute urinary infections,** it scores with its combination of soothing *demulcent, anti-inflammatory* and *antiseptic* effects. The rhizome's essential oil content is probably responsible for its good *antiseptic* action. It is a gentle, yet effective remedy that combines easily and well.

At times, Hydrangea root was historically also given for **dry cough** (like Queen's root or Mullein) and for **chronic metabolic toxicosis** presenting rheumatoid arthritis, gout and eczema. Note the saponins, glycosides and trace minerals, in this connection, that support these lesser-known usages.

Regulate Uterus Qi, Harmonize Menstruation and Relieve Pain

Uterine relaxants (uterine spasmolytics)

Motherwort Herb

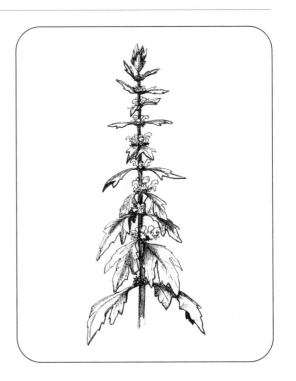

Botanical source: *Leonorus cardiaca* L.
     (Lamiaceae/Labiatae)
Pharmaceutical name: Herba Leonori
Ancient names: Agripalma, Herba pectoralis (Lat)
Other names: Cowthwort, Lion's tail, Lion's ear
     (Eng)
     Agripaume, Creneuse (Fr)
     Herzgespann, Herzgold, Löwenschwanz,
     Wolfstrapp (Ge)
Part used: the herb

NATURE

Therapeutic category: mild remedy with minimal chronic toxicity
Constituents: alkaloids (incl. leonurinine, stachydrin, betonicin, turicin), bitter glycosides, essential oil, resins, tannins 5-10%, cholin, malic/citric/vinitic acids, phosphoric acid, potassium chloride, phytosterol, stachyose, calcium, trace minerals
Effective qualities: bitter, somewhat pungent and astringent, cool, dry
     relaxing, calming, restoring, stimulating
Tropism: heart, circulation, lungs, intestines, kidneys, uterus
     Liver, Heart, Lung, Kidney meridians
     Air, Fluid bodies
Ground: Sanguine and Choleric krases
     Expressive/Jue Yin and Tough Shao Yang biotypes; all three constitutions

FUNCTIONS AND INDICATIONS

1   **REGULATES UTERUS QI AND HARMONIZES MENSTRUATION;**
     REGULATES HEART QI, RELIEVES IRRITABILITY AND PROMOTES REST;
     INHIBITS THE THYROID

     uterus Qi constraint: painful, difficult periods, tension, irritability, PMS
     SPASMODIC DYSMENORRHEA
     heart Qi constraint (Liver Yang rising): palpitations, rapid heartbeat, anxiety, irritability, stress
     NEUROCARDIAC SYNDROME, hypertension
     TACHYCARDIA
     CORONARY DISEASE with SPASMODIC ANGINA
     MENOPAUSAL SYNDROME, hot flashes, night sweats
     THYROID HYPERFUNCTIONING (hyperthyroid conditions)

intestines Qi constraint: colicky abdominal pains, flatulence, worsening with tension
INSOMNIA

2 **TONIFIES UTERUS QI, PROMOTES MENSTRUATION AND LABOR, AND ENHANCES DELIVERY**

uterus Qi stagnation: delayed or obstructed periods, abdominal lumps
AMENORRHEA, infertility
DIFFICULT, SLOW or PAINFUL LABOR
POSTPARTUM PAIN and BLEEDING
UTERINE SUBINVOLUTION

3 **TONIFIES HEART QI AND RELIEVES CHEST OPPRESSION**

heart Qi deficiency: chest oppression, palpitations
CARDIAC DEFICIENCY

4 **PROMOTES SWEATING, DISPELS WIND-HEAT, OPENS THE CHEST AND RELIEVES WHEEZING**

lung wind-heat: feverishness, chills, unrest, coughing
lung phlegm-damp: cough, expectoration of white sputum, wheezing
CHRONIC BRONCHITIS, bronchial asthma

5 **RESTORES THE KIDNEYS, PROMOTES URINATION AND RELIEVES EDEMA AND ECZEMA**

kidney water congestion: water retention (esp. in lower limbs), scanty or obstructed urination
NEPHRITIS (acute or chronic)
EDEMA (incl. cardiac), acute renal failure, albuminuria, chronic prostatitis
kidney Qi stagnation with *metabolic toxicosis:* skin rashes, pyogenic abscesses, skin ulcers
ECZEMA

6 **ASTRINGES AND STOPS DISCHARGE AND BLEEDING; PROMOTES TISSUE REPAIR**

HEMORRHAGE (incl. blood in urine or stool, menorrhagia, postpartum uterine bleeding)
DIARRHEA or LEUCORRHEA with *damp-heat* or *damp-cold*
WOUNDS, bruises, ulcers

PREPARATION

Use: Motherwort herb is taken by **infusion** or **tincture.** External preparations include **sponges** and **pessaries** for vaginal infections and discharges (including yeast), and **washes** and **poultices** for tissue trauma.
Dosage: Infusion: 8-14 g. Up to 40 g should be used for acute bleeding.
      Tincture: 2-5 ml at 1:3 strength in 45% ethanol
• *To promote labor contractions and ease pain:* take 1/2 tsp of the tincture until labor resumes.
• *To help the uterus contract after delivery, lessen afterpains and prevent, reduce or stop hemorrhage:* take 1/2-1 teaspoon of the tincture every hour or two.
Caution: Being a *uterine stimulant,* Motherwort herb is contraindicated during the main part of pregnancy. Use with caution in Yin and Blood (metabolic) deficiency conditions.

NOTES

Motherwort herb is one of many remedies that, around a hundred years ago, were destined for oblivion. According to herbalist WILLFORT, the herb was rescued from this fate by certain English doctors. In the oral, unrecorded tradition of women healers—the wise woman tradition—Motherwort was used for conditions of the mother, i.e., the uterus. Since this empirical tradition was actively supressed from the fourteenth to seventeenth centuries, all herbal remedies that belonged to it simply followed its demise. To put it plainly: Motherwort is a woman's remedy that suffered disuse with the suppression of women in general and the rise of male legislated medicine specifically.

In tandem with this development came the downward slide and, ultimately, the demise of traditional Greek medicine itself. The sixteenth to nineteenth centuries saw the final, decadent phase of Greek medicine as a vitalistic clinical science. This did not exactly encourage the use of herbs like Motherwort either. Because this remedy is mild, nontoxic, and because its action is essentially relaxing, it became lost when medicine turned to agressive *eliminant specifics* (many of them toxic minerals) from the 1600s onwards. As with many other trusted woman's allies—Cronewort, Yarrow, Lady's mantle, Sea holly and White deadnettle, among others, the knowledge of Motherwort's powers has only survived down recent centuries in the cloak of simplistic folk uses.

Today the situation has somewhat changed. Motherwort herb enjoys a degree of scientific sanction in both the West and East. Species of *Leonorus* have been traditionally used as far as Siberia, the Russian Far East and Japan. All have been scientifically analyzed. Luckily, Motherwort contains alkaloids that always carry pharmacological clout—and these are also found in Wood betony, for example. They have shown to induce uterine contractions. This fact is relevant to the herb's time-tested use for **dysmenorrhea** arising from **Qi constraint,** like the point formula Ht 7, Sp 6 and 8, Li 5, CV 3 and Bl 32, and like Cramp bark, Wild yam root and White peony root (Paeonia Bai Shao), for instance—common combining herbs here.

The remedy also acts as a *parturient* for **difficult** or **ineffective labor** because of its *uterine stimulant* action, and as a *hemostatic* for **postpartum hemorrhage.** In many Chinese hospitals, for example, Motherwort decoction is now routinely given (in huge doses) after the delivery to help the uterus contract, reduce pain and stop bleeding. We may wonder whether traditional European midwives used the remedy's twin *uterine spasmolytic/stimulant* actions when the stronger (but riskier) Rye ergot was unavailable. Motherwort is clearly also an excellent alternative to the various Native American "squaw remedies" before, during and after childbirth.

Even Motherwort herb's fabled benefits to the heart have been confirmed via its content in glycosides. The remedy is fundamentally a broad *neurocardiac relaxant* with a mild *depressant* action that is perfect for those presenting chronic symptoms of anxiety, irritability, palpitations, sleep loss and chest discomfort. The key syndrome seen here is **heart Qi constraint** with **spasmodic angina.** Complementary herbs here might be Bugleweed herb, Melissa leaf and Ligusticum Chuan Xiong.

This syndrome includes **thyroid hyperfunctioning** when present because of the herb's *thyroid-inhibitant* action (Like Bugleweed herb, in fact). Moreover, as Motherwort helps release tension caused by emotional and mental stress, it also relieves local spasms in other areas—e.g., working much like Cramp bark, Hops flower or Valerian root in the digestive tract. Because Motherwort also supports the heart muscle as a *cardiotonic* at the same time, the net effect on the heart is ultimately a regulating, supportive one, like that of Hawthorn berry. Both herbs should be taken over a long period of time for cumulative benefits here.

Motherwort herb is an important example of a plant that treats both the heart and uterus, tailor-made for women presenting PMS with anxiety, frustration, palpitations and insomnia. This type of herb *does* exist! The energetic connection between these organs is also described in most traditional medical systems. The ancient Chinese canon, the *Yellow Emperor's Classic of Internal Medicine,* for example, discusses the pathology of the Heart-Uterus meridian (*bao mai*) in Su Wen 33/321. Greek medicine describes the pathology in such terms as "uterus rising." The spiritual teacher RUDOLF STEINER in his medical lectures also commented on the close energetic relations between these two organs.

Modern China probably makes more use of this herb than other countries. Confusingly to us, here Motherwort herb is found in many experimental formulas treating **chronic glomerulonephritis,** alongside other herbs like Astragalus Huang Qi and Tripterygium Lei Gong Teng (see HOLMES 1997). Motherwort, after all is also a considerable *diuretic* that, like Goldenrod herb, over time can also act as a nice *kidney trophorestorative.*

Feverfew Herb

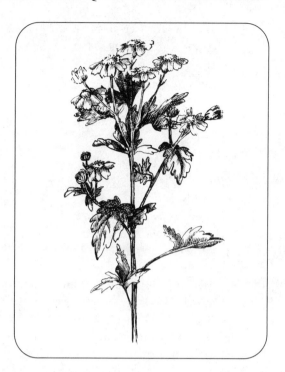

Botanical source: *Tanacetum parthenium* Schultz-Bip.
(syn. *Chrysanthemum parthenium* [L.]
Bernhardi, *Pyrethrum parthenium* Smith)
(Asteraceae/Compositae)
Pharmaceutical name: Herba Tanaceti parthenii
Ancient names: Parthenion (Gr)
Matricaria, Febrifuga (Lat)
Other names: Featherfew, Featherfowl, Motherwort,
Midsummer daisy, Bertram, Nosebleed,
Mayweed, Whitewort (Eng)
Espargoutte (Fr)
Bertram(wurzel), Mutterkraut, Metram (Ge)
Part used: the herb; also the root, Radix Chrysanthemi
parthenii

NATURE

Therapeutic category: medium-strength remedy with moderate chronic toxicity
Constituents: bitter resin, pyrethrin, essential oil (incl. lactones [parthenolide], camphor, borneol, terpenes, esters); inulin (in root), gums, tannic acid
Effective qualities: bitter, pungent, cool, dry
relaxing, stimulating, calming
Tropism: muscles, nerves, uterus and genitals, lungs
Liver, Spleen, Lung meridians
Air, Warmth bodies

FUNCTIONS AND INDICATIONS

1 **REGULATES UTERUS QI, HARMONIZES MENSTRUATION AND RELIEVES PAIN; PROMOTES MENSTRUATION AND RELIEVES AMENORRHEA**

uterus Qi constraint: painful menstrual cramps, difficult flow, PMS, swollen breasts
SPASMODIC DYSMENORRHEA
uterus Qi stagnation: scanty or delayed periods with clots, dull pain before onset
AMENORRHEA

2 **RESOLVES DAMP-COLD, RELIEVES PAIN AND REDUCES INFLAMMATION AND FEVER; CLEARS INTERNAL WIND**

damp-cold obstruction: intermittent or erratic aches and pains
NEURALGIA (incl. sciatica, trigeminal neuralgia), arthritis, insect bites
FIBROMYALGIA
MIGRAINE, TENSION HEADACHE
SEIZURES, epilepsy, paralysis, pain from *wind (-phlegm)* obstruction
FEVER (intermittent and acute)

3 **RESOLVES MUCOUS-DAMP AND STOPS DISCHARGE;**
  PROMOTES EXPECTORATION, RESOLVES PHLEGM AND RELIEVES COUGHING AND WHEEZING;
  ELIMINATES PARASITES

head damp-cold: nasal congestion, runny nose, frontal headache

SINUSITIS, rhinitis

stomach and intestines damp: indigestion, flatulence, epigastric pains

DYSPEPSIA, gastritis

INTESTINAL PARASITES

kidney and bladder damp: vaginal discharges, difficult periods

LEUCORRHEA

lung phlegm-damp: coughing, expectoration of sputum, wheezing, chest pain

CHRONIC BRONCHITIS, bronchial asthma

PREPARATION

Use: Feverfew herb is prepared by **infusion** or **tincture.**
Dosage: Infusion: 8-14 g
  Tincture: 2-4 ml at 1:4 strength in 60% ethanol
Caution: Avoid continuous or long-term use of this medium-strength herb if taken alone in high doses. Use Feverfew in formulas or intermittently. Contraindicated during pregnancy because of its *uterine stimulant* action. The fresh plant may cause allergic skin rashes in some people.

NOTES

Feverfew was originally and most widely known in England as "Featherfew" from the delicacy of its flower corolla. It is one of many composites used in herbal medicine since Greek days. Like *Leonorus,* Yarrow, Camomile and Tansy (among others), it was also called "Motherwort" in Europe as it addresses disharmonies of the mother, or womb. The herbalist JOHN PARKINSON in his major herbal of 1629 makes this clear: "Featherfew ... is chiefly used for the diseases of the mother, whether it be the stranglings or the risings of the mother, or the hardness or inflammations of the same." PARKINSON is speaking not only as a medical practitioner, but also as an extraordinary researcher of ancient texts. He typically devotes up to half a folio page or more, if necessary, to discussing the identification and taxonomy of plant remedies.

Today, we too can see Feverfew as an important woman's ally. As a *uterine spasmolytic* it treats **uterus Qi constraint** ("stranglings or risings") in the woman manifesting cramping, painful periods and PMS, and **uterus Qi stagnation** ("hardness") in the woman with irregular cycles or delayed or absent periods. PARKINSON also advises a vaginal steam for these dysmenorrheas, using a hot infusion. The same *uterine stimulant* and *spasmolytic*

actions found in the related Tansy herb are also here in evidence.

Like Tansy herb and Costmary herb, Feverfew herb is essentially a *relaxant* remedy with a secondary *mucostatic* and *heat-clearing* effect. It primarily addresses **tense** conditions that tend to **damp** and **heat.** Damp interfering with respiratory, digestive and urogenital functions is resolved and eliminated—as in catarrhal bronchitis, atonic dyspepsias and clear vaginal discharges. Under the *relaxant* heading we can put Feverfew's currently well-known *analgesic* and *anti-inflammatory* actions. The herb addresses **painful, inflammatory** conditions in general, such as **headache, neuralgia** and **(fibro-) myalgia.** Its usefulness for migraine also falls in this category, aided by *liver decongestion* on one hand and *cerebral vasoregulation* on the other.

Regarding its heat-clearing effect, Feverfew is a traditional *antipyretic* remedy—witness its name, as also its pronounced bitter taste. Containing essential oil and bitter compounds, this *relaxant diaphoretic* is best used in **intermittent fevers** (*shao yang* stage) and acute **wind-heat fevers** also presenting headaches and other aches and pains.

Blackhaw Root Bark

Botanical source: *Viburnum prunifolium* L.
(Caprifoliaceae)
Pharmaceutical name: Cortex radicis Viburni
prunifolii
Other names: Stagbush, Sweet viburnum, American
sloe, Sloe-leaf viburnum, Nannybush,
Sheepberry, Plumleaf, Sweet haw/sloe,
Arrowwood (Am)
Aubépine noire, Senelle noire (Fr)
Schlingbaum, Schneeballbaum (Ge)
Part used: the root bark

NATURE

Therapeutic category: mild remedy with minimal chronic toxicity
Constituents: amentoflavone, oleanolic and ursolic acid-like triterpenoids, sitosterol, arbutin, coumarins (incl. scopoletin, aesculetin), citric/oxalic/oleanoli/ursolic/salicylic/chlorogenic/isochlorogenic/valerianic/tannic acids, salicosides, bitter (viburnin), bitter resins, tannin, calcium chloride, magnesium, potassium, iron, trace minerals
Effective qualities: bitter, somewhat astringent, cool, dry
relaxing, calming, restoring, astringing, stabilizing,
Tropism: uterus, stomach, intestines, heart, lungs
Liver, Heart, Stomach, Small Intestine, *chong, ren* meridians
Air, Fluid bodies
Ground: Sanguine krasis; Expressive/Jue Yin biotype; Hematogenic/Sulphuric constitution

FUNCTIONS AND INDICATIONS

1 **REGULATES UTERUS QI: HARMONIZES MENSTRUATION AND RELIEVES PAIN**

uterus Qi constraint: severe cramps (esp. before onset), irritability, leg cramps at night, lumbar pains

SPASMODIC DYSMENORRHEA

OVULATION PAINS, ovarian pain, POSTPARTUM PAIN

2 **TONIFIES REPRODUCTIVE QI: RELIEVES INFERTILITY, REGULATES MENSTRUATION, PREGNANCY AND DELIVERY, AND PREVENTS MISCARRIAGE**

uterus Qi deficiency: delayed, scanty, difficult periods, long cycles

AMENORRHEA, INFERTILITY

HORMONAL (PROGESTERONE?) DEFICIENCY gynecological disorders, including:

PMS with withdrawal, sore swollen breasts, sexual disinterest, frequent urination, vaginal dryness

PROPHYLACTIC and REMEDIAL during the WHOLE of PREGNANCY

MORNING SICKNESS

HABITUAL or THREATENED MISCARRIAGE

UTERINE SUBINVOLUTION, postpartum bleeding

3   **REGULATES THE QI AND RELAXES CONSTRAINT; SETTLES THE STOMACH**

heart Qi constraint: nervousness, palpitations, stress, anxiety

NEUROCARDIAC SYNDROME, HYPERTENSION

lung Qi constraint: irritating dry cough, asthmatic breathing

stomach and intestines Qi constraint: abdominal weight, epigastric and abdominal pains, nausea, flatulence

HICCUPS (esp. severe)

4   **VITALIZES THE BLOOD: REDUCES CONGESTION AND MODERATES MENSTRUATION; ASTRINGES, REDUCES INFLAMMATION AND STOPS DISCHARGE AND BLEEDING; PROMOTES TISSUE REPAIR**

uterus blood congestion: heavy periods, bearing-down pains before onset, painful difficult flow

CONGESTIVE DYSMENORRHEA

INFLAMMATORY REPRODUCTIVE CONDITIONS (incl. PID)

MENORRHAGIA, UTERINE and MENOPAUSAL BLEEDING

LEUCORRHEA, spermatorrhea, diarrhea, dysentery

CANKER SORES, ulcers, conjunctivitis

PREPARATION

Use: Blackhaw root bark is prepared by **decoction** or **tincture.** The latter is best overall. Like Raspberry leaf, Blackhaw is a *uterine restorative* that may safely be taken in small doses throughout pregnancy to enhance every aspect of gestation, labor and delivery.

Astringent and healing washes, compresses, gargles, etc., may be prepared for ulcers and such like.

Dosage: Decoction: 8-14 g

Tincture: 2-4 ml twice daily at 1:2 strength in 40% ethanol

• *To prevent habitual miscarriage:* take medium doses starting two or three weeks before the time of the anticipated possible miscarriage until well into the second trimester.

• *To prevent threatening miscarriage:* take 1 tsp of the tincture every hour

• *To relieve false labor pains, or Braxton Hicks contractions:* take 2 ml (50 drops) of the tincture every three hours.

Caution: None

NOTES

The lovely Southern blackhaw bush, *Viburnum prunifolium,* is related to the snowball tree, *Viburnum opulus.* Both species produce the same gorgeous snowball blossoms when in season, and both carry many identical and similar names. Because they also share a large portion of therapeutic effects, much confusion surrounding their use has arisen over time. The remedy Blackhaw root bark itself has seen many changes in cultural settings. However, from its first use in the American South, which included use by Blacks, to its inclusion in European herbal practice, its main empirical application has always remained the same. This is problems related to childbirth.

Blackhaw root bark is one of the most useful all-round remedies throughout pregnancy and works on both a tissue and hormonal level. Its *rest-* *orative* action is evinced in its astringent and bitter taste. The remedy excels in managing chronic miscarriage resulting from either deficient uterine tone or hormonal deficiency. Weak conditions such as **miscarriage** and **postpartum pain** and **bleeding** can be treated prophylactically and remedially with this *astringent uterine tonic*. During the first two trimesters, in women presenting systemic Qi deficiency conditions with damp, a good *restorative* like Helonias root may be added to Blackhaw; while in tense conditions (constrained Qi), a *relaxant* like Wild yam root or White peony root. In the third trimester, Blackhaw can be combined with Partridgeberry herb and root, or Helonias root, to ensure full fetal development and to prevent premature delivery.

Because it addresses various conditions both

during and outside of pregnancy that are known to be related to insufficient progesterone, it is possible that Blackhaw possesses a *progesteronic* or progesterone-like action. However, some of these conditions can also arise from tense/spasmodic tissue, making its mode of operation uncertain. Either way, from a clinical point of view, the key conditions that always indicate the use of this remedy include **PMS, ovulation pain, infertility** and **impending miscarriage.**

Blackhaw is superlative for relaxing the central nerves and reducing nervous tension. This it does in some way by stimulating GABA. As a systemic *smooth muscle relaxant,* Blackhaw treats Qi constraint involving reproductive, cardiovascular, respiratory and gastrointestinal functions. It is an excellent *spasmolytic* to these functions. The net result energetically is a relaxing of **constrained Qi** in individuals manifesting chronic anxiety, nervous tension and its retinue of symptoms involving **pain** and **spasm.** As FINLEY ELLINGWOOD (1919) expresses it in the delicate idiom of his day: "It is the remedy for sympathetic disturbances of the heart, stomach and nervous system, common to ladies with irritable nervous systems, preceeding or during the menstrual epoch." Blackhaw can be reinforced by other remedies serving them more specifically: Motherwort herb with **heart-uterus Qi constraint** present, for example.

A simple rule of thumb differentiation between Blackhaw and Cramp bark would be the following. Whereas Blackhaw is an *autonomic nervous relaxant* that reduces smooth muscle spasm (activating the Qi), Cramp bark is a better *neuromuscular relaxant* that reduces striped muscle spasms (clearing internal wind). Another practical differentiation is that historically Blackhaw has been used more during pregnancy, while Cramp bark more during menstruation.

As an *astringent decongestant* on the tissue level, Blackhaw also addresses women presenting **uterus blood congestion** with delayed or early, heavy, painful menstrual flow—congestive dysmenorrhea in short. A good specific *anti-inflammatory* action (note the string of acids) rounds off its gynecological uses very nicely.

Cramp Bark

Botanical source: *Viburnum opulus* L., *V. edule*
    (Caprifoliaceae)
Pharmaceutical name: Cortex ramuli Viburni opuli
Other names: Guelder rose, Love roses, Water elder,
    Wayfaring tree, Pincushion (Eng)
    Snowball tree, Highbush cranberry, Pimbina,
      White dogwood, Squaw bush (Am)
    Viorne orbier, Pomme/Boule de neige, Pain
      blanc, Rose de gueldre, Sureau d'eau (Fr)
    Wasser Schneeball, Schlingbaum, Wasser-holder,
      Schwelkenbaum, Kleiner Mehlbaum, Kalinen,
      Drosselbeeren, Wasserahorn,
      Leber/Vogels/Galinken-beere (Ge)
Part used: the branch bark

NATURE
Therapeutic category: mild remedy with minimal chronic toxicity
Constituents: valerianic acid, salicosides, arbutin, bitter (viburnin), resin, tannin
Effective qualities: bitter, somewhat astringent, cool, dry
    relaxing, calming, astringing, stabilizing
Tropism: uterus, heart, lungs, neuromuscular system

Liver, Heart, Lung, Bladder, *chong, ren* meridians; Air, Fluid bodies
Ground: all krases, biotypes and constitutions for symptomatic use

FUNCTIONS AND INDICATIONS

1 **REGULATES UTERUS QI: HARMONIZES MENSTRUATION AND RELIEVES PAIN**

uterus Qi constraint: severe menstrual cramps (esp. before onset), irritability, lumbar pain
SPASMODIC DYSMENORRHEA
OVULATION PAINS, OVARIAN PAIN, fallopian pain; endometriosis, PCOS

2 **REGULATES THE QI: RELAXES CONSTRAINT AND RELIEVES PAIN;**
CLEARS INTERNAL WIND AND STOPS SPASMS

heart Qi constraint: nervousness, palpitations, stress
NEUROCARDIAC SYNDROME, HYPERTENSION
lung Qi constraint: irritating dry cough, asthmatic breathing
ASTHMA
bladder Qi constraint: difficult, painful, obstructed urination, sharp bladder pains
NEUROGENIC BLADDER, dysuria, strangury
LOWER BACK PAIN radiating down thighs
LEG CRAMPS (esp. at night, from pelvic cramps)
nerve excess with *internal wind:* tremors, twitches, convulsions
SEIZURES (incl. of pregancy)

3 **PREVENTS MISCARRIAGE AND HARMONIZES PREGNANCY AND DELIVERY**

HABITUAL or THREATENED MISCARRIAGE (esp. with rhythmical cramps)
PROPHYLACTIC and REMEDIAL during the WHOLE of PREGNANCY

4 **VITALIZES THE BLOOD: REDUCES CONGESTION AND MODERATES MENSTRUATION;**
ASTRINGES, REDUCES INFLAMMATION AND STOPS DISCHARGE AND BLEEDING;
PROMOTES TISSUE REPAIR

uterus blood congestion: heavy periods, bearing-down pains before onset, painful difficult flow
CONGESTIVE DYSMENORRHEA
MENORRHAGIA, UTERINE and MENOPAUSAL BLEEDING
INFLAMMATORY disorders of reproductive organs (esp. PID)
LEUCORRHEA, spermatorrhea
DIARRHEA, dysentery
CANKER SORES, ulcers, conjunctivitis
ULCERS (esp. indolent, chronic, cancerous)

PREPARATION

Use: Cramp bark is prepared by **decoction** or **tincture.** The latter is best overall. Like Blackhaw root bark, Cramp bark is a *uterine restorative* that may safely be taken in small doses throughout pregnancy to enhance every aspect of gestation, labor and delivery. The remedy is a specific for preventing or treating seizures during pregnancy. Cramp bark "given prior to labor … is a *partus preparator* of much value … but to an extent greatly inferior to *Viburnum prunifolium* ... " (ELLINGWOOD 1919).

Astringent and tissue healing **washes, compresses, gargles,** etc., may be prepared for ulcers, etc.
Dosage: Decoction: 8-14 g
Tincture: 2-4 ml twice daily at 1:2 strength in 40% ethanol

• *To prevent habitual miscarriage:* take medium doses starting two or three weeks before the time of the anticipated possible miscarriage and well into the second trimester.

• *To prevent threatening miscarriage:* take 1 tsp of the tincture every hour

• *To prevent seizures during the last trimester:* take medium doses during the last two months of pregancy.

Caution: None

NOTES

The inner bark of this variety of *Viburnum,* or guelder rose, was traditionally used by women of several North American tribes as both a menstrual and obstetrical remedy. Not surprisingly, the small tree among Whites acquired the names "squaw bush" and "cramp bark." In the nineteenth century, Eclectic doctors extensively used both types of *Viburnum* (*V. opulus* and *V. prunifolium)* and through clinical experience came to define their exact therapeutic area. They noted specifically when Cramp bark and Blackhaw root bark could be used interchangeably, and when not.

Essentially, Cramp bark is a *relaxant* to woman's reproductive organs, not a *restorative.* The remedy should be used mainly for **spasmodic** and **congestive dysmenorrhea** with **severe cramping,** and only secondarily as a *restorative* during pregnancy—for which Blackhaw is preferred. With its combined *spasmolytic* and *uterine decongestant* actions, Cramp bark addresses both the syndromes uterus Qi constraint and **uterus blood congestion.** This makes the remedy an ideal, uncomplicated woman's choice for menstrual pain, regardless of its origin. As such it will combine with other *uterine relaxants* such as Motherwort, Feverfew, White peony root (Paeonia Bai Shao Yao) and Pasqueflower.

Just as important, however, is to note that Cramp bark is *relaxant* not only to the smooth muscles, but also to the skeletal muscles. In Chinese medicine terms, Cramp bark not only releases **constrained Qi** (like Blackhaw), but also clears **internal wind.** In this respect, compare function 2 of Cramp bark and function 3 of Blackhaw. This is why only Cramp bark is used for treating seizures during pregnancy and childhood.

Apart from these two differences of emphasis, the two Viburnums may be used interchangeably. The reader is refered to the notes on Blackhaw for further differentiations between them.

White Peony Root

Botanical source: *Paeonia lactiflora* Pallas
    (Ranunculaceae)
Pharmaceutical name: Radix Paeoniae lactiflorae
Other names: Bai Shao Yao (Mandarin Chinese)
    Baak Cheuk Yeuk, Baak Chat Lai (Cantonese
      Chinese)
    Byakushaku (Japanese)
Part used: the root

NATURE

Therapeutic category: mild remedy with minimal chronic toxicity
Constituents: essential oil (incl. monoterpene [paeoniflorin], paeonol), paeonin, triterpenoids, alliflorine, steroids daucosterol & sitosterol, benzoic acid 5%, tannin, asparagin, glucosides, minerals (incl. zn, mg, cu)
Effective qualities: bitter, sour, astringent, cool, dry
    relaxing, restoring, astringing, decongesting, calming
Tropism: reproductive organs, stomach, intestines, nervous system
    Liver, Spleen, Lung, *chong, dai, yang wei* meridians; Air, Fluids bodies
Ground: All krases, biotypes and iris constitutions

FUNCTIONS AND INDICATIONS

1   **REGULATES UTERUS QI, HARMONIZES MENSTRUATION AND RELIEVES PAIN**

    uterus Qi constraint: severe menstrual cramps, difficult onset of flow, headache, irritability
    SPASMODIC DYSMENORRHEA, ovarian pain, polycystic ovarian syndrome
    HYPERTONIC UTERINE DYSTOCIA

2   **REGULATES THE QI, RELAXES CONSTRAINT AND RELIEVES PAIN**

    kidney/adrenal Qi constraint and *Liver Yang rising:* restlessness, headache, dizziness, abdominal
      or flank pain, painful spasms
    STRESS-RELATED CONDITIONS
    PMS with headache, irritability
    intestines Qi constraint (Liver-Spleen disharmony): abdominal pains, indigestion, colic
    COLITIS, IBS
    PAIN CONDITIONS (incl. limb spasms and cramps; uterine, abdominal and intercostal pain, colic)
    HEADACHE

3   **VITALIZES THE BLOOD, REDUCES CONGESTION AND MODERATES MENSTRUATION**

    uterus blood congestion: heavy and early onset of flow, pelvic weight and dragging, irritability
    CONGESTIVE DYSMENORRHEA, menorrhagia

4   **ASTRINGES AND STOPS DISCHARGEAND SWEATING**

genitourinary damp: clear vaginal discharges, spermatorrhea

LEUCORRHEA

CHRONIC ENTERITIS, DYSENTERY

SPONTENOUS SWEATING from external deficiency, night sweats from Yin deficiency

ACID DYSPEPSIA from HYPERCHLORHYDRIA, peptic ulcer

PREPARATION

Use: White peony root is prepared by **decoction** and **tincture.** The toasted root is traditionally said to be more astringent and better for heavy menses due to uterus blood congestion and for sweating from external wind-cold with deficiency.

Dosage: Decoction: 8-18 g

Tincture: 1-3 ml at 1:2 strength in 45% ethanol

Caution: None, except to be used with caution in diarrea in empty cold conditions.

NOTES

Far and away the "popular favorite" garden ornamental of Tang dynasty China, the peony also was and remains a highly esteemed woman's remedy. Prolifically used in many types of Chinese herb formulas, the white peony root has finally come full circle to the West.

White peony root is versatile in managing difficult and painful menstrution as it can relieve both **spasmodic** and **congestive** types of **dysmenorrhea.** Through its *nerve-relaxant* and *analgesic* action White peony root treats **uterus Qi constraint** conditions with cramping; while with its *astringency* it acts as a *pelvic decongestant* for **uterus blood congestion.**

White peony's *spasmolytic* and *analgesic* effect on the smooth muscles also indicates use for cramps and spasms of the limbs, calves as well as the digestive tract. It is a good adjunct to other remedies for IBS, for instance.

With its *mucostatic* and *antidischarge* effects, White peony's other uses include diarrheal conditions with spasms, sweating disorders of all types (day or night sweats) and, interestingly enough, excessive gastric acidity causing acid indigestion.

Tansy Herb

Botanical source: *Tanacetum vulgare* L. (syn. *Chrysanthemum vulgare*) (Compositae/Asteraceae)

Pharmaceutical name: Herba Tanaceti

Ancient name: Artemisia, Lepophyllo, Athanasia, Tanesia (Gr)

Athanasia vulgaris, Ambrosia, Sanacum (Lat)

Other names: Bitter buttons, Bachelor's buttons, English cost, Parsley/Scented fern, Ginger plant, Hindheal (Eng)

Tanaisie, Herbe amère, Barbotine, Herbe d'effort (Fr)

Rainfarn, Wurmkraut, Mutterkraut, Kraftkraut Donnerblume (Ge)

Part used: the herb; also the flowerhead, Flos Tanaceti

NATURE

Therapeutic category: medium-strength remedy with moderate chronic toxicity

Constituents: essential oil 0.12-0.18% (incl. thujone 70-90%, borneol, camphor), 3 bitter resins (incl. tanacetin), bitter extractive gum, chlorophyll, stearine, wax, tannin, lead oxydes, tanacetic/gallic/citric/malic/oxalic/arabinic acid

Effective qualities: bitter, somewhat pungent, cool, dry
> relaxing, stimulating

Tropism: stomach, intestines, liver, kidneys, bladder, nerves, skin
> Liver, Spleen, Stomach, Bladder meridians
> Air, Fluid bodies

Ground: Choleric and Sanguine krases
> Tough/Generous and Expressive/Jue Yin biotypes
> Hematogenic/Sulphuric constitution

FUNCTIONS AND INDICATIONS

1 **REGULATES UTERUS QI, HARMONIZES MENSTRUATION AND RELIEVES PAIN; PROMOTES MENSTRUATION AND RELIEVES AMENORRHEA**

uterus Qi constraint: painful menstrual cramps, difficult flow, PMS, swollen breasts
SPASMODIC DYSMENORRHEA
uterus Qi stagnation: scanty or delayed periods with clots, dull pain before onset
AMENORRHEA

2 **RELAXES CONSTRAINT, REGULATES THE QI AND RELIEVES PAIN; CLEARS INTERNAL WIND AND STOPS SPASMS**

kidney/adrenal Qi constraint: mental/emotional tension, nervous unrest, erratic pains (esp. from physical debility, chronic stress, pain)
intestines Qi constraint (Liver/Spleen disharmony): abdominal pains, indigestion, flatulence
COLITIS, COLIC, IBS
bladder Qi constraint: difficult, obstructed, or frequent scanty urination
NEUROGENIC BLADDER, dysuria
nerve excess with *internal wind:* spasms, tremors, convulsions
SEIZURES (incl. of chorea, epilepsy, infants)

3 **PROMOTES SWEATING, DISPELS WIND-HEAT AND REDUCES FEVER**

external wind-heat: fever, restlessness, irritability, aches and pains, sore throat
COLD and FLU ONSET with FEVER
REMITTENT FEVERS (*shao yang* stage)

4 **STIMULATES DIGESTION AND RESOLVES MUCOUS-DAMP; KILLS PARASITES**

liver and stomach Qi stagnation with *damp:* painful epigastrium, indigestion, appetite loss, flank pain
ACUTE DYSPEPSIA
WEAKNESS, debility, due to overwork, convalescence, etc.
kidney and bladder damp: white vaginal discharges, fatigue, backache
LEUCORRHEA
INTESTINAL and SKIN PARASITES (incl. pinworms, tapeworms [especially in children])

5 **PROMOTES URINATION, DRAINS WATER AND RELIEVES EDEMA**

liver and kidney water congestion: water retention from waist downward (or generalized), nausea
EDEMA
kidney Qi stagnation: malaise, skin rashes, smelly urine
URINARY SAND

6 **REDUCES INFLAMMATION, CONTUSION, SWELLING AND PAIN;**
   PROMOTES TISSUE REPAIR AND BENEFITS THE SKIN

INFLAMMATON and PAIN of eyes, skin; sunburn, muscle aches

BRUISES, sprains, strains

WOUNDS with pain and swelling, ulcers, abscesses, varicose veins, breast lumps

SKIN ERUPTIONS and DEFORMITIES (incl. eczema, acne, blemishes, freckles)

PREPARATION

Use: Tansy herb is prepared by **infusion** or **tincture.** Although the tincture is generally more effective than the infusion, the latter makes an invaluable bitter *digestive stimulant* for upper dyspepsia and a good *diaphoretic* for the onset of wind-heat colds and flus. **Lotions, washes, vaginal sponges** and **steams,** etc., are some further applications.

Note that either the whole herb or the flowerhead alone may be used. Tansy flowerheads contain up to 1.5% of essential oil, more than four times the amount found in the leaves and twigs alone.

With their higher essential oil content, **Tansy flower** and **seed** are both more effective than the whole herb against intestinal parasites. Infused, crushed or powdered the flower and/or seed should be taken on an empty stomach. Hot abdominal **compresses** and **suppositories** are also prepared with them for this purpose. For parasites, Tansy is often more effective when combined with another *vermifuge* such as Walnut hull, as well as with a *laxative* to flush them out.

Like numerous members of the related fragrant *Artemisia* family, Tansy herb was also traditionally used to smudge or fumigate places and people for protection and cleansing.

Dosage: Infusion of the herb: 4-10 g

   Infusion of the flowers: 3-5 g at 1:3 strength in 45% ethanol

   Tincture of the herb: 1-2 ml at 1:3 strength in 45% ethanol

For intestinal parasites: Make a long infusion with 1 teaspoon of the crushed or ground seeds. Take a single dose with warm herb tea before breakfast.

Caution: Being *uterine stimulant,* Tansy herb is contraindicated during pregnancy and breastfeeding. Do not exceed the above doses. Tansy is a medium-strength remedy with some cumulative toxicity that should mainly be used in formulas or intermittently on its own. Extremely high overdosing may cause vomiting, coma and convulsions.

Tansy essential oil is not suited for general use because of its high thujone content. Its toxicity is roughly on a par with that of Wormwood essential oil (*Artemisia absinthium*), also called Armoise oil.

Note: Costmary herb, *Chrysanthemum balsamita* L. (syn. *Tanacetum b.*) (also known as Alecost, Balsam herb and Mace), is traditionally used in a similar way to Tansy herb. However, Costmary is more pungent, *stimulant, antiseptic, antidotal, astringent* and *mucostatic* than Tansy. It is used especially for **uterus Qi stagnation** with amenorrhea, **lung phlegm-damp** with chronic bronchitis, **intestines (Spleen) damp** with painful dyspeptic disorders, **intestines damp-heat** with enteritis (dysentery), and poisonous insect bites. Originally from the Middle East, the plant migrated to South Europe and by Renaissance times was a favorite old English garden ornamental and pot herb. The fresh, aromatic spring leaves are eaten in salads and used in pot-pourris. Dose: as for Tansy herb.

NOTES

Tansy with its striking yellow "button" flowerheads is therapeutically multifaceted and has similar uses to other members of its family, like Camomile flower and Yarrow herb. However, nothing can quite replace this *relaxant* remedy when a certain combination of disharmonies come together. Tansy herb should be seen mainly as a woman's friend, and in the past was one of several plants called "motherwort" by wise woman healers. With its pungent-cool energetic qualities, the most important uses for Tansy are essentially tense conditions of the reproductive and digestive tract that tend to heat.

Essentially a good general *nervous relaxant* with *spasmolytic* and *analgesic* actions that regulate stagnant Qi, this herb addresses conditions of **Qi contraint** presenting painful **spasms** and **cramps**—especially menstrual and digestive. Note, in this connection, the pungent essential oil content with its borneol, camphor and thujone fractions.

591

Because of this, Tansy's also unfolds a *vasodilatant diaphoretic* effect in the person developing a **wind-heat** onset of a cold or flu with sore throat, fever and irritability—like Yarrow herb, Linden flower and Chrysanthemum Ju Hua. Those caught in the *shao yang* stage of remittent fevers will also benefit from its use in this connection.

Not only **spasmodic dysmenorrhea** comes under its *relaxant* effect, but also **amenorrhea, breast lumps** and **possibly tumors.** Like Yarrow herb, Tansy herb is ideal for conditions involving poor quality or backed-up estrogen. Like the acupuncture point selection Li 2, Kd 5, Sp 8, Gb 41, CV 3 and Bl 32, this herb is excellent for women presenting mental and emotional unrest as well as physical PMS symptoms. For treating spasmodic dysmenorrhea, Tansy is on a par with an White peony root or Cramp bark.

As a pungent-bitter *digestive stimulant* Tansy effectively mobilizes upper gastric stagnation with appetite loss and nausea as prominent symptoms, much like Peppermint herb. This results from the synergistic action of its essential oil, bitter resins and acids.

In traditional Greek (Western) medicine, Tansy was extensively used in ointments, plasters and such like for topical conditions. *Rubefacient, tissue-healing, anti-inflammatory* and *analgesic* to local tissues, the herb was a common pharmacy item—both single and compound—for various contusion conditions, painful wounds and local inflammation. Clearly an alternative to Arnica flower here. Because of this it also entered into many cosmetic preparations for skin care.

Pasqueflower Root and Herb

Botanical source: *Anemone pulsatilla* L.
   (syn. *Pulsatilla vulgaris* Miller), *A. patens* L.,
   A. pratensis L. and spp. (Ranunculaceae)
Pharmaceutical name: Radix et herba Pulsatillae
Ancient names: Herba ventis, Pulsatilla, Cauda
   vulpis, Nola culinaria (Lat)
Other names: Wind flower, Easter flower, Blue
   money, Dane's flower (Eng)
   Mayflower, Hartshorn plant, Goslinweed (Am)
   Pulsatille, Passefleur, Coque-lourde, Fleur de
   Pâques, Passe-velours, Teigne-oeuf,
   Coquerelle (Fr)
   Kuhschelle, Küchenschelle, Hackerkraut,
   Osterblume, Bisskraut (Ge)
Part used: the root and herb

NATURE
Therapeutic category: medium-strength remedy with moderate chronic toxicity
Constituents (*A. pulsatilla*): glycosides (incl. ranunculin [fresh], anemonin [dry], ess. oil, saponins, tannin, resin, phytosterol, fatty oil, phenols, cardiotonic substances
Effective qualities: somewhat bitter and pungent, neutral with warming and cooling potential, dry
   relaxing, calming, restoring, stimulating
Tropism: heart, lungs, kidneys, bladder, uterus and genitals, nerves
   Liver, Spleen, Heart, Lung, Large Intestine meridians
   Air, Warmth bodies

Ground: Melancholic and Sanguine krases
Burdened/Shao Yin and Expressive/Jue Yin biotypes
Biliary/Phosphoric constitution

FUNCTIONS AND INDICATIONS

1 **REGULATES UTERUS QI, HARMONIZES MENSTRUATION AND RELIEVES PAIN;**
TONIFIES UROGENITAL QI, HARMONIZES URINATION AND STOPS DISCHARGE

uterus Qi constraint: irregular, delayed or painful menstruation, worse from cold

SPASMODIC DYSMENORRHEA, ovarian pain (incl. from ovulation), salpingitis

PMS with spasmodic weeping, depression, melancholy, anxiety, withdrawal, headache

kidney and bladder Qi deficiency with damp: scanty, dribbling urination, bedwetting, delayed or
stopped periods, genital discharges, fatigue, cold limbs

AMENORRHEA, LEUCORRHEA, spermatorrhea, prostatorrhea, chronic gonorrhea

2 **RELAXES CONSTRAINT AND RELIEVES PAIN;**
RESTORES THE NERVES, LIFTS THE MIND AND RELIEVES DEPRESSION

kidney / adrenal Qi constraint: mental/nervous tension with debility, depression, cold, pain (esp. from
chronic stress, illness, mental or physical overwork) agitated depression, exhaustion, burnout

nerve and brain deficiency: weakness, depression, headache, fainting, poor vision, local paralysis

DEPRESSION, despondency, melancholy

NEURALGIAS (esp. in head and pelvic region)

HEADACHE (tension, frontal, gastric or bilious, esp. in deficiency conditions)

TOOTHACHE (jumping, esp. from abscess)

ARTHRITIC / RHEUMATIC PAIN

3 **REGULATES HEART QI AND RELIEVES ANXIETY**

heart Qi constraint (Liver Yang rising): anxiety, fear, chest pain, dizziness, impaired vision, tinnitus,
hot flashes

NEUROCARDIAC SYNDROME, cardiac hypertrophy

MENOPAUSAL ANXIETY with PALPITATIONS

INSOMNIA (esp. in deficiency conditions), mental overstimulation

4 **STIMULATES THE HEART AND CIRCULATION, AND DISPELS COLD;**
STIMULATES THE LIVER AND REDUCES CONGESTION

heart Yang deficiency: chilliness, mental depression, scanty urine, cyanosed lips, cold limbs

CIRCULATORY DEFICIENCY (incl. capillary deficiency, venous stasis), HYPOTHERMIA, FROSTBITE

liver Qi stagnation: indigestion, fat intolerance, flatulence, bad breath, heartburn, soft irregular stool,
pasty thick tongue moss

LIVER CONGESTION

5 **PROMOTES SWEATING, DISPELS WIND AND STOPS NASAL DISCHARGE**

external wind-cold/heat: chills, aches and pains, fearfulness, unrest, fatigue, sore throat, sharp earache

COLD and FLU ONSET, PHARYNGITIS

head damp-cold/heat: thick nasal discharge, frontal sinus headache, earache

ACUTE RHINITIS, OTITIS (esp. chronic, with or without discharge)

6 **CLEARS DAMP-HEAT AND REDUCES INFLAMMATION AND INFECTION;**
PROMOTES TISSUE REPAIR AND BENEFITS THE SKIN

REPRODUCTIVE ORGAN INFLAMMATIONS (incl. salpingitis, orchitis, epidydimitis, vaginitis, prostatitis)

INNER EYE INFLAMMATIONS (iritis, scleritis, conjunctivitis, stye, star)

IMPAIRMENT, threatened blindness, glaucoma, corneal opacity, amaurosis

microbial toxicosis with *damp-heat:* chronic indigestion, intestinal dysbiosis, food allergies

intestines damp-heat: painful, urgent bowel movement, bloody loose stool

DYSENTERY (amoebic and bacillary), enteritis

TRICHOMONAS vaginalis (?), candida albicans (?)

WOUNDS, ULCERS, burns, tooth abscess

SKIN ERUPTIONS and blemishes

PREPARATION

Use: Pasqueflower root and herb is used in **decoction** and **tincture** form. The whole plant should be used whenever possible; the next best is the root alone, then the herb alone (which gets a **long infusion**). To minimize potential toxicity, the root must be *completely dry* before processing in any way.

Low dilutions of the decoction or infusion are excellent for **eyewashes** (function 5), but standard dilutions apply to topical **washes, lotions,** etc., for its *vulnerary, anti-inflammatory, emollient* actions.

Low potency homeopathic preparations are also used for the very same functions as above.

Dosage: Decoction of the root and **infusion** of the herb: 3-6 g

Powder: 0.5-2 g

Tincture: 0.5-1.5 ml (12-38 drops) once or twice daily at 1:2 strength in 45% ethanol

Caution: Do not exceed dosages for this medium-strength remedy. If used daily, Pasqueflower root or herb should always be combined with other herbs as part of a formula, or else in occasional doses.

Being a *uterine stimulant,* this remedy is contraindicated during pregnancy. Also forbidden in nursing mothers because of a *gastrointestinal irritant* effect.

Note: As with the Chinese remedy, **Pulsatilla Bai Tou Weng,** in the U.S. and in Europe a variety of different *Pulsatilla/Anemone* species have always been used as source for this remedy. All have produced the same therapeutic results on both sides of the Atlantic, and so may be considered valid sources for this remedy. This especially as "the European species that are collected for medicinal use differ from each other as widely as from the variety of species indigenous to America" (URI LLOYD 1898).

NOTES

The stunningly beautiful, life-like woodcut illustration of pasqueflower by HANS WEIDITZ in OTTO BRUNFELS' herbal of 1532 is significant for being the first realistic depiction of this plant. Furthermore, it announces the first mention of Pasqueflower as a herbal remedy in any extant Western text. BRUNFELS was concerned with bringing the empirical folk remedies of the wise women into the recorded tradition, and this is one example among many. Later proponents of Pasqueflower such as VON STOERCK, CHRISTOF HUFELAND and SAMUEL HAHNEMANN would probably not even have known about this valuable remedy had BRUNFELS not decided for its inclusion among the established Western botanicals handed down from Greek and Arabic texts.

Meanwhile on the other side of the Atlantic, the American variety of pasqueflower, *Anemone patens,* "was the chief medicinal plant of the Minnesota tribe of Indians" (LLOYD 1898). In the nineteenth century the symptom pictures of the European and American species were considered virtually identical and became well known through homeopathic provings. In turn, the homeopathic symtomatology of Pasqueflower heavily influenced the Eclectic and Physiomedical use of the remedy.

For these historical reasons, Pasqueflower developed two distinct *personae.* Before HAHNEMANN's development of homeopathy, Pasqueflower root and herb was mainly used for its *antiseptic, anti-infective* and *diaphoretic* actions, as well as for treating **eye** and **vision** disorders. This usage is closely paralleled by the Chinese use of the root of *Pulsatilla chinensis,* which contains both identical and similar glycosides. After HAHNEMANN, Pasqueflower became an important *analgesic* and *mucostatic* remedy for neuralgic pain and discharges with a particular tropism for the female reproductive organs—in addition to acquiring a crusty overlay of mental/emotional symptoms as a result of homeopathic provings. No question, Pasque flower is a dyadic remedy.

In terms of the warm/cold dialectic alone, Pasqueflower root and herb is a paradoxical remedy. Essentially a drying *arterial* and *capillary stimulant* and *astringent mucostatic* in one, it can produce a bivalent warming or cooling effect, depending on the condition being treated. The first essential area of application for this remedy is **chronic damp-cold** in the **reproductive** and **digestive organs.** Here the person presents thick, bland mucus discharges, chronic indigestion, a weak, slippery, tight pulse and grey-white, greasy tongue coating. Disorders such as genital discharges, amenorrhea, dysmenorrhea and chronic intestinal dysbiosis all fall into this framework. Similar-acting *mucostatic* for combining would include Sage leaf, Helonias root, Yerba Mansa root and Kava root.

Moreover Pasqueflower's *stimulant* effect is diffusive enough to also affect the exterior as a *diaphoretic* when drunk hot. Here it can predictably treat both **external wind-cold** and **wind-heat** infections such as flu and laryngitis, typically seen in those with sore throat, pains and fearfulness. Its *mucostatic* and *anti-inflammatory* actions combine here to address both acute and chronic upper respiratory conditions, including catarrhal rhinitis and otitis media. Here Pasqueflower's action can be reinforced variously with Class 1 *diaphoretics* to promote sweating and release the exterior; Class 12 *anti-infectives* like Echinacea root and Marigold flower to reduce toxic heat and infection; and Class 15 *mucostatics* to resolve mucous-damp like Sage leaf, Plantain leaf and Lungwort lichen.

Pasqueflower's second essential area of application is **damp-heat** caused by **bacterial** and **fungal proliferation.** Here the remedy effectively works as an *anti-infective, anti-inflammatory, astringent* and *antiseptic* for dysenterial conditions, especially with blood and mucus discharge. Because Chinese experiments have successfully used *P. chinensis* for fungal and protozoal infec-

tions (e.g., candidiasis and trichomoniasis), it is worth putting these uses to the test with indigenous varieties of *Pulsatilla*.

However, for a full picture of the complex remedy, we need to consider its *restorative* action on the nervous system. The clinical experience of Eclectic doctors showed that it always works best with individuals presenting an underlying **nervous deficiency.** Pasqueflower essentially addresses **empty tense** conditions with **cold,** involving both nervous and circulatory deficiency. Regardless of the disorder or condition being treated, the remedy will always succeed best when the person shows symptoms of pain, nervous tension, exhaustion, cold, depression and fearfulness. Mental depression and insomnia from overstimulation are further classic indications here. Other *nervous restoratives* come to mind here for CNS support, such as Skullcap herb, Sage leaf, St. John's wort, Vervain herb and the Chinese Polygonum He Shou Wu.

Pasqueflower is both *restorative* and *relaxant* to the nervous system and therefore will regulate constrained Qi and relieve pain. Its *relaxant* action specifically arises from the *spasmolytic, analgesic* and somewhat *sedative* activity of the glycoside anemonin and the essential oil combined.

As a result, women in **menstrual** and **childbirth** situations presenting **pain, tension, debility and cold** are also foremost in Pasqueflower' range of clinical indications. The remedy combines well with other *spasmolytic, analgesic* women's herbs such as Motherwort herb and Black cohosh root (also in menopause), and Cramp bark, White peony root and other Chinese favorites such as Ligusticum Chuan Xiong and Cyperus Xiang Fu.

The mental symptoms associated with Pasqueflower, such as "an active imagination for disease, a fear of impending danger" (JOHN SCUDDER 1856), deep depression and inner unrest are an integral part of the Pasqueflower symptom picture. These are especially connected with the heart and kidneys. There is no doubt that Pulsatilla is effective here when the tincture is used, because the latter also incorporates a homeopathic action that will address mental and emotional states such as these (see *Tincture* in Ch. 8).

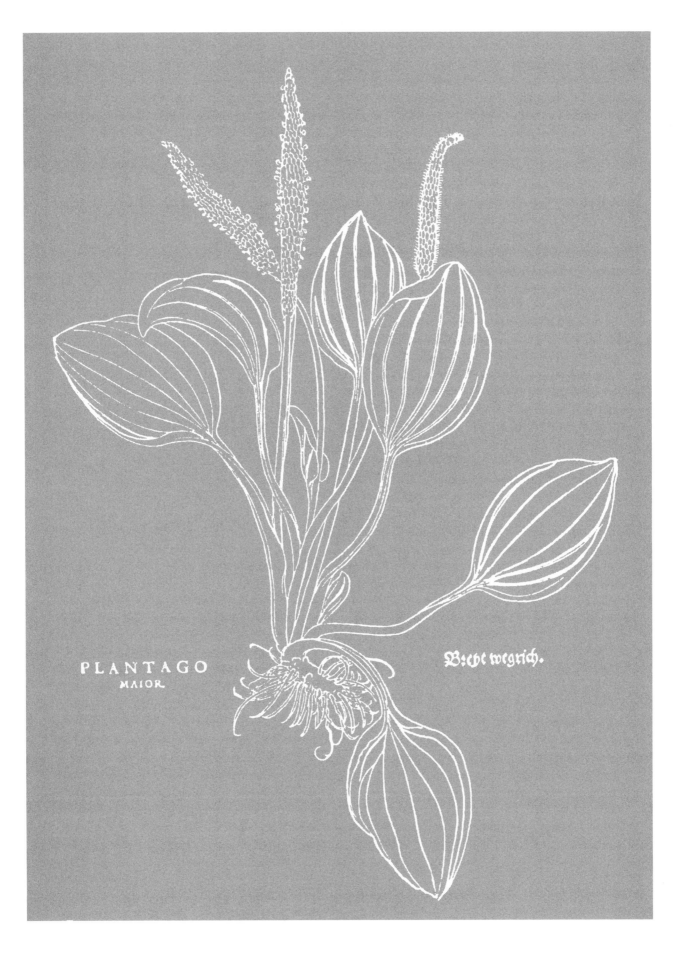

PLANTAGO
MAIOR

Brehc wegrich.

Herbs to Clear Heat and Reduce Fever and Infection

The treatment strategy of clearing heat addresses conditions known in vitalistic herbal medicine as hot conditions. These involve hyperfunctioning and may include the signs of fever (pyrexia) and inflammation, a rapid pulse and deep red tongue, as well as the subjective symptom of feelings of heat. Fever and inflammation are normal responses of the warmth body, the body's Yang, to toxic irritation by various pathogens, including exogenous micro-organisms and endogenous toxins.

Remedies that clear heat are generally called *refrigerants* or simply *cooling remedies*. They address hot conditions in two ways.

1. They reduce the heat of fever and inflammation that have become too intense or prolonged and so counterproductive to healing. As such they include *antipyretic* and *anti-inflammatory* remedies.

2. They reduce infection itself whenever this is present. As such they include *anti-infective* herbs with *detoxicant, immunostimulant* and *antimicrobial* actions.

The Nature and Dynamics of Heat and Infection

Any abnormal heat generated in the body results from a spontaneous defense mechanism of the individual's vital force, and is an expression of the warmth body. The basic purpose of this warmth response is to neutralize and remove something foreign and therefore irritant and pathogenic to the body. **Fever** and **inflammation** increase the metabolic rate and stimulate immune functions, especially antibody production, thereby helping the body resolve toxic irritation. Tissue irritation is therefore the one common factor in the etiopathology of hot conditions. It may arise from microbial proliferation (microbial toxicosis) or infection, or from various non- or para-infectious conditions such as metabolic toxicosis, intestinal dysbiosis, blood congestion, hypersensitivity disorders and tissue trauma. Despite the current steady increase of all types of hypersensitivities involving chronic infla-

mmation, **microbial infection** is still the main pathogen that causes warmth responses.

The dynamics of the warmth response involve either an increase of local blood flow to an area, producing an **inflammation,** or an increase of overall body temperature by the controlling "thermostat" in the hypothalamus, causing a **fever**. In the case of inflammation, signs of redness, swelling, pain and heat will manifest in the affected area. With fever present, symptoms such as flushed face, headache, thirst, restlessness, nausea, appetite loss, constipation, general aches and pains, scanty, dark yellow urine, a dark red tongue and a rapid, forceful pulse may appear.

Heat, dryness and **rising movement** are the general characteristics of hot conditions. The symptoms that appear will vary widely, depending on two factors. First, the nature of the irritating pathogens. Second, the predisposing ground (terrain) of the individual himself, which is dependent on the constitution. The most common types of hot conditions involve **viral and bacterial infections** such as flu, sinusitis, otitis, tonsilitis, gastroenteritis, cystitis, food poisoning, mumps, measles, chickenpox and whooping cough. More serious conditions include pneumonia, hepatitis, rheumatic fever, meningitis and septicemia.

Examples of heat disorders that may be **non-infectious** in nature include otitis (middle ear inflammation), atopic dermatitis, atopic asthma, pelvic inflammatory disease, inflammatory bowel disease (including ulcerative colitis and Crohn's disease), rheumatoid arthritis, vasculitis, lupus erythematosus and appendicitis. Many of these involve inflammation and fever caused by hypersensitivity reactions to allergens, which range from immediate allergies to autoimmune diseases. Note also that immune complex hypersensitivities (type III) may in turn generate infections presenting heat, such as chronic hepatitis B, bacterial glomerulonephritis and bacterial endocarditis.

More discussion on the nature and dynamics of infection itself is found in Class 24.

The Diagnosis and Treatment of Hot Conditions

The triggering and predisposing factors for hot conditions are certainly important diagnostic and treatment considerations. It is important to know the type, location and development of an infection that may be causing fever or inflammation. For instance:
• A rapidly spiking fever usually indicates influenza, kidney infection (pyelitis) or pneumonia.
• If the temperature is extremely high, infection or injury in the head is the most likely cause.

Because hot conditions arise from a warmth response to pathogens, on a more fundamental energetic level they must be fully evaluated and treated as such. It is thanks to this fine-tuned dialectic, vitalistic approach that traditional medicines excel at managing a large variety of hot conditions. Specifically, for a rational and skilled treatment of hot conditions, two basic assessments must be made.
1. To what extent are the heat-producing processes (i.e. the fever and inflammation) beneficial or injurious?
2. What are the relative strengths of the pathogens and the person's warmth/Yang response?

Let us consider each issue in turn.

In principle, because fever and inflammation are necessary vital responses to toxic irritation, they should be supported as far as possible, not immediately suppressed with *antipyretic* or *anti-inflammatory* drugs. This is only possible, however, by differentiating between beneficial and injurious heat. Only this primary evaluation can guide us to the correct treatment approach to hot and febrile conditions.

1. When fever or inflammation are moderate and do not cause any serious side effects, this is not considered pathological. Here the best treatment strategy is simply to assist the warmth response in resolving the toxic irritation. Treatment should aim not only to boost immune functions, but also to remove toxic debris from the conflict through the lymph, skin and kidneys. *Promoting sweating and urination* with Class 1 *diaphoretics* and Class 2 *diuretics* respectively are the two main herbal treatment methods used.

Other gentle measures that support a healthy fever are just as important, however. They include complete bedrest, drinking plenty of fluids and a light diet of cooling (or at least neutral), high water content fruits and vegetables such as apples, grapes, grapefruits, raw carrots and so on. Lemon drinks and barley waters, for example, are often drunk during fever because of their *detoxicant, refreshing* and *thirst-quenching* effects.

2. When fever and inflammation become excessive or prolonged, they become injurious and are then considered pathological. Heat can easily outlive its usefulness as an appropriate response to pathogens and get out of control!
• Any temperature above 104°F (44°C) is considered the sign of a counterproductive and therefore dangerous fever, and requires lowering with *antipyretic* herbs from this class.
• Any temperature that refuses to go down after two days, or maximum 72 hours in strong individuals, is also counterproductive and must be lowered with *antipyretics*.

Herbal *antipyretics* are superior to drug *antipyretics* because they support the liver in temperature reduction rather than in spite of it. See High Fevers below for the particular treatment.

Next, we need to assess the relative strength of the pathogens versus the person's warmth/Yang response in order to determine the *intensity* of heat-clearing treatment required in any hot condition.

1. If there are no signs of Yang deficiency, such as exhaustion, diarrhea and cold limbs, then generally speaking the warmth body/Yang is strong. In this case relatively strong heat-clearing measures can be taken. *Cold antipyretic* and/or *anti-inflammatory* remedies should be adopted to strongly reduce temperature and/or inflammation.

2. If signs of Yang deficiency are present, the heat-clearing treatment should be moderate and should include tonification of the body's warmth/Yang, using appropriate *warm, stimulant* remedies (Class 8).

Another way of understanding the body's warmth responses to pathogens or trauma is by looking at a person's constitutional biotype.
• Yang, full-blooded, sthenic (full) constitutions will produce strong, rapid warmth responses to pathogens, such as high fever and acute inflammation. The Shao Yang and Tai Yang Fire types belong in this category. For treatment they require draining, cooling kinds of remedies with a bitter, dry taste, such as Boneset herb, Gentian root,

Bogbean herb and Baikal skullcap root.

• Yin, anemic, asthenic (empty) constitutions, on the other hand, having insufficient warmth or Yang to properly respond, tend to generate symptoms of empty heat such as chronic low-level, sub-acute, catarrhal or serous inflammations. The Shao Yin and Tai Yin Earth types are good examples of these types. The Yin types require restoring, cooling remedies with a sweet, moist tatse; mostly the Class 9 *demulcents* such as Slippery elm bark, Borage leaf, Scrophularia Xuan Shen and Anemarrhena Zhi Mu, for example.

Once the cause and degree of injuriousness of a hot condition have been evaluated and the strength of the person's warmth/Yang assessed, we can then consider more specific details. We then to need look at:

1. The temporal development of the heat, and specifically of the fever
2. The physical location of the fever or inflammation

We can determine the phase and location of fevers by using the syndromes of disease progression, as well as by understanding different types of fevers.

Chinese medicine uses two basic models here, the four level stages (*si fen*) and the six meridian stages (*liu jing*). The four stages through which a fever progresses are the defensive, Qi, blood and nutritive level. The six meridian stages are the *tai yang, shao yang, yang ming, tai yin, jue yin* and *shao yin*. Both models can be matched directly with the four stages of disease used in vitalistic (herbal, naturopathic) medicine in the West, namely the acute, subacute, chronic and degenerative.

Traditional Greek medicine classifies fevers according to their periodicity, i.e., whether occurring daily, every other day or every three or four days.

The physical location of a hot condition Oriental medicine describes extensively in the *zang fu* (organ) and Triple Warmer syndromes.

Whatever model we adopt to describe and treat febrile and inflammatory conditions, the point is that these models allow us to make specific heat-clearing herbal formulas that are accurately tailored to their phase of defense response. Here we will consider the types of fevers, based on the traditional Western model of their periodicity, while integrating the Chinese medicine models of the disease stages and organ syndromes.

The Types of Fevers

In terms of their own temporal and intrinsic character, fevers can present in the following ways:
• A **continuous,** or sustained, fever: one that shows unvarying high temperature for an extended period.
• A **remittent** fever: one that presents temperature variations throughout the day.
• An **intermittent** fever: where periods of fever alternate with periods of normal temperature.

When these types of fevers are combined with the various stages of fever, four main types of fever emerge:

1. The onset of fever
2. High fever or the *fastidium*
3. Remittent fever
4. Low-grade fever

Each type of febrile condition requires a heat-clearing method specifically tailored to the phase and nature of its warmth response, using certain types of *refrigerant* or *cooling* herbs.

The Onset of Fevers: The Acute External Stage

Febrile onsets generally last one or two days at the most and show a steady increase in temeperature. They are acute conditions that present a mild fever, chills, aches and pains, headache and a floating pulse. Onset fevers are treated with *diaphoretics* that promote sweating and reduce fever (Class 1), and in the cases of Yang, sthenic types of individuals, with *diuretics* that promote urination (Class 2).

In Chinese medicine the onset of fevers is said to be at the *tai yang* stage and the **external** location. The main syndromes that present at this stage are **external wind-cold** and **external wind-heat** (see Class 1).

It is important, once again, here to support the body's heat response by promoting sweating rather than to abort the fever with simple temperature-lowering *antipyretic* herbs or drugs, which actually undermine and weaken the vital force or Qi. The *antipyretics* are brought in for the next stage of fever if, and only if, the *diaphoretics* don't work— and they usually do. If they do not, this is a sign that a more serious infection is brewing.

High Fevers: The Acute Internal Stage

A fever that fails to respond to treatment at the onset external stage will move to the the body's interior and become an acute high fever. It usually signals the presence of a more severe infection. A fever at this stage is characterized by a temperature of 102 F and higher and show symptoms such as feelings of heat, headache, thirst, unrest, irritability, insomnia, delirium, constipation, dark scanty urine, a rapid, full, forceful pulse and a yellow coating on a bright or dark red tongue. From the diagnostic perspective, these symptoms represent a condition of **internal full heat.**

A high fever belongs to the **Qi level** or *yang ming* stage of fevers in Chinese medicine, which Western medicine traditionally calls the **fastidium.** It represents an acute healing crisis in the resistance phase of adaptation. It specifically occurs as the warmth body (the Yang) attempts to overcome pathogens, i.e. microbes that are causing a serious infection of some kind. Although high fever is clearly productive in the beginning, it soon becomes counterproductive if it continues to rise (spike) instead of coming down, or if it causes secondary conditions such as delirium, spasms, or fluids deficiency with thirst—which can occur anytime, depending on the individual constitution.

A **continuous** or **sustained high fever** usually arises from a septic or abscess source involving the teeth, sinuses, tonsils, appendix or prostate. However, it may also arise from lung TB, scarlet fever, pneumonia or typhus, as well as noninfectious conditions such as liver disease and cancer.

Treatment aims to clear excess heat and reduce fever through the use of *antipyretics* with cold, bitter, sinking qualities. Belonging mainly to the composite and barberry family, these herbs include Gentian root, Barberry root bark, Chicory root, Dandelion root, Bogbean herb, Boneset herb, Goldenseal root, Asian buplever root and Yellow jessamine root. They tend to support the liver, thereby allowing the temperature to go down while the body's defenses are still fully active. Comparable Oriental *antipyretics* would be Anemarrhena Zhi Mu (Know-mother root) and Gardenia Zhi Zi (Gardenia pod).

In high fevers it may also be necessary to promote bowel movement with *stimulant laxatives* (Class 3) such as Rhubarb root, Cascara sagrada and Senna leaf. This treatment method is especially useful when heat injures the fluids, causing internal dryness with constipation and hard dry stools.

The concern when treating full heat conditions is not to clear the heat too rapidly or too soon.[3]

Should the temperature be reduced too forcibly, e.g., through the use of *antipyretic* drugs or mineral remedies such as Gypsum (Gypsum Shi Gao) used in Chinese medicine, there are two possible outcomes:

1. Injury to the Kidney Yang, the warmth body. The liver's defenses collapse and the fever then becomes adynamic (weak) and remittent (see below). The unresolved acute stage then falls back into the subacute shao yang stage halfway between the acute Yang and the chronic Yin phases. (The shao yang in classical texts is qualified as the hinge stage between the two.)

2. Exhaustion of the Kidney Yang, the warmth body. As the body's warmth response becomes exhausted, the acute stage may collapse into the chronic *shao yin* stage, producing a low-grade tidal fever (see below). If the vital resistance is still deficient at this stage, chronic conditions of the *tai yin* or *jue yin* phase ensue.

Remittent Fevers

This type of fever is also known as a hectic fever when severe. Typically it shows *temperature variations* throughout the day and is accompanied by alternating spells of chills and fever, sweating, headache, irritability, nausea, appetite loss, fullness of the chest and sides, a bitter taste in the mouth, blurred vision and a wiry, large or rapid pulse.

Remittent fever belongs to the *shao yang* stage of febrile disease and is a subacute condition located half-way between the exterior and interior. It results from an unsuccessful (or at least unresolved) healing crisis in the resistance phase of adaptation and specifically occurs when the warmth body/Yang is unable to overcome the infection during the acute high fever phase. It may occur as a result of mismanaged high fever, or may indicate an abscess, sepsis, blood poisoning (septicemia), malaria, typhoid or empyema.

Treatment aims to clear the injurious heat and reduce the fever, and to cause sweating in order to stimulate defense response. The *diaphoretic antipyretics* used generally have pungent-bitter, cool qualities and include Eucalyptus leaf, Wormwood herb, Boneset herb, Pennyroyal herb, Catnip leaf, Elderflower, Echinacea root, Hops flower, Melilot herb, Wahoo bark, Asian buplever root and Virginia snakeroot. Chinese medicine equivalents also include Artemisia Qing Hao (Celery wormwood herb).

Low-Grade Fevers

This type of fever shows a temperature of up to 101 F. It is benign if short lived and gone within two or three days. It typically occurs in the declining, or defervescent, stage of a high fever that has successfully run its course. In young children, low-grade fevers may also arise simply as a response to emotional stress.

If a low-grade fever suddenly follows a high fever during a disease crisis, it signals the exhaustion stage of adaptation, or the *shao yin* stage of disease, and the condition becomes truly chronic (see above) and popularly known as a "rotten fever."

Regardless of the cause, if a low fever persists and becomes chronic, it becomes injurious. Then it will present symptoms of **empty heat,** such as hot spells with hot sensations in the palms, sternum and soles of the feet; mental and physical fatigue and restlessness, thirst, night sweats, insomnia, a thin, rapid pulse and a scarlet, thin tongue. The cause of a chronic low fever are usually some type of chronic infection, chronic inflammation or a severe or chronic autonomic nervous or neuroendocrine dysfunction.

Low-grade fevers may be tidal or periodic in character.

• **Tidal** low-grade fevers are so called because they recur like tides in the late afternoon, and are also known as **intermittent fevers.**

• **Periodic** low-grade fevers are so called because they occur daily or periodically every few days. Greek medicine classifies them by the number of days they recur: tertian, quatan, and so on.

Treatment aims to clear empty heat and tonify the Qi with sweet, cool, *restorative antipyretics* such as Valerian root, Pipsissewa root/herb, Chicory root, Wahoo bark, Solomon's seal root, Lungwort lichen, Slippery elm bark and Cleavers herb. These are complemented by Chinese herbs such as Ophiopogon Mai Men Dong (Japanese lilyturf root), Rehmannia Sheng Di Huang (Raw rehmannia root) and Scrophularia Xuan Shen (Black figwort root). With dryness present, moist-natured *demulcents* (Class 10) are selected in complement.

Treatment Considerations

• In addition to the use of heat-clearing herbs in this chapter, there are secondary methods for clearing heat, including eliminating treatments such as promoting sweating, urination and bowel movement. These possess indirect heat-clearing effects, especially during a high fever. In the West, historically the most significant primary method of clearing heat was phlebotomy (bloodletting). This treatment method is a highly effective, although widely misunderstood therapeutic technique.[2]

The three main posible consequences of pathological heat are **dehydration, spasms** and **delirium.** These side effects result from heat injuring the fluids, nervous system and mind, respectively.

• With injury to the fluids causing dehydration, the result is **dry-heat in the intestines** with hard dry stool, constipation, hot dry skin and unslakeable thirst. *Demulcent laxatives* and *purgatives combined* (Class 3) will clear the heat, moisten the intestines and promote bowel movement.

• With the autonomic nervous system affected, spasmodic symptoms such as tremors, spasms or convulsions may arise, described in Chinese medicine as **internal wind.** The treatment priority then becomes relieveing spasms with *spasmolytics* (Class 21).

• In the case of **agitation of the mind,** delirious rambling or slurred speech may occur. *Nervous sedatives* (Class 19) are then appropriate to calm the mind and reduce delirium or manic behavior.

• In the case of **coma** from high fever, *analeptic nervous stimulants* (Class 20) should be used to revive consciousness.

The Herbs that Clear Heat and Reduce Infection

Remedies that clear heat are traditionally known as *refrigerants*. The majority of *refrigerants* possess *antipyretic, anti-inflammatory, anti-infective* and *antiseptic* functions. They present a study in taste energetics because among them are found:

• the bitter kind, dominated by plants from the composite family, such as Gentian root, Chicory root, Bogbean herb and Centaury herb;

• the bitter-astringent kind, such as Barberry bark, Willow bark, Goldenseal root and Chaparral leaf.

• the pungent kind, such as Yarrow herb, Elderflower, Catnip leaf and Boneset herb.

• the sour kind, including Lemon rind and Grapevine leaf;

• the salty kind, such as Plantain leaf, Purslane herb and Echinacea root;

• the astringent kind, which includes herbs in the rose family, such as Red root, Lady's mantle herb and Rose flower;

To summarize, *refrigerant herbs* treat hot conditions in two ways.

1. By reducing the heat of fever and inflammation. Certain *refrigerants* reduce febrile or inflammatory heat that has become too intense or prolonged and so counterproductive to healing. These are *antipyretics* and *anti-inflammatories* that can limit high fever or inflammation by specifically lowering the body's temperature through hypothalamic modulation of the heat-regulating centers. Again, in distinction to synthetic medication, they achieve this without injuring the body's Yang/warmth body. Important *antipyretics* and *anti-inflammatories* include Barberry bark, Goldenseal root, White willow bark, Boneset herb, Plantain leaf, Figwort herb, Baikal skullcap root, Asian buplever root, Yellow jessamine root, Gardenia Shan Zhi Zi (Gardenia pod) and Anemarrhena Zhi Mu (Know-mother root).

Note that these *refrigerant* remedies not only treat fever and inflammation, but often will also help relieve subjective feelings of heat without actual fever or inflammation being present. Perimenopausal hot flashes are a common example.

2. By reducing the infection itself. Certain *refrigerants* work directly to reduce infection itself whenever this is present—which it often is. These are *anti-infective* herbs that work essentially by assisting fever and inflammation in their task of resolving infection. *Anti-infectives* clear heat physiologically in three ways by:

• Supporting liver and kidney functions, especially the detoxification pathways and urine production: as such they have a *detoxicant/depurative* action, and often a good *diuretic* action.
• Directly stimulating the body's immune functions in one way or other: as such they have an *immunostimulant* action (see also Class 24).
• Promoting general asepsis, an *antiseptic* action, by directly inhibiting microbial growth. As such they are *antiseptics* that then subdivide into *antiviral, antibacterial, antifungal* and *antiprotozoal* actions.

Important *anti-infective* remedies include Echinacea root, Marigold flower, Wild indigo root, Goldenseal root, Barberry bark, Sage leaf, Chaparral leaf and Poke root, as well as Chinese herbs such as Lonicera Jin Yin Hua (Japanese honeysuckle flower) and Da Qing Ye (Woad leaf).

Note the significant overlap of *anti-infectives* with *detoxicant* herbs (Class 13) and many *eliminant* remedies (Classes 1 through 4). Highly effective herbs such as Echinacea root, Marigold flower, Chaparral leaf, Goldenseal root and Dandelion root actually belong in both categories.

The first, second and fourth subclasses below present the nature and treatment of three kinds of infectious heat involving toxicosis, mucosal inflammation and blood congestion, respectively.

Clear Toxic Heat and Reduce Fever and Infection
Cool detoxicant anti-infectives (immunostimulants, antimicrobials, antipyretics, anti-inflammatories)

Remedies of this type are used to treat the condition known in Chinese medicine as **heat toxin** or **fire toxin** (*re du, huo du*). This is an acute inflammatory and febrile condition presenting sepsis/infection and purulence. It is usually triggered by a bacterial infection arising from underlying pathogenic factors such as microbial toxicosis with immune deficiency, poor hygiene and malnutrition. **Heat toxin** syndromes generally consists of swollen glands; hot, swollen, discolored painful lesions such as boils (including furuncles and carbuncles), abscesses, pyodermia, sores, mastitis and appendicitis. These may be accompanied by remittent or continuous fever, as well as general signs of endogenous toxicosis such as headache, malaise, irritability and skin rashes.

The condition of **heat toxin** is treated by reducing acute infection, fever, inflammation, purulence and swelling. The herbs that clear toxic heat are essentially *anti-infective* and *detoxicant,* and specifically entail *antipyretic, immuostimulant, antiseptic, anti-inflammatory* and *detumescent* actions. They tend to be bitter and cooling by nature, as seen in Echinacea root, Marigold flower, Plantain leaf, Purslane herb, Usnea thallus, Wild indigo root, Dandelion root, Yellow dock root, Heartsease herb and Violet root/herb. As in the Chinese materia medica, which uses remedies like Lonicera Jin Yin Hua (Japanese honeysuckle flower) and Forsythia Lian Qiao (Forsythia valve), many of these remedies are leaves and flowers that possess a gentle raising quality of movement.

Oral internal use of these remedies should be complemented by a local application such as a compress, suppository or pessary made from the same herbs, all depending on the actual site of the infection.

Clear Damp-Heat and Reduce Infection and Discharge

Bitter, cold, dry, astringent anti-infectives

Refrigerant herbs of this type address **damp-heat** conditions, which are locally caused by infection or irritation along mucosal surfaces. Because this condition may occur in the head, eyes, lungs, stomach, intestines, bladder, kidneys or reproductive organs, the symptoms will vary according to its location. The essential features of damp-heat are invariably: redness, swelling, mucosal/catarrhal exudate and fetid purulent discharge.

Typical damp heat syndromes include:
• **intestines damp-heat,** showing urgent, frequent, loose bloody stools, seen, e.g., in chronic enteritis, dysentery and inflammatory bowel disease;
• **kidney/bladder damp-heat** displaying painful urination and purulent, fetid, yellow or blood-streaked vaginal discharge, seen in vaginitis, cervicitis, trichomoniasis, PID or venereal infections;
• **bladder damp-heat** presenting urgent, frequent burning urination, backache and thirst, seen in mucous cystitis, urethritis, prostatitis, etc.

Damp-heat is treated at root level by reducing infection, relieving irritation and encouraging mucosal tissue repair. On the symptom level this in turn will help clear toxins and reduce acute inflammation, as well as reduce or stop discharge. The remedies of choice are bitter, astringent, dry, cold *anti-infectives* that are high in tannins and/or bitter components. Their strong *anti-infective* and *anti-inflammatory* actions may be seen in Goldenseal root, Bilberry leaf, Bearberry leaf, Barberry root bark, Gentian root, Chaparral leaf and Pau d'arco bark. They are paralleled in Asian medicine by remedies such as Scutellaria Huang Qin (Baikal skullcap root), Gardenia Shan Zhi Zi (Gardenia pod) and Coptis Huang Lian (Goldthread root). They are similar to the dry *astringents* (Class 18) in that they are drying, astringing and discharge-stopping. However, dry *astringents* are not primarily bitter in taste nor heat-clearing in effect.
• Bitter, cold *anti-infectives* in this class and dry *astringents* (Class 18) may be combined for a greater *anti-discharge* and *hemostatic* action.
• *Demulcents* (Class 10), such as Marsh mallow root, Mullein leaf and Comfrey leaf, may be added for soothing the irritation present and for healing the mucus membranes.

Clear Blood Heat and Stop Bleeding

These herbs treat **internal heat** that is said in Chinese medicine to have reached the blood level, causing a syndrome known as **blood heat** (*xue re*). Blood heat is the result of two conditions, one infectious, the other non-infectious.

1. The first kind arises at an advanced stage of infection when chronic blood congestion becomes inflammatory, and for that reason could be called **blood heat congestion.** This is one type of inflammatory diathesis in Western medicine. The typical symptoms of this kind of blood heat are spontaneous bleeding—blood in the spittle, nosebleeds, blood in urine or stool, copious menstrual or intermenstrual bleeding—fever and skin rashes, as well as the more general heat signs mentioned above.

2. The non-infectious kind of blood heat occurs when pelvic congestion and internal heat (with or without inflammation) cause early or heavy menstruation (menorrhagia) or intermenstrual bleeding (metrorrhagia), with unrest, insomnia, etc. This is non-infectious blood heat. The two types of this syndrome should be clearly distinguished.

The treatment of both types of blood heat have a common basis. The treatment consists of removing blood congestion by vitalizing the blood, clearing inflammation and stopping bleeding. Most remedies that clear heat and cool the blood possess cool, dry, sour and astringent qualities because of their organic acid or tannin content. They are also specifically *anti-inflammatory* and have a tropism for the blood and capillaries.[4] These qualities together account for their *decongestant* effect.

Anti-inflammatory decongestants include Wood sorrel herb, Lady's mantle herb, Grapevine leaf, White deadnettle herb, Rose flower/essential oil, Goldenseal root, and in China, remedies such as Paeonia Mu Dan Pi (Tree peony root), Gardenia Zhi Zi (Gardenia pod). Because they are often used for treating gynecological disorders, many of these *decongestants* are found among the remedies that vitalize the blood (Class 14).
• Both types of blood heat may be reinforced by *hemostatics* to staunch acute bleeding and by other *refrigerants* in this section, depending on the particular condition.
• In the case of infectious blood heat, *anti-infectives* (Class 12) should also be selected to clear infection.
• In the case of gynecological blood heat, *hemosta-*

tics (Class 18) may be added to reduce menstrual or intermenstrual bleeding.

• According to Eclectic physician HERBERT WEBSTER (1898), if blood heat presents with acute inflammatory congestion, as with pelvic inflammation, only those herbs with a low tannin content should be used, such as Plantain leaf, Lemon rind, Rose petal, Cypress twig and Wood sorrel herb. He does not explain the reason for this, however.

A summary of remedies in this Class can be found in the Repertory under the headings of Fever, Inflammation and Infection.

NOTES

1. Heat presenting with Yang deficiency may occur in conditions of true cold with false heat. Harmful side effects include fluids depletion and internal wind. A striking case history illustrating this is given in an article by ZHENG JIAGUI ("Verfälschung der klinischen Aussagen der chinesischen Medizin unter dem Einfluss der westlichen Medizin") published in *Chinesische Medizin* No. 1/2, Munich, July 1986.

2. Far from being a primitive practice, phlebotomy (also known as bleeding, bloodletting or venesection) is a highly effective, simple and elegant treatment method used by all major medical systems, including Chinese, Tibetan, Ayurvedic and Greek. The main forms of phlebotomy are bleeding (drawing a certain quantity of blood from a vein with the use of a lancet), cupping (causing suction on the skin with cupping glasses through vacuum) and leeching (using live leeches).

Phlebotomy works according to the treatment principles of both Eliminating and Draining. It is eliminating in the sense that excess fluid is removed, as with causing sweating, urination, bowel movement, menstruation, etc. Phlebotomy is also draining because it discharges an excess of energy by globally regulating circulatory dynamics, thereby limiting excessive and counterproductive vital responses such as fever, inflammation and blood congestion. Its main uses, therefore, is for excess conditions. These include **full heat, blood congestion, toxicosis** and **Qi constraint.** Its effects can be summarized as *heat-clearing* (*anti-inflammatory* and *antipyretic* in the case of **inflammation and fever**), *decongestant* (in **blood congestion** and **blood heat**), *detoxicant* (*antidyskratic*) (in **metabolic toxicosis** and **heat toxin**), *resolvent, anticoagulant* and *blood-resorbent* (in **stagnant, thrombotic** or **ecchymotic blood**), *relaxant* (*spasmolytic* in **Qi constraint**) and *analgesic* (in excess conditions with pain).

Because it is such a direct and effective method of treatment, phlebotomy has several cautions and contraindications that must be respected. The absolute contraindications are deficiency conditions such as stomach and intestines (Spleen) Qi deficiency; Qi, blood, fluids, Essence or Yang deficiency, as well as weakness, hypotension, angina pectoris, extreme nervousness and menstruation. Phlebotomy should generally not be performed in people of the Blue Iris type. It is important to note that in simple infections without blood congestion, severe inflammation or toxicosis present, and without any signs of full internal heat, blood heat, toxic heat or metabolic toxicosis, phlebotomy is *not* indicated.

There is a clear distinction between phlebotomy used in an appropriate way based on the principles of energetic medicine, and its malpractice when used excessively or indiscriminately. Phlebotomy was often malpracticed in the past and from the 1650s onwards degenerated into an empty vampiric technique. Like all eliminating and draining treatment methods, and like the use of many modern drugs, phlebotomy can only give satisfactory results when the indications calling for its use are clearly present. Moreover, being a powerful technique, its misuse will lead to correspondingly strong negative reactions.

The historical degeneration and misuse of phlebotomy in the West may better be understood in connection with the rise of Western medicine as a legislated, male-dominant profession since the fifteenth century. This in tandem with the concomitant decline of the classic Greek medicine tradition. During this phase of traditional Western medicine, phlebotomy increasingly came to represent one of an arsenal of aggressive eliminant techniques that ignored the individual terrain and vital force. Its design, in a sense, was to drain (in both a physical and energetic sense) the patient to such an extent that illness would have no place to go except out. In the hands of its misguided and over-zealous champions—physicians such as GUY PATIN and FRANCOIS BROUSSAIS in France, and in the early nineteenth century BENJAMIN RUSH and HENRY CLUTTERBUCK in the Eastern U.S.—phlebotomy simply became another brutal do-or-die treatment strategy. It is not surprising that by the end of the 1600s phlebotomy acquired a highly questionable reputation (see the plays of MOLIERE), and by the end of the 1700s sank into downright disrepute, instilling terror even in solidly heroic American pioneers. In the late eighteenth and early nineteenth century it finally sunk to the level of a cheap medical trick, alongside megadose prescriptions of Calomel and Scammony and Jalap superpurges. It was often a fatal trick, in fact. The strongest constitutions were not able to withstand repeated lettings of over 500 cc of blood.

As a result of its widespread misuse, during the nineteenth century phlebotomy was conveniently swept away in the tide of experimental and bacteriological medicine, along with the sleazy remnants of other burdensome and embarrassing traditional Galenic luggage. Its recent legacy as a barbaric, naive treatment method has unfortunately survived virtually intact to this day. This is true in spite of the careful work of proponents such as SCHARFBILLIG (Germany) and ASCHNER (New York) in the twentieth century. Images die hard despite modern clinical trials and current renewed interest in traditional healing systems. The best presentation of phlebotomy, including documented case histories, are still to be found in ASCHNER's two volumes on constitutional therapy.

Like the external derivative or skin irritant techniques (see Class 13), phlebotomy clearly deserves renewed investigation and clinical assays, especially since the vitalistic treatment principles from traditional Chinese and Greek medicine have become widely available to guide us in its proper use. When the specific conditions that suggest its use are present, and when cautions and contraindications are given due consideration, phlebotomy may well be the most appropriate, efficient method of treatment available. This is not to say that other methods would be inefficient, but rather that they would be slower to take effect. In a situation where time is of the essence, the speed and efficiency that bloodletting provides is of incomparable value. Alone its ability to dramatically drain potentially dangerous acute conditions, such as heat in the Qi, Blood and Nutritive levels, through its powerful *heat-clearing* and *detoxicant* capacity, places it among the finest treatment methods available.

Moreover, phlebotomy is more than an Eliminating and Draining method that addresses excess

conditions. When used discriminately according to the individual biotype, constitution, season, weather, etc., and when only small amounts of blood are let, phlebotomy can also act as a restorative and preventive treatment. As such it may be used to support the righteous Qi (*fu zhen* therapy in Chinese medicine) to reinforce the individual ground and constitutional potential. This is easier to understand if we consider that phlebotomy has an *immunostimulant* and *immunoregulative* action. French research has demonstrated positive effects at the onset of infections and in allergic (hypersensitivity) disorders. GALEN and his Persian successors such as AR-RAZI and IBN SINA judiciously used phlebotomy to maintain health and prevent illness as much as to treat illness. This practice was successfully shared in the modern era by countless other medical pioneers that followed the old masters, such as THOMAS SYDENHAM, HERMANN BOERHAAVE, CHRISTOPH HUFELAND and many others. The key here, once again, is that these practitioners used phlebotomy in the context of vitalistic Greek medicine, not as a symptomatic technique.

3. This is especially true if, as in Chinese medicine, mineral remedies are used. With the use of herbs of the mild and medium-strength category, however, it is less likely that this could happen. This is not so with acutely toxic alkaloidal plants such as Belladonna, Bryonia and Veratrum that GALEN classed as cold in the 4th degree.

4. The fact that herbs must possess astringent, sour and cold qualities in order to effectively treat blood heat makes it clear that *detoxicant* remedies (*alteratives*) are particularly incompetent at this job. Class 13 *detoxicants* not only have the wrong effective energetic qualities for treating Blood heat, but their purpose by definition is entirely other than for clearing Blood heat. Blood heat is a condition that has nothing in common with toxicosis. It is simply an internal congestive condition that has become inflammatory, generates heat and causes hemmorrhage. On the other hand, an internal toxicosis condition turning hot will generate toxic heat, not Blood heat. It is the confusion between these two conditions that has lead to the misguided use of *detoxicants* for Blood heat instead of for heat toxin.

This is one example among many of the unfortunate result of mixing Western and Oriental therapeutic methods without any rational procedure.

Clear Toxic Heat and Reduce Fever and Infection

Cool, detoxicant anti-infectives (immunostimulants, antimicrobials, antipyretics, anti-inflammatories, detoxicants)

Echinacea Root

Botanical source: *Echinacea angustifolia*
      De Candolle, *E. purpurea* Moench,
      E. pallida Nuttall (Asteraceae/Compositae)
Pharmaceutical name: Radix Echinaceae
Other names: Purple coneflower, Red sunflower,
      Comb flower, Black Sampson, Hedgehog,
      Scurvy root, Indian head (Am)
      Kegelblume, Igelkopf, Stachelkopf,
      Kupferblume (Ge)
Part used: the root; also the flower

NATURE

Therapeutic category: mild remedy with minimal chronic toxicity
Constituents: glycoside echinacoside, essential oil (incl. humulene), mucopolysaccharides (incl. echinacin and inulin), isobutylamides, polyines, polyenes, echinolone, betaine, tannins, resins, oleic/cerotic/linolic/palmatic/trihydroxiphenylpropionic acids, 13 polyacetylenes (incl. echinalone), sesquiterpene, enzymes, fatty acids, phytosterols, trace minerals, vitamin C
Effective qualities: pungent, salty, cool, dry
      calming, stimulating, dissolving
Tropism: blood, lymph, skin, stomach, urogenital organs
      Lung, Large Intestine, Stomach meridians
      Air, Warmth, Fluid bodies
Ground: all krases, biotypes and constitutions for symptomatic use

FUNCTIONS AND INDICATIONS

1   **CLEARS TOXIC HEAT AND REDUCES INFECTION, FEVER AND INFLAMMATION; STIMULATES AND REGULATES IMMUNITY, ANTIDOTES POISON AND REDUCES ALLERGY**

    microbial toxicosis with *toxic heat:* boils, abscesses, pyodermia, inflammations, fevers, allergies

    BACTERIAL and VIRAL INFECTIONS (local or systemic, acute or chronic, esp. dermal, upper respiratory, urogenital; esp. with swollen glands, purulence and mucus discharges)

    LARYNGITIS, tonsillitis, adenitis, stomatitis, periodontitis, gingivitis, pyorrhea

    MENINGITIS, SEPTICEMIA, diphtheria, anthrax, tetanus, rabies, cholera, erysipelas

    HERPES, gonorrhea, vaginitis, prostatitis, peritonitis, phlebitis, mastitis, appendicitis, empyema

    PREVENTIVE in EPIDEMICS

    FEVERS (esp. adynamic, low-grade, in *shao yin* stage; with deficiency, weakness, emaciation; incl. rheumatic, typhoid and septicemic fever)

    POISONING from plants, foods or animals (incl. snake, insect and spider bites)

    ALLERGIES (immediate, incl. rhinitis, otitis, atopic dermatitis)

**2 PROMOTES DETOXIFICATION AND URINATION, REDUCES LYMPH CONGESTION,
   RELIEVES ECZEMA AND REDUCES TUMORS; STOPS DISCHARGE**

kidney Qi stagnation with *metabolic toxicosis:* malaise, headache, dry skin, irritated urination

ECZEMA, atopic dermatitis, psoriasis, erysipelas, dermatosis

LYMPHADENITIS, lymphadenoma

PROSTATE ENLARGEMENT

TUMORS (incl. cancer, esp. with mucosal involvement)

CATARRHAL DISCHARGES (simple or infectious, esp. with *damp-heat,* incl. rhinitis, bronchitis)

3 PROMOTES SWEATING, DISPELS WIND-HEAT, REDUCES FEVER AND PROMOTES ERUPTIONS

external wind-heat: chills, feverishness, sore throat, aches and pains in muscles, swollen glands

COLD and FLU ONSET with FEVER

ERUPTIVE FEVERS (incl. mumps, measles, scarlet fever, chickenpox)

4 STIMULATES DIGESTION AND RELIEVES ABDOMINAL FULLNESS

stomach Qi stagnation: indigestion, epigastric pain, flatulence, bad breath, appetite loss

GASTRIC DYSPEPSIA

5 PROMOTES TISSUE REPAIR, CLEARS DECAY AND RELIEVES PAIN AND SWELLING

WOUNDS, gangrene (with inflammation, pain, swelling, infection, purulence, putrefaction)

ULCERS (esp. chronic, septic, with sloughing; of skin, mouth, tongue, throat)

BURNS, scalds, skin inflammations and rashes (incl. dermatitis, from poison ivy/oak)

PREPARATION

Use: Echinacea root is prepared by **decoction** or **tincture.** The **decoction** is not as effective as the **tincture,** and both should be prepared from the freshly dried root if possible. Echinacea is a desirable ingredient in winter **syrups, gargles** and **douches,** and in **washes** and **compresses** for topical conditions such as injuries, ulcers, burns and skin disorders. For topical conditions, best results are achieved (as always) by simultaneous external and internal use.

Nowadays Echinacea flower is also used.

Dosage: Decoction: 6-10 g

   Tincture: 2-4 ml at 1:2 strength in 50% alcohol

For acute conditions (onset of flu and other infections), take up to 2 tablespoons of the **decoction** or 1 tsp of the **tincture** every two hours.

Caution: Although Echinacea root belongs to the mild, nontoxic category of remedies, it is quite *stimulating* by nature. In rare case it may cause mild dizziness, nausea, mild throat irritation, joint pain or gastric upset. For nausea, combine Echinacea with a little Ginger root or Peppermint leaf.

NOTES

Echinos is the Greek word for sea urchin or hedgehog. In 1794 the German botanist CONRAD MOENCH named the *purpurea* species of this plant *Echinacea*. This is an apt description of the purple coneflower's prickly dome of dark pales, its prominent feature—especially when dried. Before and since then, three distinct species of *Echinacea* have been collected to prepare the remedy known as Echinacea, namely *purpurea* (purple coneflower), *angustifolia* (narrow-leaf coneflower) and *pallida* (pale coneflower). Their chemical constituents, actions and indications vary but little. The first two species, however, are currently considered more effective than the last one.

As with most native North American remedies, Echinacea root has an extensive history of native use that was first naturally adopted by early White settlers and later actively explored by medical botanists. By the late 1880s the remedy became the most widely used of all among medics for infections, inflammations and toxicosis. This was due to the unprejudiced outlook of JOHN KING, founder of the Eclectic school of medical herbalists. His favorable predisposition towards Echinacea was influenced by the persistence of Dr. H. MEYERS, whose main objective was to market his product, *Meyer's Blood Purifier*. This remedy consisted mainly of Echinacea root, Wormwood herb and Hops flower—a formula that generally regulated digestive functions and provided a good *anti-infective* action.

Renewed interest in Echinacea root is fairly recent. It has grown in proportion to the diminishing integrity of the Western city dweller's immune system. In the scientific sector, the plant's constituents have been taken most seriously by German researchers. Today Echinacea is recognized as one of the most efficacious agents for stimulating defenses and reducing **infection.** It is certainly one of the most popular—along with the widely used Goldenseal root. The *anti-infective* action is central to its many functions and includes a nonspecific *immunostimulant* action. This in turn consists of increased T lymphocyte transformation, interferon production and macrophage cytotoxicity, as well as stimulation of lymphocytes, leukocytes and increased macrophage activity. Although the root's polysaccharides have been found to modulate immune functions, it is foolish to name any one constituent as responsible. This is especially true considering the comprehensiveness of Echinacea's pharmacokinetics. They also dynamically treat the **fever, inflammation, suppuration** and **discharge** that accompany infection.

The root's energetic qualities confirm its biochemistry. Possessing salty, cool qualities like Chaparral leaf and Plantain leaf, Echinacea root is a *refrigerant detoxicant* and *dissolvent* remedy. These indicate the possible uses of Echinacea in a wide range of conditions involving **heat, toxicosis** and **hard deposits.** These range from **heat toxin** syndromes with boils, abscesses and fever, and **damp-heat urogenital** and **skin** infections, to **tumors** benign and malignant.

However, there is an important therapeutic—not pharmacological—consideration to be made. **Bacterial** and **viral infections** and **tissue trauma** all benefit most from Echinacea root when **chronic inflammation** specifically arises from underlying Qi or blood deficiency and/or general toxicosis. In this Echinacea is similar to Wild indigo root. The remedy is especially valuable here because it stimulates capillary circulation and peripheral nerves, thereby restoring function and tone to pale, lifeless tissues, reducing mucosal oversecretion and promoting tissue detoxification. Inulin has shown *anti-inflammatory* activity here.

Among late Eclectic practitioners, Echinacea acquired the inevitable hoary patina of an "alterative blood cleanser." Taking semantic shifts of meaning into consideration, the remedy can also be seen as one that promotes systemic detoxification—no doubt about that. Its *diuretic, dermatropic, lymphatic decongestant, antitumoral* and *dissolvent* actions that address chronic, cold **skin, lymphatic** and **tumoral disorders** could be adduced towards the profile of a Class 13 *diuretic/renal detoxicant.*

However, this is only part of the whole picture. When we add Echinacea's superb bivalent *stimulating/regulating* action on immune functions (again the inulin and lignans at work), its *anti-inflammatory, antipyretic, antiseptic* and *mucostatic* effects in the presence of infections of all types (simple, suppurative and putrefactive), we must acknowledge the remedy's treatment of **heat toxin** as absolutely central. Hot, swollen possibly purulent lesions, including pyoderma, boils, abscesses, septic or ulcerative throat, mouth and skin inflammations—these are the core indications because of Echinacea's combined *refrigerant* and *detoxicant* functions.

Echinacea root also has a pungent taste, similar to that of Prickly ash bark. This quality signals a *diaphoretic* effect that dispels wind and heat from the exterior, including the skin. **Wind-heat** types of upper respiratory infections, eruptive fevers and skin eruptions also call for this remedy. Swollen lymph glands, sore throat, skin rashes and feverishness are the key symptoms here.

Regarding **allergic/atopic dermatitis,** Echinacea will clearly address both the damp-heat and the wind-heat types. Here again the gently *stimulant* nature of Echinacea extends to the urogenital organs, especially in subjects presenting with prostate enlargement and kidney deficiency.

Wild Indigo Root

Botanical source: *Baptisia tinctoria* R. Brown
      (syn. *Sophora tinctoria* L.)
      (Fabaceae/Leguminosae)
Pharmaceutical name: Radix Baptisiae tinctoriae
Other names: Indigo weed, Yellow wild indigo,
      Horsefly weed, Rattle bush, Clover/Yellow
      broom, Dyer's baptisia, False indigo (Am)
    Indigo sauvage, Indigo trèfle (Fr)
    Baptisie (Ge)
Part used: the root

NATURE

Therapeutic category: medium-strength remedy with moderate chronic toxicity
Constituents: alkaloids (incl. baptisine, baptitoxine [cytisine]), flavonoids (incl. baptin, baptisin), amino acids (incl. aspartic and glutamic acid, threonine, alanine), polysaccharides, oleoresin, albumen, calcium
Effective qualities: very bitter, somewhat pungent and astringent, cool
    calming, stimulating, restoring, decongesting
Tropism: blood, fluids, liver, gallbladder, intestines, lungs
    Liver, Lung, Large Intestine meridians
    Warmth, Air bodies
Ground: all krases, biotypes and constitutions for symptomatic use

NATURE AND FUNCTIONS

1   **CLEARS TOXIC HEAT AND REDUCES INFECTION, FEVER AND INFLAMMATION;**
    STIMULATES IMMUNITY, DECONGESTS LYMPH, ANTIDOTES POISON AND STOPS DISCHARGE

microbial toxicosis with *toxic heat:* boils, abscesses, ulcers, fevers, inflammations, food allergies

CHRONIC INFLAMMATIONS from INFECTION (esp. atonic and septic, incl. tonsilitis, laryngitis, sinusitis, stomatitis, lymphadenitis, mastitis)

ULCERATIVE INFLAMMATIONS (internal and external, incl. dysentery, mouth and nasal ulcers, breast ulcers, gangrenous skin ulcers)

TYPHOID FEVER, malaria, smallpox, scarlet fever, diptheria

REMITTENT and TIDAL FEVERS with asthenia/deficiency (*shao yang* and *shao yin* stages)

SEPTICEMIA, all septic conditions

SKIN INFECTIONS, chronic dermatitis

DISCHARGES from ulcers; leucorrhea, gonorrhea

LEUKOPENIA

LYMPHADENITIS, lymphangitis with swollen glands

SNAKEBITES

2 STIMULATES DIGESTION, PROMOTES BILE FLOW, REDUCES LIVER CONGESTION AND RELIEVES CONSTIPATION

liver Qi stagnation with *damp-heat:* flank pain/swelling, constipation, irritability, moodiness, bad breath
LIVER CONGESTION

intestines Qi stagnation: foul belching, constipation, appetite loss, indigestion, abdominal distension
CONSTIPATION

**3 DESCENDS LUNG QI, OPENS THE CHEST AND RELIEVES WHEEZING;
TONIFIES HEART AND LUNG QI**

lung Qi constraint: chest oppression, wheezing
ASTHMA (esp. when lying down)

heart and lung Qi deficiency: fatigue, palpitations, breathlessness on exertion
CARDIAC and respiratory deficiency

4 PROMOTES TISSUE REPAIR, CLEARS DECAY AND REDUCES TUMORS

CUTS, wounds, sore nipples
ULCERS, sores, gangrene (esp. chronic, septic, with discharge incl. lymphatic, laryngeal, nasal, malignant)
TUMORS (incl. of breast)

PREPARATION

Use: Wild indigo root is used in **decoction** and **tincture** form. The latter is more effective for treating infections. The remedy is an excellent topical *antiseptic* used in **compresses** and **washes** for boils, eczema, inflammations, ulcers, wounds and so on. **Douches** and **pessaries** treat infectious vaginal discharges.

Dosage: Decoction: 4-8 g
        Tincture: 0.5-2.5 ml at 1:2 strength in 60% ethanol

Small doses are *stimulant* and *laxative* (functions 2 and 3); medium doses are *anti-infective* and *cooling* (function 1), while larger than therapeutic doses are *toxic, emetic* and *cathartic*.

Caution: Contraindicated in diarrhea caused by intestines (Spleen) Qi deficiency or cold. Because of its medium-strength therapeutic status, Wild indigo root is best used in a formula or for short-term use on its own. In this case, watch for possible signs of cumulative toxicity.

NOTES

For hundreds of years Wild indigo root has been in use as a remedy for infection and fever, beginning with Native American tribes on the East coast. The Creeks, for example, used decoctions of this root to boost vitality and stimulate immunity. The remedy qualifies as an important *anti-infective, anti-inflammatory* and *antiseptic refrigerant* with similarities to the related Sophora Ku Shen in China. Leukocyte production and activity have shown to increase, toxins are removed and eliminated, fever and inflammation is reduced, and infectious, septic and putrefactive processes are halted and reversed. In energetic terms, the remedy addresses both acute and chronic **toxic heat** and **damp-heat** conditions.

This still leaves us with the question of Baptisia's specific symptom picture. For this, the traditions of Clinical medicine and Homeopathy join forces in the Eclectic tradition. Baptisia is for "dusky, leaden, purplish or livid discoloration of the tongue and mucous membranes; … dark, tar-like fetid discharges from the bowels; general putrid secretions." The remedy is ideal for individuals also presenting **liver** and **intestinal stagnation** (as with Goldenseal root), tending to generate damp-heat. Its bitter, pungent, cold qualities will break up and move downward damp-heat digestive accumulation, thereby systematically assisting the *detoxicant* actions. The resemblance here with Goldenseal root and Chaparral leaf is clear. In this connection, the use of Wild indigo for chronic **damp-heat skin eruptions**, as well as for intestinal damp-heat with enteritis deserves to be further explored. Nineteenth century physicians relied extensively on this remedy during the typhoid epidemics, and lauded its efficacy in reducing both the fever and the dysentery.

On the other hand, these same medics observed Wild indigo's good *capillary stimulant* action, noting that it worked particularly well in patients presenting a "full and purplish face, like one who has long been exposed to cold," and what we would call endogenous toxicosis with bacterial terrain (which tends to create damp-heat).

In **fevers,** Wild indigo root should specifically only be used for asthenic (deficient) ones, where *shao yang* or *yang ming* threaten to turn into *shao yin*. This is a complementary remedy to Yellow jessamine, which is only for sthenic/full fevers. This important *antipyretic* remedy's most elegant use is actually as a preventive of *shao yin* conditions at the point of the "disease crisis." This is the point when the vital response becomes increasingly low and threatens to introduce the chronic phase of illness. Here the pulse goes from full and rapid to weak and thin, the tongue from bright red to a dry dark red, and the fever threatens to become a truly "rotten" one.

It is no accident that nineteenth century Eclectic herbal medicine shows similarity to Homeopathic medicine. Wild indigo root, or Baptisia, is a good example of a remedy where, for truly effective results, signs and symptoms need to be considered as a whole gestalt. Syndromes, conditions, symptoms and Western disorders are merely ways of breaking down the remedy's specific symptomatology for convenient therapeutic and didactic purposes. This is evident both historically and pharmacologically: the use of alcohol preparations in smaller doses such as tinctures entails homeopathic as well as allopathic effects. There is really no division of the two kinds of effects. Rather, there is a common area where both preparation types share a common ground of pathology.

Marigold Flower

Botanical source: *Calendula officinalis* L.
(Asteraceae/Compositae)
Pharmaceutical name: Flos Calendulae
Ancient names: Chrysanthemon (Gr)
Solsequia, Aureola, Caltha, Solis sponsa,
Oculus Christi (Lat)
Other names: Calendula, Pot marigold, Golding,
Gold bloom, Gowlan, Golds, Ruddes,
Sunflower, Mally gowl (Eng)
Souci des jardins, Fleur de tous les mois (Fr)
Ringelblume, Goldblume, Sonnenwende,
Salbenblume (Ge)
Part used: the flower

NATURE
Therapeutic category: mild remedy with minimal chronic toxicity
Constituents: triterpenoid saponins, flavonoids (incl. kaempferol, quercetin, isorhamnetin), carotenoids (carotene, calendulin, lycopin), bitters, phytosterols, resin, mucilage, polysaccharides, essential oil (incl. alcohols, terpene lactone), trace minerals, palmitic/malic/salicylic acid, potassium chloride and sulphate, calcium sulphate
Effective qualities: somewhat bitter, sweet, salty and pungent, neutral with cooling potential, dry
calming, decongesting, astringing, stimulating, softening, dissolving

Tropism: liver, heart, uterus, skin, veins, lymphatic system, blood
      Liver, Heart, Lung, *chong, ren* meridians
      Fluid, Warmth bodies
Ground: krases, biotypes and constitutions

FUNCTIONS AND INDICATIONS

1   **CLEARS TOXIC AND DAMP-HEAT, AND REDUCES INFECTION, INFLAMMATION AND SWELLING; STIMULATES IMMUNITY, REDUCES LYMPH CONGESTION AND REDUCES LIPIDS**

    microbial toxicosis with *toxic heat:* boils, carbuncles, swollen glands, low fever

    skin wind-damp-heat: skin rashes, red eruptions (dry or wet), itching

    SKIN INFECTIONS and INFLAMMATIONS (incl. eczema, acne, cold sores); *Herpes, Staphylococcus*

    BACTERIAL, FUNGAL and AMOEBAL INFECTIONS (incl. hepatitis, lymphangitis, candidiasis, thrush, ringworm, periodontitis, gingivitis, stomatitis, laryngitis, otitis, conjunctivitis, mastitis, influenza); viral infections

    FEMALE REPRODUCTIVE INFECTIONS and inflammations (incl. yeast infections)

    HYPERLIPIDEMIA

    LYMPHADENITIS

2   **VITALIZES THE BLOOD, REDUCES CONGESTION AND MODERATES MENSTRUATION; ASTRINGES, REDUCES TUMORS AND STOPS DISCHARGE AND BLEEDING**

    uterus blood congestion: early or copious periods with pelvic weight and dull pains

    CONGESTIVE DYSMENORRHEA

    venous blood stagnation: varicosities, heavy or aching legs, leg cramps at night, fatigue, constipation

    VARICOSE VEINS, hemorrhoids, phlebitis

    MENORRHAGIA, hemorrhage (esp. uterine, fibroidal, hemorrhoidal)

    GASTRIC ULCERS, gastritis, colitis

    LEUCORRHEA (white and purulent, with *damp-cold* or *damp-heat*)

    OVARIAN CYSTS, TUMORS, CANCER (esp. of female reproductive organs, breasts, intestines)

3   **PROMOTES AND REGULATES MENSTRUATION, AND BALANCES HORMONES; PROMOTES LABOR AND ENHANCES DELIVERY**

    uterus Qi stagnation: delayed, difficult or irregular periods, cramps, clots in flow

    SPASMODIC DYSMENORRHEA

    HORMONAL IMBALANCE in women in general (esp. estrogen/progesterone deficiency)

    MENOPAUSAL SYNDROME

    DIFFICULT LABOR

    RETAINED PLACENTA

    UTERINE SUBINVOLUTION

4   **PROMOTES BILE FLOW AND DIGESTION, REDUCES LIVER CONGESTION AND RELIEVES EPIGASTRIC FULLNESS**

    liver Qi stagnation: painful digestion, epigastric or swelling, headache, constipation, poor appetite

    LIVER CONGESTION with DYSPEPSIA, jaundice, spleen congestion

5   **PROMOTES SWEATING, DISPELS WIND-HEAT, REDUCES FEVER AND PROMOTES ERUPTIONS**

    external wind-heat: aches and pains, sore throat, swollen glands, feverishness, anxiety

    COLD and FLU with FEVER

    ERUPTIVE FEVERS (incl. measles, scarlet fever, smallpox)

    REMITTENT and TIDAL FEVERS (*shao yang* and *shao yin* stages)

6 TONIFIES HEART QI

heart Qi deficiency: palpitations, wheezing on exertion, esp. in old age
CARDIAC DEFICIENCY

**7 PROMOTES TISSUE REPAIR, REDUCES INFLAMMATION, PREVENTS DECAY
AND BENEFITS THE SKIN**

WOUNDS (esp. with squashed or torn skin; slow-healing), bruises, cuts, abrasions, chafing, sprains, insect bites, frostbite, perineal tears

SKIN ULCERS, mouth ulcers (esp. chronic); gangrene

BURNS, scalds, inflammations

INFLAMMATIONS from INFECTION (incl. thrush, gingivitis, laryngitis, conjunctivitis, vaginitis, etc.)

SKIN DEFORMITIES and blemishes, warts

PREPARATION

Use: Marigold petals require careful collecting and drying without the use of artificial warmth and should be used withing one or two years of collecting. They are used in **infusion** and **tincture** form. The **infusion** is more gentle and quite adequate for children and mild cases. The **tincture** is the best point of departure for various preparations like **swabs, compresses, mouthwashes, gargles, douches, sitzbaths, creams, ointments, pessaries**—every external preparation known, in fact. In these, Marigold combines well with other remedies for topical use, like Arnica flower, St. John's Wort herb, Witch hazel leaf and Plantain leaf.

In feverish, wind-heat onset of infections with swollen glands, the infusion should be sipped hot with other *detoxicant diaphoretics* such as Yarrow flower, Elderflower and Camomile flower.

Dosage: Infusion: 8-14 g

Tincture: 2-4 ml at 1:3 strength in 25% ethanol: this low alcohol extraction favors the flavonoids and is best for all indications except for bacterial/fungal/amoebal infections.

Tincture: 2-4 ml at 1:3 strength in 90% ethanol: this high-alcohol extraction favors the antimicrobial resins and is specifically *antibacterial* and *antifungal* for treating infections.

Caution: Use Marigold flower carefully when applying to dirty or septic wounds, as it promotes rapid tissue healing. Avoid internal use during pregnancy as it is a *uterine stimulant*.

Note: Do not confuse Pot marigold, the source of this remedy, with the common Garden or African marigold, *Tagetes* spp., which has somewhat different functions and uses.

NOTES

Marigold flower is more than a simple first-aid remedy for injuries and burns. Its deeper character is a highly complex remedy for infections on one hand, and woman's ailments on the other. To fully appreciate this, we need to closely examine its two major functional aspects, *detoxicant* and *decongestant*.

Marigold flower has an important *detoxicant* action, whose applications are **wind-heat, toxic heat** and **tissue trauma.** At the onset of wind-heat respiratory infections, its *detoxicant, anti-infective, lymphatic decongestant* and *vasodilatant diaphoretic* actions work synergistically in much the same way as in the Chinese remedies Lonicera Jin Yin Hua and Forsythia Lian Qiao, and to some extent as in Echinacea root. Lymph gland swelling is prevented in the process, and fever is lowered through the *antipyretic* action. In chronic local infections manifesting heat toxin such as laryngitis, boils, abscesses and pyodermia, Marigold shows good *resorbent, anti-inflammatory* and *antiseptic* effects because of its mild, fairly neutral qualities. In skin infections, the remedy clears **wind, damp** and **heat** from the **skin** through its combined *anti-inflammatory, anti-infective* and *detoxicant* actions (topical and internal applications should, of course, be combined here). In **tissue trauma** where there is no major infection, Marigold again excells at resorbing toxins and exudates, as well as assisting tissue granulation and preventing scarring—gentle *capillary stimulant, detoxicant, astringent* and *tissue-healing* actions operating in concert.

Marigold flower also has excellent *blood-decongestant* and *astringent* properties that will benefit those tending to **venous blood stagnation, uterus blood congestion, bleeding** and **ulceration.**

Like Horsechestnut, the remedy relies on saponins and flavonoids, not tannins, for this effect. These stimulate and restore the venous and capillary circulation, thereby treating conditions of blood stagnation. Here the remedy will treat varicose veins, hemorrhoids, phlebitis, congestive dysmenorrhea, and so on, like any good Class 15 *decongestant*. The flavonoids in particular have shown *vasoprotectant* and *antioxidant* properties.

With its added *coagulant hemostatic* action, Marigold is also used to stop bleeding, especially from hemorrhoids, fibroids and the uterus—like Shepherd's purse herb and Red root, in fact. Ulcers of all kinds, internal and external, also benefit from the remedy's combined *astringent* and *tissue-healing* properties.

Because it combines *hormonal balancing* and *uterine stimulant* with *blood decongestant* actions, Marigold flower—like acupuncture points Li 13, CV 3, Bl 32, Gb 41 and Sp 8—addresses various types of dysmenorrhea caused by **liver Qi stagnation.** It stands out as a comprehensive menstrual and even premenstrual remedy. However, in contrast to herbs such as Lavender flower and Camomile flower (which help with emotional and psychological factors through their endocrine balancing effect), Marigold flower works mainly on the physiological level. It therefore works best when physiological imbalance alone underlies the condition.

When we consider the time-tested use of Marigold flower in childbirth and menopause in addition to reproductive disorders, it is not surprising that this remedy—like Dong quai root, for example—has come to be known as a foremost woman's ally.

Plantain Leaf

Botanical source: *Plantago lanceolata* L.,
       P. major L. (Plantaginaceae)
Pharmaceutical name: Folium Plantaginis
Ancient names: Polyneuron, Heptapleuron (Gr)
       Costa canina, Quinquenervia, Plantago longa,
         Vulgo lanceolata, Cynoglossum (Lat)
Other names: a) Lance-leaf plantain, Ribwort,
       Lamb's tongue, Dog's ribs, Bent, Leechwort,
       Windles (Eng)
       Plantain lancéolé (Fr)
       Spitzwegerich, Lungenkraut, Gaucheil,
        Heil/Wundwegerich (Ge)
       b) Round-leaf/Broad-leaf/Common plantain,
        Ripple grass, Waybread, Snakeweed (Eng)
       Che Qian Cao (Mand); Che Chin Chou (Cant)
Part used: the leaf

NATURE
Therapeutic category: mild remedy with minimal chronic toxicity
Constituents: a) glycoside, glucosides aucubin and catalpol, tannins up to 1.6%, mucilage (xylin), silicic acid, hexitol, minerals and trace minerals (inl. zinc, iron, calcium, sodium), organic acids (incl. phosphoric, ursolic, palmitic and chlorogenic), bitter compounds, essential oil, enzyme, vitamins A, C, K
Effective qualities: somewhat astringent, salty, bitter, cold, dry and moist potential
       calming, astringing, restoring, decongesting, stabilizing
Tropism: lungs, intestines, bladder, kidneys, blood, skin
       Lung, Large Intestine, Bladder meridians; decreases *pitta* and *kapha*
       Warmth, Fluid bodies

FUNCTIONS AND INDICATIONS

1 CLEARS TOXIC HEAT, REDUCES INFLAMMATION AND RELIEVES SWELLING; PROMOTES DETOXIFICATION, REDUCES LYMPH CONGESTION, REDUCES ALLERGY AND RELIEVES ECZEMA

microbial toxicosis with *toxic heat:* boils, inflammations, abscesses, fever, allergies

EYE, MOUTH, THROAT, GUM and MIDDLE EAR INFLAMMATIONS (esp. acute, infectious or allergic, from bacterial infection, with purulence and mucus)

SEPTICEMIA (local or systemic); malaria

VENOMOUS BITES from insects, spiders, snakes

IMMEDIATE ALLEGIES (incl. rhinitis, atopic dermatitis, asthma, otitis media)

skin wind-heat: red skin rashes, skin itching

ECZEMA, ATOPIC/ALLERGIC DERMATITIS (esp. dry, crusty)

metabolic toxicosis: dry skin, rashes, fetid body odor or urine, swollen glands, malaise, hemorrhoids

LYMPHADENITIS, lymphangitis, syphilis

2 CLEARS HEAT, RESOLVES MUCUS-DAMP AND STOPS DISCHARGE; ASTRINGES AND STOPS BLEEDING

head damp-heat: painful sinuses, thick yellowish nasal discharges

RHINITIS (acute and chronic, allergic)

intestines damp-heat: urgent painful passing of loose stool with blood, dry mouth, thirst

ENTERITIS, dysentery, diarrhea, leucorrhea (acute and chronic, with *damp-heat* or *damp-cold*)

bladder damp-heat: frequent, urgent, painful urination with mucous or blood, thirst

URINARY INFECTIONS (acute, incl. cystitis, nephritis)

blood heat: spontaneous bruising or bleeding, skin rashes, thirst, irritability, heavy periods

HEMORRHAGE (passive, esp. blood in sputum and urine)

3 TONIFIES URINARY QI, HARMONIZES URINATION AND RELIEVES INCONTINENCE

bladder Qi deficiency: incontinent, frequent, copious urination, bedwetting

URINARY INCONTINENCE

4 PROMOTES EXPECTORATION, RESOLVES PHLEGM-HEAT, RESTORES THE LUNGS AND RELIEVES COUGHING; DIFFUSES LUNG QI AND RELIEVES WHEEZING

lung phlegm-heat: full cough with copious thick yellow sputum, blood and pus in sputum

lung heat-dryness: fever, sore throat, dry mouth and nose, harsh dry difficult cough, wheezing

BRONCHITIS, LARYNGITIS (acute), lung TB

COUGH and ASTHMA in any condition

5 PROMOTES TISSUE REPAIR AND REDUCES CONTUSION AND PAIN

WOUNDS (esp. with pain, contusion or bleeding)

ULCERS (internal or external, esp. chronic, slow-healing, rodent)

TOOTHACHE, earache, headache, facial neuralgia

BURNS, scalds

THROMBOSIS (preventive)

PREPARATION

Use: The best preparations for Plantain leaf are the fresh expressed **juice** and the **freeze-dried extract,** closely followed by the **infusion** and **tincture.**

Washes, compresses and **poultices** are excellent for tissue trauma and skin conditions. **Mouth-**

washes and **gargles** serve mouth, gum and throat inflammations. **Douches** are useful for vaginal discharges. **Enemas** and **suppositories** treat intestinal infections. In all cases Plantain leaf should, as usual, also be taken internally. The above respiratory conditions will benefit from Plantain leaf **syrup,** especially with sore, inflamed or dry throat .

Freshly crushed Plantain *leaves* are highly effective for treating topical tissue trauma, skin infections, sores, ulcers, and so on, as biochemical findings have corroborated. The act of crushing the leaves releases an enzyme that, together with the glucoside aucubin, produces an amalgam, aucubigenin. It is this which is highly *bacteriostatic*. It follows that infectious conditions are best treated with a *fresh plant* preparation.

WILLIAM SALMON records a traditional "cosmetick" preparation of Plantain (2 parts), Houseleek (2 parts), Lemon (1 part) for burns, inflammations, boils, red eruptions, etc. Concerning this good cooling, *emollient* and *lenitive* formula we would only suggest that if Houseleek is unobtainable, Chickweed herb or Comfrey leaf should be substituted.

Dosage: Juice: 10 ml, or 2 tsp
      Long infusion: 8-16 g
      Tincture: 2-5 ml at 1:3 strength in 25% ethanol

Caution: None

Note: Historically, two plantain species have mainly been used: the tall, sharp-leaved variety, *Plantago lanceolata,* called lance-leaf plantain or Ribwort plantain because of its ribbed leaves, and the smaller plantain, *Plantago major,* called round-leaf or common plantain. Traditional users of Plantain in Europe — wise women, country folk, barbers and pharmacists in the main — agreed that Lance-leaf plantain was somewhat more effective than Round-leaf plantain. The essential symptomatology for both Plantain species in countless traditional texts, at any rate, is the same. Today the Lance-leaf plantain is considered more effective for treating respiratory, infectious and allergic conditions, i.e. toxic heat in general. Round-leaf plantain is thought more effective for intestinal and urinary conditions, i.e. damp-heat conditions.

NOTES

Traditionally a widely used remedy in the West, Plantain leaf presents an ancient image when we look into the past, and a modern one as we move into the future. The important seventeenth century *Schroeder's Dispensatory* defines Plantain as an *herba polychresta* — a remedy that systemically treats a broad spectrum of disorders. This description is accurate as Plantain addresses a large variety of hot conditions and acute injuries. The presence in this plant of tannins, mucilage, silicic acid and glycosides ensures a wound and pain remedy of the highest order — one that Western healers have been able to rely on for millennia. Fresh wounds with bleeding, chronic ulcers and severe toothache are the asterisk symptoms in this connection. GALEN in the second century made the interesting comment that "among all remedies that arrest bleeding, clear heat and heal ulcers, Plantain is foremost, or hardly surpassed at all. This is because it dries without biting or sharpness, and clears heat without causing heaviness or stupefaction."

Few other herbs address the variety of internal heat conditions found in clinical practice as comprehensively as Plantain leaf. This herb's salty, astringent, bitter, cold qualities determine *refrigerant, detoxicant, decongestant, hemostatic* and *lenitive* actions. As a result, its main uses are **toxicosis conditions** such as heat toxin, eczema and lymphadenitis; **acute pyogenic infections** presenting redness, swelling, pain and pus; **blood congestion** such as uterus blood congestion and blood heat; and **irritated skin** and **mucosal** conditions in general. Dry, irritated or infective **eczema** presenting **wind-damp-heat** is also high among Plantain leaf's symptomatology. Plantain is also frequently used in both traditional Greek and Chinese medicine for lung abscess, respiratory infections, active bleeding, urinary tract infections and dysentery. As a *toxic heat* and *damp-heat-clearing* remedy, it is also paralleled by the Chinese herb Houttuynia Yu Xing Cao.

Plantain leaf is versatile in addressing both dry/hot and catarrhal/damp respiratory conditions. On one hand it should be included in formulations treating those with dry, hot bronchial infections — the syndrome **lung (heat-) dryness** — accompanied by hoarseness, tickling dry cough and futile, painful expectoration. On the other hand the remedy should be part of a formula for those with acute congestive catarrhal disorders—the syndrome **lung phlegm-heat**—showing productive yellow sputum. Plantain leaf has an excellent *mucostatic* action that inhibits excessive mucus secretion, especially once the infection itself has cleared.

Because Plantain has a strong affinity for the lungs and the skin, it suggests use in **atopic** or **allergic eczema, asthma, rhinitis** and **otitis.** Its *anti-allergic* action has shown to be effective in immediate (type I) hypersensitivity disorders.

Purslane Herb

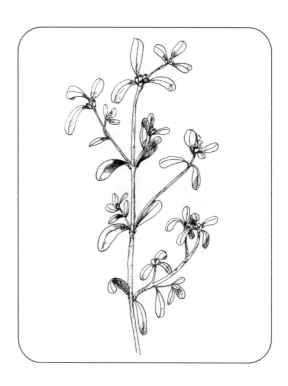

Botanical source: *Portulaca oleracea* L.
> (Portulacaceae)

Pharmaceutical name: Herba Portulaca

Ancient names: Andraken (Gr)
> Portulaca (Lat) Purupuhu (Assyrian)

Other names: Golden purslane, Pigweed (Eng)
> Pourpier, Pourcelaine (Fr)
> Portulak, Burzel, Fette Henne, Tag und
>> Nachtblüemli (Ge)
> Ma Chi Xian (Mand)
> Ma Chi Yin (Cant)

Part used: the herb

NATURE

Therapeutic category: mild remedy with minimal chronic toxicity

Constituents: mucilage, coumarins, flavones, trace minerals, alkoloids, glycosides (cardiac, anthraquinone), omega-3 fatty acids, organic acids (incl. oxalic acid), vitamins (incl. vitamin C), minerals

Effective qualities: somewhat sour, salty, sweet, cold, moist
> astringing, calming, sinking, nourishing

Tropism: stomach, intestines, fluids, blood
> Lung, Large Intestine, Bladder meridians
> Warmth, Fluid bodies

Ground: all krases, biotypes and constitutions

FUNCTIONS AND INDICATIONS

1 **CLEARS TOXIC HEAT, REDUCES INFECTION, INFLAMMATION AND FEVER, MOISTENS DRYNESS AND RELIEVES THIRST; GENERATES FLUIDS AND PROMOTES LACTATION AND SPERM PRODUCTION**

> *toxic heat:* painful boils, carbuncles, fever, local purulent infections
> EYE, MOUTH, GUM and THROAT INFLAMMATIONS/INFECTIONS; appendicitis
> LARYNGITIS, pneumonia (initial phase), lung TB
> ORGAN HEAT conditions (esp. of liver, intestines, stomach, lungs, with constipation, dry cough, fever)
> *fluids deficiency:* thirst, dehydration, dry mouth and throat
> INTERNAL DRYNESS (esp. in hot conditions)
> BREAST MILK or SPERM DEFICIENCY
> *blood heat:* thirst, spontaneous bleeding, skin rashes, menorrhagia, postpartum bleeding

2 **CLEARS DAMP-HEAT AND STOPS DISCHARGE AND BLEEDING; ELIMINATES PARASITES; REDUCES SEXUAL OVERSTIMULATION**

intestines damp-heat: chronic loose stool with blood and pus, frequent burning bowel movement

ENTERITIS (incl. dysentery, bacterial/amoebic)

INTESTINAL PARASITES (esp. hookworm)

bladder damp-heat: burning difficult urination, thirst

URINARY INFECTIONS with discharge (cystitis, urethritis)

GENITAL DISCHARGES (incl. leucorrhea, spermatorrhea)

HEMORRHAGE (passive, esp. in hot conditions, incl. menstrual and postpartum bleeding)

SEXUAL OVERSTIMULATION

PREPARATION

Use: Purslane herb (*Portulaca oleracea* and *P. sativa*) is both remedy and food, and is used as such the world over. As remedy Purslane is prepared in the form of **fresh juice, tincture** and **short decoction,** in decreasing order of strength. As a vegetable it is best eaten raw, lightly steamed or pickled.

Syrups, washes, gargles and **mouthwashes** are other useful Purslane preparations, many of which were officinal in Greek medicine—e.g., MESUE's *Compound Syrup of Purslane and Chicory.*

Dosage: Juice: 2-3 tsp

Short decoction: 6-14 g

Tincture: 2-4 ml at 1:3 strength in 30% ethanol

Caution: During pregnancy

NOTES

Purslane is good proof (if proof is needed) that a first-rate medicine can be prepared from a culinary herb. In Persia and India where it originated, Purslane has been appreciated for millennia both as a fine heat-clearing remedy and as a unique succulent vegetable. In Europe it has always been grown as a garden vegetable, being one of the few really *mucilagenous* vegetables for thickening soups, stews and hot-pots. As such it is the Western temperate equivalent to okra, or lady's fingers (brinjal) from the tropics. The indefatigable WILLIAM SALMON (1710) reported that "the leaves are preserved with salt and pickle, in Holland, as capers are ... having a pleasant and grateful taste."

The historic practice of eating purslane in salads alongside other green coolers like chickweed, dandelion and cucumber should find new adherents at this time. Cooling salads, in moderation, are certainly as appropriate for helping clear today's manufactured condition of urban empty heat as they were for reducing the full heat of high fevers in the past. During the Renaissance, the innocent-tasting purslane was processed into all kinds of cooling syrups, juleps, robs and diet drinks—a legacy from the Persian physicians who introduced Purslane to the West as a serious heat-clearing agent. In those days the taste of medicines

was "improved" to such an extent that the black, sticky, treacly preparations acquired a uniformly sickly sweet flavor.

From all available evidence Purslane herb is a moist, cooling *demulcent* with sour, salty taste qualities. It contains a series of organic acids, glycosides, trace mineral, vitamins and mucilages, and possibly some essential oil, too. Eminent Renaissance physician JEAN FERNEL in 1508 noted that "it has the unique property of tempering and containing burning and flaming bile, resisting toxin to prevent its further spread." To this the Arab *Book of Experiences* (1225) added "It quenches thirst caused by stomach, heart, liver and kidney fire." In short, Purslane is essentially a good *refrigerant* remedy for clearing **full heat** from the **internal organs.**

Today we ascribe *detoxicant, anti-inflammatory* and *antiseptic* properties to the plant, which are more active when the fresh plant is used. Purslane's *antiseptic* effect has been shown by Chinese researchers over 90% effective in acute cases and 60% in recurrent cases of bacillary dysentery. In treating toxic heat, damp-heat and blood heat conditions, Purslane is distinctive in *providing moisture* and *protecting the fluids* while clearing injurious heat. This is a great advantage in the treatment of full heat conditions. Along with Plantain leaf, Purslane is one of the very few heat-clearing herbs with marked *demulcent* properties.

Effective remedies like Purslane don't have to be special imports, and they don't have to taste bad, either. The notion that for a remedy to work it must taste awful is one peculiar to the nineteenth century Victorian era. It is based on the patriarchal belief that because disease represents suffering for past sins, the medicine to alleviate it should also entail suffering—or at least not interfere with the atonement or penitence. It is interesting to note, in this connection, that the heroic tactics of forceful sweating, purging and vomiting that Thomsonian practitioners exclusively used for treatment were ultimately based on the same approach to healing as those of the regular medics. The "regulars" only sweated, purged and vomited in *style*—using exotic tropical botanicals and toxic minerals such as calomel.

Usnea Thallus

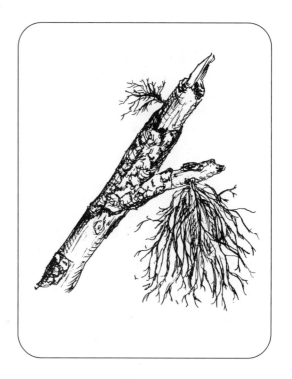

Botanical source: *Usnea diffracta* Vain,
　　　U. longissima Ach., *U. barbata* Hoffman
　　　and spp. (Usneaceae)
Pharmaceutical name: Thallus Usneae
Other names: Beard lichen, Witch's broom,
　　　Old man's beard (Eng, Am)
　　　Usnée barbue, Barbe de capucin (Fr)
　　　Bartflechte (Ge)
　　　Song Luo (Mand)
　　　Chung Lo (Cant)
Part used: the lichen thallus

NATURE
Therapeutic category: mild remedy with minimal chronic toxicity
Constituents: bitter usnic acid up to 5%, barbatic/diffractaic/evernic acids, polysaccharides, mucilage
Effective qualities: sweet, somewhat bitter, cool
　　　calming, stimulating, relaxing
Tropism: respiratory, reproductive, lymphatic, immune systems
　　　Lung, Liver meridians
　　　Air, Warmth bodies
Ground: all krases, biotypes and constitutions for symptomatic use

FUNCTIONS AND INDICATIONS
1　**CLEARS TOXIC HEAT AND REDUCES INFECTION, INFLAMMATION AND FEVER;
　　STIMULATES IMMUNITY AND PROMOTES URINATION**

toxic heat: painful boils, fever, purulent infections

BOILS, carbuncles

BACTERIAL and FUNGAL INFECTIONS (esp. respiratory, intestinal, urinary, with fever, incl. flu, cold, sinusitis, laryngitis, bronchitis, pneumonia (initial phase), pleurisy, lung TB, gastroenteritis, dermatitis, dysentery, thrush, ringworm, impetigo, cystitis, urethritis, athlete's foot, trichomonas)

external/lung wind-heat: aches and pains, headache, sore throat, nasal congestion, cough, feverishness
FEVERS (esp. with anuria)

2   **PROMOTES EXPECTORATION, OPENS THE CHEST, RESOLVES PHLEGM-HEAT AND RELIEVES WHEEZING**

lung phlegm-heat with *Qi constraint:* coughing with thick yellow sputum, sore chest, wheezing
BRONCHITIS (acute or chronic), asthma

3   **PROMOTES TISSUE REPAIR AND PREVENTS DECAY**

WOUNDS (esp. suppurative), ulcers, eczema
CERVICAL EROSION, cracked nipples, mastitis

PREPARATION

Use: Usnea lichen is prepared by **cold water infusion** (steep for at least 6 hours) or **tincture.** Good **washes, compresses, vaginal sponges, douches, gargles** and so on, are also prepared with it for the topical treatment of infections such as dermatitis, vaginitis, oral thrush, etc.

Dosage: Cold infusion: 10-20 g (up to 30 g in acute conditions)
         Tincture: 2-4 ml at 1:2 strength in 30% ethanol

Caution: None

NOTES

Usnea is one of numerous lichens found throughout the northern hemisphere growing on coniferous and other trees in grey-green, often beard-like tufts and strands. It is a traditional remedy in Europe, China and probably Russia,

In modern times Usnea lichen has shown fairly strong *antiseptic, anti-inflammatory* and *antipyretic* properties through its content in usnic acid and polysaccharides. The traditional indications have thereby been corroborated and extended by modern research, and include a large variety of bacterial and fungal infections both simple and pyogenic.

As a heat and toxin-clearing *broad-spectrum anti-infective,* Usnea specifically works well in respiratory infections presenting the syndromes **lung wind-heat** or **lung phlegm-heat.** The remedy is effective in flu, sinusitis, laryngitis (incl. streptococcal) and bronchitis at any stage, especially in individuals presenting sore throat, productive cough and wheezing. Like Morus Sang Bai Pi in Chinese medicine, Usnea will also ease the wheezing found in many bronchial conditions.

Usnea should also be used topically not just because it reduces infection, but also because of its *vulnerary* and *tissue-healing* action. Chronic and suppurative wounds, ulcers and eczema of all types will benefit from Usnea as much as they will from Marigold flower, Echinacea root or Wild indigo root.

Lemon Rind
(and Essential Oil)

Botanical source: *Citrus limonum* L. (Rutaceae)
Pharmaceutical name: Pericarpium Citri limonii
Ancient names: Limonion melon (Gr)
      Malum limonium (Lat)
Other names: Citron (Fr)
      Zitrone, Limone (Ge)
      Zagara (Ar)
Part used: the rind

NATURE

Therapeutic category: mild remedy with minimal chronic toxicity
Constituents: essential oil (incl. limonene up to 80%, terpenes, linalol, linalyl/geranyl/neryl/citronelyl acetate, citral 3.5-5%, citronellal, aldehydes, pinene, camphene, cadinene, phellandrene, methylheptone, citronol, terpineol, acetic/caprinic/lavrinic acid), citric and malic acid, citrates, glucides, large and trace minerals, albumins, flavonoids (incl. hesperidin), carotenoids, phytosterols, resins, vitamins A, B, C, K
Effective qualities: very sour, somewhat sweet and astringent, cold, dry
      decongesting, dissolving, diluting, nourishing, restoring, astringing
Tropism: stomach, intestines, liver, gallbladder, heart/circulation, fluids, nerves, pancreas, skin
      Liver, Stomach, Large Intestine, Heart, Triple Heater meridians
      Air, Warmth, Fluid bodies
Ground: all krases, biotypes and constitutions

FUNCTIONS AND INDICATIONS

1 **CLEARS TOXIC HEAT AND REDUCES INFECTION, FEVER AND INFLAMMATION; PROMOTES DETOXIFICATION, STIMULATES IMMUNITY, ANTIDOTES POISON AND ELIMINATES PARASITES**

microbial toxicosis with *toxic heat:* boils, inflammations, infections, food allergies
BACTERIAL INFECTIONS (esp. in the head, chest and skin, incl. flu, otitis, tonsilitis [streptococcal], conjunctivitis, gingivitis, glossitis, bronchitis, pneumonia, bone or lung TB, herpes, gonorrhea, dermatitis, scurvy, ringworm, mange, tinea, scabies, syphilis)
LEUKOPENIA; PREVENTIVE in EPIDEMICS
INSECT and ANIMAL BITES
INTESTINAL PARASITES
blood heat: skin rashes, spontaneous bleeding, fever, thirst
FEVERS (incl. malaria, typhoid fever)
stomach heat: thirst for cold drinks, heartburn, swollen, painful or bleeding gums, aphthous sores

2 **PROMOTES DETOXIFICATION, RESOLVES TOXICOSIS AND REDUCES PLETHORA; PROMOTES URINATION, DISSOLVES DEPOSITS AND BENEFITS THE SKIN**

metabolic toxicosis with *damp-cold:* aches and pains, headaches, dry skin with rashes, malaise
RHEUMATISM, arthritis, gout
DERMATOSES and blemishes (preventive and remedial)

HYPERLIPIDEMIA

DEPOSITORY DIATHESIS (incl. arteriosclerosis, hepatic sclerosis, urinary and biliary phosphorus stones)

general plethora: overweight, headaches, malaise, abdominal distension

METABOLIC ACIDOSIS, hypertension, obesity

3 **VITALIZES THE BLOOD, REDUCES CONGESTION AND STOPS BLEEDING;
RESOLVES MUCOUS-DAMP AND STOPS DISCHARGE;
STRENGTHENS THE CONNECTIVE TISSUE, VEINS AND CAPILLARIES**

venous blood stagnation: varicose veins, hemorrhoids, phlebitis, thrombosis, capillary fragility

HEMORRHAGE from internal organs, blood in saliva, urine; capillary fragility

head damp-cold: congested head and sinuses, watery nasal discharge

DISCHARGES (incl. diarrhea, dysentery)

ASCITES

CAPILLARY CIRCULATION DEFICIENCY

CONNECTIVE TISSUE WEAKNESS

4 **NOURISHES THE BLOOD AND REPLENISHES DEFICIENCY;
STIMULATES DIGESTION, REDUCES ACIDITY AND PROMOTES APPETITE**

blood deficiency: pale eyelids, complexion and nails, fatigue

ANEMIA, hemophilia, low WBC and RBC count

MINERAL DEFICIENCY or imbalance

HYPERGLYCEMIA, DIABETES (supportive)

liver and stomach Qi stagnation: painful, slow digestions, nausea, flatulence, constipation

UPPER GASTRIC DYSPEPSIA

GASTRIC HYPERACIDITY (with or without ulcers)

5 **RESTORES THE NERVES AND TONIFIES HEART QI**

nerve deficiency: fatigue, weakness, chronic stress, convalescence

heart Qi deficiency: palpitations, chest oppression, shortness of breath with exertion

NERVOUS and CARDIAC DEFICIENCY

6 **PROMOTES TISSUE REPAIR, REDUCES SWELLING, PREVENTS DECAY, BENEFITS THE SKIN**

WOUNDS (esp. infected and putrid; with redness and swelling), mouth ulcers, verrucas, boils, chilblains

SKIN and NAIL CARE: seborrhea, freckles, wrinkles, broken capillaries, skin itching, acne, broken nails

OILY, OVERSENSITIVE or SAGGING SKIN

SKIN ITCHING, SKIN INFECTIONS, rashes

ANT and MITE REPELLANT

PREPARATION

Use: The most essential and preventive way to benefit from Lemon is to use the **juice** in the diet. Here its excellent *nutritive, restorative, detoxicant* and *antiseptic* properties accumulate daily.

Lemon **essential oil,** which is expressed from the rind, provides the full therapeutic spectrum in a form easy to apply. The oil is massaged into the body with a base oil in a low, 1% dilution. The **essential oil** is also less painful than the acid **juice** when applied to external wounds, skin infections and hot boils. Both preparations are much used in **compresses, washes, lotions, mouthwashes,** etc. Lemon essential oil is also much used in skin care formulas treating hypersensitive, thin, sagging or oily skin types, as well as broken capillaries, acne, etc.

Lemon rind **tincture** is the next best preparation after the essential oil, followed by the short **decoction** of the rind. For all these be sure to use organic lemons.

Traditionally the Lemon **julep** was a favorite cooling, thirst-quenching sweet-sour medicinal drink. It included any number of matching *cooling* herbs such as Borage leaf, Plantain leaf, Cleavers herb, Barberry berry, Lemon balm leaf and Purslane herb.

For very detailed and useful practical suggestions on the many uses and preparations of Lemon, see *The Practice of Aromatherapy* by JEAN VALNET.

Dosage: Essential oil: 3-6 drops in a gel cap topped with some olive oil

    Short decoction: 8-14 g

    Tincture: 2-4 ml at 1:2 strength in 45% ethanol

A course of **Lemon juice**: start with 1/2 lemon a day and increase to 10 or 12 daily. After four or five weeks reduce to 1 or 2 lemons a day. Recommended for summertime or hot weather season only.

Caution: Avoid in all conditions presenting acute pain.

NOTES

The presence of sour lemons in the kitchen should not deter us from viewing this fruit as a fully-fledged botanical remedy. This all the more so if we consider that it is the essential oil, cold exp ressed from the rind, that is needed for the most satisfactory therapeutic results. From the viewpoint of energetic therapeutics, Lemon rind is a study in the sour taste: it performs all the functions sour-ness is supposed to. For a start, upper digestive stimulation and regulation that addresses several digestive disorders, notably **liver and stomach Qi stagnation** and **gastric hyperacidity.**

Containing sour organic acids and salty trace minerals, Lemon rind is first and foremost an important *detoxicant* remedy that addresses both microbial and metabolic forms of toxicosis. In addressing **microbial toxicosis** in individuals presenting signs of **toxic heat** like **inflammations** and **acute infections,** the remedy is a lead *refrigerant* remedy. Its heat-clearing effect runs like a *Leitmotif* through the labyrinth of its indications. This effect Lemon achieves through a combination of actions: *detoxicant, anti-inflammatory, antibacterial, antiparasitic, antiseptic* and *vulnerary.* Like other remedies in this class and Class 13, Lemon belongs to the most important group that could easily fit in either category. Clearing heat and promoting detoxification are very closely linked treatment strategies, after all. In energetic terms, Lemon clears both **Qi** and **blood-level heat,** and especially when the **liver, gallbladder** or stomach are involved.

In the treatment of those presenting **metabolic toxicosis** with **toxic cold,** Lemon excels in controlling and reversing **depository** and **plethoric** conditions with **metabolic acidosis.** The acids and trace minerals together perform *resolvent, dissolvent* and *hypoglycemiant* actions, thereby assisting in softening and eliminating hard deposits, and reducing high lipid/cholesterol levels in the blood.

These same minerals also ensure a *nutritive* and *neuroendocrine restorative* effect that includes tonification of **Kidney Essence** in Chinese medicine. Lemon is specifically *restorative* to cerebral and cardiac functions, thereby creating mental clarity, greater awareness and sensory acuity. These too are known functions of the sour taste quality.

Yet the effects of Lemon as a sour remedy go even beyond the pharmacological tenets of even an authoritative traditional textbook like the *Charak Samhita* (one of the most important canons of Ayurvedic medicine). Its sourness also promotes astriction, to the extent of toning connective tissue and so the veins and capillaries especially. This ensures a *mucostatic* action on the mucous membrane (especially the respiratory) for the treatment of discharges, and a *venous* and *capillary decongestant* action on the veins for individuals with **venous blood stasis** and a tendency to **hemorrhage** from atonic capillaries.

Asian Buplever Root

Botanical source: *Bupleurum chinense* De Candolle,
    B. falcatum L., *B. longiradiatum* Turchaninov
    and spp. (Apiaceae/Umbelliferae)
Pharmaceutical name: Radix Bupleuri
Other names: Hare's ear, Thoroughwax, "Kindling
    barbarian"
    Chai Hu (Mandarin Chinese)
    Chaai Wu (Cantonese Chinese)
    Saiko (Japanese)
Part used: the root

NATURE

Therapeutic category: medium-strength remedy with moderate chronic toxicity
Constituents: triterpenoid saponins (incl. sapogenin, daikogenin, saikosaponins, saikogenins), phyto-sterols (spinasterol, furfurol, bupleurumol, stigmasterols), hexanoic and pentanoic acids, adonitol, angeli-cin, oleic/linoleic/ palmitic/stearic/lignoceric acids, polysaccharides, essential oil (incl. ketone)
Effective qualities: bitter, somewhat pungent, astringent, cool, dry
Tropism: nervous, immune, cardiovascular, digestive, respiratory, reproductive systems
    calming, relaxing, dispersing, decongesting
    Liver, Gallbladder, Pericardium, *yang wei* meridians; Air, Warmth bodies

FUNCTIONS AND INDICATIONS

1   **CLEARS HEAT AND REDUCES INFECTION, FEVER AND INFLAMMATION;
    STIMULATES IMMUNITY AND PROTECTS THE LIVER**

    shao yang-stage heat: intermittent high fever, heat with chills on motion, restlessness, irritability, pain
    external wind-heat: rising fever, aches and pains, headache, chills, sore throat
    ACUTE FEVERS (most types, incl. remittent; influenza, malaria, infectious fevers in general)
    ACUTE INFLAMMATIONS (incl. gastritis, enteritis, inflammatory bowel disease, ulcerative colitis,
        appendicitis, pancreatitis, hepatitis, cholecystitis, neuritis, cerebrospinal inflammations, pleurisy)
    VIRAL and BACTERIAL INFECTIONS, ACUTE and CHRONIC (incl. common cold, flu, infectious
        hepatitis, pleurisy, peptic ulcer, polio, other chronic viral infections)
    TOXICOSIS from LIVER DISEASE and INFECTIONS

2   **REGULATES THE QI, RELAXES CONSTRAINT AND RELIEVES PAIN;
    REGULATES IMMUNITY AND REDUCES ALLERGIES**

    kidney / adrenal Qi constraint: nervous tension, unexplained pains, irritability, allergies
    NEURALGIA (incl. intercostal, trigeminal, sciatic)
    HEADACHE (tension and migraine types), tinnitus, vertigo
    PAINFUL CONDITIONS (in general, incl. neuralgias, headache, abdominal pain, menstrual, ovarian pain)
    IMMEDIATE ALLERGIES (incl. rhinitis, sinusitis, otitis, urticaria, dermatitis, asthma, some food allergies)

4 ASTRINGES TO STOP DIARRHEA AND RELIEVE PROLAPSE

ACUTE and CHRONIC DIARRHEA, gastroenteritis, IBS
Central Qi sinking: abdominal bearing down sensation, rectal and uterine prolapse
GASTROPTOSIS

PREPARATION

Use: Asian buplever root is **decocted** or used in **tincture** form. It is not generally used topically, although its astringent, cooling quality would work in non-alcoholic preparations for hot, swollen skin lesions.
Dosage: Decoction: 3-10 g
　　　　　Tincture: 1-3 ml at 1:2 strength in 45% ethanol
Caution: Because *Bupleurum* possesses cumulative toxicity, do not use on its own for more than two weeks. Signs of over-/mis-use include dry mouth, dizziness and headache. The remedy is designed to treat *acute* and *subacute* conditions, not chronic ones, and for both these reasons is always best combined with other herbs in a formula. Contraindicated in Liver Yang rising syndrome causing dizziness, tinnitus or headache, and in Yin and fluids deficiency causing symptoms of mucosal dryness.

NOTES

Asian buplever is a fragrant perennial herb in the carrot family from Northeast Asia. Favoring sunny slopes, roadsides and waste ground, it produces small spherical compound umbels of small yellow flowers in late summer and summer. The root is a traditional Chinese remedy that has found its way into the tincture bottles of Western herbalists—and with good reason.

Asian buplever root, also known as *Bupleurum* for short, has a very long and hoary history as a remedy for **fever** and **pain;** in the energetic terms of Chinese medicine, for clearing heat and relieving constrained Qi. This is clearly the place to start a modern Western evaluation of this herb.

Asian buplever is traditionally used for **acute fevers** of the **wind-heat** type presenting aches and pains and inflammation. It is indicated whenever Boneset is indicated, in fact—for the fever of a flu that does not respond to the normal *vasorelaxant diaphoretics*. Asian buplever brings *antipyretic, analgesic* and *anti-inflammatory* actions to the table, being loaded with saponins, acids and essential oil. **Intermittent fevers** is the other main usage for this herb, with similar symptoms: this is an important *antimalarial* remedy, for instance, where it is often combined with Baical skullcap, another good *antipyretic*. Today, *Bupleurum* is showing good clinical results in *any* type of fever, as long as a reduction of the temperature is what is required.

Equally important from the infection point of view, Asian buplever weighs in with a hefty *anti-infectious* effect as well. Reasearch in Hong Kong, Japan and China has shown the root to possess considerable *antiviral* and *antibacterial* actions, with additional *immune stimulation* involving an increase of antigen and interferon production. A wide range of mostly acute viral and bacterial infections have been treated with it since the 1950s. It combines superbly with the likes of Echinacea, Marigold, Plantain, Wild indigo, and so on.

Moreover, by working as a *liver-protectant,* Asian buplever can help the liver clean up the toxicosis caused by infection, and especially in hepatobiliary infections. Its use for chronic toxicosis, however, is limited (see Caution above). It is *not* a comprehensive *liver restorative* like Milk-thistle seed, Schisandra berry or Licorice root, but can certainly be combined with these if long-term liver support is needed.

Bupleurum has a nice, compassionate *nervous sedative/relaxant* effect that tops off its other actions, somewhat like Lavender. It will shine in **acute infections** where the individual shows **fever, inflammation, pain, irritability** and **restlessness.** The pain can be of any origin. If spasmodic pain is present, as in digestive colic, spasmodic dysmenorrhea, gallstone colic, and so on, Bupleurum's strong *spasmolytic* action will engage. Think of Wild yam root, Black haw bark ... Neuralgias and headaches also respond particularly well to it. Therapeutically, the key to its usage is therefore **pain, spasm, inflammation** and **fever.**

Anticomplementary polysaccharides have also been found in this remedy (Yamada and Kiyohara 1989), suggesting application to **immediate (type I) allergies** of the **wind-heat** type presenting inflammation and pain.

Yellow Jessamine Root

Botanical source: *Gelsemium sempervirens* (L.)
Persoon (syn. *G. nitidum* Michaux, *Bignonia sempervirens* L.) (Loganiaceae)
Pharmaceutical name: Rhizoma Gelsemii
Other names: Wild jessamine, Yellow jasmine,
Carolina jessamine/jasmine, Wild woodbine,
White jessamine, White poison vine (Am)
Jasmin jaune, Gelsemium (Fr)
Gelber Jasmin, Virginianischer Jasmin (Ge)
Part used: the rhizome (with rootlets)

NATURE

Therapeutic category: strong remedy with acute toxicity
Constituents: essential oil, alkaloids (gelsemine, gelseminine, gelsemoidine, sempervirine), gelsemic acid, resin, starch
Effective qualities: bitter, dry, cold
calming, relaxing, sinking
Tropism: nervous, digestive, urinary, cardiovascular, respiratory systems
Liver, Kidney, Heart, Pericardium, Stomach meridians
Warmth, Air bodies

FUNCTIONS AND INDICATIONS

1 **CLEARS FULL HEAT AND REDUCES FEVER AND INFLAMMATION;**
CALMS THE MIND, REDUCES AGITATION AND PROMOTES REST

yang ming-stage / Qi-level heat: high fever, irritability, restlessness, excitability, headache,
flushed complexion, bright eyes, contracted/pinhead pupils

shao yang-stage heat: intermittent high fever, heat with chills on motion, restlessness, irritability

ACUTE FEVERS (full or remittent, in adults and children, incl. bilious, typhoid and infectious in general;
malaria, pneumonia, pleurisy, puerperal fever, eruptive fevers, influenza)

ACUTE INFLAMMATIONS (incl. nephritis, cystitis, urethritis, asthma, bronchitis, pleuritis, laryngitis,
meningitis, cerebrospinal inflammations, enteritis, inflammatory bowel disease, appendicitis, ovaritis,
salpingitis, endometritis, peritonitis, mastitis, iritis, conjunctivitis)

CEREBRAL / SPINAL HYPEREMIA

heart fire / heart phlegm-fire: restlessness, agitation, flushed face, insomnia, palpitations, mania

AGITATION, DELIRIUM in any condition

stomach fire: epigastric feeling of rawness, heat, pain and knotty contraction; thirst, hunger

SYMPATHETIC NERVOUS HYPERFUNCTIONING

ONSET INSOMNIA with EXITABILITY (from emotions, shock, trauma, drugs, foods); stage fright

**2 REGULATES THE QI, RELAXES CONSTRAINT AND RELIEVES PAIN;
CLEARS INTERNAL WIND AND STOPS SPASMS**

kidney / adrenal Qi constraint: nervous tension, unexplained pains, spasm proneness, pinched or contracted tissues, ringing in ears, dizziness

NEURALGIA (incl. trigeminal, sciatic, intercostal)

HEADACHE (tension and migraine types), tinnitus, vertigo

PAINFUL CONDITIONS (in general, incl. neuralgias, headache, toothache, myalgia, ovarian pain, abdominal pain, bladder pain, false/true labor pains, afterbirth pains, hyperesthesia)

PRURITUS from ECZEMA

SPASMODIC CONDITIONS (incl. spasmodic dysmenorrhea, spasmodic uterine dystocia, spasmodic dysuria, spasmodic irritable bowel syndrome [tenesmus], iliocecal valve spasm, spasms of any sphincter, spasmodic asthma, glottis spasms, asthma, rigid os uteri with dry vaginal walls, hypertonic labor contractions, spasmodic stalled labor)

lung Qi constraint: wheezing, tight painful chest, coughing

WHOOPING COUGH, ASTHMA (all types)

bladder Qi constraint: scanty, irritated, difficult urination

SPASMODIC NEUROGENIC BLADDER with DYSURIA, STRANGURY (painful urethral stricture)

GONORRHEA (acute)

uterus Qi constraint: painful periods from spasms

SPASMODIC DYSMENORRHEA

HYPERTONIC LABOR CONTRACTIONS

intestines Qi constraint: indigestion, abdominal aches, pains or spasms, irregular stool

SPASMODIC IBS

SPASMS and TREMORS of peripheries from *internal wind*

FEBRILE SPASMS (esp. in children; in epilepsy, tetanus, chorea, delirium tremens, puerperal eclampsia)

SEIZURES (incl. in children, from fever, teething, gastroenteritis, food poisoning, cholera, dysentery)

PREPARATION

Use: Yellow jessamine root is prepared by **decoction** or **tincture.** The tincture is the best all-round preparation. According to the Eclectic practitioners of the nineteenth and twentieth century, the root should be collected *green* in early spring (around March) and tinctured fresh to best fulfill the above therapeutic requirements (KING, FELTER & LLOYD 1898).

Topical applications such as **compresses, liniments** and **ointments** are prepared for neuralgic, rheumatic and pruritic conditions.

Low potency homeopathic preparations (up to 30x potency) are also available under the name Gelsemium, and address some of the same as well as some different conditions (such as paralysis).

Honey derived from yellow jessamine flowers is considered poisonous, as the plant's alkaloids concentrate in the flower nectar. For the same reason, infants should be kept away from the flowers and from sucking the nectar, which have caused several reported cases of poisoning.

Dosage: Decoction: 0.5-2 g

Tincture: 0.07-0.35 ml (c. 1.5-8 drops) at 1:5 strength in 60% ethanol. Eclectic practitioners prescribed a maximum of 0.2-1 ml (c. 5-25 drops) per day taken in water.

Smaller doses are sufficient for children and most conditions in function 1, i.e., for its *sedative* and *refrigerant* actions. Larger doses are needed for conditions in function 2, i.e., for its *spasmolytic* and *anticonvulsant* actions. As a general rule, within each category begin with a smaller dose and administer increasing doses cautiously every few hours until the therapeutic effect is obtained. Administration needs to be repeated often for good results (especially in children) as the remedy is quickly eliminated by the kidneys. At the same time, watch out for any possible (but unlikely) undesirable side-effects and go back to the starting dose if neccessary. Signs of cumulative toxicity usually only occur beyond these therapeutic doses and include a slow, weak pulse, prostration, headache, dry mouth, dropping of the lower jaw, muscle weakness, sweating, nausea, brain fog, pain in the eyes and double vision.

Caution: Yellow jessamine root's therapeutic status is a toxic remedy that possesses some acute toxicity. It must be used under professional supervision, using the exact dosage protocols indicated above.

Yellow jessamine root is contraindicated in all cold and empty conditions such as all Yang deficiency, Qi deficiency, in low-grade intermittent fevers, in heart weakness of any kind, in weak people with low vital force (*zheng qi*), as well as during pregnancy and lactation (apart from the specific pregnancy and puerperal conditions indicated). Avoid using this remedy in conditions other than the full hot and tense conditions indicated. Stop use as soon as the condition improves to avoid damaging the individual's vital force (*zheng qi*) and prolonging the recuperation or convalescence phase (including when it presents empty heat with intermittent fever).

NOTES

Yellow jessamine is an evergreen climbing vine from North America's South that thrives in humid subtropical woods, thickets and swamps. Blooming February through June with yellow funnel shaped flowers, its heady sweet-floral fragrance long ago invited names such as "Carolina jessamine" and "yellow jasmine." Note that this is neither the true jessamine with thin, greenish white flowers of the *Cestrum* genus, nor the Eastern jasmines of the *Jasminum* genus with their cream white flowers. Yellow jessamine's long, slender brown rhizome is normally 3 to 10 feet long, but has been known to reach 30 feet in length.

Yellow jessamine's medicinal use was discovered by accident during the eighteenth century when a Mississippi plantation worker erroneously collected and decocted this root instead of another one, thereby quickly curing his master's bilious fever. The remedy was first mentioned in *Elliott's Botany of South Carolina and Georgia* of 1821 by STEPHEN ELLIOTT, a cornerstone work for researchers and doctors (e.g., PORCHER, RAFINESQUE) inquiring into Southern medicinal plants. Within a short forty years, Yellow jessamine root ascended to become *the primary fever remedy* bar none of both Eclectic and Regular physicians.

In the words of LLOYD and FELTER (1898), Early Eclectic practitioners "regarded Yellow jessamine as the only agent ever yet discovered capable of subduing in from 2 to 20 hours, and without the least possible injury to the patient, the most formidable and most complicated, as well as the most simple fevers incident to our country and climate." They found that it works by "quieting all nervous irritability and excitement, equalizing the circulation, promoting perspiration and rectifying the various secretions without causing nausea, vomiting or purging," noting also that "in the recent epidemics of influenza, probably no one reme-

dy was more extensively used, or more oftener indicated."

As an equivalent of the Chinese mineral remedy, Gypsum Shi Gao, but with a wider range of indications, Yellow jessamine is the classic Western *refrigerant* botanical for **high fever** and **acute inflammation.** Essentially a *nervous sedative* and *relaxant* in one, it is called for whenever the condition is unequivocally hot, tense and dry. Its *antipyretic, anti-inflammatory* and *depressant* actions address *yang ming*-**stage fevers** presenting headache, flushed red face, excitability and thirst. Containing potent alkaloids and acids, the remedy works by removing spinal and cerebral hyperemia with sympathetic hyperfunctioning, regardless of the cause. Gelsemium, as it was then known, was successfully relied on for severe conditions such as acute meningitis, nephritis and pleuritis before the advent of synthetic medication.

"Gelsemium, as an *antispasmodic,* is second to no other drug," affirm the Eclectics. Its *spasmolytic* action relaxes both smooth and striated muscles, addressing a variety of tense conditions seen in various **constrained Qi** syndromes in Chinese medicine. The remedy excels in **painful spasmodic** and **neuralgic** conditions, including those found in gynecology and obstetrics. Fairly large doses may be given for spasmodic dysmenorrhea arising from **uterus Qi constraint,** for example, and for **hypertonic, rapidly successive labor contractions** in women presenting agitation and anxiety. Its *anticonvulsant* action was a standard in treating children's seizures, especially from nervous tension and fever.

Conditions of **pain** also respond well to this remedy, especially when arising from nerve irritation, spasm or blood congestion. It focuses on neuralgias and headaches of all types, as well as the pain of striated muscle spasm in general.

Clear Damp-Heat and Reduce Infection and Discharge

Bitter, cold, dry, astringent anti-infectives

Goldenseal Root

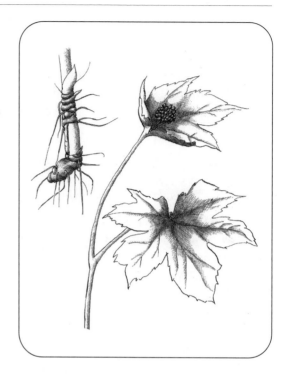

Botanical source: *Hydrastis canadensis* L.
    (Ranunculaceae)
Pharmaceutical name: Rhizoma Hydrastis
Other names: Yellow root, Indian dye,
    Yellow puccoon, Eye balm root,
    Ground raspberry (Am)
    Sceau d'or, Racine d'or, Racine orange (Fr)
    Wasserblatt, Wasserkraut, Gelbwurzel (Ge)
Part used: the rhizome

NATURE

Therapeutic category: medium-strength remedy with moderate chronic toxicity
Constituents: isoquinoline alkaloids (incl. berberine 3.5-6%, hydrastine 2-4%, berberastine 2-3%, candaline, canadine, hydrastinine), essential oil, resins, meconin, phytosterins, lipids with fatty acids, albumin, chlorogenic acid, potassium, sugar, starch
Effective qualities: bitter and astringent, cold with warming potential, dry
    decongesting, astringing, stabilizing, calming, restoring, stimulating
Tropism: stomach, intestines, lung, heart, reproductive organs, bladder, kidneys, liver, gallbladder
    Liver, Gallbladder, Stomach, Large Intestine meridians
    Fluid, Warmth bodies
Ground: all krases, biotypes and constitutions

FUNCTIONS AND INDICATIONS

1   **CLEARS DAMP-HEAT, REDUCES INFECTION AND INFLAMMATION, AND STOPS DISCHARGE; STIMULATES IMMUNITY**

   intestines damp-heat: difficult, urgent, burning bowel movement, chronic loose stool with blood and pus
   ENTERITIS, dysentery (esp. acute)

   skin wind-heat: red skin rashes, itching skin
   SKIN ERUPTIONS with itching or burning skin: acute dermatitis, measles, smallpox, etc.; oral or anal
      eczema; acne, lymphadenitis, lymphangitis, pyodermia
   BACTERIAL, FUNGAL, AMOEBIC, PARASITIC INFECTIONS (esp. acute, with *damp-heat,* incl. dermal,
      intestinal, uterine, vaginal; e.g. ringworm, cholera, dysentery, giardiasis, TB, thrush, candidiasis)
   OTITIS MEDIA with purulent discharge; EYE INFLAMMATIONS
   MOUTH, GUM, THROAT and ANAL SORENESS and INFLAMMATION (acute and chronic, esp. with
      discharge, ulcers, sores; e.g. tonsilitis, stomatitis, gingivitis, laryngitis, periodontitis)
   LEUKOPENIA

2   RESOLVES MUCOUS-DAMP CONGESTION AND STOPS DISCHARGE

head mucous-damp: sinus congestion, frontal pain, discharge of viscous tenacious mucous

SINUSITIS

intestines mucous-damp: loose stools, distended abdomen

GASTROENTERITIS, diarrhea (esp. chronic)

MICROBIAL TOXICOSIS

kidney and bladder damp: white vaginal and uterine discharges, sperm loss

LEUCORRHEA, spermatorrhea, gonorrhea

CERVICAL EROSION, uterine ulcers, cystitis, gonnorrhea

EXCESSIVE PERSPIRATION

3   VITALIZES THE BLOOD, REDUCES CONGESTION AND MODERATES MENSTRUATION;
RESTORES THE VEINS, ASTRINGES, REDUCES TUMORS AND STOPS BLEEDING

venous blood stagnation: varicosities, heavy or aching legs, leg cramps at night, fatigue, constipation

VARICOSE VEINS, phlebitis, hemorrhoids, pelvic congestion and varioceles, cerebral hyperemia

uterus blood congestion: pelvic weight and persistant dragging or cramping pain, early copious
    menstruation

CONGESTIVE DYSMENORRHEA

liver blood congestion: abdominal distension, low fat tolerance, fatigue

PORTAL CONGESTION

TUMORS, fibroids, ovarian cysts, (esp. hard, painful, of female reproductive organs, breasts, stomach)

BREAST PAIN and SWELLING

HEMORRHAGE (passive) from pelvic organs, uterine fibroids, kidneys, lungs (incl. menorrhagia,
    metrorrhagia, menopausal bleeding)

4   CLEARS DAMP-HEAT, REDUCES LIVER CONGESTION AND RELIEVES JAUNDICE

liver Qi stagnation: midback and flank pain, constipation, headache, jaundice, indigestion, muscle aches

LIVER CONGESTION with DYSPEPSIA

CHRONIC CONSTIPATION

liver / gallbladder (damp)- heat: nausea, swollen right flank, headache, bitter taste in mouth

JAUNDICE, CHOLANGITIS, cholecystitis, gallstones

5   STIMULATES DIGESTION AND APPETITE, WARMS THE STOMACH,
PROMOTES BILE FLOW AND RELIEVES FATIGUE

gallbladder and stomach Qi stagnation (stomach damp-heat): slow painful digestion, nausea, belching,
    epigastric distension and pain, flatulence, appetite loss, fatigue

GASTRIC and BILIARY DYSPEPSIA

stomach cold: sense of emptiness at pit of stomach, dull epigastric pain, vomiting clear sour liquid

CHRONIC GASTRITIS

GASTRIC ULCERS

DEBILITY from fevers, dysentery, etc.

6   PROMOTES AND ENHANCES LABOR

FAILURE to PROGRESS during LABOR

UTERINE SUBINVOLUTION

7   PROMOTES TISSUE REPAR, REDUCES INFLAMMATION AND BENEFITS THE SKIN AND EYES

ATONIC ULCERS, open sores (incl. eruptive and syphilitic sores), acne, erysipelas, oral and anal fissures

SKIN and EYE INFLAMMATIONS (incl. suppurative dermatitis, conjunctivitis, trachoma, corneal ulcer)
BOILS, abscesses

PREPARATION

Use: Goldenseal root is better used in **tincture** than in **decoction** form for the whole range of its applications. Numerous external preparations can be made on this basis. Liquid preparations of Goldenseal are preferable for topical use where irritation is present. Gynecological conditions benefit from a **douche, pessary** or **tampon** where appropriate, whereas the eye, mouth and skin inflammations and ulcers require **washes** or **compresses** in low dilutions. A **salve** or **compress** can be made for skin or breast conditions, though they require internal use first and foremost.

Goldenseal **powder** is more useful in upper gastric stagnation (function 5) and can also make a quick **infusion.** It may also be taken as a **sneezing snuff** for sinus congestion and nasal ulcers and polyps.

Dosage: Only smallest doses are neccessary when *stimulating (warming)* the liver and stomach (function 5). Medium doses are *mucostatic* and *decongestant* as well as *antiseptic* and *anti-inflammatory* (functions 1, 2, 3, 6). Larger doses are very *stimulating, laxative* and ultimately *cooling* (function 4). The full dosage ranges are as follows:

• *Small dose:*
　　Powder and **decoction:** 0.25-1 g
　　Tincture: 0.25-0.75 ml or 7-20 drops at 1:3 strength in 45% ethanol
• *Medium dose:*
　　Powder and **decoction:** 1-2 g
　　Tincture: O.75-1.5 ml or 20-40 dropsat 1:3 strength in 45% ethanol
• *Large dose:*
　　Powder and **decoction:** 2-3 g
　　Tincture: 1.5-3 ml or 40-80 drops at 1:3 strength in 45% ethanol

Caution: Contraindicated during pregnancy and in hypertension, as Goldenseal root is both *uterine stimulant* and *hypertensive*. Also forbidden in Yin deficiency conditions.

As Goldenseal root is a medium-strength remedy, exact doses should be maintained; over-dosing may eventually cause kidney and liver damage. The remedy is best used as part of a formula, or on its own for short-term use only.

Because Goldenseal tends to remove beneficial microorganisms as well as pathogenic ones, it is always a good idea to take some probiotics such as acidophilus, miso (e.g., miso soup), sauerkraut or live yoghurt while using it. Prebiotic foods and herbs containing inulin that promote healthy commensuals include onion, tomato, banana, jerusalem artichoke, cereal grains and the herbs Artichoke root, Dandelion root, Burdock root (gobo), Elecampane, Echinacea and Downy bellflower root *(Codonopsis)*. These measures will minimize damage to the intestinal flora. For this reason, and because of its slight cumulative toxicity, Goldenseal should not be taken continuously on its own for more than six weeks without a two-week break.

NOTES

In his *Collections for a Vegetable Materia Medica* of 1794 the botanist WILLIAM BARTON for the first time documents the native uses of Goldenseal root. For hundreds of years this plant had been of much value to natives and settlers alike. By the time JOHN KING writes his *American Dispensatory* in 1852, however, the remedy had finally reached the attention of practicing physicians, after which its reputation soared. Here it remains today—in orbit—in spite (or perhaps because?) of its misuse as a universal panacea.

As a *broad-spectrum anti-infective* Goldenseal root has gained new relevance with the increased incidence of epidemics such as cholera (India) and giardia (Africa, Asia, U.S.A.). When used in acute infectious, inflammatory and discharge conditions such as **intestines damp-heat** and **skin damp-heat,** it is as successful as Coptis Huang Lian and Scutellaria Huang Qin (Baikal skullcap root) are in Chinese medicine. These remedies share much both therapeutically and biochemically. Goldenseal almost comes up to Coptis' quota of the powerful alkaloid berberine. Topically the remedy's excellent *anti-inflammatory, antiseptic* and *astringent-vulnerary* actions address oozing suppurative discharges, weeping eczema, and so on.

Goldenseal root's essential functions may be summarized as *stimulating, decongesting* and *astringing*. Like other bitter, dry, cold remedies it can be used in smallest doses (see Preparation above) as a *stimulant* to all digestive organs (function 5). Goldenseal has about the same strength as Centaury herb in this respect (hence is inferior to Gentian root and Wormwood herb). As such, the root acts as a bivalent *gastric* and *biliary stimulant* with potential for either warming chronic cold, hypofunctioning gastric conditions—stomach cold —or cooling down acute, hyperfunctioning gastric conditions—stomach damp-heat—with upper digestive dyspepsia. Its strong *antibacterial* action will help treat those ulcers that involve bacterial infection.

When taken in medium doses, however, Goldenseal root acts as an effective damp-heat clearer for those with liver and biliary congestion—somewhat like Blue flag root, Butternut root bark or even Gardenia Shan Zhi Zi. Jaundice, constipation and sore muscles are the traditional key symptoms of the type of liver damp-heat that it addresses. The remedy also reduces **damp-heat** in the **intestines** arising from **intestinal dysbiosis** or its progression, systemic candidiasis. In the case of **allergic eczema** arising from this damp-heat (as in "Yin fire"), Goldenseal is still the right remedy.

Goldenseal's *anticatarrhal,* or *mucostatic,* action in the digestive tract was even more highly esteemed by past physicians. Eclectic medic HARVEY FELTER (1922) summed up this action succinctly when he recommended Goldenseal for "all catarrhal conditions of the mucous membrane without acute inflammation, with secretions of thick, viscous, yellowish muco-pus." As a Class 15 *tonic astringent* addressing both damp-cold and damp-heat conditions in the digestive, urogenital and head region, Goldenseal not simply dries, but *resolves* mucous-damp. With its use, chronic **damp-cold discharge** forms of **gastroenteritis, leucorrhea** and **rhinitis** seen in individuals presenting a bedrock terrain of **microbial toxicosis** will improve drastically with its use.

Not only a *decongestant* to hepatobiliary functions, Goldenseal is also *decongestant* to the entire vascular system. This effect has a specific application to the female reproductive organs. The brilliant biochemist JOHN URI LLOYD in 1875 accurately wrote "it may prove to be one of the chief remedies, if not *the* remedy, for chronic congestion, or more properly, stasis of the various organs of the body." He goes on to say that "it is of veritable value in chronic blood stasis in the liver, spleen, uterus, abdomen and portal system." LLOYD comments that "if it increases the tonicity of the muscle fibres of the terminal blood-vessels, it must also increase that of the large arterial and venous trunks, and even of the heart itself."

In clinical practice, Goldenseal is selected mainly for **uterus blood congestion, liver blood congestion** and **venous blood stasis** with typical signs of varicosities and menorrhagia with short cycles. As such it will combine well with other Class 14 *blood decongestants*. In situations of passive hemorrhage, the remedy shows excellent *hemostatic* power, partly from capillary astriction, partly from a *coagulant action*.

As part of its *decongestant* action, Goldenseal not only tones the veins, but also evinces an *antitumor* effect. This would go in tandem with its *antiviral* and *antiparasitic* actions. Because of Goldenseal's tropism for the pelvic organs, this action focuses on female reproductive tumors. By decreasing blood-supply, the remedy can effectively reduce hard, moveable fibroids—in addition to stopping the resultant bleeding. Still, it is likely that other pharmacological mechanisms also play a part in its *antitumor* effect.

Barberry Root Bark

Botanical source: *Berberis vulgaris* L.
    (Berberidaceae)

Pharmaceutical name: Cortex radicis Berberis

Ancient names: Crespinus, Spina acida, Oxycantha
    (Lat)

Other names: Barbaryn, Guild tree, Jaundice berry,
    Pipperidge bush, Woodsour, Maiden barberry
    (Eng)

    Epine-vinette, Vinettier commun (Fr)

    Sauerdorn, Berberize, Reisselbeeren, Versich
    (Ge)

Part used: the root bark; also the berry and leaf

NATURE

Therapeutic category: mild remedy with minimal chronic toxicity

Constituents: isoquinoline alkaloids (incl. berberine, oxycanthine, berbamine, berberrubine, palmatine, isotetrandine, jatrorrhizine, columbamine, hydrastine), chelidonic acid, tannins, gum, resin, wax

Effective qualities: bitter, astringent, cold, dry
    stimulating, astringing, decongesting, relaxing, sinking

Tropism: liver, gallbladder, spleen, intestines, blood
    Spleen, Stomch, Liver, Gallbladder meridians
    Warmth, Fluid bodies
    decreases *pitta* and *kapha,* increases *vatta*

Ground: Choleric and Sanguine krases/temperaments
    Industrious/Tai Yang, Expressive/Jue Yin and Charming/Yang Ming Earth; all three constitutions

FUNCTIONS AND INDICATIONS

1   **CLEARS DAMP-HEAT, REDUCES INFECTION AND INFLAMMATION, AND STOPS DISCHARGE**

   intestines damp-heat: urgent defecation with burning, blood in stools

   ACUTE GASTROENTERITIS, dysentery, chronic diarrhea, cholera, amoebiasis, salmonella

   CHRONIC CANDIDIASIS

   genitourinary damp-heat: veneral infections with purulent yellow discharge

   MOUTH, THROAT and GUM INFECTIONS, MOUTH ULCERS (incl. periodontal disease, stomatitis, laryngitis)

   liver and gallbladder damp-heat: nausea, headache, right subcostal pain, jaundice, irritability

   INFECTIOUS HEPATITIS, jaundice, cholecystitis, biliary colic, fever

   stomach fire: ravenous hunger, thirst for cold water, mouth ulcers, bleeding gums

2   **STIMULATES DIGESTION AND APPETITE AND REDUCES LIVER CONGESTION**

   liver and stomach Qi stagnation / stomach damp-heat: painful indigestion, constipation or diarrhea, lethargy, appetite loss, nausea, moodiness, swollen sore right flank, midback pain

   LIVER CONGESTION, JAUNDICE

   FATIGUE from liver congestion, anemia, convalescence, malnutrition, etc.

3 PROMOTES URINATION, RESOLVES TOXICOSIS AND DISSOLVES STONES

kidney Qi stagnation: skin rashes, scanty urination, static or migratory pains

kidney Qi stagnation with *metabolic toxicosis:* aches and pains, headaches, malaise, fatigue

RHEUMATISM, GALLSTONES, KIDNEY STONES, ovarian cysts, gouty arthritis

4 VITALIZES THE BLOOD, REDUCES CONGESTION AND MODERATES MENSTRUATION

venous blood stagnation: varicose veins, hemorrhoids, constipation, lethargy

VARICOSITIES

uterus blood congestion: early or heavy periods with dull pelvic pain and weight

CONGESTIVE DYSMENORRHEA

PREPARATION

Use: Barberry root bark is prepared by **decoction** and **tincture.** The **decoction** is suitable for **washes, gargling** and for *cooling* and *astringing* purposes generally. However, the **tincture** has the widest range of effects.

Barberry berry and leaf are astringent, sour cool in quality and would probably be useful in genital discharges to "contain sperm" and other discharges in deficient Qi and Yin conditions. They are also used in lung phlegm-heat syndromes with purulent yellow expectoration, etc.

Dosage: Decoction: 8-16 g

   Tincture: 2-5 ml at 1:2 strength in 45% cthanol

Smaller doses taken unsweetened are sufficient for the *digestive stimulant* action of function 1.

Caution: Contraindicated during pregnancy because of a *uterine stimulant* action. Discontinue if the tincture causes nosebleeds or dizziness. (This happens only rarely.)

Note: The Chinese remedy, **Baikal skullcap root,** *Huang Qi,* from *Scutellaria baicalensis,* has very similar qualities, tropism and applications to Barberry bark. Baikal skullcap is particularly *anti-infective* and *anti-inflamatory.* Its *antibacterial, antifungal* and *immunostimulant* actions serve **acute respiratory, intestinal, hepatobiliary, urinary** and **skin infections.** As a *bronchodilator* and *anti-inflamatory* it also addresses asthmatic conditions. The root is *antiallergic* in a range of **immediate allergies** such as allergic asthma, rhinitis, otits and food allergies. Being liver-centered and *cholagogue* like Barberry, Baikal skullcap also treats liver congestion and biliary dyspepsia.

   Dosage: Decoction: 6-18 g; tincture 1.5-3 ml at 1:2 in 60% ethanol.

See the author's *Jade Remedies* for a full presentation of this valuable remedy.

NOTES

By working on the upper digestive organs, the liver, stomach and duodenum, Barberry root bark's effect is firstly *stimulating* and *restoring,* and then secondarily *cooling.* As it stimulates gastric and other secretions when taken in small doses, this bitter *digestant* promotes digestion and generates strength. It helps break up and move out toxic intestinal accumulations in general, thereby addressing **stagnant** and **hot** conditions of the **liver, gallbladder, stomach** and **intestines.** Barberry is appropriate for treating chronic deficiency that has turned into stagnant heat. When this flares up into an acute heat episode, as in the syndromes **Stomach fire** and **Liver fire,** Barberry then acts as a pure *refrigerant,* like Lady's mantle herb.

In second place, Barberry root bark exerts an excellent *cold astringent* and *blood decongestant* effects that address Lower Warmer **damp-heat infections** with **inflammation** and **discharge.** By mobilizing venous circulation, the remedy also relieves **venous** and **pelvic blood congestion,** and lends tone to the veins themselves. The alkaloid berberin in particular is thought responsible for these effects, with some assistance from the tannins. The similarity of many of these uses with the Chinese herbs Scutellaria Huang Qi and Coptis Huang Lian, which contain a similar string of alkaloids, should not be overlooked. We can make inferences about both by considering their remaining indications. These inferences, however, await the empirical evidence of actual use before we can make any definite conclusions.

Pau d'Arco Bark

Botanical source: *Tabebuia avellanedae* Lorentz,
　　　T. impetiginosa (Martius) Stanley and spp.
　　　(syn. *Tecoma ipe, T. cassinoides,*
　　　T. ochracea) (Bignoniaceae)
Pharmaceutical name: Cortex Tabebuiae
Other names: Ipe roxo, Tahibo (Braz)
　　　Lapacho (Arg)
　　　Bowstick (Am)
Part used: the inner bark

NATURE

Therapeutic category: mild remedy with minimal chronic toxicity
Constituents: naphthoquinones (incl. lapachol 2-7%, menaquinone, deoxylapachol, alpha-lapachone, beta-lapachone, dehydro-alpha-lapachone), anthraquinones (incl. methylanthraquinone, hydroxymethylanthraquinone, acetoxymethylanthraquinone, anthraquinone aldehyde, hydroxy- and methoxyanthraquinone, hydroxymethylquinone, tabebulin), lapachenol, flavanoid quercetrin, hydroxybenzoic acid, resin, tannins, minerals (incl. calcium, iron), trace minerals (incl. cobalt, silica), vitamins
Effective qualities: astringent, bitter, cold
　　　stimulating, restoring, astringing, decongesting
Tropism: intestines, lungs, veins, kidney, bladder, prostate, fluids, blood
　　　Lung, Large Intestine, Bladder meridians
　　　Warmth, Fluid bodies
Ground: all krases, biotypes and constitutions

FUNCTIONS AND INDICATIONS

1　**CLEARS DAMP-HEAT AND TOXIC HEAT, REDUCES INFECTION AND INFLAMMATION, AND STOPS DISCHARGE; ANTIDOTES POISON**

　　intestines damp-heat: burning, urgent bowel movement, chronic diarrhea with pus and blood
　　DIARRHEA, enteritis, colitis, dysentery
　　bladder and kidney damp-heat: urgent, burning urination, orange or red urine, thirst, fever
　　URINARY INFECTIONS (incl. cystitis, nephritis)
　　toxic heat: boils, sores, fevers, infections
　　PROSTATITIS, pharyngitis
　　BACTERIAL, VIRAL, FUNGAL and PARASITIC INFECTIONS (incl. candidiasis [intestinal, vaginal], yeast
　　　　infections, tinea, lung TB, herpes, influenza, polio, vesicular stomatitis, cervicitis, vaginitis;
　　　　schistosomiasis, malaria, acid-fast mycobacteria)
　　SNAKEBITES

2　**PROMOTES DETOXIFICATION, RESOLVES DAMP-COLD AND RELIEVES ECZEMA AND PAIN;
　　REDUCES TUMORS**

metabolic toxicosis with **damp-cold** *:* joint and muscle pains, dry skin rashes, malaise
RHEUMATISM, arthritis, syphilis
ECZEMA, PSORIASIS, scrofula
TUMORS (incl. malignant, esp. of esophagus, intestines, lung, prostate)

3   **PROMOTES EXPECTORATION, RESOLVES PHLEGM AND RELIEVES COUGHING AND WHEEZING**
lung phlegm-damp/cold: coughing with copious white sputum
BRONCHITIS (esp. chronic)

4   **VITALIZES THE BLOOD, REDUCES CONGESTION, ASTRINGES AND STOPS BLEEDING; RESTORES THE BLOOD**
venous blood stagnation: varicosities, fatigue, constipation
VARICOSE VEINS, hemorrhoids
ULCERS (incl. peptic, prostate, varicose)
HEMORRHAGE
LEUCORRHEA, ENURESIS
ANEMIA, chlorosis

5   **PROMOTES TISSUE REPAIR**
WOUNDS, skin ulcers, varicose ulcers

PREPARATION

Use: Pau d'arco bark is used in **decoction** and **tincture** form. Excellent **ointments** and **compresses** can be made for topical use in skin eruptions, ulcers, tumors and tissue trauma. **Douches** and **vaginal sponges** should be prepared for genital infections, including candidiasis, vaginitis and cervicitis.

Dosage: Decoction: 12-20 g
          Tincture: 1-3 ml at 1:2 strength in 45% ethanol
Larger doses are used in cancer treatment.

Caution: None, except in larger doses where nausea and vomiting may result. Combine then with an *antiemetic* herb such as Peppermint, Ginger or Iceland moss.

Note: The taxonomy and nomenclature of the tree from which this remedy is derived are both particularly confusing. The taxonomical confusion may originate with botanists and/or harvesters, because *Tabebuia* and *Tecoma* are both given as the genus names, with numerous species to each. Today, the species *Tabebuia avellanedae* is considered by many the ideal primary source of this remedy.

In everyday language, Pau d'arco and Ipe roxo are the most common, widespread names for those species found in Brazil. Lapacho is the common name for a certain species in Argentina and Paraguay, while the name Tahibo is commonly used for Peruvian species.

According to the research of Dr. MEIER in Argentina, the purple-flowered Argentinian species of Tabebuia may be somewhat more effective than the red-flowered Brazilian species.

NOTES

The inner bark of the red or violet flowered pau d'arco tree is one of an increasing number of South American botanicals currently emerging from traditional native use into the international arena—courtesy of extensive pharmacological research. Although its main application in the West is as an *anti-infective,* the remedy carries a rich legacy of successful empirical usage.

Even as an *anti-infective,* however, Pau d'arco bark doesn't work like a simple antibiotic drug. Instead, like all *anti-infectives* of botanical origin, it addresses particular types of infections better than others. Like Scutellaria Huang Qin (Baikal Skullcap root) in Chinese medicine, Pau d'arco bark is a prime **damp-heat** remover for the **intestinal** and **urinary tract.** Bacterial and viral infections such as enteritis with diarrhea, and cystitis, recede under its bitter, cold, astringent qualities. An *anti-inflammatory* action here joins the *antiviral, antibacterial* and *antifungal* actions that extend to herpes, candidiasis and other damp-heat generating yeast infections.

On a deeper level, Pau d'arco bark shows *resolvent detoxicant, diuretic, analgesic* and *antitumoral* properties that apply not only to infections in general but more specifically to conditions of both **microbial** and **metabolic toxicosis.** The remedy is perfect for those with painful arthritic conditions, skin disorders and tumors, including cancers. Operative here, as listed above, are long strings of naphthoquinone and anthraquinone glycosides.

Pau d'arco bark's *restorative* action on the veins (note the quercetrin) is joined by an *astringent* and *hemostatic* one. Together acting as *venous decongestants,* they will treat **venous blood stagnation.** Hemorrhage resulting from congested blood or infection can also be stopped as a result. This is partly also the basis for the remedy's excellent results in tissue healing, notably in **chronic ulcers.**

Empirically, Pau d'arco bark has also been used for managing diabetes, Hodgkin's disease and Parkinson's disease.

Horsetail Herb

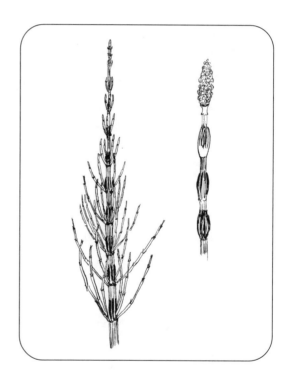

Botanical source: *Equisetum arvense* L. ,
      E. hiemale L. and spp. (Equisetaceae)
Pharmaceutical name: Herba Equiseti
Ancient names: Hippouris (Gk)
      Arcontilla, Asparilla, Corsandra (Lat)
Other names: Dutch rushes, Bottlebrush, Pewterwort
      (Eng)
      Shave grass, Joint weed, Bull pipes, Tad broom
      (Am)
      Prêle, Equisette, Queue de chat/de cheval (Fr)
      Ackerschachtelhalm, Zinnkraut, Schaftheu,
      Hermos, Katzenschwantz (Ge)
Part used: the herb

NATURE
Therapeutic category: mild remedy with minimal chronic toxicity
Constituents: silicic acid 5-8%, aconitic acid, saponin (equisetonin), flavonoids (incl. isoquercitrin, luteolin, kaempferol), alkaloids (nicotine, relustrine), bitter, equisitine, phytosterols, starch, potassium, calcium, trace minerals (incl. aluminum)
Effective qualities: somewhat bitter, astringent and bland, cold, dry
      astringing, stabilizing, dissolving, restoring, nourishing
Tropism: bladder, kidneys, lungs, intestines, bones, skin
      Kidney, Bladder, Liver, Lung, Large Intestine
      Warmth, Fluid
Ground: Melancholic krasss, biotypes and constitutions

FUNCTIONS AND INDICATIONS

1   CLEARS DAMP-HEAT, REDUCES INFECTION AND STOPS DISCHARGE

intestines damp-heat: frequent watery bloody stools, diarrhea
ENTERITIS (incl. dysentery)
bladder damp-heat: burning frequent urination, thirst
LOWER URINARY INFECTIONS (acute, incl. interstitial cystitis, prostatitis)
genitourinary damp-heat/cold: white or yellow vaginal discharges
VENEREAL INFECTIONS with DISCHARGE (e.g. vaginitis, gonorrhea)
skin damp-heat: swollen red painful sores, boils, lesions
EYE, mouth, gum and throat infections

2   ASTRINGES, REDUCES SECRETIONS AND STOPS DISCHARGE AND BLEEDING; PROMOTES TISSUE REPAIR

HEMORRHAGE (active or passive, internal or external, incl. metrorrhagia, epistaxis, hematuria, hemoptysis)
EAR, NOSE and THROAT discharges (simple or infected)
ALBUMINURIA, SEMINAL EMISSION
EXCESSIVE SWEATING from body or feet
PROSTATE ENLARGEMENT (benign)
CHRONIC ULCERS (internal and external, incl. peptic/leg/cancerous ulcers)
INJURIES (incl. wounds, fractures); chilblains

3   RESTORES MUSCULOSKELETAL AND CONNECTIVE TISSUE, REGULATES MINERAL METABOLISM, NOURISHES THE BLOOD AND RELIEVES FATIGUE; STRENGTHENS THE KIDNEYS, BLADDER, LUNGS, BONES AND CONNECTIVE TISSUE

musculoskeletal deficiency (Liver and Kidney depletion): debility, weakness and soreness, esp. of legs, knees, lower back, hair and nails; frequent fractures
SKELETAL and MUSCULAR WEAKNESS (incl. chronic arthritis, osteoporosis, lupus, muscular dystrophy)
DEMINERALIZATION, Paget's disease, mineral deficiency (incl. broken nails, split ends)
EPITHELIAL and CONNECTIVE TISSUE DEGENERATION
ANEMIA, DEBILITY
KIDNEY DEFICIENCY, glomerulonephritis
LUNG DISEASE (chronic and degenerative, incl. TB, emphysema, asthma)

4   TONIFIES URINARY QI, HARMONIZES URINATION AND RELIEVES PAIN

kidney and bladder Qi deficiency: frequent, dripping, scanty urination, lumbar pain, sperm loss
URINARY and SEMINAL INCONTINENCE, enuresis
bladder Qi constraint: urgent, difficult, irritated urination
NEUROGENIC BLADDER, DYSURIA, strangury

5   PROMOTES DETOXIFICATION, RESOLVES TOXICOSIS AND REDUCES PLETHORA; PROMOTES URINATION, DISSOLVES DEPOSITS AND BENEFITS THE SKIN

metabolic toxicosis: skin rashes, fatigue, malaise, scanty irritated urination
ECZEMA, ARTHRITIS, GOUT, CYSTS, dry skin (all chronic)
DEPOSITORY DIATHESIS with urinary stones, arteriosclerosis, atherosclerosis
general plethora: water retention, cellulite, obesity, hypertension

PREPARATION

Use: As with many other plants, the fresh expressed Horsetail herb **juice** is the most efficacious in its actions. Use only the early, green plant collected in May and June; the older plant becomes somewhat strong and toxic. The **decoction** must be simmered for up to 3 hours to extract all of Horsetail's constituents. Alchoholic preparations such as **tinctures** are not as good. The finely ground **powder** in tea or capsules may also be used internally and externally. Alternately, an **ointment** can be prepared. **Gargles, washes** and **poultices** are also effective.

In acute conditions, Horsetail should be taken internally and applied topically as powder or poultice.
Dosage: Juice: 2 tsp; **Decoction:** 2-5 g
       Tincture: 1-2 ml at 1:2 strength in 25% ethanol
Caution: When doing a course of Horsetail herb, it is advisable to ensure high vitamin B intake (e.g., nutritional or brewer's yeast), as this remedy favors breakdown of B vitamins. Beware of using Horsetail herb on its own for more than several weeks at a time, as it may cause some urinary irritation.

NOTES

A botanical relic from very ancient times, Horsetail grows the world over in different varieties. In China, for example, *Equisetum hiemale,* known as *mu zei,* is the species used in herbal medicine.

Horsetail herb presents an interesting paradox. It is a very clear example of a remedy used both for extreme *acute situations* such as inflammation, discharge and hemorrhage, and *long-term degenerative* conditions involving connective tissue metabolism, such as metabolic toxicosis, arthritis and osteoporosis.

Certainly its placement here among *astringent anti-infectives* means that it treats acute infection with discharge, in vitalistic terms damp-heat. Horsetail is an important remedy for clearing **damp-heat** involving the mucosa of the **intestines, bladder, kidneys** and **eyes.** Its cold, dry, astringent quality dries up excess mucus, reduces inflammation and clears exudates. Moreover, Horsetail can be used as an all-occasion remedy for acute discharges of many kinds, and includes *coagulant hemostatic, mucostatic* and *anhydrotic* actions. Therapeutic applications include bleeding, nasal, urinary and genital discharges and incontinence, and excessive sweating.

We will next attempt to explain Horsetail's other uses through a more unconventional route— using the priciples of plant bioenergetics as developed by RUDOLPH HAUSCHKA, WILHELM PELIKAN and others in the middle of the twentieth century. Horsetail herb's bioenergetic functions can be summed up as building up and regenerating substance, and regulating and creating surfaces. Its regenerating and nourishing effect is confirmed by its silicic acid and calcium content. Because these affect the bones, kidneys, lungs, brain and connec-

tive tissue, we may conclude that Horsetail restores Essence (*jing*). We also note the remedy's affinity for the element Earth. Here calcium and silica operate not only as substances, but also as bioenergetic activities. In the case of silica, they also enhance surfaces and promote surface tension, with the clinical result of stopping sweating, bleeding and, in fact, stopping any fluid discharge. Silica thereby also strengthens all epithelial and connective tissues—hence the use of Horsetail in all **chronic skin conditions, tissue degeneration** disorders such as arthritis, osteoporosis, peptic ulcers, and chronic lung and kidney disease. Silica is actually found in highest concentrations in these organs. It would clearly be no exageration to call Horsetail a *trophorestorative* to the **bones, kidneys, bladder, lungs** and **skin.**

The herb also helps keep all membranes flexible, especially the semi-permeable ones of the respiratory tract and kidneys. On the surface, silica energy renders the skin more supple by strengthening collagen and skin cells.

Horsetail herb's regulating effect is caused by the bioenergy aluminum. Although the plant actually contains some aluminum, the quantity present is unrelated to its effectiveness as a bioenergy on the energetic level. While harmonizing and enabling the work of silica and calcium energies, aluminum's effects are clear from Horsetail's excellent *resolvent* action with **hard deposits** and *detoxicant* action in conditions of **metabolic toxicosis** such as rheumatoid arthritis, gout and chronic eczema. The way it adjusts sweating and urination functions, and in fact all eliminative processes, is another example of its fundamental regulating character.

Bilberry Leaf and Fruit

Botanical source: *Vaccinium myrtillus* L. (Ericaeae)
Pharmaceutical name: Folium et fructus Vaccinii
Ancient names: Chamaimyrsine (Gr)
> Myrtillus, Avesperma, Mora agrestis (Lat)

Other names: Black whortleberry, Black whortle,
> Whinberrry, Dyeberry (Eng/Am)
> Myrtille, Airelle, Mourtré, Cousinier, Raisin des
> bois/de bruyère, Brimbailles, Abretier,
> Quéquénier (Fr)
> Heidelbeere, Waldbeere, Bickbeere, Mostbeere,
> Blaubeere, Besinge (Ge)

Part used: the leaf and fruit

NATURE

Therapeutic category: *leaf:* medium-strength remedy with moderate chronic toxicity
> *fruit:* mild remedy with minimal chronic toxicity

Constituents: *leaf:* tannins, glucoquinines, hydroquinone
fruit: tannins 6-20%, flavonoids (incl. arbutin, myrtillin, ericolin, anthocyanidins), hyperoside, asperuloside astragalin, coffeeic/chlorogenic/malic/citric acids, china acid 2-5%, pectin, minerals, bitter

Effective qualities: astringent, somewhat sour, cold, dry
> restoring, astringing, solidifying, stabilizing, calming, dissolving

Tropism: stomach, intestines, lungs, pancreas, eyes, arteries and capillaries, kidneys, fluids
> Large Intestine, Bladder, Stomach, Lung, Dai meridians
> Warmth, Air bodies

Ground: all for symptomatic use

FUNCTIONS AND INDICATIONS

1   **CLEARS DAMP-HEAT, REDUCES INFECTION AND INFLAMMATION, AND STOPS DISCHARGE; ELIMINATES PARASITES**

intestines damp-heat: urgent, painful passing of fetid loose stool, flatulence

ENTERITIS, dysentery, colitis

stomach damp-heat (stomach Qi stagnation): nausea, vomiting, diarrhea, swollen painful abdomen

ACUTE DYSPEPSIA, gastroenteritis

bladder damp-heat: painful urination, thirst

CYSTITIS with DYSURIA

EYE, MOUTH, GUM, TONGUE and SKIN INFLAMMATIONS (incl. conjunctivitis, gingivitis, periodontitis, stomatitis, dermatitis)

BURNS, scalds

CHRONIC DIARRHEA in all conditions

ROUNDWORMS (pinworms)

2   VITALIZES THE BLOOD, ASTRINGES, STRENGTHENS THE CAPILLARIES, RAISES CENTRAL QI AND STOPS PROLAPSE

venous blood stagnation: varicose veins, hemorrhoids, spontaneous bleeding, calf cramps, purpura

VENOUS DEFICIENCY, purpura

CAPILLARY FRAGILITY with spontaneous bleeding, periodontal disease

Central Qi sinking: heavy sinking, bearing-down sensation in lower abdomen

INTESTINAL or UTERINE PROLAPSE

EXCESSIVE SWEATING

3   RESTORES THE PANCREAS, STRENGTHENS THE LUNGS AND RELIEVES COUGHING

DIABETES, hyperglycemia (supportive)

LUNG ULCERS, LUNG TB

CHRONIC COUGHING

4   PROMOTES DETOXIFICATION, DISSOLVES DEPOSITS AND PROMOTES URINATION; RESTORES CONNECTIVE TISSUE AND BENEFITS THE SKIN AND VISION

ATHEROSCLEROSIS, hyperlipidemia

HYPERTENSION *(leaf extract),* abdominal plethora

HYPERURICEMIA, gout, rheumatoid arthritis

ECZEMA, dermatitis, dandruff

VISION IMPAIRMENT, poor night vision, near-sightedness

RETINAL/MACULAR DEGENERATION, diabetic retinopathy and cataracts

GLAUCOMA (esp. chronic)

PREPARATION

Use: Bilberry leaf and fruit are prepared by short **decoction** or **tincture.** Both plant parts have a wide range of therapeutic actions and are generally best used together to reinforce each other and to represent as much of the whole plant as possible. Having said that, however, the *dried leaf* is especially useful for hypertension (function 4), strengthening the pancreas and lowering high blood sugar (fn.3). The *dried fruit* is best for treating intestinal damp-heat conditions (fn. 1), venous blood stagnation (fn. 2), vision impairment and other ocular conditions (fn. 4). Note however that Bilberry leaf has a caution attached to its use, unlike the fruit (see below).

Chewing the dried berries for intestinal infections has been tried and tested in Europe and by Native Americans. The *fresh* berries, however, are appetite-restoring and flatus-relieving, and may be used for relief of constipation.

Bilberry juice, prepared from the fresh berries, treats inflammatory and infectious (damp-heat) intestinal conditions. Note that the juice must not be sweetened, as sweeteners render it therapeutically ineffective. For damp-heat conditions Bilberry juice combines well with quark (ricotta) as a medicinal food.

Bilberry wine is a traditional European panacea for a variety of digestive complaints. The warming quality of the wine provides effective symptom relief for indigestion with pain from damp-cold.

An excellent **mouthwash** for the mouth and gums (especially bleeding gums) can be made with the berry or juice. External **washes** are useful for inflammatory skin and eye complaints.

Dosage: Short decoction of the **leaf** (5-10 minutes): 6-10 g

      Short decoction of the **berry** (5-10 minutes): 8-12 g

      Tincture of the **leaf or berry**: 1-3 ml at 1:2 strength in 30% ethanol

      Juice of the leaf: 2 tsp

Caution: Contraindicated in stomach cold conditions and not to be used on its own with diarrhea from intestines cold (Spleen and Kidney Yang deficiency).

Bilberry *leaf* contains the toxic compound hydroquinone, making this a medium-strength remedy. If used on its own for diabetes or bladder infections, the leaf should not be taken continuously as it may cause mild toxicosis. After three weeks a break of another three weeks would be advisable before resuming use. As with most herbs in this category, Bilberry leaf is ultimately best used in a formula.

Note: According to old-time Austrian herbalist RICHARD WILLFORT, Bilberry leaves should be picked before the fruits ripen to ensure highest levels of myrtillin, one of the leaves' active glycosides.

There are many other *Vaccinium* species in the Heath family which have some of the properties of Bilberry, but none is an exact substitute for Bilberry. Most of them have been called "blueberry" at some time to the point of immense general confusion.

• *V. ovatum* is the **Huckleberry** or Blueberry of the Western States, also useful (like Bilberry) for cystitis and for hyperglycemia in juvenile-onset diabetes.

• *V. angustifolium* is the **Late lowbush blueberry** of the Eastern States, traditionally used by Native Americans for colic, labor pains and postpartum uterine tonic.

• *V. oxycoccos* is **Cranberry;** the *berry juice* is known for its ability to reduce urinary tract infections. Cranberry poultices are excellent for chronic ulcers of all types, boils, sore throat, tonsilitis and erysipela.

• *V. vitis-idaea* is the European **Cowberry,** Red whortleberry or Alpine cranberry, an edible fruit. The *leaf* of this plant, which contains ursone and arbutin, is used similarly to Uva ursi leaf for treating acute urinary tract infections with its *antiseptic* action; it is also *hypoglycemiant* in high blood sugar conditions, treats diarrhea with its astringent quality and is a traditional *detoxicant* for gout and rheumatic conditions.

NOTES

Bilberry, sometimes confusingly also known as Blueberry, was well known among healers in the distant past. Although widely used by illiterate wise woman practitioners, the remedy was first written about by the medieval herbalist, musician and mystic, HILDEGARD OF BINGEN. She recommended using Bilberry leaves and fruits for respiratory complaints, a popular use that has survived intact in Europe to the present day.

Despite the fact that Bilberry leaf today is fashionably used for treating vision disorders, its central use is still roughly the same as it was 2,000 years ago—for treating diarrhea arising from **damp-heat** in the **intestines.** The remedy's astringent, cold, dry qualities qualify it perfectly for hot or inflammatory conditions with discharges. Its considerable *antiseptic* and *anti-inflammatory* actions arise from a potent cocktail of flavonoids and tannins. Bilberry equates here with an acupuncture point complex such as CV 10, LI 4, St 44, Li 8 and St 25. It also relates to the way the bitter, yellow, berberine-rich roots of Chinese medicine, such as Coptis Huang Lian, have been used in China for an equally long time.

Bilberry is also an important digestive remedy for acute upper gastric disorders, i.e., **stomach damp-heat**—as seen in acute forms of (gastro)-enteritis. Its action here can be enhanced and deepened with bitters such as Wormwood herb and Gentian root.

Because it lifts Central Qi and treats intestinal and uterine prolapse, we can confidently assign Spleen and Stomach meridian entering properties to this valuable remedy. All tissues are restored, strengthened and solidified, including those of the pancreas, lungs and venous and capillary blood vessels. Although Bilberry leaf has had a checkered reputation in treating diabetes in particular, it will adequately serve this purpose, especially if the leaves are collected before the fruit ripens (see Note above).

In the treatment of **venous blood stagnation** with varicose veins (including hemorrhoids), Bilberry is also valuable—especially with **metabolic toxicosis** presenting high lipid counts and arthritic tendencies. Horsechestnut and Yarrow herb would be complementary remedies here.

Bilberry leaf and fruit has currently become popular for treating **vision disorders,** as well as for enhancing vision stressed by job or lifestyle-related constraints—such as working at computers for long hours, the classic example. Modern research has in fact demonstrated *antioxidant* and *capillary restorative* activity in its anthocyanic glycosides. These actions prevent free radical damage and reduce capillary fragility to strengthen and protect the retina. Combining Bilberry with Ginkgo leaf will considerably reinforce this action (see Holmes 1997).

Loosestrife Herb

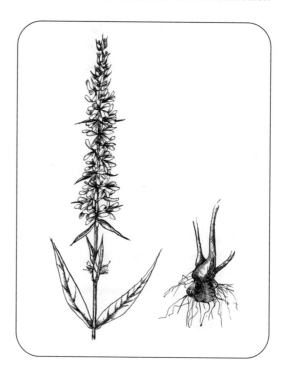

Botanical source: a) *Lythrum salicaria* L.
    b) *Lysimachia vulgaris* L. (Lythraceae)
Pharmaceutical name: Herba Lythri
Ancient names: a) Lytron (Gr)
    Salicaria, Lysimachia spicata purpurea (Lat)
    b) Lysimachion (Gr)
    Lysimachia lutea (Lat)
Other names: a) Red sally, Pong purples,
    Willow herb (Eng)
    Purple loosestrife, Sage willow (Am)
    Salicaire, Lysimaque rouge (Fr)
    Blut Weiderich, Purpurweiderich, Blutkraut,
      Katzenwendel (Ge)
    b) Yellow/Golden loosestrife, Willowwort (Eng)
    Cornéole, Soulcie d'eau, Percebosse (Fr)
    Gelber Weiderich, Gold-Weiderich,
      Gilbfelberich (Ge)
Part used: the herb

NATURE

Therapeutic category: mild remedy with minimal chronic toxicity
Constituents: a) glycosides (vitexin and salicarin), polyphenolic tannins 10%, essential oil, ellagic and other acids, narcissin, orietin, pectin, resin, mucilage, iron
b) flavonoids (incl. rutin, myricetin, quercetin, kaempferol, leucodelphinidin, leucocyanidin), caffeic acid
Effective qualities: somewhat astringent, bitter and bland, cold, both moist and dry
    astringing, restoring, stimulating
Tropism: intestines, urogenital organs, kidneys
    Large Intestine, Lung, Liver meridians
    Warmth, Air bodies
Ground: all krases, biotypes and constitutions

FUNCTIONS AND INDICATIONS

1 **CLEARS DAMP-HEAT AND REDUCES INFECTION AND INFLAMMATION; STOPS DISCHARGE AND BLEEDING**

intestines damp-heat: painful, bloody loose stools, diarrhea
ENTERITIS (incl. of breastfeeding infants; dysentery, cholera)
PASSIVE HEMORRHAGE (from all parts, esp. uterine bleeding)
GENITAL DISCHARGES with PRURITUS in all conditions (incl. vaginitis, leucorrhea, spermatorrhea)
MOUTH, GUM and THROAT INFLAMMATIONS (e.g., gingivitis, stomatitis, laryngitis)
DIARRHEA in all conditions

2 **PROMOTES URINATION, RESOLVES TOXICOSIS, AND BENEFITS THE VISION AND SINEWS**

kidney Qi stagnation: skin rashes, painful dark urination, malaise, blurred vision
VISION IMPAIRMENT or disturbances
WEAK MUSCLES and TENDONS

3 PROMOTES SWEATING, DISPELS WIND HEAT AND EASES THE THROAT

external wind-heat: chills, fever, painful swollen throat

COLD and FLU onset with fever

4 PROMOTES TISSUE REPAIR AND RESOLVES CONTUSION

WOUNDS, ulcers, sores, eczema, bites (esp. with inflammation and bruising)

PREPARATION

Use: Loosestrife herb is best used in **infusion** or **tincture** form. **Salves, washes, gargles** and **enemas** may be prepared for topical use. **Douches** and **pessaries** are excellent for genital discharges with itching.

Loosestrife herb was traditionally used for **fumigating** or **smudging** places to keep away mosquitoes, flies, insects, snakes and such. As a garden ornamental it was said to attract butterflies.

Dosage: Infusion: 6-10 g

Tincture: 1-3 ml at 1:3 strength in 30% ethanol

Caution: None

Note: While the **Purple loosestrife** is preferred medicinally in America, past European practitioners such as REMBERT DODOENS from Antwerp admonished his readers "to take none other than that with the yellow flowers [**Yellow loosestrife**], which is the true *Lysimachia,* because although others at present bear the same name, they have neither the same properties nor effects." The symptom indications for both types of Loosestrife are close enough, however, to justify using them interchangeably.

In addition to these two types, *Lysimachia numularia,* **Penny loosestrife** or **Moneywort** (Herbe aux deniers, Petite monnaie (Fr), Schlangenkraut, Wiesengold, Kreisend-Wundkraut (Ge) has also been used interchangeably. In China *Lysimachia christinae* is the main botanical sources for Jin Qian Cao, but is used more for its *cholagogue* and *stone-dissolving* effects than anything else (see HOLMES 1997).

NOTES

Every *astringent* has its advantages and disadvantages, and Loosestrife is no exception. When used in the most appropriate situation, however, it has only advantages. These are easy to see in Loosestrife, which combines good astringency with stimulation.

Like Bayberry bark, this herb is both a bitter-cold *astringent* and an *arterial stimulant.* Moreover, with its mucilage content, Loosestrife effectively prevents any drying out of tissues, especially the mucosa. **Intestines damp-heat** conditions where inflammation causes **dryness** benefit especially from its use, as well as individuals presenting constitutional dryness.

As a *stimulant diaphoretic* Loosestrife herb treats **wind-heat** onsets of flus and upper respiratory infections manifesting sore throat and fever.

With its content of rutin and other glycosides, it is worth trying out the Yellow loosestrife herb for **inflammatory** and **allergic** conditions such as rhinitis, eczema, mouth ulcers, and so on.

In Europe the herb is pervasively used to enhance vision, much like Bilberry. This is due to more than its *detoxicant* action through enhanced *diuresis.* Rutin is known to lower inner eye pressure in conditions such as glaucoma, for example, while the other glycosides may act similarly to Bilberry leaf and fruit to strengthen the eye capillaries in various vision disorders.

Wood Sorrel Herb

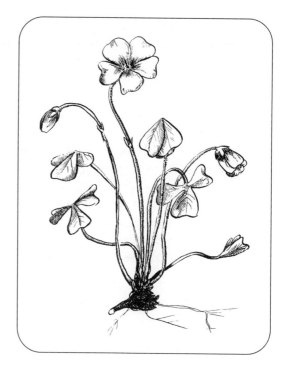

Botanical source: *Oxalis acetosella* L.,
  O. corniculata L. and spp. (Oxalidaceae)
Pharmaceutical name: Herba Oxalis
Ancient names: Oxalys (Gr)
  Acedula, Alleluia, Cuculopanis, Alaula,
   Trifolium acetosum (Lat)
Other names: Sorrel, Trefoil, Wood sour, Stickwort,
  Stabwort, Hallelujah, Cuckoo's bread,
   Fairy bells (Eng)
  Trèfle aigre, Alléluia, Pain de coucou, Surelles,
   Surettes, Aigrette, Herbe de boeuf (Fr)
  Sauerklee, Buchampfer, Hasenklee,
   Guckauchsklee, Gauchklee (Ge)
Part used: the herb

NATURE

Therapeutic category: mild remedy with minimal chronic toxicity
Constituents: potassium oxalate (0.3 - 1.25%), oxalic acid, organic acids, enzyme
Effective qualities: sour, astringent, cold, dry
  calming, sinking, astringing, restoring, dissolving
Tropism: liver, stomach, intestines, kidneys, bladder, blood
  Liver, Kidney, Stomach, Large Intestine meridians
  Warmth, Air bodies
Ground: Choleric krasis
  Tough/Shao Yang and Industrious/Tai Yang biotypes
  all three constitutions

FUNCTIONS AND INDICATIONS

1 **CLEARS DAMP-HEAT, REDUCES FEVER AND INFLAMMATION, AND RELIEVES THIRST; STOPS BLEEDING**

intestines damp-heat: urgent bowel movement, burning liquid stools, diarrhea
ENTERITIS (incl. bacterial dysentery)
liver fire: thirst, dry mouth and throat with bitter taste, intense headache, congested head and face
FEVERS, CHOLECYSTITIS, jaundice
kidney fire: high fever, blocked urination, pain in kidney region, unproductive sweating
ACUTE NEPHRITIS
stomach fire: thirst for cold water, fetid breath, mouth ulcers and sores
GASTRIC HYPERACIDITY (with or without ulcers), heartburn
blood heat: spontaneous bleeding, fever, thirst
HEMORRHAGE (internal or external, esp. in excess conditions; incl. nosebleeds, bleeding gums)

2 **REDUCES LIVER CONGESTION, STIMULATES THE APPETITE, SETTLES THE STOMACH AND STOPS VOMITING**

liver blood congestion: abdominal distension, fatigue, appetite loss, low fat tolerance

LIVER CONGESTION, hepatic or gastric dyspepsia

abdominal plethora: overweight, abdominal distension, fatigue

INTESTINAL PARASITES

stomach Qi reflux: nausea, vomiting

3   PROMOTES URINATION, PREVENTS DEPOSITS AND ANTIDOTES POISON

kidney Qi stagnation: fetid stool, poor appetite, dry skin

DEPOSITORY DIATHESIS with biliary or urinary stones, arteriosclerosis (preventive)

MERCURY and ARSENIC POISONING

4   PROMOTES TISSUE REPAIR AND REDUCES INFLAMMATION

WOUNDS (acute or chronic)

MOUTH and THROAT ULCERS (indolent or malignant), aphthous sores, scurvy

CANCEROUS ULCERS and TUMORS

heat toxin: boils, sores, abscesses, fever

SKIN and MUCOSA INFLAMMATION

PREPARATION

Use: Wood sorrel herb should be used fresh for best results because drying impairs some of its properties. The fresh herb **juice, infusion** and **tincture** are therefore the best preparations.

Sorrel herb eaten in **salads** alongside purslane, endive, lamb's lettuce and chickweed is excellent for hot/ inflammatory conditions, including mouth ulcers. These nutritious greens also make tangy, refreshing hot weather salads.

Sorrel **mouthwashes, gargles** and **compresses** are all prepared for inflammatory and infectious conditions. Paradoxically, a **compress** of the cooked leaves is also used to promote the resolution of cold abscesses. In Parkinson's disease, Wood sorrel can be taken internally and applied directly on the spine.

Dosage: Juice: 2 tsp

      Infusion: 4-8 g

      Tincture: 1-3 ml at 1:3 strength in 25% ethanol

Caution: Do not overdose, because large doses of oxalic acid may cause gastric and other upsets. Avoid using Wood sorrel herb in rheumatic and gouty disorders, as the high oxalic acid content may cause irritation in these conditions.

Note: Other sorrel types may be substituted for Wood sorrel, but are traditionally considered less effective for the above actions and indications. Other sorrels include **Sheep's sorrel,** *Rumex acetosella,* (see below), **Garden sorrel,** *Rumex acetosa,* and several other species in the *Rumex* genus.

NOTES

In the traditional Galenic pharmacy Wood sorrel herb occupied a major position in the section of cooling remedies and was represented by such preparations as the wine, distilled water, ointment, conserve and so on. In those days this plant belonged to the clover or trefoil family, which included melilot, red clover, bogbean and wild indigo. These herbs were called yellow clover, red clover, marsh clover and clover bloom, respectively. This makes complete sense, especially from the therapeutic viewpoint: all these botanicals are used in conditions of **heat, toxicosis** and **infection.** All could have been placed in this section were they not more outstanding in other functions.

Wood sorrel herb is an important *refrigerant* remedy that addresses acute hot conditions of most of the internal organs through its combined *antipyretic, anti-inflammatory, atringent* and *antiseptic* actions. The herb is a good demonstration of the heat-clearing effects of the primary energetic qualities of sour, astringent and cold, resulting from its high content in organic acids and potassium oxalate. Three conditions are particularly amenable to Wood sorrel's *refrigerant* influence. **Liver fire** with acute cholecystitis and fever; **stomach fire** presenting mouth ulcers, bleeding gums or simply gastric hyperacidity; and **intestines damp-heat** with acute enteritis such as bacterial dysentery. The herb basically addresses **Qi** and **blood-level heat** presenting intense thirst, fever and stopped urination. Acupuncture points LI 11, Sp 10, Bl 54, Kd 2 and Li 1 would be a comparable point selection.

Liver blood congestion and **abdominal plethora** involving portal blood congestion are two further important syndromes that Wood sorrel will treat. With a significant tropism for the liver and blood vessels, this remedy is a rational alternative to Goldenseal root for treating this condition.

Botanically speaking, Wood sorrel belongs to the *Oxalidaceae,* i.e., the oxalic acid forming plants. Oxalic acid results from the same bioenergies in all species of this plant genus. It is believed by some European practitioners that these bioenergetic processes present an interesting therapeutic upshot. According to this controversial perspective, all plants containing oxalic acid would be superb in preventing **mineral** and **heavy metal deposits**— for example, biliary and urinary stones, hardening of the arteries, heavy metal accumulation, and so on. Although oxalic acid-containing plants do not treat depository conditions once they are present, for individuals with this constitutional tendency they *may* provide a radical preventive treatment of the ground by stimulating oxalic acid release. In this connection, the related **Sheep's sorrel** herb is an important ingredient in the Canadian Essiac formula. which has empirically been found useful in reducing tumors, including early stage cancer.

Lady's Mantle Herb

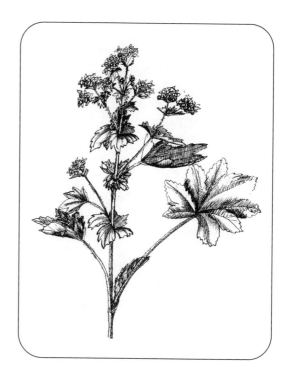

Botanical source: *Alchemilla vulgaris* L. (Rosaceae)
Pharmaceutical name: Herba Alchemillae
Ancient names: Sanicula major, Stellaria, Alchimilla,
   Pes leonis, Leontopodium, Drosera, Drosium
   (Lat)
Other names: Great sanicle, Nine hooks, Lion's foot,
   Bear's foot (Eng)
   Alchémille, Pied de lion, Manteau de Notre
   Dame/des dames, Porte-rosée, Pinou,
   Patte de lapin (Fr)
   Frauenmantel, Taumantel, Taubecher, Sinnau,
   Mutterkraut, Frauenhilf, Ohmkraut,
   Grosser Sanikel, Marienmantel (Ge)
Part used: the herb

NATURE
Therapeutic category: mild remedy with minimal chronic toxicity
Constituents: tannins 6-8%, gallotannins, tannic glycosides, salicylic acid, phytosterol, saponins, bitters, lecithin, linoleic acid, fixed oil
Effective qualities: astringent, somewhat bitter, cold, dry
   calming, astringing, stabilizing, decongesting, restoring
Tropism: blood, liver, gallbladder, intestines, urogenital organs
   Liver, Spleen, Bladder, Large Intestine, *chong, ren* meridians
   Warmth body
Ground: all krases, biotypes and constitutions

FUNCTIONS AND INDICATIONS

1 CLEARS DAMP-HEAT, REDUCES INFLAMMATION, ASTRINGES AND STOPS DISCHARGE

genitourinary damp-heat: white or yellow vaginal discharges with blood, painful urination
CERVICITIS, endometritis
bladder damp-heat: frequent, urgent painful urination, backache, fever, blood in urine
URETHRITIS, cystitis
stomach and intestines damp-heat: painful, urgent, bloody stool, diarrhea, epigastric pain
ENTERITIS (incl. dysentery); COLITIS, acute gastritis
PELVIC INFLAMMATIONS (esp. chronic, incl. salpingitis, cervicitis; vulvular pruritis)

2 CLEARS HEAT, REDUCES FEVER AND STOPS BLEEDING

liver fire: bursting headache, irritability, fever, insomnia
HIGH FEVER
liver blood congestion: abdominal distension, lethargy, fatigue, low fat tolerance
blood heat: spontaneous bleeding, early or heavy menstruation, uterine bleeding
HEMORRHAGE (incl. from lower and upper orifices, ruptures, wounds)
UTERINE BLEEDING (incl. MENORRHAGIA, intermenstrual, postpartum, perimenopausal)

3 PROMOTES URINATION, DISSOLVES DEPOSITS, REDUCES PLETHORA AND RELIEVES OVERWEIGHT

abdominal plethora: overweight, abdominal distension, sluggishness
OBESITY, weight gain
ARTERIOSCLEROSIS, ovarian cysts

4 TONIFIES REPRODUCTIVE QI, HARMONIZES MENSTRUATION AND MENOPAUSE; INCREASES HORMONES (?) AND ENHANCES LABOR

PROGESTERONE DEFICIENCY conditions (?), incl.:
PMS with swollen or lumpy breasts, irritability, withdrawal, sexual disinterest
DYSMENORRHEA with cramps before flow, heavy flow; congestive dysmenorrhea
MENOPAUSAL SYNDROME with bleeding, hot flashes, sexual disinterest
DIFFICULT LABOR, failure to progress; habitual miscarriage

5 RESTORES THE NERVES, RELIEVES PAIN AND PROMOTES REST

nerve deficiency: weakness, weak muscular force in children, headache, sleep loss
HEADACHE in deficiency conditions
INSOMNIA

6 PROMOTES TISSUE REPAIR, REDUCES INFLAMMATION AND RELIEVES PAIN

INJURIES (external and internal, esp. with bleeding, discoloration and pain, incl. wounds, ulcers
    [incl. suppurative, varicose, gangrenous], fractures, bruises)
EYE, MOUTH, THROAT and GUM INFLAMMATIONS (incl. with bleeding)
heat toxin: boils, carbuncles with heat and redness
ENLARGED BREASTS

PREPARATION

Use: Lady's mantle herb is prepared by **infusion** and **tincture.** Both are excellent bases for preparations in gynecological, genitourinary and tissue trauma conditions. **Suppositories, pessaries, douches, compresses, washes, gargles** and **ointments** are some possibles here.

For acute conditions, Lady's mantle is usually quite effective on its own but will always be enhanced with other astringents, hemostatics, anti-inflammatories and so on. The remedy may be taken extensively where chronic conditions require it—but should be discontinued if it causes constipation (courtesy of the tannins).

Dosage: Infusion: 8-14 g

Tincture: 2-5 ml at 1:3 strength in 30% ethanol

If being used to clear heat, 60-80 g of the herb (or 2-3 tsp of the tincture) may be used.

Caution: Contraindicated in stomach-intestines (Spleen) cold or damp-cold syndromes because of its cold, astringent quality.

NOTES

To the beauty-loving Humanist doctors of the 1500s, Lady's mantle was a very interesting plant. With its dark moss-green nine-rayed leaves with scalloped borders, not to mention its beleaged collection of evocative Latin names, Lady's mantle truly inspired these classicists. They delighted in conjuring up fanciful conjectures about the plant. One such anecdote is that alchemists at one time made use of the dew droplets that collect in the plant's leaves for preparing their longevity elixirs. Their imagination on a roll like the mercury dewdrops trickling down its leaves, the Humanists finally christened the herb *Alchemilla*. It would have been fascinating to discuss the origin of this story with someone like the brilliant botanist and linguist CHARLES DE L'ECLUSE.

The conceits of these *literati* were justified, however, to the extent that Lady's mantle is both an attractive garden plant and a reliable medicine. DE L'ECLUSE's portrayal of the plant's morphology is worth consulting, as "his descriptions are remarkable because of their unsurpassed precision, elegance and technique." We are quoting one of the most trustworthy and insightful of medical historians, OLIVIER DEZEIMERIS, from his 1828 *Dictionaire historique de la médecine ancienne et moderne*.

The Belgian physician REMBERT DODOENS, who was DE L'ECLUSE's contemporary, wrote extensively about Lady's mantle's medicinal values. In his 1554 herbal DODOENS states that "it strongly resembles Sanicle in its faculties, and applies to all the conditions in which Sanicle is used." In those days both herbs were reckoned among the elite of trauma remedies alongside Plantain leaf and Tormentil root. We cannot contradict this practice, especially as purulent wounds and swollen, painful injuries go. Here, as in Meadowsweet herb and Birch leaf, the salicylic acid content mingles with the tannins and acids for good *anti-inflammatory, analgesic* and *detoxicant* effects, resulting in a prime *vulnerary* herb.

Whereas past herbals class Lady's mantle as a *vulnerary,* we choose rather to place it among the *refrigerant* botanicals. With its astringent, bitter, cold qualities, this remedy specifically clears damp-heat of many kinds, especially **urogenital damp-heat** with yellow vaginal discharges, urinary infections and dysuria. Chronic and subacute **gynecological inflammations** of many kinds will also benefit, but will often need the back-up of *anti-infectives* such as Marigold flower and Echinacea root. We are also looking at a major *hemostatic* remedy for **hemorrhage, spontaneous bleeding, fever** and **skin rashes,** especially when arising from **blood heat.** In cases of perimenopausal hemmorhage, for instance, Lady's mantle can be enhanced with Birthroot (for its similar action) and Chasteberry (for hormonal regulation)

It is interesting to note that Lady's mantle was one of many plants traditionally called "Motherwort" by European wise woman healers. It was one of several remedies reputed for their wonderful action on the mother, or womb. The same bioenergies and constituents that make it a *vulnerary* also make Lady's mantle a *menstrual regulator* and *uterine toner*—an important woman's remedy, in short.

More than anything else, **menstrual flooding** in all **congestive** conditions of medium severity call for its use. When these conditions are present, possibly due to low progesterone levels, Lady's mantle is also the right remedy. Here the herb will find congenial reinforcement from Class 14 *uterine decongestants* such as Shepherd's purse, Partridgeberry, Blackhaw, Red root and many others.

This "Great sanicle" closely resembles Sanguisorba Di Yu and Sophora Huai Hua Mi in the Oriental materia medica. Like Pasqueflower, however, Lady's mantle also has a *relaxant* and *sedative* edge that is welcome in these conditions. Its reputation as a *nervous restorative* is still alive in the European folk tradition, and may find some justification in light of the lecithin content.

Small wonder that BERGZABERN's compendious herbal of 1588 devotes three large folio pages to prescriptions based on Lady's mantle.

Sanicle Herb

Botanical source: *Sanicula europaea* L. (Rosaceae)
Pharmaceutical name: Herba Saniculae
Ancient names: Sanaria, Solidago, Diapense,
      Ferraria maior (Lat)
Other names: Wood sanicle, Self-heal, Poolroot,
      March (Eng)
    Sanicle, Sanicle d'Europe (Fr)
    Sanikel, Heildolde, Wundkraut,
      St. Laurentzenkraut (Ge)
Part used: the herb

NATURE
Therapeutic category: mild remedy with minimal chonic toxicity
Constituents: ascorbic, malic, citric, oxalic acids, resin, ess. oil, tannins, bitter, allantoin, saponins
Effective qualities: somewhat astringent, bitter and pungent, cold, dry
    calming, astringing, stabilizing, restoring, stimulating

This remedy is virtually identical in nature, functions and uses to Lady's mantle herb (above), being used interchangeably with the latter in the past. The following differences should be noted, however:

1   Sanicle in addition has a *stimulant expectorant* effect useful in **lung phlegm-heat** syndromes with respiratory infections, especially at the beginning stages.
2   Unlike Lady's mantle, Sanicle is definitely not *hormonal* or *uterine stimulant* in action (function 4)

Uva Ursi Leaf

Botanical source: *Arctostaphylos uva ursi* L.
(Ericaceae)
Pharmaceutical name: Folium Arctostaphyli cum
fructu
Other names: Bearberry, Rapper dandies, Brawlins,
Cranberry, Gnashaks (Eng)
Bearberry, Kinnikinnik, Sagackhomi,
Mountain box, Sierra/Alpine bearberry,
Mealy plum vine, Hog cranberry (Am)
Busserole, Arbousier, Raisin d'ours, Olonier,
Petitbuis, Arbre aux fraises (Fr)
Bärentraube, Moosbeere, Sandbeere, Harnkraut,
Wilder Inchs, Wolfsbeere, Achelkraut, Garlen,
Granten (Ge)
Part used: the leaf and fruit

NATURE

Therapeutic category: mild remedy with moderate chronic toxicity
Constituents: flavonoids (incl. arbutin 5-18%, methylarbutin, ericolin, ericinol ursone), quercetin- and myricetin-like flavonoids, gallic and ellagic tannins (up to 15%), gallic/malic/ursolic/phenolic/ursodes-oxycholic acids, triterpenoids, myretene, resin (ursone), allantoin, uvaol, resin urvone, essential oil traces, minerals and trace minerals (incl. iron, calcium, chromium, selenium, magnesium)
Effective qualities: astringent, cold, dry; the *berry* is also somewhat sweet
astringing, solidifying, stabilizing, restoring, calming
Tropism: urogenital organs, intestines
Bladder, Kidney, Large Intestine, Liver meridians
Warmth, Air bodies
Ground: all krases, biotypes and constitutions

FUNCTIONS AND INDICATIONS

1 **CLEARS DAMP-HEAT, REDUCES INFECTION AND INFLAMMATION, AND STOPS DISCHARGE**
bladder and kidney damp-heat: frequent, urgent, painful urination, dry mouth
URINARY INFECTIONS (esp. acute, incl. urethritis, cystitis, pyelitis, glomerulonephritis); prostatitis
large intestine damp-heat: painful, urgent defecation, pus and blood in stool, scanty urine
DYSENTERY, enteritis, colitis
genitourinary damp-heat: thick, fetid purulent genital discharges, mucous and blood in urine,
frequent, scanty painful urination
VENEREAL INFECTIONS with DISCHARGE (incl. gonorrhea, cervicitis, vaginitis, candida)

2 **ASTRINGES AND STOPS DISCHARGE AND BLEEDING; PROMOTES TISSUE REPAIR**
HEMORRHAGE (acute and chronic, incl. blood in urine, stool or spittle, uterine bleeding, menorrhagia)
DIARRHEA (in excess conditions, esp. chronic)
GENITAL and URINARY DISCHARGES
HEMORRHOIDS
BLADDER ULCERATION

SPRAINS, swellings, sore spongy gums, canker sores

POSTPARTUM TISSUE TRAUMA

3   TONIFIES UROGENITAL QI, HARMONIZES URINATION AND RELIEVES IRRITATION;
RESTORES THE PANCREAS

kidney and bladder Qi deficiency with damp: lower back soreness, frequent scanty, dripping urination, bedwetting, prostate irritation, vaginal discharges, seminal emissions

URINANRY INCONTINENCE and IRRITATION from any cause

URINARY STONES (esp. with infection)

DIABETES (supportive), GLYCOSURIA

DERMATITIS

4   PROMOTES CONTRACTIONS AND ENHANCES LABOR

DIFFICULT LABOR

FAILURE to PROGRESS

PREPARATION

Use: Uva ursi leaf is prepared by **long infusion** or **tincture.** For the long infusion, steep the leaves in cool water for 12-24 hours; warm up before drinking. This method preserves the glycosides and essential oils, and is the best preparation for damp-heat conditions such as acute inflammatory bowel and urinary infections.

Uva ursi leaf should not be over nine months old, or it may have lost its arbutin content and therefore most of its medicinal value. It is then still effective for toning and astringing the urogenital organs, however. Leaves and berries gathered in autumn are the most effective overall, and alpine plants are definitely stronger than lowland ones.

Internal hemorrhoids will benefit from a Uva ursi **suppository. Sitzbaths, sponges** and **douches** are excellent for gynecological and postpartum perineal tissue trauma, where they will also prevent infection. Whole **body baths** have successfully been used for chronic TB and rheumatic conditions.

Dosage: Infusion: 4-8 g

   Tincture: 1-3 ml at 1:3 strength in 45% ethanol

Caution: Care should be taken if Uva ursi is used alone longer than just a few days, as its tannin content may slightly upset the stomach. Bearberry should be alternated every week or two with other similar remedies in this class or, better still, combined with a *demulcent* such as Licorice root, Linseed or Codonopsis Dang Shen. In the unlikely case that irritation persists, Cranberry or Pear leaf should be used instead. Although their tannin content is lower, their arbutin content is also lower.

Uva ursi leaf has been used to promote labor contractions with its *oxytocic* action, and is therefore contraindicated during pregnancy. Avoid also in kidney disease and prolonged use in children because of possible liver impairment.

Note: Uva ursi's major *antiseptic* and *anti-inflammatory* component is arbutin. Because arbutin can only be transmuted into hydroquinone in an alkaline ph environment, it is important when using this remedy to ensure alkaline conditions through a vegetarian diet high in vegetable content.

Manzanita leaf, from *Arctostaphylos* species of shrubs/trees in the North American Pacific West, may be used interchangeably with Uva ursi leaf. The chemical and energetic profile of both herbs is very similar, and their uses, dosages and cautions are the same

NOTES

The history of Uva ursi's medicinal uses demonstrates the extent to which a plant's therapeutic efficacy depends on the skill of its user rather than on the plant itself. Almost forgotten in European Galenic medicine, once introduced to the American continent, Uva ursi leaf became a top quality medicinal in the skilled hands of natives. A mention by CHARLES DE L'ECLUSE (1601), who was a botanist, not a physician, and by the pharmacist GERHARD (1763), does not alter the story. The fact remains that, until very recently, Uva ursi leaf was forgotten in Europe as a therapeutic tool. Even the encyclopedic dinosaur tomes of Renaissance apothecarist J.J. BERGZABERN (see Chapter 6) fail to show an entry for this remedy.

Uva ursi leaf was known well enough in the more distant past in Scandinavia and the British Isles. Welsh Myddfai physicians made extensive use of it, for example. It was then neglected for over a millenium and finally rediscovered on the other side of the Atlantic by Native Americans. Or did the latter receive this remedy from the early Vikings in the course of their frequent North American visits in the first centuries A.D.? Like the migration of plants around the world, the migration of herbal remedies from one continent to another often remains a mystery and a matter of speculation rather than fact.

At any rate, we do know that Native Americans used Kinnikinnik — as one tribe called this herb — for urogenital incontinence, urogenital infections and urinary stones. Native Oregonians believed the berries helped the bears, who ate massive amounts of them each fall, procure a deep, regenerating winter's sleep. This bush was appropriately known as "Bear's bilberry" and "Bear's whortleberry." Farther southeast, Spanish and French missionaries reported cures of gonorrhea with extracts prepared from the entire plant. The Cheyenne and Sioux used the whole plant for promoting labor contractions. Meanwhile, according to reports of eighteenth century fur traders of the Scottish Northwest Company, certain tribes such as the Nez Percé, Crows, Modocs, Cayuse and Yakimas were using the leaves in a longevity electuary, mixed with honey, flower pollen and other unidentified herbs.

Uva ursi is a remedy with limited, specific applications, rather than a rainbow spectrum of uses like Yarrow herb and Vervain herb. Above all, Uva ursi clears **urogenital damp-heat** and tonifies **urinary Qi deficiency.** Its dry, astringent, cold qualities, assisted by *antiseptic* and *lenitive* properties, make it more appropriate for acute than for chronic infections, and apply to both urinary and intestinal infections — and especially those with blood in the discharge.

Uva ursi leaves are very high in tannins, flavonoids and minerals, which support these two primary uses. Uva ursi's actual *diuretic* effect is minimal, which shows that promoting urination with a *diuretic* is not the only, or even main, way to clear urinary damp-heat. Therapeutically the remedy is very close to some Chinese herbs of the same class, such as Phellodendron Huang Bai and Gardenia Shan Zhi Zi (neither of which is *diuretic,* either). It could serve as an excellent replacement for these if required. For damp-heat conditions in the lower warmer, Uva ursi combines well with such cool *demulcents* as Cornsilk, Plantain leaf, Couch grass root and Hydrangea root bark, paralleling an acupuncture point combination such as Bl 53, 27 and 28, Li 8, CV 3 and Bl 17.

If we wish to apply Uva ursi's *antiseptic* and *anti-incontinence* actions for cases of **chronic damp-heat** or **chronic infections** with urinary incontinence, then the remedy should be combined with active *diuretics* that drain fluids to flush the area through: Dandelion root, Horsetail herb and Lovage root, for example. In this connection, Uva ursi also enjoys a good reputation for preventing stone formation, as an *antilithic* remedy, like Hydrangea root and Madder root.

White Willow Bark

Botanical source: *Salix alba* L. (Salicaceae)
Pharmaceutical name: Cortex Salicis albae
Ancient names: Itea (Gr)
Other names: White willow, Sallow tree, Saugh,
     Wythy, Geese and goslings (Eng)
     Saule blanc, Saule argente/commun,
      Osier blanc (Fr)
     Silberweide, Wilgenbaum, Felbinger (Ge)
Part used: the bark; also the flower (catkin),
     Flos Salicis

NATURE

Therapeutic category: mild remedy with minimal chronic toxicity
Constituents: glycoside salicin, phenolic glycosides (up to 11%), flavonoids, tannins 8-20%, resin, enzyme, salicortin, fragilin, triandrin, vimalin, bitter yellow pigment, organic acids, aromatic aldehydes
Effective qualities: astringent, somewhat bitter, cool, dry
     calming, astringing, stabilizing
Tropism: urogenital organs, liver, stomach
     Bladder, Kidney, Heart, Stomach meridians
     Warmth body
Ground: all krases, biotypes and constitutions

FUNCTIONS AND INDICATIONS

1   **CLEARS DAMP-HEAT AND REDUCES INFECTION AND INFLAMMATION;
STOPS DISCHARGE AND BLEEDING, AND RELIEVES PAIN**

     bladder damp-heat: burning dark urine, painful urination, thirst, fever
     URINARY INFECTIONS and IRRITATION
     JOINT, THROAT, MOUTH and EYE INFLAMMATIONS from INFECTION
     HEMORRHAGE (passive, from mouth, nose, wounds)
     MUCOUS DISCHARGES (chronic, esp. in dysentery, diarrhea)
     GASTRIC HYPERACIDITY
     PAIN in general (incl. headaches, rheumatic pain, neuralgia)

2   **CLEARS HEAT AND REDUCES FEVER;
REDUCES SEXUAL OVERSTIMULATION AND PROMOTES REST**

     heart and Kidney Yin deficiency (Yin deficiency* with *Kidney fire*): insomnia, restlessness, wet dreams,
      sexual overstimulation, premature ejaculation
     SEXUAL OVERSTIMULATION (nymphomania, satyriasis, erotomania)
     GENITAL DISCHARGES (incl. nocturnal emissions, vaginitis, esp. with *damp-heat* or *empty heat*)
     LOW-GRADE TIDAL FEVERS (*shao yin* stage)

3   **STIMULATES DIGESTION AND APPETITE**

stomach Qi stagnation: slow painful digestion, epigastric pain and distension, appetite loss
GASTRIC DYSPEPSIA

4   **PROMOTES TISSUE REPAIR AND REDUCES INFLAMMATION**

WOUNDS, ulcerations, eczema, gangrene
BURNS, scalds

PREPARATION

Use: White willow bark is prepared by **decoction** or **tincture.** Topical preparations such as **washes** and **compresses** are best made from the decoction.
Dosage: Decoction: 2-10 g
         Tincture: 1-4 ml at 1:2 strength in 45% ethanol
Caution: Overdosing may cause internal bleeding and excitability. Use with care during pregnancy.
Note: Black willow bark from *Salix nigra* L. (and to some extent the **berry**) is used in a similar way to this remedy. This tree is also known as Pussy willow and in German as Purpurweide, Bach-/Hand-/Rosen-/Hange-weide. It is especially *anaphrodisiac* and *nervous sedative* (function 2 above) and *antidischarge,* and is specifically given in ovarian pain (e.g., during ovulation), gonorrheal discharges, nocturnal emissions (wet dreams), premature ejaculation, and topically for chronic indolent ulcers, gangrene and poison ivy/oak dermatitis. Eclectic doctors considered Black willow "unrivalled" for these topical uses. Dose: as above.

    Black willow bud (botanically an ament) was extensively used by Eclectic practitioners for its superior *anaphrodisiac* action in conditions of sexual overstimulation, including that of adolescence. This *genital sedative* remedy is given in such conditions as premature ejaculation, wet dreams and erotic obsessions. Dose: as above.

NOTES

The bark of a large variety of Willow trees is used for two broad therapeutic actions: for its heat-clearing and pain-relieving effects. Both actions depend on a combination of several biochemical constituents, particularly the various glycosides and tannins.

As a heat-clearing *antipyretic* remedy, Willow bark is important for treating the **empty heat** of **Yin deficiency** conditions—whether the mechanism is hyperemia, inflammation or fever. Like Artemisia Qing Hao in Chinese medicine, it is one of the best agents for the *shao yin* stage of illness where vital defenses are more than just a little weak, and where fever is an exhausting, recurrent evening time flickering of empty heat. Here Willow bark will benefit from the support of other *restoring* remedies such as American ginseng root, Wahoo root bark and Elecampane root. Other congenial herbs that clear empty heat may be teamed up with it, such as Poplar bark and Pipsissewa herb.

Alternatively, Willow bark is used for chronic inflammation, infection and pain, providing good symptom relief for these conditions. Here its acids, tannins, glycosides, aldehydes and salicin conspire to produce a reliable *anti-inflammatory, analgesic, astringent* and *antiseptic* remedy that can be appropriately added to virtually any condition requiring these actions.

There is one Chinese syndrome that fits this remedy especially well: **Heart and Kidney Yin deficiency.** This syndrome can include urogenital discharges and sexual overstimulation. In the first century, DIOSKURIDES already used **Willow catkins** for treating this syndrome, a use confirmed by the clinical experience of the French herbalist physician HENRI LECLERC (1935). It is unclear whether the catkins (used more in Europe) or the bark (used more in America) is more effective in this respect. Regardless, in addressing genital emissions due to Heart and Kidney Yin deficiency with empty heat, Willow bark corresponds to acupuncture points Kd 3 and 12, Li 2 and 3, Sp 6, Bl 52, 23 and 15, and Ht 7.

Because it focuses on the urogenital tract, Willow bark can also clear **damp-heat** in this area, especially in acute urinary infections. In treating genital emissions resulting from damp-heat in the lower warmer, Willow bark is equivalent to the points St 28, CV 3 and 6, Sp 6 and 9, Li 8, Kd 3.

In addressing three types of hot conditions, Willow bark reminds us of the Chinese remedy Phellodendron Huang Bai. The difference between them is this: Huang Bai is used to treat heat toxin in addition to clearing damp-heat and empty heat, whereas Willow bark is used to relieve symptoms of pain of any kind. Keeping this difference in mind, the two remedies may be interchanged in complete confidence.

Cornsilk Style

Botanical source: *Zea mays* L. (Poaceae/Gramineae)
Pharmaceutical name: Stylus Zeae
Other names: Maize (Eng)
> Maïs, Froment des Indes, Blé de Turquie, Gaude (Fr)
> Mais, Kukurutz, Indianisches Korn (Ge)
> Yu Mi Xu, Yu Mi Rui (Mand)
> Yuk Mai So, Yuk Mai Yeui (Cant)
> Gyokumaishu (Jap)

Part used: the style

NATURE
Therapeutic category: mild remedy with minimal chronic toxicity
Constituents: saponins, glycosides, allantoin, tannins, resins, volatile alkaloid, phytosterols, fixed oil 5.25% (incl. oleic/linoleic acid), thymol, mannite, maizenic/silicic/palmitic/malic/tartaric/oxalic acid, clotting factors, vitamins C and K, albuminoids, gum, glucose, maltose, phlobaphene, calcium, potassium, trace minerals (incl. fluorine, silica)
Effective qualities: somewhat sweet and astringent, cool, drying and moistening potential
> nourishing, restoring, stimulating, dissolving, softening
Tropism: urogenital organs, gallbladder, arteries, fluids
> Bladder, Kidney, Gallbladder meridians
> Warmth, Fluid bodies
Ground: Choleric and Sanguine krases
> Tough/Shao Yang and Charming/Yang Ming Earth biotypes
> Hematogenic/Sulphuric and Biliary/Phosphoric constitutions

FUNCTIONS AND INDICATIONS
1 **CLEARS DAMP-HEAT, REDUCES INFECTION AND INFLAMMATION, AND STOPS DISCHARGE; PROMOTES BILE FLOW AND REDUCES LIVER CONGESTION**

> *bladder and kidney damp-heat:* urgent, painful urination, mucous discharges in urine
> URINARY INFECTIONS with DISCHARGE (acute and chonic, incl. nephritis, cystitis, pyelitis, urethritis, prostatitis)

gallbladder damp-heat: nausea, vomiting, flank and side pain

CHOLECYSTITIS, cholelithiasis

JAUNDICE, hepatitis from liver/gallbladder congestion

2 **PROMOTES URINATION, RESOLVES TOXICOSIS AND DRAINS WATER;
DISSOLVES DEPOSITS AND STONES, AND RELIEVES IRRITATION**

kidney Qi stagnation with *metabolic toxicosis:* urinary irritation, skin rashes, muscle or joint aches

URIC ACID DIATHESIS with urinary irritation (hyperuricemia)

DEPOSITORY DIATHESIS (incl. arteriosclerosis, stones)

URINARY STONES (oxalic, uric, phosphatic)

ALBUMINURIA

OLIGURIA, ANURIA

DYSURIA (bladder irritation or pain, in any condition)

kidney water congestion: bloating from water retention, esp. in legs

EDEMA (renal, cardiac)

PREPARATION

Use: Cornsilk style is used in **infusion** or **tincture** form. For best results, these should be made from the fresh styles, i.e., the cornsilk, picked when the corn is in milk.

Dosage: Infusion: 10-16 g

Tincture: 2-5 ml at 1:2 strength in 25% ethanol

Caution: None

NOTES

Every part of the corn has served as food and medicine among native North and Central American peoples. When some of these people's medical practices were passed on to European colonists, the knowledge of Cornsilk's reliable properties crossed over with them. Cornsilk's reputation among early pioneers as *the* remedy for acute urinary tract infections was unrivaled and has survived untainted to the present day. Since Cornsilk's introduction to China, it has maintained its reputation among doctors of Oriental medicine as well.

Cornsilk style is also versatile in herbal medicine. It is an archetypal *urinary demulcent,* providing *lenitive, anti-inflammatory* and *antiseptic* actions when required. By transforming damp-heat in the lower warmer, Cornsilk addresses **bladder damp-heat** presenting dripping, scanty, painful urination. For symptom relief, any urinary irritation will be helped, whether due to infection, excess uric acid or stones. Cornsilk is one of several bland, vaguely sweet tasting botanicals, similar to Couchgrass root, Red clover flower and Imperata Bai Mao Gen (Woolly grass root), that rely on an assortment of trace minerals, organic acids and tannins for their *refrigerant* and *urinary sedative* effect. These properties were used by the Central American Aztecs—if we can rely on the *Badianus Manuscript* to accurately reflect their extensive medical knowledge—to clear "heat in the heart" just like Dianthus Qu Mai is used in Chinese medicine.

With its heat-clearing and damp-draining energetic properties, Cornsilk style also addresses **gallbladder damp-heat** and **gallbladder fire,** e.g., in (sub)acute gallstone attack displaying sharp right flank pains. This remedy's *cholagogue* action may also be used (as in China) for simple jaundice. As a *hepatobiliary sedative* Cornsilk closely resembles Lysimachia/Desmodium Jin Qian Cao which—like Cornsilk—is routinely used throughout China for preventing and treating urinary stones.

Cornsilk style's excellent *diuretic* action has three main clinical implications. First, a *fluid-draining* effect used in **edema.** Second, a *dissolvent* action used for treating urinary stones and other **depository conditions** such as arteriosclerosis. Third, a *detoxicant* and *uric acid-clearing* action used in **hyperuricemia** and **metabolic toxicosis** with resultant rheumatic disorders.

Cornsilk style is often found in formulas because of the wide range of urinary disorders that it can treat and because of its reliable action.

PERSONATIA   Groß Kletten.

Herbs for Altering and Regulating

Herbal remedies that alter and regulate are classed as follows:

Class 13   *Resolvent detoxicants:* Promote detoxification and resolve toxicosis
Class 14   *Decongestants:* Vitalize the blood, reduce congestion and moderate menstruation
Class 15   *Mucostatics:* Resolve mucous-damp congestion and stop discharge
Class 16   *Hormonal regulators:* Regulate endocrine functions

The Nature and Dynamics of Altering and Draining

Herbs that alter and regulate are used to cause physiological changes aside from those induced by eliminating, restoring and draining remedies. They are often called *alterative* or *altering* remedies because they promote qualitative alterations or transformations in the system without promoting elimination, restoration or draining. *Detoxicants*, for example, reduce general toxicosis and thereby treat chronic skin, muscle and joint disorders. Likewise, *decongestants* reduce internal congestion of the venous circulation.

Alteratives also have *regulating* functions: bringing a balance to the fluids, the circulatory, nervous and endocrine systems They neither restore where there is deficiency, nor drain or eliminate where there is excess, but simply alter and regulate a qualitative imbalance. In traditional Greek medicine (TGM) this type of condition was called a *dyskrasia*. In essence, *alterative* remedies address a dyskrasia of either fluids, blood, mucus, nerves or hormones.

Altering and Regulating as a Principle of Treatment

Like Restoring and Draining, Altering as a treatment principle is a general one. It addresses whole patterns of disharmony and represents the third type of constitution-altering treatment method. Moreover, Altering is usually required in treating chronic, longstanding conditions. In this sense it stands polarized to Eliminating, which is primarily indicated for acute conditions. Altering focuses on transforming an internal harmful (toxic) accumulation such as metabolic wastes, mucus, stagnant blood or hormones, whereas Eliminating aims to remove a surface eliminatory obstruction such as closed pores, edema, stool or phlegm. In this sense Altering and Regulating is the equivalent of Reducing (*xiao fa*) in Oriental medicine—an appropriate term because the end-result of qualitative alteration is a reduction of stagnant toxins, blood, mucus and nerve and endocrine functions. Deep systemic changes may be effected with *alterative* remedies, for which reason they are more often combined with *restoratives* and *drainers* than are any other kinds of herbs.

We should note that the meaning of the word "alterative" in the last three hundred years has undergone several changes. Today it has been reduced to mean a "blood cleanser." Because the concept of blood cleansing has progressively been abandoned as being physiologically imprecise, the concept of an *alterative* has been jettisoned along with it. Here we are simply redefining *alteratives* in the original sense intended by GALEN, as well as in the Chinese sense of *harmonizing*. They are remedies that implement a specific treatment strategy, not a kind of physiological action—which is where the confusion arises. Class 13 remedies that promote detoxification therefore merely represent one kind of *alterative*, namely the one that works on the fluids and blood. The other *alteratives* in this section affect the circulation, mucus membrane and nervous and endocrine systems.

Class 13   Resolvent Detoxicants

Herbs to Promote Detoxification and Resolve Toxicosis

Known as *detoxicants,* herbal remedies in this class promote detoxification, also known as cleansing. They embody the treatment strategy of promoting detoxification in conditions of toxicosis, the internal accumulation of harmful toxins. Toxicosis may present conditions as varied and generalized as fatigue, headaches, insomnia, proneness to infection, eczema, fibromyalgia and arthritis. By assisting the body's innate vital defensive ability to identify and process harmful (toxic) substances, *detoxicants* promote a systemic alteration in the overall quality of the internal environment and thereby help resolve both endogenous and exogenous forms of toxicosis. Promoting detoxification is the most fundamental treatment strategy among the Altering and Regulating methods of treatment.

The Nature and Dynamics of Toxicosis— A New Approach

Because the concept of toxins has historically been so closely linked with the body's natural discharges, any discussion of body toxins is bound to reveal our basic attitude to the body and its eliminations. The attempt in the last two-hundred years of the heroic school of Western naturopathic medicine to achieve a sterile, toxin-free state through drastic elimination methods can now be seen as misguided. This attitude is actually parallelled by modern allopathic medicine, which is also based on the concept of physiological asepsis—a notion disproved as long ago as the 1920s by GÜNTHER ENDERLEIN's pleomorphic microbiology. This attempt arose mainly from the ancient patristic Judaeo-Christian notion of the need to purify the "unclean temple" of the body. It was motivated by the wish to cure the countless disorders supposedly generated by the presence of toxins (compare Note 2 in Class 1).

From the fifteenth century on, practitioners of traditional Greek medicine believed that detoxification was only possible by causing an actual elimination, such as sweat, stool, urine, sputum and even menstruation, vomiting and bloodletting. In the nineteenth century, the therapeutic emphasis on eliminating toxins was reinforced by a one-sided search-to-destroy approach to microorganisms in general. The importance of the body's own symbiotic, eubiotic bacterial and fungal hosts and the ultimately productive function of infections was entirely misunderstood and therefore ignored—as it still is in orthodox Western medicine today. This one-sided view was based on a conceptual separation of the human and nature, in which the individual was seen in isolation from the environment, with no interplay of microorganisms and energies between them.

Today we know that it is quite impossible to be totally toxin free: the intestinal microflora, the interstitial fluid and the connective tissue that it permeates are always bathed in toxins of many kinds. The microflora, liver, spleen and immune system are continuously working together to neutralize circulating toxins, while the kidneys, intestines, skin and lungs further select and eliminate them. The interstitial fluid reservoir and its hub, the intestinal microflora, is the mobile, ever-changing arena in which the opposing processes of self-toxification and self-detoxification play out their destiny. Toxification and detoxification thereby form a continuous dualistic cycle, much like the process of nutrient assimilation and toxin rejection itself. As living beings we cannot escape toxins and thrive in sterility.

Nor should we wish such a sterile, toxin-free state on ourselves. With a more gentle, trusting and inclusive view of the body's natural metabolic and elimination processes—a holistic Daoist and Wise Woman view—we can begin to accept toxins as an integral part of our wholeness. ("Love your toxins.")

The parallel here on the psychological level is the integration of the dark side of ourselves into our conscious personality ("Love your shadow self.") Ultimately, the most level-headed approach is to consider a certain level of endogenous toxicosis in the connective tissue "reservoir" entirely normal and acceptable. This is an interesting paradox, because the very definition of "toxin" is something injurious to the body.

Likewise, on the assimilation end, we also know now that our symbiotic intestinal microbes, which constitute the living organism we call the intestinal microflora, is in fact vital to our health and very survival—it's an intrinsic part of what we are. Composed of hundreds of fungal and bacterial strains, the microflora has shown to perform such essential anabolic and catabolic functions as assisting in enzyme production, helping in the production and utilisation of vitamins, regulating intestinal PH and stimulating antibody formation, as well as ensuring detoxification on a very essential level. When this living microbial organism deteriorates in quality through increased microbe multiplication and change of form (pleomorphism), it becomes toxic to us. Because this commensal organism represents an internalisation of the external world through nutrient and microbial intake, the intestinal microflora ultimately is a living emblem of our identity with the environment.

Using this holistic approach to toxins as a basis, we can then differentiate between an acceptable level of toxin accumulation and a pathological one. This differentiation is analagous to and largely represented by the difference between a normal intestinal microflora—an **intestinal eubiosis**—and an imbalanced one—an **intestinal dysbiosis.** Intestinal eubiosis therefore ultimately defines the healthy functional balance between toxin production, transformation and elimination. A pathological toxin level is simply one where disharmony or disease arises, as defined by the individual.

Because toxins may build up from endogenous (internal) or exogenous (external) origins, it's useful to divide toxicosis into these two types. **Endogenous toxicosis** commonly involves the production of microbial toxins through intestinal dysbiosis, and metabolic toxins through dysfunctions of protein, fat and calcium metabolism. **Exogenous toxicosis,** on the other hand, usually results from the accumulation of chemical and heavy metal environmental pollutants. Moreover, endogenous and exogenous forms of toxicosis can aggravate each other (not much is yet known about this), and both in turn predispose to infection, especially viral, fungal and parasitic infections. In addition, from the clinical perspective it is also necessary to consider the syndrome (symptom picture) presentation, regardless of the type of toxicosis presenting.

The Prevention and Treatment of Toxicosis

The treatment of toxicosis involves transforming rather than eliminating toxins, as the detoxification process fundamentally entails an alteration of the internal environment, not an elimination of body waste—a qualitative, not quantitative, change. Significantly, this concept is implicit in the traditional Greek medical syndrome used to denote a general state of toxicosis, **fluid dyskrasia.** This term literally denotes an imbalance among the body fluids. In terms of the body's organ functions, it would make sense then to simply assist them in their role of detoxification, not to short-circuit the toxin-transformation process by causing forced eliminations.

In all cultures physical exercise and detoxification practices have traditionally been an integral part of hygiene and health maintenance. Therapeutic food preparing and the practice of maintaining a good diet in balance with one's constitution, the environment and the seasons are also important hygiene components of most traditional cultures. These practices support assimilatory, detoxificatory and eliminatory functions through exercise, massage, nutritional therapy (dietetics), fasting and the taking of herbal remedies. There is no lack of information on these methods, either traditional or modern, available today.

Most forms of toxicosis at first may produce nothing more than low-level, minor but often chronic symptoms such as of malaise, tiredness, irritability, headaches, poor sleep, food intolerances, rough or dry skin, strong smelling urine or stool, and a proneness to infections. This would be called the preclinical phase of autotoxicosis, which corresponds to the Greek syndrome fluid dyskrasia. The syndrome presentation will jointly be determined by the type of toxic insult and the predisposing constitution. For this stage of low-level toxicosis, it is a recommended to gently and regularly stimulate internal and excretory organs— the liver, intestines, kidneys, skin and lungs especially—creating herb combinations from the *stimulants* (Class 8) and *eliminants* (Classes 1-5).

Because toxicosis so often involves deficient digestive, urinary and circulatory functions, the functional integrity of these organs, as well as of all elimination channels should always be ensured with the use of organ-specific *trophorestoratives*, whatever the condition. At the same time it is important to support the liver in its toxin-neutralizing function with Class 9 *liver-protective* remedies.

This may be all that is required at this initial subclinical stage to restore normal functioning and prevent toxicosis from progressing. As toxicosis progresses it predisposes to chronic inflammatory, infectious, hypersensitivity, depository, immunodeficiency and tumoral disorders. The constitutional ground of the individual will determine the type of disorder that actually manifests—for example, whether acute or chronic, hot or cold in nature.[1] Stronger and more specific *alterative detoxicant* remedies from this class will then need to be adopted.

Endogenous Forms of Toxicosis

At various times in the past, build-up of endogenous wastes was variously known as feculence, impure blood and sludged blood. Today endogenous toxicosis is more specifically described as a process of autotoxicosis, or self-poisoning (RECKEWEG), because the poisons found in the system are generated by the body itself.

Endogenous toxicosis assumes two primary forms, microbial and metabolic. Although these both may seem to pale in significance compared to today's rampant forms of exogenous toxins, they are actually major contributors to many of today's common disorders, including candidiasis, fibromyalgia and food allergies in general. *Clinically it is important to recognize that it is the toxicosis that is causing these diseases with its many and confusing symptoms, not the diseases that are causing the symptoms.* It is the confusion between underlying disease conditions and disease entities that leads to the erroneous belief that "such and such" is the cause of one-thousand and one diseases.

Microbial Toxicosis

Microbial toxicosis is the result of a dysbiosis of the intestinal microflora creating toxins. Here the microflora shows inhibited nutrient transformation and, in tandem, lowered capacity to transform and detoxify digestive toxins. These digestive toxins include amines, bile toxins, exotoxins, endotoxins and various carcinogenic toxins. Microbial toxicosis can also involve obstruction by mucus of the colon's lymphatic filters, causing impaired intestinal assimilation with toxin seepage into the circulation—also known as **leaky gut syndrome.** Once absorbed, the toxic byproducts of the gut's bacteria and fungi can significantly disrupt normal processes, leading to the following forms of pathology:

- **allergic,** including food allergies, atopic dermatitis, asthma and rhinitis;
- **inflammatory,** including acute fibromyalgia, pancreatitis, arthritis, pelvic inflammatory disease and ulcerative colitis; these are also often involved in hypersensitivity disorders;
- **infectious,** including candidiasis, viral and parasitic infections and duodenal ulcers;
- **autoimmune,** including psoriasis, lupus, Crohn's disease, myasthenia gravis, rheumatoid arthritis and autoimmune thyroiditis (as antibodies formed against microbial antigens cross-react with the body's own tissues);
- **tumoral** and **cancerous** forms of pathology.

In vitalistic terms, microbial toxicosis generally presents symptom patterns of either **damp-heat** or **toxic-heat,** which may be more systemic or more localized.

Treatment should proceed on various levels:

1. Regulation of the dysbiotic microflora through careful food combining, individual food selection and lactobacillus acidophilus/bifidus and colostrum supplementation is fundamental. Important also is adequate intake of dietary vegatable fiber, which constantly binds and eliminates gut toxins.

2. Elimination of toxins using *broad-spectrum anti-infective, detoxicant* herbs such as Garlic bulb, Horseradish root, Milkthistle seed, Burdock root, Oregon grape root, Marigold flower, Wormwood herb, Chaparral leaf and Pau d'arco bark. Pure essential oils such as Lemon, Grapefruit, *Juniper berry, Palmarosa, Myrrh, Thyme, Tea tree* and *Niaouli* may also be used by gel capsule or suppository administration.

3. Liver support to reduce hepatic toxicosis with Class 9 *liver protectives* such as Licorice root, Dandelion root, Milkthistle seed, Artichoke leaf, Turmeric root and Schisandra berry, as well as through *liver detoxicants* that clear damp-heat (see below).

4. Reduction of the free radical burden using *antioxidant* remedies and supplements, such as

Turmeric root, Bilberry leaf, Ginkgo leaf, Reishi mushroom, pycnogenol, coconut oil, and so on.

Metabolic Toxicosis

Metabolic toxicosis arises primarily from metabolic dysfunctions in the interstitial fluid environment that involve disorders of protein, fat and calcium metabolism. The main precursors of inefficient nutrient breakdown, transportation and utilization, and toxin elimination, is Liver insufficiency with congestion, biliary and pancreatic enzyme deficiency, and kidney insufficiency. The resultant toxic metabolites that remain in the system include uric acid, urea, chlorides, ammonia, and fatty and mineral deposits in general. These metabolic toxins then create various chronic types of pathology:

• **immunodeficiency** conditions, including herpes, chronic fatigue syndrome (CFS) and AIDS.

• **catarrhal (mucousy), disorders,** including lymphadenopathies, chronic bronchitis and chronic eczema.

• **inflammatory** conditions such as gouty arthritis, dermatitis, psoriasis, fibromyalgia and various other rheumatic conditions.

• **depository** conditions, including fatty deposits causing e.g., atherosclerosis and cellulite, and mineral deposits causing arteriosclerosis and urinary and biliary stone formation.

In syndrome terms, metabolic toxicosis presents **damp** and **toxic-cold.**

Treatment aims to enhance protein metabolism at both the digestive assimilation and the kidney elimination end:

1. Increased protein breakdown with bitter *digestive stimulants* such as Dandelion root, Barberry bark, Centaury herb, Wormwood herb and Gentian root generally aid in protein breakdown by increasing digestive enzyme release.

2. Elimination of metabolites like uric acid and urea, using d*iuretic kidney restoratives,* i.e., the *diuretic detoxicants* that drain damp (see below), such as Cleavers herb, Goldenrod herb and Dandelion leaf, to increase kidney efficiency.

3. Other remedies should be chosen according to the type of pathology presenting (see the summary of conditions above and the *detoxicant* herb actions below).

Exogenous Forms of Toxicosis

In the case of toxicosis arising from environmental pollutants, the causes are external as opposed to self-generated. The main types of toxicosis are chemical accumulation, heavy metal accumulation, radiation accumulation and food toxicosis (causing food allergies). Heavy metal and chemical toxins are particularly ubiquitous—in the air, in food and water. Although exogenous toxins are nothing new —they have always existed in every civilization to some extent—there are two new factors that are making their onslaught on physiological balance particularly damaging. First is the large range of chemical compounds now present in the soil and food chain since the rise of carbon chemistry. Second is the contamination of air and food with the heavy metals produced by modern industry. Chemical and heavy metal toxic factors then both combine with the microbial and metabolic forms of toxicosis to systemically disrupt internal homeostasis in a vicious interplay of the organic and inorganic. For the modern practitioner, untangling the predisposing and triggering toxic causes of contemporary disorders such as chronic fatigue syndrome or candidiasis often becomes a nightmare of injurious relationships and vicious cycles.

Fortunately, there *are* methods available to anyone for protection from exogenous toxicosis, as well as treatment of its resultant disorders—once the toxic factors have successfully been identified. Foremost among these are fasting and elimination diets involving vegetable and/or fruit juice. Fasting is an important treatment well known for enhancing the body's ability to neutralize and eliminate all forms of toxins—chemical, metallic, microbial and metabolic. Good references for fasting and elimination methods are generally available.

For quicker and often safer results in detoxifying chemicals and heavy metals, there is an increasing number of herbs and nutritional supplements now available. Garlic, Milk thistle seed and Lovage root have shown good protective effects against heavy metal and chemical poisoning, and the latter two may help with heavy metal chelation and elimination. Modified citrus pectin and the broken-down cell wall of *Chlorella* and other microalgae also are known to chelate exogenous toxins. Coriander (Cilantro) herb may also be helpful, but is still unproven from the scientific perspective. Herbs and amino acids are also important for providing specific support of tissues and organs directly affected by toxic insult. With symptoms and disorders actually present, herbal remedies from this section again provide superlative specific treatment.

Chemical Toxicosis

The types of chemical toxins at large range from pesticides, herbicides, organichlorides, food, perfume, cosmetic and tobacco additives, to medical and pleasure drugs (including alcohol and nicotine) and chemical solvents (including formaldehyde, benzene, toluene and various cleaning materials). Exposure to these mainly affects two body systems: the nervous system and the liver. Chemicals act as both neurotoxins and hepatotoxins.

1. Chemical toxins directly inhibit brain and nervous functioning. Signs of chemical toxicosis include such neurological and psychological symptoms as chronic headaches, mental depression, mental confusion, various mental disorders, tingling or numbness in the extremities and abnormal nerve reflexes. **Reproductive disorders** such as impotence, infertility and low sperm count have recently also shown to be implicated. Most of these symptoms can be classified under the syndromes **nerve and brain deficiency** and **reproductive Qi deficiency,** both of which correspond in Oriental medicine to a **Kidney Essence deficiency.**

In addition to the natural chelating agents mentioned above (e.g. Coriander, Chlorella) to address the chemical toxicosis, the following should be selected, depending on the situation:
• *Nervous restoratives*, including Gotu kola herb, Sage leaf, Rosemary leaf, Basil herb, Milky oat berry, St. John's wort, Gotu kola herb, Schisandra berry and Polygonum He Shou Wu root.
• *Reproductive restoratives* are Oat berry, Saw palmetto berry, Blue cohosh root and Flower pollen, as well as the Chinese herbs Polygonum He Shou Wu and Alisma Ze Xie.

2. Chemical toxins directly affect their conjugation/breakdown by the liver, leading to chronic low-grade **liver Yin deficiency** (see p. 411). This in turn lays extra stress on the spleen and immune systems. Not suprisingly, typical disorders of chemical toxicosis therefore also include immediate hypersensitivity disorders, i.e, **allergic disorders** such as rhinitis, middle ear inflammation (otitis), atopic eczema and asthma. These often present as **wind-heat** or **toxic-heat** conditions.

Liver Yin restoratives with *liver-protective* action are here the remedies of choice (Class 9).

Examples would be Licorice root, Milk thistle seed, Dandelion root, Artichoke leaf, Schisandra berry (Wu Wei Zi), Astragalus root (Huang Qi) and Prepared rehmannia root (Shu Di Huang). For metabolic support, remedies with *antioxidant* action are also essential, such as Licorice root, American ginseng root, Eleuthero root, Chaparral leaf, Turmeric root and Reishi mushroom (Ganoderma Ling Zhi). Important *antiallergic* remedies include Flower pollen, Goldenrod herb, Camomile flower, Nettle herb, Garlic bulb, Baical skullcap, Schisandra berry and Ephedra herb.

Heavy Metal Toxicosis

Environmental heavy metals currently present include lead, mercury, fluoride, arsenic, thallium, asbestos, carbon monoxide and many others (a fairly comprenehensive list with disorders they may cause is available elsewhere (e.g., SCHECHTER 1990, MURRAY and PIZZORNO 1991). In heavy metal toxicosis it is again the nervous system (especially the brain) and the liver that take the main brunt. Here, however, a wide range of other tissues and organs are also affected secondarily. Typical signs of subclinical heavy metal toxicosis are fatigue, headaches, dizziness, absent-mindedness, concentration difficulties, loss of coordination, muscle pains, indigestion and constipation. A wide range of disorders, including eczema, hair loss, visual disorders, cancers, anemia, bone disease, hypertension, kidney disease and learning disabilities (including ADD), has also shown to be directly related to heavy metal toxicosis. The main Chinese syndrome presentation here is **Liver and Kidney Essence deficiency.**

The treatment of heavy metal toxicosis involves first, managment of the resultant disorder itself; second, liver and nervous system support as outlined above using *liver Yin restoratives* with *detoxicant* and *antioxidant* actions; and third, use of the natural chelating agents mentioned above. Increasing trace minerals (e.g., from seaweeds, nettle and alfalfa) in the diet or through supplementation, have also proved helpful in eliminating heavy metals. Amino acid and vitamin supplementation here also plays an important part. Saunas with their dry heat have also shown to help with heavy metal toxicosis specifically.

The Herbs that Promote Detoxification

The plant remedies that treat toxicosis conditions have a long history. In traditional Greek/European medicine they have variously been called *antidyskratics, resolvents, alteratives, detoxicants, depuratives* and *blood cleansers*. In this text they are properly known as *resolvent detoxicants*. They include more specialized actions that focus on particular aspects or types of toxicosis, such as *lymphatic decongestant, dermatropic, antiallergic, antiarthritic, antilithic, dissolvent, choleretic, antitumoral* and other actions (see below). Most importantly, however, *resolvent detoxicants* address a large variety of disorders by altering and regulating the ground of disease. They do not possess a single, drug-like action that works only in specific areas, such as the lymphatic circulation or the skin, or on specific pathgologies, such as inflammatory bowel disease, psoriasis or tumors. Their action rather is general, systemic and broad-spectrum.

Treatment Considerations

• As seen above, causing alterative changes in the system also involves restoring and eliminating. As a result, *detoxicant* herbs are in a pivotal position between *restoratives* and *eliminants*. In the long run therefore, *detoxicants* are conversely able to enhance the actions of *restoratives* and *eliminants*. *Detoxicants* should be used as adjuncts to treat longstanding deficiency or excess conditions as well as to speed up the resolution of acute infections and fevers.
• When *restoratives* are used for treating chronic deficiency conditions, for instance, an additional detoxification element will usually enhance results.
• The same is true when *detoxicant* remedies are used to enhance *eliminants* in the treatment of chronic excess conditions with acute accumulations, such as edema, food accumulation, phlegm obstruction and menstrual obstruction.

Summary of Detoxicant Herb Actions

What follows is a synopsis of the different kinds of specific actions exhibited by both types of *resolvent detoxicants* in general, and regardless of whether they treat damp-heat or damp conditions from the energetic point of view.

• ***Dermatropic detoxicant*** action. In both sections above, some *detoxicants* more than others possess a particular affinity for treating skin problems. They are often used for dermatological conditions, including the many forms of eczema/dermatitis, psoriasis and acne. They include Burdock root, Yellow dock root, Walnut leaf, Heartsease herb, Jamaica sarsaparilla root, Cleavers herb, red clover flower, Figwort herb and (in Chinese medicine) Lithospermum Zi Cao, Smilax Tu Fu Ling and Dictamnus Bai Xian Pi. Saponins figure prominently in the action of *dermatropic* remedies and help focus on the skin. Flavonoids, including genistein, often lend support in this direction.

• ***Lymphatic detoxicant*** action. Many *detoxicants* improve lymphatic tissue drainage and reduce gland swelling; some also specifically treat inflammatory lymphatic disorders. They are given for lymphadenitis, lymphangitis, scrofula and other such disorders. Burdock root, Marigold flower, Walnut leaf, Figwort root/herb, Echinacea root, Blue flag root and Poke root are highly effective *lymphatic detoxicant* remedies—as are the Asian remedies Forsythia Lian Qiao, Lonicera Jin Yin Hua and Smilax Tu Fu Ling. Minerals such as calcium, trace minerals such as iodine and magnesium, and organic acids such as oxalic acid help account for the *resolvent* effect of these remedies on the lymphatic circulation.

• ***Antiarthritic detoxicant*** action. *Diuretic detoxicants* in particular promote the removal of uric acid (*uricosuric diuretics*), urea and other toxic metabolites by increasing renal efficiency. They are used for rheumatoid arthritis and other rheumatic conditions, and include Birch leaf, Celerey seed, Parslay seed, Red clover flower, Juniper berry, Horsetail herb, Cowslip root and Pipsissewa or Wintergreen herb. Salicylic acid is usually found in those *detoxicants* traditionally given for joint or muscle pain—for instance in Cowslip root, Birch leaf, Pipsissewa herb, Meadowsweet herb and Hearts-ease herb. Comparable *antiarthritic detoxicant* Chinese remedies include Acanthopanax Wu Jia Pi, Eucommia Du Zhong and Loranthus Sang Ji Sheng.

• ***Dissolvent detoxicant*** action. There are several types of remedies able to soften and dissolve depositions, or hard deposits. In Greek medicine they are said to possess softening and dissolving effective qualities in addition to promoting resorption and elimination. *Dissolvent detoxicants* exhibit the following more specific actions:

• ***Antilithic*** action. Many *dissolvent detoxicants* (especially the *diuretic* kind) can help resolve

665

mineral deposits in the system, including stones and arterial mineral deposits. They are divided into *antilithics* that treat urinary and biliary stones, and *arterial resolvents* (or *antiarteriosclerotics*) that treat arteriosclerosis. Pellitory of the wall, Gravel root, Cornsilk style, Horsetail herb, Cleavers herb, Celery seed or root, Madder root, Parsley piert herb, Kelp thallus, Red clover flower, Hydrangea root and the Asian remedies Lysimachia/Desmodium Jin Qian Cao and Rubia Qian Cao Gen are some examples of good *antilithic* remedies. These herbs contain significant amounts of trace mineral and/or organic acids, and often have a correspondingly salty taste.

• *Antilipemic* action. Some *dissolvent detoxicants* help resolve fat deposits in the system, and also possess softening and dissolving qualities. They can treat atherosclerosis and other conditions with hyperlipidemia present—high lipid levels (including cholesterol, triglycerides, etc.) in the blood. Examples would be Dandelion root, Chicory root, Alfalfa herb, Artichoke leaf, Hawthorn berry, Dong quai root, Linden flower and the Chinese remedies Polygonum He Shou Wu, Bupleurum Chai Hu and Alisma Ze Xie.

• *Antitumoral detoxicant* action. Certain *detoxicants* in general possess an *antitumoral* action in the sense that they can prevent or reduce tumor formation, both benign and malignant. This does not mean that *antitumorals* treat cancer of all types and at any stage. It simply means that the tendency to neoplasms is checked through their systemic, multifaceted *detoxicant* action. Some have, in fact, had specific *antitumor* compounds isolated from them—certainly helpful in a scientific rationalization of their effect. However, many have not. It should be stressed that the major contributing factor to their inhibiting effect is their systemic *detoxification* and *resolvent* functions—their action of altering the ground (terrain) and rebalancing the dyskratic diathesis in which tumors develop. This accounts for their preventive as well as remedial use where, for example, a hereditary predisposition may be present.

Important *antitumoral detoxicants* include Echinacea root/flower, Chaparral leaf, Cleavers herb, Red clover flower, Violet root/herb, Poke root, Mistletoe herb, Celandine herb, Garlic bulb, Yellow dock root, Thuja, Pau d'arco and the essential oils of *Geranium, Lemon* and *Bergamot*. Comparable Chinese *antitumorals* include Solanum Long Kui, Sophora Ku Shen and Oldenlandia Bai Hua She She Cao (see HOLMES 1997).

From the perspective of the syndromes that they address, *resolvent detoxicants* can be divided into two broad categories, regardless of the type of toxicosis they treat:
• *liver decongestants* that clear damp-heat
• *urinary dissolvents* that resolve damp

Herbs to Promote Detoxification, Clear Damp-Heat and Relieve Eczema
Bitter, cold laxative depurant detoxicants (liver decongestants)

Remedies in this category address chronic toxicosis conditions that are characterized by **damp-heat.** Damp-heat toxicosis typically presents such symptoms as red skin rashes, swollen lymph glands, joint pain, swelling and redness (arthritis), rheumatic pains, malaise, indigestion with abdominal distension, constipation, thirst, dark fetid urine, a red tongue with possible oily yellow or grey fur, and a rapid pulse.

Bitter, dry, cool and sinking by nature, these *detoxicants* specifically work by treating the digestive deficiency at the root of the toxicosis condition. They essentially address **liver congestion, intestinal microbial toxicosis** and **constipation with food accumulation**—major signs of stagnant **damp-heat** in the **liver,** and the key components of **damp-heat toxicosis.** They are essentially *detoxicants* that act as *laxative liver decongestants*. As such they can help resolve inflammatory, eczematous, lymphatic, arthritic and rheumatic disorders characterized by damp-heat and, secondarily, toxic heat.

Important *laxative detoxicant* herbs include Dandelion root, Yellow dock root, Figwort root and herb, Blue flag root, Butternut root bark, Bur-dock root, Fringe tree bark, Barberry bark and, from Chinese medicine, Scutellaria Huang Qin, Sophora Ku Shen and Polygonum Hu Zhang.
These and other *laxative detoxicants* also display important *cholagogue, lymphatic deconges-tant, dermatropic* and *anti-rheumatic/arthritic* actions that are simply particular aspects of their concerted *resolvent detoxicant* effect. The majority are used in various skin disorders, lymphadenopathies and arthritic conditions in addition to con-gestive liver disorders, digestive disorders and actual liver disease. Pharmacologically the effect of *hepatic*

detoxicants largely depends on glycosides (including *laxative* anthraquinones and *dermatropic* saponins) and alkaloids, both of which also impart their typical bitter taste and cooling effect.

Herbs to Promote Detoxification, Resolve Damp and Dissolve Deposits
Cool diuretic depurant detoxicants
(urinary dissolvents, antilithics)

Remedies in this section treat toxicosis conditions characterized by **damp** or **deposition.** Damp and deposition forms of toxicosis often present symptoms such as chronic skin rashes, dry scaly eczema, swollen glands, joint pain and stiffness, muscle aches, urinary stones and other deposits (such as arteriosclerosis, calcium spurs, skin nodules, liver cirrhosis and gouty deposits), irritated, scanty or obstructed urination, pale urine, a pale (often furless) tongue, and a slow, deep or thin pulse.

Diuretic detoxicants specifically operate by addressing a weakness of the kidneys' selective eliminative activity that underlies the toxicosis. As *renal depurants* they specifically address kidney deficiency with irritation, urinary mineral deposits and urination difficulties, as these are involved with stone formation and other hard deposits. *Diuretic detoxicants* thereby help resolve chronic, **degenerative eczematous, lymphatic, depository, arthritic** and **rheumatic** conditions typified by **damp.**

Examples of significant *diuretic depurant detoxicants* include Cleavers herb, Burdock root, Nettle herb, Celery seed, Parsley peirt herb, Gravel root, Juniper berry, Silver birch leaf and bark, Heartsease herb and Meadowsweet herb. In Chinese medicine they include Smilax Tu Fu Ling, Dioscorea Bi Xie, Phytolacca Shang Lu, Dianthus Qu Mai, Polygonum Bian Xu. Dandelion leaf and Lobelia Ban Bian Lian are two of the very few remedies that belong both to the *laxative* and the *diuretic* group of *resolvent detoxicants*.

Detoxicant diuretics are distinct from *draining diuretics* (Class 2) whose main function is to relieve water congestion with edema. Although both types of *diuretics* increase the amount and frequency of urination, their systemic, contextual actions are very different.

Local and Topical Treatment of Toxicosis Conditions

Traditional Greek medicine also uses a variety of topical methods in the treatment of toxicosis conditions.[2] These methods consist mainly of derivative, or skin irritating, techniques. Down the ages they have shown documented success, especially (but not solely) in the treatment of myalgic, neuralgic and arthritic disorders, i.e., conditions known as **wind-damp-cold obstruction** in Chinese medicine.

The basic technique used is to cause mechanical counterirritation and increase local blood flow in order to draw or derive the blood away from the locale of pain and inflammation. This method is therefore called derivation. Although derivation can be produced through nonirritant techniques such as cupping and bloodletting, it is the irritating ones that have historically proven the most beneficial. These range from mild derivation methods using *rubefacients* that stimulate local circulation and *vesicants* that provoke blister formation around the joints, to stronger techniques like causing artificial eruptions (exanthema) such as boils, and pustules using *pustulants*. These three types of topical remedies, then, are all classed as *counterirritants*.

• *Rubefacients* include fresh Nettles, Mustard seed, Horseradish root, Cayenne pepper, Poke root, Mayapple root, Ammonia salts, Petroleum (used by the Seneca Indians of the Eastern plains, for example) and various essential oils (mostly from conifers) such as *Thuja, Pine, Larch, Spruce, Turpentine, Cinnamon, Thyme* and *Oregano.* These are applied locally in the form of a poultice or liniment.

• *Vesicants* remedies are *rubefacients* (except for Cayenne) that are retained on the skin until blisters form. Although traditional Greek medicine uses a variety of botanical (e.g., Pulsatilla, Clematis), animal and mineral remedies, the Cantharides plaster is the most effective blistering technique. It uses *Cantharis,* or the ground beetle, Spanish fly. This was the most universally used vesicant technique, and from Renaissance times onwards was routinely applied by eminent physicians such as PARACELSUS, FYENS, SYDENHAM, RIVERIUS, BAGLIVI, TISSOT, HUFELAND and REVILLOUD, as well as many in the twentieth century.

The **cantharides plaster** is one of the most effective topical treatments not only for cold obstruction (osteoarthritic disorders), but also damp and wind obstruction (myalgic/rheumatic and neuralgic disorders). With its *anti-inflammatory, analgesic* and *spasmolytic* actions, it is probably the single most versatile and therefore most employed derivative technique. Its applications as a *vesicant* go beyond use for toxicosis alone, and include nervous diseases such as meningitis, paralysis, apoplexy; eye, throat and ear conditions; lung conditions such as pleuritis (pleurisy), pneumonia, lung TB, bronchial asthma; heart conditions such as angina pectoris, endo- and pericarditis; as well as all types of acute and chronic painful obstruction conditions (see HOLMES 1997 for a full presentation of Cantharides and the plaster). Note that counterirritants in general are contraindicated in heated rheumatic joint pains (wind-damp-heat obstruction).

• *Pustulant* remedies produce boils or pustules for a derivative effect. They are a major part of exanthematous (eruption-promoting) treatment. BRAUN-SCHEIDT's method is the most common, but not the only such technique currently employed. Pustule causing treatment is generally far more efficacious than the simple counterirritation produced by *rubefacients;* it has the advantage of being less painful than the blistering technique. *Pustulants* can also be applied over a much larger skin surface than vesicants.

The pustulant method is said to be very effective for damp obstruction presenting neuralgia/neuritis (e.g., sciatica), and also in spinal arthritis. It was, and to some extent still is, routinely used for its *spasmolytic, analgesic* and *anti-inflammatory* actions in meningitis, encephalitis, migraine, apoplexy, epilepsy, chorea, Menière's disease, tinnitus, eye inflammations, asthma, local cramps and tendinitis. *Pustulant remedies* include Cantharides powder, Tartar emetic, Croton oil and Mayapple root; they are applied in ointments or liniments, singly or mixed, with other *counterirritant* substances such as *Turpentine,* Petroleum, *Cajeput, Oregano,* Mezereum and Anacardium extract *(cardol).* In addition, the formic acid from fresh nettles or the stings of live ants and bees can also cause pustules and can be used in this way.

It is important to realize that causing blisters with *vesicants* and pustules with *pustulants* are skilled techniques. They are worth considering only if properly and safely performed by professionally trained practitioners.

The reasons for the general demise of these techniques in Western medicine is not because they lack efficacy. On the contrary, they are still used today by a small but growing number of Western practitioners with the same success that these methods enjoyed for thousands of years—and still currently enjoy in mainstream Ayurvedic medicine. Instead, the reasons are to be found in the radical change of philosophy that Greek/Western medicine underwent with the rise of experimental cellular pathology during the nineteenth century. In a classic example of throwing out the baby with the bathwater, counterirritant derivation techniques were ousted simply because they were part of the whole vitalistic Greek-Galenic package based on the four fluids. They were seen as primitive, unscientific methods that had nothing at all to do with the new explanations of disease on a cellular and microbiological level. Of course, the derivation methods had nothing in common with the four fluids theory anyway, and in hindsight it is clear that the scientists' dislike of the simple, traditional methods had more to do with their enthusiasm for modern science and technology than their ability to prove them ineffective or wrong. Little did they realize the major alterative effects on a cellular and immune level of the methods they were jettisoning.

Now that the enthusiasm for fictitious chemical miracle drugs has definitely waned and that even antibiotics are becoming as unpopular—and at times ineffective—as bloodletting was in the nineteenth century, it is appropriate to foster a renewed appreciation for these simple, low-tech yet effective topical treatment methods for toxicosis and other related conditions. Their time-tested, documented efficacy calls for renewed investigation, just as maggots are now used to clean wounds in specialized burn centers, and leeches are used to promote post-surgical tissue repair and reduce bleeding.

The traditional derivative techniques are described in full detail in the works of BERNHARD ASCHNER, especially in *Lehrbuch der Konstitutionstherapie* (1928) and in *The Treatment of Arthritis and Rheumatism in General Practice, Particularly in Women* (1946). Because of his lifetime experience with these methods as a Western doctor, ASCHNER is able to present them with their full functions, indications and contraindications, along with detailed case histories from his own practice (Austrian-born ASCHNER maintained a busy practice in New York City from 1938 to 1960, the year of his death).

A complete list of remedies for all types of toxicosis is found under Toxicosis in the Repertory.

Notes

1. Toxicosis conditions are found in many variations and are an integral component of many different types of conditions both excess and deficient, hot and cold, dry and moist. It therefore makes no sense to simplistically label any toxicosis as a blood heat condition—an unfortunate tendency found today. If we are to integrate Oriental and Western therapeutic concepts, we need to include concepts that describe the substantial states of tissues as well as their dysfunctions. In the case of the blood, for example, in addition to heat, cold or stagnation affecting the blood (all concepts describing mainly its functions), we need to make an assessment of its tissue condition, i.e., whether toxicosic, thin, viscous, and so on. Clearly then, because the concepts blood heat and toxic blood belong to different classes, no one-to-one equation can be made between them.

2. Traditional Greek and Ayurvedic medical systems use a variety of inorganic compounds to treat many types of fluid dyskrasias. Until about the turn of the century, in fact, Western physicians considered inorganic compounds among the most rapid-acting *resolvent detoxicants*. Foremost among these are various preparations of sulphur, phosphorus, arsenic, mercury and antimony—but they also included the more commonly used volatile/alkaline salts such as sodium and potassium carbonate, potassium tartrate, cream of tartar, sodium bitartrate, potassium acetate, potassium and sodium sulfate, and ammoniac salts such as ammonium chloride. Mercury in the form of calomel was used both internally and externally— with especial success, apparently—in treating chronic goiter, lymphadenopathies (incl. scrofula), eczema, chronic inflammations, chronic mastitis and hyperthyroidism. However, because cinnabar and calomel preparations are both strong and highly toxic *resolvents,* they should only be used as a last resort. A good alternative would be to use them in homeopathic preparation. All traditional pharmaceutical systems—and Chinese and Ayurvedic medicine still today—also utilize *resolvent* animal products such as Cuttlefish bone, Oyster shell, Pearl crab stone and Red and White coral. Many of these inorganic remedies of mineral and animal origin deserve further investigation.

Promote Detoxification, Clear Damp-Heat and Relieve Eczema

Bitter, cold laxative depurant detoxicants (liver decongestants)

Dandelion Root

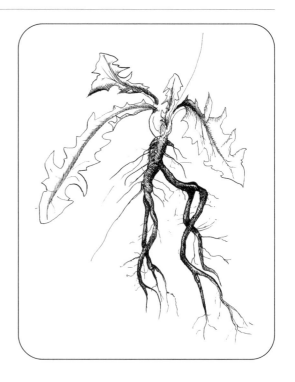

Botanical source: *Taraxacum officinale* Weber
    (Asteraceae/Compositae)
Pharmaceutical name: Radix Taraxaci
Ancient names: Calendula agreste, Leontodon,
    Taraxacum (Lat)
Other names: Wild succory, Puffball, Gowan,
    Swinesnout, Lion's tooth (Eng)
    Pissenlit, Chicorée sauvage, Dent-de-lion (Fr)
    Löwenzahn, Kuhblume, Röhrleinkraut,
    Butterblume (Ge)
Part used: the root

NATURE

Therapeutic category: mild remedy with minimal chronic toxicity
Constituents: bitter glycosides, bitter resin taraxacerin, phytosterols (incl. sitosterol, taraxerol), fatty acids, tannins, essential oil, triterpenes, inulin, levulin, saponin, enzyme, citric and silicic acid, minerals (incl. potassium, calcium, sodium, phosphorus, iron), carotenoids, levulose, glutin, gum, vitamins A, C, choline, niacin, mannite/mannitol (in spring root)
Effective qualities: bitter, somewhat salty and sweet, cold, dry
    softening, dissolving, restoring, decongesting, calming, sinking
Tropism: liver, gallbladder, spleen, pancreas, intestines, kidneys, interstitial fluids, blood
    Liver, Gallbladder, Spleen, Bladder meridians
    Fluid, Warmth, Air bodies
Ground: all krases, biotypes and constitutions

FUNCTIONS AND INDICATIONS

1 **PROMOTES DETOXIFICATION AND CLEARS DAMP-HEAT;**
    PROMOTES BILE, REDUCES LIVER CONGESTION, RELIEVES JAUNDICE AND CONSTIPATION
    microbial toxicosis with *damp-heat:* proneness to inflammations, food allergies, malaise
    liver and gallbladder Qi stagnation with *damp-heat:* indigestion, right hypochondriac pain,
        constipation, appetite loss
    LIVER CONGESTION, JAUNDICE, HEPATITIS
    liver/gallbladder fire: fever, headache, nausea, bitter taste in mouth, right flank pain
    CHOLECYSTITIS, cholangitis, gallstone colic

2 **PROMOTES DETOXIFICATION AND CLEARS TOXIC HEAT;**
    REDUCES INFECTION AND INFLAMMATION, AND STIMULATES IMMUNITY

microbial toxicosis with *toxic heat:* boils, abscesses, sores, ulcers, fevers

INFECTIONS (acute, inflammatory, pyogenic, incl. acne, tonsilitis, pharyngitis, mastitis, appendicitis, P.I.D., urinary tract infections, herpes simplex, lymphangitis)

3 RESOLVES DAMP AND DISSOLVES DEPOSITS;
PROMOTES URINATION, DRAINS WATER AND RELIEVES IRRITATION;
RELIEVES ECZEMA AND REDUCES LYMPH CONGESTION

liver and kidney water congestion: generalized water retention, nausea, fatigue

EDEMA (general, renal, cardiac), dropsy

DYSURIA, oliguria, polyuria

DEPOSITORY DIATHESIS with liver cirrhosis, arteriosclerosis

BILIARY and URINARY STONES, crystals

skin damp: chronic skin eruptions, malaise

ECZEMA (esp. chronic); herpes

LYMPHADENITIS, scrofula

ARTHRITIS, rheumatism, gout (all chronic); hyperuricemia

general plethora: overweight, abdominal distension, malaise

HYPERLIPIDEMIA, hypertension

4 ENRICHES LIVER YIN, NOURISHES THE BLOOD AND RELIEVES FATIGUE;
RESTORES AND PROTECTS THE LIVER, PANCREAS AND SPLEEN, AND ENHANCES IMMUNITY;
STRENGTHENS CONNECTIVE TISSUE AND REDUCES BLOOD CONGESTION;
PROMOTES LACTATION

liver and pancreas Yin deficiency: loss of stamina and motivation, fatigue, weight loss, appetite loss, frequent infections

METABOLIC DISORDERS (all chronic and degenerative, esp. involving liver, pancreas, spleen, incl. hypoglycemia, anemia, cirrhosis, liver disease)

IMMUNE DEFICIENCY (chronic)

CONNECTIVE TISSUE DEGENERATION (esp. with toxicosis)

venous and liver blood stagnation: varicose veins, hemorrhoids, fatigue, overweight, abdominal distension

DIABETES (supportive)

INSUFFICIENT LACTATION

5 RELIEVES WHEEZING AND COUGHING

ASTHMATIC conditions with cough

PREPARATION

Use: Dandelion root is best prepared in **decoction** or **tincture,** using either the fresh or dried root. Dandelion **leaf** is found in Class 2, a much stronger *diuretic* for draining water in edema (function 3).

The roasted root is used for a coffee-like drink that retains some of its properties.

Dandelion flower stems are traditionally infused to lower blood sugar; their milky juice is applied directly to warts.

Dosage: Decoction: 6-16 g

Tincture: 2-5 ml at 1:2 strength in 35% ethanol

While Dandelion is *detoxicant* at all doses, smaller doses are suitable for restoring (function 4), while larger doses are for cooling and draining (functions 1, 2 and 3).

Caution: Continuous large doses may cause minor symptoms such as loose stool, heartburn and nausea. Contraindicated with acute gastric inflammation present (stomach fire) as it is a *gastric acid stimulant.*

NOTES

Surprisingly, no earlier reference to Dandelion has been found than in the herbal of HIERONYMUS BOCK (1534). At a time when classical medicine was mainly practiced by university physicians and licensed apothecaries, BOCK was noted for researching the practical uses of plants among wise women practitioners. He thereby helped to integrate this knowledge into official medicine. It is safe to assume, therefore, that women healers had known and used this plant for a long time.

Today, the innocent Dandelion with its punkish bright yellow flowerheads stands squarely in the crosscurrents of different herbal traditions: Western, Chinese and Ayurvedic. This alone is proof of its status as an important remedy, and past country healers would have been heartily amused at the heated scholastic debates this simple plant generates today. The point is that, although Dandelion is virtually the same plant the world over, its functions and uses differ widely, depending on which medical tradition one belongs to.

In the Western tradition, Dandelion is mainly used as a bitter *digestive stimulant, liver tropho-restorative, diuretic* and *antidyskratic detoxicant*. Its bitter taste stimulates digestive secretions such as bile, gastric and pancreatic enzymes. In other words, its *cholagogue* action is effective for those presenting **liver and gallbladder Qi stagnation,** especially when it generates damp-heat. These functions are more pronounced in the spring-harvested root, which are lower in sugars than the fall-harvested root, which accumulates the sugars of summer's photosynthesis.

Dandelion's sweet taste quality, on the other hand, restores liver tissue and, partly through the inulin content, restores pancreatic functioning. The root collected in autumn, being more moist and sweet, is especially useful for enriching liver Yin and blood, thereby generating physical stamina, weight gain and immune strength. There are echoes here of Chicory root and Alfalfa herb. Already we see a picture of Dandelion as a liver-oriented remedy emerging.

This root's high mineral content also gives it a salty taste that produces *detoxicant* and *regulating* effects on the whole fluids. Chronic and degenerative **toxicosis** conditions involving the **connec-**tive tissue and **interstitial fluids** are addressed— here as with Horsetail, for instance. Dandelion works undramatically yet, given time and consistency, deeply in altering mode. The root's *resolvent* action is tailor-made for those with systemic **metabolic** and **microbial toxicoses** presenting **damp-heat** or **damp** with hyperuricemia, depositions (such as stones) or eczema. Because it covers more ground more effectively here than anywhere else, Dandelion has a strong place in this section of remedies. It will combine easily with most of the other herbs in this category.

In contrast, Chinese medicine presents quite a different picture of this plant. It values the *anti-inflammatory* action of this heat and toxins-clearing remedy, and applies them to **heat toxin** symptoms such as boils, internal abscesses and throat inflammations. The *cooling* and *detoxicant* effects of the root's bitter taste are here put into effect. Modern research supports these uses for Dandelion root and, moreover, has demonstrated *immunostimulant (phagocyte stimulant)* and *antiviral* activity. This underscores use in acute local infections as well as in chronic viral conditions such as herpes simplex presenting cold sores. The root gathered in spring is the most bitter and drying, and is best for these conditions. Where is the unity underlying these disparate Western and Oriental uses?

The answer may be found in Ayurvedic pharmacology, where the bitter taste is said to stimulate digestive functions, reduce accumulations and promote detoxification. In this light Dandelion's bitter and salty tastes merge to produce a single movement or process—*detoxicant, draining* and *refrigerant*. Moreover it becomes clear that, because Dandelion addresses the liver and gallbladder, it also clears liver fire. In Western terms, Dandelion is a classic *antiplethoric* remedy indicated for individuals with portal and venous blood congestion, high blood cholesterol, overweight, and gallbladder inflammations and stones. Culver's root, Artichoke leaf and Kelp come to mind here as compatible therapeutic support.

The portrait of Dandelion as an important *detoxicant hepatic* remedy that treats both deficiency and excess conditions is thereby complete.

Bogbean Leaf

Botanical source: *Menyanthes trifoliata* L.
    (Menyanthaceae/Gentianaceae)
Pharmaceutical name: Folium Menyanthis
Ancient names: Menyanthion (Gr)
    Trifolium palustre, Lotus palustris (Lat)
    Monatsblume, Zitterblume (Old Ge)
Other names: Buckbean, Bog myrtle, Marsh clover,
    Water trefoil/Shamrock (Eng)
    Trèfle d'eau, Ménianthe trifolié, Trèfle des
      marais (Fr)
    Fieberklee, Bitterklee, Bocksbohne,
      Scharbocksklee, Ziegenklappen,
      Monatsblume (Ge)
Part used: the leaf

NATURE

Therapeutic category: mild remedy with minimal chronic toxicity
Constituents: alkaloids (incl. gentianine, gentialutine), bitter glycoside menyanthin, rutin, hyperin, cholin, trifolioside, phytosterin, menyanthol, meliatin, essential oil (incl. terpenes, hexanals, pentenols), ceryl alcohol, carotene, ascorbic and other acid, tannins, acids, saponins, fatty oil with palmitinic acids, trace minerals (incl. manganese, iodine)
Effective qualities: very bitter, somewhat pungent, cold, dry
    stimulating, sinking
Tropism: liver, galbladder, stomach, intestines, lungs, kidneys, uterus
    Liver, Lung, Large Intestine meridians
    Warmth, Fluid bodies
Ground: Sanguine krasis; Charming/Yang Ming Earth biotype
    Hematogenic/Brown Iris and Biliary/Mixed Iris

FUNCTIONS AND INDICATIONS

1   **PROMOTES DETOXIFICATION AND CLEARS DAMP-HEAT;**
    PROMOTES BILE FLOW, REDUCES LIVER CONGESTION, HARMONIZES THE MIDDLE,
    STOPS VOMITING AND RELIEVES CONSTIPATION; ELIMINATES PARASITES

microbial toxicosis with ***damp-heat:*** proneness to digestive problems, malaise, food allergies
liver and gallbladder damp-heat: nauseous headache, swollen painful flanks, sides and glands
HEPATITIS (acute)
MIGRAINES (biliary headaches, esp. after meals, from food intolerances/allergies, with vomiting)
gallbladder, stomach and intestines Qi stagnation (stomach damp-heat): fatigue, appetite loss, nausea,
    vomiting, epigastric pain and distension, constipation
LIVER CONGESTION (esp. with constipation)
DYSPEPSIA (biliary, gastric, intestinal, esp. with nausea, vomiting)
DEBILITY from overwork, anemia, fever, chronic illness, etc.
CONSTIPATION
INTESTINAL PARASITES

2 PROMOTES DETOXIFICATION AND CLEARS TOXIC HEAT; REDUCES FEVER AND INFLAMMATION

microbial toxicosis with *toxic heat:* sores, boils, abscesses, fevers, inflammations

liver fire: throbbing headache, red face and eyes, fever, flank pain, irritability

FEVERS (high, remittent; esp. in *yang ming* and *shao yang* stage)

3 RESOLVES DAMP, PROMOTES URINATION AND RELIEVES IRRITATION AND ECZEMA; PROMOTES MENSTRUATION AND RELIEVES AMENORRHEA

metabolic toxicosis with *damp:* skin eruptions, malaise, fatigue, smelly urine

ECZEMA, SCURVY

RHEUMATISM (myalgia, esp. chronic); gout, rheumatoid arthritis

EDEMA

uterus Qi stagnation: delayed or stopped periods, fatigue, scanty flow

DYSMENORRHEA, AMENORRHEA

4 DESCENDS LUNG QI AND RELIEVES WHEEZING; PROMOTES EXPECTORATION AND RESOLVES PHLEGM

lung Qi constraint: wheezing, tight sore chest

ASTHMA

lung phlegm-damp: coughing with copious sputum wheezing

BRONCHITIS (esp. chronic)

PREPARATION

Use: Bogbean leaf is prepared in **infusion** or **tincture** form. The tincture should be made from the fresh leaf (the best) or the dried herb under six months old (it loses much of its potency after that). Bogbean **syrup** for chronic bronchial conditions was found in the old European pharmacies. **Washes** are beneficial for skin conditions.

Dosage: Infusion: 4-6 g

        Tincture: 2-7 ml at 1:3 strength in 45% ethanol

The larger the dose, the more effective Bogbean is for draining damp-heat. Smaller doses simply stimulate digestive functions and thereby resolve gallbladder/stomach/intestines Qi stasis.

Caution: Contraindicated in the syndromes intestines (Spleen) Qi deficiency presenting diarrhea, and in stomach fire with acute inflammation.

NOTES

Indigenous to both Europe and the U.S., bogbean is a valuable member of the gentian family, usually seen in boggy, swampy and other damp temperate terrains. Its other very descriptive, although botanically inaccurate, names include "bog myrtle" and "marsh clover." Although traditionally both the rhizome and leaves (i.e. the whole plant) were used for medicine making, current ecological practice favors using the leaves alone. These should be "completely adequate" from the therapeutic point of view (MOORE 1993).

Bogbean leaf is primarily a *cooling, detoxicant* remedy with many similarities to Butternut root bark, but more heat-clearing and less astringent. Both remedies achieve their cooling effect largely through a combination of digestive stimulation and intrinsic *anti-inflammatory* and *antipyretic* actions. One of Bogbean's main European names is "fever trefoil/clover" (*Fieberklee* in German), witness to its long-term Greek medicine use for **remittent** or **intermittent fevers.** Greek medical texts cryptically state that the herb excels at clearing **heat** and **toxic heat** caused by stagnant bile, mucus and lymph.

As with the related Gentian root, Bogbean leaf resolves conditions of **liver damp-heat** and **intestinal accumulations** through its bitter-pungent, downward-moving energetic effect. This results from the activity of glycosides, alkaloids and essential oils in concert, causing *cholagogue, gastro-*

intestinal stimulant and *laxative* actions. Bogbean has been found very useful in particular for individuals with poor food-combining abilities suffering from **food sensitivities** or **allergies, constipation** and chronic forms of upper or lower indigestion. In Europe the herb is a specific for biliary migraines after liver-unfriendly meals, much like Blue flag root in the U.S.

Taken in small quantities, Bogbean leaf can act as a bitter *digestive stimulant* for **liver and stomach Qi stagnation** with fatigue and poor appetite. Its bitter glycosides, although not quite as intense as those found in Gentian root and Wormwood herb, are active here. Bogbean leaf also carries out detoxification on the kidney/liver/blood level and to some extent the interstitial level for dermal, rheumatic and arthritic complaints arising from **metabolic toxicosis.**

One of the German names for this herb is *Monatsblume,* or "Moonflower," is a reminder of its regional use for dysmenorrhea and amenorrhea. This *emmenagogue* effect is likely due to its *liver-stimulant laxative* action.

As a cooling *stimulant expectorant* and *anti-asthmatic* remedy, Bogbean leaf has much in common with the Chinese herb Belamcanda Shi Gan. .

Yellow Dock Root

Botanical source: *Rumex crispus* L., *R. patienta* L.,
    R. acutus L., *R. alpina* L. and spp.
    (Polygonaceae)
Pharmaceutical name: Radix Rumicis
Ancient names: Lapathon (Gk)
Other names: Curled dock, Narrow-leaf dock,
    Phorams (Eng)
    Patience, Parielle, Rhubarbe sauvage, Churelle,
    Oseille aquatique, Oreille de vache (Fr)
    Grindampfer, Krauser Ampfer, Mengelwurz,
    Wilder Mangolt, Zitterwurz (Ge)
Part used: the root

NATURE

Therapeutic category: mild remedy with minimal chronic toxicity
Constituents: anthraquinones (incl. emodin and chrysophanol), quercetrin, tannins, essential oil, calcium oxalate, resin, rumicin, brassidinic/lapathinic/chrysophanic/oxalic acids, minerals (incl. calcium, phosphorus, iron), vitamins A, B, C, thiamine, riboflavin, niacin
Effective qualities: somewhat bitter and astringent, cold, dry
    dissolving, decongesting, restoring, astringing
Tropism: fluids, blood, lymph, intestines, pancreas, kidneys, liver, skin
    Liver, Kidney, Large Intestine meridians
    Fluid body
Ground: all krases, biotypes and constitutions

FUNCTIONS AND INDICATIONS

1 **PROMOTES DETOXIFICATION AND CLEARS DAMP-HEAT;**
 REDUCES LIVER CONGESTION AND RELIEVES CONSTIPATION

 microbial toxicosis with *damp-heat:* proneness to inflammations, malaise, food allergies

 liver Qi stagnation with *damp-heat:* bitter taste in mouth, indigestion, moodiness, headache,
   fat intolerance, constipation

 LIVER CONGESTION, JAUNDICE

 intestines Qi stagnation: chronic constipation, fatigue, abdominal distension

 CONSTIPATION (esp. chronic)

2 **CLEARS TOXIC HEAT AND REDUCES INFLAMMATION AND DISCHARGE**

 microbial toxicosis with *toxic heat:* boils, furuncles, abscesses, suppurating ulcers

 SORE THROAT, laryngitis, pharyngitis, bronchitis

 INFLAMMATIONS (acute)

 PEPTIC ULCER (?)

 intestines damp-heat: diarrhea, burning stools

 ENTERITIS, dysentery

3 **RESOLVES DAMP AND DISSOLVES STONES;**
 REDUCES LYMPH CONGESTION AND RELIEVES ECZEMA;
 PROMOTES URINATION, REDUCES ACIDOSIS AND RELIEVES IRRITATION

 metabolic toxicosis with *damp:* dry skin with rashes, urinary infections or irritation

 METABOLIC ACIDOSIS with frequent irritated urination, dry itching skin, deep breathing, yawning

 LYMPHADENITIS with swollen glands, scrofula

 OVARIAN CYSTS

 URINARY STONES (esp. with urinary irritation)

 skin damp: red skin rashes, wetness, itching, malaise, fatigue

 ECZEMA (chronic), urticaria, scurvy, syphilis

 GOUT, chronic arthritis

4 **VITALIZES THE BLOOD, REDUCES CONGESTION AND MODERATES MENSTRUATION;**
 REDUCES TUMORS

 uterus blood congestion: abdominal fullness, pelvic weight and dragging before the periods,
   constipation, early copious flow with pain and dark clots

 CONGESTIVE DYSMENORRHEA, hemorrhoids

 liver blood congestion: low fat tolerance, abdominal distension, malaise

 PORTAL CONGESTION

 abdominal plethora: constipation, overweight, fatigue

 TUMORS (esp. female reproductive)

5 **RESTORES THE BLOOD**

 ANEMIA, hemoglobin deficiency, chlorosis

 DIABETES (supportive)

6 **PROMOTES TISSUE REPAIR AND REDUCES INFLAMATION AND SUPPURATION**

 WOUNDS and ULCERS (atonic, chronic, suppurative, incl. of skin, leg, mouth)

 INFLAMMATIONS of skin, mouth, gums, throat, eyes

PREPARATION

Use: Yellow dock root is used in **decoction** and **tincture** form. **Compresses, washes** and **ointments** are used topically for skin conditions and surface traumas. **Mouthwashes** and **gargles** are excellent for mouth, gum and throat inflammations. **Vaginal sponges** and **pessaries** should be used to stop leucorrhea and reduce fibroids.

Dosage: Decoction: 3-5 g

Tincture: 2-4 ml at 1:2 strength in 30% ethanol

These doses may be safely increased without risk of detoxification reactions.

Caution: Forbidden in diarrhea caused by intestines (Spleen) Qi deficiency.

Note: The root of the **Red dock** (also known as Water dock), from *Rumex aquaticus* L., may be used instead of Yellow dock root, with similar results.

NOTES

Yellow dock is one of many members of the valuable knotweed family found worldwide. Like them, the root of various species of the yellow or narrow-leaf dock is used as an important *resolvent detoxicant* remedy. Because Yellow dock chooses a variety of pathways for accomplishing the job of detoxification, it ensures good results across a broad spectrum of **toxicosis** conditions. Toxin elimination is comprehensively favored through the liver, the kidneys and bladder, and the colon.

Primarily, however, Yellow dock root is a bitter *digestive stimulant* (and *cholagogue)* that operates by reducing **Qi stagnation** of the **liver, gallbladder** and **intestines.** Because of its dry, cold nature, the root is best used in individuals presenting **liver congestion** that tends to generate **damp-heat,** typically seen with symptoms such as bilious headache, jaundice, fatty indigestion, chronic constipation and a tendency to food allergies. Its moderate yet certain *laxative* action is signaled by the anthraquinone glycosides. In addressing these conditions, Yellow dock will find good support with many other herbs in this subsection, e.g. with Bogbean leaf (with food allergies involved); with Butternut root bark (with constipation); with Blue flag (with bilious headaches), with Barberry (with fatty indigestion); with Figwort (with eczema); with Queen's root (with chronic sore throats), and so on.

For the same reason the remedy relieves symptoms of **toxic heat, intestines damp-heat** and **gastric ulcer,** where Yellow dock's *anti-inflammatory* and *astringent* actions engage.

Yellow dock root at the same time is a *kidney stimulant* that reduces acidosis and bladder deposits, and promotes urination—where the anthraquinones are active. Its *detoxicant* and *depurant diuretic* action here reinforces the *detoxicant digestive* effect. The net result: an effective remedy for congestive disorders of the skin and lymph. Yellow dock eliminates **wind-damp** and **heat in the skin** and so addresses a wide range of **eczemas** presenting itching, redness and vesicular suppuration. Swollen lymph glands likewise benefit from the remedy's ultimate *lymphatic decongestant* action. Sympathetic herbs here would include Marigold flower, Cleavers herb and Birch leaf.

In the West Yellow dock root has a particular reputation for treating **anemia.** It is also a fact that the root is high in minerals, including iron. However, we must guard against making the statement that Yellow dock "nourishes the Blood" in the TCM sense of tonifying metabolic functions. Nothing could be further from the truth. The fact is that Yellow dock is clearly a *draining, detoxicant* remedy for prime use in congestive, hot and damp-heat conditions—the exact opposite of the qualities required for treating TCM Blood deficiency, which is essentially a weak/deficiency condition. Therefore, if you *must* use it for anemia, please combine this cold remedy with a warming *restorative* and/or *stimulant* herb from Classes 7 through 9.

Butternut Root Bark

Botanical source: *Juglans cinerea* L. (syn.
   J. cathartica Michaux, *J. oblonga* Miller)
   (Juglandaceae)
Pharmaceutical name: Cortex radicis Juglandis
   cinereae
Other names: White walnut, Oil nut (Am)
   Noyer gris (Fr)
   Graue Wallnuss (Ge)
Part used: the root bark; also the bark

NATURE

Therapeutic category: mild remedy with minimal chronic toxicity
Constituents: bitter compound, naphthoquinones (incl. juglone, juglandin and juglandic acid), lipids,
essential oil, tannins
Effective qualities: bitter, astringent, somewhat pungent, cold, dry
   stimulating, decongesting, astringing, sedating
Tropism: liver, gallbladder, stomach, intestines, rectum, skin, muscles
   Liver, Stomach, Large Intestine meridians
   Fluid, Warmth bodies

FUNCTIONS AND INDICATIONS

1   **PROMOTES DETOXIFICATION AND CLEARS DAMP-HEAT;**
   REDUCES LIVER CONGESTION AND RELIEVES CONSTIPATION;
   REDUCES PLETHORA AND RELIEVES ECZEMA

   microbial toxicosis with *damp-heat:* proneness to malaise, skin rashes, food intolerances or allergies
   liver Qi stagnation with *damp-heat:* indigestion, low fat tolerance, abdominal distension, constipation
   LIVER DYSPEPSIA, chronic jaundice
   stomach and intestines Qi stagnation (stomach damp-heat): indigestion, flatulence, appetite loss,
      epigastric or abdominal distension, sour eructations, habitual constipation, dry clay-colored stools
   CHRONIC CONSTIPATION
   abdominal plethora with *liver blood congestion:* indigestion, constipation, abd. distension, hemorrhoids
   PORTAL CONGESTION, pelvic congestion
   skin damp / -heat: skin rashes with vesicles, pustules or scales
   ECZEMA (chronic, wet oozing or dry scaly), acne, impetigo, pemphigus, lichen
   ULCERS (chronic, incl. mouth ulcers)
   TAPEWORM in children age 6 and over

2   **CLEARS DAMP-HEAT, REDUCES INFLAMMATION AND STOPS DISCHARGE; REDUCES FEVER**

   intestines damp-heat: diarrhea, burning, fetid stool, tenesmus
   ENTERITIS, dysentery
   INFLAMMATORY BOWEL DISEASE (incl. colorectitis, ulcerative colitis, Crohn's disease)
   FEVER (remittent, intermittent)
   REHUMATISM (esp. of lower back muscles)

PREPARATION

Use: Butternut root bark is prepared by **decoction** or **tincture.** The **syrup** is a good preparation for mild constipation, especially in children and elderly. Skin rashes, ulcers and wounds need topical/local use, as in **compresses, mouthwashes** and such like, in addition to internal administration.

Butternut *leaves* when powdered are *rubefacient* and were used in the past as a topical Cantharides subsitute in derivation treatment. Presumably they're less effective.

Dosage: Infusion: 8-16 g

Tincture: 2-5 ml at 1:2 strength in 30% ethanol

Note that the smaller dose is a gentle *bitter stimulant* in stomach Qi stagnation with appetite loss (etc.) (function 1) and an *intestinal sedative* in intestines damp-heat conditions with diarrhea (function 2). The average dose is actively *laxative*.

Caution: None

NOTES

Butternut is a common North American tree in the walnut family, related to the black walnut, the English walnut, the hickory, pecan and others. The tree thrives in rich woods along river banks, and provides a valuable hardwood—light, strong and free of worms. Like other walnuts it also yields an edible oil. The half ripe fruits were formerly pickled, and butternut sap after boiling is said to makes a sweet syrup equal to maple syrup.

As with most other native American plants, Butternut root bark was already a remedy among American Indians long before it ever became a physician's remedy in the early 1800s. It found use for rheumatism, headache, toothache and topically for wounds.

On a symptom treatment level, Butternut has always been used for the simple relief of constipation—and was praised by patients and even medics for its smooth operation, free of any griping or diarrhea side effects.

Butternut root bark is a *stimulating decongestant* to all digestive functions, from the gallbladder and stomach all the way to the large intestine, specifically *choleretic, stomachic, gastrointestinal stimulant* and *laxative*—a milder version of Mayapple root in that sense. The remedy is tailor-made for individuals with chronic **damp-heat** in the **liver/gallbladder/stomach** and **accumulation** in the gastrointestinal tract, with prominent symptoms of constipation, epigastric fullness and general malaise and dry skin. Beyond that, however, Butternut treats **microbial toxicosis** resulting from this stagnant atonic condition, accompanied by intestinal dysbiosis. In addition, its juglone content treats any dysbiotic gut organisms that may be present directly.

Because it is so liver-centered, Butternut root bark also addresses the congestive aspect of the liver and portal vein. Through its *portal decongestant* effect the remedy addresses the syndromes **liver blood congestion** and **abdominal plethora** in general, typified by abdominal distension, a tendency to constipation and hemorrhoids, and (more often in women) pelvic congestion. Here Butternut acts like a milder, gentler version of Goldenseal root or Madder root.

True to form in this section of *detoxicants,* Butternut also helps resolve **skin eruptions** dependant on microbial toxicosis. Like Yellow dock root or Barberry bark, moreover, Butternut can also be used as an *intestinal sedative* for **intestines damp-heat,** for infectious or inflammatory bowel conditions. A good *anti-inflammatory* effect is obtained here through a combination of naphthoquinones and tannins.

Figwort Root and Herb

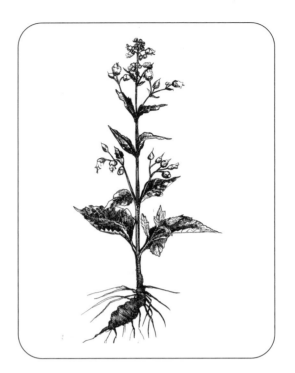

Botanical source: *Scrophularia nodosa* L.,
 S. marylandica, S. californica, S. lanceolata,
 S. aquatica and spp. (Scrophulariaceae)
Pharmaceutical name: Herba Scrophulariae
Ancient names: Millemorbia, Ficaria, Castrangula,
 Galeopsis (Lat)
Other names: Kernelwort, Throatwort, Great
 pilewort, Brownwort (Eng)
 Carpenter's square, Healall, Scrofula plant (Am)
 Herbe du siège, Scrofulaire (noueuse) (Fr)
 Knoten-braunwurz, Skrofelkraut, Feigenkraut,
 Wurmkraut, Rauchwurz (Ge)
Part used: the root and herb (i.e. the whole plant)

NATURE

Therapeutic category: mild remedy with minimal chronic toxicity
Constituents: harpagophytum iridoid glycosides (incl. verbascoside, aucubin), cardioactive glycosides, saponins, flavonoids (incl. diosmin, hesperidin), alkaloid, phenolic acids, organic acids, pectin
Effective qualities: bitter, somewhat pungent, cool, dry
 dissolving, decongesting
Tropism: kidneys, liver, intestines, heart, pancreas, fluids, blood, lymph
 Liver, Heart, Large Intestine meridians
 Fluid, Air bodies
Ground: all krases, biotypes and constitutions

FUNCTIONS AND INDICATIONS

1 **PROMOTES DETOXIFICATION AND CLEARS DAMP-HEAT;**
 REDUCES LIVER CONGESTION AND RELIEVES CONSTIPATION;
 RELIEVES ECZEMA AND REDUCES ALLERGY, LYMPH CONGESTION AND TUMORS

 metabolic toxicosis with *damp-heat:* proneness to skin rashes and swellings, malaise
 liver and intestines Qi stagnation with *damp-heat:* chronic constipation, abdominal distension,
 indigestion, skin rashes
 LIVER CONGESTION
 CONSTIPATION (chronic)
 skin damp-heat: wet, red skin rashes, vesicles, itching
 ECZEMA, atopic dermatitis, hives, erysipelas
 LYMPHADENITIS (chronic), SCROFULA
 TUMORS (incl. lymphoma)

2 **CLEARS TOXIC HEAT AND REDUCES INFLAMMATION;**
 PROMOTES URINATION, DRAINS WATER AND RELIEVES EDEMA

 microbial toxicosis with *toxic heat:* chronic low-grade sores, swollen boils, abscesses, low-grade fever
 INFLAMMATORY suppurative lesions and swellings (esp. dermatitis, mastitis, orchitis, lymphangitis)

FUNGAL/PARASITIC SKIN INFECTIONS (incl. tinea/ringworm, scabies, lice, scurf, scrofula)

HEMORRHOIDS (esp. when hot, painful)

KIDNEY INFLAMMATIONS (incl. nephritis)

GOITER (struma)

liver and kidney water congestion: general or local water retention, fatigue

EDEMA

RHEUMATIC, arthritic, gouty conditions, esp. psoriatic arthritis; hyperuricemia

3 **PROMOTES MENSTRUATION AND EXPELS THE AFTERBIRTH**

uterus Qi stagnation: delayed, scanty, clotted periods, cramps

DYSMENORRHEA

RETAINED PLACENTA

4 **TONIFIES HEART QI;**
RESTORES THE PANCREAS

heart Qi deficiency: precordial oppression, palpitations

HEART WEAKNESS

PANCREATIC INSUFFICIENCY

DIABETES (supportive)

5 **PROMOTES TISSUE REPAIR AND REDUCES INFLAMMATION, SWELLING AND CLOTTING**

WOUNDS and ULCERS (esp. atonic/chronic, with redness, swelling and pain; around eyes/ears/nose/face)

BURNS, scalds, stings, erysipelas, diaper rash and other skin inflammations/infections/irritations

CONTUSION (bruising) from injury, PMS breast pain, menstrual clots

PREPARATION

Use: Figwort root and/or herb is prepared by **infusion** or **tincture. Washes, compresses** and **ointments** containing Figwort are (or should be) often used for topical application in the treatment of wounds, sores, scalds, burns, skin inflammations, bruising and so on. A good complement to Marigold, Plantain, St. John's wort and Gotu kola here.

Dosage: Infusion: 8-16 g

   Tincture: 2-5 ml at 1:3 strength in 45% ethanol

   These doses may be safely increased if neccessary in more serious conditions (e.g., tumors).

Caution: Because of some mild *cardiotonic* action, Figwort herb should not be used with tachycardia or a rapid pulse. Avoid during pregancy and taking with heart medication. Monitor any detox reactions such as (increased) skin rashes when using this remedy.

NOTES

Figwort root and herb is another example of a *detoxicant* remedy that operates by altering the fluid environment in tissues, lymph and skin. The remedy qualifies as one of the finest systemic *detoxicant* and may safely be used in many types of **toxicosis** conditions.

This property is due to two *anti-inflammatory* iridoids that also found in Devil's claw, *Harpago-phytum procumbens,* and several other plants such as Mullein (all of which belong to the same plant family). The two saponins also contribute a major skin-specific *detoxicant* and *anti-inflammatory*

action. From the vitalistic viewpoint, Figwort releases **wind, damp** and **heat** from the **skin** and **meridians,** and clears **damp-heat** from the **liver.**

Like any remedy, Figwort herb excels at certain functions more than others. It is a prime agent for the glandular system as a whole, and should be used in any disorder involving it. The lymphatic system especially is *stimulated, decongested* and *cleansed.* Through a combination of *lymphatic detoxification, capillary stimulation* and *liver stim-ulation,* Figwort addresses a variety of eczemas, especially with redness and itching present. Here it will find support with the likes of Cleavers and Burdock, for instance. Figwort's many names (in European languages) allude to its reliable *detumescent* action on lumps and tumors, including lymph node swelling from lymphadenitis.

Because it works at the ground level of the fluid body and connective tissue, Figwort excels at altering disharmonies at the chronic and degenerative stage of disease. As with the similar Chinese remedy, Trachelospermum Luo Shi Teng, **inflammation** of any kind also calls for Figwort, whether due to chronic conditions such as lymphangitis and arthritis, or due to acute ones from injury. The iridoid glycosides are thought active here.

Figwort is superlative for symptom relief and **first-aid use** in general. Burns, injuries, sprains, irritations and swellings of many kinds can quickly be relieved with it.

As a *cardiotonic* for heart Qi deficiency (note

the glycosides), Figwort root and herb is also very useful for chronic weak heart conditions. As such it should be combined with Hawthorn berry or Lily of the Valley herb for enhancement.

There are some similarities between this species of Figwort, used in Western phytotherapy, and the Black figwort, Scrophularia Xuan Shen *(Scrophularia nodosa)*, commonly used in China. Both remedies are given in formulas for their *refrigerant, anti-inflammatory* and *detoxicant* properties. These address **heat toxin** such as low-grade, chronic infectious sores and boils.

Their uses also divide, however. Black figwort possesses *sedative* and *hypotensive* properties used in Yin deficiency syndromes; Figwort does not. This effectively shifts the overall therapeutic emphasis of the Chinese Black figwort from a *detoxicant, alterant* type remedy to a *draining* one.

Blue Flag Root

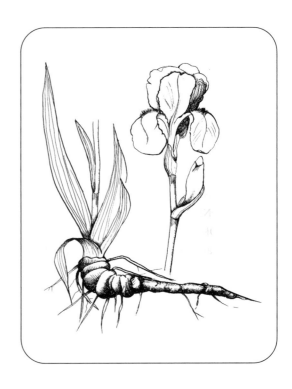

Botanical source: *Iris versicolor, I. germanica* L.
    (Liliaceae)
Pharmaceutical name: Rhizoma Iridis
Ancient names: Ireus, Iris (Gr)
    Affrodisia, Gladiolus, Illiria (Lat)
Other names: Flower-de-luce (Eng)
    Flag lily, Liver lily, Snake lily, Wild iris (Am)
    Iris d'Allemagne, Glaieul bleu, Flambe, Lis (Fr)
    Schwertlilie, Blaue Schwertel, Lilgen,
       Veilchenwurzel, Himmelschwertel (Ge)
Part used: the rhizome

NATURE
Therapeutic category: medium-strength remedy with moderate chronic toxicity
Constituents: alkaloid, salicylic and isophthalic acids, essential oil (incl. ketone, irone), polysaccharide, iridin, phytosterol, heptacosane, myric alcohol, ipuranol, gum, resin, mucilage, tannin, saccharides
Effective qualities: pungent, somewhat bitter and sweet, cold, dry
    stimulating, decongesting, dissolving
Tropism: liver, stomach, spleen, intestines, lungs, bladder, blood, lymph
    Gallbladder, Liver, Lung, Bladder meridians; Warmth, Fluid bodies
Ground: Phlegmatic and Sanguine krasis
    Self-reliant/Yang Ming Metal, Expressive/Jue Yin biotypes; Hematogenic/Brown Iris constitutions

FUNCTIONS AND INDICATIONS

1 PROMOTES DETOXIFICATION AND CLEARS DAMP-HEAT; STIMULATES THE GALLBLADDER, PANCREAS, INTESTINES AND THYROID; REDUCES LIVER CONGESTION AND RELIEVES CONSTIPATION

microbial toxicosis with *damp-heat:* proneness to malaise, skin rashes, food allergies, headaches

liver and gallbladder damp-heat: nauseating headache, bitter vomiting, swollen painful flanks / sides, distaste for rich foods, bitter taste in mouth

ACUTE HEPATITIS, cholecystitis

liver Qi stagnation: distended right flank with sharp pains mid-back pain, clay colored stools, constipation, scanty urine, jaundice

LIVER CONGESTION, SPLEEN and LIVER ENLARGEMENT, biliary and pancreatic insufficiency

stomach and intestines Qi stagnation: swollen, painful abdomen, acid belching, nausea, vomiting of sour semidigested food, constipation, sick headache

CHRONIC CONSTIPATION

BILIARY, PANCREATIC and THYROID DEFICIENCY

2 CLEARS TOXIC HEAT, PROMOTES URINATION, DRAINS WATER AND REDUCES PLETHORA

microbial toxicosis with *toxic heat:* abscesses, sores, urinary infections, fetid vaginal discharges

bladder damp-heat: urgent painful burning urination, thirst

genitourinary damp-heat: venereal infections with purulent discharge (incl. syphilis)

URINARY and GENITAL INFECTIONS (incl. cystitis, vaginitis, yellow leucorrhea, PID, endometriosis)

liver water congestion: generalized edema, heaviness of body, shortness of breath

FATTY LIVER INFILTRATION, EDEMA, ascites

ACUTE GASTRITIS

abdominal plethora: overweight, abdominal distension, chronic lethargy, malaise

3 REDUCES LYMPH CONGESTION, RELIEVES ECZEMA AND REDUCES TUMORS

LYMPHOMA, LYMPHADENITIS with soft swollen glands, scrofula

CHRONIC ECZEMA, HERPES, psoriasis, ringworm (tinea)

CHRONIC ARTHRITIS, gout, rheumatism

TUMORS, UTERINE FIBROIDS; polyps, ovarian cysts, uterine and ovarian enlargement, goiter (thyroid enlargment)

4 PROMOTES EXPECTORATION, RESOLVES PHLEGM AND RELIEVES COUGHING; PROMOTES MENSTRUATION

lung phlegm-heat: full cough with thick yellow sputum, sore throat, hoarseness

ACUTE BRONCHITIS, coughing

uterus Qi stagnation: delayed painful periods with purple clots, sore breasts

DYSMENORRHEA, estrogen accumulation

PREPARATION

Use: Blue flag root is used in **tincture** or **decoction** form. The dried root should be used by preference. The fresh root is somewhat toxic and as a result causes purging.

Topical preparations such as washes and compresses are prepared for skin conditions and wounds. Venereal infections should be addressed with **vaginal sponges, pessaries** and **douches.**

Historical preparations of Blue Flag include **syrups, gargles** and medicinal **snuffs.** SCHROEDER (1611), for example, gives a 15-ingredient **bronchial syrup** for "cold coughs and cold lung conditions." MATTIOLI (1610) presents an *expectorant* and *laxative* **wine** of Blue flag, Agrimony, Holy thistle, Centaury, Wormwood, Betony, Anise, Fennel, Tamarind, Senna, Rhubarb and Scabious, which "cleanses the body of all pernicious damp, assists those with phlegm in the lungs and chest, and with coughing and difficult breathing ... "

Dosage: Smaller doses are sufficient for *stimulating* and *detoxicant* actions. Larger doses are more *purging, detoxicant, heat clearing* and *phlegm resolving.*

Smaller dose:
> **Decoction:** 4-8 g
> **Tincture:** 0.5-2 ml at 1:2 strength in 55% ethanol

Larger dose:
> **Decoction:** 8-16 g
> **Tincture:** 2-4 ml at 1:2 strength in 55% ethanol

Caution: Blue flag root should never be used in deficiency conditions of any kind. Use cautiously during pregnancy. If Blue flag is taken alone it is for short-term use only. When used as part of a formula, this medium-strength remedy rarely causes any problems.

NOTES

At one time, Blue flag root was not only a standard remedy in the European pharmacy, but also the most widely used medicine of all among Native Americans (VOGEL 1970). Of course, it was also eventually taken up by the American medical profession during the nineteenth century. As with many indigenous herbs, this remedy only drew the attention of practising physicians when the pioneering work of Philadelphia botanist WILLIAM BARTON was published in the early 1800s. From then on we see the familiar influence of clinical medicine (originally from Paris) and homeopathy mature and refine its clinical indications to the classic Eclectic medicinal that it became by the 1880s.

Eclectic medical prescribing at that time, like that of contemporary homeopathy, was very specific with respect to remedy symptomatology. This was only partly due to the bleed-through of homeopathy to forms of allopathic medicine during this period. With Blue flag, for example, the type of liver-congested individual best served would typically show clay-colored stools, scanty urine, a thin, narrow red tongue with yellow moss in the center, palpitations and inactive, jaundiced skin. These specific symptoms immediately paint a picture of the particular type of liver congestion addressed. In the same vein we may say, using Chinese medical terminology, that the remedy's use in **liver/gallbladder damp-heat** is characterized by "a neuralgic pain over one eye, or involving one side of the face, usually the right side" (ELLINGWOOD 1919).

Blue flag root essentially clears various kinds of **damp-heat—congestive** and **infectious catarrhal** conditions of the **chest, upper digestive** and **urogenital** areas. Its *stimulating, decongestant* (and *choleretic*) influence is centered on the liver, stomach, gallbladder and small intestines. The remedy works especially well in those suffering from chronic hepatic, gastric and intestinal stasis that periodically causes episodes of acid belching, sick headache, jaundice and constipation. Here the root combines well with other cold *cholagogue laxatives,* such as Cascara sagrada bark, Dandelion root and Bogbean herb.

In this respect the bitter-pungent root covers the therapeutic ground of the Chinese herb Artemisia Yin Chen Hao more than adequately, corresponding to the acupuncture points Gb 34 and 44, Si 4, Bl 18 and 19, and Li 13. As a result, overall catabolism is also enhanced, with evident benefits in chronic **blood, lymph, fluids** and **skin** conditions resulting from high toxin levels. In this context Blue flag can also help resolve gynecological tumors, perhaps with the support of Poke root, for example.

Inasmuch as Blue flag root clears damp-heat in the lower warmer, drains water and dispels wind damp heat obstruction, it shows therapeutic similarities with Stephania Han Fang Ji in the Chinese materia medica.

Mayapple Root

Botanical source: *Podophyllum peltatum* L.
        (Berberidaceae/Podophyllaceae))
Pharmaceutical name: Rhizoma Podophylli
Other names: American mandrake, Racoonberry, Hog
        apple, Indian apple, Wild lemon, Duck's foot,
        Wild jalap (Am)
        Citron (Fr)
Part used: the rhizome

NATURE

Therapeutic category: medium-strength remedy with medium chronic toxicity
Constituents: resin podophyllin (incl. lignan glycosides podophyllotoxin 20%, alpha-/beta-peltatins),
picropodophyllinic and gallic acid, podophylloquercitin, glycosides, tannin, calcium oxalate, essential oil
Effective qualities: bitter, sweet, pungent, cool, dry
        stimulating, decongesting
Tropism: liver, gallbladder,stomach, intestines, uterus, kidneys, bladder
        Liver, Gallbladder meridians
        Fluid, Warmth bodies
Ground: Phlegmatic krasis
        Self-reliant/Yang Ming Metal biotype
        Hematogenic/Sulphuric/Brown Iris constitution

FUNCTIONS AND INDICATIONS

1   **PROMOTES DETOXIFICATION AND CLEARS DAMP-HEAT;**
     PROMOTES BILE FLOW, REDUCES LIVER AND BLOOD CONGESTION, AND
     RELIEVES PLETHORA AND CONSTIPATION

microbial toxicosis with *damp-heat:* food intolerances or allergies, malaise, chronic headaches
gallbladder and stomach damp-heat: appetite loss, dizziness, heavy headache, fatigue, lethargy
CHRONIC BILIARY / GASTRIC DYSPEPSIA
liver / gallbladder Qi stagnation with *damp-heat:* pain beneath right scapula, painful distended
    flanks/sides, hard, dry, clay-colored stools, bitter vomiting, nauseating headache, dizziness
HEPATITIS, JAUNDICE (acute, chronic), hepatomegaly
CHRONIC CONSTIPATION
abdominal plethora with *liver blood congestion:* indigestion, constipation, abdominal distension,
    hemorrhoids
PORTAL CONGESTION, pelvic congestion

**2 PROMOTES DETOXIFICATION AND CLEARS TOXIC HEAT;
RESOLVES ECZEMA AND REDUCES TUMORS**

microbial toxicosis with *toxic heat:* boils, furuncles, skin rashes, pustules

ECZEMA (esp. infantile), fissures, pustules

CHRONIC RHEUMATISM, SYPHILIS, TUMORS

**3 PROMOTES URINATION AND REDUCES EDEMA AND INCONTINENCE;
MODERATES MENSTRUATION**

liver and kidney water congestion: water retention, tissue swelling, sluggishness

EDEMA (dropsy)

URINARY INCONTINENCE

uterus blood congestion: heavy menstrual flow, bearing-down pains, cramps, hemorrhoids

CONGESTIVE DYSMENORRHEA, amenorrhea

PREPARATION

Use: Mayapple root is prepared in **decoction** and **tincture.** The root should always be used dried to reduce its strong irritant quality and reduce its ever-present *emetic* and *diarrheal* potential. The powdered root is a strong skin and mucosal irritant, and should be avoided unless pustulant treatment is desired (see p. 675).

Dosage: Decoction: 2-5 g

Tincture: 0.25-1 ml (10-25 drops) at 1:3 strength in 60% ethanol

The small dose acts as a bitter *digestive stimulant,* the medium one as a *liver decongestant* and *detoxicant,* the large one and over as an *emetic* and *purgative.*

Caution: Contraindicated in all deficiency or weak conditions, during pregnancy and with gallstones present. Mayapple root should always be combined with a *carminative* to relieve the intestinal griping it tends to cause.

Mayapple root is a medium-strength remedy with cumulative toxicity. Doses larger than those indicated will cause vomiting and profuse diarrhea, and were traditionally used in emetic therapy (see Class 6). The remedy is best used in a maximum 10% proportion as part of a formula. It could also be used occasionally or very short-term within the above doses, watching for any signs of toxicity.

Mayapple fruits are edible and are sometimes called "wild lemon" because of their sweet-sour taste.

NOTES

Favoring moist, marshy terrain and wet, wooded areas in the Eastern States, mayapple has fragrant, mawkish white flowers and a lemon-like edible fruit. Mayapple root was a common medicine among Eastern plains American Indians and early White settlers, and was also called Mandrake after the European mandrake of similar action.

In two ways Mayapple epitomized the popular heroic medicine of those days. First, as a botanical *emetic,* alongside the beloved Lobelia and Ipecac; second, as a botanical *purgative,* alongside the exotic Jalap. Early Eclectics nicknamed Mayapple root "vegetable Calomel" because it caused salivation in these larger heroic doses. Although this name was intended as a compliment at the time, today it merely reminds us of the embarassing heroic late Galenic legacy of drastic elimination carried out by mineral remedies such as Calomel.

ELLINGWOOD in his clinical notes (1919) describes the particulars that indicate the use of Mayapple root. The pulse is "full, large, sluggish and oppressed;" the tongue is "pale and flabby, heavily coated, uniformly yellowish, [with a] yellow center, a thick dirty coat, especially at the back;" the skin is "of a dingy hue, dull, soggy, yellowish, flabby, cool, and inclined to eruptions;" there is "fullness of the superficial veins, cool extremities, oppressed heart action, occasionally an irregular or intermittent pulse." This symptom picture could be summed up as a **systemic plethora,** and is typically seen in Sulphuric and Brown Iris constitutions, or "liver types."

Taking this phenomenological information clinically one step further in the direction of therapeutics, we can then define these indications in energetic terms. Mayapple root essentially addresses **damp-heat** conditions centered in the **liver** with secondary **blood congestion.** Physiologically there is **microbial toxicosis** and poor nutrient transformation involving a dysbiotic microflora, liver congestion, portal congestion, venous and capillary insufficiency, as well as sytemic digestive atony causing digestive accumu-lations. This person will present symptoms of bilious, heavy, nauseous headaches, dingy flabby skin with tendencies to boils and cold extremities, chronic indigestion with right flank pain, nausea and constipation, and heavy periods with cramps from chronic pelvic congestion.

There is no doubt that Mayapple is one of the strongest botanical *liver decongestant* and *cholagogues* around, which is why it must only be used in the small doses above. Its increasing scarcity is another reason to reserve this important medicinal not only for chronic, but also severe cases — conditions that are beyond the likes of Butternut, Barberry and even Blue flag. The remedy was, and still can be, used as part of a gallstone flush protocol if gallstones have been diagnosed, as well as a *biliary detoxicant/depurative,* where it stimulates fresh bile flow, liquifies existing hyperviscous bile and promotes gallstone evacuation. Mayapple is not known as a *dissolvent antilithic* remedy, however, unlike Cornsilk or Cleavers.

Modern pharmacological research has shown at least two of Mayapple's chemical constituents to possess *antiviral* and *antitumoral* actions. These are the lignans podophyllotoxin and peltatin, which are currently used in the treatment of warts, especially venereal warts such as HPV. Internal low dosage use of the whole herb or another *antitumoral* remedy should, if possible, complement the topical protocol with these components or their semisynthetic derivatives.

Chaparral Leaf

Botanical source: *Larrea divaricata* L.,
      L. tridentata, L. mexicana L., *L. glutinosa* L.
      (Zygophyllaceae)
Pharmaceutical name: Folium Larreae
Other names: Creosote bush, Greasewood,
      Stinkweed, Black bush (Am)
      Gobernadora, Hediondilla, Tasajo (Sp)
Part used: the leaf (sometimes with the stem)

NATURE

Therapeutic category: medium-strength remedy with moderate chronic toxicity
Constituents: two guaiuretic acids lignins (incl. nordihydroguaiaretic acid [NDGA] 1-1.5%), essential oil (incl. limonene, pinene, eudesmol, calametene), 18 flavonoids (incl. quercetin), larreic acid, free steroids (incl. cholesterol, stigmasterol, campestrol, sitosterol), gums, resin, protein, acids, alcohol, sucrose
Effective qualities: very bitter, pungent, salty, astringent, cold, dry
      stimulating, softening, dissolving, restoring, astringing, stabilizing
Tropism: liver, stomach, urogenital organs
      Liver, Kidney, Bladder meridians
      Warmth, Air bodies
Ground: all krases, biotypes and constitutions for symptomatic use

FUNCTIONS AND INDICATIONS

1   **PROMOTES DETOXIFICATION AND CLEARS DAMP-HEAT;**
      PROTECTS THE LIVER, REDUCES LIVER CONGESTION AND PLETHORA, AND
      RELIEVES CONSTIPATION

      microbial toxicosis with *damp-heat:* proneness to malaise, food allergies
      liver and stomach Qi stagnation with *damp-heat:* epigastric distension, constipation, indigestion,
         appetite loss,biliousness, nausea, vomiting, bitter taste in mouth, dry skin
      UPPER GASTRIC DYSPEPSIA (esp. from fats, proteins)
      HEPATITIS, LIVER TOXICOSIS (from faulty diet, drugs, pollution, disease)
      general plethora: overweight, painful or irregular menstruation, hemorrhoids, malaise

2   **CLEARS TOXIC HEAT AND REDUCES INFECTION, INFLAMMATION AND FEVER;**
      STIMULATES IMMUNITY AND ANTIDOTES POISON

      microbial toxicosis with *toxic heat:* boils, pyodermia, abscesses, fever, acute infections
      VIRAL, BACTERIAL and FUNGAL INFECTIONS (local or systemic, esp. dermal, respiratory, urogenital,
         digestive; incl. herpes, dermatitis, scabies, acne, boils, furuncles, warts, venereal infections,
         bronchitis, hepatitis, candidiasis, athlete's foot, thrush)

PREVENTIVE in EPIDEMICS

REMITTENT FEVERS (*shao yang* stage)

NEURITIS, NEURALGIA (incl. sciatica, lumbago)

POISONING from snakebites, herb or food

3 TONIFIES URINARY QI, HARMONIZES URINATION, DISSOLVES STONES AND ENHANCES VISION; REDUCES TUMORS; RAISES CENTRAL QI AND RELIEVES PROLAPSE

genitourinary (Kidney) Qi deficiency: chronic backache, fatigue, irregular, dripping, irritated urination, dysmenorrha, amenorrhea

URINARY INCONTINENCE, dysuria

URINARY STONES

VISION IMPAIRMENT

ARTHRITIS, RHEUMATISM, ECZEMA (esp. chronic)

TUMORS (benign and malignant, esp. of skin, stomach, liver, kidney)

Central Qi sinking: heavy dragging sensation in lower abdomen

UTERINE PROLAPSE

4 PROMOTES TISSUE REPAIR AND PREVENTS DECAY

WOUNDS, bruises, hemorrhoids

ULCERS, sores

TOOTH DECAY, cavities, gingivitis, periodontitis

PREPARATION

Use: Chaparral leaf is prepared by **cold infusion, long infusion** and **tincture** are the best preparations for Chaparral leaf. A **short decoction** extracts more resins and increases its *antiseptic* property. These may irritate the kidneys, however. On balance, use with care.

Antiseptic, anti-inflammatory and *astringent* **liniments, ointments, washes** and **compresses** are all excellent for topical use, which includes skin eruptions, tumors (incl. cancer), boils, ulcers, wounds and hemorrhoids. Chaparral **mouthwashes** will prevent or treat tooth decay, cavities and gum disorders, and should be used on a daily basis after brushing and flossing (especially by those prone to caries).

Vaginal **douches** and **sponges** are effective for vaginal infections and disharges of most types, as well as for uterine prolapse. These may also be helpful for dysmenorrhea and amenorrhea.

Dosage: Cold infusion, long infusion and **short decoction:** 4-8 g

        Tincture: 1-2.5 ml at 1:2 strength in 45% ethanol

Only small doses are needed for the *digestive stimulant* action (function 4).

Caution: Because of its medium-strength status, Chaparral leaf should not be used on its own (if ever) for more than three weeks. The herb is best given as part of a formula.

Contraindicated in diarrhea from intestines Qi deficiency or cold (Spleen Qi deficiency or Spleen cold). Also forbidden with a history of liver damage present because of possible hepatotoxicity. Some individuals may be hypersensitive to the herb or its resin.

NOTES

Native to the North American Southwest, the chaparral bush in the hot desert sun exudes a characteristic fresh, camphoraceous-green scent with a creosote-like undertone. These signal its high essential oil and resin content. Local Hispanics have appropriately named the shrub *hediondilla,* meaning "little stinker." Despite this superficial disadvantage, however, Chaparral has always been highly valued by native tribes and Hispanics as a good *anti-infective* and *antiseptic* remedy. The same plant that protects itself from predators and microbes through its essentil oil also provides protection for us in the presence of pathogens.

Chaparral leaf is an important remedy for internal and external use in a wide range of infectious and preinfectious conditions. It both improves immune response and inhibits pathogens on direct contact. The substance NDGA, flavonoids and essential oils are active here with *antibacterial* and *antiviral* actions. *Anti-inflammatory, antipyre-tic* and *detoxicant* actions combine here to produce a major remedy for **heat toxin** and other **bacterial/ viral infections,** especially with **fever** present. The *anti-inflammatory* and *antihistamine* action is said to be due to NDGA's inhibition of enzyme systems (including cyclooxygenase and lipogenase).

Moreover, the acid NDGA has also shown *antioxidant,* or free radical-inhibiting, activity. But this in itself is insufficient to explain the remedy's superb *detoxicant* effect in subjects suffering from chronic **microbial** and **metabolic** forms of **toxico-sis.** Typical symptoms here are skin rashes (allergic or otherwise), arthritis, tumors and various forms of neuralgia. While Chaparral improves liver functions, glandular secretions and general metabolism through its stimulating bitter taste, the pungent

essential oil also increases peristalsis (among other things). More than one person has aptly described this remedy as an "industrial-strength liver clean-ser" that radically mobilizes liver congestion.

In energetic terms, Chaparral's bitter, cold, sinking energies effectively clear **liver damp-heat** with **constipation.** In this respect the herb is a good equivalent to Baikal skullcap root. Like So-phora Ku Shen, however, Chaparral also dispels **wind-heat** and **damp-heat** drom the **skin** and **meridians,** thereby treating both dry and suppura-tive eczema.

Chaparral leaf could be used to tonify urogen-ital (Kidney) Qi and relieve incontinence and stone formation. However, in this case it should always be combined with warming herbs to counteract its cold, sinking nature. The remedy on the whole is best used in **damp-heat urinary infections** with dripping, irritated urination.

Oregon Grape Root

Botanical source: *Mahonia aquifolia, M. repens* Webber, *M. nervosa, M. pinnata* (syn. *Berberis* spp. Pursh) (Berberidaceae)
Pharmaceutical name: Cortex radicis Mahoniae
Other names: Mountain holly/grape, Holly grape, Creeping/Trailing mahonia, California barberry (Am)
Yerba de Sangre (Sp)
Part used: the root bark

NATURE
Therapeutic category: mild remedy with minimal chronic toxicity
Constituents: isoquinoline alkaloids (incl. berberine, oxyberberine, oxyacanthine, berbamine, canadine, mahonine, magnoflorine, jatrorrhizine), tannins, resins
Effective qualities: bitter, cold, dry
stimulating, restoring, astringing
Tropism: liver, gallbladder, stomach, intestines, skin
Liver, Gallbladder meridians
Warmth, Fluid bodies
Ground: all constitutions and biotypes

FUNCTIONS AND INDICATIONS

1 PROMOTES DETOXIFICATION, CLEARS DAMP-HEAT AND RELIEVES ECZEMA; REGULATES BILE FLOW AND REDUCES LIVER CONGESTION

microbial toxicosis with *damp-heat:* proneness to dry or poorly healing skin, food allergies

ECZEMA, dermatosis, dry skin eruptions (scaly, pustular), dandruff, pimples, rough complexion

ACNE, psoriasis

LIVER CONGESTION, hepatitis

liver and stomach Qi stagnation with *damp-heat:* indigestion (esp. from fats), right subcostal pain/swelling, bad breath, constipation, appetite loss, fat intolerance, constipation

BILIARY / GASTRIC / PANCREATIC DYSPEPSIA

2 CLEARS DAMP-HEAT, REDUCES INFECTION AND INFLAMMATION

intestines damp-heat: diarrhea, urgent painful stool

ENTERITIS (mild, incl. food poisoning, mild dysentery [bacterial, amoebic])

PREPARATION

Use: Oregon grape root is prepared by **decoction** and **tincture**. Topical preparations such as **salves** or **compresses** are made for skin abrasions as well as for the above skin disorders.

Dosage: **Decoction**: 8-16 g

   Tincture: 2-4 ml at 1:2 strength in 35% ethanol

Caution: Avoid using this remedy during pregnancy, and in hyperthyroid conditions.

NOTES

Closely related to the common barberry and often put under the *Berberis* genus is the Oregon grape. This "mountain holly" or "mountain grape" is a true Western States native and barberry look-alike which, however, should be clearly differentiated from it both in appearance and therapeutic effects.

It is true that both Oregon grape root and Barberry root bark are *liver stimulants* and *gastrointestinal sedatives* with bitter, cold, dry qualities. They also count similar isoquinoline alkaloids from the biochemical point of view, which are also found in Goldenseal root and related Chinese genera. Still, as with other "look-alikes" and "analogs," it is important to consider their differences as much as their similarities, especially when we consider the perspective of clinical practice rather than theoretical pharmacognosy.

In the case of Oregon grape root, its tropism for the skin and its specific ability to handle various skin problems stands out. The remedy could simply be labeled a "specific" for skin problems, much like Burdock root and Heartsease, one that generally improves skin quality. In particular, it is helpful for individuals presenting chronic **dry skin eruptions** arising from liver congestion, especially with excess alkalinity present.

Secondly, Oregon grape root will also treat suppurative dermatitis, acne and various other skin conditions—where it should preferably be combined with other *dermatropic* remedies from this section. The root is said to stimulate the liver and skin metabolism of dietary and blood proteins (MOORE 1993).

From the energetic perspective, Oregon grape root clears **damp-heat**—from the liver, the skin and the middle warmer. Like the other herbs in this section, it should be used for individuals with a basic terrain of **microbial toxicosis** who tend to food allergies and dry skin, and for the central syndrome **liver and stomach Qi stagnation** with its typical dyspeptic acolyte symptoms.

It is true that Oregon grape root will treat mild infectious enteritic conditions with damp-heat. However, were we to rely just on a biochemical comparison of this plant, Barberry root bark and Goldenseal root, we might be misled into thinking that these remedies were completely interchangeable. Nothing could be further from the truth of clinical experience. In reality, Oregon grape root is only a mild *anti-infective* when compared to Barberry, itself a mild *anti-infective* compared to Goldenseal. In the final analysis, Oregon grape is an ideal remedy for milder cases of food poisoning or dysentery, as well as for children.

Fumitory Herb

Botanical source: *Fumaria officinalis* L.
(Papaveraceae/Fumariaceae)
Pharmaceutical name: Herba Fumariae
Ancient names: Kapnos, Phoumaria (Gk)
Fumus terrae (Lat)
Other names: Beggary, Wax dolls, Earth smoke,
Snapdragon (Eng)
Fumeterre, Herbe à la jaunisse, Fiel de terre (Fr)
Erdrauch, Taubenkropf, Katzenkörbel (Ge)
Part used: the herb

NATURE

Therapeutic category: medium-strength remedy with moderate chronic toxicity
Constituents: alkaloids (incl. fumarine, cryptocavine, corydaline, sinactine, aurotensine), fumaric acid, hydroxycinnamic acid esters, cholin, flavonoids (incl. rutin, quercitin), mucilage, resin, bitter
Effective qualities: bitter, somewhat salty, cold, dry
stimulating, diluting, sinking
Tropism: liver, gallbladder, intestines, uterus, blood, skin, nervous system
Liver, Gallbladder, Triple Heater meridians
Warmth, Fluid bodies
Ground: Choleric and Sanguine krases
Tough/Shao Yang and Expressive/Jue Yin biotypes
Hematogenic/Sulphuric/Brown Iris constitution

FUNCTIONS AND INDICATIONS

1 **PROMOTES DETOXIFICATION AND CLEARS DAMP-HEAT;**
   REGULATES BILE FLOW, REDUCES LIVER CONGESTION AND PLETHORA, AND
   RELIEVES ECZEMA

   microbial toxicosis with *damp-heat:* dry skin rashes, malaise, food intolerances/allergies
   liver and stomach Qi stagnation with *damp-heat:* indigestion, right subcostal pain/swelling,
      constipation, appetite loss, fat intolerance, irritability, mood swings
   LIVER CONGESTION, JAUNDICE, gastritis
   gallbladder Yang excess: gastric indigestion soon after eating, acute gastric distress with right rib pain,
      right scapula pain, epigastric distension, overconfidence
   BILIARY / GASTRIC DYSPEPSIA
   CHRONIC BILIARY DYSKINESIA (insufficient or excessive bile flow)
   general plethora: overweight, abdominal distension, malaise
   OBESITY
   ECZEMA, psoriasis, dermatosis

2 STIMULATES DIGESTION AND RESOLVES MUCUS-DAMP; PROMOTES MENSTRUATION

intestines mucous-damp : alternating constipation and diarrhea, indigestion, abdominal distension
CHRONIC DYSPEPSIA (most kinds)
uterus Qi stagnation: delayed painful menstruation, dark clots
DYSMENORRHEA

3 RESOLVES CONTUSIONS

CONTUSIONS, bruising, ecchymosis

PREPARATION

Use: Fumitory herb is prepared as **infusion** and **tincture.** The herb is used in topical **compresses,** etc. for contusions.
Dosage: Infusion: 4-10 g
          Tincture: 1-3 ml at 1:3 strength in 35% ethanol
Caution: If used over about ten days, Fumitory will begin to show a *nervous sedative* effect that can escalate and end up acting like the related California poppy (*Eschscholtzia*) or Bleeding heart (*Dicentra*). This medium-strength remedy generates slight cumulative toxicity over time. Use with discretion or for the short-term only, or combine with other herbs. Avoid use with prescription medication.

Fumitory is forbidden during pregnancy not only because of possible teratogenic effects, but also because of its general stimulant action on all the pelvic organs. Contraindicated in stomach or intestines cold (Spleen cold), especially with diarrhea present.

NOTES

Fumitory is one of those classic Greek medicine herbs that has been used successfully for both acute and chronic digestive conditions since pre-Greek days. Its Latin name means "earth smoke."

Fumitory belongs to the poppy family, like celandine, blood root and corydalis, and evinces an impressive array of seven alkaloids. These provide a systemic relaxing and cooling effect via the nervous system, which becomes centrally sedating with continuous use. With its bitter, salty and sinking taste effects, Fumitory herb is definitely a cooling remedy that should be used mainly for individuals who easily generate heat—red-faced, overweight and irritable types that look "like they're about to throw a fit."

Like Celandine herb, Fumitory is and important hepatic and biliary remedy in particular. Unlike it, however, Fumitory possesses an amphoteric regulating action on bile production and release. It is unique among the gallbladder herbs in this respect. The herb has a solid empirical tradition of use for all conditions of **liver, gallbladder** and **stomach Qi stagnation** arising from either deficient or, as is sometimes the case, excessive bile flow (WEISS 1972). The syndrome **gallbladder Yang ex-**cess presents the typical symptom picture involved with excessive discharge of thin, low quality bile.

But we should also take a more wide-angle perspective of this herb's effects when taken over a longer time period, and when combined with the likes of Figwort herb, Dandelion root or Butternut root bark. Fumitory herb is excellent for those presenting **toxicosis** and **general plethora** involving **mucus-damp accumulation** and **gallbladder** dysfunction. The individual symptom picture here includes irritability, skin rashes, weight gain, recurring digestive problems and, for women, late, painful, clotted periods. From the energetic perspective, GALEN's summary statement that the remedy "de-obstructs the liver, evacuates burnt bile and cools the blood" cannot be bettered.

This therapeutic profile suggests the disharmonies of the Shao Yang biotype with their constitutional sympathetic nervous excess, which are basically those of the Gallbladder and Triple Heater meridians. In usage patterns of, say, ten days on, four days off, Fumitory could well be a good preventive ground tonic for this constitutional type.

Promote Detoxification, Resolve Damp and Dissolve Deposits

Cool diuretic depurant detoxicants (urinary dissolvents, antilithics)

Cleavers Herb

Botanical source: *Galium aparine* L. (Rubiaceae)
Pharmaceutical name: Herba Galii aparinis
Ancient names: Galion, Gallerion, Aparine,
        Philanthropos (Gk)
    Rubea minor (Lat)
Other names: Goosegrass, Clites, Cleaverwort,
        Goslingweed, Hedgeriff, Hayruff,
        Sticky-willie (Eng)
    Gratteron, Gaillet accrochant, Caille-lait,
        Petit muguet (Fr)
    Kletten-Labkraut, Klebkraut, Vogelheu, Klimme
        (Ge)
Part used: the herb

NATURE

Therapeutic category: mild remedy with minimal chronic toxicity
Constituents: citric/rubichloric/galitannic acids, red dye with anthraquinones (incl. galiosin), saponins, asperuloside, coumarins, chlorophyll, tannins, trace minerals
Effective qualities: somewhat bitter, sweet, salty, cold, dry
        softening, dissolving, diluting, decongesting, restoring
Tropism: liver, bladder, prostate, blood, fluids, lymph, skin
        Kidney, Bladder meridians
        Fluid, Warmth bodies
Ground: Sanguine krasis
        Charming/Yang Ming Earth biotype
        all three constitutions

FUNCTIONS AND INDICATIONS

1 **PROMOTES DETOXIFICATION, RESOLVES DAMP AND DISSOLVES DEPOSITS;**
    REDUCES LYMPH CONGESTION, ECZEMA AND TUMORS;
    THINS THE BLOOD AND LYMPH, AND DISSOLVES CLOTS

    metabolic toxicosis with *damp:* skin rashes, swollen glands, nodules in skin, malaise
    URINARY DEPOSITS (incl. stones)
    LYMPHADENITIS, tonsilitis, scrofula
    skin damp (-heat): dry itching skin, chronic rashes, dry scales
    ECZEMA, psoriasis, lichen (chronic)
    TUMORS (incl. malignant, esp. of skin; lymphoma, breast tumors)
    THROMBOSIS (blood clots)

2   **PROMOTES URINATION, DRAINS WATER AND RELIEVES EDEMA;
HARMONIZES URINATION AND RELIEVES IRRITATION**

kidney and liver water congestion: general or local water retention, thirst
EDEMA (incl. with fever)
bladder Qi constraint: painful or dripping urination
BLADDER / KIDNEY / PROSTATE IRRITATION, dysuria, neurogenic bladder

3   **CLEARS DAMP-HEAT AND REDUCES FEVER AND INFLAMMATION;
REDUCES LIVER CONGESTION**

bladder damp-heat: dribbling urination, bladder pains, scalding orange urine, thirst
URINARY INFECTIONS (esp. acute cystitis); prostatitis
INTERMITTENT FEVERS with empty heat (*shao yin* stage)
ERUPTIVE SKIN CONDITIONS (incl. scarlet fever, measles, erysipelas)
liver damp-heat: right hypochondriac soreness and swelling, nausea, jaundice
LIVER CONGESTION, HEPATITIS
heat toxin: boils, sores, ulcers, fever
LYMPHANGITIS

4   **REDUCES INFLAMMATION AND PROMOTES TISSUE REPAIR**

BURNS, sunburn, inflammations, blemishes
FRESH WOUNDS

PREPARATION

Use: Cleavers herb is used in fresh **juice, infusion** and **tincture** form. Never boil or decoct Cleavers, as this destroys much of its biological activity.

Cooling, soothing, healing external preparations like **swabs, compresses** and **ointments** are effective topically for burns, skin inflammations, wounds, skin blemishes, etc. They are also useful for skin and lymph cancers, in conjunction with internal use.

Dosage: Juice: 2 tsp
        Infusion: 8-16 g
        Tincture: 2-5 ml at 1:3 strength in 25% ethanol
Caution: None
Note: In chronic conditions, best results are obtained when Cleavers herb is given over a long period.

NOTES

From the energetic viewpoint, this sticky, ubiquitous wayside plant posesses two main therapeutic themes. First, Cleavers as a *refrigerant* herb, and second as a *detoxicant* herb. Herbal medicine uses these two primary functions in a very specific way. These become clearer when we consider its particular tropism for the skin, lymphatic system and urinary tract.

Thanks to the tannins, trace minerals and organic acids, we can today still apply Cleavers' heat-clearing effect to **intermittent fevers** presenting **Yin deficiency** with **empty heat.** The remedy is a true *refrigerant,* cooling and refreshing in summer like Borage leaf and Chickweed herb, and lowering the temperature in the case of fevers. Greek medicine in Europe extensively used Cleavers in this way.

Cleavers herb is also an important *urinary sedative* remedy for clearing damp-heat from the urinary system and the liver. Its strong *detoxicant diuretic* and *stone-dissolvent* actions address **edema, jaundice, urinary stones** and acute **urinary tract infections** with painful dripping urination in a **damp-heat** presentation. The herb can also be used as a simple—yet effective—*lenitive urinary demulcent,* like Cornsilk or Marsh mallow root, for bladder irritation from any cause. In most of these respects Cleavers especially resembles the Chinese herb Desmodium Jin Qian Cao.

Perhaps better known and documented by today's biochemical standards is Cleavers' systemic *detoxicant* function. This causes a qualitative alteration of the fluid and blood environment (saponins, acids) involving increased urinary and lymphatic dredging of toxins. By enhancing catabolic resorption processes involving exudates and wastes, a *resolvent* effect becomes prominent and includes valuable *anti-inflammatory, skin* and *lymph-detoxicant* and *antitumoral* actions.

Cleavers is important for individuals with chronic **skin eruptions** or **lymphatic disorders**— dermatitis and lymphangitis among them. In short, the herb essentially dispels **damp-heat** and **toxic heat** from the skin. In the experience of Eclectic doctors, the remedy was also useful for "nodulated growths or deposits in the skin or mucous membranes" (JOHN SCUDDER 1874).

Cleavers herb will clearly combine well with other *refrigerants* (Class 12) as well as *detoxicants* from this class in general. Its combined actions make the herb a good assistant remedy in formulas for any type of infection. In overall gestalt, Cleavers is close to the herb Polygonum Hu Zhang (Japanese knotweed) used in Chinese medicine.

London pharmacist JOHN QUINCY's lament in the early eighteenth century that "modern Practice hath no regard for it" is fortunately no longer true. Herbal medicine clearly has greatly evolved its treatment strategies since those days of simplistic heroic treatment.

Burdock Root

Botanical source: *Arctium lappa* L.
  (Asteraceae/Compositae)
Pharmaceutical name: Radix Arctii
Ancient names: Arkeion, Prosopis (Gk)
  Bardana, Lappa (Lat)
Other names: Beggar's/Cockle buttons, Cocklebur,
  Bazzies, Eldin, Hare lock (Eng)
  Bardane, Glatteron, Napolier, Teignons (Fr)
  Grosse Klette, Klisse, Dackenkraut, Grindwurzel
  (Ge)
Part used: the root; also the seed, Fructus Arctii

NATURE
Therapeutic category: mild remedy with minimal chronic toxicity
Constituents: bitter glycosides (incl. arctiopicrin), flavonoids (incl. arctiin, arctigenin), polysaccharides, two lignans (lignaol A and B), arctic/volatile/norhydroxy/phosphoric/tannic acids, alkaloid, antibiotic substances, inulin (up to 45%), tannin, resin, fixed oil, mucilage 5-12%, condensed tannins, essential oil traces, polyacetylenes, vitamins A, C, minerals (incl. calcium, phosphorus, iron, sodium, iodine, chromium, magnesium, silicon, cobalt, zinc, selenium, manganese), thiamine, riboflavin, niacin
Effective qualities: somewhat bitter and pungent, cool, dry
  dissolving, stimulating, restoring
Tropism: kidneys, bladder, liver
  Kidney, Bladder, Liver, Gallbladder, Lung meridians
  Fluid, Air bodies
Ground: all krases, biotypes and constitutions for symptomatic use

FUNCTIONS AND INDICATIONS

1 PROMOTES DETOXIFICATION, RESOLVES DAMP AND DISSOLVES DEPOSITS; REDUCES LYMPH CONGESTION AND RELIEVES ECZEMA AND IRRITATION

metabolic toxicosis with *damp:* skin rashes, swollen glands, joint pains and stiffness, muscle aches, headaches, dry skin, frequent urinary infections, bladder irritation

URINARY DEPOSITS (incl. stones)

BLADDER IRRITATION, DYSURIA (incl. difficult, dribbling, irregular urination)

LYMPHADENITIS, scrofula, ovarian cysts

skin damp / heat: lumps, swellings, rashes, dry scales, weeping purulent eruptions

ECZEMA, PSORIASIS, scurvy, itch, syphilis, hives (urticaria) (esp. chronic)

ARTHRITIS, GOUT, rheumatism; hyperuricemia

TUMORS (incl. malignant)

2 CLEARS TOXIC HEAT, REDUCES INFECTION AND INFLAMMATION; STIMULATES IMMUNITY AND ANTIDOTES POISON; REGULATES IMMUNITY TO REDUCE ALLERGY

microbial toxicosis with *toxic heat:* purulent sores and boils, carbuncles, furuncles, abscesses, anthrax

INFECTIONS (bacterial, fungal, incl. flu, venereal/yeast infections, ringworm, candidiasis, herpes)

POISONING from food, herbs or bites (incl. snakebite)

PREVENTIVE in EPIDEMICS

ALLERGIES (incl. eczema, hives/urticaria), autoimmune disorders

3 TONIFIES UROGENITAL QI, HARMONIZES URINATION AND RELIEVES INCONTINENCE; HARMONIZES MENSTRUATION

genitourinary (Kidney) Qi deficiency: clear, frequent urination (scanty or copious), delayed, difficult menstruation

URINARY INCONTINENCE, enuresis

uterus Qi stagnation: delayed, irregular, painful periods

DYSMENORRHEA

4 PROMOTES SWEATING, DISPELS WIND-HEAT, REDUCES FEVER AND PROMOTES ERUPTIONS

external wind-heat: feverishness, sore throat, dry skin, thirst

COLD and FLU ONSET

ERUPTIVE FEVER (incl. measles, scarlet fever, typhus, chickenpox)

5 STIMULATES DIGESTION, PROMOTES BILE FLOW AND RELIEVES FULLNESS; RAISES CENTRAL QI AND RELIEVES PROLAPSE

gallbladder and stomach Qi deficiency: epigastric distension and pain, indigestion, flatulence

UPPER DIGESTIVE DYSPEPSIA, intestinal dysbiosis

Central Qi sinking: dragging sensation in lower abdomen

PROLAPSE of internal organs (esp. uterus)

DIABETES (supportive)

6 PROMOTES TISSUE REPAIR AND BENEFITS THE SKIN AND HAIR

WOUNDS, ULCERS (esp. atonic, chronic, purulent); burns, caries

HERPES SORES

SKIN, SCALP and HAIR conditions in general (incl. balding)

PREPARATION

Use: Burdock root **juice, decoction** and **tincture** are the best preparations. The fresh root makes the most active *antibacterial* and *antifungal* remedy.

Used in **ointments** and **creams,** Burdock comes into its own for all skin conditions (function 6). A **medicated oil** with Burdock root is used for hair and scalp conditions.

Burdock seed is more effective for urinary and skin conditions than the root because of its additional *diaphoretic* action. The seed also treats wind-heat conditions with sore throat.

The fresh root or seed are best for lowering blood sugar in diabetes.

Dosage: Decoction: 6-12 g

Tincture: 1-4 ml at 1:2 strength in 25% ethanol

Caution: Watch for possible cleansing reactions and only increase the dose gradually. In chronic conditions of toxicosis begin with a low dose of this remedy and/or combine with stronger *diuretics* such as Cleavers herb or Dandelion root/leaf to ensure better toxin elimination through the urine.

Being a gentle *uterine stimulant,* Burdock root is contraindicated in pregnancy except during the last trimester.

NOTES

There are certain remedies that are not particularly dramatic, but which over time prove particularly effective. These herbs tend to treat a broad range of disharmonies with equal success. Herbs such as Yarrow, Agrimony, Speedwell and Vervain are examples. Burdock root also belongs to this group.

Although also an *eliminant,* Burdock root is essentially *regulating* in the widest sense. Its numerous and multifaceted actions are equally *restoring, altering* and *eliminating.* Burdock can clear both **damp-heat** and **damp** from the **skin** and **channels,** and treats **bladder Qi deficiency** with either incontinence or irritation present (especially when caused by **urinary deposits**).

Burdock is very useful for those presenting chronic, multi-layered disharmonies, especially when they involve urinary, digestive and epidermal systems. With its multipronged *diuretic, diaphoretic* and *detoxicant* actions, Burdock both corrects these underlying dysfunctions and relieves the particular symptoms presenting. Remembering Burdock as a skin and bladder remedy is a terse but useful rule of thumb.

The dynamics of Burdock root's *detoxicant* functions are interesting. The root specifically retrieves toxins from the connective tissue and shunts them into the bloodstream. Remember, though, that an excess of toxins in the bloodstream can cause low-level skin eruptions, fatigue, headaches and general malaise. When using a *resolvent detoxicant* such as this one, it is crucial to achieve a nice balance between tissue detoxification and toxin elimination. And because Burdock root is not a significant *diuretic* or *diaphoretic,* support from a *draining diuretic* such as Cleavers herb or Birch leaf or Wild carrot seed, or a *stimulant diaphoretic* such as Ginger root or Jamaica sarsaparilla root (depending on the type of toxicosis being treated) is usually welcome. Burdock's reputation for treating malignant **tumors** is supported by the finding that arctigenin has shown *antitumoral* activity.

If, as in Chinese medicine, the *seed* of this plant is used (Arctium Niu Bang Zi), Burdock has a greater ability to cause sweating and resolve **wind-heat** onsets of upper respiratory infections. In the process, sore throats are relieved, chronic skin conditions are cleared up and eruptions are promoted in the course of measles. Burdock root's polysaccharides modulate immune functions and add the final touch in the treatment of wind-heat colds and flus—more evidence that if several parts of an herb are used medicinally, best results are usually achieved by combining them into one remedy.

Burdock root's content in inulin and two lignans has been related to *anti-inflammatory* and *immunoregulatory,* activities. These find application on one hand to **inflammatory conditions** (i.e. heat toxin), including acute laryngitis and pyoderma. On the other hand, they apply to **immune hypersensitivity disorders** such as allergic/atopic dermatitis, food allergies and angioedema. In these conditions Burdock root clearly strikes as contemporary a note today as it it did with toxicosis disorders in the past.

Pipsissewa (Wintergreen) Herb and Root

Botanical source: *Chimaphila umbellata* Nuttall
　　(syn. *Pyrola umbellata* L.), *C. maculata* Pursh
　　and spp. (Ericaceae)
Pharmaceutical name: Herba et radix Chimaphilae
Other names: a) Ground holly, Prince's pine, Bitter
　　wintergreen, King's cure, Rheumatism
　　weed, Fire-flower (Am)
　b) Spotted wintergreen (Am)
　Wood lily, Wintergreen (Eng)
　Doldenblütiges Wintergrün, Harnkraut,
　　Winterlieb, Nabel/Gichtkraut, Waldmangold,
　　Waldholde (Ge)
Part used: the herb and root

NATURE

Therapeutic category: mild remedy with minimal chronic toxicity
Constituents: a) flavonoids (incl. hyperoside, arbutin 7.5%, isohomoarbutin, ericolin), taraxasterol and sitosterol, crystal chimaphilin (2%), hemtriancontane, ursolic/silicic/sulphuric acid, salicylic acid, epicatechin gallate, tannins (4%), bitters, minerals (incl. iron, calcium, potassium, magnesium)
Effective qualities: astringent, somewhat bitter and sweet, cold, dry
　　dissolving, stimulating, decongesting, restoring, astringing, stabilizing
Tropism: bladder, kidneys, liver, circulation, skin, blood and lymph, breasts
　　Kidney, Bladder, Liver meridians
　　Fluid body
Ground: Melancholic krasis
　　Burdened/Shao Yin and Sensitive/Tai Yin Metal biotypes
　　Lymphatic/Carbonic and Biliary/Phosphoric constitutions

FUNCTIONS AND INDICATIONS

1　**PROMOTES DETOXIFICATION, RESOLVES DAMP AND DISSOLVES DEPOSITS;**
　　REDUCES LYMPH CONGESTION, RESOLVES ECZEMA AND REDUCES TUMORS;
　　RELIEVES PAIN

　　metabolic toxicosis with *damp:* chronic skin rashes, swollen glands, joint stiffness and pains, muscle
　　　aches and pains
　　URINARY DEPOSITS (incl. stones)
　　LYMPHADENITIS with hard, swollen glands, with ulcers; scrofula
　　skin damp / heat: skin rashes (dry or wet with vesicles)
　　ECZEMA
　　RHEUMATISM, arthritis, gout (chronic); hyperuricemia
　　TUMORS, ovarian cysts; breast lumps, enlarged breasts
　　POSTPARTUM PAIN

2 CLEARS TOXIC- AND DAMP-HEAT, AND REDUCES INFECTION, INFLAMMATION AND FEVER; ASTRINGES AND STOPS DISCHARGE

microbial toxicosis with *toxic heat:* fever, chronic abscesses, sores, ulcers, boils, lymphangitis, mastitis

bladder and kidney damp-heat: frequent, urgent, difficult, burning urination, dark urine, thirst, lumbar aches, nausea, fever

URINARY INFECTIONS (incl. cystitis [incl. interstitial], urethritis, nephritis; esp. chronic); prostatitis

genitourinary damp-heat: painful urination, fetid purulent yellow vaginal discharges

VENEREAL INFECTIONS (incl. gonorrhea)

INTERMITTENT FEVERS (*shao yin* stage)

LEUCORRHEA (white or yellow)

3 TONIFIES UROGENITAL QI, HARMONIZES URINATION AND RELIEVES INCONTINENCE AND IRRITATION; PROMOTES URINATION, DRAINS WATER AND RELIEVES EDEMA

genitourinary (Kidney) Qi deficiency with *damp:* fatigue, frequent, scanty, dripping urination, bedwetting, cloudy turbid urine, clear vaginal discharges, delayed or absent periods

URINARY INCONTINENCE

DYSURIA, ENURESIS

MUCUS, pus or blood in urine

CHRONIC NEPHRITIS, NEPHROSIS

AMENORRHEA due to pregnancy, constitution, overwork

PROSTATE CONGESTION with irritation

CHRONIC URINARY and PROSTATIC IRRITATION

kidney water congestion: ankle or leg swelling progressing to rest of body, fatigue, poor appetite

EDEMA, ascites

4 PROMOTES TISSUE REPAIR, BENEFITS THE SKIN AND RELIEVES SWELLING AND PAIN

WOUNDS (fresh and chronic), sores

SKIN conditions in general

PREPARATION

Use: Pipsissewa herb and root is prepared by **long infusion,** 10 minute **short decoction** or **tincture** (the most effective). External uses include **pessaries** and **douches** for gynecological complaints, and **salves, lotions** or **compresses** applied for skin, lymph and all painful conditions.

Fresh **Pipsissewa leaf,** bruised and applied to the skin, is *rubefacient* and *vesicant.* By causing counterirritation (and eventually blistering) it is useful in painful conditions such as arthritis (see p. 675).

Dosage: Long infusion and **short decoction:** 6-12 g

Tincture: 2-4 ml at 1:3 strength in 30% ethanol

Caution: None

NOTES

Pipsissewa is the Native American name for a small plant in the heather family. It has little pink or white flowers and grows extensively in the cool, shady pine and larch forests of North America. The plant has always enjoyed a variety of therapeutic uses, having been used by Native Americans, Pennsylvania Germans and Thomsonian and Eclectic practitioners alike. The main European species of *Chimaphila* is closely related to the American one, contains almost identical chemical compo-

nents and is used therapeutically in exactly the same way. Both species will therefore be discussed under the name of Pipsissewa.

Pipsissewa's history goes back to ancient times through the unrecorded, empirical tradition of European wise women healers. They very likely made extensive use of its multifaceted healing properties. Its reputation among these healers must have been stellar for two reasons. First, because—as the Italian medic PIERANDREA MATTIOLI reports around 1570—it was a stock-in-trade *detergent* (wound-cleanser) and *vulnerary* among the up-and-coming barber-surgeons during the sixteenth century. Barber-surgeons were essentially folk healers who, like all folk healers, only used plant remedies that really worked.

The second reason lies among the writings of Paracelsus. This brilliant Renaissance therapist asserted that "for wounds, for old weeping injuries/ to stop abdominal fluxes/and for fresh wounds, there is hardly any remedy in greater repute for healing these." This statement comes from a physician who openly boasted that he had learned more herbal medicine from witches and midwives than from his entire readings of the Greek medical classics. Although in those days this was a dangerous conceit, more importantly for us today, it was also a brutally honest one.

Clearly, we are looking at a botanical with a solid, if largely unwritten, reputation.

Today we can only fully appreciate Pipsissewa's therapeutic scope by examining its energetic qualities. Its taste properties are cool, astringent and dry. The outcome on the skin and mucous membrane is *antiseptic, anti-inflammatory, detoxicant* and *mucostatic*. This indicates the use of Pipsissewa in conditions of **damp-heat** and **toxic heat,** i.e., suppurative infectious accompanied by purulent discharge. As it powerfully promotes resorbtion, Pipsissewa (like Elderflower and Poke root) treats many kinds of swelling, including lipomas and tumors. As a *lymphatic decongestant* it can reduce swollen lymph glands.

Harnkraut (urine weed) is one of Pipsissewa's names in German. It points to the remedy's important cluster of actions on the urinary tract. These become more understandable when we note the similar flavonoids component (including arbutin) to Bearberry leaf and Bilberry leaf from the same family. Because it clears **damp-heat** in the **lower warmer,** Pipsissewa is for those tending to acute urinary infections, prostatitis, vaginal discharges and urinary stones—especially when accompanied by painful, frequent, scanty urination containing mucus or blood. In this respect it would be a good stand-in for a *damp-drainig diuretic* from the Chinese materia medica such as Dianthus Qu Mai. The herb's associated *antipyretic* action was used by Pennsylvania Germans to reduce fever: they took their cue from Native Americans, as the English had also done centuries before them.

In the past Pipsissewa was called "Rheumatism weed" because its systemic *detoxicant* action has long been used for syndromes of **metabolic toxicosis** with rheumatic pains, and eczemas with dry or wet eruptions. In Chinese medical terms, this herb clears **wind-damp** obstructing the **skin** and **channels.** The remedy's salicylic acid content signals a useful *analgesic* effect, in this respect.

Speedwell Herb

Botanical source: *Veronica officinalis* L.
     (Scrophulariaceae)
Pharmaceutical name: Herba Veronicae officinalis
Ancient names: Veronica, Betonica (Lat)
Other names: Paul's betony, Groundheal, Fluellin
     (Eng)
     Véronique, Herbe aux ladres, Thé d'Europe (Fr)
     Echter Ehrenpreis, Grindheil, Ausschlagkraut,
      Heil aller Schäden (Ge)
Part used: the herb

NATURE

Therapeutic category: mild remedy with minimal chronic toxicity
Constituents: bitter, tannin, saponin, alkaloid, acrid compound, resin, malic/tartaric/citric/lactic/acetic acids
Effective qualities: somewhat bitter and astringent, cold, dry
dissolving, decongesting, stimulating, astringing, restoring

This remedy is virtually identical in its nature, functions, indications and preparations to **Pipsissewa herb and root** (p. 699). However, the following differences should be noted:

1   Because Speedwell herb is a *resolvent detoxicant* that contains saponin, its focus is the skin more than the joints or muscles. Like Heartsease herb and Burdock root, Speedwell excells at treating **chronic skin disorders** of many kinds.
2   Unlike Pipsissewa herb and root, Speedwell herb is a *stimulant* and *mucolytic expectorant* used for chronic **lung phlegm-damp** and **lung phlegm-dryness** syndromes in bronchitis, bronchial asthma, etc.
3   Speedwell herb is more *astringent* and *hemostatic* than Pipsissewa herb and root, and is given in **internal** and **external bleeding**—including blood in the urine and stool in damp-heat conditions of the intestines and bladder.
4   Unlike Pipsissewa herb and root, Speedwell herb is not used for pain relief of any kind.

Heartsease Herb

Botanical source: *Viola tricolor* L. subsp. *arvensis* Gaudin, *V. vulgaris* Koch (Violaceae)
Pharmaceutical name: Herba Violae tricoloris
Ancient names: Herba Jaceae (Lat)
Other names: Wild pansy, Wild Johnny jump-up, Love in idleness, Herb trinity, Stepmother (Eng, Am)
Pensé sauvage, Violette tricolore/des champs, Herbe de la Trinité (Fr)
Wilde Stiefmütterchen, Ackerveilchen, Siebenfarbenblume (Ge)
Part used: the flowering herb

NATURE

Therapeutic category: mild remedy with minimal chronic toxicity
Constituents: saponins, flavonoids (incl. violaquercitrin, anthocyanidins [violanin]), salicylic acid, methylsalicylate, alkaloid, mucilage, tannin, essential oil, minerals (incl. calcium, magnesium)
Effective qualities: somewhat pungent, sweet and salty, neutral, moist
stimulating, decongesting, dissolving
Tropism: lungs, nerves, fluids, skin, joints
Kidney, Bladder, Lung, Heart meridians
Fluid body
Ground: all krases and biotypes

FUNCTIONS AND INDICATIONS

1 **PROMOTES DETOXIFICATION, RESOLVES DAMP AND DISSOLVES DEPOSITS;**
REDUCES LYMPH CONGESTION AND RELIEVES ECZEMA;
REDUCES ALLERGY AND INFLAMMATION, AND RELIEVES ITCHING AND PAIN

metabolic toxicosis with *damp:* chronic skin rashes, swollen glands, frequent urinary infections, chronic aches and pains

skin (wind-) damp: skin rashes (esp. with oozing vesicles, scales or itching)

ECZEMA (incl. allergic, infantile), cradle cap, impetigo, psoriasis, acne, hives, scabies, syphilis, herpes

PRURITUS in general

URINARY DEPOSITS (incl. stones); arteriosclerosis

LYMPHADENITIS (esp. infantile), scrofula

RHEUMATISM (all types); gout, neuritis

VARICOSITIES, phlebitis, hemorrhoids

IMMEDIATE ALLERGIES (incl. atopic eczema, otitis, rhinitis, asthma, drug reactions)

2 **TONIFIES URINARY QI, HARMONIZES URINATION AND RELIEVES INCONTINENCE;**
PROMOTES URINATION AND RELIEVES IRRITATION

genitourinary (Kidney) Qi deficiency: scanty/dripping/difficult urination, bedwetting, cloudy urine

URINARY INCONTINENCE, ENURESIS, mucus in urine

BLADDER IRRITATION, dysuria, strangury

3 **PROMOTES SWEATING AND EXPECTORATION, DISPELS WIND-HEAT,**
STIMULATES IMMUNITY AND REDUCES INFECTION

lung wind-heat: fever, coughing with hard sputum, muscle aches

COLD and FLU ONSET

BRONCHITIS (esp. chronic), croup

INFECTIONS in general (esp. chronic)

4 **RESTORES AND RELAXES THE NERVES, AND RELIEVES FATIGUE;**
CLEARS INTERNAL WIND AND STOPS SPASMS

nerve deficiency: chronic fatigue, nervous exhaustion, weakness

NEURASTHENIA, SPASMS, tremors, cramps

NEUROGENIC BLADDER with STRANGURY

NERVOUS PALPITATIONS with *heart Qi constraint*

ASTHMA with *lung Qi constraint*

5 **PROMOTES TISSUE REPAIR**

WOUNDS, sores, ulcers

PREPARATION

Use: Heartsease herb is prepared by **infusion** or by an eight-hour **cold infusion. Compresses** of the dried, **powdered herb** are used for injuries, while the **ointment** is for itchy skin eruptions and wounds.

Long-term use is indicated for chronic rheumatism or eczema, and for neuritis. **Heartease root** may be used for its *emetic* effect in emetic therapy.

Dosage: Infusion: 8-16 g

Tincture: 3-5 ml at 1:3 strength in 45% ethanol

Caution: Because Heartsease herb is very high in saponins, prolonged full dose use in some people may cause mild diarrhea, nausea or vomiting. It is best to combine this herb with others from the start, or simply switch to another single herb if this should happen.

Note: The cultivated, common garden variety of heartsease or Johnny jump-up is not a valid botanical source for this remedy; only the wild heartsease is fully effective.

Heartsease growing in rye fields is therapeutically superior to any other kind because of the symbiotic relationship between heartsease and rye. In the past, skin eruptions caused by excessive amounts of rye in the diet were cured by Heartsease herb.

Blue violet herb and root is obtained from a related species of the same genus, *Viola odorata* L. (or *V. pedata* L.), also known as sweet/garden/blue violet. It is used in essentially the same way as Heartsease herb. Its chemical composition and energetic qualities are also very similar. The two remedies may be used interchangeably, with two considerations.

First, Blue violet herb and root is more frequently used for its *expectorant, mucolytic* action (function 3) than Heartsease herb. With its added *bronchial antiseptic* and *antitussive* effects, this remedy is given in chronic bronchial syndromes such as **lung phlegm-damp, lung phlegm-dryness** and **lung phlegm-heat** (which include whooping cough).

Second, Blue violet herb and root has an *antitumoral* action, especially in the treatment of lung, breast, pharyngeal, gastric and intestinal cancer. Two to three times the standard dose is taken in tumoral/cancerous conditions of these types.

Blue violet seed is especially used to treat painful uric acid retention and urinary deposits with sand or stones that cause urinary irritation, urgency or obstruction.

NOTES

In the biochemical classification system of today's pharmacology, Heartsease herb is considered a saponin remedy. By this theoretical logic it has a general tropism for the skin and a *dissolving* action on tissue. True enough, this plant by all traditional European accounts was considered one of the most effective remedies for **skin conditions.** It was also seen as a general *antidyskratic detoxicant*. However, from the clinical point of view, its *resolvent* and *dissolvent diuretic* properties, addressing depository conditions such as arteriosclerosis, are comparatively minor—especially in the face of more comprehensive, effective *detoxicant* urinary remedies like Hydrangea root, Cleavers herb and Pipsissewa herb.

For therapeutic purposes the biochemical approach, while often helpful, by itself is insufficient. This becomes especially clear when, as unfortunately often happens today, a plant remedy is seen as a drug and reduced to the theoretical *in vitro* activities of its known and purported primary chemical constituents. For one thing, we should always consider the whole gamut of substances that compose a remedy, as well as their synergistic effects—about which we know very little. In the case of Heartsease herb, the sum of its constituents has in the Greek medical tradition of the last 2,000 years empirically shown properties as varied as *vulnerary, diaphoretic, lymphatic decongestant, diuretic* and *spasmolytic.*

More fundamentally, we need to rediscover the real identity of an herb as a remedy, or thera-peutic tool—a status it has retained in the unbroken Oriental herbal tradition. The challenge in the West is to make the most efficacious medicinal use of local plants. For this search, rather than limit ourselves to the analytical findings of biochemistry, we also need to draw on energetic pharmacology and its historical context, the Greek medicine tradition. Biochemistry can be a helpful tool, but it can only take us so far in understanding plants as healing agents.

Lucky for us that Chinese and Ayurvedic medicine have gained Western acceptance as classical medical systems, so that the vitalistic roots of Western medicine can now be approached with an unjaundiced eye. The *salty/dissolving, pungent/mobilizing* and *sweet/tonifying* effective taste qualities of Heartsease address conditions of **toxicosis** and **hard deposits, lymph stagnation** and **nervous deficiency,** respectively. The herb's reputation for **chronic dry skin** conditions is all the more understandable in light of its *diaphoretic* and *diuretic* actions.

Historically, this versatile remedy was often used for the treatment of individuals with urinary disorders arising from **bladder Qi deficiency** or **bladder Qi constraint,** such as dripping, difficult, painful urination. Today however, with the rise of immune disorders caused by different types of toxicosis, its use as an *immune-stimulating* and *immune-regulating* remedy for **immune deficiency** and **allergic** disorders has come to the fore. Heartsease has shown excellent results with allergic infantile eczema triggered by the intake of cow's milk, for example, and acts like an *antihis-* *tamine* remedy. Another significant traditional use was asthma. It deserves further experimentation with hypersensitivity disorders in general.

Birch Leaf and Bark

Botanical source: *Betula alba* L., *B. pendula* Roth, *B. lenta* L., *B. fontinalis, B. papyracea* and spp. (Betulaceae)
Pharmaceutical name: Folium et cortex Betulae
Ancient names: Semuda (Gr)
Other names: Silver birch, White birch, Lady birch, Ribbon tree (Eng)
　　Black birch, Paper birch, Water birch, etc. (Am)
　　Bouleau, Bouleau blanc, Arbre de la sagesse (Fr)
　　Birke, Weissbirke (Ge)
Part used: the leaf and bark; also the bud, Gemma Betulae, and the sap, Succus Betulae

NATURE
Therapeutic category: mild remedy with minimal chronic toxicity
Constituents: saponins (leaf), bitter (leaf), flavonoids (hyperosides, bark), sesquiterpenes, tannins 4-15%, resin, salicylic acid methylester, gallic acid, betulalbic acid, betulin, phytosterol, pentosane, albumin, essential oil (incl. camphoraceous betulin), minerals (incl. potassium, calcium, phosphorus)
Effective qualities: somewhat bitter, astringent and pungent, cool, dry
　　dissolving, stimulating, astringing
Tropism: liver, kidneys, bladder, heart, fluids, skin
　　Kidney, Bladder, Liver meridians
　　Fluid body
Ground: all krases and biotypes for symptomatic use

FUNCTIONS AND INDICATIONS
1　**PROMOTES DETOXIFICATION, RESOLVES DAMP AND DISSOLVES DEPOSITS; RELIEVES ECZEMA AND PLETHORA, AND REDUCES PAIN**

metabolic toxicosis with *damp :* skin eruptions, joint or muscle pains, swollen joints, frequent bladder infections, urinary irritation
URINARY DEPOSITS (incl. urinary sand, stones and other deposit), arteriosclerosis
ARTHRITIS, gout, fibromyalgia (esp. chronic, painful)
HYPERURICEMIA, chlorides or urea retention
ATHEROSCLEROSIS, hyperlipidemia
skin damp / heat: chronic skin eruptions
ECZEMA (chronic), acne
general plethora: overweight, abdominal distension, fatigue
OBESITY

2 PROMOTES URINATION, DRAINS WATER AND RELIEVES EDEMA; STIMULATES BILE FLOW AND RELIEVES CONSTIPATION; ELIMINATES PARASITES

kidney and liver water congestion: general or local water retention

EDEMA (incl. cardiac); OLIGURIA, anuria

HYPERTENSION with dizziness, visual disturbances, headaches

gallbladder and stomach Qi stagnation: constipation, painful digestion, epigastric distension

UPPER GASTRIC DYSPEPSIA

INTESTINAL PARASITES

3 CLEARS DAMP-HEAT, REDUCES INFECTION AND INFLAMMATION, AND STOPS DISCHARGE

bladder damp-heat: cloudy or dark urine, painful, dribbling urination, fever

URINARY INFECTIONS (esp. chronic, incl. mucous cystitis, interstitial cystitis)

intestines damp-heat: burning bowel movement, pus and blood in stool, chronic diarrhea

ENTERITIS, dysentery, cholera

ALBUMINURIA, mucus in urine

4 PROMOTES SWEATING, DISPELS WIND-HEAT AND REDUCES FEVER

external wind heat: fever, irritability, aches and pains, headache, misery

FEVERS in general (at intial external stage [*tai yang*] and at all later stages [*shao yang, shao yin*])

5 PROMOTES HAIR GROWTH AND BENEFITS THE SKIN

HAIR LOSS

ECZEMA, swollen glands, wounds, itch, mouth sores

PREPARATION

Use: Birch leaf and bark are prepared in **decoction** or **tincture**. If the leaf or bud alone is used, the **long** or **cold infusion** is best. **Poultices**, **liniments** and other topical preparations are prepared from all parts of the birch. Add 1/2 tsp of bicarbonate of soda to the leaf infusion to enhance its effect.

While **Birch leaf** acts more strongly on the urinary tract, **Birch bark** is more active on the liver— but this is only a matter of emphasis. Birch leaf alone is *diaphoeretic,* however (function 4), and Birch bark is more *astringent* and *antidiarrheal* (function 3). The leaf and bark together work better than do either used separately. In addition to its basic functions, **Birch bud** is also given to reduce congested/ swollen lymph glands. **Birch sap** is used in a similar way to the bark and leaf, but has a milder effect; it is also considered best for dissolving urinary stones and relieving resultant kidney colic.

Experience shows that an alternation every three days of Birch leaf/bark/bud and Nettle herb produces superior results in chronic conditions. This also holds true when they are combined in a formula.

Dosage: Decoction: 8-14 g

Tincture: 2-5 ml at 1:3 strength in 30% ethanol

Caution: None

Note: The North American **Black birch,** *Betula lenta* L. (also known as Cherry birch, Sweet birch or Mahogany birch), is an important botanical source for this remedy; the leaf and bark are also used. Black birch leaf yields an essential oil with *diaphoretic, anti-inflammatory* and *analgesic* actions. Black birch oil is commercially often added to, or sold under the name of, Wintergreen oil, which it resembles.

NOTES

Although Birch leaf on the whole is a gentle remedy, its effectiveness in managing most types of conditions caused by an imbalance of the fluid body has been proven time and again. These conditions include chronic forms of **water congestion with edema, urinary deposits, uric acid accumulation** and simple **metabolic toxicosis** arising from catabolic stasis. Birch has not been abandoned by natural therapists. For one thing, its *hair-growth stimulant* property is still being used—today as ever—by the cosmetics industry. Experimental pharmacology, moreover, has confirmed *analgesic, anti-inflammatory, antipyretic, diuretic* and *choleretic* components of one kind or another in the leaf, bud and bark. This pharmacological confirmation justifies the same functions and uses for all parts equally. Clinically the leaf and bark together represents the most effective remedy—regardless of the particular ailment being treated. This usage is reinforced by the use of all parts of various birch species by numerous Native American tribes.

With its slender silvery grace, the airy birch tree has always been emblematic of the feminine, or the Goddess. In Nordic countries the birch is an emblem of a legendary princess, while in Mediterranean countries it belongs to her aspect of Aphrodite. Thriving in Yin quality cool, moist environments (what else?) and served by airiness and spaciousness, birch radiates light. We may describe this light energy as a bioenergetic light process. On the physical level, these light bioenergies leave their marks in the the form of the compound known as salicylic acid.

Understanding the energetic processes of an herb helps us contact its inner nature, or spirit being. More importantly for therapy, it allows us to appreciate to the fullest the spiritual source of the healing effects. In the case of Birch, the light-filled salicylic acid helps explain its use for **painful inflammations** (e.g., in the joints), **fevers, infections** (e.g. intestinal and urinary) and **biliary congestion.** Acute conditions mainly are addressed here.

On the other hand, Birch's saponins, potassium and minerals—resulting from different bioenergies—ensure a gentle *diuretic detoxicant* and *resolvent* action in those presenting chronic imbalances (dyskrasias) of the fluid environment. **Hard, fatty deposits** are dissolved and uric acid is eliminated. **Gout** is the strongest indication of all.

Celery Seed

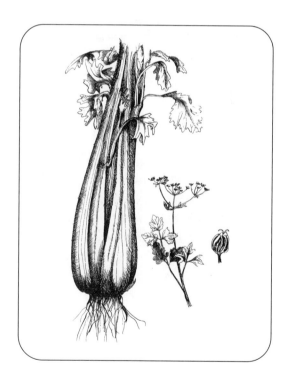

Botanical source: *Apium graveolens* L.
    (Umbelliferae)
Pharmaceutical name: Fructus Apii
Ancient names: Eleioselinon, Ydroselinon (Gk)
    Paludapium (Lat)
Other names: Smallage, Ache, Marsh/Water parsley
    (Eng)
    Céléri, Persil/Ache des marais (Fr)
    Sellerie, Zellerie, Wassereppich, Gailwurz,
    Schoppenkraut (Ge)
Part used: the fruit; also the root, Radix Apii

NATURE
Therapeutic category: mild remedy with minimal chronic toxicity
Constituents: essential oil 2-3% (incl. apiol, furanocoumarin [bergapten]), flavonoids, fixed oil, asparagin, cholin, alkaloid (apiin), tyrosin, many minerals and trace minerals (incl. sodium, potassium, phosphorus, magnesium, iodine, chlorine, manganese), vitamins A, B, C, E

Effective qualities: somewhat bitter, sweet and pungent, neutral to cool, moist
    dissolving, stimulating, restoring, nourishing
Tropism: kidneys, bladder, liver, stomach, intestines, pancreas, fluids
    Fluid, Warmth, Air bodies
    Kidney, Bladder, Lung, *chong, ren* meridians
Ground: all krases, biotypes and constitutions

FUNCTIONS AND INDICATIONS

1 **PROMOTES DETOXIFICATION, RESOLVES DAMP, DISSOLVES DEPOSITS AND RELIEVES PAIN; PROMOTES URINATION, DRAINS WATER AND RELIEVES EDEMA**

metabolic toxicosis with *damp (-heat):* joint stiffness, pain and swelling, muscle aches, malaise, dribbling uriation, frequent urinary infections
ARTHRITIS, gout, rheumatism, fibromyalgia, calcium bone spurs, sciatica, neuralgia (acute and chronic)
URINARY DEPOSITS (incl. urinary stones and sand); arteriosclerosis
ANURIA
kidney and liver water congestion: generalised edema, fatigue, nausea, possibly fever
EDEMA (esp. of lower limbs, face)

2 **CLEARS DAMP-HEAT AND REDUCES INFECTION, FEVER AND INFLAMMATION**

bladder damp-heat: frequent, painful, dribbling urination, lower backache, thirst
URINARY INFECTIONS (esp. acute)
REMITTENT FEVERS (esp. *shao yin* stage)

3 **TONIFIES REPRODUCTIVE QI AND PROMOTES MENSTRUATION; PROMOTES LACTATION**

genitourinary/uterus cold (Kidney Yang deficiency): loss of sexual interest, fatigue, delayed or irregular periods, urinary difficulties
FRIGIDITY, IMPOTENCE
AMENORRHEA
POSTPARTUM UTERINE WEAKNESS
INSUFFICIENT LACTATION

4 **RESTORES THE NERVES AND ADRENALS, RELIEVES FATIGUE AND WHEEZING, AND SOOTHES THE THROAT; LOWERS BLOOD SUGAR**

nerve and adrenal deficiency: fatigue, weakness, loss of stamina, frequent infections
NEURASTHENIA, ADRENAL DEFICIENCY
DEBILITY or BURNOUT from chronic disease, stress, overwork, childbirth, trauma
lung and Kidney Yang deficiency: wheezing, chronic exhaustion, backache, sexual disinterest
WHEEZING in *deficient Qi* or *Yang* conditions (incl. asthma, bronchitis, with *phlegm*)
HOARSENESS
HYPERGLYCEMIA, DIABETES (supportive)

5 **STIMULATES AND HARMONIZES DIGESTION, AND RELIEVES BLOATING**

liver and stomach Qi stagnation: appetite loss, indigestion with pain, flatulence, epigastric bloating
LIVER CONGESTION, DYSPEPSIA, hemorrhoids
intestines Qi constraint: indigestion, flatulence, abdominal pain and distension
INTESTINAL COLIC, IBS

PREPARATION

Use: Celery seed is prepared in **short decoction** or **tincture** form. The **fresh juice** expressed from the whole plant is also bioactive. Celery seed **essential oil** is also effective and available.

The refreshing, cooling **celery stalk** eaten regularly has a slower *restoring, nourishing* and *detoxicant* action.

Dosage: Juice: 2 tsp or 10 ml
>**Short decoction:** 8-14 g
>**Tincture:** 2-5 ml at 1:2 strength in 40% ethanol
>**Essential oil:** 1-2 drops in a gel cap topped with some olive oil

Caution: Avoid using during pregnancy, as Celery is *uterine stimulant*. Forbidden with organic kidney disease present.

NOTES

Celery is one of the food remedies which, like Kelp, Artichoke and others in Class 9, is both *restorative* and *detoxicant* at the same time. Celery seed is the remedy of choice for the individual in a chronic deficiency condition presenting other pathogens, such as metabolic toxicosis, bladder damp-heat, as well as kidney and digestive stagnation arising from the deficiency itself.

Specifically, Celery seed provides ideal support for those with **chronic disorders** that involve **deficient autonomic nervous, adrenocortical, digestive** and **reproductive** functions with functional stagnation. The traditional name for this condition is **neurasthenia** and involves both systemic Qi and Yang deficiency. Key symptoms presenting would be chronic tiredness, low stamina or endurance, atonic indigestion and low sex drive—symptoms commonly seen in today's multifactorial diseases such as chronic fatigue syndrome, fibromyalgia, and so on. The remedy is a good choice in *any* form of chronic unproductive stress with adrenal burnout. In advanced-onset asthma or chronic bronchitis for example, Celery is an important remedy, not least because of its specific ability to relieve wheezing in these conditions.

For these chronic neurasthenic conditions, the combining choices with Celery are numerous, and depend on the exact symptom presentation. Some other *neuroendocrine restoratives* that will complement Celery include Sage leaf, Rosemary leaf, Milky oat berry, Eleuthero root, Asian ginseng root and Rhodiola root. Celery would be chosen because of its specific action on urinary and respiratory functions, as well as its superb systemic *detoxicant/depurative* effect.

The Chinese syndromes addressed here are **Kidney Qi/Yang deficiency,** eventually leading to **Lung and Kidney Yang deficiency** as the Kidney fails to grasp the Qi. Because Celery is a regenerating *restorative* to the reproductive organs, it should be taken in liberal doses after childbirth, when it will ensures plentiful breast milk as a *galactagogue* (like Fennel seed).

The main pathogens arising from these deficiencies that Celery seed treats is endogenous **metabolic toxicosis** with either **arthritis, urinary dysfunctions** or **edema.** The accumulation of toxins itself presents as **damp painful obstruction,** and can lodge in the muscles and nerves as well joints. Celery here is not just an excellent *detoxicant diuretic,* but a prime *anti-inflammatory* and *analgesic* as well, especially for painful red swollen joints, neuralgic pains, and so on. It is especially indicated in chronic conditions presenting acute flare-ups, like fibromyalgia with its fundamental kidney-adrenal deficiency.

In terms of the urinary dysfunctions, Celery is a strong *urinary stimulant diuretic* for both anuria and **water retention.** In addition, the remedy acts as a *dissolvent* for **urinary deposits,** like Burdock root and Madder root.

Celery seed empirically was also found useful for acute heart attacks with crampy chest pains, panicky feelings and so on.

Blackcurrant Leaf

Botanical source: *Ribes nigrum* L., *R. americanum*
    Miller (Saxifragaceae)
Pharmaceutical name: Folium Ribis nigri
Other names: Quinsy berry, Squinancy berry (Eng)
    Cassis, Groseillier noir (Fr)
    Schwarze Johannisbeere, Albeere, Gichtbeere,
      Bocksbeere (Ge)
Part used: the leaf; also the fruit, Fructus Ribis nigri

NATURE

Therapeutic category: mild remedy with minimal chronic toxicity
Constituents: anthocyanins, essential oil (incl. polyphenols), quinic acid, oxydase, emulsin, tannin, organic acids (incl. malic and citric acid), pectin, purple dye, gamma-linolenic acid (in seeds), vitamin C, trace minerals
Effective qualities: pungent, sweet, astringent, cool, dry
    dissolving, stimulating
Tropism: kidney, liver, prostate, skin, fluids
    Kidney, Liver, Large Intestine meridians; Fluid, Warmth bodies
Ground: all krases, biotypes and constitutions

FUNCTIONS AND INDICATIONS

1   **PROMOTES DETOXIFICATION, RESOLVES DAMP AND DISSOLVES DEPOSITS;
RELIEVES ECZEMA AND REDUCES PLETHORA**

    metabolic toxicosis with *damp-cold:* muscle and joint aches, urinary irritation, skin rashes

    DEPOSITORY DIATHESIS with urinary deposits (alkaline, phosphatic), urinary sand or stones,
        arteriosclerosis

    skin damp-heat: chronic skin rashes

    CHRONIC ECZEMA, swollen glands

    RHEUMATISM, gout, arthritis;

    URIC ACID DIATHESIS (hyperuricemia)

    general plethora: overweight, malaise, aches and pains

2   **PROMOTES URINATION, DRAINS WATER AND RELIEVES EDEMA;
BENEFITS THE PROSTATE AND RELIEVES IRRITATION; REDUCES BLOOD PRESSURE**

    liver and kidney water congestion: local or general bloating

    EDEMA, urinary irritation

    PROSTATE ENLARGEMENT, prostatitis

    HYPERTENSION

3 **CLEARS DAMP-HEAT, REDUCES LIVER CONGESTION, ASTRINGES AND STOPS DISCHARGE; ELIMINATES PARASITES; STRENGTHENS THE CAPILLARIES**

liver damp-heat: jaundice, right flank pain and swelling, nausea, bilious headaches

LIVER CONGESTION, jaundice, migraine

intestines damp-heat: loose stool, burning, urgent bowel movement, thirst

DIARRHEA, enteritis, dysentery (acute or chronic)

INTESTINAL PARASITES

MENOPAUSAL BLEEDING

SCURVY, MALARIA

COLDS, flus (esp. preventive)

4 **REGULATES THE QI AND RELIEVES PAIN AND COUGHING**

lung Qi constraint: spasmodic, tight cough, painful chest

CROUP, whooping cough

RESPIRATORY INFECTIONS

COLIC PAINS, painful diarrhea

5 **PROMOTES TISSUE REPAIR, REDUCES SWELLING AND SOOTHES THE THROAT**

WOUNDS, sores, swellings

SORE SWOLLEN THROAT, laryngitis

BLEEDING GUMS

PREPARATION

Use: Blackcurrant leaf is prepared in **short decoction** and **tincture** form for all purposes.

Astringent, anti-inflammatory **compresses, mouthwashes, gargles** and **sitzbaths** are prepared for injuries, gum and throat problems, and for postpartum tissue trauma.

The medicinal drink, fresh **blackcurrant juice,** prepared from the fresh berries, is valuable for preventing colds and flus, and useful in fevers and diarrhea. It is very high in vitamin C, tannic acid, rutin and potassium, and should be drunk hot as a preventive or treatment for colds.

Dosage: Short decoction: 8-12 g

       Tincture: 2-3 ml at 1:3 strength in 35% ethanol

Caution: After ten days or so alternate with other *astringent* remedies if using for chronic diarrhea or, better still, combine in a formula from the very beginning.

Note: Black currant root or **root bark** may be used in standard decoction for a stronger *astringent* effect in acute or chronic diarrheal disorders (function 3).

The **fruit/berry** of the **Red currant**, *Ribes rubrum* L., is used similarly to Blackcurrant berry (see Use above), and is also usually taken as a medicinal **juice.** Although considered less effective all around than Blackcurrant juice, Red currant juice is especially cooling, refreshing and thirst-relieving. It is traditonally drunk in fevers and generally preferred during the summer months. As an appetite-promoting drink it is taken before or with meals. The rule of thumb is then: Black current juice in the winter, Red currant juice in the summer.

NOTES

Blackcurrant has enjoyed thousands of years of European use as a medicinal plant. Its main action is on the body's fluids and the urinary tract. From the taste quality perspective an astringent, cool remedy, Blaccurrant leaf clears **damp-heat** in the **liver, urinary tract** and **intestines,** like Lysimachia Jin Qian Cao in Chinese medicine. *Liver de-congestant, anti-inflammatory, astringent* and *diuretic* actions operate here as they do in the treatment of water congestion and prostatitis. In particular, the remedy reduces **urinary deposits** of all kinds accumulating from damp.

Blackcurrant's *astringent* action can be used in acute enteric infections, including with bloody discharge present.

In most of Europe, however, this remedy is seen primarily as a *resolvent detoxicant* addressing chronic forms of **metabolic toxicosis** presenting arthritic joints, rheumatism, eczema and other similar disorders. Here Blackcurrant leaf is usually reserved for individuals presenting edema, weight gain and hypertension—a syndrome called **general plethora** in traditional Greek medicine. In conditions of **hyperuricemia**, Blackcurrant leaf, like Birch leaf and bark, carries out the specific function of eliminating uric acid from the system: it is believed to be one of the most effective remedies in this respect.

Red Clover Flower

Botanical source: *Trifolium pratense* L.
       (Leguminosae)
Pharmaceutical name: Flos Trifolii
Ancient names: Triphyllon (Gr)
       Cithysus, Calta (Lat)
Other names: Purple clover, Field claver, Suckles,
       Meadow trefoil (Eng and Am)
       Trèfle rose, Trèfle des prés (Fr)
       Wiesenklee, Harzklee, Rotklee, Fleischblume
       (Ge)
Parts used: the flowerhead

NATURE
Therapeutic category: mild remedy with minimal chronic toxicity
Constituents: caffeic, silicic, oxalic, salicylic and other acids, essential oil with furfurol, myricyl alcohol, phenolic and cyanogenic glycosides, coumarins, flavonoids (incl. genistein, isorhamnetin, daidzein), isoflavones, phytosterols (incl. trifolianol, trifolin, trifolitin), anthocyane (violanin), prateniol, resins, tannins, malvidin, cyanidin, sitosterol, heptacosane, hentracontane, bitter, chlorophyll, minerals (incl. iron, chromium, molybdenum), vitamin C, tocopherol
Effective qualities: somewhat sweet and bland, neutral with cooling potential, moist
      softening, dissolving, diluting, nourishing, astringing, relaxing
Tropism: fluids (including plasma), skin, lungs, bladder, nerves
      Kidney, Bladder, Lung, Large intestine meridians; Fluid, Air bodies
Ground: Melancholic krases, biotypes and constitutions

FUNCTIONS AND INDICATIONS
1   **PROMOTES DETOXIFICATION, RESOLVES DAMP AND DISSOLVES DEPOSITS;**
    PROMOTES URINATION AND RELIEVES IRRITATION;
    RELIEVES ECZEMA AND REDUCES TUMORS

    metabolic toxicosis with *damp:* skin eruptions, joint pains and redness, fatigue, skin rashes, urinary irritation

    BLADDER IRRITATION, vaginal or rectal irritation from any cause

    URINARY DEPOSITS, arteriosclerosis

    GOUT, rheumatism, arthritis (chronic)

HEAVY METAL and CHEMICAL TOXICOSIS (incl. drug residues)

skin damp-heat: skin rashes, scales, swellings

CHRONIC ECZEMA (esp. from *Yin* or *blood deficiency*), leg ulcers

TUMORS (incl. malignant, esp. of skin, breasts, ovaries; incl. estrogen-induced)

2   CLEARS TOXIC HEAT, REDUCES INFLAMMATION AND STOPS DISCHARGE

bladder damp-heat: painful, frequent urination, dark or cloudy urine, thirst

URINARY INFECTIONS (esp. acute cystitis)

MUCUS in urine

WHITE LEUCORRHEA, spermatorrhea

3   DESCENDS LUNG QI, OPENS THE CHEST AND RELIEVES WHEEZING AND COUGHING; REGULATES BLADDER QI, HARMONIZES URINATION AND RELIEVES URGENCY

lung Qi constraint: irritable spasmodic cough, wheezing

ASTHMA, whooping cough (spasmodic)

SPASMODIC COUGHING (uncontrollable; in whooping cough, measles, bronchitis, laryngitis, etc.)

bladder Qi constraint: urgent, frequent, difficult, irritated scanty urination

NEUROGENIC BLADDER, STRANGURY

4   NOURISHES THE YIN, GENERATES FLUIDS AND MOISTENS DRYNESS; INCREASES ESTROGEN

Yin and fluids deficiency: dehydration, thirst, hot spells, fatigue, constipation

lung (heat-) dryness: hard dry cough, sore throat, dry mouth, nose and throat, thirst

BRONCHITIS, whooping cough, croup

intestines (heat-) dryness: small, hard, dry stool, constipation, difficult bowel movement, thirst

CONSTIPATION from internal dryness

NUTRITIONAL DEFICIENCIES (incl. anemias, demineralisation)

ESTROGEN DEFICIENCY conditions (incl. PMS, dysmenorrhea, menopausal syndrome)

5   PROMOTES TISSUE REPAIR AND REDUCES INFLAMMATION AND PAIN

WOUNDS, ulcers, sores (esp. chronic, indolent, malignant)

BURNS, EYE INFLAMMATIONS

heat toxin: boils, sores, abscesses, low fever

INSECT BITES and stings

PAIN from arthritis, gout, etc.

PREPARATION

Use: Red clover flower is prepared as **fresh juice, infusion** or **tincture.** These may be used topically in **swabs, ointments, creams,** etc., for skin-related conditions, neuralgias and arthritic pain.

Suppositories/enemas should be taken for rectal irritation, and **pessaries** or **sponges** for vaginal itching.

As a major remedy for internal use, Red clover flower must be taken consistently for months to achieve its deep *detoxicant* and *tumor-resolvent* effects (which include cancer).

Red clover syrup is of immediate help in dry, spasmodic coughs, possibly alongside other moistening and soothing *respiratory demulcents* such as Marshmallow root, Licorice root or Iceland moss.

Dosage: Juice: 2 tsp

Infusion: 10-16 g

Tincture: 2-5 ml at 1:3 strength in 30% ethanol

For severe conditions, two to four times these quantities may safely be taken.

Caution: None

NOTES

Red clover flower is no easy remedy to classify. Its multifaceted nature makes it a strong contender for three different therapeutic categories. A glance at the sheer variety of the chemical constituents found by research confirms its subtle, complex character. However, knowing this only goes so far in helping us understand the herb's therapeutic uses. And it is those practical therapeutic uses that largely determine its character, or the way we commonly think of it.

Most of Red clover flower's functions have in common an application to chronic and degenerative conditions, and especially to conditions found in children and older people. We are looking at a mild, yet deeply acting remedy. We may summarize its main functions as being systemically *detoxicant* and *nutritive,* and *respiratory relaxant.*

Red clover's general *detoxicant* action makes it an important remedy for **metabolic** and **heavy metal toxicosis.** As such it addresses **chronic skin** conditions with either **dryness** or **heat**—without the help of saponins—as well as **tumoral** diatheses, including cancer (for which it has an outstanding reputation). A good synergistic remedy in this arena would be Cleavers herb. In this connection, **urinary** and other **deposits,** including heavy metals, are also slowly removed from the system.

Red clover possesses sweet, moist, cool energetic qualities. This is the crucial information we need to grasp the essential quality and functions of this valuable herb. It means that Red clover is a *restorative, moistening* and *nourishing* remedy. Its Yin-, fluids- and blood-nourishing effects are perfect for individuals presenting long-term dry /irritated and hot/inflamed conditions of the skin and mucosa, as well as actual secretory and nutritional deficiencies. In these people Red clover will act as a soothing *demulcent, anti-inflammatory, secretory* and *nutritive* herb. This also includes an *estrogenic* action in the case of a woman, but mainly benefits the respiratory and urinary membranes.

Yin deficiency, heat-dryness and **Qi constraint** in these areas are the main energetic indications. When used to treat Yin and fluids deficiency with dryness, as well as lung heat-dryness, for example. Red clover flower closely resembles the Chinese *Yin tonic* Asparagus Tian Men Dong. Western *Yin tonics* such as Chickweed herb, Iceland moss and Solomon's seal root will also combine well with it.

Ultimately, however, Red clover will succeed best in individuals with blood/fluids/Yin deficiency with elements of toxicosis affecting the skin (with Heartsease herb, Burdock root and/or Gotu kola herb for instance) or the urinary tract (with Nettle herb, Celery seed and/or Cleavers herb). Turning this concept around, we can also say that Red clover is excellent for chronic toxicosis from chemical, drugs or metabolites with some heat and dryness lodging in the chest, gut and skin. Clearly a mod-ern urban remedy, if ever there was one.

Walnut Leaf and Hull

Botanical source: a) *Juglans regia* L., b) *J. nigra* L.
    (Juglandaceae)
Pharmaceutical name: Folium et pericarpium
    Juglandis
Ancient names: Karya, Basilika (Gr)
    Nux persica/regia, Jovis glans (Lat)
Other names: a) Persian/Common walnut (Eng)
    Noix (Fr)
    Walnuss, Welschnuss, Steinnuss (Ge)
    b) Black walnut (Am)
Part used: the leaf and ripe fruit rind (hull)

NATURE

Therapeutic category: mild remedy with minimal chronic toxicity

Constituents: flavonoids, tannins, ellagic, tannic and gallic acids, bitter (juglone), essential oil, naphtho-quinones, serotonin, juglandine, alkaloids, protein, emulsin, peroxydase, malic/citric/oxalic acid, calcium phosphate and oxalate, potassium and calcium chloride, magnesium and potassium sulphate, sulphur, sulphur iodide, calcium, potassium, trace minerals (incl. magnesium, iodine, copper, silicon, zinc), vitamins (incl. C)

Effective qualities: astringent, somewhat bitter and pungent, neutral (leaf) with cooling potential (hull), dry
dissolving, astringing, solidifying, stabilizing, stimulating

Tropism: stomach, intestines, pancreas, skin, veins, bones, nerves
Large Intestine, Spleen, Kidney meridians
Warmth, Fluid bodies

Ground: Phlegmatic and Melancholic krases
all biotypes; Lymphatic/Carbonic and Mixed/Phosphoric constitutions

FUNCTIONS AND INDICATIONS

1   **PROMOTES DETOXIFICATION AND RESOLVES DAMP;**
    REDUCES LYMPH CONGESTION, ECZEMA AND TUMORS;
    REDUCES ACCUMULATION AND RELIEVES CONSTIPATION

    metabolic toxicosis with *damp:* dry skin, skin rashes, tiredness, aches and pains, constipation

    skin wind-damp: skin rashes with oozing, itching

    ECZEMA (esp. chronic, suppurative), pruritus, impetigo, herpes, tinea (ringworm), syphilis, TB

    LYMPHADENITIS (chronic), scrofula

    GOUT, rheumatism, osteoarthritis

    TUMORS (incl. malignant)

    intestines Qi stagnation: abdominal distension and pain, constipation

    CONSTIPATION (esp. chronic, of pregnancy)

2   **NOURISHES THE BLOOD AND RELIEVES FATIGUE;**
    GENERATES GROWTH, NOURISHES AND STRENGTHENS THE BONES, SINEWS, SKIN AND HAIR,
    AND RELIEVES WEAKNESS

    blood deficiency: fatigue, weakness, pale complexion

    ANEMIA, DEMINERALIZATION

    CHRONIC FATIGUE or DEBILITY

    musculoskeletal deficiency (Liver and Kidney depletion): fatigue, lower back/knee/leg weakness

    SLOW PHYSICAL and MENTAL DEVELOPMENT in INFANTS and CHILDREN

    BONE, SINEW or CARTILAGE WEAKNESS

    BONE DISEASE (incl. rickets, scoliosis, osteomalacia, osteoporosis, osteoma)

    WEAK or BRITTLE HAIR, hair loss, dry skin

3   **ASTRINGES, STOPS SECRETIONS, DISCHARGE AND BLEEDING;**
    RAISES CENTRAL QI AND RELIEVES PROLAPSE;
    ELIMINATES PARASITES

    CHRONIC DIARRHEA in *intestines damp-cold/heat* conditions, with intestinal dysbiosis/toxicosis
        (esp. with alternating diarrhea and constipation)

    GASTROENTERITIS, dysentery, mucous colitis, IBS, peptic ulcer, candidiasis (esp. chronic, with subacute
        inflammation)

    LEUCORRHEA, yeast infections

    HEMORRHAGE in any part

EXCESSIVE SWEATING (incl. from palms and soles)

Central Qi sinking: heavy dragging sensation in lower abdomen, fatigue

PROLAPSE (uterine, intestinal)

DIABETES (supportive)

INTESTINAL PARASITES (esp. tapeworm, roundworm)

4   **PROMOTES TISSUE REPAIR, REDUCES INFLAMMTION AND INFECTION, AND BENEFITS THE SKIN AND BONE**

WOUNDS, ulcers, cervical erosion, boils, abscesses, acne, varicose veins (esp. Yin/atonic cold type, incl. leg ulcers)

MOUTH, GUM, THROAT and EYE INFLAMMATIONS

SKIN CONDITIONS (incl. dry skin, eczema, wrinkles, dandruff, freckles)

BACTERIAL and FUNGAL SKIN INFECTIONS (incl. dermatitis, tinea, candidiasis), yeast infections

BONE DEGENERATION or SWELLING (incl. DENTAL CARIES)

PREPARATION

Use: Walnut leaf and hull are both prepared by **long infusion, short decoction** or **tincture.** For best results, the leaf and hull should be used together. **Baths** and local **compresses** are used with excellent results for such conditions as debility, frostbite, skin and lymph gland disorders, boils and conjunctivitis. **Vaginal sponges, pessaries** and such like are good in white vaginal discharges, yeast infections and cervical ulcers/erosion, while **mouthwashes** and **gargles** will help gum disease, tooth decay and throat inflammations.

Used in a restoring, cleansing **hair rinse,** Walnut hull treats hairloss, lacklustre or brittle hair and dandruff. The green hull is best for darkening hair tone.

Walnut liqueur, made from the green nut (meat) is a traditional European aperitive drink taken in between or before meals for digestive problems.

Dosage: Infusion and **short decoction:** 8-16 g

Tincture: 2-3 ml at 1:2 strength in 45% ethanol

Caution: Avoid using Walnut leaf and hull with tinnitus (ringing in the ears) present. If taken internally on its own for longer than about ten days, alternate weekly with a complementry *astringent* remedy such as Tormentil root, Blackberry leaf or Geranium essential oil.

Note: Walnut leaf contains an essential oil, an alkaloid and a bitter substance in addition to tannins, minerals, etc. It has bitter, pungent, astringent and dry qualities, and is therefore more *stimulating* and *spasmolytic* than Walnut hull alone. Walnut leaf is best for treating **digestive disorders** arising from **stagnant Qi** or **damp cold** (in functions 1 and 3).

Walnut hull contains malic, citric and oxalic acids, hydrojuglone, peroxydase and emulsin in addition to tannins, minerals, etc. It has astringent, dry, cool qualities, and is therefore more *astringent* and *anti-inflammatory.* Walnut hull is better at treating chronic inflammatory and infectious conditions, especially chronic **intestinal** and **urogenital infections** with damp heat presenting discharges with mucus and blood, as well as **intestinal parasites** (function 3).

NOTES

The Walnut tree has Asian origins, and has always been revered not only for cultish reasons, but also for the many practical uses that its wood, fruit, leaf and flower provide. Greeks and Romans especially esteemed the products of this "imperial nut", and Walnut oil and meat were extensively used for both culinary and medicinal purposes.

As intense as the walnut tree is in its very earthy, concentrated and enduring type of vitality (evident in its dense, hard wood, for example), so are its therapeutic effects strengthening on the whole organism. The meat of the nuts has always been considered highly *nutritive,* and today we know of its high content in minerals and trace minerals. Possibly based on the suggestion or omen given by its appearance, the walnut was said to feed the brain, to be a brain food.

By the same logic however, the walnut visually also suggests the intestines. This may actually be more relevant from the therapeutic vantage point. While sidestepping any need at this point to endorse a doctrine of signatures, it is worth considering for a moment that the mind does not create links of this kind gratuitously: we should definitely recognize the essentially spontaneous, synmorphous nature of such associations when they occur. Whether we go on to deduce natural laws from repeated observation of such things, as did many Renaissance scientists and physicians, is another matter entirely. Likewise if we then label this phenomenon the "doctrine of signatures." In any case, noticing such links first hand with the imagistic mind or right brain is often very useful therapeutically and should not be rejected offhand on principle—any more than they should be accepted without some screening from the rational mind or left brain, in fact.

Walnut's radical *detoxicant* influence on a wide range of **skin disorders,** especially with **lymphatic stagnation** present, has a long and reputable European history. With its astringent, bitter and dry primary qualities, Walnut is a drying and somewhat cooling remedy. In energetic terms the remedy effectively eliminates **wind-damp** (and to some extent **heat**) from the **skin** and **channels.** Its deep systemic *alterative* effect causes more superficial *anti-inflammatory, antiseptic, tissue-healing* and *detergent* actions on surface tissues such as the skin and mucus membranes.

Walnut is often combined with plants like Hearstease herb, Burdock root or Gotu kola herb for individuals suffering from chronic suppurative (damp) skin eruptions, for example. The bitter naphthoquinones found in the leaf have specifically shown *antifungal* and *antiparasitic* activity useful both topically and internally for fungal and parasitic infections, including candidiasis, yeast infections and ringworm.

Because of its generous content in minerals, trace elements and amino acids, Walnut possesses an outstanding tropism for chronic or degenerative-stage deficiencies of mesenchymal tissues such as skin, bone, nail and hair. This may be part of the explanation for its traditional *antitumoral* use, which is also best applied to **tumors** of the **skin, mucosa** and **bone.** The remedy can be considered *trophorestorative* to the musculoskeletal and epidermal system. Like Loranthus Sang Ji Sheng in Chinese medicine, it addresses patterns of **musculoskeletal deficiency,** more commonly known in TCM as **Liver and Kidney depletion.**

Walnut should in particular be given in those presenting **bone disorders, mineral deficiencies** and **anemias,** especially with exhaustion and muscular or skeletal weakness present. By altering the internal fluid environment of the connective tissue, Walnut is also able to build and nourish the blood and fluids, both in the physiological and Oriental energetic sense of these terms. Like Loranthus Sang Ji Sheng, Walnut will also nourish the skin and clear up skin dryness from blood/metabolic deficiency. Interestingly, Walnut has also been explored as a *growth stimulant,* perhaps as a *protein anabolism stimulant,* in those with metabolic disorders such as retarded children's development.

From a broad therapeutic perspective, Walnut exerts an *intestinal stimulant* and *laxative* action that will improve conditions of toxicosis aggravated by **intestines Qi stasis** presenting as **chronic constipation.** Walnut hull in particular also has a good reputation as an *antiparasitic* for tapeworm and roundworm.

Walnut leaf and hull are both well known as *astringent antidischarge* remedies (Class 18) and possess considerable astringency. Typically, it is able to raise prolapsed conditions, stop excessive sweating *(anhydrotic),* stop bleeding *(hemostatic* and *styptic)* and relieve diarrhea and other discharges of the intestines, reproductive organs and skin. See the many preparations above for a sampling of some reliable internal and topical preparations for these conditions.

Queen's Root

Botanical source: *Stillingia sylvatica* L.
(Euphorbiaceae)
Pharmaceutical name: Radix Stillingiae
Other names: Stillingia, Queen's delight, Yaw root,
Silver leaf (Am)
Stillingia (Fr)
Stillingie (Ge)
Part used: the root

NATURE

Therapeutic category: mild remedy with minimal chronic toxicity
Constituents: essential oil up to 3.25%, fatty oil, resin, alkaloids (incl. stillingine), tannins, gum, starch
Effective qualities: bitter, pungent, cool, dry
stimulating, calming, softening
Tropism: lymph, blood, fluids, lungs, liver, intestines
Liver, Lung meridians
Fluid, Warmth bodies
Ground: Lymphatic/Carbonic constitution

FUNCTIONS AND INDICATIONS

1 **PROMOTES DETOXIFICATION AND RESOLVES DAMP;**
REDUCES LYMPH CONGESTION AND RELIEVES ECZEMA;
REDUCES LIVER CONGESTION

metabolic toxicosis with *damp:* dry skin with rashes, discharges, swollen glands

skin (wind) damp: chronic skin rashes, oozing, irritation

ECZEMA (esp. chronic, obstinate skin conditions with pruritus and weeping); ulcers

LYMPHADENITIS, scrofula

SYPHILIS, scurvy, struma

TUBERCULOSIS (incl. scrofulitic)

TUMORS (incl. malignant)

liver Qi stagnation: indigestion, abdominal distension, fatigue, dry itchy skin

LIVER CONGESTION with toxicosis

2 **REDUCES INFLAMMATION, RELIEVES PAIN AND BENEFITS THE PERIOSTEUM**

RHEUMATIC conditions

PERIOSTITIS

EXOSTOSIS (osteoma), nodes (e.g. of tibia, head, face), periostoma

INFLAMMATIONS (chronic, incl. arthritis, dermatitis, lymphangitis, laryngitis, pharyngitis)

3 CLEARS LUNG HEAT, RELIEVES COUGHING AND SOOTHES THE THROAT

lung heat-dryness: constant dry barking cough, tight chest, dry irritated throat, thirst
BRONCHITIS, CROUP
COUGH (incl. chronic, esp. hoarse, paroxysmal, barking, with throat irritation, in winter)
LARYNGITIS (chronic), pharyngeal, tracheal irritation with cough

PREPARATION

Use: Queen's root is prepared by **decoction** or **tincture.** It's best to use the freshly dried root, which loses its potency after a few months. Discard roots over six months old, especially if not kept in airtight containers. **Compresses** and **liniments** relieve rheumatic pain, while **syrups** are excellent for the chest and throat conditions in function 3.
Dosage: Decoction: 6-14 g
        Tincture: 2-4 ml at 1:2 strength in 60% ethanol
Caution: Use cautiously in Yin deficiency conditions. Be cautious about using large doses continuously as in some people the remedy may cause nausea and loose stool.

NOTES

Indigenous to North America, queen's root from the spurge family grows in sandy soils and pine barrens from Maryland through to Mississippi and Louisiana in the gulf of Mexico. The plant is named after the eighteenth century botanist BENJAMIN STILLINGFLEET and was an official U.S. Pharmacopeia botanical from 1842 to 1916. Among Eclectic doctors the remedy had a glowing reputation, in particular for treating syphilis and struma with resultant periostitis. Its essentially *alterative (anti-dyskratic)* function was widely recognized and often utilized in the treatment of skin diseases and throat inflammations.

Bitter, pungent in taste qualities, Queen's root is essentially *altering* and *draining* by nature. The *resolvent detoxicant* action is best displayed in individuals with chronic conditions of **metabolic toxicosis** presenting **damp skin eruptions,** especially when this involves lymphatic stasis and liver congestion. The remedy is particularly appropriate for those in whom connective tissue weakness causes slow metabolite removal and poor tissue regeneration. **Wind-damp eczema** benefits here the most, especially when presenting itching, irritation and ichorous wet discharge.

Chronic throat inflammation with irritation is the other area in which Queen's root excells, particularly when scanty secretions and swollen, red, glistening mucosa are seen. The combined *detoxicant, anti-inflammatory, anti-infective* and somewhat *analgesic* actions of the root's very high essential oil content make this an important remedy for both chronic and acute laryngeal and pharyngeal infections—somewhat like the Chinese Belamcanda She Gan. The *respiratory sedative* action effectively addresses "irritative disorders of the fauces, trachea and bronchiae" (JOHN KING 1898).

Because of its cooling nature, Queen's root also works successfully on **lung heat-dryness.** Nineteenth century medics would declare that "the cases for its exhibition" are bronchial and croupy conditions of winter displaying a barking, hoarse, throaty cough. The fact that Queen's root for a long time was the main remedy for **croup** points to the possibility that an *antiviral* action may in fact be involved.

Poke Root

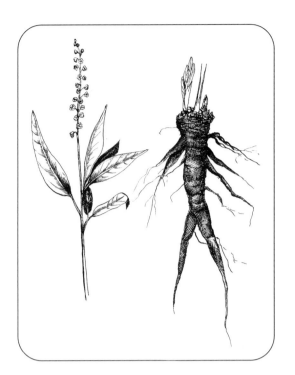

Botanical source: *Phytolacca decandra* L.
(Chenopodiaceae)
Pharmaceutical name: Radix Phytolaccae decandrae
Other names: Pokeweed, Garget, Scoke, Crowberry,
American nightshade, Pigeonberry, Coakum,
Inkberry (Am)
Morelle à grappes, Mechoucan du Canada,
Raisin d'Amérique (Fr)
Kermesbeere, Amerikanische Scharlachbeere
(Ge)
Part used: the root; also the fruit, Fructus Phytolaccae

NATURE

Therapeutic category: medium-strength remedy with moderate chronic toxicity
Constituents: triterpenoid saponins (phytolaccosides), alkaloid (phytolaccine), bitter resins, phytolaccic acid, formic and oleanolic acids, amino acids, tannin, saccharides, potassium, potassium formate, calcium oxalate
Effective qualities: somewhat pungent and sweet, neutral
softening, dissolving, stimulating
Tropism: digestive, lymphatic, musculoskeletal systems
Liver, Kidney, Bladder meridians
Fluid, Warmth bodies
Ground: Lymphatic/Carbonic and Hydrogenoid Iris constitutions

FUNCTIONS AND INDICATIONS

1   **PROMOTES DETOXIFICATION AND RESOLVES DAMP;**
    REDUCES LYMPH CONGESTION, DEPOSITION, ECZEMA AND TUMORS;
    BENEFITS THE BREASTS, SPINE AND BONES, AND RELIEVES PAIN

metabolic toxicosis with *damp:* muscle aches and pains, dry skin with rashes, swollen glands
LYMPHADENITIS with painful, swollen, hard glands (incl. from infections, scrofula)
DEPOSITION DISORDERS (incl. liver cirrhosis, fibrocystic breasts, hard lymph glands, exostosis,
    ovarian cysts, polyps)
FIBROCYSTIC BREASTS (incl. swelling, oversensitivity with PMS and during menstruation)
BREAST CONDITIONS in general (incl. engorgement, inflammation)
skin wind-damp-cold: skin rashes, itching, wetness, vesicles, pustules, malaise
ECZEMA (chronic, with dryness, irritation, fissures, incl. psoriasis, children's dry eczema)
RHEUMATISM (synovial, ligamental), arthritis, gout, neuralgia
TUMORS (incl. breast, lymphatic [lymphoma], skin, female reproductive fibroids)
ALBUMINURIA, edema
BONE and SPINE DISEASE, HEADACHE

2 **PROMOTES DETOXIFICATION AND CLEARS TOXIC HEAT;**
  REDUCES INFECTION AND INFLAMMATION, AND STIMULATES (/REGULATES?) IMMUNITY

microbial toxicosis with *toxic heat:* pyodermia, boils, carbuncles, skin abscesses, sores
VIRAL INFECTIONS (incl. herpes simplex, cold sores, aphthous sores, warts)
FUNGAL and PARASITIC INFECTIONS (incl. scabies, tinea, sycosis, yeast infections)
INFLAMMATIONS (acute, with pain and swelling, esp. lymphangitis, laryngitis, sinusitis, conjunctivitis,
    otitis media, stomatitis, parotitis, orchitis, mastitis, ovaritis, osteomyelitis)
DIPHTHERIA (non-malignant, with deposits and false membrane)
AUTOIMMUNE DISORDERS (?)

3 **REDUCES LIVER CONGESTION AND PLETHORA;**
  REDUCES GASTRIC ACIDITY

liver Qi stagnation: bilious headache, nausea, constipation, abdominal distension, midback pain
LIVER CONGESTION
abdominal plethora: overweight, constipation, low fat tolerance, abdominal distension
ADIPOSITY
GASTRIC HYPERACIDITY, peptic ulcers

4 **PROMOTES TISSUE REPAIR, REDUCES INFLAMMATION AND RELIEVES PAIN**

SKIN and GENITAL ULCERS (incl. varicose and chancrous; fissures, wounds)
ULCERS and INFLAMMATION of mucosa in rheumatic conditions
BURNS, scalds

PREPARATION

Use: Poke root **tincture** prepared from the dried root is the most reliable preparation. Avoid using the fresh root, which is somewhat toxic internally and caustic/escharotic topically. Internal use is still necessary when treating topical conditions such as skin rashes, ulcers and tumors, and will more than halve recovery time. For these external uses, **liniments, lotions, salves** and **poultices** are prepared.

Poke leaf prepared in a strong **decoction** or **suppository** is useful in hemorrhoids and chronic constipation; topical applications improve chronic skin ulcers. A **thickened juice** of the leaves was traditionally used as a folk remedy for skin cancers and chronic indolent ulcers.

Dosage: Decoction: 1-2 g

Tincture: 0.1-1 ml, or 3-25 drops (the average is 0.4 ml or 9 drops. Prepare at 1:5 strength in 45% ethanol. The maximum weekly dose is 8 ml.

The larger the dose, the more *purgative* this remedy becomes.

Be sure to decrease the dosage up to 1/4 the normal dose for children and elderly.

Caution: Poke root belongs to the medium-strength category of remedies that have cumulative toxicity. The dosage must be respected. The remedy is for short-term use only. Never use for more than two weeks at a stretch, whether on its own or, as is usual, in a formula.

Poke root is forbidden during pregnancy because of possible *teratogenic* effects.

Note: Known as poke salad in the American South, the tender young shoots of this plant make an excellent spring green vegetable. Boil, discard the liquid, and then simmer or prepare as tempura.

Fresh poke root should only be handled with rubber gloves as it is a mitogen that can cause blood changes.

NOTES

Because in late summer its clusters of hyacinth berries hang like heavy, ripe grapes, pokeweed in the American Midwest was aptly known by early French explorers as "morelle à grappes." Native Americans taught them how to use the root for external conditions, and early eighteenth century travellers like the Swede PETER KALM and the Englishman JONATHAN CARVER wisely recorded their observations of native uses in their detailed travelogues.

Since those days, however, Poke root has become a remedy for internal use above all. Early Eclectic practitioners in the 1840s launched Poke root—like so many other valuable native botanicals—as a superior *alterative* remedy. By the late nineteenth century Phytolacca, as it was known, was firmly classified as an "alterative influencing the glands" (ELLINGWOOD 1919).

Like Yellow dock root, Figwort root and herb, Burdock root and others in this section, Poke root is a systemic *resolvent detoxicant* remedy with particular affinity for the exocrine glandular system, especially the lymphatic circulation. Hydrogenoid iris constitutions, take note. Containing triterpenoid saponins and generous amounts of potassium, the root's *detoxicant* action is deep and powerful. It radically addresses several types of **metabolic toxicosis** syndromes, namely, **lymphatic, depository** (hardening) and **tumoral diatheses.** This is where it excels. With assistance from its *liver stimulant* and *laxative* actions, Poke enhances the catabolic phase of metabolism and resorption, with particular benefits to the glandular, integumentary and musculoskeletal systems.

The remedy is especially useful for subjects that badly need resolution of **chronically enlarged,** painful, hard **lymph glands, eczema** with **chronic dryness** and **irritation,** and **hardening/ depository disorders** such as cirrhosis, fibrocystic breasts and lipomas. In Chinese medical terms, Poke essentially dispels **wind-damp** and **phlegm** from the **skin** and **channels.** Eclectic doctors found

the root to work best for individuals presenting pale mucosa, ulceration and swollen glands.

Poke root's effects are enhanced when combined with a more strongly *diuretic detoxicant* such as Birch leaf, Cleavers herb or Burdock root in this subsection. In any event, because of its powerful action, Poke root should only be used in small quantities and in combination with other remedies rather than alone.

Three of Poke root's specific effects cause widespread benefits, especially in the soft tissues. The first is an excellent *anti-inflammatory* action that has been used for **inflammatory conditions** as diverse as lymphadenitis, laryngitis, otitis, pericarditis and burns.

Second, *immunostimulant, antiviral* and *antifungal* actions useful in a variety of **infections,** which make sense in view of the formic and oleanolic acid content (Poke has demonstrated *lymphocyte stimulant* activity).

Third, a *tissue-repairing* effect especially useful in the treatment of **peptic ulcers** resulting from gastric hyperacidity, as well as for skin ulcers of various kinds.

Eclectic doctors during the second half of the nineteenth century observed the particular affinity of this remedy for the female breast and the skeletal system—and for the spine in particular. Poke root was routinely included in formulas for numerous **breast disorders** ranging from acute mastitis to chronic lumps (benign and cancerous), as well as for conditions of the **bones** and **spine** in general. This definitely brings up echoes of Horsetail herb and Walnut leaf/bark, also used in bone and spine disorders.

Soapwort Root

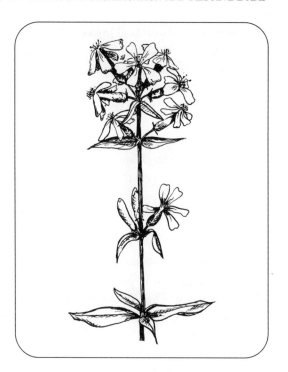

Botanical source: *Saponaria officinalis* L.
      (Caryophyllaceae)
Pharmaceutical name: Radix Saponariae
Ancient names: Saponaria (Lat)
Other names: Soaproot, Bouncing bet, Bruisewort,
      Latherwort, Fuller's herb, Sweet bettie,
      Crow soap, Old maid's pink, Dog cloves
      (Eng and Am)
      Saponaire, Herba à foulon, Savonnière,
       Savon de fossé (Fr)
      Seifenkraut, Seifenwurzel, Speichelwurz,
       Waschkraut, Hundsnelke (Ge)
Parts used: the root

NATURE

Therapeutic category: mild remedy with minimal chronic toxicity
Constituents: saponins 4% (incl. saporubin), resin, gum, mucilage, calcium oxalate, trace minerals
leaves: flavonoids (vitexin, saponarin), vitamin C
Effective qualities: sweet, bitter, somewhat pungent, cool, moist
      restoring, softening, dissolving, diluting, stimulating
Tropism: fluids (including plasma), skin, lungs, bladder; Lung, Spleen, Liver meridians

FUNCTIONS AND INDICATIONS

1   **PROMOTES DETOXIFICATION AND RESOLVES DAMP;**
    PROMOTES URINATION AND RELIEVES IRRITATION; REDUCES ECZEMA AND TUMORS

    metabolic toxicosis with *damp:* skin rashes, aches and pains, fatigue, urinary irritation
    BLADDER IRRITATION (dysuria)
    skin wind-damp: skin rashes with itching, scales
    ECZEMA (chronic), leg ulcers, syphilis
    LYMPHADENITIS, scrofula
    GOUT, rheumatism (chronic); leprosy
    TUMORS (incl. malignant)

2   **PROMOTES SWEATING, DISPELS WARM-DRYNESS AND REDUCES FEVER;**
    PROMOTES EXPECTORATION, RESOLVES VISCOUS PHLEGM AND RELIEVES COUGHING

    external warm-dryness: fever, thirst, dry cough, headache
    COLD or BRONCHITIS onset
    lung heat-dryness: dry throat, dry rasping cough, feverishness, constipation
    lung phlegm-dryness: hard unproductive cough, difficult expectoration with scanty viscous sputum
    BRONCHITIS, emphysema, pneumonia; CHRONIC DRY COUGH

3   **TONIFIES DIGESTIVE QI, PROMOTES ABSORPTION AND RELIEVES FATIGUE;**
    REDUCES LIVER CONGESTION, JAUNDICE AND CONSTIPATION; ELIMINATES PARASITES

stomach and intestines (Spleen) Qi deficiency: poor digestion, loose stool, appetite loss, weight loss
MALABSORPTION, metabolic acidosis, anemia, anorexia, DEBILITY in general
liver Qi stagnation: indigestion, constipation, right flank soreness
LIVER CONGESTION, jaundice, spleen congestion
PIN- or THREADWORMS (oxyuriasis)

4   **VITALIZES THE BLOOD, REDUCES CONGESTION AND REGULATES MENSTRUATION**

uterus blood stagnation: dull, heavy pains in lower abdomen, premenstrual pains, heavy or late periods
CONGESTIVE DYSMENORRHEA, PELVIC VARICOCELES

5   **BENEFITS THE SKIN AND HAIR, AND REDUCES ITCHING**

ECZEMA, acne, boils, pruritus, tumors, poison ivy/oak rash; HAIR CARE

PREPARATION

Use: Soapwort root is prepared by **decoction** or **tincture.** Topical applications such as **ointments, poultices** and **washes** (including hair rinses) are excellent for skin conditions. **Suppositories** and **pessaries** may be used for congestive pelvic conditions with pain and dysmenorrhea. The whole mature plant was also traditionally **juiced.**

Soapwort leaf has similar functions as the root, but is weaker. The leaves have been used since ancient days as a washing soap.

Dosage: Decoction: 10-16 g; **Tincture:** 2-4 ml at 1:2 strength in 30% ethanol

Caution: Contraindicated during pregnancy because of the *uterine stimulant* and *laxative* actions. Contraindicated in diarrhea from cold or damp in the intestines (Spleen), and in lung (phlegm-) cold.

NOTES

True to its name, the pretty soapwort of the roadsides and waste places has been used since prehistory as an emulsifying and lathering agent. Untold thousands of tons of washing were done with soapwort. The same saponin glycosides that emulsify fat are responsible for the plant's therapeutic effects when given under certain conditions. However, although soapwort root is virtually a study in the actions of saponins, we cannot explain all of its actions through these alone. The root's effective qualities—sweet, bitter and somewhat pungent—inform us as much about its clinical applications.

A traditional European remedy, Soapwort root is essentially an *alterative* with *restorative* properties. While improving the quality of the fluid and blood environment, the herb also enhances overall energy production. In altering mode, Soapwort operates as a *resolvent detoxicant* with *diuretic, lymphatic detoxicant, liver detoxicant, laxative* and *antitumoral* actions. It succeeds best in individuals suffering from chronic forms of eczema and swollen glands with underlying kidney and liver deficiency—especially when they complain of always feeling tired and run-down. Soapwort clears **wind-damp** in the **skin** and **meridians** and tonifies the Qi at the same time.

On the blood level, Soapwort is a *pelvic venous decongestant* that benefits women with congestive dysmenorrhea and even varicoceles—the syndrome **uterus blood congestion.**

Soapwort root may be used for its *restorative* functions alone, however. Like the Chinese Pseudostellaria Tai Zi Shen, also in the pink family and loaded with saponins, Soapwort addresses **intestines (Spleen) Qi deficiency.** Forms of digestive malabsorption and anemia therefore respond well to it.

Soapwort's therapeutic profile would not be complete without mention of its respiratory and surface functions. Its combined saponins and mucilage ensure a good *mucolytic expectorant* action in **lung phlegm-dryness** conditions. Here the person presents a dry cough with difficult, scanty expectoration—as in chronic bronchial disorders. At the onset of respiratory infections, this remedy is simultaneously gently *diaphoretic* (the pungent taste) and *demulcent* (the sweet taste), and thereby able to resolve **external warm-dryness** conditions with fever, thirst and dry cough.

Pellitory of the Wall Herb

Botanical source: *Parietaria officinalis* L.
(Urticaceae)
Pharmaceutical name: Herba Parietariae
Ancient names: (Lat)
Other names: Wallwort, Lichwort, Hammerwort,
Billie beatie (Eng)
Pariétaire, Casse-pierre, Herbe au verre,
Perce-muraille (Fr)
Parts used: the herb

NATURE

Therapeutic category: mild remedy with minimal chronic toxicity
Constituents: flavonoids (incl. quercetrin glycosides and rhamnoside, kaempferol, isorhamnetin, sophorosides, neohesperidosides), potassium nitrate, tannins, bitter compound, glucoproteins
Effective qualities: somewhat bitter, cool, dry
restoring, softening, dissolving
Tropism: kidneys, bladder, muscles; Fluid body
Kidney, Bladder meridians
Ground: all krases, biotypes and constitutions

FUNCTIONS AND INDICATIONS

1   **PROMOTES DETOXIFICATION AND RESOLVES DAMP;**
   PROMOTES URINATION, DISSOLVES DEPOSITS, REDUCES INFLAMMATION AND IRRITATION
   metabolic toxicosis with *damp:* aches and pains, morning mid-back pains, malaise
   URINARY DEPOSITS (incl. stones, sand); bile stones
   RHEUMATISM
   KIDNEY EDEMA
   bladder and kidney damp-heat: urgent, difficult, burning scanty urination, dark urine, thirst
   KIDNEY COLIC, strangury
   URINARY INFECTIONS (incl. cystitis [incl. interstitial], urethritis, pyelitis, nephritis)

2   **REDUCES HEMORRHOIDS AND CONTUSION**
   HEMMORRHOIDS
   CONTUSIONS, sore throat, skin spots, sunburn

PREPARATION

Use: Pellitory of the wall herb is prepared by **infusion** or **tincture.** The fresh herb is said to be more potent. **Compresses** and **ointments** could contain this herb in treating topical conditions, especially hemorroids.
Dosage: Infusion: 10-16 g

Tincture: 1-3 ml at 1:3 strength in 45% ethanol

Caution: None

Note: Parsley piert herb, from *Alchemilla arvensis* (L.) Scopoli (Rosaceae), is used in a very similar way to Pellitory of the wall herb. Other names common for this herbaceous plant common in the northern hemisphere include Parsley breakstone, Piercestone, Field lady's mantle, Colickwort, Firegrass and Bowel-hive. With an astringent taste and containing tannins and mucilage, the remedy is a highly effective *diuretic* that stimulates liver and kidney functions, and dissolves urinary sand and stones. Cold and moist by nature, it is also a *refrigerant* and *demulcent*. Prime applications include urinary deposits, strangury, acute urinary tract inflammation, edema and jaundice. Use and dose: As for Pellitory of the wall above.

Wild strawberry fruit, from *Fragaria vesca* (Rosaceae), is another specific remedy for dissolving urinary stones. Only the wild strawberry is medicinal. Its *detoxicant diuretic, laxative* and *nutritive* effects may be used for treating urinary stones, kidney disorders, rheumatic and gouty conditions, and dysentery. The botanist CARL LINNEUS is one of many who in the past successfully treated attacks of gout with extended strawberry fasts alone—he set quite a trend in the late eighteenth century. Strawberries are very digestible and promote weight gain in deficiency and wasting conditions.

NOTES

A member of the nettle family, Pellitory of the wall is a common native European herb. Most of its names describe its liking for stony habitats like stone walls and other stony places. As luck would have it though, this remedy does "pierce" urinary stones as well. Pellitory is a classic Western stone-dissolving remedy, a *dissolvent* and *detoxicant diuretic* that also works on other deposits such as biliary stones and rheumatic conditions generally. Add to this a good *anti-inflammatory* and a mild *demulcent* effect, and we find a remedy that addresses tense and hot urinary conditions with bladder irritation and strangury. With its combination of actions therefore, Pellitory is an important remedy for those presenting **urinary stones, infection** or **neurogenic bladder** with **bladder irritation** or **pain.** For other than mild urinary infections, a good *urinary anti-infective* remedy like Echinacea root should definitely be combined with it.

Gotu Kola Herb

Botanical source: *Centella asiatica* L. Urban
  (Umbelliferae/Apiaeae)
Other names: Ji Xue Cao (Mandarin Chinese),
  Jik Syut Chou (Cantonese Chinese)
Part used: the herb

Therapeutic category: mild remedy w. no toxicity
Constituents: glycosides, alkaloid hydrocotylin, bitter, triterpenic & hydrocyanic acids, tannins
Effective qualities: somewhat sweet, bitter & pungent

Notes On Its Functions and Indications

Gotu kola herb is a well known subtropical East Asian herb also much used in Ayurvedic medicine for its superlative *detoxifying* action with respect to skin conditions. **Chronic eczema/dermatitis** with pruritus, psoriasis, boils and lymphadenitis benefit the most here, particularly as the herb is also a *connective tissue restorative*. Cellulite and varicose veins will also do well as a result. In tandem with this action is a *venous decongestant* and *astringent restorative* effect that applies to **venous insufficiency** with varicose veins, including hemorroids, and **pelvic congestion** with dysmenorrhea.

Besides being *alterative* on the fluid-lymph-tissue level, Gotu kola also has a *broad-spectrum anti-infective* action, especially on **respiratory infections.** However, more distinctive is its *central nervous, adrenal cortex* and *immune restorative* effect. This puts the herb on a par with Sage leaf, Milky oat berry and others in Class 7, e.g.in **cerebral/nervous deficiencies (neurasthenia)** with depression, mental and physical fatigue and stress-related disorders in general. Along with all this, we can consider Gotu kola mildly *adaptogenic*. (See the author's *Jade Remedies* for the full monograph).

Dosage: Infusion and **decoction:** 10-30g

Tincture: 2-5 ml at 1:3 strength in 45% eth.

Caution: None within these dosage ranges

Herbs to Vitalize the Blood, Reduce Congestion and Moderate Menstruation

Called *decongestants,* remedies in this class are used to vitalize the blood to relieve passive blood congestion usually found in the lower limbs and pelvic basin. They are selected in conditions of congested blood or hyperemia caused by deficient venous circulation, in which the quality of blood and lymph circulation are compromised. *Decongestants* are also frequently used to reduce excessive menstrual bleeding, which is a common manifestation of blood congestion in the pelvis.

The Nature, Dynamics and Treatment of Blood Congestion

Blood congestion may be active or passive by nature and occurs either as a local or systemic condition. Active blood congestion usually results from local irritation or infection, and always involves inflammation. Passive blood congestion is usually connected with general insufficient venous return. Instead of smoothly moving up and back towards the heart, the venous blood stagnates and tends to thicken. Over time, a passive blood congestion may become an active, localized one, and vice versa. An example of this is pelvic blood congestion that predisposes to fibroid tumors, endometriosis or pelvic inflammatory disease.

Active blood congestion is discussed among the remedies that clear heat, cool the blood and stop bleeding in Class 12. **Coronary congestion** is a special case and is discussed in Class 7. Passive congestion is seen in two main syndromes, **venous blood stagnation** and **uterus blood congestion.** Both syndromes originate in factors such as lack of exercise, shallow breathing, emotional imbalance, excessive intake of dairy products, chronic constipation and constitutional circulatory weakness.

Venous blood stagnation typically presents fatigue, internal varicosities, varicose veins (including hemorrhoids), a sensation of heaviness in the legs or a dull aching after prolonged standing, edema and pigmentation around the ankles, leg cramps at night, nodules, phlebitis and skin rashes (eczema). The sublingual tongue veins are large and purple; the pulse may be slippery or forceful.

The core treatment principle for venous blood stagnation is to vitalize the blood. Sluggish venous return is specifically corrected by restoring the tone of the veins and by increasing venous circulation and capillary perfusion. Both actions together encourage the blood to rise against gravity, thereby relieving the congestion.

The syndrome **uterus blood congestion** arises from pelvic blood congestion and leads to congestive dysmenorrhea. Because woman's pelvic basin is built to accomodate her reproductive organs and is normally saturated with arterial and venous blood, it is anatomically predisposed to this condition. This syndrome presents a feeling of heaviness and dragging pains in the pelvis, a constant dull pain in the lower abdomen (these "cramps" are seen especially during the progesteronic phase of approaching menstruation), early, heavy or prolonged menstrual bleeding with bright red blood (menorrhagia) and sometimes intermenstrual bleeding (metrorrhagia). The tongue may have a purple tinge and the pulse is tight, deep.

The basic treatment for uterus blood congestion is to vitalize pelvic/uterine blood specifically. It cannot be ove-remphsized how important it is for female health to treat this condition while still in the functional stage. This will effectively prevent a host of other reproductive pathologies from developing, including uterine fibroid tumors, endometriosis and cervical dysplasia. These all have their source in stagnant pelvic/uterus blood, despite the fact that they also include a hormonal imbalance, usually estrogen accumulation.

Note that excessive menstrual and intermenstrual bleeding may have specific causes that should be assessed, preferably through an internal exam. Causes include the use of IUD's, the presence of polyps, fibroid tumors, cancer, pelvic inflammatory disease and infections such as acute endometritis and salpingitis. Most of these disorders result from long-term uterus blood congestion involving estrogen accumulation in the system. They should be treated alongside the blood congestion and menorrhagia.

Blood congestion is clinically often associated with one of two other syndromes, which may be primary or secondary. The first is **liver blood congestion** where the prominent symptoms are lethargy, abdominal distension, flank pain and distension, constipation, delayed, clotted menses and a tight or sunken pulse. This syndrome includes portal congestion and, in some cases, water congestion with general edema, or abdominal plethora with damp-heat in the middle warmer. The other syndrome is **Kidney Yang deficiency,** typically presenting dreaminess, mental stupor, a lack of feeling response, cold limbs, hypotension, possible urogenital symptoms and a deep, weak pulse. Both of these associated syndromes are often seen in perimenopause, for instance.

The Herbs that Vitalize the Blood

The herbs that vitalize the blood in the treatment of **venous blood stagnation** are called *venous decongestants*. Astringent, dry and cool in quality, they tend to contain significant amounts of tannins, organic acids and flavonoids; some also contain saponins that would explain their action. Important *venous decongestants* include Horsechestnut seed, Butcher's broom herb, Yarrow herb, Witch hazel leaf, Grapevine leaf and the Oriental herb Sophora Huai Hua (Japanese pagoda tree flower). The majority of these reduce congestion in two ways.
1. By increasing the capillary and venous circulation. Here their astringency tightens dilated capillaries and veins, thereby shunting stagnant blood foreward in the venous circulation.
2. By enhancing the tissue tone of the veins and capillaries themselves. *Antioxidant* bioflavonoids are known to strengthen the blood vessels and are also high in Bilberry fruit, green tea, etc.

Hyperviscous blood and **thrombosis** commonly result from venous blood congestion when toxicosis or other pathogenic factors are present— a potentially dangerous condition. Treatment here aims to thin the blood, reduce blood hyperviscosity and prevent or treat thrombosis using *anticoagulant (thrombolytic)* remedies. *Anticoagulants* were called *attenuants* and *antiplastics* in the past, and are often high in blood-thinning coumarins. They include Melilot herb, Horsechestnut, Garlic bulb, Linden flower, Cleavers herb, Goldenrod herb,

Cayenne pepper, Ginger root, Onion bulb and Helichrysum essential oil, as well as the Oriental remedies Panax San Qi (Pseudo-ginseng root) and Ligusticum Chuan Xiong (Sich-uan lovage root). Internal use of these should be supplemented by topical applications of *anti-contusion* herbs such as Arnica flower, Horseradish root, Garlic bulb and Tansy herb. There is a clear difference between *decongestants,* which reduces venous congestion, and *anticoagulants,* which reduce hyperviscous blood.

Uterus blood congestion specifically is treated first, by promoting general venous return using the *venous decongestants;* and second, by decongesting pelvic blood specifically, which will reduce excessive menstrual flow. Important *uterine decongestants* include Lady's mantle herb, White deadnettle herb, Yarrow herb, Shepherd's purse herb, Partridgeberry herb, Mugwort herb, Pasqueflower root/herb, Helonias root and Madder root.

Note that some of these herbs are also general *venous decongestants,* although the majority exert a greater action on the pelvic basin itself with a resultant *uterine decongestant* effect.

Because in uterus blood congestion the pelvic capillaries especially become engorged, it is also necessary here to stimulate arterial circulation with *diffusive arterial stimulants* such as Ginger root, Prickly ash bark and Cayenne (Class 8). A good formula for this condition will therefore include *venous decongestants, uterine decongestants* and *arterial stimulants* in various proportions, depending on the relative emphasis required.

If **uterine bleeding** is severe or prolonged, *hemostatic* or *coagulant* reinforcements (Class 18) should be added, despite the fact that many *uterine decongestants* are also *hemostatic. Hemostatics* help stop bleeding either by causing capillary astriction and/or by speeding up blood clotting—a *coagulant* action.

Caution: In the case of uterine bleeding during or between the periods, it is important to determine the cause by an internal exam. This is especially important for women past menopause.

Anticoagulant remedies that thin the blood should not be used before surgery and contact sports, and are forbidden in infants.

A summary list of remedies that address blood congestion is found in the Repertory under Circulation, insufficient venous, and Pelvic congestion.

Vitalize the Blood, Reduce Congestion and Moderate Menstruation

Astringent venous and uterine decongestants

Horsechestnut Seed

Botanical source: *Aesculus hippocastanum* L.,
    A. glabra L., *A. californica* (Hippocastanaceae)
Pharmaceutical name: Semen Aesculi
Ancient names: Kassana (Gr)
    Castanea equina (Lat)
Other names: Lambs, Konker tree, Bongay (Eng)
    Buckeye, Spanish chestnut (Am)
    Marron d'Inde, Chataignier de cheval, Faux
      chataignier (Fr)
    Rosskastanie, Kestenbaum (Ge)
Part used: the seed; also the leaf, Folium Aesculi,
    and the branch bark, Cortex rami Aesculi

NATURE

Therapeutic category: medium-strength remedy with moderate chronic toxicity
Constituents: triterpenoid saponins (incl. aescin), flavonoids (incl. aesculetin, fraxin, argyrin), esculetol, coumarin aesculin, tannins, fatty oil, protein, phytosterin, fraxin, allantoin, starch 35%
Effective qualities: somewhat bitter, astringent and pungent, cool, dry
    decongesting, astringing, restoring, diluting, dissolving
Tropism: venous system, uterus, liver, blood
    Liver, Lung, Large Intestine meridians
    Fluid body
Ground: all krases, biotypes and constitutions for symptomatic use

FUNCTIONS AND INDICATIONS

1 **VITALIZES THE BLOOD, REDUCES CONGESTION AND MODERATES MENSTRUATION;**
   RESTORES THE VEINS AND THINS THE BLOOD; BENEFITS THE PROSTATE

   venous blood stagnation: varicosities, heavy or aching legs, leg cramps at night, dull abdominal aches,
      lethargy
   VARICOSE VEINS, varicocele, thrombophlebitis, pelvic congestion
   HEMORRHOIDS (with or without bleeding)
   THROMBOSIS, HYPERLIPIDEMIA (blood hyperviscosity), frostbite
   uterus blood congestion: abundant, early periods, pelvic weight, dragging or pains
   CONGESTIVE DYSMENORRHEA, MENORRHAGIA
   PROSTATE CONGESTION (hyperplasia) with dysuria

2 **ASTRINGES AND STOPS DISCHARGE AND BLEEDING;**
   RESOLVES VISCOUS PHLEGM AND STOPS COUGHING

   DIARRHEA, enteritis, leucorrhea with *damp*
   HEMORRHAGE (internal and external, incl. intermenstrual and postpartum uterine bleeding)

lung phlegm-dryness: cough with difficult expectoration, viscous scanty sputum
BRONCHITIS

3 PROMOTES URINATION, DRAINS PLETHORA AND RELIEVES OVERWEIGHT; REDUCES FEVER

liver Qi and blood stagnation: fatigue, constipation, headache, low fat tolerance, abdominal distension,
   water retention
LIVER CONGESTION with EDEMA
abdominal plethora: abdominal distension, overweight, right flank pain
OBESITY, CELLULITE
REMITTENT FEVER (*shao yang* stage)

4 BENEFITS THE SKIN

SKIN ERUPTIONS and blemishes, frostbite, warts

PREPARATION

Use: Horsechestnut seed (the hard brown fruit without the rind) is used for all functions above. **Horsechestnut seed** or **bark** are prepared by **decoction** and **tincture.** Applied topically, Horsechestnut seed **washes** and **ointments** are excellent for skin eruptions, skin blemishes and frostbite. **Pessaries** and **suppositories,** which are also prepared from the seed, should be used to complement internal use in conditions of rectal, pelvic and uterine congestion.

   Horsechestnut bark is more astringent, bitter and cold in quality than the seed. It is mainly used for its *astringent* and *antipyretic* actions that address a variety of discharges arising from damp-heat and damp, as well as remittent fevers (functions 2 and 4).

   Horsechestnut flower preparations are used in **liniments** for neuralgic, rheumatic and gouty disorders. The flower **tincture,** taken in 10-15 drop doses, is taken internally for relief of abdominal cramps and fainting.

   The extracted glycoside aesculin is used in sun-protective preparations, such as sun lotions.

Dosage: Decoction: 2-4 g   ·
   Tincture: 0.5-1.5. The average dose is 0.5 ml. Prepare at 1:2 strength in 35% ethanol

Caution: Being a medium-strength remedy with moderate cumulative toxicity, Horsechestnut if used on its own is for short-term use only. The best use is to combine the remedy with others in a formula. Contraindicated before surgery or with bleeding disorders present because of its *anticoagulant* action.

NOTES

The seed of the magnificent horsechestnut tree has been exploited in Europe by the pharmaceutical industry for aescin, an acid saponin that is thought to generate the main effects of this remedy. Extracted aescin has proven important in the treatment of varicose veins, thrombophlebitis, local edemas, cellulite and bleeding. It works by decreasing capillary permeability through *vasoconstriction,* and by toning the vein walls and valves. For this reason Horsechestnut is called a *venous trophorestorative.*

   Herbal medicine, however, prefers to utilize the whole plant with its rich complex of components rather than an isolated extract. In the case of Horsechestnut, flavonoids and other glycosides play an important assistant role in enhancing aescin's total field of action. Consequently, Horse-

chestnut addresses a wider range of disorders than just the ones described.

   Like Cypress twig and leaf, Horsechestnut is a *venous restorative, astringent* and *anticoagulant* all in one. The three actions merge comfortably with each other, creating a single *blood decongestant,* or *blood-vitalizing* effect. **Congestion** of the **venous blood** is the remedy's main area of application, and includes **liver (portal)/pelvic/uterine/prostate blood congestion. In this connection,** Horsechestnut is an important woman's remedy that moderates menstrual flooding, thereby treating congestive dysmenorrhea—like the similar Chinese remedies Rubia Qian Cao Gen and Biota Ce Bai Ye, and the acupuncture points Sp 8 and 10, Li 5 and Bl 17.

   Horsechestnut is especially indicated when

liver Qi and blood stagnation presenting **abdominal plethora and pelvic congestion** is part of the overall condition. The remedy's *liver stimulant/ decongestant* and *diuretic* action will enhance portal circulation and liver Yang functions in individuals prone to chronic headaches, water retention, abdominal bloating, weight gain, hemorrhoids, nausea and skin rashes.

In the respiratory tract the remedy's saponins exert a *mucolytic expectorant* action that effectively loosens hard dry sputum in chronic bronchial conditions entailing **lung phlegm-dryness.** The triterpenoid saponins here work in a similar way to the saponins found in Birthroot and Anemarrhena Zhi Mu.

Because it is highly effective, Horsechestnut rarely needs support from other remedies for the congestive conditions it treats. Still, to fully address a particular condition, this remedy like any other should routinely be combined with other remedies to create an individualized formula.

Stoneroot

Botanical source: *Collinsonia canadensis* L.
　　　(Lamiaceae/Labiatae)
Pharmaceutical name: Radix Collinsoniae
Other names: Horsebalm, Canada horsemint,
　　　Horseweed, Richweed, Richleaf, Knotroot,
　　　Knobroot, (Am)
　　　Herbe/baume de cheval, Guérit tout (Fr)
　　　Griesswurzel, Steinwurzel (Ge)
Part used: the root

NATURE
Therapeutic category: mild remedy with minimal chronic toxicity
Constituents: rosmarinic acid, alkaloid, resin, tannins, saponin, essential oil, organic acids, wax, starch, mucilage, magnesium
Effective qualities: somewhat bitter and sweet, cool, dry
　　　decongesting, astringing, stabilizing, restoring, relaxing
Tropism: veins, lungs, heart, stomach, intestines, bladder
　　　Liver, Spleen, Lung, Bladder, Dai meridians
　　　Fluid, Air bodies
Ground: all krases, biotypersa and constitutions

FUNCTIONS AND INDICATIONS
1　**VITALIZES THE BLOOD, REDUCES CONGESTION AND MODERATES MENSTRUATION**
　　venous blood stagnation: varicosities, heavy or aching legs, leg cramps at night, fatigue, constipation
　　VARICOSE VEINS, varicoceles, pelvic congestion
　　HEMORRHOIDS (esp. with constipation)

731

liver blood congestion: right subcostal pain, hemorrhoids, constipation

uterus blood congestion: pelvic weight and fullness with dull pains, heavy or early periods, constipation, hemorrhoids

CONGESTIVE DYSMENORRHEA

2 ASTRINGES TO STOPS DISCHARGE AND BLEEDING, AND RELIEVES IRRITATION;
RAISES CENTRAL QI, RELIEVES PROLAPSE AND BENEFITS THE RECTUM;
STIMULATES DIGESTION AND APPETITE

stomach-intestines (Spleen) Qi deficiency: watery stools, abdominal distension, fatigue, appetite loss

DIARRHEA, gastroenteritis, dysentery, colitis, IBS (esp. chronic)

genitourinary damp: white vaginal discharges, spermatorrhea

LEUCORRHEA, mucus cystitis, urinary incontinence and irritation

HEMORRHAGE (passive), MENORRHAGIA

Central Qi sinking: abdominal bearing down sensation, intestinal prolapse

GASTRIC AND INTESTINAL PROLAPSE

RECTAL PAIN, WEIGHT, CONSTRICTION or HEAT (incl. of pregnancy)

3 PROMOTES EXPECTORATION, RESOLVES PHLEGM AND RELIEVES COUGHING;
BENEFITS THE THROAT AND OPENS THE VOICE

lung phlegm-damp: cough, expectoration of copious white sputum, wheezing

CHRONIC BRONCHITIS, LARYNGITIS, pharyngitis, otitis (esp. chronic)

HOARSENESS, VOICE LOSS, throat irritation and constriction

4 REGULATES THE QI, RELAXES CONSTRAINT AND RELIEVES PAIN;
TONIFIES HEART QI

heart Qi constraint: sticking chest pains, shortness of breath, nervousness, cough

NEUROCARDIAC SYNDROME, heart disease

intestines Qi constraint (liver/Spleen disharmony): indigestion, flatulence, epigastric or abdominal pain

INTESTINAL COLIC, IBS

heart Qi deficiency: fatigue, dyspnea, low stamina in chronic disease, old age, overexercise

5 PROMOTES TISSUE REPAIR AND REDUCES CONTUSION

WOUNDS, bruises, sprains, sores, ulcers, burns

ANAL FISTULAS and ulcers

PREPARATION

Use: Stoneroot is prepared in **decoction** or **tincture** form. **Compresses** and **poultices** can be made from these for wounds, sores, sprains, bruises and burns. **Suppositories** and **pessaries** are excellent for treating congestive conditions of the pelvic organs and rectum.

Dosage: Decoction: 8-14 g

  Tincture: 1-4 ml at 1:2 strength in 40% ethanol

Caution: Do not use the leaves of Stoneroot, as even small doses may cause vomiting.

Note: The reputation that Stoneroot enjoys for treating hemorroids is shared in Europe and North Africa by **Pilewort herb,** from *Ranunculus ficaria* L. This plant is also known as lesser celandine, figwort and smallwort. Pilewort herb is in the mild therapeutic category. Very little is known about it other than its consistent historical and current usage for safely reducing hemorrhoidal congestion and pain.

An **infusion** is taken internally and/or the remedy may be applied topically in an **ointment** or **suppository.** Other topical applications address boils and abscesses.

  Dose: Infusion: 8-14 g. Tincture: 3-5 ml. Caution: None.

NOTES

An unusual remedy, Stoneroot is one of the very few plants in the lipflower/mint family whose root is used in herbal medicine. It's a knobbly root at that, hard as stone. Because of its versatility, Stoneroot long ago became known by Anglo settlers in the Blue Ridge Mountains of Virginia as a "Healall," a "Richweed." Already the Native Americans had extensively used it as an internal and external remedy. In the nineteenth century, Homeopathic and Eclectic practitioners experimented widely with the plant in tincture and fluid extract form. Stoneroot's specific symptom-atology is a direct result of their experiments. Because of this sound basis of empirical therapeu-tic use, it is now possible to define the remedy's energetic qualities, functions and uses, as well as its pharmacological actions.

Stoneroot combines an unusual set of properties that essentially addresses three very different types of conditions among reproductive, respiratory and neurological functions. As a dry, astringent *decongestant*, this remedy addresses conditions of **venous and liver (portal) blood stagnation** and **uterus blood congestion.** Varicosities anywhere, and especially **hemorrhoids,** respond to it very well, and congestive dysmenorrhea is relieved as the remedy reduces pelvic congestion. In addition to the more common and general symptoms of pelvic congestion, Stoneroot is especially beneficial for those presenting the specific symptoms of **rectal pain, weight** and **constriction.** In Chinese medicine this points to a weakness of the Central Qi failing in its raising action.

In tandem with this chief area of pathology is Stoneroot's *mucostatic (anticatarrhal)* action. **Damp-cold urogenital** and **intestinal discharges** are the most appropriate conditions it addresses. One of the remedy's Pennsylvanian German names, *Griesswurzel,* is a historical reminder of its reputation for clear white leucorrhea. In this respect, Stoneroot functions like Terminalia He Zi (Myrobalan fruit) which is used in Chinese and Ayurvedic medicine.

The root's essential oil content supports its traditional use as an *expectorant* in bronchial congestion. In this connection, chronic bronchial, throat and middle ear inflammation are also said to respond well to it. Here addressing damp, congestive conditions as always, Stoneroot treats **lung phlegm-damp** with copious sputum production and throat irritation. The remedy has also always enjoyed a special reputation for treating **hoarseness** and **voice loss,** whether from laryngitis or simply from excessive use—as in "minister's voice."

Stoneroot is indicated then as a long-term and perhaps constitutional remedy in individuals with three forms of congestion: chronic venous congestion, mucous congestion and phlegm congestion.

Red Root

Botanical source: *Ceanothus americanus* L.,
    C. cuneatus, C. integerrimus, C. velutinus
    and spp. (Rhamnaceae)
Pharmaceutical name: Cortex radicis Ceanothi
Other names: Mountain lilac, Wild snowball,
    New Jersey tea, Buckbrush, California lilac,
    Walpole tea, Snowbrush, Deerbrush,
    Tobaccobrush, Oregon tea tree (Am)
    Palo colorado, Chaquerilla (Sp)
    Wilder Schneeball, Säckelblume,
    Hundsbeerbaum (Ge)
Part used: the root bark

NATURE

Therapeutic category: mild remedy with minimal chronic toxicity
Constituents: alkaloids (incl. ceanothine A/B/C/D/E, frangularine, adonetine-X/Y, ceanothamine, integeressine, integerrine, integerrenine, americine), ceanothic/succinic/oxalic/malonic/malic/orthophos-phoric/pyrophosphoric/betulinic acids, quercetrin, pungent oil, methylsalicilate, resin, tannin
Effective qualities: astringent, somewhat bitter, cold, dry
    decongesting, stimulating, astringing, stabilizing, relaxing
Tropism: liver, spleen, lungs, uterus, blood
    Liver, Spleen, Lung meridians
    Fluid body
Ground: Sanguine and Phlegmatic krases/biotypes
    Expressive/Jue Yin and Dependant/Tai Yin biotypes
    Lymphatic/Carbonic constitution

FUNCTIONS AND INDICATIONS

1   **VITALIZES THE BLOOD AND LYMPH, REDUCES CONGESTION AND MODERATES MENSTRUATION;**
    ASTRINGES AND STOPS DISCHARGE AND BLEEDING

uterus blood congestion: pelvic weight and dragging, heavy periods
CONGESTIVE DYSMENORRHEA
liver blood congestion: fatigue, low fat tolerance, abdominal distension, hemorrhoids
PORTAL CONGESTION, BLOOD CONGESTION (chronic, anywhere)
LYMPHADENITIS, adenoid enlargement
SPLEEN ENLARGEMENT with left flank pain, sallow doughy skin (incl. from hepatitis, mononucleosis)
NONFIBROUS CYSTS (incl. of ovaries, breasts), hydrocele
HEMORRHAGE (incl. uterine bleeding, nosebleeds, bleeding hemorrhoids, capillary ruptures)
MENORRHAGIA, metrorrhagia
LEUCORRHEA with *damp-heat* or *damp-cold*
VENEREAL DISCHARGES

2   **CLEARS DAMP-HEAT, DECONGESTS THE LIVER AND REDUCES INFLAMMATION**

liver Qi stagnation with *damp-heat:* bilious headache, right flank soreness, constipation, irritability,
    nausea, painful flanks and sides
LIVER CONGESTION

abdominal plethora: malaise, fatigue, overweight, abdominal distension
HYPERTENSION
DIPHTHERIA
INFLAMMATION of the MOUTH, GUM, THROAT, TONSILS, SINUSES and MIDDLE EAR

3 DESCENDS LUNG QI, OPENS THE CHEST AND RELIEVES WHEEZING

lung Qi constraint: difficult breathing, wheezing
WHOOPING COUGH, asthma
lung phlegm-heat: cough, expectoration of white or yellow sputum, wheezing
BRONCHITIS

PREPARATION

Use: Red root bark is used by **tincture** or **decoction.** When used to stop bleeding, Red root should be given every 1/2 hour for 6 hours, then hourly if still needed. **Gargles** and **mouthwashes** may also be prepared. **Red root leaves** may be used for a bracing hair rinse.
Dosage: Decoction or cold infusion: 6-10 g
          Tincture: 1-3 ml at 1:2 strength in 60% ethanol
Caution: Contraindicated in intestines (Spleen) Qi deficiency presenting loose stool.

NOTES

Also called "wild snowball" and "mountain lilac," this remedy is obtained from the root bark of a shrub that superficially looks much like the snowball tree, or guelder rose. Native Americans in the past used its leaves to brew a stimulating tea, and to make hair rinses.

As an internal remedy, Red root bark is essentially a highly effective *cooling astringent* that addresses conditions of **blood congestion** and **heat.** As a blood *decongestant* and *hemostatic,* this remedy acts mainly by tightening the veins, capillaries and lymphatics. **Uterine** and **liver/portal blood congestion** are the specific syndromes here calling for its use, and include the treatment of congestive dysmenorrhea, menorrhagia as well as hemmorrhage in general.

Red root bark is perfect for treating symptoms arising from chronic forms of **heat**—specifically, heat at the blood or nutritive level in Chinese medicine. The remedy is especially useful in those that tend to heat and tension, as its *refrigerant* and *nervous relaxant* effect relieves irritability and restlessness. This is not surprising, seeing its phalanx of alkaloids and acids. It is these that also make

Red root an excellent *anti-inflammatory* agent that should be used for acute inflammations of the special senses and upper respiratory organs, with swelling and possibly discharge.

Red root bark resembles the Chinese herb Biota Ce Bai Ye. In both botanicals the emphasis is on stopping uterine bleeding and removing blood congestion. Although the herb Salvia Dan Shen also literally means "red root," the latter has a much wider and different spectrum of therapeutic functions than the North American Red root (see HOLMES 1997).

Plethoric, stagnant conditions of the Middle Warmer is Red root bark's second main area of application. These are described in traditional Greek medicine as **abdominal plethora,** usually involving the stagnation of water that generates damp-heat. Whenever **damp-heat** is generated by **chronic liver congestion, portal vein congestion, lymphatic stagnation** and **mucus accumulation,** Red root is the right remedy. Here it acts with thoroughness, like Blue flag root or Goldenseal root.

Yarrow Herb

Botanical source: *Achillea millefolium* L.,
    A. lanulosa Nuttall and spp. (Asteraceae/
    Compositae)
Pharmaceutical name: Herba Achilleae
Ancient names: Chiliophyllon (Gr)
    Ambrosia, Ballusticum, Centifolia, Supercilium
      veneris, Sideritis (Lat)
Other names: Milfoil, Thousandleaf, Nosebleed,
    Devil's nettle, Cammock (Eng)
    Millefeuille, Achillée, Herbe aux charpentiers,
      Herbe aux coupures (Fr)
    Schafgarbe, Garbenkraut, Tausendblatt,
      Jungfernaugen, Blutstillkraut (Ge)
Part used: the herb

NATURE

Therapeutic category: mild remedy with minimal chronic toxicity
Constituents: essential oil 0.1-1.4% (incl. pinenes 16%, 1.8 cineol 10%, ketones [incl. thujone], azulene 0-51%, sabinene, camphene, eugenol, lactones), alkaloids (achilleine, betaine, trigonelline, betonicine, stachydrine), anthocyane, apigenin with glucoside, tannins, resin, aconitic/acetic/isovalerianic acid, succinic acid, salicylic acid, asparagin, inulin, ferment, cyanogenic glycosides, phytosterols (stigmasterol, sitosterol), polysaccharides, lactones (achillin, millefin, deacetylmatricarine), flavonoids (incl. quercitrin, kaempferol, apigenin, luteolin), rutin, hydroxycoumarins, saponins, alkanes (tricosane, pentacosane, heptadecane), fluorescent substance, fatty acids (linoleic, palmatic, oleic), chlorophyll, minerals (incl. potassium 48%, calcium, magnesium, iron, phosphorus, silicon), vitamin C
Effective qualities: somewhat bitter, astringent and sweet, cool, dry
    decongesting, astringing, restoring, stimulating, relaxing
Tropism: circulation, liver, spleen, intestines, kidney, bladder, uterus, blood, endocrine system
    Liver, Kidney, Bladder, Spleen, Heart, *chong, ren* meridians
    Air, Fluid bodies
Ground: all krases, biotypes and constitutions

FUNCTIONS AND INDICATIONS

1   **VITALIZES THE BLOOD, REDUCES CONGESTION AND MODERATES MENSTRUATION;
    ASTRINGES, RESOLVES MUCOUS-DAMP AND STOPS DISCHARGE AND BLEEDING**

    venous blood stagnation: varicosities, heavy or aching legs, leg cramps at night, fatigue
    VARICOSE VEINS, hemorrhoids, phlebitis
    uterus blood congestion: pelvic weight and dull pain, copious or prolonged menstruation
    MENORRHAGIA, CONGESTIVE DYSMENORRHEA, fibroids
    HEMORRHAGE (passive, internally and external, incl. from mouth and nose, in urine or stool)
    UTERINE BLEEDING, incl. FIBROIDAL
    LEUCORRHEA (esp. in young women), cervical erosion, spermatorrhea
    DIARRHEA

2 PROMOTES AND REGULATES MENSTRUATION, AND BALANCES HORMONES; REGULATES PREGNANCY AND MENOPAUSE

uterus Qi stagnation: irregular, delayed, scanty or stopped periods

AMENORRHEA (esp. from emotions, exposure to cold)

HORMONAL IMBALANCE in women in general (esp. estrogen/progesterone deficiency)

PMS with sore swollen breasts, irritability, moodiness, cramps

MENOPAUSAL SYNDROME with bleeding, varicose vains, hot flashes

3 TONIFIES URINARY QI, HARMONIZES URINATION AND RELIEVES IRRITATION; RESTORES THE KIDNEYS, PROMOTES URINATION AND RESOLVES TOXICOSIS

kidney and bladder Qi deficiency: frequent scanty urination, lumbar pain, irregular/difficult periods

URINARY INCONTINENCE, DYSURIA

URINARY STONES, gallstones

CHRONIC NEPHROSIS

BONE-MARROW DISEASE

kidney Qi stagnation: headache, fetid stool and urine, aches and pains

RHEUMATISM of back and shoulders, gout

4 REGULATES THE QI, RELAXES CONSTRAINT AND RELIEVES PAIN AND SPASMS

heart Qi constraint (Liver Yang rising): chest pains, palpitations, shortness of breath, dizziness, headache

ANGINA PECTORIS, neurogenic heart disorders, hypertension

intestines Qi constraint: abdominal pain and distention, flatulence

DIGESTIVE COLIC, IBS

bladder Qi constraint: scanty, dribling and frequent urination, anxiety, bedwetting

uterus Qi constraint: tension and irritability before onset of periods, dysmenorrhea, PMS

SPASMODIC DYSMENORRHEA

INFANTILE FITS and SEIZURES

5 STIMULATES DIGESTION, PROMOTES BILE FLOW AND AWAKENS APPETITE

liver/gallbladder and stomach Qi stagnation: painful, slow digestion, appetite loss, epigastric distension

GASTROENTERITIS, colitis

6 PROMOTES SWEATING, DISPELS WIND, REDUCES FEVER AND PROMOTES ERUPTIONS

external wind cold / heat: chills, sneezing, feverishness, aches and pains

COLD or FLU ONSET

ERUPTIVE and INTERMITTENT FEVERS (incl. measles, chickenpox)

7 PROMOTES TISSUE REPAIR, REDUCES INFLAMMATION, STOPS BLEEDING AND BENEFITS THE SKIN

WOUNDS (most types, esp. with pus); local bleeding from cuts, scrapes

ULCERS (incl. mouth, throat, leg, peptic ulcers); fistulas, cracked nipples

EYE IRRITATION/INFLAMMATION (pinkeye, conjunctivitis)

SKIN CONDITIONS in general; dandruff, hairloss

PREPARATION

Use: Yarrow herb is used in **fresh juice, infusion** or **tincture** form. The tincture serves best for general purposes. The hot infusion prepared with the lid *on* is excellent for causing sweating at the start of respiratory infections, and is also much used in various preparations for women's problems (**sitzbath, pessary, sponge**), as well as for wounds and ulcers (**swabs, compresses,** etc.). In topical conditions, the best results are obtained from combined internal and external use, with repeated small doses. This is especially true of acute situations like hemorrhage.

Dosage: Juice: 2 tsp

> **Infusion:** 8-14 g
>
> **Tincture:** 3-9 ml at 1:3 strength in 45% ethanol

Caution: Avoid using Yarrow during the first trimester of pregnancy because of the *uterine stimulant* effect. Sensitive people in rare cases may be allergic to Yarrow and develop skin rashes (because of the sesquiterpene lactone content). Prolonged and/or high-dosage use on its own over several months may lead to increased skin photosensitivity. Should this occur, exposure to direct sunlight should be avoided.

NOTES

A ubiquitous wayside plant, Yarrow herb is one of those very versatile, multi-directional remedies that years ago would have been thought of as simply another "old wives' tale" had it not consistently proved effective. Whereas past herbalists such as JOHANN SCHROEDER (1611) valued Yarrow as "among the *wound remedies* one of the most egregious," its full scope has only been fully appreciated in modern times. Considering the generously wide spectrum of its chemical components, pharmacologists have had quite a field day enumerating all the plant's potential activities in the system.

Still, using Yarrow herb is no excuse for bailing out under the wide parachute canopy of its constituents and functions. Yarrow is an outstanding gynecological remedy. Like White deadnettle herb, it qualifies as a universal regulator of female reproductive functions from pre-puberty to post-menopause. *Ambrosia,* as this herb was also called, is a gentle and reliable woman's ally, constant like the plant itself that continues to flower well into the autumn months.

Besides the hormonal influence (note the phytosterol content), Yarrow achieves this regulating effect through a comprehensive action on the uterus, blood and circulation. As an *astringent venous* and *uterine decongestant,* Yarrow vitalizes the venous circulation and removes **pelvic/uterine congestion,** thereby reducing flooding menses (rutin, tannins). In cases of functional **uterine bleeding,** Yarrow's provides a *hemostatic* action, like Shepherd's purse and Lady's mantle.

As a *uterine stimulant,* the remedy relieves delayed, painful periods with swollen breasts (essential oil). The *spasmolytic* action, meanwhile, addresses painful spasmodic dysmenorrhea (azu-

lene, alkaloids). The net result of all these actions is a systemic harmonizing of menstrual functions, bringing relief to the long retinue of PMS symptoms of whatever type.

In vitalistic terms, Yarrow's bitter, sweet and astringent tastes are evidence of general *relaxant* and *stimulant* effects. Yarrow is a gentle *nervous* and *smooth muscle relaxant* that also systemically addresses tense conditions of the digestive, cardiovascular and urinary systems. In syndrome terms, the herb promotes good Qi circulation, thereby mainly treating **Liver/Spleen disharmony, heart Qi constraint** and **bladder Qi constraint.** With its achillein content, for example, the remedy relieves vascular spasms and neurogenic heart disorders. Where Liver Yang rises to the head causing visual and other neurological disturbances, Yarrow can also be helpful, like Selfheal spike.

True to its carrot family, Yarrow herb excels at regulating digestive functions as much as menstrual ones. Its *mucostatic astringent* effect (tannins), for instance, resolves damp-caused diarrhea and intestinal and genital mucous discharges.

As a *diaphoretic,* Yarrow herb should be combined for **wind-cold** fevers with *arterial stimulants* like Ginger and Cinnamon, and in **wind-heat** fevers with *vasorelaxants* like Elder-/Linden-/Lavender flower. Not to be outdone, this remedy also contains polysaccharides that have shown *immunostimulant* and thus activity.

Yarrow's *diaphoretic* and *diuretic* actions, together with its gamut of trace elements, help explain its traditional use for rheumatic and neuralgic complaints, especially of the upper trunk—like a milder version of Lungwort lichen or Notopterygium Qiang Huo, perhaps.

Shepherd's Purse Herb

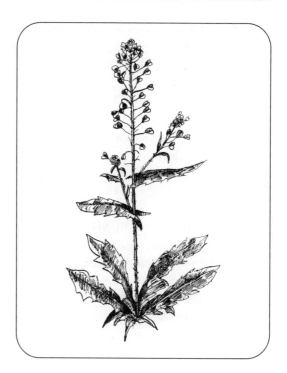

Botanical source: *Capsella bursa-pastoris* Medicus
   (Cruciferae)
Pharmaceutical name: Herba Capsellae
Ancient names: Balistrum, Crispula, Gallitricum,
   Sanguinaria, Nasturcium (Lat)
Other names: Sanguinary, Pickpurse, Mother's heart,
   Witches pouches, Ward seed (Eng)
   Bourse à pasteur, Capselle, Tabouret, Molette
   de berger (Fr)
   Hirtentäschel, Blutkraut, Gerwell, Gänsbross,
   Säckelkraut (Ge)
Part used: the herb

NATURE

Therapeutic category: mild remedy with minimal chronic toxicity
Constituents: amino-alcohols (choline, acetylcholine, aminophenols, tyramine), flavonoid (diosmin), saponins, mustard glycoside, tannins, alkaloid (bursine), essential oil, malic/phosphoric/silicic/citric/acetic acids, minerals (incl. calcium, iron, potassium, sodium, sulphur, zinc), vitamins K, C
Effective qualities: somewhat bitter, astringent and pungent, cool, dry
   decongesting, astringing, stabilizing, stimulating, restoring
Tropism: veins, uterus, urogenital organs, kidneys, heart, intestines
   Liver, Heart, Large Intestine meridians
   Fluid, Air bodies

FUNCTIONS AND INDICATIONS

1 **VITALIZES THE BLOOD, REDUCES CONGESTION AND MODERATES MENSTRUATION; ASTRINGES AND STOPS DISCHARGE AND BLEEDING**

venous blood stagnation: varicosities, heavy or aching legs, leg cramps at night, fatigue
VARICOSE VEINS, hemorrhoids, hypotension
uterus blood congestion: early copious periods, pelvic dragging sensation, constipation
CONGESTIVE DYSMENORRHEA, MENORRHAGIA, irregular cycles (esp. chronic)
HEMORRHAGES (passive and active, esp. chronic, from upper and lower orifices, incl. from kidneys, uterus, ulcers, fibroids, hemorrhoids, varicose veins)
UTERINE BLEEDING (incl. during and after childbirth, puberty, menopause)
CHRONIC DIARRHEA, inguinal hernia
GENITAL DISCHARGES (incl. leucorrhea, spermatorrhea)

2 **CLEARS DAMP-HEAT, REDUCES INFLAMMATION AND FEVER**

intestines damp-heat: urgent defecation with mucus and blood, chronic diarrhea, thirst
ENTERITIS, dysentery
REMITTENT FEVERS, malaria, typhus, lung TB

3   **TONIFES HEART QI AND BALANCES CIRCULATION**

heart Qi deficiency: fatigue, frequent sweating, palpitations worse on exertion, chest oppression
HYPER- or HYPOTENSION

4   **STIMULATES DIGESTION AND RELIEVES CONSTIPATION;**
    PROMOTES URINATION AND DISSOLVES STONES

intestines Qi stagnation: slow, painful digestion, abdominal distension, constipation
CONSTIPATION
kidney Qi stagnation: dry skin, pus or mucous in urine, bladder irritation, frequent urgent urination
URINARY STONES

5   **PROMOTES MENSTRUATION AND LABOR**

uterus Qi stagnation: delayed, difficult periods
FAILURE to PROGRESS during LABOR

6   **PROMOTES TISSUE REPAIR AND REDUCES CONTUSION**

FRESH WOUNDS, bruises, contusions, strains, sores
SCURVY

PREPARATION

Use: Sheperd's purse herb is equally good as **infusion** and **tincture.** In acute situations such as bleeding or dysentery it should be taken intermittently.
Dosage: Infusion: 10-15 g
       Tincture: 2-5 ml at 1:3 strength in 30% ethanol
       Up to twice the high doses can be given for acute hemorrhage.
Caution: Being *uterine stimulant,* Shepherd's purse herb is contraindicated during pregancy, unless used just before or during labor.
Note: Never use Shepherd's purse herb that is over twelve months old, because it severely loses potency.

NOTES

Shepherd's purse is a common weed on which relatively little pharmacological research has been done. This should not intimidate us, however, into making a low-grade assessment of its medicinal value. While the recorded history of the herb's medical use goes back to Greek times, we can assume that the extent of its empirical use is in keeping with its ubiquitous presence.

Although well known as a simple, effective *hemostatic,* Shepherd's purse specifically focuses on the circulation and female reproductive organs. Like others in this category, it is an important *astringent decongestant* that affects the entire venous circulation. It is both an effective *venous* and *uterine decongestant.* As such it mainly addresses **venous blood stagnation** and **uterus blood congestion.**

Apart from its vitamin K content, it is difficult to exactly pinpoint the chemical components involved in this action. However, we can always experience the herb's astringent, bitter, cool qualities for ourselves. From the energetic standpoint, these are the qualities responsible for its action.

On the symptom treatment front, **hemorrhage** of any type, anywhere, calls for this remedy. Its excellent *hemostatic* effect results from both a *vasoconstrictive* action (courtesy of the tannins and saponins) and a *coagulant* action that makes blood clotting factors more efficient.

Shepherd's purse herb's *restoring* effect on the veins and capillaries make an ideal complement in those presenting congested blood conditions with **heart Qi deficiency** and either hypertension or hypotension present. Being a *sympathetic nervous system stimulant*, the remedy first increases blood pressure and then decreases it, resulting in a net regulating effect (WILLFORT 1974).

Like the Chinese remedies Sophora Huai Hua and Biota Ce Bai Ye, Shepherd's purse also helps resolve acute intestinal infections presenting damp-heat. The herb's pungent taste signals a stimulating influence that promotes uterine, colonic and bronchial contractions. This again reinforces its use in gynecology first and foremost.

Partridgeberry Herb

Botanical name: *Mitchella repens* L. (Rubiaceae)
Pharmaceutical source: Herba seu radix Mitchellae
Other names: Squaw vine/plum/flower, Winter clover,
      Deerberry, Oneberry, Running box,
      Squawberry vine (Am)
    Herbe à la perdrix (Fr)
    Rebhuhnbeere (Ge)
Part used: the herb (and/or root)

NATURE

Therapeutic category: mild remedy with minimal chronic toxicity
Constituents: saponins, resins, bitter glycoside, tryptophan, tannin, mucilage, dextrin, wax, emodin (?)
Effective qualities: somewhat bitter and astringent, cool, dry
    restoring, astringing, decongesting
Tropism: uterus, kidneys, bladder, veins
    Liver, Kidney, *chong, ren* meridians
    Air, Fluid bodies
Ground: all krases, biotypes and constitutions

FUNCTIONS AND INDICATIONS

1   **VITALIZES THE BLOOD, REDUCES CONGESTION AND MODERATES MENSTRUATION; ASTRINGES AND STOPS DISCHARGE**

uterus blood congestion: early or heavy periods, dull or heavy lower abdominal pain before onset
CONGESTIVE DYSMENORRHEA from PELVIC CONGESTION
HEMORRHOIDS
MENORRHAGIA, ovarian cysts
GENITAL DISCHARGES with *damp-heat/cold* (incl. leucorrhea, spermatorrhea, mucous cystitis)
DIARRHEA, CATARRHAL COLITIS

2   **TONIFIES REPRODUCTIVE QI, REGULATES PREGNANCY & LABOR, PREVENTS MISCARRIAGE; PROMOTES LABOR AND LACTATION**

uterus Qi deficiency: late or absent periods, long cycles
AMENORRHEA
PROPHYLACTIC and REMEDIAL in the THIRD TRIMESTER of PREGNANCY and during LABOR
HABITUAL or THREATENED MISCARRIAGE from the sixth month onwards
FAILURE to PROGRESS during LABOR
INSUFFICIENT BREAST MILK

3   PROMOTES URINATION, DRAINS WATER AND RELIEVES EDEMA

kidney water congestion: edema of ankles or legs, puffy eyes in morning, fatigue

EDEMA

ANURIA, OLIGURIA

DYSURIA

PREPARATION

Use: Partridgeberry herb (and root) is prepared by **long infusion** and **tincture.** Topical preparations such as **salves** and **washes** may be prepared for sore nipples during breast-feeding, swellings, hives and rheumatic and arthritic conditions.

Dosage: Long infusion: 8-14 g

       Tincture: 2-4 ml at 1:3 strength in 30% ethanol

To tone the uterus in preparation for labor and delivery: take 1 to 2 ml (dropperfuls) of the tincture once a day, starting 8-12 weeks before the due date (see also under Use above).

Partridgeberry is an effective *astringent uterine restorative* and *pelvic decongestant* when taken as early as the sixth month of pregnancy onwards. In this capacity the remedy helps prevent miscarriage and premature delivery in women with previous histories of these. ELLINGWOOD 1919: "Once or twice daily for the sixth and seventh month of pregnancy, three times daily for the eighth month, and in larger doses as confinement approaches." Nearer the due date, Partridgeberry induces full-term fetal development and ensures a smoother labor and delivery. Like Raspberry leaf and Helonias root, it makes for happier, healthier and more cooperative babies during and after childbirth.

Caution: Avoid using Partridgeberry herb on its own for the first five months of pregnancy.

NOTES

Partridgeberry is a running perennial herb from the madder family that inhabits mostly the dry woods of North America's Eastern and Central temperate regions. Its evergreen dark leaves have earned it the name "winter clover." The herb's faintly fragrant white or sometimes pink flowers open in late spring and then bear large scarlet drupes. These edible but nearly tasteless, dry berries remain fresh most of the fall and winter and are food for partridges and other grazing animals.

Partridgeberry herb is an important woman's remedy for both gynecological and obstetrical conditions, acting mainly as an *astringent uterine restorative.* This saponin-rich herb exerts a *pelvic/ uterine blood decongestant* effect that addresses primarily **congestive dysmenorrhea,** and secondarily other symptoms of pelvic congestion such as **hemorrhoids.** Partridgeberry is for the woman with the syndrome **uterus blood stagnation** presenting heavy pressure pains before menstrual onset, a heavy clotted flow, general water retention and scanty urination. Being dry and mildly cooling by nature, the remedy is particularly appropriate for women tending to damp or damp-heat in the pelvis with chronic vaginal discharges (not acute vaginitis).

Among the herbs used during pregnancy, labor and delivery, Partridgeberry herb occupies a special place. In the eyes of Eclectic practitioners of the last century, this remedy was "par excellence the *partus preparator.*" They considered Partridgeberry herb a specific and superior *uterine restorative* in preparing for labor, despite rivalry from Blackhaw bark, Helonias root, Black cohosh root and Blue cohosh root. Having enumerated the symptoms it relieves during pregnancy itself, such as "erratic pains," "unsatisfied longings," and "imperfect digestion," ELLINGWOOD (1919) states that with this remedy's prophylactic use "labor approaches, devoid of the irritating, aggravating complications; the preparatory stage is simple, the dilatation is completed quickly, the expulsive contractions are strong, unirritating and effectual, and are much less painful than without the remedy; involution is rapid and perfect, there are no subsequent complicating conditions to contend with, the patient's strength is not abated, and the function of lactation is in its best condition." ELLINGWOOD is speaking from his own clinical experience, backed by that of numerous colleagues.

For pelvic congestion and uterine toning during late pregnancy, Partridgeberry could be seen essentially as a milder version of Helonias root *sans* the steroidal hormonal action. The herb can be used whenever a formula calls for the possibly endangered Helonias, as long as no hormonal action is required of it. Being called a "Helonias substitute" is not demeaning at all.

Because of its significant *diuretic* action, Partridgeberry herb may also be used (both during and outside of childbirth) in conditions of **water congestion** arising from kidney deficiency. This and its *astringent mucostatic* action are confirmed both physically by its chemical constituents and energetically by its astringent, dry and somewhat bitter, cool qualities. When treating women with cold or damp-cold conditions, therefore, Partridgeberry should be balanced with a suitable warm remedy like Rosemary leaf, Lovage root, Blue cohosh root or Ginger root—all depending on the type of gynecological condition being treated.

Butcher's Broom Root

Botanical source: *Ruscus aculeatus* L. (Liliaceae)
Pharmaceutical name: Rhizoma Rusci aculeati
Other names: Knee holly, Sweet broom, Jew's myrtle, Pettigree (Eng
    Petit houx, Fragon épineux, Fragon piquant (Fr)
    Mäusedorn, Stechender Mäusedorn, Stechmyrte (Ge)
Part used: the rhizome

NATURE

Therapeutic category: mild remedy with minimal chronic toxicity
Constituents: steroidal saponins (ruscogenin, neoruscogenin), saponins, essential oil, resin, potassium, rutin, trace minerals
Effective qualities: sweet, pungent, cool, dry
    decongesting, restoring, astringing, dissolving
Tropism: uterus, kidneys, bladder, veins
    Kidney, Bladder, Lung meridians
    Fluid, Air bodies
Ground: all krases, biotypes and constitutions

FUNCTIONS AND INDICATIONS

1 **VITALIZES THE BLOOD, REDUCES CONGESTION, MODERATES MENSTRUATION AND RELIEVES PAIN**

venous blood stagnation: varicosities, heavy or aching legs, leg cramps at night, fatigue

VARICOSE VEINS, phlebitis, venous insufficiency

HEMORRHOIDS (esp. chronic, menopausal)

uterus blood congestion and *Qi constraint:* early or copious periods, heavy, cramping or dull lower abdominal pain

DYSMENORRHEA (esp. congestive), menorrhagia

liver blood congestion: low fat tolerance, fatigue, right flank pains, abdominal distension
PORTAL CONGESTION

2   **TONIFIES REPRODUCTIVE QI AND REGULATES MENSTRUATION AND MENOPAUSE;
     INCREASES HORMONES**

reproductive (Kidney) Qi deficiency: fatigue, sexual disinterest, frigidity, infertility
ESTROGEN DEFICIENCY disorders incl.:
PMS with loss of self-esteem, withdrawal, thirst, frequent urination
MENOPAUSAL SYNDROME with hot flashes, fatigue
VAGINAL DRYNESS, frigidity, infertility

3   **PROMOTES URINATION, DRAINS WATER AND RELIEVES EDEMA;
     RESOLVES TOXICOSIS AND REDUCES STONES**

kidney water congestion: edema of ankles or legs, puffy eyes in morning, fatigue
EDEMA (esp. of ankles and legs)
ANURIA, jaundice
kidney Qi stagnation with *metabolic toxicosis:* fatigue, malaise, headaches, aches and pains
URINARY SAND and STONES
GOUT, uremia, lymphadenitis

PREPARATION

Use: Butcher's broom root is prepared by **decoction** (best to fully extract the rutin) and **tincture.**
Pessaries and **suppositories** treat congestive pelvic and rectal conditions of many kinds, including
hemorrhoids.
Dosage: Decoction: 8-16 g
          Tincture: 2-4 ml twice daily at 1:2 strength in 45% ethanol
Caution: None

NOTES

Butcher's broom is a thorny evergreen shrub found around the Mediterranean sea. In Mediterranean countries the shrub's rhizome has served as an extremely reliable *draining diuretic* for preventing and treating a variety of water and urinary disorders. Edema of the lower limbs arising from kidney deficiency, urinary stones and anuria are the main conditions that Greek medicine has treated with this remedy. Butcher's broom root is high in potassium, resins and saponins that biochemically support the empirical *diuretic* effect. The saponins in addition exert a steroidal *detoxicant* action that has served well in gouty and uremic conditions.

Earlier in the twentieth century French researchers put much energy into assessing Butcher's broom root's *vasoconstrictant* action. They discovered that it was stronger than Horsechestnut (the standard European *vasoconstrictant* at the time), and possibly the best generally available. Since then, Butcher's broom has emerged as an important remedy for treating **varicosities** (including hemor-rhoids and phlebitis) and **congestive menstrual disorders** with heavy, painful menstruation.

From the vitalistic perspective, the remedy is a blood-vitalizer that addresses **stagnation** of **venous blood.** In terms of the six conditions, it addresses the two primary forms of congestion: **blood congestion** and **water congestion.** Obstinate chronic hemorrhoids in particular have responded very well through combined internal and topical use to its *vein* and *capillary-astringing* action.

In gynecology, Butcher's broom treats both congestive and spasmodic forms of dysmenorrhea in exactly the same way that Cramp bark, Black-haw root and White peony root address **uterus blood congestion** and **uterus Qi constraint.**

The saponins in this plant are not only active in the *diuretic* and *vasoconstrictant* effects, some of them also posess a hormonal action. These are steroidal by nature, like those found in Wild yam root and Birth root. As a result, numerous women's disorders, especially those involving deficient estrogen, have successfully been treated with this remedy. The combination of the its *estrogenic, blood-decongestant* and *anti-inflammatory* actions in a woman amount to a tonifying effect of **reproductive (Kidney) Qi,** with good results in PMS and menopausal disorders in particular.

Cypress Tip

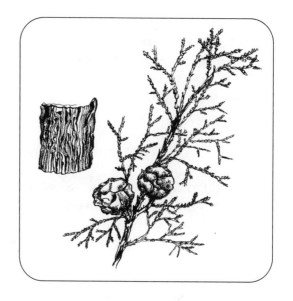

Botanical source: *Cupressus sempervirens* L.
(Cupressaceae)
Pharmaceutical name: Cacumen Cupressi
Ancient names: Kuparios (Gr)
Other names: Cyprès (Fr)
Zypressbaum (Ge)
Part used: the leafy end twig or tip; also the cone
(fruit), Fructus Cupressi

NATURE
Therapeutic category: mild remedy with minimal chronic toxicity
Constituents: essential oil (incl. alpha-pinene 45%, carene 25%, cedrol 7%, cedrine, cadinine, manool, sempervirol, neocupressic acids, camphene, sylvestrene, cymene, ketone, sabinol, terpineol, valerianic acid, cypressic camphor furfurol), tannins
Effective qualities: bitter, somewhat sweet, sour and astringent, cool, dry
decongesting, astringing, stabilizing, relaxing, dissolving
Tropism: genital organs, bladder, kidneys, lungs, stomach, blood veins
Liver, Lung, Bladder, *chong, ren* meridians
Fluid, Air bodies
Ground: all krases, biotypes and constitutions

FUNCTIONS AND INDICATIONS
1 **VITALIZES THE BLOOD AND LYMPH, REDUCES CONGESTION AND MODERATES MENSTRUATION; ASTRINGES, RESTORES THE VEINS AND STOPS BLEEDING, DISCHARGE AND SWEATING; STRENGTHENS CONNECTIVE TISSUE**

venous blood stagnation: varicosities, heavy or aching legs, leg cramps at night, fatigue
VARICOSE VEINS, venous deficiency
uterus blood congestion: pelvic weight and dull aching, early heavy periods, clots in flow
CONGESTIVE DYSMENORRHEA
LYMPHATIC CONGESTION
PROSTATE CONGESTION (hyperplasia)
HEMORRHAGE (incl. uterine bleeding, bleeding gums, coughing up blood, blood in stool)
MENORRHAGIA, metrorrhagia
DIARRHEA, dysentery with fatigue
COPIOUS PERSPIRATION (especially from feet)

2 TONIFIES REPRODUCTIVE QI AND REGULATES MENSTRUATION AND MENOPAUSE; INCREASES HORMONES AND RELIEVES FATIGUE

uterus Qi stagnation: delayed, scanty periods, difficult periods, dry skin, fatigue

HORMONAL / ESTROGEN (?) DEFICIENCY with DYSMENORRHEA, PMS

MENOPAUSAL SYNDROME with tiredness, hot flashes, varicosities, mood swings

3 PROMOTES URINATION AND DETOXIFICATION, AND DRAINS WATER; CLEARS TOXIC HEAT AND REDUCES INFLAMMATION AND TUMORS

kidney Qi stagnation with *metabolic toxicosis:* malaise, irritability, intermittent muscle or joint pains

RHEUMATISM (chronic)

EDEMA of LOWER LIMBS

heat toxin: boils, carbuncles, abscesses (internal and superficial)

PELVIC INFLAMMATORY DISEASE

TUMORS, CYSTS (incl. fibroids, polyps, esp. reproductive); prostate adenoma

4 REGULATES THE QI, RELAXES CONSTRAINT AND RELIEVES PAIN; RELIEVES WHEEZING AND COUGHING, AND HARMONIZES URINATION AND MENSTRUATION

lung Qi constraint: nervous or irritating dry cough, wheezing, irritabiliy

ASTHMA, whooping cough (spasmodic), lung TB, pleurisy

COUGH, VOICE LOSS

uterus Qi constraint: irregular menstruation, cramps with onset of flow, PMS

SPASMODIC DYSMENORRHEA

bladder Qi constraint: difficult, dripping, painful urination, bedwetting

NEUROGENIC BLADDER, STRANGURY, DYSURIA, ENURESIS

IRRITABILITY in general

5 SETTLES THE STOMACH AND STOPS VOMITING

stomach Qi reflux: nausea, queasiness, vomiting

VOMITING

6 BENEFITS THE SKIN AND REPELS INSECTS

SKIN CONDITIONS: oily skin, acne, dandruff, hairloss; sagging, weak skin

INSECT REPELLENT

PREPARATION

Use: The most practical, effective administration method for Cypress tip is the distilled **essential oil,** followed by the **tincture.** Both are suitable for internal and topical use.

External preparations include **pessaries** for gynecological disorders such as dysmenorrhea, uterine bleeding, cysts and fibroids, **inhalations** for spasmodic cough and asthma, **footbaths** for sweating feet, **suppositories** for hemorrhoids, and **ointments** and **washes** for skin conditions.

Traditional European pharmacies also used to carry **Cypress cone, bark** and **wood,** from which water and alcohol-based preparations were made.

Dosage: Essential oil: 1-3 drops in a gel cap topped with some olive oil

Tincture: 1-4 ml at 1:2 strength in 60% ethanol

Caution: None

NOTES

The tall, slender, dark evergreen cypress tree from the Eastern Mediterranean shores traditionally provided many herbal remedies, including the cone (fruit), leafy tips, bark and heartwood. Today the essential oil distilled from the leafy twigs is emerging as an important woman's remedy. This is because its comprehensive action—endocrine, neural and tissular—engages in a number of gynecological conditions characterized by blood congestion, fluid congestion and tension.

Cypress is one of several essential oil remedies with a *decongestant* action on the venous circulation. Basically *astringent* by nature, it gives a lift to the side of the circulation liable to congestive stasis, thereby relieving disorders of **blood stagnation** such as heavy periods and intermenstrual bleeding. Part of Cypress' blood-activating effect is a toning action on the veins and a *hemostatic* action. This makes the remedy useful for ailments ranging from hemorrhoids, varicose veins and phlebitis to uterine and other forms of bleeding. In women presenting **pelvic blood congestion** with fibroids or cysts causing prolonged menstruation (as often happens), Cypress is still in the league. The remedy has demonstrated *antitumoral, diuretic* and *resolvent detoxicant* actions that result from its catabolic effect through the connective tissue and interstitial fluids.

Because of its good *anti-inflammatory* action,

Cypress is also relevant in **inflammatory conditions** involving elements of blood congestion and toxicosis. These include phlebitis, endometritis, pelvic inflammatory disease and heat toxin such as boils, abscesses, and so on.

Cypress' profile as a woman's remedy is enhanced when we consider the neuroendocrine context of its therapeutic effects. Cypress essentially inhibits parasympathetic nervous functioning and therefore should be considered for **gynecological conditions** arising from **emotional causes.** When psychological imbalances cause or aggravate PMS, menopausal syndrome, dysmenorrhea or reproductive tumors, Cypress is one of the best remedies available. Its *parasympathetic-inhibiting* action is the basis for a broad-spectrum *spasmolytic* action that relaxes the bladder and bronchi as much as it does the uterus.

In energetic terms, by regulating Qi flow, Cypress relaxes constrained Qi in the uterus, bladder and lungs. The remedy's benefits for women with tense conditions of emotional origin, such as spasmodic dysmenorrhea, spasmodic asthma and neurogenic bladder, should now be clearer.

Two other remedies derived from closely related conifers, Arborvitae tip (Thuja occidentalis) and the Oriental arborvitae tip (Thuja/Biota orientalis or Ce Bai Ye) have very similar uses.

Witch Hazel Leaf

Botanical source: *Hamamelis virginiana* L.
  (Saxifragaceae)
Pharmaceutical name: Folium Hamamelis
Other names: Black Virginian pistachia,
  Spotted/Striped alder, Winterbloom, Snapping
  hazelnut (Am)
   Hamamélis de Virginie, Noisetier des sorcières
   (Fr)
   Virginischer Zauberstrauch/-nuss (Ge)
Part used: the leaf; also the twig bark, Cortex ramuli
  Hamamelis

NATURE

Therapeutic category: mild remedy with minimal chronic toxicity
Constituents: tannins 6% (incl. hamamelitannin, gallotannin, digallyhamamelose), gallic acid up to 65%, saponin, bitter, essential oil (incl. eugenol-like compound), flavonoids (incl. kaempferol, quercetin, astragalin), hamamelose, resins (c. 7% hamalin and hamamelin), choline, safrole
Effective qualities: astringent, cool, dry
  decongesting, astringing, solidifying, raising, stabilizing
Tropism: veins, capillaries, blood, uterus
  Liver, Spleen, *dai* meridians
  Fluid body
Ground: all for symptomatic use

FUNCTIONS AND INDICATIONS

1   **VITALIZES THE BLOOD, REDUCES CONGESTION AND MODERATES MENSTRUATION;**
   ASTRINGES, RESTORES THE VEINS AND STOPS BLEEDING

  venous blood stagnation: varicosities, heavy or aching legs, leg cramps at night, fatigue
  VARICOSE VEINS, phlebitis, hemorrhoids
  uterus blood congestion: pelvic weight and fullness, heavy or early periods, dull ovarian pains
  CONGESTIVE DYSMENORRHEA
  MENORRHAGIA, metrorrhagia, postpartum bleeding
  HEMORRHAGE (passive, esp. from nose, lungs, stomach, kidneys, uterus, hemorrhoids)

2   **RESOLVES MUCOUS-DAMP, RELIEVES ALLERGY AND STOPS DISCHARGE;**
   RAISES CENTRAL QI TO RELIEVE PROLAPSE

  head damp-cold: clear nasal discharges, nasal congestion
  SINUSITIS, ALLERGIC RHINITIS
  DIARRHEA (chronic and acute, incl. dysentery)
  LEUCORRHEA
  BLENNURIA, DYSURIA
  Central Qi sinking: heavy dragging sensation in lower abdomen, aching rectal pain
  PROLAPSE (intestinal, uterine)

3 PROMOTES TISSUE REPAIR, REDUCES INFLAMMATION AND INFECTION, AND RELIEVES PAIN AND SWELLING

ULCERS of mouth, throat, skin, legs (esp. chronic, fetid)

WOUNDS, abrasions, sores, variocele, cuts, bruises, sprains, swelling, postpartum trauma

THROAT INFLAMMATION (e.g. laryngitis, esp. chronic)

TONSILITIS, conjunctivitis, mammitis (esp. acute)

ACHING muscles (from any cause, incl. backache)

BURNS, scalds, inflammations with swellings (incl. mammitis, mastitis); freckles, facial capillaries

PREPARATION

Use: Witch hazel leaf is prepared by **infusion** or **tincture.** Witch hazel often enters into **salves, swabs, compresses, gargles** and **mouthwashes. Sitzbaths** will heal postpartum perineal tissue trauma. **Pessaries** and **suppositories** are excellent for congestive pelvic conditions.

Witch hazel twig bark is prepared by **decoction** or **tincture.** Being higher in hydrolysable tannins, it exerts a superior *systemically astringent* action than the leaf, as these are more easily absorbed in the gut.

Dosage: Infusion: 6-10 g

Tincture: 1-3 ml at 1:3 strength in 45% ethanol

Caution: Avoid continuous use of this very *astringent* remedy.

Note: A similar yet less effective remedy to Witch hazel leaf is **Hazel leaf,** from *Corylus avellana* L. (in Europe), *C. americana* and *C. cornuta* (both in the U.S.) (Cupuliferae). Hazel leaf has astringent, dry qualities. It is a *venous restorative, vasoconstrictor* and *hemostatic* that reduces venous blood stagnation. Conditions treated include varicose veins, leg edema and hemorrhage. Again like Witch hazel leaf, the remedy topically promotes tissue healing in atonic wounds, ulcers and sores, and chronic eczema.

Dose and caution: As for Witch hazel leaf above

Hazel twig bark is considered *antipyretic* in fevers, and externally is used in the same way as the leaf. **Hazel catkin** (i.e., the soft unopened bud) is traditionally used for promoting weightloss.

NOTES

What Horsechestnut is to European herbal medicine, Witch hazel is to American. Although a simplification, this comparison is essentially valid. The main function of both remedies is to astringe, relieve **blood congestion** and reduce excessive menstruation. Both remedies are *venous vasoconstrictors* and *restoratives* of a systemic kind. Both apply to conditions of hyper-relaxed tissue causing copious secretions, and to "catarrhal discharge from relaxed mucous membranes with tendency to passive hemorrhages of dark blood." This is another of FELTER's typically pithy statements from his terse *Eclectic Materia Medica* (1922). In Chinese medical terms, it translates simply as a **weakness** of **Spleen Qi** with the production of **damp.** Sinusitis, mucousy diarrhea and leucorrhea are the main conditions that can manifest here.

But whereas Horsechestnut is also a *liver decongestant,* Witch hazel leaf is a superior general *astringent* and *anti-inflammatory* remedy that contains generous amounts of tannins and flavonoids. In addition to their well-documented *anti-inflammatory* action, many flavonoids are also thought to strengthen collagen matrix and therefore tone the veins and capillaries. As a *capillary stimulant,* Witch hazel should therefore also be used for treating irritated or inflamed dermal and mucosal surfaces. Moreover like Birth root, for example, Witch hazel posesses *stabilizing* and *solidifying* effective qualities that tighten up **Central Qi**—useful where a tendency to prolapse exists. In particular, Witch hazel excells for individuals presenting *dull, aching, sore pains* in the pelvis, reproductive organs or rectum—other signs that the remedy strengthens the Spleen.

We can now summarise this remedy's action by using the six condition assessment. Witch hazel essentially addresses **blood congestion, weakness** and **mucous-damp** seen mainly in the Lower Warmer, or pelvis.

When we relate Witch hazel's leaf's content in quercetin, kaempferol and other flavonoids with its use for sinusitis, there is a clear possibility that **immediate allergies** such as hayfever will also be helped. These glycosides have shown *anti-*

histamine activity in the labs, and may do the same in the body. Together with the tannins and essential oils, they add to Witch hazel's superior *vulnerary* effect. The combined *anti-inflammatory, tissue healing, astringent, antiseptic* and *analgesic* actions make this leaf one of the finest topical first-aid remedies around. Sore, aching muscles from overexertion or other causes will also benefit in particular from combined internal and topical use. Sports medicine enthusiasts, take note.

Red Grapevine Leaf

Botanical source: *Vitis vinifera* L. var. *tinctoria*
      and spp. (Vitaceae)
Pharmaceutical name: Folium Vitis
Ancient names: Oinophoros, Ampelo (Gr)
      Vitis, Lambrusca, Pampinus (Lat)
Other names: Vigne rouge (Fr)
      Edle Weinrebe, Weinstock (Ge)
Part used: the leaf (including the stem)

NATURE

Therapeutic category: mild remedy with minimal chronic toxicity
Constituents: potassium bitartrates and other tartrates up to 2%, tannins, flavonoid quercetrin, anthocyanic glycosides, tartaric/malic/acetic/bernstein acids, levulose, saccharose, dextrose, choline, inositol, vitamin C
Effective qualities: astringent, sour, bitter, cold, dry
      restoring, astringing, stabilizing, decongesting, diluting
Tropism: liver, urinary system, uterus, blood, veins
      Liver, Bladder, Large Intestine meridians
      Warmth, Air bodies
Ground: Choleric and Sanguine krases
      Industrious/Tai Yang and Expressive/Jue Yin biotypes; Hematogenic/Sulphuric Iris

FUNCTIONS AND INDICATIONS

1 **VITALIZES THE BLOOD, REDUCES CONGESTION AND MODERATES MENSTRUATION; RESTORES THE VEINS**

   venous blood stagnation: varicosities, heavy or aching legs, leg cramps at night, fatigue
   VARICOSE VEINS, hemoroids, phlebitis, varicocele
   uterus blood congestion: painful, early periods, heavy flow, dull pelvic pains before onset
   CONGESTIVE DYSMENORRHEA, menorrhagia
   liver blood congestion: right flank pain, low fat tolerance, overweight, abdominal distension
   PORTAL CONGESTION

2 **CLEARS HEAT, REDUCES FEVER, STOPS BLEEDING AND RELIEVES THIRST; DRAINS PLETHORA AND PROMOTES URINATION**

blood heat: spontaneous bleeding, skin rashes, heavy menstrual bleeding

HEMORRHAGE from upper or lower orifices (esp. in hot condition; uterine and menopausal bleeding)

FEVERS with thirst, scanty urination (*yang ming*/Qi level heat)

general plethora: overweight, abdominal distension, fatigue

OBESITY, HYPERTENSION

HYPERLIPIDEMIA

3 **CLEARS DAMP-HEAT, REDUCES INFLAMMATION AND INFECTION; ASTRINGES AND STOPS DISCHARGE**

intestines damp-heat: blood in stool, urgent defecation, diarrhea

ENTERITIS

bladder damp-heat: painful, difficult, scanty urination, orange or red urine, thirst

URINARY INFECTIONS with DYSURIA

MOUTH, GUM, THROAT, EYE and SKIN INFLAMMATIONS

LEUCORRHEA, seminal emission, spermatorrhea

PREPARATION

Use: Red grapevine leaf is prepared in **decoctions** and **tincture.** *Astringent* and *anti-inflammatory* **washes, gargles, mouthwashes** and **eyebaths** are among the external preparations made with this remedy for hot, swollen, painful mouth, gum, throat, tongue and eye conditions.

Only the dark red leaves collected in autumn should be used to prepare this remedy.

Dosage: Decoction: 6-12 g

　　　　　Tincture: 2-4 ml at 1:3 strength in 30% ethanol

Caution: None

NOTES

The large, deep-magenta leaves of the climbing grapevine from the sun-soaked vineyards of Southern Europe, North Africa and the Middle East are used both in cooking and medicine. In these countries they have cooled fevers and inflammations for many a millenium. Throughout Europe this remedy has been used in pharmacy as an outstanding draining remedy that addresses conditions of heat and blood congestion.

Red grapevine leaf should currently find renewed use as a heat-clearing botanical with a very specific focus. It is one of the few *astringent venous decongestants* that is really cold in quality (like Red root) and, conversely, one of the few *refrigerants* that is also sour-astringent in taste (like Wood sorrel). Central to these two polar functions is the remedy's *blood-decongestant* action, whose dynamic is activation of both capillary and venous circulation. Note, in this connection, the *blood vessel-toning* anthocyanidins and the *anti-inflammatory, colla-gen matrix-building* flavonoid quercetrin. Grapevine excels at relieving chronic **blood congestion,** especially with inflammation, fever or bleeding present. The traditional Chinese syndrome **blood heat** best describes this condition—as found, for example, in menorrhagia or metrorrhagia resulting from uterine/pelvic blood congestion, as well as in febrile infectious diseases in general. An acupuncturist here would select points such as Li 1, Sp 10 and 6 and Ht 5.

Moreover, Red grapevine also clears heat at the Qi level. In western terms its *antilipemic, hypotensive* and *antiplethoric* properties are perfect for those with **full heat** and **general plethora** displaying chronic irritability, thirst, abdominal distension and overweight, and typically involving hypertension and high blood lipid counts.

Tartrates, acids and tannins testify to bioenergetic processes that have created a cold *astringent* remedy of the best kind. The energy of these constituents creates *anti-inflammatory* and *antiseptic* actions when applied to **damp-heat intestinal** and **urinary infections.** All inflamed or infected mucosal and skin surfaces also benefit. Although the bioenergetics of a Chinese heat-clearing herb like Phellodendron Huang Bai are different, its properties are similar enough to justify interchanging these two herbs whenever neccessary.

The North American continent has wild grapevines gowing in a natural profusion. It is curious then to consider that the country famed as the "land of the wild grapes" by its earliest Viking visitors around two thousand years ago has never made much medicinal use of this ubiquitous climber. We are faced with a paradox. Vinland, as the Scandinavians called this continent, has not honored this natural resource beyond the culinary creation of grape jelly, wild grape pie and wild grape conserve. The whole range of effects evinced by the cultivated Grapevine leaf may not be entirely reproducible in the wild varieties. Nevertheless, it is surely time to start experimenting therapeutically with the Wild grape leaf.

Madder Root

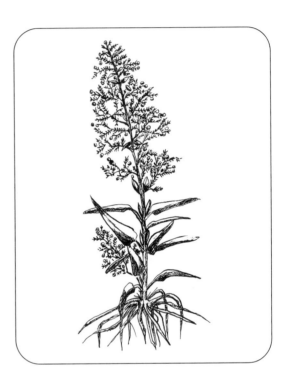

Botanical source: *Rubia tinctoria* L. and spp.
   (Rubiaceae
Pharmaceutical name: Radix Rubiae
Ancient names: — (Gr)
   — (Lat)
Other names: Warence (Eng)
   Garance (Fr)
   Krapp, Färberröte (Ge)
   Qian Cao Gen (Mand); Chan Chou Gan (Cant)
Part used: the root

NATURE
Therapeutic category: mild remedy with minimal chronic toxicity
Constituents: anthraquinones (incl. purpurin, pseudopurpurin, alizarin, munjistin, purpuroxanthin, rubimallin), tannins, sitosterol, daucosterol
Effective qualities: bitter, astringent, cold, dry
   decongesting, astringing, thickening, stimulating, dissolving
Tropism: reproductive, respiratory, vascular, nervous systems
   Heart, Liver, Lung, *dai, yang wei* meridians
   Fluid, Air bodies
Ground: all krases and constitutions

FUNCTIONS AND INDICATIONS
1   **VITALIZES THE BLOOD, REDUCES CONGESTION AND MODERATES MENSTRUATION;**
   DECONGESTS THE LIVER AND PROMOTES BILE FLOW;
   ASTRINGES AND STOPS BLEEDING AND DISCHARGE
   uterus blood congestion: heavy or prolonged periods, clotted flow, intermenstrual bleeding,
      lower abdominal pressure
   CONGESTIVE DYSMENORRHEA, MENORRHAGIA

liver blood and Qi stagnation: acute indigestion, epigastric and abdominal bloating, constipation
LIVER CONGESTION, JAUNDICE
LIVER and SPLEEN ENLARGEMENT, chronic hepatitis
PORTAL CONGESTION, bleeding hemorrhoids
HEMORRHAGE (incl. uterine bleeding, bleeding hemorrhoids, blood in stool or urine, coughing or vomiting blood, nosebleeds)
DIARRHEA, dysentery, leucorrhea

2 **TONIFIES UROGENITAL QI, HARMONIZES URINATION AND RELIEVES INCONTINENCE;**
PROMOTES URINATION AND DETOXIFICATION, AND DISSOLVES DEPOSITS

bladder Qi deficiency: frequent, scanty, dripping urination, bedwetting, cloudy turbid urine, clear vaginal discharges, delayed periods
URINARY INCONTINENCE, prostate congestion, enuresis
HYPERURICEMIA, albuminuria
HARD DEPOSITS (incl. urinary stones [especially phosphate stones], gallstones)

3 **PROMOTES MENSTRUATION AND RELIEVES AMENORRHEA;**
PROMOTES EXPECTORATION AND RELIEVES COUGHING

uterus Qi stagnation: delayed or absent periods, abdominal pain
AMENORRHEA
PROLONGED PREGNANCY (stalled labor), retained placenta, uterine subinvolution
BRONCHITIS, COUGH (chronic)

4 **REDUCES PAIN AND INFECTION**

PAIN (incl. chest and flank pain, joint pain, urinary pain, abdominal pain, trauma pain)
TRAUMATIC INJURIES (incl. fractures)
INFECTIONS (viral, bacterial, incl. influenza, hepatitis)

PREPARATION

Use: Madder root is prepared by **decoction** or **tincture. Vaginal sponges** and **douches** may be prepared for discharges, and **suppositories** and **ointments** for hemorrhoids.
Dosage: Decoction: 8-16 g
  Tincture: 2-4 ml at 1:2 strength in 45% ethanol
Caution: Contraindicated during pregnancy because of the *uterine stimulant* action, and in empty cold conditions, especially with indigestion present. Harmless orange discoloration of the urine may be caused by the dye alizarin contained in the root.

NOTES

Madder is an old European dye plant that tradition-al Greek medicine used for a variety of menstrual, urinary and liver problems, especially for conges-tive conditions in the abdominal and pelvic region. It finds an interesting parallel in its Oriental cousin, *Rubia cordifolia,* Qian Cao Gen, which is used in much the same way (see HOLMES 1997). Farther West, Madder root has a desert analog, Ocotillo bark (see below).

Madder essentially addresses conditions of blood congestion in the liver and pelvis. **Uterus blood congestion** with pelvic pressure and heavy, clotted periods; **liver blood congestion** with portal congestion and abdominal distension; and **liver** and **spleen enlargement** are the three classic syndromes that will benefit from the remedy's combined *decongestant* and *astringent* effects. Imagine an herb acting virtually like Ocotillo and Red root in one! Its specific *cholagogue* and *stimu-lant laxative* actions—note the anthraquinones—are also helpful in individuals with Qi stagnation of upper digestive functions, causing epigastric dyspepsia and, further down, constipation. Like Red root, Madder is also an important *hemostatic* and *coagulant* for uterine bleeding and for any kind of vicarious blood in the pelvis.

Like Ocotillo bark, Birthroot and Red peony root in Chinese medicine (Paeonia Chi Shao), Madder root is also a *uterine stimulant* as well as *uterine decongestant*, and may be used as a *parturient* for prolonged pregnancy as well as for simple relief of amenorrhea.

Because it contains similar anthraquinones to those in Cascara sagrada bark, Madder root is also an important maintenance remedy for those predisposed to **urinary deposits.** As fine a *urinary restorative* as any, Madder specifically addresses urinary stones, incontinence and uric acid diathesis with its *uricosuric diuretic* and *urinary dissolvent (antilithic)* actions. The remedy's *analgesic* action will reduce any pain involved in these conditions.

There is every chance that Madder would find successful application in tumoral conditions, including cancer, as its Oriental analog does. It certainly has the right preconditions for a *pelvic antitumoral:* strongly *astringent, coagulant* and *antiviral*. **Reproductive fibroids** with bleeding from long-standing pelvic congestion here stand to benefit generously from its use.

Ocotillo Bark

Botanical source: *Fouquieria splendens*
    (Fouquieriaceae)
Other names: Candlewood, Couchwhip
Part used: the woody stem bark

Therapeutic category: mild remedy w. no toxicity
Constituents: iridoid glycosides, monotropein methylester, loganin, adoxoside, waxes, resins
Effective qualities: bitter, astringent, dry, cool

Notes On Its Functions and Indications

Like Madder root, this desert plant of the American Southwest and Northern Mexico is an excellent *uterine decongestant* and *uterine stimulant*. Ocotillo bark's main function is to treat **uterus blood congestion** with heavy, clotted periods with slow, difficult onset. As a simple *emmenagogue* it could also be used for short-term amenorrhea.

By mobilizing venous return in the pelvis and the lower limbs, Ocotillo is a *pelvic* and *portal blood* and *lymph decongestant*. The herb also helps resolve **pelvic varicosities** such as cervical varicosities, hemorrhoids and ovarian cysts, **benign prostate congestion** (hyperplasia) in men, and **portal blood congestion** with chronic abdominal distension. Combining possibilities with this herb are therefore many, but include especially Horsechestnut and Red root.

Ocotillo can also be used for its systemic *lymphatic stimulant/decongestant* action alone. Here it will address swollen glands or lymphadenitis in particular. It is also known to help resolve benign tumors, especially the **female reproductive fibroids** seen in pelvic congestion. Echinacea, Marigold and Chaparral would be nice enhancements here to start building a formula with.

Dosage: Infusion and **decoction:** 6-10 g
    Tincture: 1-4 ml at 1:2 strength in 50% eth.
Caution: Contraindicated during pregnancy because of its *uterine stimulant* action, and with organic disorders of the lymphatics or pelvic organs.

Herbs to Resolve Mucous-Damp Congestion and Stop Discharge

Remedies in this class are used to treat congestion of mucous, a treatment strategy traditionally described as resolving mucous-damp. They are called *mucostatics* or *mucus decongestants* because they stop abnormal or excessive mucus (catarrh) production and thereby relieve mucus discharges such as nasal discharge (rhinorrhea), vaginal discharge (leucorrhea) and intestinal discharge (mucous in the stool). Resolving mucous-damp is an Altering and Regulating treatment strategy because the condition is changed or resolved primarily without any actual elimination or drainage taking place.

The Nature and Dynamics of Mucous-Damp

In all traditional medical systems, the accumulation of mucus-damp is considered pathological—a type of pathogen. Mucus is called *phlegmon* in Greek medicine, *tan yin* (phlegm-mucous) and *tan shi* (mucous- damp) in Chinese medicine, and *ama* in Ayurvedic medicine. Greek medicine sees mucus as arising from a combination of the damp and cold effective qualities (*dynameis*) (see Appendix A). Greek and Chinese medicine treat this condition by drawing it to the intestines and the stomach, "preparing" it by softening, and then eliminating it through bowel movement or vomiting. This procedure is still favored in traditional Greek (Tibb Unani) and Ayurvedic medicine today.

Also known as a catarrhal condition, mucus congestion physiologically arises from excessive mucus production as the mucous membrane loses its normal tone and oversecretes, thereby tending to cause discharges. Mucus congestion can be caused by various factors such as chronic unproductive or sudden severe stress, excessive intake of dairy foods, hypersensitivities or allergies to foods, molds, pollens or drugs, chronic intestinal dysbiosis (an imbalance of the microflora), chronic infection (including candidiasis), chronic illness, old age and excessive purging or colonic therapy. Predisposing constitutional factors, such as we find

in blue iris types (e.g., Lymphatic and Hydrogenoid iris constitutions) also contribute significantly to a fertile mucous-damp terrain.

Mucus congestion typically produce signs of damp among the mucosa-lined organs, typically with a clear mucus discharge, and when chronic is described as a damp-cold condition.

• In the sinus passages mucus oversecretion may cause the syndrome **head damp-cold** presenting sinus congestion, runny nose and postnasal drip— as seen in viral or allergic sinusitis and rhinitis.

• In the bronchi, mucus oversecretion is called sputum and leads to the syndromes **lung phlegm-damp**—as in chronic bronchitis and emphysema.

• In the digestive tract, mucus oversecretion may generate **intestines mucous-damp** (known as Spleen/Middle Warmer turbid-damp in Chinese medicine). This syndrome manifests irregular, mucousy stool, indigestion with abdominal gurgling and distension, and typically involves chronic gastroenteritis, IBS/colitis or candidiasis.

• In the reproductive system, oversecretion may generate **genitourinary damp** displaying clear, inoffensive vaginal discharges and itching, as seen in vaginitis and cervicitis with leucorrhea, including fungal/candidiasal vaginitis.

The Treatment of Congested Mucous-Damp

The treatment of mucous-damp congestion has two aspects. First, clearing the body of any accumulated mucus present by expelling it upward or downward, depending on where it presents. Because the mucous membrane is found from the head to the colon, lining the entire G.I. tract, removing stagnant mucus also requires additional remedies, depending on its location. As a result, *mucostatics* are routinely combined with the following other herb categories to address the particular mucous-damp conditions discussed above:

• Congested mucus in the sinuses is removed by *mucostatics* combined with *nasal decongestants* with pungent, warm qualities, found among the *stimulant diaphoretics* in Classes 1 and 8. Steam inhalations with essential oils are an important treatment method here (see Ch. 8).

• Bronchial sputum is eliminated by combining *mucostatics* with pungent, warm *expectorants* for promoting expectoration of congested bronchial sputum (Class 4).

• When mucus is oversecreted in the digestive tract, causing intestines mucous-damp, it is treated with the addition of pungent, warm *digestive stimulants* (Class 8). If it also causes Qi stagnation in the intestines, causing pain, irregular stools, and so on, *intestinal relaxants* from Class 12 should additionally be selected

• For severe or acute discharges, *mucostatics* may be combined with *antidischarge* remedies (Class 18).

• When treating any fungal/viral/bacterial terrain that may be present, *mucostatics* should be combined with *detoxicant anti-infective* remedies (Class 12, first subclass).

• Over time, mucus and other toxins may congeal and adhere to the colon walls, forming the dark viscous bands sometimes eliminated in colonic irrigation therapy. This chronic type of mucus should be eliminated not only through colonic treatment, but also with the judicious use of *laxative* herbs (Class 3), as well as with suitable essential oils.

• Mucous congestion, being generally a chronic damp-cold condition, can also become an acute damp-heat condition presenting purulence, fetor and pain as well as discharge. Here the *mucostatics* should be combined with *anti-infective astringents* (Class 12), and/or Class 18 *astringents* if the discharge is severe.

• In the case of an underlying intestines Qi deficiency to the mucous-damp, *digestive restoratives* (Class 7) should be added to the *mucostatics*.

• In the case of underlying Yin deficiency or dryness, *mucostatics* should be complemented by sweet, moist Yin tonics (Class 10), and the *non-astringent mucostatics* above should be selected by preference to avoid aggravating the condition.

Preventing excessive mucus from being generated in the first place is the more fundamental task. This may be difficult because it usually requires treating the mucous-damp ground or terrain of the whole individual, involving the identification and removal of predisposing factors among diet, lifestyle, attitude and other disorders such as infections and preinfectious viral/fungal/bacterial terrain, as well as inherited constitutional weaknesses. Unproductive stress in the individual's life is often a major cause of mucous-damp. This is a condition that requires truly holistic treatment, if ever there was one.

The Herbs that Resolve Mucous-Damp

Also known as *mucus decongestants* and *anticatarrhals*, there are basically two types of *mucostatics:*

1. *Astringent mucostatics* that resolve mucus congestion through their astringent, dry quality, which tones and tightens mucosal cells. These herbs are usually high in tannins or tannic acid, and include Goldenrod herb, Agrimony herb, Thyme herb, Sage leaf, Cinnamon bark, Goldenseal root and Birthroot. Note that these should not be combined with Class 10 *demulcents* that nourish the Yin.

2. *Non-astringent mucostatics* that resolve mucus congestion in other ways than using tannins. Many are high in essential oils or glycosides, through which they achieve the same *mucus decongestant* effect by means that are not exactly clear. They include: Elderflower, Plantain leaf, Eyebright herb, Cayenne, Yerba mansa, Myrrh resin, Sandalwood and Arborvitae twig. In Chinese medicine, Cuscuta Tu Si Zi (Asian dodder seed) and Euryale Qian Shi (Foxnut) are examples of important non-astringent *mucostatics*.

Other *non-astringent mucostatics* may work through their high polysaccharide content, notably Lungwort thallus and Iceland moss thallus.

Mucostatics are mainly effective when taken internally. However, in the case of local inflammations and discharges such as stomatitis, gingivitis, laryngitis, enteritis, vaginitis and dermatitis they are also often prepared in the forms of mouthwashes, gargles, enemas, pessaries (vaginal suppositaries) and douches in addition to internal use, to maximize local contact.

Although *mucostatic* remedies can address both chronic (damp-cold) and acute (damp-heat) conditions along the mucus membrane, they are more effective for the chronic, damp-cold conditions discussed above.

A summary list of remedies in this class is found in the Repertory under Mucous membrane.

Resolve Mucous-Damp Congestion and Stop Discharge
Astringent mucostatics (mucus decongestants)

Eyebright Herb

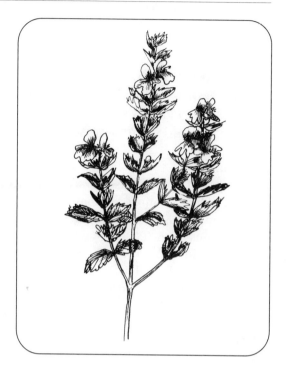

Botanical source: *Euphrasia rostkoviana* Hayne
      and spp. (Scrophulariaceae)
Pharmaceutical name: Herba Euphrasiae
Ancient name: Frasia, Luminella, Ambrosia, Eufragia
      (Lat)
Other name: Euphrasy, Adhib, Ewfras (Eng)
      Euphraise, Brise-lunettes (Fr)
      Augstenzieger, Wiesenaugentrost, Schabab,
        Hirnkraut, Weisses Ruhrkraut, Zwangkraut
      (Ge)
Part used: the whole herb

NATURE
Therapeutic category: mild remedy with minimal chronic toxicity
Constituents: resins, tannins, essential oil, glycosides (incl. aucubin, aneobin, rhynanthin), bitter, trace elements, euphrastanic acid
Effective qualities: somewhat astringent, pungent and bitter, cool, dry
      astringing, restoring, decongesting, dissolving
Tropism: eyes, lungs, stomach, intestines, kidneys
      Lung, Spleen, Bladder meridians; Fluid body
Ground: all krases, biotypes and constitutions

FUNCTIONS AND INDICATIONS
1   **RESOLVES MUCOUS-DAMP CONGESTION AND STOPS DISCHARGE;**
     REDUCES INFLAMMATION AND INFECTION, DECONGESTS THE SINUSES AND PROMOTES REST

     head damp-cold and *external wind-cold:* headache, earache, sinus congestion, watery nasal discharge, postnasal drip, chills, sneezing, restlessness

     RHINITIS, COLD (acute and chronic, infectious or allergic)

     SINUS and THROAT INFECTIONS with profuse catarrhal watery discharge (with or without acute inflammation, incl. sinusitis, pharyngitis)

     EYE INFECTIONS with red, swollen, stinging or burning eyes and eyelids, thin watery or thick yellow discharge (incl. styes, conjunctivitis, blepharitis, keratitis, iritis, pinkeye)

     intestines (Spleen) mucous-damp: indigestion, appetite loss, loose stool, abdominal distension

     CHRONIC GASTROENTERITIS

     LEUCORRHEA

     TENSION HEADACHE, insomnia

2 STRENGTHENS VISION AND CLEARS AND HEALS THE EYES

VISION IMPAIRMENT from strain of close work, reading, etc.

CORNEAL NEBULA and MACULA; cataracts, glaucoma

MUCUS FILM, CLOUD or DUST in eyes; bloodshot eye

SCRATCHES on the EYE SURFACE (mild to severe)

3 PROMOTES URINATION, SOFTENS STONES AND HARMONIZES URINATION; ANTIDOTES POISON

kidney Qi stagnation: tiredness, headaches, pus in urine, painful urination

DYSURIA, URINARY STONES

ALCOHOL and NICOTINE POISONING

PREPARATION

Use: Eyebright herb is **infused** or taken in **tincture** form. In many cases internal and external application go hand in hand. **Lotions, eyebaths,** cotton (-wool) **eye swabs, vaginal sponges** and **douches** are the main external applications that make use of Eyebright.

Dosage: Infusion: 6-16 g

Tincture: 2-5 ml at 1:3 strength in 40% ethanol

For an **eye bath,** briefly decoct 1.5 g (about 1/2 tsp) of the herb in 50 ml (1 cup) of water for 10 minutes. Strain and refrigerate the liquid in an airtight, sterilized container. Use within two days.

Caution: None

NOTES

With its pretty eye-like flowers, Eyebright is the delight of those addicted to the doctrine of signatures. True enough, the herb is a specific eye remedy that treats various conditions of that delicate organ.

The traditional association of Eyebright herb and the eyes goes back a long way. Quite apart from the perennial wise women's silent, unwritten tradition, eminent natural physicians from BOCK, FUCHS, HALLER and HOFFMAN in Europe to KING and FELTER in the U.S. have recorded their success with it. In the early 1300s, the Spanish neoplatonic radical ARNALD DE VILLANOVA wrote a booklet about this remedy called *Luminella.* Its title means "little light," and refers to the vision it is said to promote. As late as the nineteenth century, the medic WOODVILLE—waxing lyrical in the style of the Italian Schola Salernita herb poems of the twelfth century—epitomized Eyebright as the *verum oculorum solamen,* the "eyes' true solace."

Despite this solid partisanship we should remember that Eyebright herb is not intrinsically superior to any other efficient remedy. It just *seems* like a miracle producer when relieving eye conditions that entail "exquisite pain," as seventeenth century textbooks describe.

Eyebright herb enjoys a traditional reputation for restoring poor vision from strain and old age. Although difficult to prove scientifically, its renal/urinary *detoxicant* action would help in this regard. We should be cautious about being reductionist about Eyebright's purpoted *vision-enhancing* action. In addition, and especially when applied topically as a wash or compress, the remedy removes surface obstructions from the eyes, such as corneal macula and nebula, and may slow down cataracts. Celandine and Bilberry would make a good synergy here, as well as Ginkgo for actual vision impairment.

Another application for Eyebright herb that was popular among traditional herbalists up to the present day was as a cooling *astringent.* Because of its dry, cool qualities Eyebright has good, yet gentle *astringent, antiseptic* and *anti-inflammatory* actions that especially reveal themselves in **eye, nose** and **throat** conditions, usually seen in **external wind-cold** syndromes. The remedy addresses **acute inflammation** of these delicate organs with discharge and exudate—especially when involving the conjunctiva and the sinus mucosa. Here Eyebright can make more aggressive—and expensive—herbs like Goldenseal quite unnecessary. Its excellent *mucostatic (anticatarrhal)* action is always a boon to those with catarrhal head colds—

rhinitis, hayfever, etc., especially when seen with thin watery discharges from the nose and eyes, sore throat, headache and complete misery. Eyebright's mild *nervous sedative* action is of course a welcome bonus here.

BOCK (1532), ever the ardent spokesman for common garden plants, recommends combining Eyebright herb with Fennel seed and Vervain herb in all catarrhal, inflammatory eye conditions. This is another nice combination, and also makes us think of Camomile flower and Chrysanthemum flower as further possibilities.

Lungwort Thallus

Botanical source: *Sticta pulmonaria* Hook.,
syn. *Lobaria pulmonaria* (L.) Hoffman
(Stictaceae)
Pharmaceutical name: Thallus Stictae
Ancient names: Pulmonaria arborea (Lat)
Other names: Lungmoss, Mossy/tree lungwort,
Lungwort lichen, Oak lungwort (Eng)
Lichen pulmonaire, Pulmonaire du chêne, Herbe
aux poumons (Fr)
Lungenflechte, Lungenmoos, Lungengrass (Ge)
Part used: the lichen thallus

NATURE
Therapeutic category: mild remedy with minimal chronic toxicity
Constituents: mucilage, polysaccharides, tannins, bitter stictic acid, amino acids, trace minerals, vitamins
Effective qualities: somewhat sweet, salty, bitter and astringent, cool, moist and dry
restoring, astringing, calming
Tropism: sinuses, lungs, chest, muscles, nerves
Lung, Liver meridians; Fluid, Air bodies
Ground: all krases and biotypes

FUNCTIONS AND INDICATIONS

1   **RESOLVES MUCOUS-DAMP CONGESTION AND STOPS DISCHARGE;**
    REDUCES INFECTION, ALLERGY AND FEVER, AND STIMULATES IMMUNITY

head wind/damp/cold: frontal pressure or pain, occipital headache, sinus congestion, watery nasal
discharge (thin-hot turning thick-green), postnasal drip, chills, sneezing, muscle aches and pains
SINUSITIS, RHINITIS (chronic and acute, infectious or allergic); otitis, asthma
HEAD COLD, FLU with FEVER (esp. in summer and change of seasons)
PREVENTIVE in EPIDEMICS

2   **NOURISHES LUNG YIN, MOISTENS DRYNESS, CLEARS EMPTY HEAT AND STOPS COUGHING**

lung Yin deficiency: low-grade afternoon (hectic) fever, night sweats, dry unproductive cough
lung heat- / wind-dryness: dry throat, rasping cough, chest or shoulder soreness or dull pain, headache
WHOOPING COUGH, croup, bronchitis, bronchial asthma, lung TB (consumption)
lung wind-heat: irritating cough, sore throat, feverishness, muscle and head aches and pains
COUGH (all types, acute or chronic, esp. irritating, dry, painful, tight, wheezing, rasping, persistent;
with tracheal irritation)
INTERMITTENT FEVERS (*shao yin* stage, esp. with night sweats)

3   REDUCES PAINFUL OBSTRUCTION

PAIN in the nape of the neck (cervicals), shoulders, beneath scapulae, back of head (occiput)

FIBROMYALGIA, rheumatic pain (esp. in shoulders, chest walls), arthralgia (esp. in small joints)

PREPARATION

Use: Lungwort thallus is prepared by **short decoction** or **tincture.**

Dosage: Short decoction: 6-14 g

Tincture: 2-5 ml at 1:3 strength in 25% ethanol

At the onset of a head cold with watery nasal discharges and frontal headache: take 3 ml of tincture or one cup of the decoction every three hours.

Caution: None

Note: Many lichens possess similar *anti-infective* and sometimes *mucostatic* properties to Lungwort, chief among them **Usnea** (Class 12), **Iceland moss** (Class 10) and **Rock tripe,** *Umbilicaria* spp., also known as Blistered rock tripe.

   Rock tripe in the past doubled as medicinal plant and survival food for Native American tribes, explorers and early settlers in the northern U.S. and Canada. The Arctic explorers FRANKLIN and RICHARD-SON, for example, survived on it for months at a stretch. In addition to its *anti-infective* action (especially on gram-positive bacteria), Rock tripe **decoction** was taken as a bitter *digestive stimulant, nutritive, moist demulcent* and *antidiarrheal.* **Mouthwashes** were prepared with it for canker sores and tender gums.

NOTES

A lichen is a unique form of plant growth because it consists of an alga developing in symbiosis with a fungus. Originally from Scandinavian countries, the lichen lungwort today is also found growing on trees and rocks in the mountainous areas of the Eastern U.S. Thick, coriaceous and almost crust-aceous, this lichen is green and reticulated on the upper surface, resembling lung tissue, and downy beneath.

   An excellent remedy is prepared from Lungwort that is similar to, and yet distinct from, the other two lichens used in herbal medicine, Iceland moss and Usnea. Its past domestic uses included decocting the chopped thallus in milk to prepare a thick cough drink, and making even thicker, smoother lichen hot chocolate. Can we imagine a nicer Victorian bedtime drink for the cold, infection-rife winter months? Difficult.

   Because it combines *anti-infective* and *muco-static* actions, Lungwort thallus (or *Sticta,* as the remedy was known in the past), has always been used for **upper respiratory infections.** When the energies of **wind** and **damp** invade the nasal passa-ges presenting frontal headache, watery discharge and muscle aches and pains, Lungwort is the right remedy. Today we note the presence of *immune-stimulating* mucopolysaccharides to help explain this use.

   More difficult to explain, however, is Lung-wort's reputation for **allergic forms of rhinitis.**

Likewise, those in whom infections go directly to the chest, causing an irritating dry cough, aching muscles, headache, sore throat and possibly fever —the syndrome **lung wind-heat**—will benefit from the remedy's added *anti-inflammatory, anti-tussive* and *antipyretic* actions. In the past, **fevers** of many sorts (including those producing night sweats) were successfully resolved with Lungwort. Its combination of mild sweet, bitter and salty qualities here engage.

   Lungwort thallus comprehensively combines *restorative, relaxant* and *sedative* functions in the respiratory system. The *restorative* effect does not stop at toning the nasal mucosa, but extends to moistening the bronchi in **lung Yin deficiency** conditions, much like Slippery elm bark, Borage leaf or Ophiopogon Mai Men Dong.

   Because this *bronchial demulcent* action is supported by *bronchodilatant* and *antitussive* ac-tions, Lungwort may be used for various bacterial and viral bronchial conditions presenting **lung heat-dryness** and **lung wind-dryness.** The key-note symptoms the individual presents are dry throat, painful tight cough in the tracheal region with throat constriction, and "dull pains in the chest increased upon taking a deep breath, and a sense of soreness like that from a bruise or muscu-lar overexertion." (JOHN KING 1852). Until compa-ratively recently, Lungwort was in fact *the* major remedy for whooping cough and croup. Pointing to an element of constrained lung Qi caused by vagus nerve hyperfunctioning, the Eclectic professor notes that "the Sticta pulse is soft but has a peculiar wiry thrill." Talk about fine-tuned diagnosis and herb prescribing!

Downright *antirheumatic* and *analgesic* actions are also evident in Lungwort, which may be given for various types of **pain,** especially when

occuring in the area between the scapulae, shoulders and occiput, or in the chest and shoulders. In TCM terms these would be forms of **wind-damp-cold obstruction**. Concluding his extensive monograph, the Eclectic grand-master JOHN KING outdoes even himself in pithyness by stating that "Sticta is a remedy for pain and cough."

Birthroot

Botanical source: *Trillium erectum* L.,
    T. pendulum Aiton, *T. ovatum* and spp.
    (Liliaceae)
Pharmaceutical name: Rhizoma Trillii
Other names: Bethroot, Squaw flower, Cough root,
    Wakerobin, Indian shamrock, Lamb's quarter,
    Indian balm, Ground lily, Rattlesnakeroot
    (Am)
    Waldlilie, Dreiblatt (Ge)
Part used: the rhizome

NATURE
Therapeutic category: mild remedy with minimal chronic toxicity
Constituents: steroidal saponins (incl. trillarin, diosgenin), steroidal cardiac glycosides, tannins, resin, fixed oil, trilline, essential oil, bitter compound, starch, vitamin D
Effective qualities: sour, somewhat pungent, sweet, oily and astringent, neutral, moist
    astringing, stabilizing, solidifying, restoring, stimulating, relaxing
Tropism: reproductive organs, intestines, lungs
    Spleen, Lung, Kidney, *chong, ren, dai* meridians
    Air, Fluid bodies
Ground: Melancholic *krasis*; Burdened/Shao Yin biotype; all three constitutions

FUNCTIONS AND INDICATIONS
1   **RESOLVES MUCOUS-DAMP CONGESTION AND STOPS LEAKAGE, DISCHARGE AND BLEEDING; ASTRINGES TO RAISE CENTRAL QI AND RELIEVES PROLAPSE**

   kidney and bladder Qi deficiency with damp: chronic genital mucous discharges, scanty dribbling urination, seminal loss, frigidity, infertility

   LEUCORRHEA, cervicitis, cystitis

   URINARY INCONTINENCE (urinary, seminal)

   PROSTATE CONGESTION with painful urination

intestines (Spleen) Qi deficiency): chronic loose stool, fatigue

DIARRHEA, dysentery

HEMORRHAGE (passive, esp. from uterus, uterine fibroids [short-term only!], hemorrhoids, diverticula, lungs); blood in urine, stool or spittle

POSTPARTUM and MENOPAUSAL UTERINE BLEEDING

Central Qi sinking: heavy dragging feeling in lower abdomen

UTERINE and VAGINAL PROLAPSE

DIABETES (supportive)

2 **TONIFIES REPRODUCTIVE QI AND REGULATES MENSTRUATION AND MENOPAUSE; INCREASES HORMONES; REDUCES BLOOD CONGESTION AND MODERATES MENSTRUATION**

uterus Qi deficiency with *blood congestion:* long menstrual cycles, heavy flow, cramps before onset, pelvic weight and fullness

CONGESTIVE DYSMENORRHEA

MENORRHAGIA, metrorrhagia

ESTROGEN / PROGESTERONE (?) DEFICIENCY conditions, incl.:

AMENORRHEA, INFERTILITY, PMS with oversensitivity, introversion, vaginal dryness

MENOPAUSAL SYNDROME with vaginal dryness, figidity, hot flashes, fatigue

3 **STIMULATES THE UTERUS, PROMOTES LABOR AND ENHANCES DELIVERY**

PROPHYLACTIC and REMEDIAL during LABOR, DELIVERY and POSTPARTUM

FAILURE to PROGRESS during LABOR

RETAINED PLACENTA, POSTPARTUM BLEEDING

4 **PROMOTES EXPECTORATION, RESOLVES VISCOUS PHLEGM AND RELIEVES COUGHING; OPENS THE CHEST AND RELIEVES WHEEZING**

lung phlegm-damp/dryness: coughing with scanty or copious clear sputum, wheezing, dry hard cough

CHRONIC BRONCHITIS, emphysema

lung Qi constraint: wheezing, tight chest, palpitations

BRONCHIAL ASTHMA

UNPRODUCTIVE COUGH

5 **PROMOTES TISSUE REPAIR AND REDUCES INFLAMMATION AND TUMORS**

ULCERS, wounds, sores, perineal tears

SKIN INFLAMMATIONS, insect stings, gangrene, anthrax

TUMORS

PREPARATION

Use: Birthroot is best used in **decoction** or **tincture** form, prepared from the *dried* root. **Washes, compresses** and the like are good topical preparations for sores, inflammations and so on. **Sitzbaths** are excellent for healing perineal tissues after childbirth. **Suppositories** should be helpful for internal organ prolapse. **Vaginal sponges** and **pessaries** can be applied in chronic mucous discharges and should be taken for an extended period.

Dosage: Decoction: 6-10 g

Tincture: 1-4 ml at 1:2 strength in 60% ethanol

• *To prime the uterus for labor starting a few days before the due date:* take 10-30 drops of the tincture once a day.

• *To promote contractions in stalled labor:* take 1/4-1/2 tsp of the tincture hourly until labor resumes.

• *To stop uterine bleeding from fibroids, heavy periods or after delivery:* take 2-4 ml (40-80 drops) of the tincture frequently or several times a day, as appropriate. In severe cases combine with Shepherd's purse herb or Cotton root bark to make up that dosage. See also Caution below.

Caution: This *uterine stimulant* is contraindicated during pregnancy unless given just before labor. Contraindicated for long-term use in fibroids because of its estrogenic saponin content; for acute, short-term treatment of fibroids only. Avoid in Braxton-Hicks contractions. Avoid using in Yin deficiency with empty heat, acute gastritis and peptic ulcer.

Note: Species of *Trillium* vary in their astringency and pungency (acridity). Those that are more astringent are better *hemostatics,* while those that are more pungent are better *mucolytic expectorants* and *bronchodilators. Trillium erectum* is the most *astringent* and *hemostatic.*

NOTES

This common herbaceous plant from the lily family has long been used by Canadian and American Natives in gynecological conditions. Their medicine men deemed the white blossomed variety best for these. Because of this, early European explorers and settlers later named the plant "Birthroot" and "Squaw weed." Birthroot was first publicly introduced to the Western medical community in 1830 by botanist and herbalist CONSTANTINE RAFINESQUE in his landmark materia medica, *Medical Flora.*

Birthroot is complex both as a plant and remedy. Like other important remedies such as Rhubarb root and Tree peony root bark (Paeonia Mu Dan Pi) it is polarized between the astringency of tannins and the stimulation of saponins, essential oils and resins.

As an *astringent,* Birthroot effectively stops discharges and bleeding. Its *mucostatic, antidiarrheal* and *hemostatic* actions were long used by Native Americans for treating urinary, genital and intestinal **discharges** presenting **damp,** as well as to stop bleeding. Birthroot mainly affects urogenital and respiratory functions. Conditions such as **chronic leucorrhea, uterine bleeding** from pelvic congestion, **blood in the urine** and **coughing up of blood** benefit most from its use. For chronic loose stool (diarrhea), the remedy has the unique advantage of reducing discharge without causing internal dryness, as the *secretory* saponins maintain internal moisture. This is especially useful for individuals with the commonly seen Yin and fluids deficiency displaying dryness and diarrhea together, which would worsen by the simple high-tannin *astringents* normally used (in Class 18).

Like Helonias root, Birthroot has stabilizing, consolidating effective qualities that raise Central Qi, thereby effectively preventing and treating sinking phenomena such as **internal organ prolapse**—especially of the uterus. In Chinese medical terms, Birthroot relies on its tonification of Spleen and Kidney Qi for its effects.

There is a whole other aspect to this plant, however, that until very recently has received very little attention in research or therapy. This is Birthroot's *uterine restorative, decongestant* and *stimulant* actions, as well as its estrogenic *hormonal* effect in general. The plant contain steroidal saponins, including the diosgenin of Wild yam fame, and some essential oils. Its *uterine stimulant* action has historically mainly been used in **childbirth** for promoting smooth, vigorous contractions during the first stage of labor. **Infrequent** or **ineffective** (i.e. hypotonic) **contractions** are especially helped through the plant's *oxytocic* action. After delivery, Birthroot's combined *astringent,* solidifying and *hemostatic* actions reliably help the mother's uterus contract, prevent or reduce hemorrhage, tone her pelvic tissues and promote healing of cervical and perineal tears.

In the eighteenth and nineteenth centuries this "Cough root" also had a good reputation for bronchial disorders. We can now see why. Saponins are known to have a softening effect on hardened bronchial sputum, as well as an *anti-inflammatory* action. Together with the essential oil they exert a *mucolytic expectorant* action on the bronchi. This is especially valuable in the syndrome **lung phlegm-dryness** manifesting difficult, dry cough with scanty, viscous sputum. Congenial herbs here would be certain *Yin tonics* of Class 10, especially Solomon's seal root, Mullein leaf and Chickweed herb. When this syndrome is seen in asthmatic conditions, it is accompanied by wheezing and a feeling of constriction at the sternum. Birthroot accomodates here with a resin that shows a *bronchodilatant* effect.

There is a particular resemblance between Birthroot and the milkworts, also in the lily family, including Seneca snakeroot (*Polygala seneca*) and the Asian Thin-leaf milkwort (Polygala Yuan Zhi, *Polygala tenuifolia*). Birthroot and Polygala Yuan Zhi in particular both share that typical sweet-pungent-sour taste quality that is the vitalistic basis of their actions.

Arborvitae Tip

Botanical source: *Thuja occidentalis* L.
    (Cupressaceae)
Pharmaceutical name: Cacumen Thujae
Ancient names: Thuya (Gr)
Other names: Yellow cedar, False cedar, Northern
    white cedar, Tree of life
    Thuya, Arbre de vie (Fr)
    Lebensbaum, Thuja (Ge)
Part used: the leafy end twig or tip

NATURE
Therapeutic category: medium-strength remedy with moderate chronic toxicity
Constituents: essential oil up to 1% (incl. monoterpenes [incl. sabinene, limonene], monoterpenones [incl. thujone 30-60%, isothujone 8-14%, fenchone 7-14%, camphor, piperitone], terpenoid esters [incl. bornylacetate 3-12%], sesquiterpenols [occidentalol, occidol, eudesmol], monoterpenols [incl. terpinene], sesquiterpenes), tannins, glycosides (incl. pinipicrin, yellow coloring matter thujin), thujetin, thujetic acid
Effective qualities: pungent, bitter, astringent, cool, dry
    astringing, restoring, decongesting, dissolving
Tropism: bladder, lungs, genitals, skin, mucosa
    Lung, Kidney, Liver, Spleen, *dai* meridians
    Fluid, Warmth bodies
Ground: Lymphatic/Carbonic constitution

FUNCTIONS AND INDICATIONS

1   **RESOLVES MUCOUS-DAMP CONGESTION AND STOPS DISCHARGE; PROMOTES EXPECTORATION, RESOLVES PHLEGM AND REDUCES FETOR**

kidney and bladder Qi deficiency with damp: white vaginal discharges, scanty or absent periods, scanty dribbling urination, sperm loss, fatigue
LEUCORRHEA, gonorrhea, spermatorrhea
URETHRITIS with GLEET
head damp-cold: chronic nasal discharges with pain
RHINITIS (chronic, atrophic)
lung phlegm-damp: coughing with expectoration of fetid sputum, fatigue
BRONCHITIS (esp. chronic, purulent, fetid, incl. viral, with hemoptysis)

DIPHTHERIA (faucial and pharyngeal), croup
DIARRHEA, CHRONIC MUCOUS COLITIS

**2   TONIFIES URINARY QI, CLEARS DAMP-HEAT, HARMONIZES URINATION AND
RELIEVES INCONTINENCE AND PAIN; PROMOTES MENSTRUATION;
RAISES CENTRAL QI TO STOP PROLAPSE; BENEFITS THE RECTUM**

kidney and bladder Qi deficiency: scanty dribbling, difficult or painful urination, fatigue
URINARY INCONTINENCE (esp. in plethoric women and older men, with slight muscular exertion
    or coughing, with urethral soreness), nocturnal enuresis, children's bedwetting
ATONIC NEUROGENIC BLADDER
PROSTATE CONGESTION, chronic prostatitis with dribbling urine, bladder irritation
HYDROCELE
bladder damp-heat: urinary irritation and pain, dark dripping urine, thirst
CYSTITIS with scalding dysuria; balanitis with polyuria
AMENORRHEA
Central Qi sinking: heavy dragging sensations in lower abdomen, fatigue
PROLAPSE (esp. from paralysis, of rectum, intestines, uterus, vagina)
RECTAL PAINS (sharp, with itching, with slimy discharges); anal fissures with hemorrhoids

**3   REDUCES DEPOSITIONS, TUMORS, VEGETATIONS, INFECTION AND INFLAMMATION;
RELIEVES ECZEMA, SWELLING AND ITCHING**

DEPOSITIONS (incl. cyst, myoma, hydrocele, clavus, polyp, lymphoma, scar tissue)
TUMORS (esp. of skin and mucosa, benign or malignant, incl. with bleeding, incl. pterygium, nevus,
    myoma, adenoma, lymphadenoma, epithelioma, condyloma, adenoid hypertrophy, keratosis,
    epithelioma, squamous cell carcinoma)
VEGETATIONS and WARTS (viral and fungal, esp. of skin and mucosa, on hands, face, eyes, throat,
    genitals, rectum, incl. condyloma, papilloma (HPV), verruca, fungal and ulcerous epithelioma,
    trachoma, lichen planus, urethral caruncle, leprosis)
ECZEMA (esp. chronic dermatosis, eruptions with tendency to vegetations or warts)
HERPES SIMPLEX vesicles and ulcers
SCLERITIS, episcleritis, sclerochoroiditis, syphilitic iritis, conjunctivitis (esp. chronic)
LYMPHADENITIS (scrofulous), tonsilitis with swollen glands, prostate hypertrophy
GENITAL PRURITUS (esp. with fissures)
INTESTINAL PARASITES

**4   PROMOTES TISSUE REPAIR, CLEARS DECAY AND REDUCES EXUDATE AND PAIN;
RESOLVES SCAR TISSUE**

WOUNDS, ULCERS, FISSURES, GANGRENE (esp. chronic, indolent, sloughing, bleeding, gangrenous,
    incl. cold sores, decubitus ulcers, soft chancres [venereal ulcers], phagadena, mouth and throat ulcers)
RHEUMATIC PAIN
SCAR TISSUE

PREPARATION

Use: Arborvitae tip is prepared by **long infusion** or **tincture.** For the majority of the above indications, internal and topical use should always go together.

Vaginal sponges are excellent for mucous damp in the lower warmer with discharges (use low dilutions). **Pessaries** should be the first choice for all above genital and urinary conditions, including vaginitis (all types), warts, tumors, cysts, amenorrhea, prolapse and urinary dysfunctions. **Suppositories**

address rectal, intestinal and genital conditions, including painful hemorrhoids, hydrocele and protatitis.

    Gargles should be used for ulcers, growths or vegetations in the throat region, **mouthwashes** for the same in the mouth. **Inhalations** serve rhinitis, bronchitis, croup, diphtheria, etc. **Nasal insufflations** or **sprays** are appropriate for treating postnasal drip, nasal polyps and tumors of the nasopharynx.

    Washes, compresses, swabs, etc., are also applied to most conditions listed under functions 2, 3 and 4. When applying to open sores or wounds there is tingling or stinging at first before relief and healing sets in—be sure to dilute the decoction or tincture with 2-4 parts of water. Venereal infections and other S.T.D.s can be prevented by applications right after intercourse.

    For safety reasons, Thuja **essential oil,** extracted from Arborvitae tip, is restricted to topical use only in all the above-mentioned preparations. Essential oil textbooks should be consulted for the appropriate dilutions to be used in various conditions.

Dosage: Long infusion/short decoction: 3-6 g per day

        Tincture: 0.5-1.5 ml at 1:4 strength in 60% ethanol

Caution: Arborvitae tip has medium-strength status and on its own should not be taken continuously, nor the doses exceeded. The herb is safer when combined in a formula. Contraindicated in pregnant women, children and infants because of the *uterine stimulant* and highly neurotoxic nature of its essential oil (due to the content of the toxic ketone thujone). For this reason Thuja essential oil is strictly appropriate for topical use only.

NOTES

Belonging to the cypress family, arborvitae is an evergreen coniferous tree commonly found in the Northern U.S., especially in cold, wet areas with swampy terrain. In Europe the leafy end twigs were used in Greek medicine for over two millennia. PARKINSON, for example, recommends using the leaves and young shoots to cause "expectoration of tenacious and vitiated humours." On the other side of the Atlantic, the eighteenth century Swedish traveller PETER KALM saw natives use "the bruised leaves for rheumatism," while the industrious compiler SCHOEPF in addition records usage for scurvy, fevers and cough. In the early 1800s HAHNEMANN developed the use of Arborvitae, or Thuja, in his system of homeopathy. The essential oil too was at that time extracted and given internally for parasites, among other things —not a currently recommended practice, however.

    Given the combined and distilled experiences of thousands of Eclectic and Homeopathic doctors in the nineteenth and early twentieth centuries, we now have an excellent picture of this remedy's true scope. In terms of the traditional remedy classifications, Arborvitae tip is an important remedy for transforming mucous-damp. Its reliable *restorative* effect on the mucosa reduces **vaginal, urinary, bronchial** and **nasal mucus discharges** of the chronic, cold variety. In the chest the remedy acts not only as a *mucostatic (anticatarrhal),* but also (note its pungent taste) as an *expectorant.*

    One of the main symptom pictures addressed by Arborvitae is **genitourinary damp,** or **Kidney/bladder Qi deficiency** with **damp,** seen in individuals with *dai mai* weakness. Urogenital incontinence arising from an atonic neurogenic bladder is here the key symptom. Because it enters the Kidney and Liver meridians, Arborvitae also relieves **pain** found in this general area: bladder irritation (especially from prostatitis), urinary pain (especially from cystitis) and rectal pains being foremost.

    From a different perspective, Arborvitae tip shows a *resolvent detoxicant* effect that focuses on clearing stagnation of the **lymphatic circulation** (with swollen glands) and reducing **abnormal tissue growth** and **degeneration** (function 3). Arborvitae squarely addresses the important connection between insufficient lymphatic drainage and cancer, especially when compounded by chronic mucosal weakness. The remedy essentially operates in the deposition, impregnation and degeneration phases of disorders when the skin and mucosa (entodermal tissues) are involved. Arborvitae's *antitumoral, antifungal* and *antiviral* actions should therefore be understood in the larger context of its systemic *resolvent* and *dissolvent* functions at these particular disease stages.

    It now becomes clearer why more kinds of **depositions, vegetations** and **tumors** may be resolved with this remedy than with any other. In this connection, Arborvitae is useful for those with chronic forms of eczema with fungal and viral involvement presenting **vegetations** and **warts.** The *antiviral* action can be seen in application to trachoma, lichen planus, verrucas, warts, canker sores and, to some extent, herpes.

For all this, Arborvitae is not an inferior topical remedy. On the contrary, the remedy here addresses the ultimate stages of tissue injury, namely **ulceration, decay, fissuring** and **gangrene.** Soft, wet venereal chancres with painful discharges respond especially well to it. *Analgesic, antiseptic, anti-inflammatory, capillary stimulant* and *vulnerary/tissue-healing* actions work here in seamless concert.

Agrimony Herb

Botanical source: *Agrimonia eupatoria* L. (Rosaceae)

Pharmaceutical name: Herba Agrimoniae

Ancient names: Eupatorion, Epatrion (Gk) Concordia, Marmorella, Ferraria (Lat)

Other names: Sticklewort, Church steeples, Cockeburr, Harvest lice (Eng)
Aigremoine, Eupatoire/Euphorbe des Grecs (Fr)
Odermenning, Leberkletten, Königskraut, Bruchwurz (Ge)

Part used: the herb; also the root and seed, Radix Agrimoniae, Fructus Agrimoniae

NATURE

Therapeutic category: mild remedy with minimal chronic toxicity

Constituents: tannins, bitter compound, flavonoids, essential oil, nicotinic and silicic acids, phytosterol, vitamins B and K, minerals and trace minerals (incl. iron, silica)

Effective qualities: somewhat bitter and astringent, cool, dry
astringing, restoring, stimulating, softening

Tropism: liver, gallbladder, intestines, urogenital organs, lungs, kidneys, pancreas, stomach, blood
Liver, Gallbladder, Lung, Kidney meridians
Warmth, Air bodies

Ground: all krases, biotypes and constitutions

FUNCTIONS AND INDICATIONS

1 **RESOLVES MUCOUS-DAMP CONGESTION AND STOPS DISCHARGE AND BLEEDING;
RELIEVES WHEEZING AND BENEFITS THE THROAT**

lung phlegm-damp / heat: wheezing, coughing up much sputum, full cough with pain under lower ribs

BRONCHITIS, asthma, lung TB with blood-streaked sputum

VOICE LOSS, hoarseness

genitourinary damp: chronic vaginal and urinary discharges, lumbar pain

LEUCORRHEA, gonorrhea, cervicitis, vaginitis (esp. chronic)

DIARRHEA (esp. chronic, mucousy, incl. infectious/enteritic)

MUCOUS CYSTITIS, albuminuria, urethritis

HEMORRHAGE (passive, chronic, incl. metrorrhagia, hematuria, hemoptysis, hemafecia)

DIABETES (supportive)

2 CLEARS HEAT AND REDUCES FEVER AND INFLAMMATION

kidney fire: cutting kidney or lumbar pain radiating to umbilicus, blocked urination, fever

NEPHRITIS and other acute kidney infections, kidney colic

gallbladder fire: acute right flank pain, nausea

CHOLECYSTITIS, cholangitis

3 PROMOTES AND HARMONIZES URINATION, DISSOLVES STONES AND RELIEVES IRRITATION

kidney Qi stagnation: painful, scanty dripping urination, muddy or dark fetid urine, dingy skin

ANURIA

DYSURIA, INCONTINENCE (esp. chronic, from toxicosis, stones, infection)

URINARY STONES

4 STIMULATES DIGESTION, REDUCES LIVER CONGESTION AND RELIEVES FULLNESS

liver and stomach Qi stagnation: slow, difficult, painful digestion, right flank pain, appetite loss

LIVER CONGESTION, jaundice, hepatitis, liver cirrhosis

5 ASTRINGES AND PROMOTES TISSUE REPAIR, AND REDUCES INFLAMMATION

ULCERS (skin, gastric, mouth, throat; esp. chronic or rodent)

WOUNDS (external and internal, esp. infected, inflamed), cuts, punctures, fistulas, strains, sprains

EYE, MOUTH, THROAT INFLAMMATIONS (incl. conjunctivitis, laryngitis, gingivitis); neuritis, myalgia, arthritis; burns, scalds

CALLUSES and CORNS

PREPARATION

Use: Agrimony herb is **infused** or taken in **tincture** form. Always use the freshly-dried herb if possible. The simple infusion of Agrimony herb has a general, mild action—just right for resolving damp disorders with catarrhal discharge, and for making external preparations. The tincture releases the full spectrum of actions above.

Washes, compresses, gargles, douches, pessaries and **eye baths** are examples of external preparations that use Agrimony for stopping discharges and reducing inflammation, as prepared by people as different as the Native American and Renaissance Italians.

RYFF (1573) notes that Agrimony **syrup** was one of the essential remedies in stock at the apothecaries of his day. His formula consists of nineteen herbal ingredients, and treats a combination of liver Qi stagnation and intestines damp cold.

Dosage: Infusion: 8-16 g

Tincture: 1-4 ml at 1:3 strength in 45% ethanol

Caution: Because of its astringent quality, Agrimony herb should not be used with constipation present.

NOTES

Agrimony herb is one of the many gentle herbal remedies used in the West whose therapeutic role is often misunderstood by those who view herbs as simple substitutes for drugs or chemical components. Among herbalists, too, Agrimony is often seen as your typical characterless remedy that, because it seems to do everything, ends up doing nothing. Because herbal remedies only act as a result of their interaction with a person's life force, the gentler the herb, the wider its potential spectrum of uses. Consider Camomile flower, Yarrow herb and St. John's wort herb, in this connection, with their very wide area of potential uses. Unfortunately, the credibility of these thereby sinks all the more easily in the eyes of those faced with long lists of historically and empirically evident functions and indications—as is the case with Agrimony herb.

What is really needed to understand the true power and beauty of remedies such as Agrimony is a focus on its individual nature, its specific symptomatology. Eclectic practitioners of the nineteenth century perhaps came closest to realizing this goal for remedies in general. With Agrimony, however, there is perhaps more to the whole picture than even they realized.

Ultimately, because of both its gentleness and breadth of action, Agrimony herb is ideal for mixed or complex disharmonies typified by **damp** and **stagnation** that tend to **heat.** Essentially, this botanical is suited to cases of mild to medium severity, sensitive people, children and the elderly. It is inappropriate for most severe cases in adults, where stronger remedies apply. However, the real point is this. When used appropriately according to its specific indications—the totality of syndromes, symptoms and disorders that indicate its use—Agrimony is as effective a remedy as any.

Agrimony herb is one of several *refrigerant* herbs belonging to the harmony-loving rose family, and is closely related to Lady's mantle herb botanically, pharmacologically and therapeutically. As such, Agrimony achieves that delicate union of restoring and draining, which ultimately results in an altering/regulating function.

In restoring mode, Agrimony is an excellent *tonic astringent* with *mucostatic, hemostatic, antidiarrheal, antidischarge* and *expectorant* actions.

Mucous-damp and **phlegm-damp** conditions presenting **chronic mucus discharges** (including coughing up of sputum) are those best served. Of course, Agrimony infusion can always be used effectively for symptom relief of diarrhea, bladder irritation, hoarseness, gastric ulcers, wounds, and so on, both chronic and acute. In terms of systemic or constitutional treatment, however, Eclectic practitioners always considered its action on chronically congested, damp mucosa profoundly *alterative* and *restorative*. We would add that the remedy essentially works best for individuals with underlying functional **stasis** of the **kidneys, liver** and **stomach,** especially when presenting irritated or dribbling urination, or chronic indigestion of liver origin. *Diuretic* and *digestive stimulant* actions here come into play.

Agrimony's generous supply of the trace element silica also ensures tissue restoration in those areas of its tropism—especially in the bronchi and mucosa in general. Like Horsetail herb, Agrimony herb can provide valuable support for those suffering from longstanding respiratory disorders. **Chronic ulcers,** internal and external, in particular benefit from the *tissue-healing* combination of silica, tannin and flavonoids.

In draining mode, the cooling Agrimony herb possesses a *heat-clearing* effect that involves *anti-inflammatory* and *antipyretic* actions. Eclectic physicians often relied on the herb for treating acute urinary and biliary inflammations and infections, which may be expressed in the syndromes **kidney fire** and **gallbladder fire.** Acute mucosal inflammation, especially in the mouth and throat, also greatly benefit from internal and topical use com-bined.

Kava Root

Botanical source: *Piper methysticum* Forster
  (Piperaceae)
Pharmaceutical name: Rhizoma Piperis methystici
Other names: Kava kava, Ava, Ava pepper,
  Intoxicating long pepper (Eng)
  Kava, Ava, Arwa, Ava kava (Pol)
  Kava-kava (Fr)
  Rauschpfeffer (Ge)
Part used: the rhizome

NATURE

Therapeutic category: mild remedy with minimal chronic toxicity
Constituents: lactones (kava pyrones, incl. kavaine, dihydrokavaine, methysticine, yangonin, dihidro-methystecine), pungent resins 2% (alpharesin, betaresin), piperdine alkaloids (incl. kavaine), methylene protocatechuic aldehyde (kavahin), yangonic and cinnamic acids, yangono
Effective qualities: pungent, somewhat astringent and bitter, warm, dry
  restoring, astringing, stimulating, calming
Tropism: bladder, kidney, intestines, skeletal muscles, nerves
  Kidney, Bladder, Spleen, Heart meridians
  Fluid, Warmth bodies
Ground: all krases, biotypes and constitutions for symptomatic use

FUNCTIONS AND INDICATIONS

1 **RESOLVES MUCOUS-DAMP CONGESTION, STOPS DISCHARGE AND RELIEVES ITCHING;
TONIFIES URINARY QI, STRENTHENS THE BLADDER, HARMONIZES URINATION
AND RELIEVES PAIN AND INCONTINENCE**

kidney and bladder Qi deficiency with damp: genital and urinary discharges, irregular scanty urination, dribbling or irritated urination, cloudy urine, fatigue

BLENORRHEA (esp. chronic, incl. leucorrhea, gonorrhea, gleet, blennuria, mucous cystitis)

INCONTINENCE, ENURESIS (esp. in children, elderly), atonic neurogenic bladder

IRRITATION or PAIN on URINATION, urethral pain extending to perineum (in all conditions, incl. from uricosuria, acute urinary infections)

VAGINITIS with PRURITUS (vaginal, anal), urethritis

CYSTITIS (chronic and acute, incl. interstitial cystitis)

PROSTATITIS, epipidymitis, prostate hyperplasia

HEMORRHOIDS

2 **PROMOTES URINATION, DRAINS WATER AND RELIEVES EDEMA;
RESOLVES TOXICOSIS AND RELIEVES PAIN**

kidney water congestion: edema, esp. of legs and ankles, facial edema

EDEMA (esp. in lower limbs)

kidney Qi stagnation with *metabolic toxicosis:* painful, scanty dribbling urination, malaise, fatigue

RHEUMATISM, gout

NEURALGIA (esp. trigeminal); abdominal pain, menstrual pain, toothache, earache, eye pain

DYSMENORRHEA

3 **STIMULATES DIGESTION AND APPETITE, RESOLVES MUCOUS-DAMP
AND RELIEVES CONSTIPATION**

intestines (Spleen) mucous-damp: indigestion, irregular mucousy stool, distended painful abdomen,
water retention, lethargy, fatigue

CHRONIC GASTROENTERITIS

stomach and intestines Qi stagnation: difficult, painful digestion, appetite loss, fatigue, constipation

GASTROINTESTINAL DYSPEPSIA

4 **RELIEVES ANXIETY, RELAXES THE MUSCLES AND PROMOTES REST**

ANXIETY (with or without depression), INSOMNIA

MILD TRANSIENT DEPRESSION (esp. with anxiety)

MUSCLE TENSION and PAIN

PREPARATION

Use: Kava root is prepared by **decoction** or **tincture. Vaginal sponges, pessaries, douches** and
suppositories can be prepared from these for a variety of urogenital conditions.

Dosage: Decoction: 8-12 g

Tincture: 1-3 ml twice daily at 1:2 strength in 50% ethanol

Smaller doses are *restoring* and *stimulating,* while larger doses are more *sedating (calming).*

Caution: Contraindicated in chronic depression with no anxiety present, as kava is a nervous *sedative* as
well as *euphoric.* Also contraindicated during pregnancy and nursing. Kava *may* also be contraindicated in
liver disease as the alkaloids *may* over time cause some cumulative toxicity (the jury is still out on this
one). Use cautiously in Yin deficiency conditions with dryness or empty heat present.

NOTES

Kava in the pepper family is a woody creeper
found throughout most of Polynesia, Melanesia
and Micronesia, including Hawai'i, whose root is a
traditional remedy. The rhizomes are traditionally
also chewed and used to make a fermented drink
that is used both socially and ritually. This drink
produces a euphoric but clear-minded state as the
plant acts as a selective *nervous sedative* and *stimulant* combined, resulting in an *euphoric* action
similar to endorphin stimulation. Today in the
West, Kava has joined the league of "big hitters"
like St. John's wort and Ginkgo, although for different reasons. No other popular medicinal quite fits
the bill of the West's epidemic of anxiety *and*
depression combined quite as well. *Cerebral restoratives* such as Ginkgo leaf, Sage herb, Milky oat

berry and Rhodiola address depression from cerebral deficiency; but only St. John's wort comes
close to Kava in being able to treat **depression
with anxiety.** The root may in fact have some
neurocardiac sedative effect.

However, this has never been Kava's main
medical use, either in Oceania or in the West.
According to anthropologist DIEHL (1932), in the
South Pacific Kava's "chief medical use is in the
cure of chronic cystitis and gleet ..." Presumably
following this empirical lead, nineteenth century
Eclectic physicians also firmly established Kava as
an important urinary remedy in Western herbal
medicine. Despite current popular usage as a one-
stop *euphoric,* therefore, Kava has historically and
empirically many more medical applications to

disorders of urinary and genital functions. Complex, multi-symptom conditions of the body's waterworks are this remedy's prime domain.

From all available evidence, Kava root acts as a *urinary restorative, relaxant* and *stimulant*. Its *urinary restorative* effect includes an excellent *astringent mucostatic* (or *mucus decongestant*) action. Pungent, dry, astringent and slightly warm in quality, the remedy transforms **mucous-damp** in the **lower warmer,** thereby reducing **urinary** and **genital mucus discharges** (blenorrhea).

For those with simple, chronic urinary incontinence with dribbling, irritated urination arising from an underlying **bladder Qi deficiency,** Kava is absolutely pertinent. Think of Buchu leaf and Fennel seed here. *Anti-incontinent, analgesic* and *anti-inflammatory* actions here successfully operate in concert. The remedy is also one of the best for women with chronic vaginitis, leucorrhea and vaginal pruritus, especially in a damp-cold constitution. Think of Gravel root and Helonias root, which also treat **genitourinary damp.**

As a soothing *relaxant* to urinary functions, Kava root will also reduce urinary **irritation** and **pain,** whatever the cause, including prostate congestion, cystitis, uricosuria or just plain stress. Severe vaginal and anal itching are also included in its action here. Think of Hydrangea root, St. John's wort herb and Marjoram herb.

As a *urinary stimulant,* Kava root works as a *draining* and *detoxicant diuretic* in one—another way that this drying remedy reduces damp in the whole system. In **painful toxicosis** conditions such as rheumatism and fibromyalgia, the *analgesic* action (mainly neurological) is added reinforcement.

The root's high content in pungent resins nicely complement the bitter lactones in creating a good *digestive stimulant* action. This predictably addresses **mucous-damp** conditions of the **intestines** with such key symptoms as loose, mucousy, irregular stool, as well as **stagnant Qi** conditions presenting appetite loss and constipation—again like Buchu leaf, or like Angelica root, or Saussurea Mu Xiang in Chinese medicine.

Yerba Mansa Root

Botanical source: *Anemopsis californica*
      (Saururaceae)
Pharmaceutical names: Rhizoma Anemopsis
Other names: Swamp root, Lizard's tail (Am)
      Yerba mansa, Yerba del manso, Manso (Sp)
Part used: the rhizome

NATURE
Therapeutic category: mild remedy with slight chronic toxicity
Constituents: essential oil (incl. methyleugenol, estragol, thymol methylether, linalool, p-cymene, asarinine)
Effective qualities: very bitter, somewhat pungent, astringent, cool, dry
      restoring, astringing, decongesting

Tropism: respiratory, digestive, urinary systems
Lung, Spleen, Bladder meridians
Fluid body

FUNCTIONS AND INDICATIONS

1 **RESOLVES MUCOUS-DAMP CONGESTION AND STOPS DISCHARGE; REDUCES INFECTION**

head damp-cold: chronic nasal catarrh, sinus congestion and pain, nasal discharge

SINUSITIS, rhinitis, pharyngitis (esp. chronic)

lung phlegm-damp: coughing, expectoration of copious wet or sticky sputum, sore chest

CHRONIC BRONCHITIS, laryngitis

intestines damp: indigestion, flatulence, loose irregular stool

CHRONIC DYSPEPSIA, ENTERITIS (incl. food poisoning, giardiasis, amoebic dysentery)

genitourinary damp: chronic white or clear vaginal discharges

CHRONIC VAGINITIS with LEUCORRHEA, CYSTITIS, urethritis

CHRONIC INFECTIONS (bacterial, fungal)

2 **PROMOTES DETOXIFICATION, RESOLVES TOXICOSIS AND RELIEVES SWELLING; PROMOTES URINATION AND RELIEVES INFLAMMATION**

metabolic toxicosis with *damp:* scanty urination, joint aches and pains and swelling, malaise

RHEUMATOID ARTHRITIS, RHEUMATISM, gout

HYPERURICEMIA

3 **PROMOTES TISSUE REPAIR AND RELIEVES PAIN AND SWELLING**

ATONIC, INDOLENT ULCERS, sores, wounds, fissures (incl. of mouth, throat, gums, stomach, duodenum, rectum)

CONTUSIONS, abrasions, chafes, diaper rash

PREPARATION

Use: Yerba mansa root is prepared by **decoction** or **tincture. Mouthwashes, gargles, vaginal sponges, pessaries** and **douches** can be prepared from these for a variety of chronic conditions. Chronic catarrhal head colds require the *decongestant, antiseptic* **nasal spray** for best results (combine with 20% glycerine and 10% alcohol). The **powdered root** can be applied to fungal skin conditions such as athlete's foot.

Dosage: Decoction: 5-10 g

Tincture: 1-3 ml at 1:2 strength in 45% ethanol

Caution: Avoid using with sedative medication as a potentiating effect with methyleugenol may occur.

NOTES

Like bogbean, yerba mansa is a low-growing herbaceous plant with a yen for low, damp places. Loamy, alkaline terrain, marshes and swamps throughout North America's Southwest is where it is mainly seen. Although the whole plant looks superficially like plantain, it bears conical flowers of "white, starry blossoms resting on a bed of pale green leaves" (J.A. MUNK 1909) that look like anemones or cone-flowers. The whole plant is very aromatic, especially the root which, due to its essential oil content, exudes a fresh, pungent-cool, camphoraceous fragrance.

Yerba mansa's earliest medical uses include primary application as a *nasal decongestant* with *mucostatic* and *analgesic* action. Eclectic practitioners used Yerba mansa from the early 1900s until the 1920s mainly for "nasal catarrh" in a nasal spray. Today, interim experience tells us that the remedy shines, above all, at transforming **mucous damp.** It is equally successful in resolving congested mucosa in the sinuses, bronchi and digestive tract, especially when involving chronic infection at the bacterial or fungal stage of ENDERLEIN's cyclogeny. Yerba mansa is both a *resolvent mucosal restorative* (*anticatarrhal*) remedy and an *anti-infective* one—yes, like Goldenseal at the medium dosage range, or Sage leaf.

As a *uricosuric diuretic* and *anti-inflammatory,* Yerba mansa is a traditional remedy in the Southwest for **gouty arthritic** and **rheumatic** complaints—again **damp** lodging in the superficial tissues. It is somewhat *alterative* here, but perhaps not as profound as Dandelion root, Pipsissewa herb or Blackcurrant leaf, for instance.

Myrrh Resin

Botanical source: *Commiphora myrrha* L.
    (syn. *Commiphora molmol* Engler)
    (Burseraceae)
Pharmaceutical name: Resina Commiphorae
Ancient names: Myrra (Gr)
    Smyrna (Lat)
Other names: Myrrhe (Fr and Ge)
    Mo Yao (Mand)
    Mut Yeuk (Cant)
Part used: the tree resin and the essential oil

NATURE

Therapeutic category: mild remedy with minimal chronic toxicity
Constituents: essential oil 2.5-10% (incl. hydrocarbon methylisopropenyl furane 4%, sesquiterpenes [elemene, copaene, curzerene], methylisobutyl keetone, aldehyde [methylbutenal]), resin 25-40% (incl. commiphoric acid, commiphorinic acid, heerabomyrrhol), gums 50-60%, salts, sulphates, oxydase, xylose, galactose
Effective qualities: bitter, somewhat pungent, warm, dry
    decongesting, stimulating, restoring, astringing
Tropism: arterial circulation, lungs, intestines, uterus, urinary organs
    Spleen, Lung, Liver meridians
    Warmth, Fluid bodies
Ground: Phlegmatic and Melancholic krases
    Dependant/Tai Yin Earth and Burdened/Shao Yin biotype
    Lymphatic/Carbonic constitution

FUNCTIONS AND INDICATIONS

1 **RESOLVES MUCOUS DAMP CONGESTION AND STOPS DISCHARGE;
STIMULATES DIGESTION AND ELIMINATES PARASITES;
PROMOTES EXPECTORATION AND RESOLVES PHLEGM**

    intestines (Spleen) mucous-damp: gurgling abdomen, indigestion, loose stool, flatulence, appetite loss
    CHRONIC GASTRITIS, DIARRHEA, DYSPEPSIA (esp. chronic, with abdominal pain, including from
        enteritis, dysentery)

INTESTINAL DYSBIOSIS and PARASITES (esp. roundworm)
MICROBIAL DYSBIOSIS
lung phlegm-damp: coughing up copious sputum, difficult cough, wheezing, fatigue
CHRONIC BRONCHITIS, asthma
genitourinary damp: white vaginal or urinary discharges
LEUCORRHEA, blennuria, vaginitis, gonorrhea (chronic)

2 **STIMULATES CIRCULATION, DISPELS COLD AND RELIEVES CHILLS; REDUCES FEVER**
arterial blood and Qi deficiency with *cold:* weakness, fatigue, cold limbs, chills
REMITTENT FEVERS (*shao yang* stage), eruptive fevers

3 **PROMOTES MENSTRUATION AND RELIEVES AMENORRHEA;**
PROMOTES LABOR AND ENHANCES DELIVERY
uterus cold: delayed or painful periods, pelvic dragging and pain, absent periods
AMENORRHEA, spasmodic dysmenorrhea
PAINFUL, DIFFICULT LABOR in deficiency conditions (hypotonic uterine dystocia)
FAILURE to PROGRESS DURING LABOR
RETAINED PLACENTA

4 **INHIBITS THE THYROID; REDUCES SEXUAL OVERSTIMULATION**
THYROID HYPERFUNCTIONING
SEXUAL OVERSTIMULATION

5 **REDUCES INFECTION, INFLAMMATION AND DECAY**
VIRAL, BACTERIAL and FUNGAL INFECTIONS (esp. of mouth, gum, throat, vagina, with chronic
    inflammation, sepsis and putrefaction, incl. periodontitis, stomatitis, gingivitis, vaginitis, candidiasis,
    lung TB)
BOILS, carbuncles, abscesses

6 **PROMOTES TISSUE REPAIR AND RELIEVES PAIN, SWELLING, CLOTTING AND DECAY;**
BENEFITS THE THROAT, GUMS AND TEETH
CHRONIC SKIN ULCERS, wounds, sores (esp. with pain, swelling, putrefaction/gangrene)
CHRONIC PHARYNGITIS, throat ulcers, aphthous and sloughing sore throat, hoarseness, voice loss
MOUTH ULCERS (aphthae)
LOOSE TEETH, spongy or ulcerous gums, caries

PREPARATION
Use: Myrrh resin is prepared by **tincture** and the extracted **essential oil**—both good preparations. Although Myrrh is systemically warming, locally cooling and soothing **gargles, mouthwashes** and **douches** are used for infections and ulcers involving the mucosa. **Swabs, liniments** and **compresses** are prepared for injuries, ulcers and the like. Myrrh is used worldwide as an important topical *vulnerary, anti-inflammatory* and *antiseptic* remedy for tissue trauma.
Dosage: Tincture: 0.5-1.5 ml at 1:5 strength in 90% ethanol
        Essential oil: 2-3 drops in a gel cap topped with some olive oil
    As oxytocic parturient during the first stage of labor: take above doses of the tincture (or essential oil) every 30 minutes until labor resumes.
Caution: Myrrh is contraindicated during pregnancy as it is a *uterine stimulant*. There is no evidence to suggest that the remedy is *progesteronic* and therefore safe during pregnancy—regardless of whether used in resin, tincture or essential oil form.

NOTES

Myrrh resin, like Frankincense resin, is another time-honored remedy from the Middle East that has been adopted by each of the world's three traditional medical systems, the Greek, Ayurvedic and Chinese.

Myrrh applies essentially to **damp** conditions arising from **Yang deficiency.** Where stagnant mucous-damp obstruct digestive, respiratory and genitourinary functions, Myrrh is the appropriate remedy. Its superb *mucosal stimulant* and *decongestant* actions address chronically swollen, pale, catarrhal mucosal tissue. The main indications here are **chronic enteritic disorders** with diarrhea, **intestinal dsybiotic conditions** with candida-like disorders, and longstanding **bronchial infections** with productive yet painful, difficult cough.

Amenorrhea produced by the energy of cold is another worldwide use for the resin. In women of the Tai Yin Earth and Shao Yin type especially, Myrrh is an effective *oxytocic parturient* that promotes contractions, relieves pain and helps eliminate the afterbirth.

Myrrh resin is also a highly effective *antibacterial* and *antifungal* agent that has recently also shown *antiviral* activity (FRANCHOMME 1990). Like Garlic bulb, Cinnamon oil and Clove oil, it belongs to the *warming, stimulant* type of *antiseptic* remedies. In addition to its application in **chronic catarrhal infections** of the **mouth, bronchial** and **genitals,** Myrrh is also much used for acute and chronic topical conditions such as **tissue trauma** with painful, swollen tissues; skin and throat ulcers, sore throat and voice loss. Its strong *antiseptic, tissue-healing, anti-inflammatory, analgesic* and *anticontusion* actions here work here in seamless concert.

White Pond Lily Root

Botanical source: *Nymphaea odorata* [Dryander] Aiton) (Liliaceae)
Other names: Sweet/fragrant water lily
Part used: the herb

Therapeutic category: mild remedy w. no toxicity
Constituents: alkaloids (including nupharine), phytoestrogen, tannins, gallic and tartaric acids, mucilage, starch, gum, resin, saccharides, ammonia
Effective qualities: bitter, astringent, dry, cool

Notes On Its Functions and Indications

White pond lily is a perennial aquatic plant found in shallow, muddy North American ponds, bogs and sluggish streams (especially along the coasts).

This *astringent mucostatic* restores the tone of the mucous membrane and therefore resolves mucous-damp. The root reduces **digestive** and **urogenital discharges** such as diarrhea (including of dysentery), leucorrhea, venereal discharges and spermatorrhea. Secondary uses include urinary infections, prostate irritation, nephritis and cough. The main syndrome indication is genitourinary (Kidney) Qi deficiency.

Because of its *nervous* and *reproductive sedative* effect, White pond lily root also addresses irritability, anxiety and insomnia. Because of its *sedative* action on reproductive functions, it is also used for sexual overstimulation with premature ejaculation, wet dreams, etc. In Chinese medical terms the remedy reduces Kidney fire and calms the mind.

Topical preparations include **compresses** and **poultices** for ulcers, boils, skin inflammations, swollen glands and tumors. **Mouthwashes** and **gargles** may be used for mouth and throat ulcers, thrush, gingivitis with sore gums, and laryngitis with sore throat. **Vaginal sponges** and **douches** should be used consistently for chronic gleet, vaginal discharges and irritation, uterine and vaginal prolapse, uterine cancer and cervical ulcer.

Dose: Short decoction: 4-8 g.
Tincture: 2-4 ml at 1:2 strength in 45% ethan.
Caution: Avoid use with constipation present.
Note: Yellow pond lily root (also known as Spatterdock root), from *Nuphar luteum* (L.) Sibthorp and Smith (syn. *Nymphaea lutea* L)., and **European white pond lily root,** from *Nymphaea alba* L., are used interchangeably with White pond lily root.

Sandalwood

Botanical source: *Santalum album* L. (Santalaceae)
Pharmaceutical name: Lignum Santali
Other names: Santal, Santal citrin (Fr)
       Weisses Sandelholz (Ge)
Part used: the heartwood

NATURE

Therapeutic category: mild remedy with minimal chronic toxicity
Constituents: essential oil (incl. sesquiterpinol santalol 67%, santenonol, teresantalal, nortricyclosan-talol, fusenol, borneol, isovaleraldehyde, alpha and beta santalenes, santalal, santalone, santalic acid, tersantalic acid, santenone, carbides), pterocarpin
Effective qualities: bitter, astringent, somewhat sweet, cold, dry with moistening potential
      astringing, restoring, relaxing
Tropism: urogenital organs, venous and lymphatic circultion, intestines, heart, lungs
      Large Intestine, Heart, Lung meridians
      Warmth, Fluid, Air bodies

FUNCTIONS AND INDICATIONS

1 RESOLVES MUCOUS-DAMP CONGESTION AND STOPS DISCHARGE

damp-heat / cold conditions of the urogenital organs, lungs, intestines (esp. with white or purulent discharges)
INFECTIONS (acute and chronic, incl. cystitis, gonorrhea, vaginitis, enteritis, bronchitis, laryngitis)
CHRONIC DIARRHEA, dysentery, gastritis, colitis
skin damp-heat: red skin eruptions
SKIN INFLAMMATION (dermatitis)
GENITAL DISCHARGES (e.g. leucorrhea, spermatorrhea)

**2 RESTORES THE HEART, LIFTS THE MIND AND RELIEVES DEPRESSION;
TONIFIES REPRODUCTIVE QI AND RELIEVES IMPOTENCE**

heart Qi deficiency: palpitations, loss of endurance, depression, chest pains
CARDIAC DEFICIENCY
DEPRESSION and melancholy in all conditions
IMPOTENCE, frigidity, infertility

3 NOURISHES LUNG YIN, MOISTENS DRYNESS AND RELIEVES COUGHING

lung Yin deficiency: night sweats, fever, chest pain, dry cough
LUNG TB
lung dryness: chronic dry cough

| 4 | **VITALIZES THE BLOOD AND LYMPH, AND REDUCES CONGESTION** |

venous blood stagnation: fatigue, varicose veins

VARICOSE VEINS (incl.) hemorrhoids, LYMPHADENITIS

| 5 | **REGULATES THE QI, RELAXES CONSTRAINT AND RELIEVES PAIN** |

Qi constraint: conditions of the lungs, heart and intestines with pain

ANGINA with chest pains

NEURALGIA, neuritis (incl. sciatica)

| 6 | **MOISTENS AND BENEFITS THE SKIN** |

DRY and DEHYDRATED SKIN conditions

PREPARATION

Use: Sandalwood heartwood is prepared by **decoction, tincture** or **essential oil.** The decoction and tincture of the wood itself is more *astringent* and *analgesic,* and therefore suited for intestinal infections and chronic diarrhea with pain (function 1).

The **essential oil,** distilled from the heartwood, is today the most practical preparation in terms of availability. The oil may be **massaged** into the affected part with a base oil at a low dilution (2-3%) or taken internally. **Compresses** and **liniments** of the diluted oil are used externally for skin conditions.

Dosage: Decoction: 2-4 g. Up to 12 g are used for infectious conditions.

Tincture: 0.5-2 ml at 1:2 strength in 45% ethanol

Essential oil: 4-8 drops in a gelatin capsule with some olive oil

Caution: Forbidden in hot conditions arising from Yin deficiency.

NOTES

More than any other remedy, Sandalwood vividly demonstrates how dry and moist qualities can coexist, evident from their different functions. Sandalwood is intrinsically a drying remedy, an *astringent restorative* suitable for those with mucosal bogginess with copious discharges. Its prime target organs are the reproductive and respiratory systems. Here the heartwood probably restores the membrane on a more long-term basis. It addresses not only chronic conditions but also acute infectious/inflammatory situations involving **damp-heat.** In this connection Sandalwood has an outstanding reputation for treating venereal infections, for which it has been combined with Myrrh or Kava root, for instance.

When used in essential oil form, Sandalwood's moist quality engages, turning this remedy into a *soothing, lenitive emollient.* It is one of the very best for **dry, dehydrated, itching** or **inflamed skin** conditions. Dry bronchial conditions will likewise benefit from the essential oil's *demulcent* property, whether the dryness is due to Qi constraint and nervous tension, a dry climate or consumptive Yin-deficient conditions (where its *antiseptic* and *anti-inflammatory* actions also contribute benefits).

With its bitter and astringent taste and *heat-reducing, detoxicant* action, Sandalwood is incontrovertibly a cold remedy. This judgement is borne out by a glance at Arab texts that classify this botanical as cold and dry in the third degree. ISHAK IBN AMRAN (tenth century) notes that "it clears headaches due to heat," while later European texts always include Sandalwood in heat-clearing formulas for Liver fire syndromes, along with other "coolers" such as Purslane herb, Selfheal spike (*Prunella*), Chicory root and the Four Cooling Seeds (GALEN). LI SHI-ZHEN himself, one of the most prominent herbalists that China has produced, recommends the remedy for cholera—essentially a damp-heat condition.

Sandalwood oil also calms the mind, allowing overall relaxation. By working on the heart, it specifically also lifts the spirit out of states of gloom and depression—a different type of bogginess.

PHV GER-
MANICVM.

Gemein Baldrion.

Herbs to Regulate Endocrine Functions

In addition to their effects on the organs and tissues, many herbal remedies are known to affect the two systems of long- and medium-term systemic physiological control, the endocrine and nervous systems. Together these two systems are also known as the neuroendocrine system; they are steered as one by the hypothalamus. Through hypothalamic control of the pituitary, the endocrine and nervous systems constantly interact through hormonal and neurotransmitter communication.

Herbs can act as *hormonal* and *autonomic nervous system (ANS) regulators* because of their stimulating or inhibiting effect on these two systems. As such they usually address long-term and constitutional syndromes of imbalance rather than acute dysfunctions. In clinical practice, they are usually used in formulas as adjunct rather than as primary remedies. Rarely does a condition require the treatment strategy of hormonal or nervous regulation without organ or tissue dysfunctions also being addressed. The only exception to this would be systemic constitutional therapy in someone already in relatively good health.

The Nature and Treatment of Endocrine and Autonomic Nervous Dysfunctions

The dynamics of neuroendocrine functions are tightly interactive in maintaining overall homeostasis in the individual. When this precision timepiece of hormonal and neural functions is modulated and regulated in some way, systemic, long-term effects will result, never just local or short-term ones. Considering the small-scale, high-sensitivity nature of these functions and their systemic and constitutional influence, this treatment method is best used in the context of long-term and/or constitutional therapies. This is why the four basic ANS imbalances especially are often said to describe four constitutional nervous system types.

Hormonal imbalance is usually seen in chronic types of disorders and usually involves more than just one endocrine gland. When one gland is hyper- or hypo-functioning/secreting, the glands immediately related tend to become imbalanced either in sympathy or in opposition. While the predisposing and triggering causes of hormonal disorders are too numerous to list, it is nevertheless true that they often involve a mental or emotional component that is genetically embedded in the individual constitution. This is because on a constitutional level the endocrine and nervous systems are the physical substrates of the individual self and the psyche (see Appendix C). Diagnostically it is therefore important to consider a person's attitude and lifestyle imbalances and their effect on mental and affective processes if more permanent changes are to be established. Witness the newly emerging field of psychoneuroimmunology.

Gynecological problems are the prime (but not the only) examples of the neuroendocrine influence on tissues and organs via the hormonal and neurotransmitter messaging system. In gynecology an essential diagnostic consideration is whether a woman's condition involves an endocrine disturbance or tissue pathology, or both. In the case of endocrine imbalances, selecting hormonal remedies for treating menstrual, menopausal or other problems can therefore refine other treatment methods and considerably shorten treatment time. Problems with normal growth development in infants and children, and with the aging process in general, can also be treated with hormonal remedies.

Like the internal organs, most endocrine glands and the ANS itself can present hyperfunctioning and hypofunctioning types of symptom pictures in reaction to internal and external stressors. This symptomatology includes pulse and tongue findings, as well as more general character and personality traits. Because of the hierarchy of functional relationships among the endocrine glands, it is also important to understand their larger group patterns of imbalance.

Using herbs for hormonal and ANS dysfunctions successfully depends mainly on knowledge of endocrine and nervous system syndromes and the biotype profiles of the individuals that present these imbalances. Various tests such as blood, saliva and hair analysis can also be very useful when based on a neuroendocrine model.

The Herbs that Regulate Hormones

Because the remedies that are *hormonal regulators* are more often used for other treatment strategies, they are found scattered throughout the Materia Medica. *Hormonal regulators* essentially operate by either stimulating or inhibiting the release (or at least the presence or availability) of certain hormonal secretions. A large number work on the glands themselves to alter their secretions. However, despite the precise knowledge we have about the hormonal action of certain remedies, we should not forget that in this respect modern pharmacology knows very little about the majority of available remedies. For sheer lack of scientific research and because of the complexities of human pharmacokinetics, the hormonal actions of many herbal remedies is still only known to us in terms of their secondary effects on organs and tissues. Consequently we often have no certain way of telling if any and what endocrine activity may be present in a plant. Some of the known hormonal actions of plant remedies are frankly empirical rather than scientific.

Certain remedies are known to have a *bivalent hormonal action* of one kind or another, one that goes beyond the simple actions below.
• Chastetree berry and Dong quai root are general hormonal balancers used to balance the estrogen-progesterone ratio in women. Chastetree is thought to modulate pituitary functions to achieve this effect.
• Yarrow herb and Marigold flower are also hormonally balancing in women with a possible *estrogenic* or *progesteronic* action.
• Alfalfa herb and Red Clover flower are *estrogenic* but can also act in an *anti-estrogenic* way.

These are just a few examples of the way herbs work in conjunction with the body's life force. In terms of information theory, the body will always try to take what it needs from the array of chemical and electromagnetic information a remedy may provide. With some remedies it can do this better than with others.

Likewise, many remedies listed below only have the *potential* for stimulating or inhibiting a certain hormone. Because of other or opposing physiological needs, in a certain condition or constitution this action may never occur. So Angelica root, for example, may under certain conditions act as an *adrenocortical inhibitor*. However, when given in the majority of conditions found in clinical practice it will not act in this way. The body to varying degrees can selectively shut off certain metabolic pathways, as required. In this sense all herbal remedy actions are ultimately potential, not actual actions. This is perhaps the key factor that distinguishes herbal remedies from synthetic medication, which always exhibit *actual* actions, rather than potential actions. While synthetic drugs exert their actions regardless of the body's needs, hence causing the myriad "side-effects" that are a part of its primary actions, herbs always exert their actions in interplay with the body's needs, based on the inherent wisdom of the Qi/vital force. This is especially true of the remedies in the mild, non-toxic category, and increasinly less true as the herb carried greater cumulative toxicity with ingestion.

The following are the most important types and examples of *hormonal regulators*. As everywhere else in this text, those remedies that may be used in essential oil form are given *in italics* at the end of the list. A question mark after the remedy indicates that the related action is possible, but not proven.

• **adrenocortical stimulants (pituitary-adrenal stimulants/regulators)** that promote the production/quality/availability of the hormones of the adrenal cortex (e.g., gluco- and mineralcorticoids): Asian/American ginseng, Eleuthero root, Licorice root, Nettle herb, Walnut seed, Celery seed/root, Blackcurrant leaf, Black figwort root (Scrophularia Xuan Shen), Eucomia bark (Eucomia Du Zhong), Rehmannia root (Rehmannia Shu Di Huang), Rhodiola, *Black spruce, Cinnamon, Scotch pine, Fir, Rosemary, Sage, Thyme, Basil, Geranium, Winter savory, Turpentine*
• **adrenocortical inhibitors** that decrease the production/quality/availability of the hormones of the adrenal cortex: Angelica root, Mousear herb, Vervain herb, *Ylang ylang*
• **adrenomedullary stimulants** that promote the production of the hormones of the adrenal medulla (e.g., epinephrine and norepinephrine): Broom herb, Damiana herb, Ephedra herb, Cereus stem,

Asian/American ginseng, Eleuthero root, Aconitum Fu Zi, *Lemon, Thyme, Rosemary, Thyme, Winter savory, Fir, Black spruce, Scotch pine*

• **adrenomedullary inhibitors** that decrease production of the hormones of the adrenal medulla: Angelica root, *Ylang ylang*

• **androgen/testosterone stimulants** that increase production/quality/availability of certain hormones of the adrenal cortex and ovarian stroma (e.g., testosterone, DHEA and androstenedione): Ginseng root (all types), Flower pollen, Saw palmetto berry, Damiana leaf, Epimedium Yin Yang Huo, Maca (?), *Lemon, Basil, Niaouli, Winter savory*

• **estrogen stimulants** that increase the production/quality/availability of ovarian (and later in life adrenal) hormones (e.g., estrol, estradiol, estriol): Alfalfa herb, Black cohosh root, Fennel root/ seed, Fenugreek seed, Ginseng root (all types), Licorice root, Marigold herb, Hops flower, Red clover flower, Wild yam root, Common ivy leaf, Angelica root/seed(?), Lovage root(?), Parsley root(?), Elecampane root(?), Oat berry(?), Flower pollen(?), Suma root(?), Sichuan lovage root (Ligusticum Chuan Xiong)(?), *Fennel, Clary sage, Rose, Aniseed, Sage, Niaouli*

• **estrogen inhibitors** that decrease the production/quality/availability of ovarian (and later in life adrenal) hormones: Alfalfa herb, Gromwell herb, Red clover flower, Watercress herb(?), Pasqueflower root/herb(?), Poppy flower(?), *Cumin*

• **gonadotropic hormonal regulators (pituitary-gonadal stimulants)** that regulate (balance) pituitary hormones reaching the gonads: Chastetree berry, Damiana herb, Watercress herb, Kelp thallus, Bladderwrack thallus, Rehmannia root, Evening primrose oil, Borage seed oil, Blackcurrant oil, *Clary sage, Niaouli, Sage, Vetiver*

• **insulin stimulants** (including **hypoglycemiants**) that promote the production/quality/availability of the hormones of the pancreas tail (insulin and glucagon), thereby controlling and lowering high blood sugar: Artichoke leaf, Bilberry leaf, Goat's rue herb, Fenugreek seed, Eleuthero root, Watercress herb, Carrot root/seed, Chicory root, Dandelion root, Elecampane root, Nettle herb, Oat berry, Devil's club, Walnut leaf/ hull, Suma root, Rehmannia root, *Geranium, Lemon, Eucalyptus, Sage, Fennel, Juniper, Onion*

• **insulin inhibitors** that decrease the production/

quality/availability of the hormones of the pancreas tail: Angelica root, Arnica flower, Barberry bark, Bogbean herb, Centaury herb, Devil's club, Gentian root, Blessed thistle herb, Wormwood herb, Southernwood herb

• **progesterone stimulants** that increase the production/quality/availability of the ovarian hormone of the corpus luteus (progesterone): Chastetree berry is the only herb scientifically proven to exert this effect.

However, clinical experience shows that a *progesteronic* action may possibly be achieved with the following: Elecampane root, Helonias root, Marigold flower, Wild yam root, Blackhaw root bark, Cramp bark, Saw palmetto berry, Turmeric root, Damiana herb, Jasmine flower, Birthroot, *Geranium, Rose, Vetiver*

• **progesterone inhibitors** that decrease production/quality/availability of the ovarian hormone of the corpus luteus: *estrogen stimulants* in general tend to inhibit progesterone.

• **thyrotropic growth hormone stimulants** that promote production/quality/availability of the pituitary's growth hormone: Eleuthero root, Oat berry and straw, Walnut leaf/hull, Kelp thallus, Bladderwrack thallus, Watercress herb, Flower pollen(?), Microalgae(?), [Tortoise shell], [Velvet deer antler]

• **thyroxine stimulants** that promote the efficiency of thyroid functions, including that of the hormone thyroxine: Artichoke leaf, Garlic bulb, Kelp thallus, Bladderwrack thallus, Damiana leaf, Coconut oil, Nettle seed and herb(?), Chickweed herb(?), Rhodiola(?), Saw palmetto berry(?)

• **thyroxine inhibitors** that decrease efficiency of thyroid functions, especially that of the hormone thyroxine: Motherwort herb, Shepherd's purse herb, Bugleweed herb, Melissa leaf, Gromwell herb, Watercress herb, Cabbage leaf, Horseradish root, Radish root, Turnip root, Mistletoe herb, *Myrrh, Fennel, Cumin*

• **parathormone stimulants** that promote efficiency of parathyroid functions, especially that of the hormone parathormone: It is possible that herbs high in trace minerals will improve parathyroid functions, e.g. Horsetail herb, Nettle herb and seaweeds in general, including Hijiki, Wakame, Kelp, and so on.

Herbs for Symptom Treatment

Herbal remedies that treat symptoms are classed as follows:

Class 17   *Pregnancy enhancers:* Enhance pregnancy and childbirth
Class 18   *Astringents:* Astringe and stop discharge, leakage and bleeding
Class 19   *Nervous sedatives:* Calm the mind and relieve anxiety
Class 20   *Nervous stimulants:* Lift the mind and relieve depression
Class 21   *Spasmolytics:* Clear internal wind and reduce spasms
Class 22   *Analgesics:* Relieve pain
Class 23   *Vulneraries:* Promote tissue repair and relieve pain and swelling
Class 24   *Anti-infectives:* Reduce infection
Class 25   *Antiparasitics:* Eliminate parasites

The focus of remedies in these classes is symptom management, irrespective of the underlying condition or disorder. As such these classes are distinct from all others, which are organized according to the syndromes or conditions they address.

Symptom Treatment as a Principle of Treatment

In herbal medicine, treating the symptom is just as important as treating the systemic condition: these are two complementary treatment principles. It should not be thought that symptomatic treatment does not support systematic rebalancing on an energetic level—it does. This is because all natural remedies still work in conjunction with the individual life force (Qi or *physis*). There is a world of difference between the direct, aggressive action of a synthetic drug, which essentially suppresses a symptom, and the more indirect, subtle action of a natural remedy, which tends to provide symptom relief while yet allowing the whole system to remain in balance. Herbs in this section are therefore perfect complements to herbs in the Eliminating, Restoring, Draining and Altering sections when the branch, or manifestation, of a disorder needs as much attention as its root, or source.

The types of conditions that require symptom treatment are often **acute** and **local.** Typically they involve pain, infection, hemorrhage or injury. In infectious conditions, for example, *anti-infectives* that reduce infection (Class 24) are often selected alongside *diaphoretics* (Class 1), *expectorants* (Class 4), *antipyretics* (Class 12) and *mucostatics* (Class 15), depending on the type and stage of infection, the organs/parts involved and the symptoms presenting. Typical examples of combined systemic and symptom treatment are given at the end of the discussion on each herb class in the other four sections of the text.

The same herbs that treat systemic conditions, or syndromes, treat particular symptoms as well. Goldenseal root, for example, is an important *anti-infective* for reducing infection and clearing toxins. However, it is found in Class 12 because it is a superior bitter, cold *astringent* for clearing damp-heat and stopping discharge. Likewise, Valerian root is a major *nervous sedative* remedy for calming the mind and reducing anxiety (Class 19). It is presented in Class 11 because of its important role in regulating the Qi. Because it promotes astriction, Birthroot is frequently used to stop any kind of discharge, including bleeding (Class 18), but is better viewed as the superb *mucostatic* for resolving mucous-damp that it is. The majority of important and often used remedies may therefore be used on the level of systemic treatment (i.e. eliminating, restoring, draining or altering) or on the level of symptom relief.

Class 17

Herbs to Enhance Pregnancy and Childbirth

Throughout history, midwives, doctors and healers have successfully used herbal remedies during pregnancy and childbirth. Certain herbal remedies can support both the mother and growing foetus during this special time, while others may be used for particular preclinical and clinical disorders that may arise during this time. We will consider the various phases of childbirth to illustrate the many ways in which herbal remedies may safely be used.

Conception

Today, infertility is a major issue in many Western countries. Fortunately there are many remedies with a traditional reputation for treating infertility or, at the very least, simply increasing a woman's chances of conceiving. Infertility remedies address this problem first, by enhancing and regulating sexual hormones; second, by restoring the tone of the uterus. Note that *neuroendocrine restoratives* (Class 7) and certain *hormonal regulators* (Class 16) themselves promote a normal sexual appetite, an effect that is an integral part of their efficacy. The following remedies have all, at one time or another, been used to treat infertility: Ginseng root (all types), Flower pollen, Saw palmetto berry, Damiana leaf, Chasteberry, Helonias root, Birthroot, Black cohosh root, Mugwort herb, Rose flower, Marjoram herb and Oat berry. These work mainly by increasing and regulating estrogen and/or progesterone levels.

Pregnancy: The Herbs that Support and Enhance Pregnancy

Gestation is a time of nourishment and growth for both foetus and mother, and so herbs high in nutritional value are especially important—the Class 9 *nutritives*. For the whole of pregnancy and childbirth, the single most important factor that ensures well-being and freedom from complications is adequate nutrition for two. Many problems, whether relatively minor, such as morning sickness, or major, such as pre-eclampsia, can be traced back directly to poor quality or irregular food and supplemental nutrient intake. Whether we view them as **nutritional supplements, superfoods** or plain **power-weeds,** *nutritives* such as flower pollen, microalgae such as chlorella and spirulina, sea vegetables (e.g., kelp, bladderwrack, dulse, hijiki), barley grass, nettle herb, oat berry, alfalfa herb can fairly quickly provide the extra minerals and proteins vitally needed during this time. They are all the more essential these days considering the increasingly poor quality of commercially available foods (including organic produce), which is largely due to soil mineral depletion.

In addition to these *nutritives,* there are several more specific remedies that particularly enhance the whole of pregnancy and beyond to delivery and breastfeeding. These are **endocrine/hormonal remedies** that possess a selective affinity for a woman's reproductive organs, and that operate mainly by regulating hormones and toning the uterine muscle. They are **Raspberry leaf, Blackhaw root bark** and **Cramp bark.** These should be drunk freely every day in tea form throughout pregnancy. Taking one or two of these potent pregnancy allies should be seen as a simple but major investment in preventing complications during both pregnancy and labor.

In Europe, Blackberry leaf and Strawberry leaf were traditionally also used to enhance pregnancy, like Raspberry leaf, but are today considered less effective, if only for lack of research. In the U.S., nineteenth and early-twentieth century Eclectic doctors mainly employed the following remedies for pregnancy support:
• Blackhaw root bark and Cramp bark: especially in the first and second trimester in women with a history of past miscarriage and dysmenorrhea (spasmodic and congestive).
• Gravel root: especially in the first trimester and with urinary disorders present.
• Helonias root: especially in the second and third

trimester; in women with discharges and past miscarriage; amd presenting low estrogen levels and pre-labor pains.
• Partridgeberry herb: especially in the last trimester and in women with venous blood stagnation

Whatever herbs are chosen, it is important to select those that most closely match the mother's constitutional tendency to disharmony. Individual herb selection during pregnancy can prevent complications not only during pregnancy, but especially during labor, delivery and breast-feeding. The main challenge here is education of the mother (and her mate) in the incalculable preventive value of regular, consistent herb use.

If these supportive remedies are taken in tincture form (which they can be), only low doses—e.g., 1 ml [about 25 drops]—may be taken once or twice daily. Even the gentle Raspberry leaf has been known to bring on Braxton-Hicks contractions and possibly premature labor contractions.

Herbs for Problems Arising During Pregnancy

Whatever its nature, any problem arising during pregnancy should be addressed immediately. Minor complaints that may arise include morning sickness (nausea and vomiting), lower backaches, varicose veins, constipation, heartburn, mood swings, fatigue, anemia and high blood pressure. These conditions should be treated systemically and are often seen in syndromes such as venous blood stagnation, intestines mucous damp, stomach Qi reflux, blood deficiency and liver blood and Qi stagnation. On the psychological side, worry and anxiety may need to be addressed.

Note that the herbs used include some mild *uterine stimulants* that are generally considered unsafe during pregnancy. These *can* be used as part of a formula to address a particular disorder as long as the mother doesn't have a tendency to prolapse or chronic miscarriages. They should of course be discontinued as soon as possible.
• **Morning sickness** is caused either by the increased hormone levels or hypoglycemia (low blood sugar). Both conditions are exacerbated in women with liver congestion with reduced ability to break down hormones. Helpful (but not always effective) herbs include Peppermint herb, Ginger root, Wild yam root, Black horehound herb, Blackhaw root and Iceland moss tea (see also Nausea in the Repertory).

Eating protein with each meal is a sensible recommendation, as well as eating snacks between meals in the cae of hypoglycemia.

If a systemic syndrome is present, nausea will be alleviated more effectively if the functional imbalance is addressed concurrently.
• **Pain,** including postpartum pain, may involve a variety of factors and energetic imbalances, mainly connected with patterns of deficiency and constrained Qi. Blackhaw bark and Wild yam root (both Class 11 *relaxants*) are two remedies generally excellent for many types of pain during pregnancy.
• **Fatigue** is very common and caused by poor quality/inappropriate nutrition and lack of rest and sleep. In the case of actual anemia, intake of Nettle herb, Dandelion root, Chicory root, Alfalfa herb Oat berry and seaweeds in any shape or form is recommended; generally the Class 9 *nutritives*.
• **Constipation** is also very common, especially if pelvic blood congestion, Qi/Yang deficiency or internal dryness is already present. In addition to high-fiber foods, only gentle *laxatives (aperients)* should be used primarily, e.g. Dandelion root, Burdock root, Nettle herb and Tamarind pulp, not *stimulant laxatives* like Senna and Rhubarb.
• **Hemorrhage** is a common liability, for which *hemostatic* herbs (Class 18) should be used. Because it is a potentially serious situation, however, bleeding during pregnancy should only be treated by a competent practitioner. If severe, medical emergency treatment may be necessary.
• **Varicose veins** in the legs and groin area is common in the late part of pregnancy. The increased weight of the uterus in the pelvis effectively slows down the return circulation to the heart, thereby causing a back-up of stagnant venous blood with varicose veins. In addition, the veins themselves may be weaker in pregnancy because of increased levels of hormones.

Varicose veins should be treated with *venous decongestants* (Class 14). Marigold flower, Shepherd's purse herb and Butcher's broom root should be used with caution because they are normally contraindicated during pregnancy. Eating plenty of protein and fresh, flavonoid-rich fruits is also helpful—as well the practical advice of putting the feet up as much as possible (higher than the heart).
• **Miscarriage** and **premature delivery** are both serious problems that are far better prevented than treated. **Chronic miscarriage** can only be preven-

ted by ensuring that the woman's overall condition is as balanced as possible, hormonally and otherwise, *before,* not after conception. In Chinese medical terms, Central Qi and *dai mai* channel deficiency are the most common syndromes seen.

In general, Blackhaw root bark, Cramp bark, Helonias root, Partridgeberry herb and Raspberry leaf are the main remedies that specifically address recurring miscarriage. The particular remedy chosen depends mainly on which phase of pregnancy the miscarriage is liable to occur. Once pregnancy is underway, the herb should be taken daily, beginning with small doses about three weeks before the habitual miscarriage, with increasing doses during the last week. In this condition it is particularly important also to minimize toxic irritants to the mother, such as chemical pollutants and heavy metals, including pesticides, herbicides, cigarettes, toxic house-building materials, exposure to industrial fumes, amalgam tooth fillings, and so on. These can create toxic heat which is transferred to the growing fetus, which may then cause immune dysfunctions such as allergies in the newborn.

• **Threatening miscarriage** calls for *fetal relaxants* that calm the fetus and stop imminent abortion. The following, singly or in combination, may be used: Blackhaw root bark, Wild yam root, Raspberry leaf, Partridgeberry herb (after the sixth month). A standard to large dose of these (e.g., 1/2 to 1 teaspoon of the tincture) should be taken every 30 minutes. If miscarriage does occur, the appropriate herbs to complete the process, i.e., clean out the uterus (*uterine stimulants*) and stop abnormal bleeding (*hemostatics*) should be used.

The Chinese remedies Artemisia Ai Ye, Scutellaria Huang Qin, Amomum Sha Ren, Phellodendron Huang Bai, Dipsacus Xu Duan, Cuscuta Tu Si Zi, Psoralea Bu Gu Zhi and Eucomia Du Zhong are also known to be *fetal relaxants* that treat impending miscarriage (see HOLMES 1997).

• **Anxiety** and **worry** during pregnancy is common nowadays and can add mental and emotional stress to the body's increased physiological needs. In turn they can cause other symptoms such as insomnia, poor sleep, fatigue and so on. It is important for the mother to have her own "down time," get plenty of rest and deep relaxation, as well as nurturing support from her partner and a good social fabric of emotional support in general. A specific fear of pregnancy can be relieved, for instance, by taking natural childbirth classes.

Class 11 *nervous relaxants* that will help with these symptoms include Linden flower, Camomile flower, Melissa herb, Passionflower herb and California poppy herb. Diffusing calming and euphoric essential oils such as *Neroli, Rose* and *Jasmine* may also be highly beneficial.

Herbs Contraindicated During Pregnancy

In general, only remedies supportive (or at least noninvasive) of the gestation process should be taken on a regular basis. Remedies antagonistic to this process should not be used in tincture, herbal tea or any other form. There are two types of plant remedies that are contraindicated, i.e., generally forbidden for use, during pregnancy.

1. Remedies in the medium-strength and strong therapeutic category, which possess some toxicity that may be injurious to both the mother and fetus. Goldenseal root and Hyssop herb, for example, specifcally contain *teratogenic* (fetus injuring) compounds. Ephedra herb, Rue herb and Sassafras bark, for example are *neurotoxic*. Both types of herbs are also forbidden during breast-feeding, as the toxic compounds may contaminate breast milk.

2. *Uterine stimulants,* such as Angelica root, Dong quai root and Blue cohosh root. Their effective qualities are totally contrary to the physiological processes of pregnancy. Their active, downward-moving effects, usually signaled by a pungent or acrid taste, can precipitate miscarriage—again, especially in women with a constitutional Central Qi or *dai mai* deficiency.

There are two exceptions to this rule, however.

1. The harmless use of cooking herbs such as marjoram, thyme and sage, which in medicinal doses would act as *uterine stimulants*.

2. The second exception, as discussed above, is when pregnancy-related complications occur. In this case, mild *uterine stimulants* may be used in small amounts as part of an herbal formula *on the condition that the mother has no history of past miscarriage or uterine prolapse*. Both these point to a Central Qi and *dai mai* deficiency which (as just noted) prohibits the use of even mild *uterine stimulants* in treating minor pregnancy problems. Barring this, however, Wild yam root, Vervain herb and Lobelia root/herb, for example, could be selected for their specific ability to secure the fetus in the case of threatening miscarriage.

The following remedies are **contraindicated**

or **used with caution** for internal use during pregnancy. Those to be used cautiously during pregnancy are best given as part of a whole formula as well as short-term only.

Herbs in italics are often used in essential oil form as well as in extract form (e.g. tincture). Note that the *topical* application of these essential oils in a standard 1-2% dilution in a vegetable carrier oil is generally not contraindicated, as none are *teratogenic*.

Contraindicated Herbs

Achyranthes (Huai) Niu Xi, Adonis, Akebia Mu Tong, Alder buckthorn, Aloe, American ginseng, Angelica, Angelica Dang Gui, Arborvitae, Arisaema Tian Nan Xing, Arnica, Asarum Xi Xin, Barberry, Belamcanda She Gan, Belladonna, Biota Ce Bai Ye, Birth root, Birthwort, Black cohosh, Bloodroot, Blue cohosh, Boldo, Broom, Buckthorn, Caesalpinia Su Mu, Calamus, *Camphor*, Campsis Ling Xiao Hua, Cascara sagrada, Castor bean, Cayenne, Celandine, Citrus Zhi Shi, Coffee, Coix Yi Yi Ren, Coltsfoot, Colocynth, Corydalis Yan Hu Suo, Cotton root bark (Gossypium Mian Hua Gen), Crocus, Croton seed, Culver's root, Cyathula Chuan Niu Xi, Dianthus Qu Mai, Dong quai, Ephedra Ma Huang, *Fennel*, Feverfew, Flax seed, Garlic, Ginseng (all types), Goldenseal, Golden groundsel, Hazelwort, Hedge hyssop, Horseradish, *Hyssop*, Jaborandi, Jamaica dogwood, *Jasmine, Lavender,* Leonorus Yi Mu Cao, Licorice, Ligusticum Chuan Xiong, Linseed, Lindera Wu Yao, Madder root, {Manis Chuan Shan Jia}, *Marjoram*, Mayapple, Male fern, Milettia Ji Xue Teng, Mistletoe, Motherwort, Mugwort, Nasturtium, *Nutmeg, Onion,* Opium poppy, Oregon grape, Oshá, Papaver Ying Su Ke, Pasqueflower, Passionflower, Paeonia Mu Dan Pi, Parsley, Pennyroyal, Peruvian bark, Pleurisy root, Poke root, Pomegranate, Prunus Tao Ren, Rhubarb (Rheum Da Huang), Rosa Yue Ji Hua, Rubia Qian Cao Gen, Rue, Rye ergot, Safflower (Carthamus Hong Hua), *Sage,* Saffron, Salvia Dan Shen, Sassafras, Saussurea Xue Lian, Senna leaf, Shepherd's purse, Southernwood, Sparganium San Leng, [Talcum], Tansy, Thuja, *Thyme,* {Trogopterum Wu Ling Zhi}, Vaccaria Wang Bu Liu Xing, {Vespertilius}, *Vetiver,* Virginia snakeroot, Water eryngo, Wild carrot, Wild cherry, Wild ginger, Wild yam, *Winter savory,* Wormseed, Wormwood, Yarrow, Yellow jessamine

Herbs to be Used with Caution

Prepared aconite (all types), Agave, Artemisia Ai Ye, Asafoetida, *Basil,* Bearberry, Beet, *Black pepper,* Blue flag, Buchu, Bugleweed, Burdock, *Camomile,* Cubeb, Cassia, Catnip, Celery, Chasteberry, Chicory, Cinnamon (all types), Columba, Columbine, *Coriander,* Cornsilk, Cow parsnip, Cyperus Xiang Fu, Damiana, Dong quai, Dittany, Elecampane, Ephedra, Epimedium Yin Yang Huo, Evodia, Fenugreek, Feverfew, Ginger, Gotu cola, *Grapefruit,* Ground ivy, Helonias, Hops, Horehound, Ipecac, Juniper, Knotgrass, Lady's mantle, *Lemon,* Licorice, Lily of the valley, Lobelia, Lovage, Lycopus Ze Lan, Marigold, *Marjoram,* Marsh marigold, Mate, Meadowsweet, *Melissa,* Mercury, Milk thistle, Motherwort, *Myrrh,* Nettle, Ocotillo, Paeonia Chi Shao Yao, Papaya, Periwinkle, Plantain, Pleurisy root, Plum kernel, *Peppermint,* Peony, Peach kernel and leaf, Plantain, Polygala Yuan Zhi, Queen's root, Red clover, Red peony, *Roman camomile, Rosemary, Sandalwood,* Scabious, Schizandra Wu Wei Zi, Sea holly, Seneca snakeroot, Silverweed, Skullcap, Squill, Stavesacre, St. John's wort, Thyme, Uva ursi, Vervain, Watercress, White bryony, Wild carrot, Wood betony, Wood sorrel, Yellow dock

Before the Due Date

A small group of herbs called *childbirth preparers* (or *partus preparators*) are used to enhance the final phase of pregnancy. They prime the uterus and fetus in a non-specific way in preparation for the birthing process. Essentially *uterine restoratives,* specific functions include encouraging the fetus to come to full term and the cervix to completely mature (ripen) before true labor begins. *Childbirth preparers* can thereby specifically prevent premature delivery, as well as generally promote a problem-free delivery and postpartum time.

Childbirth preparers include Black cohosh root, Blackhaw root bark, Blue cohosh root, Cramp bark, Gravel root, Lady's mantle herb, Melissa herb, Raspberry leaf, Sea holly root and Partridgeberry herb. These may be taken in small quantities starting two or three weeks before the due date. Once again, the choice of remedy or remedies is directly related to the woman's overall condition and constitution. There isn't one all-round prelabor *uterine tonic* for all women. During Braxton-Hicks contractions it is best to stop use of any remedy.

Labor and Delivery

In the first stage of labor, the cervix dilates and effaces in preparation for the delivery. If this fails to occur and uterine contractions don't start, **prolonged pregnancy** ensues. Labor-promoting remedies, known as *parturients,* can promote the onset of labor by stimulating contractions, thereby making the first two stages of labor shorter and less tiring and painful. In summary, *parturients* may be used effectively both for prolonged pregnancy with delayed onset of labor, as well as for ineffective contractions and stalled labor (functional uterine dystocia) once labor is underway.

There are two basic types of *parturients:* the *stimulant* and the *relaxant* kind.

• *Stimulant parturients* are used for promoting labor when contractions are hypotonic, i.e., weak and ineffective. **Hypotonic contractions** can cause a prolonged, exhausting, painful and sometimes, stalled labor. *Stimulant parturients* include Angelica root, Lovage root, Blue cohosh root, Dong quai root, Birthroot, Lavender flower, Elecampane root, White horehound herb, Cotton root bark and Garlic bulb, as well as the Chinese remedies Achyranthes Niu Xi, Ligusticum Chuan Xiong, Lonicera Jin Yin Hua, Tricosanthes Tian Hua Fen and Dryopteris Guan Zhong.

• *Relaxant parturients,* on the other hand, are used for **hypertonic contractions,** i.e., when these are spasmodic and irregular, causing prolonged or painful labor, and possibly stalled labor. By relaxing the smooth muscles, *relaxant parturients* ensure full cervical dilation and therefore more effective contractions. Some also exert a useful *nervous sedative* effect which helps the mother stay as relaxed and focused as possible. Examples of these remedies are Motherwort herb, Blackhaw root bark, Black cohosh root, Cramp bark, *Lavender* flower, Melissa herb, *Sage* leaf and Vervain herb as well as the Chinese herb Ligusticum Chuan Xiong.

Certain *parturients* act by stimulating release of the hormone *oxytocin,* which strongly causes contractions. These are known as *oxytocic parturients,* and include Motherwort herb, *Sage* leaf, Birth root, Blue cohosh root, Cotton root bark, Schisandra berry (Wu Wei Zi) and Achyranthes Niu Xi.

Emotionally the mother's main signs at this stage may be **anxiety, worry** and **apprehension.** *Nervous sedatives* and *relaxants* (Classes 19 and 11, respectively) play a useful role here on both a physiological and mental/emotional level. Environmental aromatherapy with essential oils should also be considered for its effectiveness in promoting calm and focus. Useful essential oils at this stage include *Palmarosa, Geranium, Mandarin, Bergamot, Neroli, May chang* and *Lavender.*

During the third and fourth stages of labor, other remedies may be used for any complication that may arise, such as placental retention (adhered or detached), uterine subinvolution, uterine bleeding, infection, pain and exhaustion. These are treated as they arise with the remedies appropriate for such conditions. The reader is referred to the Repertory for a complete list of useful herbs.

Postpartum

Throughout the puerperium (postpartum period), which lasts six weeks or more after delivery, various symptoms are commonly seen, to a greater or lesser degree.

• **Exhaustion** and **weakness** are common postpartum. The mother should be given restoring remedies, including *nutritives* (Class 9), *restoratives* (Class 7) and *stimulants* (Class 8), all depending on the nature of her deficiency and her dominant symptoms. Bedrest, nurturing friends and much sleep are also vital for recouping strength, for ensuring proper uterine involution (thereby preventing future prolapse) and for minimizing uterine bleeding. In Chinese medical terms, the blood, fluids and Yin, the Kidney and Spleen Qi, Central Qi and *dai mai* all need tonification, while *chong* and *ren mai* need regulation. Massages with restorative essential oils in a 3-5% dilution are also very beneficial. The oils of *Grand fir, Silver fir, Pine, Black spruce, Ravintsara, Rosemary* and *Basil* are good examples of these.

• **Dehydration** with thirst in particular signal a fluid deficiency. *Demulcents* (Class 10) are chosen here, usually in combination with one or more types of *restoratives* above.

• **Hypersensitivity** and **irritability** are also common postpartum symptoms, and should be treated with gentle *nervous relaxants/restoratives* (Class 11) like Skullcap herb, Melissa leaf, Lady's slipper root and Valerian root. These can be very useful in helping the mother totally relax and so recuperate and complete the birthing experience psychologically as well as physiologically. In terms of essential oils, calming and grounding oils like Vetiver, Patchouli, Clary sage, Lavender and Marjoram should be used by room diffusion or diluted 3-5% in a massage lotion.

• **Postpartum depression** is best addressed with either *nervous relaxants* with an *antidepressant* action (Class 11), such as St. John's wort, Vervain herb (European and American types) and Melissa leaf; or with *nervous stimulants* with an *antidepressant* action (Class 20), such as Rosemary herb, Basil herb, Damiana leaf and American/Asian ginseng root. Aromatherapy is again excellent and usually fast-acting here: diffusor or tissue inhalations should be done of *euphoric* oils that stimulate thalamus enkephalins, such as *Jasmine, Ylang ylang, Rose, Clary sage, Bergamot* and *Neroli*. Citrus oils such as Grapefruit, Mandarin and Bergamot also have good mood-lifting and mood-balancing properties.

Sitzbaths to heal the perineum should also be taken for about a week, using *tissue repairers* such as Marigold flower, Bearberry leaf, Lady's mantle herb, Plantain leaf and Comfrey leaf. The essential oils of *Geranium, Lavender, Lemon* and *Cistus* (5-10 drops per session) are also very effective for promoting perineal healing.

SANGVISORBA
MINOR.

Klein Kölbleskraut.

Herbs to Astringe and Stop Discharge, Leakage and Bleeding

Herbal remedies in this class promote an astriction, bracing or tightening of tissues, thereby reducing or stopping abnormal fluid leakage and discharges. They are called *astringents* and *anti-discharge* remedies. *Astringents* are given in both acute and chronic forms of leakage and discharge, such as diarrhea, urinary leakage, leucorrhea, functional bleeding, and so on.

The Herbs that Astringe

The unusually high content in tannins or tannic acids of *astringents* imparts a dry quality; they are also known as *dry astringents*. Some of them, such as Sumac root bark and Birth root, are also sour in quality, an echo of Chinese *astringents* such as Schisandra berry (Schisandra WuWei Zi) and Japanese dogwood berry (Cornus Shan Zhu Yu).

Dry astringents operate mainly through their high content in tannins, which locally curdle or precipitate mucous membrane proteins, tighten connective tissue and reduce local hyperfunctioning. They thereby reduce any tendency to fluid leakages and discharges.

• Gentle *atsringents* include Agrimony herb, Witch hazel leaf/bark, Sage leaf, Lady's mantle herb and Eyebright herb. Many of these are also *vulneraries*.

• Strong *astringents* include Cranebill root, Oak bark, Tormentil root, Bistort root and Madder root.

Dry astringents should be distinguished from the Class 15 *mucostatic astringents*, which include Plantain leaf, Eyebright herb, White deadnettle and Ground ivy herb. These do not neccessarily work because of any tannin content, and are primarily employed for treating discharge or catarrhal conditions resulting from congested mucous-damp.

Dry astringents vary greatly not only in strength, but also in their focus of action. Consequently they are also known by their more specific function:

• *Antidiarrheals* are *astringents* that work best with **chronic diarrhea.** They include Tormentil root, Cranesbill root and Loosestrife herb. *Antidiarrheals* address both simple and infectious diarrhea, but should be reserved mainly for chronic, not acute, cases. The main syndrome they address is **intestines damp-cold,** which results from chronic intestines (Spleen) Qi deficiency.

• *Antileucorrheals* are *astringents* that focus on stopping **genital discharges.** Grapevine leaf, Yarrow herb, White deadnettle herb, Lady's mantle, Tormentil root and Kava root are good examples. This includes vaginal and seminal discharges (leucorrhea, spermatorrhea), as well as premature ejaculation, as seen in **genitourinary damp.**

• *Anti-incontinence astringents* such as Sumac root bark, Poplar bark and Horsetail herb treat **urinary incontinence** or leakage, with or without other symptoms of urinary dysfunction. These *astringents* address the syndromes **genitourinary damp** and **bladder Qi deficiency.**

• *Anhydrotics* are *astringents* that specifically stop **excessive sweating** (hyperhydrosis). They include Sage leaf, Cranesbill root and Cypress twig. They are often found in formulas addressing Qi deficiency (Class 7) and Yin deficiency (Class 10) conditions that present sweating as a major symptom.

• *Hemostatics* are *astringents* that specialize in stopping **bleeding** when taken internally. They treat a variety of hemmorrhagic conditions, such as uterine bleeding (metrorrhagia), blood in the stool (hamafecia), blood in the urine (hematuria), hemoptysis (coughing up of blood) and so on. When used externally, these herbs are called *styptics*. They include Plantain leaf, Shepherd's purse herb, Periwinkle herb, Witch hazel leaf, Lady's mantle herb Nettle herb and Cinnamon bark, as well as the essential oils of *Cistus, Geranium, Lemon* and *Rose*. *Hemostatics* generally work by shrinking capillaries, although some *hemostatics* are also *coagulant* in that they speed up blood-clotting time.

• *Antiprolapse astringents* treat intestinal, rectal or uterine prolapse specifically, and include Tormentil root and Birth root. Energetically speaking, this condition is caused by a **central Qi deficiency.**

A summary listing of remedies in this class is found in the Repertory under symptoms such as Diarrhea, Discharge, Gingivitis, Leucorrhea, etc.

Astringe and Stop Discharge, Leakage and Bleeding

Dry astringents (antidiarrheals, hemostatics, styptics)

Tormentil Root

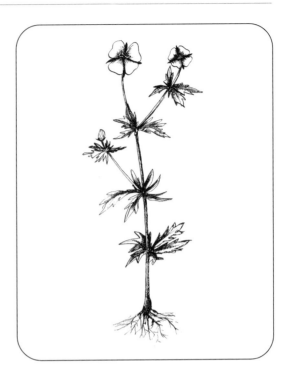

Botanical source: *Potentilla erecta* Räuschel
　　　(syn. *Potentilla tormentilla* Necker),
　　　P. anserina L. and spp. (Rosaceae)
Pharmaceutical name: Rhizoma Potentillae
Ancient names: Heptaphullon, Chrysogonon (Gr)
　　　Tormentilla, Septifolium (Lat)
Other names: a) Potentilla, Setfoil, Seven leaves,
　　　Shepherd's knot, Blood root, Ewe daisy,
　　　Biscuit (Eng and Am)
　　　Blutwurz, Ruhrwurz, Siebenfünffingerkraut,
　　　Abbiss, Retterwurzel, Birkwurz,
　　　Gewaltskraut, Heydecker (Ge)
　　　b) Cinquefoil, Silverweed/feather, Goose tansy,
　　　Wild agrimony, Marsh corn, Moss crops,
　　　Crampwort (Eng)
　　　Argentine, Cameroche (Fr)
　　　Gänsefingerkraut, Krampfkraut, Gänserich (Ge)
Part used: the rhizome

NATURE

Therapeutic category: mild remedy with minimal chronic toxicity
Constituents: catechin tannins 17-25%, tormentoside yielding termantinic acid and glucose, catechin-dimers, quinoric acid, glycoside, organic acids, resin, gum, essential oil, calcium oxalate
Effective qualities: astringent, somewhat sweet and bitter, cool, dry
　　　astringing, restoring, solidifying, stabilizing
Tropism: stomach, intestines, skin, blood
　　　Spleen, Large Intestine, Heart, Bladder, *dai* meridians
　　　Fluid, Warmth bodies
　　　decreases *kapha* and *pitta*
Ground: all krases, biotypes and constitutions

FUNCTIONS AND INDICATIONS

1　**ASTRINGES AND STOPS DISCHARGE, LEAKAGE AND BLEEDING;
　　RAISES CENTRAL QI AND RELIEVES PROLAPSE**

CHRONIC DIARRHEA in ***intestines damp-cold / heat*** conditions (esp. with alternating diarrhea and constipation)

GASTROENTERITIS, dysentery, colitis, peptic ulcer

CHRONIC LEUCORRHEA in ***genitourinary damp / -heat*** conditions

CHRONIC URINARY and GENITAL INCONTINENCE (incl. enuresis, leucorrhea, spermatorrhea, urethritis)

HEMORRHAGE from lungs, uterus, bleeding from mouth or nose, or from wounds

MENORRHAGIA, metrorrhagia

Central Qi sinking: heavy dragging feeling in lower abdomen

UTERINE and INTESTINAL PROLAPSE

HEMORRHOIDS

DIABETES (supportive)

2 **TONIFIES DIGESTIVE QI, PROMOTES ABSORPTION AND RELIEVES FATIGUE;
TONIFIES HEART QI**

stomach and intestines (Spleen) Qi deficiency: appetite loss, loose stool, fatigue, indigestion

MALABSORPTION

heart Qi deficiency: palpitations and shortness of breath worse on exertion

3 **CLEARS TOXIC HEAT AND REDUCES INFLAMMATION AND INFECTION;
ANTIDOTES POISON AND RELIEVES PAIN**

INFECTIONS of MOUTH, THROAT, GUMS and TONSILS; loose, spongy or bleeding gums (stomatitis, gingivitis, etc.)

EYE INFLAMMATION, sore eyes, pinkeye

BURNS, scalds, sunburn

heat toxin: boils, inflammations, dermatoses

INTERMITTENT FEVERS

SEPTICEMIA, venereal infections

POISONING from food or herb

HEADACHE, ARTHRITIS, GOUT, URINARY STONES

4 **PROMOTES TISSUE REPAIR AND BENEFITS THE SKIN**

WOUNDS, CUTS, abrasions, atonic ulcers, running sores

SKIN ERUPTIONS (dry or weeping, incl. dermatoses, poison oak/ivy rashes)

PREPARATION

Use: Tormentil root is used in **decoction** or **tincture** form. This remedy lends itself to the whole variety of external preparations: **mouthwashes, gargles, douches** and **suppositories** for inflammations and infections of the upper and lower mucous membrane; **washes, lotions, compresses** and **ointments** where external surfaces are involved (including for conjunctivitis and hemorrhoids). For internal conditions presenting bleeding or discharge, Tormentil root should be taken internally.

Dosage: Decoction: 6-10 g

Tincture: 1-3 g at 1:2 strength in 30% ethanol

Caution: Use cautiously in acute diarrhea. In the unlikely case that Tormentil root is used continuously for more than three weeks, it should be discontinued for a week, because of its high tannin content.

Note: Tormentil root and Silverweed root are two varieties of *Potentilla* and can be used interchangeably. However, **Silverweed root,** from *Potentilla anserina,* is also an intestinal *relaxant/spasmolytic,* and is also called Crampwort. It is especially efficacious for these digestive conditions (function 1) when accompanied by spasms and cramps.

The three types of **Five-finger grass,** *Potentilla reptans, P. canadensis* and *P. grandiflora* are considered inferior to the two species of *Potentilla* mentioned above.

NOTES

Tormentil is one of many remedies that arrives with a full history of *anti-infective* uses from the Middle Ages, when epidemics were rife. Today we know it as one of the most ideal tannin containing remedies for causing tissue astriction, and so the root is used instead for localized mucosal infec- tions. Containing condensed tannins rather than hydrolysable ones, Tormentil is absolutely safe and reliable. This remedy excels in treating **chronic infections** of the **digestive tract** involving suba- cute or chronic **inflammation.** By soothing and calming the intestines, its *antiseptic* and *anti-infla-*

mmatory actions can end both **damp-heat** and **damp-cold** intestinal conditions with discharges. Its astringency also helps genital discharges and urinary incontinence.

Tormentil root has another reason for being preferred over other *astringents* in the treatment of intestinal damp conditions. Its sweet, bitter taste gently restores and stimulates digestive functions, thereby enhancing its *astringent* action. As a *restorative astringent* therefore, Tormentil should be used for individuals with chronic constitutional **stomach and intestines (Spleen) Qi deficiency,** presenting tendencies to loose stool and fatigue— along the lines of acupuncture points Bl 20 and 38, Sp 3, St 36 and CV 12.

Scientifically speaking, this plant has more mysteries to reveal. The Dutch Renaissance botanist MATHIAS DE LOBEL (1570) reported that French physician RONDELET from Lyon had in the previous century successfully used Tormentil root for **rheumatoid arthritis.** This use survives in European country areas today. **Diabetes** is another traditional indication based on purely empirical experience. These uses, among others, suggest that at one time, and for thousands of years past, Tormentil was a very versatile, popular healing remedy.

Cranesbill Root

Botanical source: a) *Geranium maculatum* L.,
    b) *G. robertianum* L. and spp. (Geraniaceae)
Pharmaceutical name: Radix Geranii
Other names: a) Wild geranium, Crowfoot,
    Chocolate flower, Wild alum root,
    Spotted geranium (Am)
    b) Herb Robert, Bloodwort, Dragons blood (Eng)
    Herbe Robert, Bec de grue, Aiguille du berger
    (Fr)
    Ruprechtskraut, Rotlaufkraut, Kranich-schnabel
    (Ge)
Part used: the root

NATURE
Therapeutic category: mild remedy with minimal chronic toxicity
Constituents: a) tannins 10 to 25% (phlobaphenetannin), gallic acid, potassium sulfates, calcium oxalate, resin, pectin, starch, gum
Effective qualities: astringent, somewhat sweet, cool, dry
    astringing, restoring, solidifying
Tropism: stomach, intestines, urogenital organs
    Small Intestine, Large Intestine, Kidney meridians
    Fluid body

FUNCTIONS AND INDICATIONS
1   **ASTRINGES AND STOPS DISCHARGE, LEAKAGE AND BLEEDING**

    CHRONIC DIARRHEA (in *damp-cold / heat* conditions)

ENTERITIS (esp. chronic or subacute, incl. dysentery, cholera)

GENITAL INCONTINENCE, incl. leucorrhea/vaginitis, mucous cystitis, urethritis

HEMORRHAGE (passive) from nose, mouth, internal organs; copious periods (menorhagia) or intermenstrual uterine bleeding (metrorrhagia), hematuria, hemafecia

HEMORRHOIDS (including with bleeding)

DIABETES (supportive)

2   REDUCES SECRETIONS AND RELIEVES HYPERACIDITY AND PAIN

PEPTIC ULCERS from hyperacidity, heartburn

EXCESSIVE LACTATION

EXCESSIVE PERSPIRATION (day or night)

3   PROMOTES URINATION AND CLEARS HEAT

kidney fire: obstructed urination, kidney pain, diarrhea

ACUTE NEPHRITIS, ANURIA

4   PROMOTES TISSUE REPAIR

WOUNDS, sores, ulcers, pyorrhea (including with bleeding)

INDOLENT ULCERS of mouth (aphthous sores), bladder, intestines, skin

PREPARATION

Use: Cranesbill root is prepared by **decoction** and **tincture.** An **infusion** of the less astringent **Herb Robert herb** is also prepared. Good **mouthwashes, gargles** and **douches** are prepared from either herb. **Suppositories, enemas** and **pessaries** are recommended for bleeding hemorrhoids and diarrheal disorders. **Washes** and other topical preparations are applied for skin ulcers and injuries, and eczema.

Dosage: Decoction: 4-8 g

       Infusion (Herb Robert): 6-12 g

       Tincture: 1-3 ml at 1:2 strength in 30% ethanol

   Up to three times normal doses may be used in severe or acute cases.

Caution: Use with care if constipation is present, and in acute diarrhea.

Note: Herb Robert is a Cranesbill type common in Europe, and one of many in the geranium family. Along with most other Cranesbills such as **Common dovesfoot,** it may be used interchageably with American Cranesbill. It is considered somewhat less strong.

NOTES

Cranesbill root is a reliable, average strength *astringent* remedy with *mucostatic* and *hemostatic* effect. It has a long history of Native American use. Despite its *refrigerant* action in acute inflammatory conditions with damp-heat, the remedy is nevertheless more suited to **chronic mucosal infections.** Cranesbill's best application is for those presenting lingering cases of **damp** with non-suppurative **discharges** of the **urogenital** or **digestive** organs. Cranesbill treats simple damp diarrhea, for example, in much the same way as acupuncture points Sp 4 and 9, CV 9, St 25 and Bl 20.

As an *astringent* with *antisecretory* action, Cranesbill root is also specifically indicated in cases of gastric hyperacidity, peptic ulcers and hemorrhoids.

Interestingly, both Cranesbill and Herb Robert are also used in a similar way that Galla Wu Bei Zi is used in China: to stop excessive sweating and passive bleeding in deficiency conditions.

Oak Bark

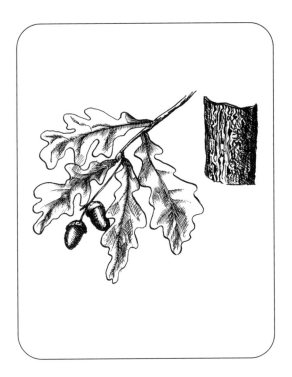

Botanical source: *Quercus alba* L., *Q. robur,*
      Q. rubra, Q. tinctoria and spp. (Fagaceae)
Pharmaceutical name: Cortex Querci
Other names: a) White oak (Am)
     b) English oak, European oak, Tanner's oak,
     Acorn tree (Eng)
     Chêne (Fr)
     Eiche, Eichenrinde (Ge)
Part used: the inner bark

NATURE

Therapeutic category: mild remedy with minimal chronic toxicity
Constituents: tannic acids 10-20% (incl. gallitannic and quercetannic acid)
Effective qualities: very astringent, cool, dry
     astringing, restoring, solidifying
Tropism: digestive, urogenital systems
     Large Intestine, Spleen, Dai meridians
Ground: all krases and biotypes for symptomatic use

FUNCTIONS AND INDICATIONS

1 **ASTRINGES AND STOPS DISCHARGE, LEAKAGE AND BLEEDING;**
  RAISES CENTRAL QI AND RELIEVES PROLAPSE

CHRONIC DIARRHEA (in ***damp-cold / heat*** conditions)

ENTERITIS (esp. chronic or subacute, incl. dysentery, cholera)

GENITAL INCONTINENCE (incl. leucorrhea, mucous cystitis, urethritis, vaginitis)

HEMORRHAGE (passive, esp. from nose, mouth, internal organs; copious periods, hematuria)

HEMORRHOIDS (including with bleeding)

DIABETES, LUNG TB (supportive)

SPLEEN ENLARGEMENT

Central Qi sinking: heavy dragging sensation in lower abdomen

PROLAPSE (intestinal, uterine, vaginal

2 **REDUCES FEVER AND SWEATING, PROMOTES URINATION AND RELIEVES FATIGUE**

REMITTENT FEVERS (Yang Ming stage)

NIGHT SWEATS (e.g. in ***Yin-deficient*** conditions); sweating feet

DEBILITY in general

3   **PROMOTES TISSUE REPAIR**

WOUNDS, sores, (atonic, including with bleeding), pyorrhea

ULCERS of mouth, bladder, intestines, skin; anal fistulas (chronic, indolent)

PREPARATION

Use: Oak bark is used in **decoction** and **tincture** form. **Baths** can be prepared with good results in deficient, weak conditions with any of the above symptoms. **Gargles, washes,** and so on, are often given for topical applications (see function 3).

Dosage: Decoction: 3-8 g

Tincture: 0.5-2.5 ml (12-60 drops) at 1:2 strength in 30% ethanol

Caution: Oak bark is contraindicated with acute diarrhea or constipation present. Avoid continuous use of this strong *astringent* remedy, and use cautiously in empty cold conditions.

NOTES

The inner bark of a variety of oak trees is used in herbal medicine for its strong *anti-discharge* and *astringent* effect. In the U.S., the white oak in particular is the type preferred. With its severe astringency Oak bark treats many types of **discharges** and **passive bleeding. Organ prolapse** arising from a sinking of the body's Central Qi, and **sweating disorders,** are two other particular conditions the bark addresses.

In the nineteenth century, White oak bark found successful use as an *astringent restorative* in weak conditions presenting debility and physical exhaustion. Those with Qi deficiency and Yin deficiency conditions presenting discharges would here seem ideal candidates for its selection.

Bistort Root

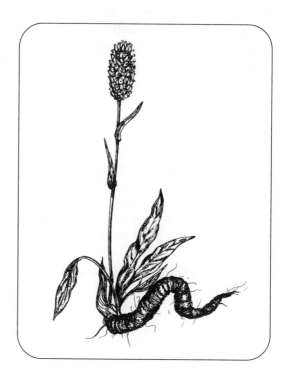

Botanical source: a) *Polygonum bistorta* L.,
b) *P. bistortoides* L. (Polygonaceae)

Pharmaceutical name: Rhizoma Polygoni bistortae

Other names: a) Snakeweed, Oderwort, Osterick, Adderwort (Eng)
b) American bistort, Western bistort,
a) Sweet dock, Dragonwort, Easter giant (Am)
Bistorte, Serpentaire femelle, Serpentaire bistordue, Langue de boeuf (Fr)
a) Wiesenknöterich, Krebswurz, Natterwurz/ -knöterich, Schlangenwurz, Lämmerzunge (Ge)

Part used: the rhizome

NATURE

Therapeutic category: mild remedy with minimal chronic toxicity

Constituents: tannins 15-20%, resin, saccharides, starch, mucilage, gallic and oxalic acids, red pigment

Effective qualities: very astringent, cool, dry
astringing, solidifying, stabilizing

Tropism: bladder, intestines; Bladder, Lung meridians; Fluid body

Ground: all krases, biotypes and constitutions

FUNCTIONS AND INDICATIONS

1 ASTRINGES AND STOPS DISCHARGE, LEAKAGE AND BLEEDING

CHRONIC DIARRHEA (from *damp-heat / cold*, including enteritis, dysentery, cholera [incl. children's])

URINARY and GENITAL INCONTINENCE (incl. enuresis, polyuria, leucorrhea, chronic urethritis)

HEMORRHAGE (passive, from all internal parts; epistaxis, hemoptysis)

MENORRHAGIA, metrorrhagia

HEMORRHOIDS (esp. with bleeding)

2 PROMOTES TISSUE REPAIR, REDUCES INFLAMMATION AND ANTIDOTES POISON

WOUNDS, ULCERS, mouth sores, weak gums

MOUTH / THROAT INFLAMMATIONS (incl. stomatitis, laryngitis), burns, scalds

INSECT STINGS and bites

PREPARATION

Use: Bistort root is used in **decoction** or **tincture** form. **Compresses, washes, gargles, suppositories, douches,** etc. are very useful for topical and mucous membrane disorders (function 2).

Dosage: Infusion: 6-12 g

Tincture: 2-4 ml at 1:2 strength in 30% ethanol

Caution: Contraindicated in acute diarrhea. Avoid in empty cold conditions and continuous use because of the very high *astringent* tannin content, and not with constipation present (barring emergencies).

Note: Great burnet root, a mild category remedy from the herbaceous *Sanguisorba officinalis* L. in the rose family, is used in virtually the same way as Bistort root; the two remedies may be interchanged. Great burnet root is especially effective at stopping bleeding of many types, and is considered a *coagulant hemostatic* and *styptic*. Its *anti-inflammatory* effect is very useful in burns and scalds. Minor uses include vomiting and eczema.

Dose: Decoction: 8-16 g. Tincture: 2-5 ml. Contraindicated in empty cold conditions.

NOTES

Bistort is a member of the dock family found in swampy areas throughout the northern hemisphere. The name refers to its bistorted root, meaning "twice-turned": The rhizome is S-shaped (see illustration) and has given rise to other evocative names such as "Snakeweed," "Adderwort" and "Dragonwort."

Bistort root is one of the simplest, safest and strongest remedies for stopping **discharges.** Like others in this section it is mainly a symptom relief remedy that may be given in the whole range of discharges, including hemorrhage. With its combination of tannins, mucilage and acids, Bistort resolves **chronic diarrhea** with blood and mucus particularly well. These would be **damp-cold** or **damp-heat intestinal** (enteritic) conditions. Not only *hemostatic* when taken internally, Bistort also makes an excellent *styptic* and *anti-inflammatory* agent when applied topically for tissue injury, bleeding and inflammation (see Preparation).

Knotgrass Herb

Botanical source: *Polygonum aviculare* L.
(Polygonaceae)
Pharmaceutical name: Herba Polygoni aviculari
Other names: Nine joints, Ninety knot, Allseed,
Bird's tongue, Red robin, Hogweed,
Cowgrass, Pigrush (Eng)
Knotweed, Birdweed, Crawlgrass, Beggarweed,
Doorweed (Am)
Renouée (des oiseaux), Sanguinaire, Herbe à
cents noeuds, Herbe des Saints-Innocents (F)
Vogelknöterich, Wegtritt, Vogelkraut,
Augenkraut, Blutkraut, Jungferntritt,
Tausendknoten, Zehrgrass (Ge)
Bian Xu (Mand); Bin Chok (Cant)
Part used: the herb

NATURE

Therapeutic category: mild remedy with minimal chronic toxicity
Constituents: anthraquinones, glucotannins, silica, essential oil, flavonoids (incl. quercetrin, rutin, avicularin), gallic/caffeic/oxalix/silicic/chlorogenic acids, mucilage, catechol, glucose, saccharides
Effective qualities: astringent, bitter, cold dry
astringing, solidifying, calming, stimulating
Tropism: lungs, kidneys, bladder, intestines
Bladder, Lung meridians
Fluid, Air bodies
Ground: all krases, biotypes and constitutions

FUNCTIONS AND INDICATIONS

1 **ASTRINGES AND STOPS DISCHARGE, LEAKAGE AND BLEEDING; RESTORES THE LUNGS**

DIARRHEA (due to *damp-heat / cold,* esp. chronic, including enteritis, dysentery)

GENITAL INCONTINENCE (incl. leucorrhea, chronic urethritis, cystitis)

HEMORRHAGE (passive, from all internal parts, incl. hemoptysis, bleeding hemorrhoids, hematuria, metrorrhagia)

DIABETES (supportive)

LUNG TB

2 **PROMOTES URINATION, RESOLVES TOXICOSIS AND DISSOLVES STONES; CLEARS DAMP HEAT, RELIEVES ITCHING AND HARMONIZES URINATION**

kidney Qi stagnation with *metabolic toxicosis:* skin rashes, painful urination, bladder infections

CHRONIC ARTHRITIS, gout, rheumatism

ALBUMINURIA

URINARY STONES, GALLSTONES

ANURIA, OLIGURIA

skin wind-damp: skin eruptions, wet sores, itching

WEEPING ECZEMA with PRURITUS

801

PRURITUS (dermal, vaginal)
bladder damp-heat: painful, burning, scanty urination, thirst
ACUTE URINARY INFECTIONS with DYSURIA

3   KILLS PARASITES AND PROMOTES TISSUE REPAIR

PARASITES (incl. tapeworm, hookworm, pinworm, roundworm; scabies, tinea, trichomonas vaginalis)
VENEREAL ULCERS with PRURITUS

PREPARATION

Use: Knotgrass herb is used in **infusion** or **tincture** form. **Washes, compresses, douches, sponges**, etc. are used for itching, ulcerative and parasitic skin conditions.

Dosage: Infusion: 8-16 g
  Tincture: 2-4 ml at 1:3 strength in 35% ethanol

Caution: Use cautiously in difficult urination arising from abdominal weakness, and in empty cold.
  Contraindicated during pregnancy due to a possible *abortifacient* action.

NOTES

A common and worldwide member of the valuable dock family, Knotgrass is used in both Western and Oriental herbal medicine as a *refrigerant astringent* with a particular tropism for the urinary tract.

As a simple *astringent* and *hemostatic* remedy, Knotgrass herb is useful for controlling a variety of **discharges** and **hemorrhages.** When used under the condition of acute urinary tract infections, these actions operate together with an excellent *diuretic* effect to clear **damp-heat** in the **lower warmer.** Painful, scanty and obstructed urination here are the key symptoms to the remedy's successful use. In this connection note Knotgrass' content in flavo-noids, acids and tannins.

Resolvent detoxicant properties in Knotgrass herb have been utilized in the Western tradition for millenniums, particularly for **urinary** and **gallstones** (like Lysimachia Jin Qian Cao in China), and for chronic arthritic and eczematous conditions. Note the operative anthraquinones and flavonoids, in this connection. Itching skin eruptions with oozing vesicles caused by **wind-damp** in the **skin** is here the most classic indication.

Knotgrass herb is traditionally also given as a *broad-spectrum antiparasitic* for both internal and topical parasites.

Canada Fleabane Herb

Botanical source: *Erigeron canadensis* L.
   (Asteraceae/Compositae)
Pharmaceutical name: Herba Erigerontis
Other names: Coltstail, Prideweed, Scabious
   [Horseweed, Butterweed] (Am)
   Vergerette du Canada (Fr)
   Kanadisches Berufskraut, Hexenbesen,
   Wilder Hanf (Ge)
Part used: the herb

NATURE

Therapeutic category: mild remedy with minimal chronic toxicity
Constituents: bitter, tannic and gallic acids, esential oil, flavonoids, choline
Effective qualities: somewhat astringent, bitter and sour, cool, dry
   astringing, solidifying, stabilizing, simulating, relaxing
Tropism: lungs, kidneys, bladder, intestines, nerves
   Spleen, Large Intestines, Bladder, Lung, Dai meridians
   Fluid, Air bodies
Ground: all krases, biotypes and constitutions

FUNCTIONS AND INDICATIONS

1 **ASTRINGES AND STOPS DISCHARGE, LEAKAGE AND BLEEDING;**
   RAISES CENTRAL QI AND RELIEVES PROLAPSE

   DIARRHEA (due to ***damp-heat / cold,*** esp. chronic, including enteritis, dysentery, cholera [incl. children's])

   GENITAL INCONTINENCE (incl. leucorrhea, chronic urethritis, cystitis, gonorrhea)

   PASSIVE HEMORRHAGE from all internal parts; hemoptysis

   UTERINE BLEEDING, menorrhagia, postpartum hemorrhage

   Central Qi sinking: heavy dragging sensation in lower abdomen

   PROLAPSE of uterus, intestines or rectum

   DIABETES (supportive)

2 **PROMOTES URINATION, RESOLVES TOXICOSIS AND DISSOLVES STONES**

   kidney Qi stagnation with ***general toxicosis:*** cystitis, skin rashes, painful urination

   URIC ACID DIATHESIS

   CHRONIC ARTHRITIS, gout, rheumatism

   NEPHROSIS, chronic nephritis, albuminuria

   DYSURIA, URINARY STONES

3 PROMOTES EXPECTORATION, RESOLVES PHLEGM AND OPENS THE CHEST

lung phlegm-damp: coughing copious white phlegm, wheezing, cold extremities, fatigue

CHRONIC BRONCHITIS

4 REGULATES THE QI, RELAXES CONSTRAINT AND STOPS SPASMS

Qi constraint: unrest, irritability, intestinal colic

SPASTIC NEUROGENIC BLADDER

PREPARATION

Use: Canada fleabane herb is used in **infusion** or **tincture** form. Sponges, pessaries, **douches, supposi-tories** and **enemas** may be prepared for vaginal and intestinal discharges. If available, the **essential oil** may be used internally only or, equally good, can also be **massaged** topically with a carrier oil.

Dosage: Infusion: 4-10 g

Tincture: 2-4 ml at 1:3 strength in 30% ethanol

Essential oil: 4-6 drops in a gel cap topped with some olive oil. Do not take more often than once an hour in acute situations.

Caution: None

Note: A similar plant used interchangeably with Canada fleabane up to the eigteenth and nineteenth centuries is **Fleawort herb,** *Pulicaria dysenterica* L. (Compositae). It was known as Kunuza in Greek, Conyza, Cunilago, Pulicaria, etc. in Latin; Fleabane or Cammock in English; Herbe des puces in French; and Flohkraut, Dürrwurz, Hundsauge and Ruhrkraut in German. See the Notes for further uses.

NOTES

The various Fleabanes and the Europen fleawort *(Pulicaria dysenterica)* share the same uses. Nature's permutations of plants and therapeutic effects are highly playful. Whereas the same plant often finds different uses on different continents (e.g., Cleavers, Shepherd's purse, Raspberry), here we have an example of the reverse: two different plants from different continents with identical uses. It proves that the natural forces that engender plant life care little about botanical subdividions of the phyla. They create similar and identical consti-tuents, qualities and effects within one family wherever and whenever they please, regardless of tribe, genus and species subdivisions. These bio-energies, being active and configurative and there-fore Yang by nature, latch on to any susceptible plant family or class. Because the latter are structive and Yin they fulfill their creative fantasies through plant types. Humans unconsciously join in this experiment by using different plants in exactly the same way, going as far as giving them similar names—as in the case of Fleabane and Fleawort.

Canada fleabane herb is not only a gentle ast-ringent, but also a fairly good *hemostatic* and *ute-rine decongestant.* When used in gynecology for heavy periods and intermenstrual bleeding it para-llels acupuncture points Sp 1, 8 and 10, Li 2 and St 29. Hemorrhages and discharges of many kinds are controlled by Fleabane's use. In the case of severe infection and inflammation, Canada Flea-bane should be reinforced by more *antiseptic* and *cooling* remedies that clear damp-heat or toxic heat, as needed. For uterine bleeding it is best to combine it with other *hemostatics* such as Shep-herd's purse herb, Greater periwinkle herb, Lady's mantle herb and Nettle herb.

Fleawort herb, on the other hand, was espou-sed by Italian natural physician PIERANDREA MATTIOLI (1611). Along with Goldenrod herb, he considered it an important *restorative* and *stimu-lant* to urogenital functions. He prescribed the herb for patients with chronic kidney Qi deficiency displaying painful urination and urinary stones, and for women with delayed or stopped menstruation.

Both Fleabanes are also mild *nervous relax-ants,* a clear advantage nowadays.

Sumac Root Bark

Botanical source: *Rhus glabra* L. (Anacardiaceae)
Pharmacological name: Cortex radicis Rhudis
Ancient names: Rhous (Gr)
      Rhus, Coggyria (Lat)
Other names: Purple/Smooth/Mountain/Upland/
      Scarlet/Sleek sumac (Am)
      Sumac, Pincentroyale (Fr)
      Sumach, Gerberbaum, Galgel (Ge)
Part used: the root bark; also the bark

NATURE

Therapeutic category: mild remedy with minimal chronic toxicity
Constituents: gallotannic acid, calcium bimalate, fixed oil, resin, gum, starch
Effective qualities: somewhat astringent and sour, cold, dry
      astringing, restoring, stabilizing, solidifying
Tropism: urogenital organs, lungs, throat
      Kidney, Bladder, Lung meridians; Fluid body
Ground: all krases, biotypes and constitutions

FUNCTIONS AND INDICATIONS

1   **ASTRINGES AND STOPS DISCHARGE, LEAKAGE AND BLEEDING;**
    STOPS SWEATING

    CHRONIC DIARRHEA (with *damp-cold / heat*, incl. enteritis, dysentery)

    GENITAL INCONTINENCE (incl. leucorrhea, gonorrhea (*damp-cold / heat*)

    PASSIVE HEMORRHAGE from uterus, lungs

    NIGHT SWEATS in deficiency conditions

2   **TONIFIES URINARY QI, HARMONIZES URINATION AND RELIEVES INCONTINENCE**

    genitourinary (Kidney) Qi deficiency: dripping or frequent scanty urination

    URINARY INCONTINENCE (incl. polyuria, enuresis; esp. in diabetes and interstitial nephritis)

3   **PROMOTES TISSUE REPAIR AND BENEFITS THE THROAT AND SKIN**

    SORE THROAT, throat ulcers with fetid secretions,

    TISSUE FLABBINESS OR ULCERATION, wet skin rashes

    SKIN and MOUTH ULCERS, ulcerative stomatitis

    BLEEDING or SPONGY GUMS

PREPARATION

Use: The root bark is the best part of the Sumac tree to use for this remedy. Whether the root bark, tree bark or berry is used (the last two are weaker), the **decoction, tincture** or **powder** forms are best. **Gargles, mouthwashes, swabs** and **compresses** are used where a good *astringent* effect is required.

Dosage: Decoction: 6-12 g

       Tincture: 1-3 ml at 1:2 strength in 30% ethanol

       Powder: 2-4 g

Caution: Contraindicated in acute diarrhea and empty cold conditions.

Note: Sumac berry is sour, astringent, dry, cold in quality and posesses *antipyretic, astringent* and *vulnerary* actions. The decoction and tincture mainly treat hot and weak conditions such as **bladder damp-heat** presenting dripping urination and fever, and **intestines damp-heat** with diarrhea. Topical preparations are prepared for mouth and throat ulcers, and for ringworm. Dosages: as for the root bark above.

NOTES

Sumac root bark is one of numerous botanicals from the Native American repertoire that was adopted by the U.S. pharmacopoeia during the nineteenth century. Its moderating effect on urination is specific and outstanding in its function as an herb that causes astriction. This is underpinned by a *restorative* influence on bladder tone, resulting in greater urinary control. Sumac root bark is more than an excellent adjunct for reinforcing other remedies in this class in a variety of acute discharge conditions. It also achieves specific *anti-incontinence* results in treating **genitourinary (Kidney) Qi deficiency.** This astringent, sour and dry remedy achieves the same results as do Rubus Fu Pen Zi and Euryale Qian Shi, or as combined acupuncture points Sp 6, Bl 28, St 28 and CV 3.

Raspberry Leaf

Botanical source: *Rubus idaeus* L., *R. strigosus*

       Michaux (Rosaceae)

Pharmaceutical name: Folium Rubi idaei

Ancient names: Batos idaia (Gr)

       Frambones, Framboses (Lat)

Other names: Red raspberry, Hineberry, Roiseberry,

       Rasp (Eng)

       Framboisier (Fr)

       Himbeer, Bocksbeer, Harbeere, Moolbeere (Ge)

Part used: the leaf

NATURE

Therapeutic category: mild remedy with minimal chronic toxicity

Constituents: tannin with gallic and ellager acids, bernstein and lactic acid, ferric citrate, alkaloid (fragarine), flavone farfarin, vitamins C, A, calcium, phosphorus, iron, trace minerals

Effective qualities: astringent, cool, dry

       restoring, astringing, stimulating

Tropism: uterus, stomach, intestines, lungs; Stomach, Lung, Bladder, *chong, ren, dai* meridians; Air body

Ground: all for symptomatic use

FUNCTIONS AND INDICATIONS

1 **ASTRINGES, RESOLVES MUCOUS-DAMP AND STOPS DISCHARGE AND BLEEDING**

DIARRHEA (mild, esp. of infants)

LEUCORRHEA in all conditions

MILD HEMORRHAGES or menorrhagia in *Qi deficiency* conditions

UTERINE PROLAPSE from *Central Qi deficiency*

2 **TONIFIES REPRODUCTIVE QI, RESTORES THE UTERUS AND HARMONIZES MENSTRUATION, PREGNANCY AND DELIVERY;**
 PREVENTS MISCARRIAGE, REDUCES VOMITING AND BLEEDING, AND PROMOTES LACTATION

uterus Qi deficiency / stagnation: delayed, scanty, difficult, painful periods

DYSMENORRHEA

PROPHYLACTIC and REMEDIAL during the WHOLE of PREGNANCY

HABITUAL MISCARRIAGE

MORNING SICKNESS

POSTPARTUM BLEEDING and SWELLING

INSUFFICIENT LACTATION, poor quality milk

3 **PROMOTES AND HARMONIZES URINATION, AND RELIEVES IRRITATION**

DIFFICULT or SCANTY URINATION

BLADDER or PROSTATE IRRITATION

4 **STIMULATES AND HARMONIZES DIGESTION**

stomach Qi stagnation (damp-heat): indigestion, sour regurgitation, diarrhea or constipation

MILD CONSTIPATION

ABDOMINAL PAIN

5 **REDUCES INFLAMMATION AND PROMOTES TISSUE REPAIR;**
 BENEFITS THE LUNGS AND THROAT

EYE, GUM, MOUTH and THROAT INFLAMMATIONS

WOUNDS, burns, skin eruptions

SPONGY GUMS, mouth ulcers

HOARSENESS, voice loss

BRONCHITIS in all conditions

PREPARATION

Use: Raspberry leaf is prepared by **long infusion** and **tincture.** The long infusion is versatile and suited to mild digestive conditions from the simplest indigestion to diarrhea and constipation—ideal for children and babies. The infusion or tincture are used for **gargles,** as a **mouthwash, eyewash, vaginal sponge, douche** or **sitzbath** where inflammation, swelling and discharge are present.

During pregnancy Raspberry leaf tea may be used as a substitute for all liquid intake, with cumulative benefits for the uterus and the upcoming birth. In the unlikely event that Raspberry leaf should cause or present with excessive Braxton Hicks contractions, take a day's break and then reduce the dose to 1-2 cups of Raspberry leaf tea per day.

Dosage: Long infusion: 8-14 g

Tincture: 2-4 ml at 1:3 strength in 25% ethanol

Caution: None

Note: Raspberry root may be used for a stronger *astringent* and *hemostatic* effect (function 1 only) that is comparable to Blackberry root bark and Strawberry root (see below).

NOTES

Raspberry leaf is a good example of the principle, basic to herbal medicine, that to be effective, remedies need not be strong. This remedy, in fact, exhibits a long-lasting range of effects. One of its strength is the *restorative* and *harmonizing* effects on uterine functions. These are unique: unlike other remedies, Raspberry actually helps build as well as restore uterine tissue. As such, it is considered a *uterus trophorestorative* with a wide *nutritive* content. The alkaloid fragarine focuses attention on the pelvic and, specifically, on the uterine muscles.

As a result, Raspberry leaf is one of the few remedies that can be strongly recommended during the whole of pregnancy (see also Cl. 17). The herb enhances every aspect of gestation and the birthing process. The possibility for miscarriage and hemo-rrhage is reduced, morning sickness is moderated, labor and afterbirth pain is lessened, and delivery is made easier and freer of complications. Like Black haw bark and Gravel root, Raspberry leaf is an important preventive *uterine restorative* remedy for pregnancy.

Raspberry leaf should also be seen as a gentle, all-purpose domestic digestive remedy. It can relieve both mild diarrhea and constipation, as well as colic. Its mildly cool, astringent nature treats the initial stages of infants' diarrhea, before Agrimony herb or Bearberry leaf are called in. Like other fruit-bearing remedies in the rose family, Raspberry leaf is a wide-spectrum *astringent anti-discharge* remedy when prompt and gentle symptom relief is all that's needed.

Blackberry Leaf

Botanical source: *Rubus fruticosus* L., *R. villosus* Aiton and spp. (Rosaceae)
Pharmaceutical name: Folium Rubi fruticosi
Ancient names: Batos (Gr)
    Mora rubi, Vepres, Dumus (Lat)
Other names: Bramble, Black brier, Brummel-kites, Thevethorn (Eng)
    Ronce, Mûrier, Mûrier sauvage/des haies (Fr)
    Brombeere, Heckenbeere, More (Ge)
Part used: the leaf

NOTES

Therapeutic category: mild remedy with minimal chronic toxicity
Constituents: tannin, tannic/citric/malic/succinic/oxalic/lactic acids, methylsalicylate, glucoside, resin, fixed oils, wax, pectin, potassium, calcium sulphate, traces essential oil, trace minerals
Effective qualities: astringent, cool, dry
    astringing. restoring, dissolving
Tropism: stomach, intestines, lungs, throat, urogenital tract
    Lung, Bladder, Large Intestine, *chong, ren* meridians
    Warmth, Fluid bodies
Ground: all krases, biotypes and constitutions

FUNCTIONS AND INDICATIONS

1 **ASTRINGES AND STOPS DISCHARGE AND BLEEDING**

DIARRHEA (with *damp-heat / cold,* incl. enteritis, children's cholera)

LEUCORRHEA and prostate discharge in *damp* conditions

PASSIVE HEMORRHAGE from urinary tract, intestines, uterus; hemoptysis, metrorrhagia, epistaxis

HEMORRHOIDS (esp. with bleeding)

DIABETES (supportive)

2 **PROMOTES URINATON, RELIEVES IRRITATION AND DISSOLVES STONES; RESOLVES VISCOUS PHLEGM**

OLIGURIA, ANURIA

URINARY IRRITATION in all conditions (esp. with gout)

URINARY STONES

VISCOUS SPUTUM (incl. with blood)

3 **TONIFIES REPRODUCTIVE QI, STRENGTHENS THE UTERUS AND ENHANCES DELIVERY**

PROPHYLACTIC and REMEDIAL during the WHOLE of PREGNANCY and in LABOR and DELIVERY

4 **PROMOTES TISSUE REPAIR, REDUCES INFLAMMATION AND BENEFITS THE THROAT**

WOUNDS, SORES, ulcers; animal bites (esp. chronic)

THROAT, MOUTH, GUM and SKIN INFLAMMATIONS, infections and lesions; toothache

VOICE LOSS

PREPARATION

Use: Blackberry leaf **infusion** and **tincture** are used. This herb makes an ideal **gargle** and **mouthwash** for painful, hot, swollen and bleeding conditions of the mouth, gums and throat. **Swabs** and **compresses** are used on external surfaces. **Douches** and **enemas** are appropriate in conditions presenting discharges.

The leaf infusion may be used throughout pregnancy (function 4), but is considered weaker in effect than Respberry leaf.

Blackberry root bark is more *astringent* and *hemostatic* than the leaf, and should be **decocted** or **tinctured.** The root bark is traditionally more used in the U.S. than in Europe. Unlike the leaf, howewer, the root bark has not been used to perform functions 2, 3 and 4 above.

Dosage: Long infusion: 6-10 g

Tincture: 2-4 ml at 1:3 strength in 30% ethanol

Caution: To avoid constipation, discontinue once symptoms clear. If used preventively during pregnancy to tone the uterus, take frequent breaks to avoid constipation.

Note: Wild strawberry leaf and root, *Fragaria vesca* L., can be used interchangeably with Blackberry leaf and root. Both share *astringent, mucostatic* and *hemostatic* properties (functions 1 and 5 above). Strawberry leaf, however, is also a good *diuretic detoxicant* useful in rheumatic disorders, gout, urinary gravel and stones, gout, urinary irritation, hematuria and kidney colic. Other traditionl uses include liver congestion, jaundice and asthma. The leaves contain a series of organic acids, silicic acid, tannin, mucilage, saccharides, calcium, iron, trace minerals and some essential oil. Their primary qualities are somewhat bitter, astringent, dry and cool. **Wild strawberry root** is better than the leaf as an *antidiarrheal, hemostatic* and *styptic* remedy for severe diarrhea and internal or local bleeding.

Avens root is a remedy in the mild category prepared from *Geum rivale* L. (Water avens or Purple avens), *G. virginiana* (also known as Throat root and Chocolate root), *G. triflorum* (Three-flower avens) and many other North American and European species. It is another *astringent* remedy from the rose family with extensive use for stopping discharges. In addition to tannins, the root contains resins; the European *G. urbanum* also contains essential oils (including the phenol eugenol).

Astringent, bitter, dry and cool in quality, Avens root treats diarrhea arising from gastroenteritis or dysentery (especially chronic), including with bloody stool present. Its additional *hemostatic,* general *restorative* and somewhat *diaphoretic* actions make it particularly useful in lung TB with debility, night sweats and coughing up of blood. Hemorrhages and vaginal discharges in general respond well to it. In the past the remedy was also given in intermittent fevers (*shao yin* stage) with debility.

G. urbanum is additionally *analgesic* and is used internally and topically for headache, toothache, abdominal pain and painful outer eye infections, etc. **Washes** and **compresses** are applied to painful wounds, sores, conjunctivitis and such like. **Dose:** Decoction: 5-10 g. Tincture: 2-4 ml.

NOTES

Being fairly gentle yet effective, as an internal remedy Blackberry leaf is ideal for treating mild conditions, children and infants. The herb focuses on treating symptoms rather than syndromes. Its dry, astringent quality can relieve symptoms of mucus discharge as effectively as other remedies in this section, and can produce good *hemostatic* effect, especially for blood in the sputum. With its overriding tannin and acids content, Blackberry is also an excellent *anti-inflammatory* for throat, tonsil, gum and skin conditions in particular. Moreover, the remedy also tones the mucosal surfaces that it touches, thereby resolving mucus and thereby preventing a recurrence of inflammation and catarrh. In short, Blackberry leaf is a *mucostatic (anticatarrhal) astringent.*

Because of its tropism for the urinary and respiratory tracts, Blackberry leaf has shown success in treating obstructed urination (from febrile infections, for example) and helping with urinary stones. Second, it has a *mucolytic expectorant* action for treating bronchial sputum of the viscous kind.

Greater Periwinkle Herb

Botanical source: a) *Vinca major* L. (Apocynaceae)
Other names: Grande pervenche, Violette de
   sorcier (Fr), Sinngrün (Ge), Pervinca (Sp)
Part used: the herb

Therapeutic category: mild remedy w. no toxicity
Constituents: indole alkaloids (incl. majdine, reserpinine, ervine, majoridine), tannins
Effective qualities: somewhat bitter and pungent

Notes On Its Functions and Indications

Originally from southern Europe, the Greater periwinkle is a reliable *astringent* and *mucous decongestant* herb with a siginificant *hemostatic* action, especially (but not solely) for **menorrhagia** and **metrorrhagia.** It will also stop leakage and discharge from the digestive and urogenital organs and is also used in formulas for diarrhea, leucorrhea and urinary leakage, including enuresis. Topical preparations have been applied to hemorrhoids, ulcers and dermatitis, and gargles for sore throat and tonsillitis. Fresh Periwinkle **fower syrup** is a nice *laxative* in occasional constipation.

Dosage: Infusion: 8-30g
     Tincture: 2-5 ml at 1:3 strength in 30% eth.
Caution: None within these dosage ranges
Note: The **Lesser periwinkle,** *Vinca minor* L., has somewhat different applications. The herb and root are both employed, which contain the alkaloid vincamine as well as tannins. This bitter, pungent remedy is used as a *restorative* for anemia and anorexia, and as a pungent *carminative* for damp intestinal conditions with dyspeptic flatulence, indigestion and belching. Its *astringent* action will treat discharges and hemorrhage, especially diarrhea, leucorrhea and hemoptysis. Lesser periwinkle is also *hypotensive* in hypertension (an African medicine use) and *antidiabetic.* Like Ginkgo leaf, this remedy also mildly increases cerebral circulation (an action of vincamine), indicating use for loss of mental focus and memory, dizziness, headache, tinnitus, peripheral arterial deficiency and so on.

Dosage for the infusion and tincture: as for Greater periwinkle. Contraindicated in brain tumors.

Herbs to Calm the Mind and Relieve Anxiety

Herbal remedies that calm the mind are used to treat conditions presenting anxiety and agitation, and are called *nervous sedatives*. Symptoms such as anxiety, insomnia, restlessness, agitation and nightmares are the manifestations of an agitated mind (spirit). In Western terms they are classified as anxiety disorders, but may also be seen in ADHD and panic disorder, for instance. Physiologically these conditions usually involve neuroendocrine dysfunctions.

Although *nervous sedatives* (including *anxiolytics*) in this section may be used on their own for acute symptom relief, they should also be used in the context of formulas that address a systemic imbalance, or pattern of disharmony, giving rise to anxiety, agitation or any other of these symptoms.

The Nature, Dynamics and Treatment of Mind Agitation and Anxiety

Mind agitation is one of the three types of pathological mind conditions that Chinese medicine recognizes. Here the mind becomes restless, agitated and floating, which is a condition of mental hyperfunctioning. In addition to the above mental symptoms, there is often an emotional component that feeds it. This consists mainly of:
• Hyper-emotivity, e.g. excessive anger, fear or joy
• Intense emotions of all types
• Hypermotivation in general

The syndromes involved in mind agitation are various, and are generally divided into hypo- and hyper-functioning types.
• **Mind agitation with hypofunctioning** creates constrained Qi types of syndromes that are essentially tense and weak conditions (see Class 11). In Chinese medicine they also include the patterns of Heart Blood deficiency and Heart Yin deficiency.
• **Mind agitation with hyperfunctioning** creates floating Yang types of syndromes, which are essentially hot and tense types of conditions (see Class 12). In Chinese medicine they include Heart/Liver/Kidney fire (including empty heat).

Mind agitation is physiologically underpinned by an array of possible processes. These include neurotransmitter anomalies (including dopamine and glutamate excess, serotonin and GABA insufficiency, and endorphin insufficiency); prostaglandin imbalance; hormonal excesses (especially thyroidal, pituitary, andrenocortical/-medullary and gonadal hormones); and autonomic nervous imbalance. These usually need to be addressed separately with herbs and nutrition.

The origins of mind agitation include acute mental, emotional or physical trauma; high fever; sudden physical exertion or exercise; heating foods and drinks, including spices and alcohol; and limited use of drugs, including nicotine, caffeine, cannabis, cocaine, and so on.

Mind agitation can therefore be treated in two ways. First, as a symptom with the use of *nervous sedative* herbs in general. Second, as a systemic condition that is differentiated into the hyper- and hypo-functioning types of syndromes above.

The Herbs that Calm the Mind

In modern herbal medicine, herbs that address anxiety and agitation tend to be referred to as *sedatives* and *hypnotics*. Modern drug pharmacology, moreover, defines a variety of sedative actions on the central nervous system, such as *depressant, hypnotic, soporific, tranquilizing, anxiolytic, anticonvulsant* and so on. Herbal remedies, too, convey these actions, but with less definition. It is therefore ultimately more useful to categorize them by the treatment strategy they embody.

*Nervous sedative*s owe their effect mainly to their content in alkaloids and essential oils, both of which variously affect neuroendocrine functions (see also the Class 11 and16 remedies).

Relax Constraint and Calm the Mind
Nervous sedatives and relaxants (anxiolytics)

Herbs of this type treat mind agitation and anxiety seen in the context of **Qi constraint** syndromes.

This can include the Chinese medicine patterns Heart Yin deficiency and Heart Blood deficiency. The key symptoms here are nervous tension, insomnia, anxiety and, in more chronic conditions, depression. This is often seen in constrained Qi stemming from overwork, chronic physical or emotional stress or illness, or simply from constitutional factors.

Remedies include gentle *nervous sedatives* that are also general *relaxants*, and are also found in Class 11. Their sedative effect is relatively mild compared to that of drugs, but cumulatively they exert deep relaxation and thereby relief from symptoms. They include Camomile flower, Melissa leaf, Lavender flower, Passionflower herb, Marjoram herb, Linden flower, Wild lettuce leaf, California poppy root and herb, Valerian root and Kava root. Equivalent Chinese herbs include Polygonatum Yu Zhu (Fragrant Solomon's seal root) and Zizyphus Suan Zao Ren (Wild jujube seed).

In chronic Qi constraint with deficiency present, depression becomes a key symptom. Then *nervous restorative relaxants* should be chosen (p. 504), such as Skullcap herb, St. John's wort herb, Sage leaf, Vervain herb, Pasqueflower root/herb and Milky oat berry. These *nervous trophorestoratives* provide badly-needed nutritive support to the nervous system in chronic anxiety or agitation as they do in depressive conditions.

In both the traditional European and Chinese tradition, certain mineral remedies were, and still are, commonly used for their strong *neurocardiac sedative* effects. Magnetitum Ci Shi (Magnetite), Ostrea Mu Li (Oyster shell) and Stegodon Long Gu (Dragon bone) are among these.

Clear Heat and Calm the Mind
Cooling nervous sedatives (depressant hynotics)

Herbs of this type treat mind agitation and anxiety in the context of heat conditions, including Liver/Heart/Kidney fire in Chinese medicine, which also include actual fever. The main symptoms are the same as before, but are more intense, with irritability and restlessness becoming more prominent, as well as a more rapid, forceful or flooding pulse.

Nervous sedatives/hypnotics with bitter, cold, sinking qualities can treat mind agitation arising from heat. They include *refrigerant* (heat-clearing) herbs from this class and from Class 12, including Hops flower, Melilot herb, Wild lettuce leaf and Mistletoe herb. The most effective, however,

especially in the case of fever with mental agitation, are the strong-category remedies: Yellow jessamine herb, Black hellebore root, Bryony root and Henbane herb. These contain alkaloids active in toxic as well as *depressant* effects and should only be used with the neccessary skills of professional herbal medicine. Very precise dosing and preparation methods are as crucial when using these plants as is exact therapeutic knowledge itself.

Cleverly, Chinese medicine bypasses the use of toxic plants for causing nervous sedation and clearing heat by turning to animal products such as Bubalus Shui Niu Jiao (Water buffalo horn). These, too, may be used as long as the animals themselves remain safe from the danger of cruelty and depopulation (which is no longer the case with the rhinoceros, for example).

Treatment Considerations
Because herbs that calm the mind mainly address symptoms (the branch of a condition), they are mainly useful for acute conditions of mind agitation and as such are used short-term. When applied to treat more chronic conditions, however, they should be combined with other herbs to treat the general syndrome presenting.

Nervous sedatives are then routinely combined as follows:
• With *relaxants* (Class 11) for treating constrained Qi conditions with pronounced anxiety, palpitations and various types of pain;
• With *refrigerants* (Class 12) for treating hot conditions with irritability and agitation;
• With *restoratives* and *nutritives* (Classes 7 and 9) for treating chronic deficiency conditions involving anxiety and insomnia;
• With *spasmolytics* (Class 21) for treating tremors, spasms and convulsions;
• With *nervous trophorestoratives* (p. 504) in general when the condition is longstanding, and especially with pronounced anxiety as main symptom.
• Caution should be used if *nervous sedatives* are used in conjunction with medication such as sleeping pills, etc. The two types of sedatives will potentiate each other so that usually less of the Western drug need actually be used to achieve the same effect.

A summary of remedies in this class is found in the Repertory under Anxiety, Delirium, Insomnia and Nervous tension.

Calm the Mind and Relieve Anxiety

Nervous sedatives (depressant hypnotics, neurocardiac sedatives, anxiolytics)

Passionflower Herb

Botanical source: *Passiflora incarnata* L., *P. lutea* L.
and spp. (Passifloraceae)
Pharmaceutical name: Herba Passiflorae
Other names: Passion vine, Love in a mist, Maypop,
Apricot vine (Am)
Passiflore, Fleur de la passion (Fr)
Passionsblume, Leiden Christi,
Muttergottessternli (Ge)
Part used: the herb

NATURE
Therapeutic category: medium-strength remedy with moderate chronic toxicity
Constituents: indole alkaloids (passiflorine, harman, harmine, harmaline, harmol, harmalol), flavonoids, cyanogenic glycoside (gynocardin), sterols, catechol, gum, pectin, saccharides, minerals (incl. iron, calcium, phosphorus)
Effective qualities: somewhat bitter, bland, cool, dry
calming, relaxing, sinking
Tropism: cardiovascular and nervous system, kidneys, lungs
Heart, Liver, Lung meridians
Air, Warmth bodies
Ground: Choleric krasis
Industrious/Tai Yang and Tough/Shao Yang biotypes; Hematogenic/Sulphuric constitution

FUNCTIONS AND INDICATIONS
1   **SINKS THE YANG, CALMS THE MIND, RELIEVES ANXIETY AND PROMOTES REST**
floating Yang (Yang excess): head congestion, headache, muscle tension, sleep loss, irritability
INSOMNIA, restlessness, agitation (esp. in children, elderly, convalescents, during menopause,
from physical or mental causes)
heart Qi constraint / Yin deficiency: palpitations, irritability, anxiety, restless sleep
STRESS-RELATED CONDITIONS, ANXIETY, palpitations from shock or excitement
DIARRHEA (esp. from stress)
HYPERTENSION

2 **RELAXES CONSTRAINT AND RELIEVES PAIN;**
CLEARS INTERNAL WIND AND STOPS SPASMS

kidney / adrenal Qi constraint: mental/nervous tension (esp. from stress, anxiety, pain, burn-out, chronic disease), agitated depression, unrest, abdominal, kidney or sacral pains

PAIN (incl. headache, earache, neuralgia [esp. facial], cardiacl/rectal pain, pains of dysmenorrhea, pregnancy and menopause, of flu, facial erysipelas, teething pain)

nerve excess with *internal wind:* twitching, trembling, convulsions

SEIZURES, SPASMS (incl. of infants, chorea, epilepsy, hysteria, Parkinson's disease, whooping cough, heat cramps, tetanus)

3 **DESCENDS LUNG QI, OPENS THE CHEST AND RELIEVES WHEEZING AND COUGHING;**
REDUCES INFLAMMATION AND PAIN

lung Qi constraint: dry nervous cough, throat irritation or tickle, wheezing, obsessive thinking

SPASMODIC ASTHMA, whooping cough; all excess conditions affecting the lungs

BOILS, skin inflammations, burns, scalds, hemorrhoids

PAINFUL SKIN ULCERS (incl. malignant), chancres, sores, toothache

PREPARATION

Use: Passionflower herb is prepared by **infusion** and **tincture.** The infusion is just right for children presenting excess conditions, whatever the cause, and for the adult with occasional spells of stress-induced insomnia or unrest. The tincture is best for most other uses. Topical **washes, compresses**, etc., are successful in painful inflammatory, ulcerative topical conditions.

In the syndromes above (which include hypertension), Passionflower can be used together with other herbs for cumulative benefits over longer periods (see below).

Dosage: Infusion: 6-10 g

Tincture: 1-3 ml at 1:3 strength in 45% ethanol

Caution: Passionflower herb is contraindicated during pregnancy as its alkaloids tend to stimulate the uterus, and because of a teratogenic glycoside (gynocardin).

This herb is a medium-strength remedy that possesses slight cumulative toxicity. It is therefore best used for occasional or short-term use only. It also works very well in combination with other herbs in a formula, which can then be taken over a longer time if necessary.

Very small doses of Passionflower herb have been known to cause nausea and vomiting.

NOTES

Meanwhile, over in the newly discovered Americas, the Spaniards were anxious to take advantage of the wealth of new plant cures their territories promised. They sought out Indian shamans, healers and herbalists to get them. After all, in 1569 the Seville physician Nicolas Monardes had written a glowing and very detailed account of the new exotics in Dos Libros *... he had esteemed Guaiac gum, Sarsa-parilla root and China root as specifics for the latest European scourge, syphilis. Within a few decades, bales of these, as well as tobacco and coca leaves, cacao and vanilla pods, sabadilla seeds, sassafras wood and various balsams were regularly unloaded from the Spanish galleons. The search for specific cures, for miracle remedies, was begun. It was a quest that led to the discovery of the remedy to rid all fevers, Peruvian bark; the remedy to bring on a tremendous sweat, Virginia Snakeroot; the remedy to induce vomit, Ipecacuanha root; the remedy to provoke a purge, Jalap root. The Jesuit missionaries who spearheaded these botanical explorations could pride themselves, by the early 1600s, on having adequately filled the bill for all current eliminative treatment strategies. In their clemency, perhaps, they felt obliged to offer yet another remedy for the evacuation-plagued patient in Europe: the remedy to pacify the mind: Passionflower herb.*

In 1605 a newly-discovered plant was sent to Pope Paul V from a Jesuit mission in Peru. Accompanying it was a letter from the Father Superior containing the fanciful suggestion that the flower-

head with its distinctive star-like corona and petals represented the Passion of Christ. With this symbolism it may be easy to accept Passionflower herb as yet another specific remedy for the treatment of yet another symptom.

Certainly, Passionflower herb is a widely applicable remedy in the treatment of anxiety states, insomnia, pains of various origins, spasms and seizures. It will bring relief to these symptoms regardless of whether they arise from acute, excess causes (such as shock, fear, acute disease or teething) or chronic, deficiency ones (such as emotional or physical burnout, chronic disease, chronic pain or childbirth). In this case there is no need to combine the remedy with a string of others identical to it, namely the *nervous sedatives* in this class. This Western "shotgun" approach to treatment is strictly unnecessary if all that's needed is symptom relief. In relieving insomnia, for example, regardless of how intransigent, Passionflower doe not need to be propped up with Hops, Valerian or California poppy: given the chance, it will do the job perfectly well on its own.

However, if we are looking for more than symptom relief and wish to treat the systemic underlying condition, then we may may want to combine Passionflower herb with other remedies. Again, the "shotgun" approach is inapropriate, as it simply amounts to nothing more than shooting in the dark. Passionflower itself also addresses particular syndromes that frequently give rise to the symptoms above—**floating Yang, heart Yin deficiency** and **kidney/adrenal Qi constraint** especially. Through its *sympathetic nervous inhibitant* and *hypotensive* action and bitter, cool energetic qualities, the remedy specifically is a good match for individuals whose Yang energies tend to float to the surface. They will find relief of tight muscles, congestive headaches, sleep disorders and other resultant symptoms. At the same time Passionflower will nourishes their heart Yin, thereby relieving anxiety, palpitations and so on. These are the energetic underpinnings of the herb's specific *muscle-relaxant, cerebral decongestant* and *analgesic* actions.

Passionflower herb's most fundamental action, however, is to regulate the Qi and clear internal wind. The remedy thereby systemically treats spasms, pains and seizures arising from **rising Liver Yang.** In the past, Passionflower was highly esteemed for treating convulsive disorders ranging from pediatric seizures through to Huntington's disease and epilepsy. The remedy, after all, contains indole alkaloids considered active in its *spasmolytic* and *anticonvulsant* effects.

In particular, Passionflower herb was also much used for individuals presenting tense bronchial conditions such as whooping cough and spasmodic asthma, as well as palpitations arising from shock, excitement or chronic neurological disorders. Here we see a tendency for this *respiratory relaxant* and *neurocardiac relaxant* to regulate constrained Qi in the Upper Warmer and to exert a sinking effect in symptoms that tend to rise.

It is interesting to note that the prominent early Eclectice doctor JOHN SCUDDER also used Passionflower herb for **liver congestion** accompanied by **hemorrhoids,** i.e., with **portal congestion** present. Equally, he applied the remedy to painful **congestive ovarian** and **uterine** conditions. However, for reasons unknown these uses never really caught on, and they remain secondary to this day. Once again, more experimentation is called for to either support or disprove this documented early nineteenth century usage.

Wild Lettuce Leaf

Botanical source: *Lactuca virosa* L., *L. canadensis* L.,
 L. scariola L., *L. altissima* Bieberstein and
 spp. (Asteraceae/Compositae)
Pharmaceutical names: Folium Lactucae,
 Lactucarium
Other names: a) Prickly lettuce, Acrid lettuce
  b) Lettuce opium, Little opium (Eng/Am)
 Laitue vireuse, Laitue sauvage (Fr)
 Giftlattich, Leberdistel, Sausalat, Stinksalat (Ge)
Part used: the leaf or milky latex

NATURE

Therapeutic category: mild remedy with minimal chronic toxicity
Constituents: milky latex (incl. bitter lactucin 0.2%, lactucone 50-60%, lactupicrin, lactucic and pectic acids, caotchouc, essential oil [incl. camphor], mannite, resins, gum albumen, saccharides, oxalic acid), triterpenes (incl. lactucerol), alkaloid hyoscamine or similar, potassium nitrate, polyacetylenes
Effective qualities: bitter, cold
 calming, relaxing, sinking
Tropism: nerves, brain, digestive organs, lungs, urinary organs
 Liver, Lung, Heart meridians
 Air, Warmth, Fluid bodies
Ground: all krases, biotypes and constitutions for symptomatic use

FUNCTIONS AND INDICATIONS

1 **SINKS THE YANG, CALMS THE MIND, RELIEVES PAIN AND PROMOTES REST;**
 DIFFUSES LUNG QI, CLEARS HEAT AND RELIEVES COUGHING

 floating Yang (Yang excess): head congestion, headache, muscle tension, sleep loss, irritability
 INSOMNIA, restlessness, agitation (esp. in children, elderly, convalescents, during menopause,
  from mental causes)
 PAIN (esp. visceral, colic)
 lung Qi constraint with *heat:* nervous, dry or uncontrollable cough, tight, painful chest
 COUGH (esp. dry, irritating, spasmodic, in whooping cough, bronchitis, TB, emphysema)
 SEXUAL OVERSTIMULATION, priapism (from *Kidney fire*)

2 **PROMOTES URINATION, DRAINS WATER AND RELIEVES EDEMA;**
 PROMOTES MENSTRUATION AND RELIEVES AMENORRHEA

 liver and kidney water congestion: swelling in extremities or trunk
 EDEMA
 AMENORRHEA

3   REDUCES INFLAMMATION AND IRRITATION

BURNS, scalds, skin inflammations and irritations
WARTS, pimples

PREPARATION

Use: Wild lettuce leaf is prepared by short **decoction** or **tincture** (the most effective preparation). The central leaf vein and stem of the plant contains a milky latex that can be mechanically extracted at flowering time. The **fresh latex** can be squeezed directly onto burns and other skin inflammations, as well as taken internally in some warm water. In Europe the *diuretic* latex was traditionally also drunk with apple cider vinegar and honey to promote urination for edema. Unless being used right away, however, it is best to dry the latex immediately to prevent enzymatic decomposition (see KING 1898 for the best extraction methods). In pharmacy the dried latex is called **Lactucarium** and was formerly much used in Europe and the U.S. The remedy Lactucarium came in small, brown cookie-shaped disks.

Topical applications are made for warts, skin inflammations and such like.

Dosage: Decoction: 8-16 g
> **Tincture:** 2-5 ml at 1:3 strength in 45% ethanol
> **Lactucarium:** 0.3-1.3 g (5-20 grains)

Caution: Do not use Wild lettuce or Lactucarium on its own indefinitely at maximum doses, if ever, because of the remedy's mild cumulative toxicity. A week's break would be advised after four weeks of continuous use. However, it should be emphasized that the remedy is non-addictive and free of the other after-effects of Opium, such as constipation, insomnia, irritability and so on. Wild lettuce leaf and Lactucarium may be used almost continuously when part of a formula, e.g., for chronic cough, pain or sleep disorder.

Note: Most species of *Lactuca* can be used for this remedy, as all contain the same latex components. In the late nineteenth century U.S. the species *scariola, altissima* and *virosa* were considered strongest.

Black horehound herb, from *Ballota foetida* L. in the mint family, is similar to Wild lettuce leaf in that it calms the mind and regulates the Qi. This remedy has bitter, pungent, cool, dry qualities and contains a bitter compound, tannins, essential oils and minerals. Its *nervous sedative* and *relaxant* effect is *depressant* and *spasmolytic* in floating Yang disorders presenting agitation, insomnia and anxiety, and in constrained Qi conditions with ringing ears. Because of combined *stimulant expectorant* and *antitussive* actions, secondary uses for Black horehound herb include spasmodic coughs (e.g., in whooping cough) and bronchial conditions arising from lung (phlegm) heat with constrained lung Qi. Topically, surface wounds and ulcers are improved from a *vulnerary* and *detergent* effect.

Dose: Infusion: 4-8 g. Tincture: 1-3 ml. *Large* doses (e.g., 3-5 ml of the tincture) are *diaphoretic* and may be used for the syndrome lung wind-heat presenting coughing, agitation and fever.

Avoid using Black horehound herb in empty cold conditions.

NOTES

There are many medicinal plants that by the nineteenth century had for a long time already been dismissed as old wives' tales. Many of these, however, then made an astonishing comeback when reintroduced into mainstream medicine by an authority figure. Wild lettuce, a relative of the domesticated garden lettuce, is a typical case in point. In 1771 the Viennese medic J. COLLIN announced the fruits of his experiences with Wild lettuce leaf and its latex extract to the medical community. The remedy could be used like Opium, but was gentler, safer and, above all, non-addictive.

This announcement opened the door to its widespread use in Western medicine, and this use continued until comparatively recently.

Wild lettuce came to be called "Little opium" or "Lettuce opium" because the plant's extracted latex looked, smelt and felt much like the original thing. The dried latex itself was known as among pharmacists and doctors as Lactucarium. Lactucarium has a sweet, intoxicating, opium-like smell, although a bitter taste. The reddish-brown rectangles or cakes of Lactucarium were mainly produced in France, Germany, Austria, Scotland

and England, some of which were imported into the U.S. The best varieties were deemed to be the Scotch and English. With the mass production of synthetic tranquilizers, however, the use of this valuable *sedative* remedy was (predictably enough) eventually discontinued.

Wild lettuce leaf and Lactucarium are both average-strength *nervous sedatives* whose mind-calming property is described as *hypnotic* and *nervous depressant*. The remedy contains on one hand the latex, rich in various compounds such as essential oil, the bitter lactucin (*sedative* and *hypoglycemiant*) and lactucone (reminiscent of cynanchol found in the dogbanes and euphorbone in the spurges). On the other hand, an alkaloid similar to hyoscamine (of henbane fame) has been determined, with purported *neuromuscular sedative/relaxant* activity. This alkaloid is a *parasympathetic nervous stimulant*. Specifically, *spasmolytic, analgesic* and *anti-inflammatory* actions have been confirmed in the remedy.

From the therapeutic viewpoint, Wild lettuce leaf also has a fairly specific profile. Its first use is for those with cerebral or nervous hyperfunctioning presenting symptoms such as mental overexcitement, anxiety, insomnia and pain. Because of its bitter, cold, sinking qualities, the remedy will work best in context of **tense** and **hot** conditions, i.e., **Yang excess** and **constrained Qi** conditions.

Next, because of its neural tropism for the respiratory system, Wild lettuce leaf is particularly effective at relieving uncontrollable, nervous, irritating **coughs** arising from **constrained lung Qi,** especially with **lung heat** present. The remedy is therefore a true *antitussive* suitable for long-term cough as well as pain managment in conditions as different as whooping cough, emphysema and lung TB.

For difficult cases, the remedy can be combined with Jamaica dogwood root bark, Black horehound herb or others in this class. Like Hops flower, Wild lettuce leaf is also a *sexual sedative:* it is somewhat *anaphrodisiac* in cases of sexual overstimulation.

California Poppy Root and Herb

Botanical name: *Eschscholtzia californica* L.
     (syn. *E. mexicana, E. arizonica*)
     (Papaveraceae)
Pharmaceutical name: Radix et herba Eschscholtziae
Other names: Gold poppy, Yellow poppy (Am)
     Dormidera, Amapola amarilla, Copa de oro,
       Amapola de California (Sp)
     Coquelicot de Californie (Fr)
     Kalifornischer (Gold)mohn (Ge)
Part used: the root and herb (i.e. the whole plant)

NATURE

Therapeutic category: mild remedy with minimal chronic toxicity
Constituents: isoquinoline alkaloids (incl. protopine, chelerythine, chelirubine, sanguinarine, macarpine, ionidine, eschscholtzine, californidine, cryptopine, alpha- and beta-homochelidonine), yellow essential oil (eschscholtzione), glycoside

Effective qualities: somewhat bitter, cool
> calming, relaxing

Tropism: brain, nerves, heart, viscera
> Heart, Liver meridians
> Air body

Ground: all krases, biotypes and constitutions for symptomatic use

FUNCTIONS AND INDICATIONS

1 **SINKS THE YANG, CALMS THE MIND, RELIEVES PAIN AND ANXIETY, AND PROMOTES REST; REGULATES HEART QI AND RELIEVES PALPITATIONS**

floating Yang (Yang excess): head congestion, headache, muscle tension, sleep loss, irritability

INSOMNIA, IRRITABILITY (esp. in children, elderly, convalescents, during menopause, from mental causes)

PAIN (incl. headache, toothache, intestinal and biliary colic, menstrual cramps)

ANXIETY STATES

heart Qi constraint: palpitations, rapid heart beats, anxiety, sleep loss

NEUROCARDIAC SYNDROME, TACHYCARDIA

HYPERTENSION

PREPARATION

Use: California poppy root and herb is prepared by **long infusion** or **tincture.** The latter is considerably more effective. Native Americans made **compresses** of the herb/ root for promoting tissue repair.

Dosage: Long infusion: 6-12 g
> **Tincture:** 2-4 ml at 1:3 strength in 45% ethanol

Caution: Forbidden in glaucoma becuause of the remedy's content in sanguinarine. Use with caution or avoid during pregnancy because of a theoretically *uterine stimulant* effect of the alkaloid crypropine.

Note: California poppy root was also used by Native Americans for treating headache, abdominal pain, excessive breast milk in nursing mothers, and topically for sores.

The red **Corn poppy flower** from *Papaver rhoeas* is also used as a mild *nervous sedative*, especially in infants, children and elderly. Cooling and moistening by nature, the remedy also has *antitussive* and *demulcent* properties useful in spasmodic, dry coughing of bronchitis, asthma and whooping cough, and in **lung heat** conditions such as pleurisy and pneumonia. Its additional gentle *diaphoretic* action makes it useful in **external dryness** syndrome with thirst, coughing, headache and irritability. **Gargles** for sore throat and **eyebaths** are good. **Dose:** 4-10 g by infusion, 2-4 ml by tincture at 1:3 strength in 45% ethanol

NOTES

This member of the poppy family looks like a miniature opium poppy with cup-like, golden-yellow flowers. Although California poppy is a widely distributed garden ornamental, the plant originally *does* come from California. Appropriately enough, it is the Golden State's state flower.

When the Spaniards first arrived in California, they noted numerous Native tribes had been using the plant as a gentle *sedative* for children. As these explorers forged their way up the coast they kept records of their experiences and communications, these being among them. According to one report, Spanish sailors soon learned to use the extensive fields of shimmering poppies found in the Los

Angeles basin near Mount Wilson as a natural landmark for guiding them into Los Angeles harbor (now Long Beach harbor). In 1820 a Russian expedition to California landed several botanists who named the plant after the ship's surgeon and naturalist, ESCHSCHOLTZ. After returning specimens to Europe they must have been gratified to see California poppy take off throughout Europe as both garden ornamental and botanical medicine.

The therapeutic applications of California poppy are as straightforward today as they were one or even two hundred years ago—despite the scientific revelations of poppy alkaloids. As a gentle, cool-natured *nervous sedative* and *neuromuscular relax-*

ant, the remedy reduces **floating Yang** and activates **constrained Qi** affecting the **heart.** Insomnia, pain and anxiety are thereby the main symptoms treated, especially in those prone to deficiency conditions, such as children and elderly. The remedy is said to have *hypnotic* but not *depressant* actions on cerebral functions, although (predictably) there is disagreement on this point. The alkaloids protopine and sanguinarine in particular have shown heart-slowing and *hypotensive* activity. This remedy's alkaloids are generally similar to those found in Celandine herb, and here also effect *analgesic* and *spasmolytic* actions, particularly in the digestive and biliary tract.

Jamaica Dogwood Root Bark

Botanical source: *Piscidia erythrina* Jacquin
       (Fabaceae/Leguminosae)
Pharmaceutical name: Cortex radicis Piscidiae
Other names: — (Fr)
       Jamaica Hornstrauch/Hartriegel (Ge)
Part used: the root bark

NATURE
Therapeutic category: medium-strength remedy with moderate chronic toxicity
Constituents: glycosides (incl. piscidin, jamaicin, ichthyone), flavonoids (incl. sumatrol, lisetin, rotenone, piscerythrone, piscidon, ichthynonee), piscidic acid, amorphous alkaloid, resin, starch, wax, lipids, calcium phosphate
Effective qualities: pungent, astringent, cool
       calming, relaxing
Tropism: nervous system, lungs
       Liver, Lung meridians
       Air, Warmth bodies
Ground: all krases, biotypes and constitutions

FUNCTIONS AND INDICATIONS
1   **SINKS THE YANG AND CALMS THE MIND; RELAXES CONSTRAINT AND RELIEVES ANXIETY**

    floating Yang (Yang excess): head congestion, headache, pains, muscle tension, sleep loss, irritability
    INSOMNIA, agitation
    kidney / adrenal Qi constraint: nervous/mental tension (esp. from anxiety, stress, pain), agitation, pains
    ANXIETY

**2 REGULATES THE QI AND RELIEVES PAIN;
DIFFUSES LUNG QI AND STOPS COUGHING;
CLEARS INTERNAL WIND AND STOPS SPASMS**

PAIN from NEURALGIA and SPASM (incl. sciatica, trigeminal/optical/supraorbital neuralgia, violent toothache, headache, migraine, arthritis, abdominal and kidney pain/colic, pain of muscular spasms, dysmenorrhea, cancer, fractures, cholera)

lung Qi constraint: nervous, dry or uncontrollable cough, tight, painful chest

COUGH (esp. irritating, spasmodic, in whooping cough, croup, bronchitis, TB)

internal wind: nervous unrest, abdominal pains or spasms, twitches

SEIZURES (esp. in children and women), delirium tremens, tremors, ticks

3 CLEARS HEAT AND REDUCES INFLAMMATION

INFLAMMATIONS (incl. iritis, conjunctivitis, panophthalmitis)

BURNS, scalds

PREPARATION

Use: Jamaica dogwood root bark is prepared in **decoction** or **tincture** form. The latter is more effective. **Swabs** and other applications may be used in painful or inflamed dental and skin conditions

Dosage: Decoction: 3-6 g

Tincture: 0.5-2 ml at 1:2 strength in 45% ethanol

Caution: Because of its medium-strength status that may produce idiosyncratic reactions, this remedy should be given in the lowest dose to begin with, and increased only gradually. For the same reason, do not use Jamaica dogwood continuously, especially on its own. Reactions occur especially when the remedy is used alone rather than in a formula, and may include nausea, indigestion and headache. Licorice root in particular can mitigate these reactions. Reduce the dosage or discontinue if necessary.

Contraindicated in children and elderly because of its *nervous depressant* action.

NOTES

Jamaica dogwood is a small tree native to the West Indies, sporadically also seen in northern Florida, Texas, Mexico and Central America. Its botanical name, *Piscidia,* denotes "fish-killing" and originates in the fact that in the West Indies the leaves and young branches of this shrub are used as a poisonous narcotic to fish. As a remedy, the root bark of this dogwood species surfaced in North America during the mid-nineteenth century. Doctors often used the remedy for patients generally prone to nervous system disorders, seeing its good *analgesic* and *sedative* actions.

Although a poorly researched remedy from the scientific point of view, Jamaica dogwood root bark performs essentially as a *nervous sedative* for conditions presenting **pain, spasm** and **inflammation.** Its glycosides piscidin and others in the lab have shown considerable *nervous sedative* (*hypnotic, depressant*) and *analgesic* activity, with a tendency to parasympathetic nervous stimulation. Individuals presenting neuralgia, spasmodic pain, anxiety, agitation and insomnia benefit here in particular—whatever the reason for their symptoms. In vitalistic terms, this heat-clearing remedy sinks **floating Yang,** releases **constrained Qi** and subdues resultant **internal wind.** It is one of the best remedies available for children's seizures and is an important *antitussive* remedy for stopping uncontrollable, spasmodic coughing.

Bitter Orange Flower

(Neroli Essential Oil)

Botanical source: *Citrus aurantium* L. ssp. *aurantium*
 (syn. *Citrus bigaradia* L.) (Rutaceae)
Pharmaceutical name: Flos Citri aurantium
Ancient names: Melon Naranzion (Gr)
 Malum nerantium, Pomum arangiae (Lat)
Other names: Oranger amère, Bigaradier; Néroli
 bigarade (Fr)
 Bitter-Orange, Pomerantze (Ge)
Part used: the flower

NATURE

Therapeutic category: mild remedy with minimal chronic toxicity
Constituents: essential oil 1.25-2.5% (incl. monoterpenes 35% [pinenes, limonene], phenols, camphene, dipentene, ocimene, farnesol, linalool 30%, geraniol, nerol, nerolidol, phenylethylic and benzylic alcohols, linalyleacetate, nerylacetate, geranylacetate, jasmone, indole, benzoic/acetic/anthranilic acid), organic acids, citrannin, mamnose, pectin, vitamins A, B, C
Effective qualities: bitter, somewhat pungent, cooling and warming potential
 calming, relaxing, restoring, sinking
Tropism: cardiovascular and central nervous system, stomach, intestines,
 Heart, Pericardium, Liver meridians
 Air, Warmth bodies
Ground: Choleric krasis
 Tough/Shao Yang and Industrious/Tai Yang biotypes
 Hematogenic/Phosphoric constitution

NATURE AND INDICATIONS

1   **SINKS THE YANG, CALMS THE MIND AND RELIEVES ANXIETY;
    REGULATES HEART QI AND RELIEVES PALPITATIONS**

   floating Yang (Yang excess) with Heart fire: agitation, irritability, palpitations, head congestion,
    headache, sleep loss
   INSOMNIA, agitation, irritability (esp. in excess or hot conditions)
   ANXIETY STATES
   heart Qi constraint: palpitations, rapid heart beats, sleep loss, anxiety
   NEUROCARDIAC SYNDROME, TACHYCARDIA, cardiac spasms
   HYPERTENSION

2   **STIMULATES DIGESTION AND RELIEVES APPETITE LOSS**
   liver-gallbladder and stomach Qi stagnation: appetite loss, indigestion, epigastric pain, belching
   UPPER GASTRIC DEFICIENCY, pancreatic deficiency

3   RESTORES THE NERVES, LIFTS THE MIND AND RELIEVES DEPRESSION; PROMOTES SEXUAL DESIRE

nerve and brain deficiency: chronic depression, fatigue, absent-mindedness

DEPRESSION (nervous)

SEXUAL DISINTEREST, impotence, frigidity

4   REDUCES INFECTION AND ELIMINATES PARASITES; BENEFITS THE SKIN

INFECTIONS (esp. bronchitis, pleurisy, lung TB, gastroenteritis)

INTESTINAL PARASITES

SKIN IRRITATION, broken veins, e.g. with dryness and redness

PREPARATION

Use: Bitter orange flower is prepared by **infusion, tincture** or **essential oil,** in ascending order of strength. The infusion is mainly used to calm and relax infants and small children with emotional or physical upset from colic, teething pains and so on. For infants use two tablespoons per bottle.

Sweet orange flowers may be substituted for bitter orange flowers, but are less effective. Both bitter and sweet orange flowers are beneficial, sweet, aromatic ingredients for herbal tea blends.

The tincture is a good general preparation, while the essential oil is the most effective of all. For historical reasons this essential oil is known as Neroli oil after the eighteenth-century French Princesse de Nérole. It is used internally and topically in a 2% carrier oil dilution. Tincture and essential oil are also excellent in **ointments** and **creams** for dry, red, irritated skin.

Dosage: Infusion: 8-12 g

Tincture: 2-4 ml at 1:3 strength in 40% ethanol

Essential oil: 1 drop in a gelatin cap topped with some olive oil

Caution: None

NOTES

The fragrant white flowers of the bitter orange have been used in East Asia, where the tree originates, and in the West for many a millennium. The flower is therapeutically more versatile than any of the orange's other parts (such as the fruit rind, leaf or seed). *Sedative* and *relaxant* at the same time, Orange flower has a particular affinity for the cardiovascular and nervous systems. Insomnia and anxiety states (including with hypertension present) are treated as the remedy addresses heart syndromes presenting Qi constraint and heat.

Working in *stimulant* and *restorative* mode, Bitter orange flower is also an excellent remedy for **stagnation** of **gallbladder, pancreas** and **stomach Qi.** It is a *cholagogue digestive stimulant* like Mandarin rind (Citrus Chen Pi). The *restorative* action of the flower's essential oils on cerebral functions is also much employed, especially in the treatment of **chronic depression.** Here the oil works physiologically in much the same way as it does when inhaled in extracted form, i.e., when used in aromatherapy.

OCIMVM
MAGNVM.

Groß Basilien.

Herbs to Lift the Mind and Relieve Depression

Herbal remedies that lift the mind are used to treat conditions of mind weakness that present depression as a chief symptom, and are called *nervous* or *nervine restoratives/stimulants*. When used to address clinical depression in particular, they are called *antidepressants*. Symptoms of a weakened mind (spirit) include depression, pessimism, loss of mental focus, fatigue, insomnia and often low motivation and self-esteem. Emotionally there may be grief and insufficient emotional responses in general. In Western terms this syndrome is traditionally called neurasthenia.

Although these herbs may be used on their own for acute symptom relief, they are more often found in the context of formulas that address the mind weakness that gives rise to depression.

The Nature, Dynamics and Treatment of Mind Weakness/Neurasthenia and Depression

Mind weakness is one of the three types of pathological conditions of the mind that Chinese medicine defines. Here the mind becomes reduced, sluggish and depressed—a mental hypofunctioning condition. In addition to the above mental symptoms, there is often an emotional component that feeds or results from it. This consists mainly of:
• Hypoemotivity or insufficient emotional responses
• Sorrow, grief, despair, fear or anxious depression
• Emotional conflict in general

The syndromes involved in mind weakness are mainly hypofunctioning types.
• **Mind weakness with hypofunctioning** creates Qi deficiency types of syndromes that are essentially weak conditions, often with cold. In Chinese medicine they include the syndromes Lung and Heart Qi deficiency, Heart and/or Liver Blood deficiency and Phlegm misting the mind.
• **Mind weakness with hyperfunctioning** creates Qi stagnation syndromes, chiefly Qi constraint.

Mind weakness is physiologically underpinned by various possible processes. These include neurotransmitter deficiency (including dopamine, vasopressin and substance P insufficiency), serotonin and GABA excess; hormonal insufficiencies, e.g. thyroidal, pituitary, adrenal and gonadal hormones; progesterone excess and autonomic nervous imbalance. These usually need to be addressed separately with herbs and nutrition.

The origins of mind weakness include chronic mental, emotional and physical stress, including chronic illness itself; chronic overwork and over-exercise and excessive sex; foods and drinks that cause damp and phlegm in the system, including dairy and low-mineral content foods; and long-term usage of medical or recreational drugs.

Mind weakness is treated in two basic ways. First, as a symptom with the use of *nervous stimulant* herbs in general. Second, as a systemic condition that is differentiated into the hyper- and hypofunctioning types of syndromes.

The Herbs that Lift the Mind

The herbs that address neurasthenia and depression owe their effect mainly to their content in alkaloids and essential oils, both of which variously affect neuroendocrine functions (see also Class 16).

Tonify Deficiency and Strengthen the Mind
Nervous restoratives/stimulants, antidepressants

Herbs of this type treat mind weakness and depression seen in the context of **mind weakness with Qi deficiency,** involving **nerve and brain deficiency.** The key symptoms here are of cerebral insufficiency with poor cognition, including fatigue, loss of concentration and memory, sleeping problems (insomnia or somnolence), depression and low self-confidence. This is often seen in conditions arising from chronic mental, physical and emotional stress; chronic illness, chronic overwork and excessive exercising and sexual activity; inadequate nutrition and long-term usage of medical or recreational drugs. This syndrome is also found outside of depression in such disorders as Parkinson's disease, Alzheimer's disease and Guillain-Barré syndrome. Unless treated, this condition over time may lead to other disorders such as neuralgia, neuritis, myelitis and chronic viral infections (e.g. shingles, herpes).

The classic *nervous restoratives* that treat mind weakness work by enhancing neural and cerebral functions. Found mostly in Classes 8 and 11, they include St. John's wort herb, Skullcap herb, Sage leaf, Vervain herb, Melissa leaf, Ginkgo leaf, Milky oat berry, Gotu kola herb, American ginseng root, Wood betony herb, Rhodiola root, Schisandra berry and—again from Chinese medicine— Polygonum He Shou Wu (Flowery knotweed root) and Acorus Shi Chang Pu and Polygala Yuan Zhi. The majority of these are also *nervous trophorestoratives* because they nourish and help rebuild actual nerve and brain cells. Long-term treatment with these is usually needed for their full *antidepressant* action to unfold (a minimum of six weeks). Usually they are combined with other *restoratives* or *relaxants,* depending on whether Qi deficiency or Qi constraint is present, to comprehensively address the whole imbalance presenting.

In severe cases involving depression, one may resort to *nervous stimulants*. These produce quicker but more short-lived results. They consist of two pharmacological categories:
• *Focused nervous stimulants* that produce a focused stimulation of attention, such as Rosemary leaf, Hyssop herb, Basil leaf, Winter savory herb, Gotu kola herb and Asian ginseng root. These can be called *psychogenics* as they gently stimulate the mind and elevate the mood, inducing increased awareness and alertness. On their own, without the use of the above *nervous restoratives,* however, they will not bring about permanent results.
• *Diffusive nervous stimulants* that create a diffuse, superficial nervous/mental stimulation and short-term energy increase. They include botanicals such as Kola nut, Maté leaf, Tea leaf, Coffee bean, Nutmeg seed, Ephedra herb and Coca leaf. These are not designed for long-term or systemic treatment. They are only appropriate for a short-term symptomatic relief of depression and other symptoms related to nervous deficiency. Misused, *diffusive nervous stimulants* will produce the very opposite effect—an inhibition of nervous functioning causing depression, fatigue and so on. On the whole this does not condemn the occasional use of these herbs for making stimulating leisure drinks,

however—as long as the quantities used remain moderate. These herbs definitely represent a crossover zone between herbal medicine and hedonics.

Reduce Qi Stagnation and Lift the Mind
Nervous restoratives, antidepressants

Herbs in this section address **mind weakness with liver Qi stgnation,** whose key symptoms are depression, mood swings, irritability, anger, feelings of hopelessness, labile motivation and inability to get going in the morning or perform normal daily activities. This is traditionally termed a **liver depression,** and often includes liver organ congestion with indigestion, right hypochondriac tenderness, and so on.

This syndrome is addressed with a combination of *antidepressant nervous restoratives* (Classes 8 and 11), such as St. John's wort herb, Melissa leaf, Gotu kola herb, Oat berry and American ginseng root, and *liver decongestants* such as Wormwood herb, Celandine herb, Fringe tree root bark and Turmeric root. Long-term treatment with routine relapses is the norm in this condition, especially with a history of chronic disease present.

Analeptic Herbs

Another type of remedy that is related to the *nervous restorative* is the *nervous stimulant,* also known as an *analeptic. Analeptics* have a more focused cerebral action that revives consciousness. They awaken the mind in acute cerebral deficiency involving dizziness, drowsiness, coma, collapse, paresthesia and paralysis, often the reult of concussion, cerebral contusion, catatonic stupor, Yin-type schizophrenia, cerebrovascular accident, heat exhaustion, myelitis, peripheral neuritis, ataxic cerebral palsy, Bell's palsy, Guillain-barré syndrome and myasthenia gravis.

Analeptic herbs include Basil herb, Sage leaf, Rosemary leaf, Ravintsara oil, Arnica flower, Lobelia herb, Lily-of-the-valley herb, and in Chinese medicine Acorus Shi Chang Pu, Bos Niu Huang and Moschus She Xiang. These are typically described in Chinese medicine as "opening the orifices and awakening the mind."

A summary list of remedies in this class is found in the Repertory under Cerebral insufficiency, Cerebral concussion, Coma, Depression, Insomnia and Nervous debility.

Class 21   Spasmolytics (Anticonvulsants)

Herbs to Clear Internal Wind and Reduce Spasms

Herbal remedies that clear internal wind are used in the treatment of spasms. Called *spasmolytics,* they address conditions dominated by striated muscle spasms producing tremors, twitches, shaking and convulsions. Because they reduce convulsions (seizures), they are specifically also known as *anticonvulsants. Spasmolytics* are usually used in combination with other remedies to address a systemic condition, rather than on their own. They have been relied on for millennia, and in much of the world still are, when synthetic drugs are unavailable.

In vitalistic medicine, visible spasms of the muscles or limbs are considered manifestations of **internal wind.** In Western terms they are a neurological symptom found in a number of preclinical and clinical disorders, including heat cramps, hypocalcemia, cerebral palsy, febrile diseases such as tetanus, eclampsia and encephalitis, and nervous system disorders such as epilepsy, tetany, meningitis with opisthotonos, Parkinson's disease and Huntington's disease (chorea). When spasms turn into paralytic and hemiplegic conditions, this is described as a **wind-phlegm obstruction.**

The Herbs that Clear Internal Wind

The majority of herbs that clear internal wind are cold by nature and chemically rely on components such as alkaloids, essential oils and glycosides for their spasm-reducing effect. Important *spasmolytics* include Passionflower herb, Hops flower, Valerian root, Yellow jessamine root, Lobelia root/seed/ herb, Jamaica dogwood root bark, Black cohosh root, Mistletoe herb, Lily of the valley herb and Camomile flower (both types). The essential oils of *Camomile* (all types) and *Valerian* may also be used for this purpose. Chinese medicine includes several *spasmolytics* that are found in numerous formulas for relieving spasms, including Uncaria Gou Teng (Gambir vine twig) and Gastrodia Tian Ma (Celestial hemp corm). Moreover, Chinese medicine relies extensively on mineral-rich animal

products for managing a large variety of spasmodic and convulsive neurological disorders. Examples are the fairly common Cryptotympana Chan Tui (Cicada slough) and the very strong Buthus Quan Xie (Scorpion) (See HOLMES 1997, 2002).

Spasmolytics in this class should be carefully distinguished from those remedies that treat spasms and pain of the smooth muscles—also called *spasmolytics* (Class 11). Although both herb types clearly reduce spasms, in practice they are applied very differently. *Anticonvulsant spasmolytics* are used to treat spasms of the striated muscles (e.g., involving the extremities) and seizures (whole body spasms, in a sense); they are therefore said to clear internal wind. Class 11 *analgesic spasmolytics,* on the other hand, reduce spasms of the smooth muscles (e.g., of the bronchi, intestines, uterus, bladder or arteries). They are more broadly known as *relaxants* and therefore are said to regulate the Qi and relax constraint.

Spasmolytics that clear internal wind usually exert other neurological actions, such as *analgesic, relaxant-spasmolytic, nervous depressant* and *nervous stimulant.* In treating conditions of internal wind, therefore, it is usually only a matter of finding the remedy with the right combination of neurological actions to perfectly match the disorder presenting.

Nevertheless, because factors such as inflammation, infection, fever (hot conditions) or, conversely, neurasthenia, Yang, blood, Yin or fluids deficiency (deficiency conditions) are commonly involved in spasms and convulsions, a comprehensive treatment formula that includes several different types of remedies is usually necessary. *Spasmolytics* are therefore routinely combined with herbs from other treatment categories to address the overall syndrome.

A summary list of remedies in this class is found in the Repertory under Spasm and Seizure.

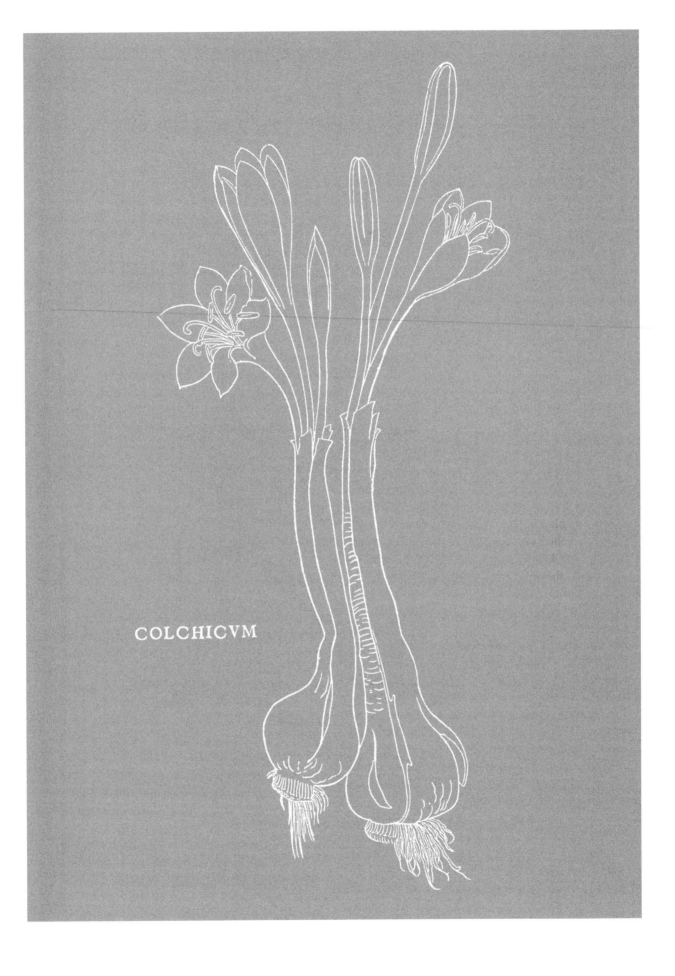

COLCHICVM

Herbs to Relieve Pain

This class consists of remedies used primarily for pain-relief, *analgesics*—also called *anodynes* in herbal medicine. They are used alone or, more commonly, as part of a formula for treating conditions involving pain. Typically, *analgesics* are not all equal. Some exert a better action on certain pain locations than others, or work better in certain types of disorders than in others. The majority of herbal *analgesics* also include effects that naturally address painful conditions in a comprehensive way, namely *nervous sedative, anti-inflammatory* and *spasmolytic* actions.

The Treatment of Pain

Much is known in Western pharmacology about the physiological dynamics of pain-relief of major *analgesic* plants such as opium poppy and hemlock. We know that alkaloids and essential oils are the major components responsible for *analgesic* activity in plants. However, relatively little information of the empirical, practical kind on pain managment has survived in the Greek medical tradition of the West. This is for two reasons. First, the collapse of traditional Greek medicine from the seventeenth to nineteenth centuries along with the rise of experimental, bacteriological and drug-based styles of modern medicine. Second, the systemic extermination of the Wise Woman tradition in the fifteenth and sixteenth centuries in tandem with the rise of the professional patriarchal medical system. Both these factors—the loss of our energetics-based medical system and the loss of empirical healing skills accumulated over millennia—have resulted in a pathetic dearth of knowledge about the specific *types* and *locations* of pain relieved by herbal remedies.

We may take for granted that the Wise Woman practitioners—essentially empirical folk healers passing on a living tradition—knew all about pain relief. Beyond the limited written information available about their use of Rye ergot for labor pains, for example, very little is directly known about the plants they used, the techniques they applied and the results they obtained.

Our consolation prize in the West is the advent of Oriental medicine. Here the empirical tradition of folk medicine—although wonderfully rationalized over the ages in the intricate terminology of Chinese medical theory by the official circles of Imperial Court Medicine—has remained intact. Practical, specific therapeutic information regarding certain plant remedies for treating certain types and locations of pain is still available. The numerous formulas and external preparations (salves, plasters, liniments, and so on) available in Chinese medicine are the practical tools of this living tradition.

In the context of modern drug-based medicine there is not much incentive for developing the same level of sophistication with herbal remedies in the area of pain relief. Yet this is exactly what is currently required. Because of the ongoing modern medical crisis and the upcoming shortage of planetary fossil fuels on which all synthetic drugs are chemically based, we actually have no choice but to start reinventing the wheel of empirical knowledge that we recently destroyed. We have allies in this task: the models of Chinese and Ayurvedic medicine, examples of what can be achieved with natural plants, minerals and animal parts alone, and the presence of essential oils, powerful plant extracts that we are only in the beginning stages of exploring, clinically and pharmacologically.

The crux of pain relief in any holistic system of therapy is not primarily the pharmacological strength of a remedy's *analgesic* action. This approach works best in drug medicine, not natural herbal medicine. The question here is, once again, What type of pain will a remedy best relieve? The answer to this question is an ongoing exploration based on the type of condition presenting pain and the nature of the pain. The main factors to be considered here are the syndrome, or symptom picture, and the person's constitution.

The Herbs that Treat Pain

The main energetic imbalances that entail pain are **Yang deficiency, Qi deficiency, blood stagnation, Qi constraint** and infectious conditions presenting **heat, damp-heat** or **toxic-heat.** The numerous syndromes that may present pain as part of their symptomatology are merely subdivisions of these main types. Here are some examples:

• Rheumatic and arthritic pain involving **wind/-damp/cold** obstruction, for example, is fundamentally due to a combination of **Yang deficiency** involving poor circulation and chronic **toxicosis** of one kind or another. The appropriate remedies include Prickly ash bark, Rosemary leaf, Juniper berry and Sassafras root bark (Class 8).

• Painful urination caused by **kidney dryness** with alkaline urine, for instance, arises from a **bladder Qi deficiency** and is treated with herbs such as Poplar bark, Gravel root, St. John's wort herb, Birch leaf, Hydrangea root and Meadowsweet herb.

• Dysmenorrhea, or menstrual cramps, may arise from **constrained Qi** with emotional/hormonal factors present. This calls for remedies such as Motherwort herb, Blackhaw bark, Cramp bark, Black cohosh root, Camomile flower, Lavender flower and Tansy herb. Dysmenorrhea presenting heaviness, down-ward pressure and cramps in the lower abdomen before menstrual onset, on the other hand, is caused by **blood congestion.** Marigold flower, Yarrow herb, Patridgeberry herb, Blackhaw bark and Lady's mantle herb are here among the right botanicals.

• Sore throat caused by an infection is usually found in the context of **wind-heat** or **toxic-heat,** for which such herbs as Burdock seed, Sage leaf, Elder flower and Bayberry bark are appropriate.

• Painful defecation with diarrhea and mucousy, bloody stool caused by infection may be found in **intestines damp-heat,** and will be treated with Horsetail herb, Bilberry leaf, Barberry root bark, Goldenseal root or Loosestrife herb, for instance.

Like any other condition, pain relief clearly may be carried out based on the symptom or the whole condition.

Still, there is a group of remedies known for their broad general *analgesic* effect that is able to reduce pain in a wide range of conditions. They include flu with painful throat and muscle pains, peripheral neuritis, arthritis, fibromyalgia, ostalgia, toothache, abdominal, lumbar, biliary, menstrual and renal pain. *Analgesics* can therefore be used in addition to the remedies addressing the main presenting condition, as in the examples above. These herbs exert a *sedative,* i.e., *hypnotic* action on the central nervous system and usually sedate other selective aspects of nervous functioning. They are often used in the syndrome **Qi constraint** presenting insomnia, dizzinesss and agitation in addition to actual pain, thereby supplementing Class 13 *relaxants* in general. *Analgesics* include Willow bark, Meadowsweet herb, Hops flower, Wild lettuce leaf, Passionflower herb, Jamaica dogwood root bark, Yellow jessamine root, Black cohosh root, Asian buplever root and Lavender essential oil. Equivalent remedies in Oriental medicine include Corydalis Yan Hu Suo (Asian corydalis root) and Vitex Man Jing Zi (Seashore chastetree berry).

A summary list of remedies in this class is found in the Repertory under Pain.

Herbs to Promote Tissue Repair and Relieve Pain and Swelling

Called *vulneraries*, remedies in this class are used to treat tissue trauma. They work by promoting the healing of injured tissue, and reducing inflammation, hematoma, pain, red/purple discoloration and swelling. *Vulneraries* are applied mainly to external injuries such as open trauma wounds (e.g., cuts, abrasions, crush wounds), sprains, strains, contusions (bruises) and fractures. However, they may also be used for internal injuries, including ulcers of the mucous membrane.

Vulneraries variously contain tannins, silica, zinc, essential oils, mucilages or other constituents that comprehensively address tissue trauma. They possess *tissue-repairing, anti-inflammatory, antipyretic, analgesic* and *detumescent* actions. Foremost among the *vulneraries* are Marigold flower, Plantain leaf, Lady's mantle herb, Sanicle herb, Echinacea root, Walnut leaf, Arnica flower, Gotu kola herb, Selfheal spike, Comfrey leaf, Iceland moss, Ground ivy herb, Madder root and Grapevine leaf. Among the most effective *vulneraries* in Chinese medicine are Panax San Qi (Pseudoginseng root), Bletilla Bai Ji and Drynaria Gu Sui Bu.

Certain essential oils also have excellent *vulnerary, detergent* and *tissue-healing* properties. These include *Lavender, Camomile* (all types), *Geranium, Myrrh, Frankincense, Bergamot, Juniper, Rosemary, Eucalyptus, Hyssop, Patchouli, Rose, Spearmint* and *Thuja.* These should be diluted in a low dilution (2-3%) in water for making swabs, compresses and other similar topical preparations.

The Treatment of Tissue Trauma

For external tissue trauma, *vulnerary* remedies are applied to the affected part in the form of a compress, poultice, ointment or cream. Initially, moist compresses, poultices or cotton swabs, often renewed, are the most effective (see Chapter 8). In the case of dirty scrapes, wounds, etc., an *antiseptic detergent* herb should be used to clean up and disinfect the area before using a *vulnerary* that promotes tissue repair. Once healing is underway, one may change over to ointments, lotions or creams.

If nothing else is at hand for treatment, e.g., while hiking, the crushed leaves of certain *vulnerary* plants (which tend to be conveniently large) may be applied fresh to a wound, bruise or bite. Secure this poultice firmly with a handkerchief or scarf. Examples of good poultice herbs are Comfrey leaf or root, Plantain leaf, Coltsfoot leaf, Butterbur leaf, Lady's mantle leaf and Gotu kola herb. Several of these plants are often found as garden ornamentals. Also on the domestic front, Aloe leaf gel from the common aloe plant is often a good vulnerary standby. Apply the gelatinous face of a piece of the broken leaf directly onto scrapes, cuts, scalds or burns.

Finally, when treating any injury it is important to complement external application with simultaneous internal use of the same remedies in decoction, infusion or tincture form. This substantially speeds up the healing process and will also treat any hidden internal injury that may have occurred (after a moving accident, for example).

Treatment Considerations

• With **bleeding** present, or if internal hemorrhage is suspected, large doses of *hemostatics* (Class 15) should be added to *vulneraries*. However, as most *hemostatics* are tannin-based *astringents,* they preclude the simultaneous use of *vulneraries* rich in mucilage, as tannins will precipitate mucilages. In case of mild bleeding, most *vulneraries* alone will be effective.

• With **bruising** or **contusion** present, *anticontusion* remedies should also be applied topically in the way most appropriate. Arnica flower and *Helichrysum* and *Frankincense* essential oil are all highly effective *anticontusion* remedies.

• With **infection** present, *anti-infectives* (Classes 12 and 24) should also be taken internally to stimulate immune activity. At the same time, *rubefacients* should be applied topically to strongly stimulate local defenses.

A summary list of remedies in this class is found in the Repertory under Wounds.

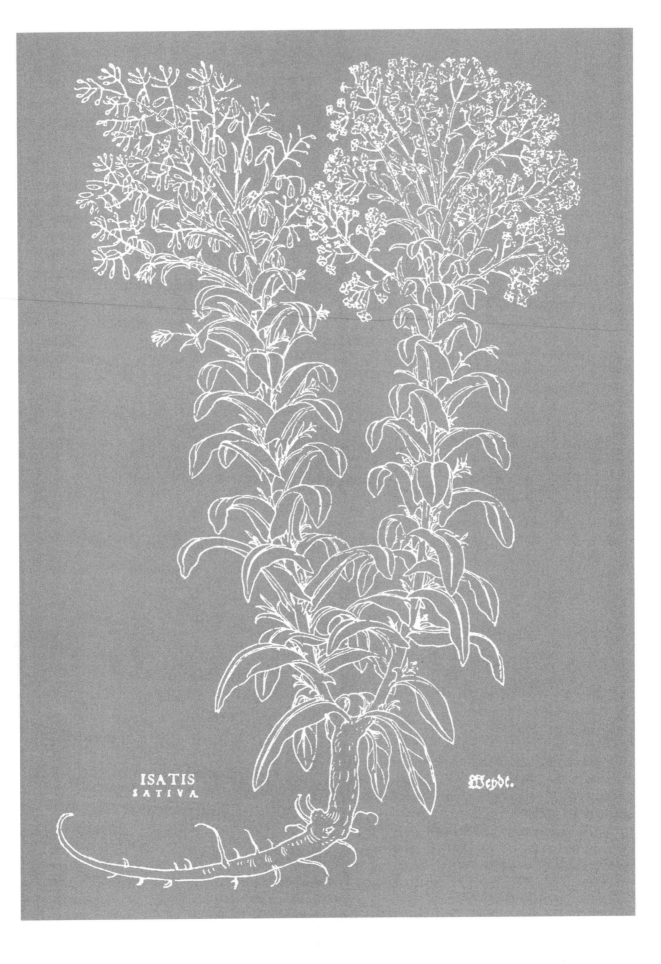

ISATIS
SATIVA

Weydt.

Herbs to Reduce Infection

Known as *anti-infectives,* botanical remedies in this class are used to treat infection, which essentially is pathology arising from the presence of injurious (toxic) microorganisms. *Anti-infective* herbs address many kinds of infections, including bacterial, viral, fungal, spirochetal, amoebal and protozoal infections. They work in four fundamental ways wherever appropriate:
1. They reduce toxicosis, the basic ground or terrain of infection; this is a *detoxicant* action.
2. They clear pathogenic heat by reducing fever and inflammation; i.e. they are *refrigerant.*
3. They stimulate immune activity and enhance defense response to pathogens; i.e. they are *immunostimulant.*
4. They disinfect at the site of the infection itself; i.e. they are *antiseptic.*

Clearly, rather than constituting a single treatment strategy therefore, reducing infection really requires several herb actions working in concert.

The Nature and Dynamics of Infection

Generally speaking, the successful management of infectious conditions in herbal medicine closely depends primarily on balancing and boosting the individual ground (terrain). Reducing infection is not simply a matter of wiping out the presumed offending pathogen seen to be involved in these conditions, as was blithely believed in past bacteriological medicine. For infection to develop, both a triggering cause—the pathogen—and a predisposing cause—the individual ground of disharmony—usually needs to be present. Whereas the triggering causes of infection are well known in modern epidemiology, less is generally understood about the body's own predispositions to infection.

Today we know that a major factor involved in the development of infection is compromised immunity. Freedom from infection depends on the integrity and strength of the individual's own vital defense responses (*wei qi*), which are an essential function of the life force (*qi*). Moreover, traditional medical systems tell us that in turn, the efficiency of the body's defenses intimately depend on the integrity of the individual ground, which in turn is shaped by both physiological and psychological factors. This is currently the study of psychoneuroendocrine-immunology. On the physiological level, toxicosis—the pathological accumulation in the system of various types of toxins—can be pinpointed as the major systemic disruptor of immune efficiency (see the introduction to Class 13). On the psychological level, we can single out chronic unproductive stress and unconscious fear and anxiety as the primary offenders (see the introduction to Class 11).

A fresh look at the nature of microbes will help us understand the difference between a healthy human ground and an unhealthy or deficient one. It will specifically also give us an insight into the origins of toxicosis as an infection-predisposing factor. Today it is becoming clearer from the emerging "new biology" that the body possesses its own ecosystem of beneficial microbes, whose job it is to maintain internal homeostasis and freedom from infection. When this commensal ecosystem is healthy it creates the ideal balanced internal condition known as **microbial eubiosis.** When the body's own microbial environment is imbalanced or insufficient, this becomes a state of **microbial dysbiosis.** In this predisposing condition, external pathogens are then far more likely to trigger an infection.

While current medical science still focuses on identifying and eliminating the external microbes involved, traditional medical systems, as just noted, emphasize correcting the ground of disease—including the body's own internal microbial environment. The vitality of this ground specifically depends on the health of the intestinal microflora, which is the hub of the body's whole microbial ecosystem. In health, this intestinal microecology is balanced or eubiotic in both quantity and quality of fungal and bacterial blooms. When this floral ecosystem becomes disrupted, intestinal dysbiosis ensues, which increases the production and retention of toxins of different types (i.e., toxicosis), thereby predisposing the individual to a status of lowered resistance to infection.

Stated another way, microorganisms are fundamentally opportunistic entities. The largest proportion of the body's bacteria, viruses and fungi actually remain harmless as part of its healthy symbiotic commensal microbial ecology, as these microorganisms go about their various positive tasks within the body's complex ecosystem. Put in a positive sense, on the contrary the body's microbes play an entirely active beneficial role, the most important of which is the maintenance of a healthy, vital immunity by regulating intestinal symbiosis and optimizing eubiosis.

The essential reason why beneficial commensal microbes multiply, diversify, colonize and so become toxic, i.e., infectious, is when the body's own defense functions break down in one way or another. In other words, microbes only become pathogenic in the presence of compromised immunity arising from toxicosis, intestinal dysbiosis, chronic unproductive stress or anxiety. This can occur, e.g. with excessive use of broad-spectrum antibiotics, which cause an overgrowth of harmful gut bacteria and candida. In this sense, all infections have an endogenous prodisposing cause as well as immediate exogenous triggering factors.

The only exception to this rule is epidemics and pandemics caused by potent microbes that can overwhelm even healthy individuals. Today we see many pertinent examples of microbial opportunism. The influenza viruses, for instance, fast-mutating viruses that are becoming more difficult to treat; various gastrointestinal viruses that fail to respond to the latest antibiotics; the herpes viruses that often cause hidden infections that lie dormant and undetected for years before causing any symptoms; and the fragile HIV viruses that, given the right predispositions such as candidiasis (an outgrowth of intestinal dysbiosis) and immune deficiency will generate the autoimmune-based AIDS syndrome.

The especially unfortunate part of this modern scenario is that Western medicine actually encourages, albeit unwittingly, the creation of antibiotics-resistant strains of microbes. This could be called iatrogenic microbiogenesis. The overuse of antibiotics can stimulate the mutation of bacteria and other microbes into various forms hitherto unknown. Likewise, an incomplete or prematurely withdrawn course of antibiotics can also create the same result by promoting the multiplication of more resistant strains. Part of the microbes' opportunism is their ability to adapt—by changing their physical form and then by increasing in number. Their natural and endless adaptability makes them more toxic and less responsive to antibiotics, as they constantly outwit the most sophisticated designer drugs. Clearly, microbial dysbiosis and the iatrogenic appearance (individual or pandemic) of more virulent microbes *together* are making commonplace infections such as flu and bronchitis increasingly difficult to treat using the conventional pathogen-reduction approach with antibiotics. These are the two key factors in the ongoing antibiotics crisis.

Another consideration must be factored into the nature of infection. The condition of microbial eubiosis and specifically of intestinal eubiosis is largely dependent on the individual's healthy relationship to the environment. This is a crucial relationship that depends on the daily intake of probiotic fermented foods used in various traditional cultures—foods such as live yoghurt, sauerkraut pickles, miso (fermented soybean paste) and tempeh (fermented soybean patties). By implanting naturally-occuring bacterial end fungal strains from the environment into the system to continuously renew and build the commensal intestinal microflora, the body acquires and maintains a natural immunity that can potentially resist virulent microbial strains if and when they arise. The problem today is that the relationship between humans and the environment has become strained because of environmental degradation and destruction on one hand, and the related imbalanced intake of food on the other. The quantitative reduction and qualitative weakening of probiotic foods has led to increased immune deficiency and intestinal dysbiosis with a resultant rise in chronic, often untreated infections. This is why the intake of the natural fermented foods just mentioned is essential for health maintenance, as well as supplementation with probiotic products like *lactobacillus acidophilus* and *l. bifidus*, and bovine colostrum.

By addressing the predisposing causes to infection, and by addressing the individual ground, herbal medicine (along with other holistic treatment modalities) can decrease the very conditions favorable for the damaging proliferation and/or invasion of microbial pathogens. The approach here is clearly dialectic and preventive rather than linear and repair-oriented.

The Prevention and Treatment of Infection

Two major approaches for managing infectious conditions exist, the first preventive, the second curative or remedial. It is important to distinguish these and use them appropriately according to the needs of the particular situation.

As just seen, the first, most fundamental strategy is to maximize immune potential by re-establishing an optimum balance with our natural environment. This approach should be used when a person's condition is either relatively eubiosic or dysbiotic with possible chronic or recurring infections present. This preventive approach assists non-specific immunity by correcting the imbalanced ground (terrain) that underlies most infections. Among the many ways that immune potential can be maximized, the most prominent are a balanced wholefood diet rich in natural fermented foods, the use of *adaptogenic* and other *restorative* herbs, regular exercise (including deep diaphragmatic breathing) and various meditation and psychological practices. This treatment method and the relevant herbs are discussed in the introductions to Classes 7, 9 and 13.

The second approach is to reduce infection itself though a combination of immune stimulation and promotion of tissue asepsis. This method should be used when the individual is in the toxicosis phase with acute or subacute infection present. This remedial approach utilizes *immunostimulant*, *anti-infective* and *detoxicant* remedies of various types to treat the infection itself.

In vitalistic medicine, infectious conditions are categorized by the specific types of conditions they generate. It follows then that herb selection for treating infections is carried out according to three presenting factors:

1. The syndrome. Acute infections tend to create patterns of **wind-heat, damp-heat** and **toxic-heat,** while chronic infections will cause **damp-cold** conditions.
• **Wind-heat** infections require herbs that promote sweating and reduce fever (Class 1).

• **Damp-heat** infections require herbs that clear damp-heat and stop discharge (Class 12).
• **Toxic heat** infections require herbs that clear fire toxin and relieve swelling (Class 12).
• **Damp-cold** infections require herbs that transform damp and stop discharge (Class 15).

2. The tissue condition. Using the criteria of the tissue condition, when a terrain of **toxicosis,** especially **microbial toxicosis,** underpins an infection, this must be addressed with remedies that promote detoxification and resolve toxicosis (Class 13).

3. The specific symptoms. For example:
• **Anxiety** and **agitation** require herbs that release constraint (Class 11) or calm the mind (Class 19).
• **Fever** requires *antipyretics* (Class 12).
• **Discharges** require *antidischarge* and *mucostatic* herbs (Class and 15).

The Herbs that Reduce Infection

Anti-infective remedies vary in their ability to counteract microbes. The most effective in general can be termed *broad-spectrum anti-infectives,* because they counteract a wide variety of microbes, especially bacterial, viral and fungal. The majority will be found in Class 12 They operate in two ways: One, by stimulating immune functions and increasing defense response to pathogens. Second, by disinfecting locally at the site of infection. Because their *anti-infective* action consists, for the most part, of a combined systemic *immunostimulant* action and a local *antiseptic* or *disinfectant* one, their efficiency in terminating infections is very high.

Anti-infective remedies are additionally generally *antipyretic, anti-inflammatory* and *detoxicant.* That is to say, they reduce fever, inflammation and toxins—functions entirely appropriate and synergistic in promoting a resolution of infection. The multifaceted action of these herbs results from a spontaneous, self-regulating synergism with the individual's own vital capacity to keep (potential) pathogens under control and maintain homeostasis. This occurs regardless of whether microbial dysbiosis is generated endogenously or exogenously, or by a combination of these two.
• Among the most prominent *broad-spectrum anti-infectives* are Garlic bulb, Echinacea root, Marigold flower, Wild indigo root, Goldenseal root, and the essential oils of *Thyme, Oregano, Manuka, Tea*

835

tree, *Niaouli, Palmarosa, Cinnamon* and *Clove*. The majority of these are pungent in taste and stimulant by nature, but can conveniently be divided into cooling and warming types.

• *Cold anti-infectives* are far more common and address infections presenting **heat** of some kind, i.e., fever and inflammation, especially **damp-heat** and **toxic-heat** syndromes. *Cold anti-infectives* are typically very bitter, astringent, dry, cold and sinking in quality—witness Goldenseal root, Chaparral leaf, Wild indigo root and (from East Asia) Coptis Huang Lian (Goldthread root) and Sophora Ku Shen (Yellow pagoda tree root).

• *Warming anti-infectives*, which include Garlic bulb and *Thyme, Myrrh, Cinnamon* and *Clove* essential oil, ideally treat infections presenting **damp-cold.**

Treatment and Administration Considerations

Broad-spectrum anti-infectives are used in one of two ways: preventively or curatively. First, they can prevent contagion during an acute epidemic caused by an exogenous pathogen, such as influenza. They should be taken as soon as a person feels an infection coming on. At the onset of an infection, the immune system can mount a more effective defense, and the chances of a speedy resolution are much higher. Second, they can cure an already established infection.

Anti-infective remedies should not be taken, as they sometimes mistakenly are, for the purpose of strengthening immune functions in times of relative good health. They do not have the endocrine depth of action that *immune enhancers* alone possess, a type of action necessary for building general non-specific resistance. As seen above, in a predisposed environment, infection can ultimately only be prevented from flaring up by strengthening neuroendocrine-immune functions, balancing the intestinal flora and regulating the overall ecology of beneficial microorganisms.

Several administration protocols need to be adhered to for *anti-infectives* to work best in acute infections in general.

• **Higher-than-normal dosages** are the rule for unfolding an *antimicrobial* action in these plants. 20-50g of a dried herb formula should be used for a single dose, repeated four to six times throughout the day. In tincture form the right average dosage is one teaspoon or more, i.e. 5-7 ml.

• **Repeating the dosage** of the herb or tincture formula several times a day is crucial in acute infections. In moderate to severe cases, one dose should be taken *every two hours*.

• **Judicious herb combining** is neccessary to achieve best *anti-infective* results, as thousands of years of experience also shown, rather than by using a single remedy alone. In the phenomenon of herb synergy, taking two or more plants together potentiate (increase) their individual actions, resulting in a greater, more powerful effect.

The Pharmacology of Anti-Infective Herbs

From the biochemical viewpoint, a variety of constituents are presumed responsible for the *anti-infective* actions found in plants. Chief among them are polysaccharides, alkaloids, glycosides, and essential oil fractions, and vitamin C. Immune-stimulating polysaccharides are found, for instance, in Echinacea root, Microalgae, Reishi mushroom and such lichens as Usnea and Lungwort. A series of *anti-infective* isoquinoline alkaloids are present in Barberry bark, Goldenseal root and Goldthread root (Coptis Huang Lian for example. *Immunostimulant* essential oils include *Lavender, Eucalyptus, Ravensara, Niaouli, Frankincense* and *Tea tree*.

Local and specific *antiseptic* activity among plants is provided by such components as essential oils, tannins, resins and alkaloids. The essential oils of certain plants in particular are the most powerful natural *antiseptic* substances known: *Thyme, Winter savory, Oregano, Cinnamon, Tea tree, Niaouli, Cajeput, Ravensara, Eucalyptus, Palmarosa* and *Clove* are among the strongest in this respect. All have natural affinities for treating certain types of infections—*Thyme, Ravensara* and *Eucalyptus* for respiratory infections, *Juniper, Fennel, Bergamot* for urinary infections, *Tea tree, Niaouli* and *Myrrh* for gastrointestinal and genital infections, and so on. Essential oils are used both internally and externally in compresses, vaginal douches and sponges, and a variety of other administration forms (see Chapter 8). However, it must be stressed here that for reasons of safety *and* efficacy, only genuine and authentic essential oils should be used for these purposes. Furthermore, because essential oils are inherently strong and intense by nature, they should only be used in the correct dosages and dilutions. Moreover, some oils are irritating to the skin and/or mucous membrane and should only be administered in specific preparations, such as gel caps for oral use.

In modern times, *in vitro* (laboratory) and *in vivo* (clinical) studies both have shown that certain herbs are more effective against certain types of microorganisms than they are against others. *Tea tree* essential oil, for instance, works best for gram-negative bacilli such as enterobacterial infections and influenza. Goldenseal root and Barberry root, for example, are known to be more effective in treating gram-negative bacilli than gram-positive ones, and more effective with influenza viruses than with others. Again, certain remedies are more *antiviral,* such as Echinacea root, Garlic bulb, Arborvitae tip and the essential oils of *Ravensara, Palmarosa, Thuja, Clove, Cinnamon, Tea tree, Niaouli, Cistus* and *Eucalyptus radiata.* Others are specifically *antifungal,* including Marigold flower and the essential oils of *Myrrh, Palmarosa, Clove, Winter savory, Cinnamon, Tea tree* and *Thyme.*

It is important to remember that, unlike syn-thetic antibiotic drugs, plant *anti-infectives* work *with* the organism's own defense functions, not against them. By engaging the individual's life for-ce rather than overriding it, they avoid the familiar "side effects" of antibiotics, such as weakened intestinal flora and diminished immune function-ing. Ultimately, their ease of use makes them superior to synthetic antibiotics, life-saving though these can sometimes be. It is known that antibiotics progressively weaken the organism as they carry out their "search and destroy" mission with mech-anical disregard for the organism's own defensive efforts. Besides, in working in cooperation with the organism rather than in spite of it, herbal *anti-infectives* also preserve the ecology of beneficial microorganisms that are needed to maintain the integrity of a person's eubiosis, or optimal balance of beneficial microorganisms.

A summary list of the different types of *anti-infective* remedies in this class—*antibacterials, antifungals, antiparasitics* and *antivirals*—is found in the Repertory under Infection and Infections, chronic.

CVCVRBITA
MAIOR
Groß Kürbß.

Herbs to Eliminate Parasites

Remedies in this class are used to treat parasitosis, infection or infestation by parasites—basically microorganisms exhibiting parasitic behavior. *Antiparasitic* remedies work by killing and/or expelling both internal and external types of parasites. Internal parasites include helminths (worms) such as roundworm, tapeworm, pinworm, hookworm and blood flukes, mycoses (fungi) such as candida, and protozoa such as trichomonas, malaria, amoeba and giardia. Parasites found on external body surfaces include fungi such as tinea (e.g., ringworm), scabies, pedicula and hookworm and roundworm. Traditional medical systems worldwide have relied more or less successfully on botanical *antiparasitics* for many millennia. Oriental and Ayurvedic medicine in particular incorporate many safe and fairly effective *antiparasitics,* not only because of the long-term development of these empirical medical systems, but also because of the sheer number of plant species available to them in East Asia and India, respectively.

The Nature and Treatment of Parasitosis

Apart from the commonly-found intestinal parasites, there is a whole universe of possible parasites that require specific diagnosis through a stool culture test, for example, and treatment with specific types of *antiparasitic* remedies. Therefore, in the treatment of parasitosis it is important first to consider the body's systemic presenting terrain. Like all microorganisms, parasites do not arise in a vacuum. They thrive in the system only when the body is unable to remove them. It is therefore often necessary to address an underlying deficiency of the person's systemic terrain in addition to eliminating the parasites themselves. This underscores the importance of the Restoring treatment methods for preventing and treating parasites, using remedies that tonify the Qi, tonify the Yang, nourish the blood and nourish the Yin (Classes 7-10).

The treatment of parasitic infection is compli-
cated by two facts. First, the presence of parasites is often asymptomatic, difficult to determine through tests, or masked by symptoms that could result from a number of different conditions. These symptoms include fatigue, sugar cravings, rectal itch, postprandial drowsiness, nervousness, irritability, depression, insomnia, clenching of teeth at night, night terrors, gingivitis, bluish sclera and ridges in the fingernails. Rarely presenting on its own, parasitosis is usually accompanied by functional internal disorders, especially of a metabolic nature. These include dyslexia, attention deficit disorder (ADD), hyperactivity, eczema, psoriasis, herpes, asthma, allergic sinusitis, chronic respiratory and ear infections, nasal polyps, irritable bowel syndrome, inflammatory bowel disease, candidiasis, chronic urinary infections, prostatitis, chronic pelvic inflammatory disease, cervical dysplasia, impotence, frigidity, chronic fatigue syndrome, AIDS, chronic hepatitis and cancer. Often the possibility of parasites is only considered after many other disease causes have been ruled out, or after many different treatment strategies have vainly been attempted. As a result, diagnosis and treatment for parasites often occurs by default rather than through positive diagnosis. Nevertheless, if parasites *are* the cause or major component of a syndrome, then results with *antiparasitic* remedies will often be good.

Second, there is a commonly little understood relationship between infestation by parasites and infection by other microorganisms such as viruses, fungi and bacteria. This may be because ultimately all microbes that create an infection have the potential for becoming parasitic. It is fairly well established, if not widely known, that there are common interactions between one type of infection and another. This may be explained in microbiological terms through the phenomenon of pleomorphic mutation (change of form and multiplication) that all microorganisms are known to perform (see the work of Antoine Béchamp, Günther Enderlein, Gaston Naessens and many others in the 19th and 20th centuries). Regardless of theory and the often controversial findings of various microbiologists, it is a fact of clinical experience that infection by one type of microbe usually predisposes to infection by another. The influenza virus causing a secondary bacterial sinus, throat or bronchial infection is a common example. But so is the presence of fungal infection such as candidiasis leading to a fully-developed HIV infection. Because of the endless relationship possibilities among microorganisms, it is important to let no infection go unresolved, however minor, and, if in doubt, to treat for a wide spectrum of infection rather than just one specific type. Fortunately, most herbal remedies possess a variety of *antiparasitic* actions, not just a single one.

The Herbs that Treat Internal Parasites

Although most *antiparasitic* remedies will treat a variety of parasitic conditions, all have specific applications that produce best results. The remedies that treat internal parasites are often called *anthelmintics* because the main type of parasite they treat are helminths, or worms. Western *anthelmintic* remedies that treat intestinal parasites include the following:
• Pumpkin seed, Walnut hull, Pineappleweed herb, Wormwood herb, Knotgrass herb, Male fern root, Garlic bulb, Clove bulb, Cinnamon bark, European and American wormseed, Rue herb, Tansy flower, Pink root and Annual wormwood herb.
• Chinese medicine counts *anthelmintics* such as Areca Bing Lang (Betel nut), Brucea Ya Dan Zi (Java brucea berry), Quisqualis Shi Jun Zi (Rangoon creeper nut) and Dichroa Chang Shan (Feverflower root). We should note that because of the sheer number of plant species available in East Asia, Oriental medicine has at its disposal a far greater number of effective yet safe *antiparasitic* remedies than we do in the West (HOLMES 1997, 2002).

The majority of good *anthelmintics* work in two ways: they are *vermicides* because they are believed to kill the parasites; and they are *vermi-*

fuges, as they also flush the parasites out. However, there is little reliable information available on this topic, except that certain remedies are definitely known to destroy parasites in general (and helminths in partiular), including Ipecac root, Gentian root, Rue herb, Boldo leaf and the essential oils of *Thyme linalool, Cinnamon, Cassia, Oregano, Black spruce, Clove, Niaouli, Eucalyptus, Cajeput* and *Boldo.* These essential oils are often used for treating intestinal parasites, for instance. They depend primarily on their content in phenols, monoterpene alcohols, oxydes, lactones and ketones for their *antiparasitic* activity (FRANCHOMME and PENOEL 1990).

Remedies known for their specifically *antiprotozoal* action include Oak bark, Gentian root and Garlic bulb. Berberis is a specific remedy for Leishmaniasis donorenii.

Because some of these remedies contain compounds that produce cumulative toxicity when taken every day, care should be taken with respect to dosage, administration and number of days ingested. The directions and cautions given at the end of each remedy presentation should be read and followed carefully.

The Herbs that Treat External Parasites

Remedies for external parasites are called *parasiticides,* and include Aloe gel, Alum root, Camphor, and the essential oils of *Thyme, Lemon, Eucalyptus* and *Lavender.* Chinese medicine relies on herbs such as Cnidium She Chuang Zi, Sophora Ku Shen and Melia Ku Lian Pi. In addition, both Western and Chinese herbal medicine made or still make extensive use of mineral and other inorganic substances for external parasites—such as Alum, Realgar, Litharge, Sulphur and Calomel. On the whole these are more effective than plant remedies and, alongside essential oils, should also be considered as a first line of treatment.

A summary of remedies in this class is found in the Repertory under Intestinal parasites and Parasites, skin.

Source Books

This listing represents a selection of the more significant Greek medical texts on botanical medicine in the last two thousand years, covering both pharmacognosy and pharmacology. For ease of reference it is divided into two periods, before 1450 and after 1450, a date that marks the end of the medieval and the beginning of the modern period.

These sources by themselves in no way represent the main texts of traditional Greek medicine. The majority of texts are on pathology and therapeutics, as well as various branches of internal medicine. They are omitted from this bibliography.

Although the greatest number of medical texts of all kinds were written in the Muslim-Arabic (Tibb Unani) phase of Greek medicine between 700 and 1300 A.D., this bibliography lists more texts written after 1450 for the purely practical reason of accessability. Only a small selection of the most important pre-1450 writings have been included. The largest portion of Greek, Hebrew, Persian, Arabic and Latin materia medicas, formularies, toxicology works, synonymic treatises and synoptic texts have therefore necessarily been omitted. However, they may be found in the only truly reliable work on Islamic-Greek medicine, Manfred Ullmann's *Die Medizin im Islam*.

Likewise, most European pharmacopoeias that that were issued from the fifteenth century onwards have been omitted; their inclusion would have been repetitious.

In addition to the works listed, numerous historical and travel books containing incidental information on herbs and their uses since the Renaissance were consulted. Their inclusion would have extended this list unnecessarily. Most pertaining to North America may be found in the bibliography of one of the leading texts on the subject, Virgil Vogel's *American Indian Medicine*.

Greek, Roman, Alexandrian and Arab Phase to 1450

Where translations in a Western language are available, no reference to the location of the original manuscript(s) is usually given. References to these may be found in studies listed under "Works on the History of Herbal Medicine" below.

abu Mansur Muwaffaq. *Kitab al-abniya 'an haqa'iq al-adwiya [Book of the Foundations of the True (Properties) of Remedies]*. 10th cent. (tr. F. R. Seligman, Wien, 1838)

al-Samarqandi. *Aqrabadin*. (tr. Latin, Venezia, 1471)

Ar-Razi, Abu bekr Mohammad ben Zakaria [Rhazes]. *Al-Kitab al-hawi [The Comprehensive Work, Liber Continens]*. Bagdhad, 9th cent.

———. *Al-kitab al-mansuri [Liber almansoris]*. tr. Latin, Milano, 1481

———. *Aqrabadin [Antidotarium]*. (tr. Hebrew 1257; tr. Latin, Venezia 1497)

Az-Zahrawi, abul-Qasim. *Kitab al-tasrif liman 'ajiza it-ta'alif [Book of Explanations for Those Weak in Nourishment]*. Cordova 10th cent. (partly tr. S.K. Harmaneh and G. Sonnedecker in *A Pharmaceutical View of Abulcasis al-Zahrawi in Moorish Spain*)

Bingen, Hildegard von. *Physica*. 11th cent. (publ. Strassburg, 1533; tr. into German, Basel, 1985

Celsus, Cornelius. *De medicina*. Rome 1st cent. (tr. W.G. Spencer, Cambridge, 1935; tr. into French A. Chaales des Étangs as *Oeuvres complètes*. Paris, 1850)

Dioskurides, Pedanios. *Peri hyles iatrikes [On Simple Remedies]*. c. 78 A.D. (tr. John Goodyer 1655, ed. R.T. Gunther, Oxford, 1934)

Galenos, Claudios [Galen]. *Peri kraseos kai dynameos ton haplon pharmakon [On the Mixture and*

Effective Qualities of Simple Remedies]. Roma, 2nd cent. A.D. (tr. as *De simplicium medicamentorum temperamentis et facultatibus); tr. into French as *Deux livres des simples de Galien*. Lyon, 1542)

———. *Peri trophon dynameon [On the Effective Qualities of Food]*. (tr. J. Martinius as *De alimentorum facultatibus*. Paris, 1530

———. *Peri syntheseos pharmakon [On the Composition of Remedies]*.

Hippokrates. *Corpus Hippocraticum*. 4th cent. B.C. (tr. Emile Littré as *Oeuvres complètes*. Paris, 1839)

ibn Ahmad al-Biruni, abu r-Raihan Muhammad. *Kitab as-saidana fit-tibb [Medical Pharmacognosy]*. 12th cent. (tr. Fritz Krenkow as *The Drug Book of Biruni* in Islamic Culture 20, 1946)

ibn al-Baitar, Diya' ad-Din abu Mohammad 'Abd Allah ibn Ahmad. *Kitab al-gami' li-mufradat al-adwiya wa-l-agdiya [Collection of Simple Remedies and Foods]*. Sevilla, c. 1225 (tr. Louis Leclerc as *Traité des simples*. Paris, 1877-83)

———. *Kitab al-mugni fi l-adwiya al-mufrada [Concerning Simple Remedies and Foods]*. Cordoba, c. 1239 (Ms. e.g. Bodleian I 588 (= Hunt.183)

ibn abi Halid al-Gazzar, Abu Ga'far Ahmad ibn Ibrahim. *Kitab al-I'timad fi l-adwiya al-mufrada [The Reliability Concerning Simple Remedies]*. 11th cent. (tr. Stephanus di Saragossa as *Adminiculum, sive liber fiduciae*. ed. Lothar Volger, Berlin, 1941)

ibn Biklaris, Yusuf ibn Ishaq. *Kitab al-musta'ini*. Almeria, ca. 1100 (partly tr. M. Levey and S. Souryal in *Janus*, 1968)

ibn Gazla. *Kitab minhag al-bayan fi-ma yasta'-miluhu l-insan [The Way of Clarification of That Used by Man]*. 11th cent. (tr. Pieter de Konings, ed. Eugen Mittwoch in *Quellen und Studien zur Geschichte der Naturwissenschaften und der Medizin 3*, 1933)

ibn Masawaih, abu Zakariya' Yuhanna [Mesuë Senior, Joannes Damascenus]. *Kitab jawahir al-tibb al-mufrada [On Simple Aromatic Substances]*. (tr. Martin Levey, *Journal Hist. Med. 16*, 394-410, 1961)

ibn Muhammad al-Gafiqi, Abu Ga'far Ahmad. *Kitab al-adwiya al-mufrada [Book of Medicinal Simples]*. Cordoba, 12th cent. (Ms. e.g. Osler Library Montreal, no. 7508)

ibn Muhammad al-Qalanisi, Badr al-Din Muhammad ibn Bahram. *Aqrabadin*. 590 (Ms. e.g. Wellcome Catalogue, p. 79)

ibn Rushd, Abu 'I-Walid Muhammad [Averroes]. *Kitab al-kulliyat fil-tibb [Compendium of Medical Kowledge]*. Marrakech, 1162.

ibn Samagun, Abu Bakr Hamid. *Kitab al-gami' li-aqwal al-qudama wa'l-mutahaddiatin mina l-atibba' wa-l-mutafalsifin fi l-adwiya al-mufrada [Collection of Statements of Older and Recent Physicians and Philosophers on Simple Remedies]*. Cordoba,10th cent. (partly tr. Paul Kahle in *Ibn Samagun und sein Drogenbuch in Documenta Islamica Inedita*. Berlin, 1952)

ibn Sina, Abu Ali Alhossain [Avicenna]. *Al qanun fi al-tibb [Canon of Medicine]*. Bagdhad, 11th cent. (tr. Vopisco Fortunato Plempio, 1658; book 1 tr. O.C. Gruner as *The Canon of Medicine of Avicenna*. London, 1930; tr. M.H. Shaw, *Avicenna's Canon…* Karachi, 1966)

Moses ben Maimon [Maimonides]. *Maimonidis medici ... Specimen diaeteticum*. 12th cent., tr. E.L. Kirschbaum, Berlin, 1822

Oreibasios. *Synagogai iatrikai pros Iulianon [Collection of Remedies for Julianus]*. 4th cent. (tr. U.C. Bussemaker and Charles Daremberg in *Oeuvres d'Oribase*. Paris, 1851-76, 6 vols.)

Paulus of Aegina. *Hypomynema*. 7th cent. (tr. Hunain ibn Ishaq into Arabic as *Kunnas at-turaiya, Handbook of the Pleiades*, tr. F. Adams into English as *The Seven Books of Paulus Aegina*, 3 vols., London, 1845-47; tr. I. Berendes as *Paulus' von Aegina des besten Arztes Sieben Bücher, Leiden, 1914)

Pseudo-Yuhanna ibn Masawaih [Joannes Mesuë]. *Antidotarium sive grabaddin medicamentum compositorium [Antidotary of Compound Medications]*. publ. Venezia, 1471

Rufus of Ephesos. *Peri thanasimon pharmakon [On Toxic Remedies]*. 1st cent. (tr. Charles Daremberg and Charles Emile Ruelle in *Oeuvres de Rufus d'Ephèse*. Paris, 1879)

Salernitatus, Nicolaus. *Antidotarium Nicolai*. 11th cent. (partly tr. by M. Steinschneider in *Virchow's*

Archiv 40, 96, 1867)

Theophrastus of Eresos. *Peri phyton historias [De historia plantarum, Enquiry into Plants]*. ca. 260 B.C. (tr. Curt Sprengel as *Theophrast's Naturgeschichte der Gewächse*. Altona, 1822)

Renaissance and Modern Phase (after 1450)

Ballard, E. *Elements of Therapeutics and Materia Medica*. Philadelphia, 1846

Barham, Henry. *Hortus Americanus*. London, 1794

Bartholow, R. *A Practical Treatise on Materia Medica and Therapeutics*. 1885

Barton, Benjamin S. *Collections Towards a Materia Medica of the United States*. Philadelphia, 1798

Barton, William P.C. *Vegetable Materia Medica of the United States*. Philadelphia, 1817-18

Bauhin, Jean. *Historia plantarum universalis*. Yverdon, Switzerland, 1650

Beach, Wooster. *American Practice*. New York, 1842

———. *The Family Physician*. Philadelphia, 1846

Bergzabern, Johann Jakob Theodor von. *Neu Kreuterbuch*. Francfurth am Main, 1588

Bernatzic, and Von Vogl. *Arzneimittellehre*. Wien, 1900

Bézanger-Beauquesne, L., M. Pinkas and M. Torck. *Les plantes dans la thérapeutique moderne*. Paris, 1975

Bigelow, Jacob. *American Medical Botany*. Boston, 1817-20

Bock, Hieronimus. *New Kreutter Buch*. Strassburg, 1532

Boerhaave, Hermann. *De viribus medicamentorum*. (tr. J. Martyn as *A Treatise on the Power of Medecines*. London, 1740; tr. as *Herman Boerhaave's Materia Medica*. London, 1741)

Brinker, Francis J. (compiler). *An Introduction to the Toxicology of Common medicinal Substances*. Portland, 1983

Britten, James, and Holland, Robert. *A Dictionary of English Plant-Names*. London, 1878

Brunfels, Otto. *Herbarum vivae eicones*. Strassburg, 1530

———. *Contrafayt Kreutterbuch*. Strassburg, 1532

Butler, G.F.. *A Text-Book of Materia Medica, Pharmacology and Therapeutics*. 1910

Cazin, F.-J. *Traité pratique et raisonné des plantes médicinales indigènes et acclimatisées*. Paris, 1886

Carrichter, Bartholomeus. *Kreutterbuch*. Strassburg, 1672

Chapman, N. *Elements of Materia Medica and Therapeutics*. Philadelphia, 1825

Charas, Moyse. *Pharmacopée royale galénique et chimique*. Lyons, 1693

Clute, Willard N. *American Plant Names*. 1940

Cole, William. *Adam in Eden*. London, 1657

———. *The Art of Simpling*. London, 1656

Cook, William H. *The Physiomedical Dispensatory*. 1869

Cullen, William. *A Treatise of the Materia Medica* (2 vols.). Philadelphia, 1808

Culbreth, David M.R. *A Manual of Materia Medica and Pharmacology*. 1927

Culpeper, Nicholas. *The English Physician*. London, 1652

Curtin, L.S.M. *Healing Herbs of the Upper Rio Grande*. Santa Fe, 1947

Da Legnano, L.P. *Le piante medicinali*. Roma, 1973

Desportes, Pouppé. *Traité ou abrégé des plantes usuelles des domingues*. Paris, 1770

Diers Rau, Henrietta A. *Healing with Herbs*. New York, 1977

Dinand, August Paul. *Handbuch der Heilpflanzenkunde*. München, 1929

Dodoens, Rembert. *Cruydeboek*. Antwerp, 1554

Duke, James A. *CRC Handbook of Medicinal Herbs*. Boca Raton, 1985

Duraffourd, C., L. D'Hervicourt and J.C. Lapraz. *Cahiers de phytothérapie clinique* (4 vols.). Paris, 1982

Eberle, John. *A Treatise on the Materia Medica and Therapeutics*. Philadelphia, 1834

Ellingwood, Finley. *American Materia Medica, Therapeutics and Pharmacognosy*. Evanston, 1919

Ellis, John. *Catalogue of Plants that may be Useful in America*. 1769

Emmons, S.B. *The Vegetable Family Physician*. 1836

Felter, Harvey Wickes. *The Eclectic Materia Medica, Pharmacology and Therapeutics*. Cincinnati, 1922

Flamm-Kroeber-Seel. *Die Heilkräfte der Pflanzen*. Stuttgart, 1942

Floridus, Macer. *De viribus herbarum*. 1477

Foster, Steven. *Herbal Renaissance*. Salt Lake City, 1993

Franchomme, Pierre, and Daniel Penoël. *L'aromatherapie exactement*. Limoges, 1990

Frawley, David, and Vasant Lad. *The Yoga of Herbs*. Santa Fe, 1986

Fuchs, Leonhardt. *De historia stirpium*. Basel, 1542

Fuller, Thomas. *Pharmacopoeia extemporanea*. London, 1730

Funke, Hans. *Die Welt der Heilpflanzen*. München, 1980

Fyfe. *Specific Diagnosis and Medication*. Cincinnati, 1909

Gerard, John. *Herball*. London, 1597

Gessner, Otto. *Die Gift und Arzneipflanzen von Mitteleuropa*. Heidelberg, 1953

Gmelin, J.F. *Onomatologia botanica*. Nürnberg, 1772

Goss. *Materia Medica and Therapeutics*. 1877

Gree, J.H. *The Physician in the House*. Chicago, 1897

Grieve, Maud. *A Modern Herbal*. London, 1931

Grohmann, Gerbert. *The Living World of Plants*. London, 1978

Hagen, Karl G. *Pharmacopoea Germanica*. Leipzig, 1872

Hänsel, R. *Pharmazeutische Biologie*. Berlin/Heidelberg/New York, 1980

Hänsel, R., and H.Haas. *Therapie mit Phytopharmaka*. Berlin/Heidelberg/New York, 1983

Harding, A.R. *Ginseng and Other Medicinal Plants*. Columbus, 1972

Hare, H.A., C. Caspari and H.H. Rusby. *The National Standard Dispensatory* (3rd ed.). 1916

Harvey, Gideon. *The Family Physician and the House-Apothecary*. London, 1678

Hegi, Gustav. *Illustrierte Flora von Mitteleuropa*. München, 1939

Heinerman, John. *Aloe Vera, Jojoba and Yucca*. New Canaan, 1982

Henry, Samuel. *New and Complete American Medical Family Herbal*. New York, 1814

Hollemback. *American Eclectic Materia Medica*. 1865

Holzner, W. ed., *Das Kritische Kräuterbuch*. Wien, 1986

Howard, Horton. *Howard's Domestic Medicine*. 1873

Hughes, William. *The American Physician*. London, 1672

Hutchens, Alma R. *Indian Herbalogy of North America*. Merco, Canada, 1973

Jones, Eli, and Scudder, John. *Materia Medica and Therapeutics*. Cincinnati, 1886

Josselyn, John. *New England's Rarities Discover'd*. London, 1672

Kindscher, Kelly. *Medicinal Plants of the Prairie*. Lawrence. Kansas, 1992

King, John. *The Eclectic Dispensatory of the United States of America*. Cincinnati 1852. Reprint: Portland, 1986

Krutch, Joseph Wood. *Herbal*. Boston, 1976

Leclerc, Henri. *Précis de phytothérapie*. Paris, 1935

L'Ecluse, Charles de. *Antidotarium*. Lyon, 1561

Lehamau, P.-J.-L. *Plantes, remèdes et maladies*. Paris, 1893

Lémery, Nicolas. *Pharmacopée universelle,* Paris, 1691

Leunis, Johannes. *Synopsis der Pflanzenkunde*. Hannover, 1877

Leyel, C.F. *Elixirs of Life*. London, 1948

———. *Compassionate Herbs*. London, 1946

List, P.H., and Hörhammer (ed.). *Hager's Handbuch der Pharmazeutischen Praxis*. Berlin/Heidelberg/New York, 1967

Lloyd, John Uri. *Drugs and Medicines of North America*. Vol 1, Cincinnati, 1884

L'Obel, Matthias de. *Stirpium adversaria nova*. Antwerp, 1570

Lonicer, Adam. *Kreuterbuch*. Francfort, 1557

Lovell, Robert. *Compleat Herball*. London, 1659

Lyle, T.J. *Physio-Medical Therapeutics, Materia Medica and Pharmacy*. Salem, 1897

Marzell, Heinrich. *Wörterbuch der Deutschen Pflanzennamen* (4 vols.). Leipzig, 1943

Mattioli, Pierandrea (ed. J. Verzascha). *Kreutterbuch*. Basel, 1611

Meddygon Myddfai (ed. Pughe). London, 1861

Mentzel, Christian. *Index Nominum Plantaris*. Berlin, 1682

Mésségué. *Of Men and Plants*. London, 1970

Meyer, Joseph E. *The Herbalist and Herb Doctor*. Hammond, 1918

Meyrick, William. *The New Family Herbal*. Birmingham, England, 1789

Miller, Joseph. *Botanicum Officinale*. London, 1722

Mills, Simon. *One Year Course of the National Institute of Medical Herbalist*. Tunbridge Wells, England, 1981

Millspaugh, Charles F. *American Medicinal Plants*. New York, 1887

Mitchell, T.D. *Materia Medica and Therapeutics*. 1850

Monardes, Nicolas. *Historia medicinal de las cosas que se traea de nuestras Indias Occidentales, que sirven en medicina*. Sevilla, 1574 (tr. John Frampton as *Joyfull Newes out of the Newe Founde Worlde*, London, 1577)

Moore, Michael. *Medicinal Plants of the Mountain West*. Albuquerque, New Mexico, 1979

———. *Medicinal Plants of the Desert and Canyon West*. Santa Fe, 1989

———. Medicinal Plants of the Pacific West. Santa Fe, 1993

Mowrey, Daniel B. *The Scientific Validation of Herbal Medicine*. 1986

Newton, James. *A Complete Herbal*. London, 1752

Paracelsus, Philipus Aureolus Theophrastus Bombastus von Hohenheim, *Herbal*. Basel, 1570

Pareira, J. *The Elements of Materia Medica and Therapeutics*. Philadelphia, 1843

Parkinson, John. *Theatrum botanicum*. London, 1629

Paulli, Simon. *Flora Danica*. Köbnhavn, 1648

Pelikan, Wilhelm. *Heilpflanzenkunde*. Dornach, 1962

Franchomme, Pierre, and Pénoël, Daniel. *L'Aromathérapie Exactement*. Limoges, 1990

Piso, Guialmo. *De medicina Brasilensi libri 4*. Amsterdam, 1648

Pomet, Pierre. *Histoire générale des drogues*. Paris, 1694

Priest, A.W., and L.R. Priest. *Herbal Medication*. London, 1982

Quincy, John. *Complete English Dispensatory*. London, 1736

Rafinesque, Constantine S. *Medical Flora or Manual of Medical Botany of the United States of America* (2 vols.). Philadelphia, 1830

Ratzenberger, Caspar. *Herbarius*. 1598

Reuss, Christian Friedrich. *Dictionarium botanicum*. Leipzig, 1781

Ripperger, W. *Grundlagen zur praktischen Pflanzenheilkunde*. Stuttgart, 1937

Rishel, Jonas. *The Indian Physician*. New Berlin, 1828

Rolland, Eugène. *Flore populaire*, 4 vols. Paris, 1896-1914

Rosmareinbüchlein…für Curen und Arzeneyen. 1675

Röszlin, Eucharius. *Kreutterbuch*. Francfurth, 1533

Ryff, Walther Hermann. *Confect Buch und Haus Apotheck*. Basel, 1548

———. *Reformierte Deutsche Apotheck*. Strassburg, 1573

———. *New Kochbuch für die Krancken*. Strassburg, 1545

Salmon, William. *Botanologia*. London, 1710

Schauenberg, Paul, and Ferdinand Paris. *Guide to Medicinal Plants*. London, 1977

Schöpf, Johann David. *Materia Medica Americana*. Erlangen, 1787

Schroeder, Johann. *Vollständige Chemical-Galenik und nutzreiche Apotheke*. Nürnberg, 1611

Schulz, H. *Vorlesungen über die Wirkungen und Anwendung der Deutschen Heilpflanzen*. Leipzig, 1921

Scudder, John Milton. *Specific Medication*. 1870

———. *Specific Diagnosis*. 1874

Scully, Virginia. *A Treasury of American Indian Herbs*. New York, 1970

Sherman, John A. *The Complete Botanical Prescriber*. Corvallis, Oregon, 1979

Shoemaker, J.V. *A Treatise on Materia Medica, Pharmacology and Therapeutics*. 1889

Shook, Edward. *A Treatise in Herbology*. Chicago, 1955

Short, Thomas. *Medicina Britannica*. Philadelphia, 1749

Simonis, Werner Christian. *Die Wunderwelt der Heilpflanzen*. Stuttgart, 1958

Smith, Arthur W. (ed.). Medicinal Plants of North America, Vol. 1, 1914

Smith, Daniel. *The Reformed Botanic and Indian Physician*. Utica, 1855

Smith, Elisha. *The Botanic Physician*. New York, 1830

Smith, Peter. *The Indian Doctor's Dispensatory*. Cincinnati, 1813

Spielman, J.R. *Pharmacopoeia universalis*. Strassburg, 1749

Stearns, Samuel. *The American Herbal or Materia Medica*. Walpole, 1772

Stille, A. *Therapeutics and Materia Medica*. 1874

Stuhr, Ernst T. *Manual of Pacific Coast Plants*. Oregon, 1933

Surya, G.W. *Die Verborgenen Heilkräfte der Heilpflanzen*. Freiburg in Breisgau, 1978

Tennent, J. *Every Man his own Doctor: or, The Poor Planter's Physician*. Williamsburg and Annapolis, 1734

Thomson, Samuel. *New Guide to Health, Or, Botanic Family Physician*. Boston, 1835

———. *The Thomsonian Materia Medica*. Boston, 1841

Tisserand, Robert. *The Art of Aromatherapy*. London, 1977

Tournefort, Pitton de. *Corollarium institutionem rei*. Paris, 1686

Triller, D.W. *Dispensatorium pharmacopoeia universale*. Frankfurth am Main, 1764

Trousseau, A. and Pidoux, H. *Treatise on Therapeutics*. New York, 1880

Turner, William. *A New Herball*. London, 1568

Usteri, Alfred. *Pflanzen, Menschen, Sterne*. Basel, 1925

———. *Mensch und Pflanze*. Basel, 1937

Valnet, Jean. *Phytothérapie*. Paris, 1972

———. *Aromathérapie*. Paris, 1976

———. *Traitement des maladies par les légumes, les fruits et les céréales*. Paris, 1977

van Wijk, Gerth H. *A Dictionary of Plant Names*. Den Haag, 1911

Wade, Carlson. *Bee Pollen and Your Health*. New Canaan, 1978

Waring, E.J. *A Manual of Practical Therapeutics*. 1886

Watts, Frank L. "The Multidimensional Ultramolecular Concept of Endocrine Nutrition", unpublished paper. San Diego, 1986

Weed, Susun. *Wise Woman Herbal for the Childbearing Year*. New York, 1986

———. *Healing Wise*. Woodstock, 1989

Weisenberg, A. *Handwörterbuch der Gesamten Arzneimittel*. Jena, 1853

Weiss, Rudolf Fritz. *Lehrbuch der Phytotherapie*. Stuttgart, 1944

Willard, Terry. *The Wild Rose Scientific Herbal.*. Calgary, 1991

Willfort, Richard. *Gesundheit durch Heilkräuter*. Linz, 1959

Books on Western Herbal Medicine

This is a selection of the more stimulating and reliable literature written down the ages; many works in languages other than English have again been omitted for practical reasons.

Aschner, Bernhard. *Lehrbuch der Konstitutionstherapie*. Stuttgart, 1928

Barrough, Phillip. *The Method of Physicke*. London, 1583

Beach, Wooster. *The American Practice of Medicine, or the Family Physician*. New York, 1833

Boyle, Robert. *The Sceptical Chymist*. London, 1661

Buchan, W. *The New Domestic Medicine*. London, 1820

Comfort, John W. *The Practice of Medicine on Thomsonian Principles*. Philadelphia, 1843

Commiers, de. *La médecine universelle, ou l'art de se conserver en santé et de prolonger la vie*. Paris, 1687

Cook, William H. *The Science and Practice of Medicine*. Chicago, 1879

Ellingwood, Finley. *A Systematic Treatise on Materia Medica and Therapeutics*. Chicago, 1898

———. *The Eclectic Practice of Medicine*. Chicago, 1910

Ettmueller, Michael. *Opera pharmaceutico-chymica*. Lugduni, 1686

Floyer, John, *The Touchstone of Medicines*. London, 1687

———. *The Physician's Pulse-Watch*. London, 1707

Galenos, Claudios [Galen]. *Techne iatrike [Ars magna, or Megategni]* (tr. Gerard of Cremona as *Ars*, 1487; tr. Nicholas Culpeper as *Galen's Art of Physick*, London, 1652)

———, *Therapeutike methodos (Ars magna* or *Megategni*, tr. Thomas Linnacre as *Methodus medendi*, Paris, 1519; tr. P. English as *Galen's Method of Physick*, Edinburgh, 1656)

Harig, Georg. *Bestimmung der Intesität im Medizinischem System Galen's*. Berlin, 1974

Hauschka, Rudolf. *Heilmittellehre*. Stuttgart, 1958

———, *Substanzlehre*. Stuttgart, 1956

Helvetius, Johann Friedrich. *Ein Edelgestein der Artzeney*. Heidelberg, 1661

Howard, H. *An Improved System of Botanic Medicine*. Cincinnati, 1832

Husemann, Friedrich, and Otto Wolf. *Das Bild des Menschen als Grundlage der Heilkunst*, 3 vols. Stuttgart, 1975-86

ibn Butlan. *Taqwim al-sihha* (tr. as *Tacuini sanitatis eluchasem elimithar medici de Baldath*. Strassburg, 1531)

ibn Gazla. *Taqwim al-abdan fi tadbir al-insan [Table of Bodies with Regard to their Constitution]* (tr. as *Tacuini aegritudinem cet. Buhahylyha byngezla autore*. Strassburg, 1582)

Institute of History of Medicine and Medical Research, *Theories and Philosophies of Medicine*. New Delhi, 1973

Lemnie, Levine. *The Touchstone of Complexions*. London, 1570

Levey, Martin. *Early Arabic Pharmacology*. Leiden, 1973

———. *Medieval Arabic Toxicology*. Leiden, 1978

Mills, Simon Y. *Out of the Earth*. London, 1991

Murray, Michael, and Pizzorno, Joseph. *Encyclopedia of Natural Medicine*. Rocklin, 1991

Nedham, Marchamont. *Medela medicinae*. London, 1665

Peterson, F.J. *Materia Medica and Clinical Therapeutics*. 1905

Rademacher, J.G. *Erfahrungsheillehre*. Berlin, 1851

Richter, Christian Friedrich. *Kurtzer and Deutlicher Unterricht von der Leibe Haus, Reis und Feld Apothecke*. 1705

Riddle, John M. *Dioscorides on Pharmacy and Medicine*. Austin, 1985

Salmon, William. *Synopsis medicinae*. London, 1702

Schechther, Steven R. *Fighting Radiation and Chemical Pollutants with Foods, Herbs and Vitamins*. Encinitas, 1988

Schenck, Johann Th. *Syntagma componendi et praescribendi medicamenta*. Jena, 1672

Schnaubelt, Kurt. *A Correspondence Course in Aromatherapy*. San Rafael, 1985

Schnepf, Walther. *Grundlagen zu einem geisteswissenschaftlich orientierten System der Pflanzenwelt*. Freiburg im Breisgau, 1951

Sennertus, Danielus. *Epitome Institutionum Medicorum*. Wittenberg, 1643

Shisti, Hakim. *The Natural Healer*. San Fransisco, 1989

Skelton, John. *Science and Practice of Botanic Medicine*. 1870

Siewecke, Herbert. *Anthroposophische Medizin*. Dornach, Switzerland, 1959

Silvaticum. *Liber pandectorum medicinae*. Taurini, 1526

Thurston, Joseph M. *The Philosophy of Physiomedicalism*. Richmond, Indiana, 1900

Villanova, Arnald de. *De regimine sanitatis*. Lausanne, 1482

———. *De conservanda juventute et retardanda senectute*. Paris, 1617

Vogel, Virgil J. *American Indian Medicine*. Norman, 1970

Webster, Herbert Tracy. *The Principles of Medicine as Applied to Dynamical Therapeutics*. Oakland, 1891

———. *Dynamical Therapeutics*. San Francisco, 1898

Books on Chinese Herbal and General Medicine in European Languages

Bensky, Dan, and Gamble, Andrew, comp. and trans. *Chinese Herbal Medicine: Materia Medica*. Seattle, 1986

Bensky, Dan, and Barolet, Randall, comp. and trans. *Chinese Herbal Medicine: Formulas and Strategies*. Seattle, 1991

Chang, S.S., and Chang, P.S. "Pharmacological actions of *Cordyceps chinensis* Zacc. Acta Pharm. Sinica 6(3), 1958

Cheung, C.S., and U Aik-kaw, comp. and trans. *Synopsis of The Pharmacopeia*. San Francisco, 1984

Cleyer, Andreas. *Medicamenta Simplicia Chinensium*. 1682

Duke, James A., and Ayensu, Edward S. *Medicinal Plants of China*. Algonac, 1985

Foster, Steven, and Yue Chonxi. *Herbal Emissaries*. Rochester, 1992

Fulder, Stephen. *The Tao of Medicine*. Rutland, 1985

Gauger, G. "Chinesische Roharzneiwaaren." Repertorium fur Pharmacie und praktische Chemie in Russland, Vol. VII. 1848

Halstead, Bruce, and Hood, Loretta L. *Eleutherococcus senticosus*. Los Angeles, 1984

Hanbury, Daniel. "Notes on Chinese Materia Medica." Pharmaceutical Journal. 1860-61

Holmes, Peter. *Jade Remedies: A Chinese Herbal Reference for the West* (2 vols.). Boulder, 1997

Hsu Hong-yen, Chen, Yuh-pan and Hong, Mina. *The Chemical Constituents of Oriental Herbs*. Los Angeles, 1982

————— . *Oriental Materia Medica: A Concise Guide*. Los Angeles, 1980

————— . *Treating Cancer with Chinese Herbs*. Los Angeles, 1982

Hunan Health Committee. *A Barefoot Doctor's Manual*. London, 1978

Kariyone, T., and Kimura, Y. *Japanese-Chinese Medicinal Plants*. 1949

Kong, Y.C., and But, Paul Pui-hai, comp. and trans. *An Enumeration of Chinese Materia Medica*. Hong Kong, 1980

Laufer, Berthold. *Sino-Iranica*. Chicago, 1919

Li Ning-hon et al. *Chinese Medicinal Plants of Hong Kong*. Hong Kong, 1984

Liu, Frank, and Liu Wan-mau. *Chinese Medical Terminology*. Hong Kong, 1980

Lu, Henry C. Correspondence Course in Chinese Herbal Medicine. Vancouver, 1977

National Institute for the Control of Pharmaceutical and Biological Products, ed. *Color Atlas of Chinese Traditional Drugs*. Beijing, 1987

Perrot, E., and Hurrier, P. *Matiere medicale et pharmacopee sino-annamites*. Paris, 1907

Porkert, Manfred. *Klassische Chinesische Pharmakologie*. Heidelberg, 1978

Porter Smith, Frederick. *Contributions towards the Materia Medica and Natural History of China*. Shanghai, 1871

Read, Bernard E. *Chinese Medicinal Plants from the Pen Ts'ao Kang Mu*. Shanghai, 1936

Roi, Jacques. *Traite des plantes medicinales chinoises*. Paris, 1955

Schatz, Jean, Larre, Claude and Elisabeth de la Roche Valee. *Survey of Traditional Chinese Medicine*. 1985

Soubeiran. *La matiere medicale chez les chinois*. Paris, 1874

Stewart, G.A. *Chinese Materia Medica, Vegetable Kingdom*. Shanghai, 1911

Tsung Pi-kwang. *Immune System and Chinese Herbs*. Irvine, 1989

Unschuld, Paul U. Medicine in China: *History of Pharmaceutics*. Boston, 198

Willard, Terry. *Reishi Mushroom: Herb of Spiritual Potency*. Washington, 1990

Wiseman, Nigel. *A Complete Chinese Materia Medica*. Watertown, 1993

Wong Ming. *La medecine chinoise par les plantes*. Paris, 1980

Yeung Him-che. *Handbook of Chinese Herbs and Formulas* (2 vols.). Los Angeles, 1985

Books on the History of Western Herbal Medicine
From the copious literature in this area, the following are the most reliable and comprehensive.

Achterberg, Jeanne. *Woman as Healer*. Boston, 1990

Arber, Agnes. *Herbals: Their Origin and Evolution*. Cambridge, England, 1938

Berendes, Johann. *Das Apothekerwesen*. Stuttgart, 1907

Chamberlain, Mary. *Old Wives' Tales, Their History, Remedies and Spells*. London, 1981

Dezeimeris, Olivier. *Dictionnaire historique de la médecine ancienne et moderne* (4 vols). Paris, 1828-39

Diegpen, Paul. *Kultur und Medizin*. Stuttgart, 1925

Ehrenreich, Barbara, and Deidre English. *Witches, Midwives and Nurses*. New York, 1973

Felter, Harvey Wickes. *The Genesis of the American Materia Medica,* Bulletin of the Lloyd Library of Botany, No. 20. Cincinnati, 1927

Fischer, Hermann. *Mittelälterliche Pflanzenkunde*. Munich, 1929

Kremers, E., and G. Urdang. *History of Pharmacy*. Philadelphia, 1940

Lewis, W. *An Experimental History of the Materia Medica*. London, 1791

Lichtenthäler, Charles. *Geschichte der Medizin*. Stuttgart, 1982

———. *La médecine hippocratique*. Neuchâtel, 1957

Lloyd, John Uri. *Origin and History of all the Pharmacopoeia Vegetable Drugs, Chemicals and Preparations*. Cincinnati, 1929

Meyerhof, M. *Quellen und Studien zur Geschichte der Naturwissenschaften und der Medizin*. Stuttgart

Müller-Jancke, Wolf-Dieter. *Astrologisch Magische Theorie und Praxis in der Heilkunde der frühen Medizin*. Stuttgart, 1985

Neuburger, Max. *Geschichte der Medizin*. Stuttgart, 1906-11

Riddle, John M. *Dioscorides on Pharmacy and Medicine*. Austin, 1985

Sachs, Julius. *Geschichte der Botanik*. München, 1875

Schelenz, Hermann. *Geschichte der Pharmazie*. Berlin, 1904

Sigerist, Henry. *Great Doctors*. New York/London, 1933

———. *A History of Medicine*. New York, 1938

———. *American Medicine*. New York, 1934

Singer, Charles. *A Short History of Medicine*. Oxford, 1928

Sprengel, Curt. *Geschichte der Botanik*. Altenberg, 1817

———. *Geschichte der Medizin*. Halle, 1800-3

Stone, Eric. *Medicine Among the American Indians*. New York, 1962

Südhoff, Karl. *Kurzes Handbuch der Geschichte der Medizin*. Berlin, 1922

Tschirch, Alexander. *Handbuch der Pharmakognosie* (3 vols.). Leipzig, 1909-25

Ullmann, Manfred. *Die Medizin im Islam*. Leiden/Köln, 1970

Whitington, E.T.W. *Medical History from the Earliest Times*. London, 1894

Wilder, Alexander. *History of Medicine*. 1904

Lexicographical Books
Choulant, L. *Handbuch der Bücherkunde für die ältere Medizin*. Leipzig, 1841

Current Works in the History of Medicine, an International Bibliography, Vols. XXX-XL, The Wellcome Historical Medical Library. London, 1962-63

Haller, Albrecht von. *Bibliotheca botanica qua scripta ad rem herbarium* (2 vols.). Zürich, 1771

Koudelka, Janet B., (ed.). "Bibliography of the History of Medicine in the United States and Canada, 1964" in *Bulletin of the History of Medicine,* Vol XXXIX, No.6 (Nov.-Dec. 1965)

Lloyd, John Uri, Theodor Just and Corinne Miller Simons. *Catalogue of the Pharmacopoeias, Dispensatories, Formularies and Allied Publications [1493-1957],* reprinted from *Lloydia,* Vol XX, No. 1 (March 1957), for the Llyod Library and Museum. Cincinnati, 1957

Schneider, Wofgang. *Lexicon der Arzneimittelgeschichte*. Stuttgart, 1975

Sonnedecker, Glenn, J. Hampton Hoch and Wolfgang Schneider. *Some Pharmaco-Historical Guidelines to the Literature,* American Institute of the History of Pharmacy. Madison, 1959

Glossary of Terms

Items in italics denote remedy actions.

adaptogenic — enhances adaptation response to stress

Air organism — one of the four organisms, dealing with movement and response, having the nervous system as its main substrate

alterative — promotes systemic changes

Altering —one of the five treatment principles according to which hernal remedies are classified; Altering defines the four treatment methods that cause systemic alteration or change, namely, promoting detoxification, vitalizing the blood, resolving mucous damp and regulating endocrine and autonomic nervous functions

analeptic — revives from shock or poisoning

analgesic — relieves pain internally

anesthetic — deadens local sensation or pain

anhydrotic — stops sweating

anodyne — relieves pain

antacid — reduces gastric acid

anthelmintic — treats worms

antiabortive — prevents miscarriage

antiaging — retards aging

antiallergic — treats allergies or hypersensitivities

antiarthritic — treats arthritis

antiasthmatic — treats asthma

antibacterial — treats bacteria

anticatarrhal — reduces catarrh (excessive mucus production)

anticoagulant — prevents blood clotting

anticonvulsant — treats convulsions

antidepressant — relieves depression

antidiarrheal — treats diarrhea

antidyskratic — rebalances the fluids in the presence of a fluids dyskrasia (disharmony)

antiemetic — treats vomiting

antienuretic — treats enuresis (involuntary urination)

antifungal — treats fungus

antigenic — reduces antibody production

anti-infective — treats infection

anti-inflammatory — reduces inflammation

antileucorrheal — treats leucorrhea

antilipemic — lowers blood lipid levels in the presence of hyperlipemia

antilithic — prevents or dissolves and flushes out stones

antineoplastic — treats neoplasm or cancer

antioxidant — reduces oxidation

antiparasitic — treats parasites

antipruritic — relieves skin itching

antipyretic — reduces fever by lowering temperature

antirheumatic —treats rheumatism

antisecretory — reduces secretions

antiseptic — topically prevents or restrains infection or putrefaction

antispasmodic — relieves spasm or cramp

antitumoral — treats tumors

antitussive — relieves coughing

antiviral — treats viruses

aperitive — stimulates the appetite

aphrodisiac — promotes sexuality

astriction — a tightening effect

astringent — astricts or tightens tissue

bioenergies — natural forces that create and sustain living things

biotype — an individual psychosomatic type; in Greek medicine a manifestation of a person's physis (natural condition) according to their krasis (quality) and fluid balance

blood — structive physiological force grounded in the blood fluid; also known in Chinese medicine as *xue*

bronchodilatant — dilates the bronchi

cardiac — relating to the heart

carminative — relieves intestinal flatus

coagulant — promotes blood clotting

cholagogue — promotes bile flow

choleretic — enhances bile quality and quantity

cicatrisant — promotes tissue repair and reduces scarring

cold — one of the four qualities; a qualitative concept used in pharmacognosy, diagnostics and pathology to designate an effective quality; in pathology it defines a condition with insufficient objective or subjective warmth, as in hypothermia with feeling cold

congestion — a pathological condition involving stasis of one of the fluids, i.e. blood, mucous, interstitial or other fluid

constraint — a pathological condition involving mental or emotional, and therefore nervous, tension.

contraceptive — prevents conception

counterirritant — irritates to cause derivation

damp — one of the four qualities; a qualitative concept used in pharmacognosy, nosology and pathology to mean an effective quality; in pathology defining a condition caused by a stagnation of one of the pure or impure fluids, and therefore often qualified, e.g. mucous damp, water damp, phlegm damp; if unqualified, then usually referring to excessive mucous secretion (catarrh)

decongestant — relieves fluid or blood congestion

deficiency — a pathological condition presenting a functional or structural insufficiency or weakness

demulcent — soothes the mucous membrane

depressant — reducing mental/cerebral functions

derivation — a therapeutic technique that uses counterirritation to draw blood away from an area of disease to another body part, usually through the methods of cupping or bloodletting, or the topical use of *rubefacient, vesicant* or *pustulant* remedies

dermal — relating to the skin

dermatropic — having a tropism for the skin

detergent — cleans and disinfects wounds

detumescent — reduces swelling

detoxicant — resolves and clears toxin(s)

diaphoretic — promotes sweating

diathesis — an individual tendency or predisposition for disharmony inherent in an individual's physis (natural condition)

digestant — promotes digestion

discutient — resolves tumors

dissolvent — promotes solution (dissolving) of hard deposits, tissues or exudates *diuretic* — promotes increased urination

Draining — one of the five treatment principles according to which remedies are classified, in which excess energy is drained or discharged; the two Draining methods are: circulating the Qi and clearing heat

draining diuretic — relieves fluid congestion (edema) and increases urination

dryness — one of the four qualities; a qualitative concept used in pharmacognoscy, diagnostics and pathology to denote an effective quality; in pathology designating a condition with insufficient mucous or other fluid secretion present

dyskrasia — a Greek medical term literally meaning a poor mixture (in quantity or quality) of the fluids, the result on the Fluid organism level of an individual's imbalanced physis (natural condition); today referring more specifically to chronic rheumatic, arthritic or gouty conditions (as in general fluids dyskrasia), for which antidyskratic botanicals are used

effective qualities — qualitative aspects of the nature of any substance—mineral, herbal, animal or human; applied to remedies, they consist of taste, warmth and moisture; they are effective since they produce physiological therapeutic effects (see four qualities below).

eliminant — promotes elimination through an excretory channel

Eliminating — one of the five treatment principles according to which remedies are classified, used to promote a discharge of a eliminatory fluid; the six Eliminating methods are: promoting sweating, promoting urination, promoting bowel movement, promoting expectoration, promoting menstruation, causing vomiting

emetic — causes vomiting

emmenagogue — promotes menstrual discharge

emollient — soothes and moistens the skin

essence — an etheric or vital force governing growth, regeneration and reproduction; known as *jing* in Chinese medicine

eukrasia — a Greek medical term denoting a balanced mixture (condition) of the four fluids and qualities in accordance with an individual's physis (innate nature)

excess — a pathological condition presenting a redundancy of function or substance

expectorant — promotes phlegm expulsion

external — (also exterior); a pathological condition at the initial or alarm stage of the three stages of general adaptation to stressors, and at the Tai Yang phase of the Chinese six disease stages; external conditions occur on the superficial body levels and present acute symptoms

febrifuge — reduces fever

fetal relaxant — relaxing/calming to the fetus and therefore reducing abnormal fetal movement

Fluid organism — one of the four organisms, dealing with metabolic (i.e. transformative) activities and mediated by the body fluids

four fluids — also known as four humors; in Greek medicine the four basic fluid substances responsible for maintaining balance (or eukrasia, literally "good mixture"); they are phlegm, yellow bile, black bile and blood; when imbalanced they cause a dyskrasia, or poor (fluid) mixture, synonymous with disharmony

four level stages — the Chinese medical theory of the progression of disease according to four levels, namely the defensive, Qi, blood and nutritive levels

four organisms — four physiological systems corresponding to the four elements: the Warmth, Air, Fluid and Physical organisms. Each is housed and regulated by certain organ systems, having specific qualities and functions, and dealing with specific forms of energy.

four qualities — energetic, dynamic, effective qualities used to describe substances and processes such as remedies (pharmacognosy) and pathological conditions (pathology); hot/cold, dry/damp are the four qualities

free radical inhibitor — reduces free radicals

galactagogue — produces milk flow

ground — the place where disease occurs, whether the whole person, constitution or particular tissue heat — (also hot); one of the four qualities; a qualitative concept used in pharmacology, diagnostics and pathology; in pathology designating a condition with excessive warmth response, such as fever or inflammation, as well as subjective feelings of excessive warmth, and properly known   as injurious heat.

hemogenic — builds blood (cells)

hemolytic — destroys blood (cells)

hemostatic — stops bleeding

hydragogue — expells water through the bowels

hydrogenic — retains fluids

hypertensive — increases blood pressure

hypnotic — calming the mind and spirit

hypoglycemiant — lowers blood sugar levels

hypotensive — reduces blood pressure

immune enhancer — enhances immune potential

immune potential — the potential of the immune system for effective response to pathogen

immune regulator — regulates immunity in hypersensitivity (i.e. allergic and autoimmune) disorders

immunostimulant — stimulates immune functions

interferon inducent — produces interferon

internal — (also interior); a pathological condition at the exhaustion phase of adaptation to stressors, and at any of the three Yin phases of the Chinese six meridian stages of disease (Tai Yin, Jue Yin, Shao Yin); internal conditions occur in the internal organs or systems and manifest chronic or degenerative symptoms

krasis — an individual's particular constitutional mixture (balance) of effective qualities and fluids; when appropriately balanced said to be in state of eukrasia, and if imbalanced producing a dyskrasia; synonymous with temperament.

laxative — promotes gentle bowel movement

lenify — to soothe or mitigate

lenitive — reduces irritation

leukocytogenic — increases white blood cells

lymphocyte stimulant — increases T-lymphocytes and lymphocyte transformation rate

mucogenic — produces mucus

mucolytic — softens hardened bronchial phlegm or intestinal mucus

mucostatic —stops mucus/catarrhal discharge

mucus — mucosal fluid

nervine — having an affinity for the nervous system

nutritive — promotes nutrition or provides nourishment

optitropic — having a tropism for the eyes and vision

oxytocic — promotes labor contractions by releasing oxytocin hormone

parasiticide — kills parasites

parturient — promotes labor

pattern of disharmony — a syndrome, consisting of a complex of specific signs and symptoms

phagocyte stimulant — enhances phagocyte functions

pharmacognosy — the study of the nature of remedies

pharmacology — the study of the physiological effects of remedies

phenomenology — the study of empirically observed phenomena

phlegm — bronchial mucous/sputum

physical organism — one of the four organisms; physical body tissue as a whole

physis — a Greek medical term denoting an individual's innate, authentic and normal condition composed of inborn and acquired characteristics; the physis determines the general quality of the ground, his/her particular krasis (temperament) or balance of qualities and fluids, as well as one's particular diathesis (predisposition) to disease

puerperal — relating to childbirth

purgative — promotes copious bowel movement

pustulant — causes pustules

Qi — a Chinese medical term denoting active physiological energy

rash-promoting — promoting eruptions in eruptive fever

refrigerant — promotes a cooling down and clears heat

relaxant — promotes relaxation

resolvent — resolves toxicosis

resorbant — promotes catabolic resorption

restorative — restores and strengthens

Restoring — one of the five treatment principles; it classifies remedies used to enhance functional and structural physiological integrity; the Restoring methods are: tonifying the Qi, tonifying the Yang, nourishing the blood and nourishing the Yin

righteous Qi —a Chinese medical term denoting the sum of "righteous" (*zheng*) Qi available to a person. It is also defined by its opposite, "injurious" or "pathogenic" (*xie*) Qi. In practice it can be reconciled with the Greek medical concept of vital spirit(s)

rubefacient — causes skin reddening through hyperemia

secretory — promotes secretions

sedative — reduces activity

simple — a single remedy

six meridian stages — the Chinese medical theory of stages of disease according to the six meridian pairs; exogenous illness begins in the Tai Yang stage and progresses to the Yang Ming, Shao Yang, Tai Yin, Shao Yin and Jue Yin stages

spasmolytic — reduces spasm or cramp

spermicidal — kills sperm

Stages of adaptation — the theory of the three stages of adaptation to stressors, being the alarm, resistance and exhaustion stages; also known as the general adaptation syndrome

Stages of disease — the theory of the four stages of disease according to vital activity; illness begins in the acute stage and progresses to the subacute, chronic and degenerative

Stagnation — a pathological condition denoting a slowing down of normal processes and buildup of injurious or toxic substances (e.g. mucus, sputum, endotoxins, fatty and mineral deposits, etc.)

stimulant — increases activity and promotes warmth

structive — producing substance and form; the opposite/complementary of active

styptic — stops bleeding through topical application

syndrome — a specific complex of signs and symptoms presenting a symptom picture; synonymous with "pattern of disharmony"

temperament — krasis (which see)

teratogenic — injures the fetus

tonic — restores and strengthens

toxicosis — (also "toxemia" and "autotoxicosis"); a pathological condition involving the accumulation of endogenous or exogenous toxins

toxins — injurious (pathological) substances generated internally or accumulated from the environment

Tri Dosas — the three fundamental energies in Ayurvedic (Indian) medical physiopathology

trophorestorative — nourishes and builds tissue

tropism — the property of a remedy of having an affinity or bias for treating certain organs, systems or body parts

vasoconstrictor — tightens blood vessels

vasodilator — expands blood vessels

vermicide — kills intestinal parasites

vermifuge — expels intestinal parasites

vesicant — causes watery blisters

vital spirit(s) — a Greek medical term denoting the total potential of a person's active response to stressors; virtually identical with the Chinese term righteous Qi (*zheng qi*)

vulnerary — promotes tissue healing

Warmth organism — one of the four organisms, dealing with warmth responses, such as inflammation, fever or dislike of heat; or a lack of these, as in hypothermia or fear of cold

Yang — physiological energies of the Yang type

Yin — physiological energies of the Yin type

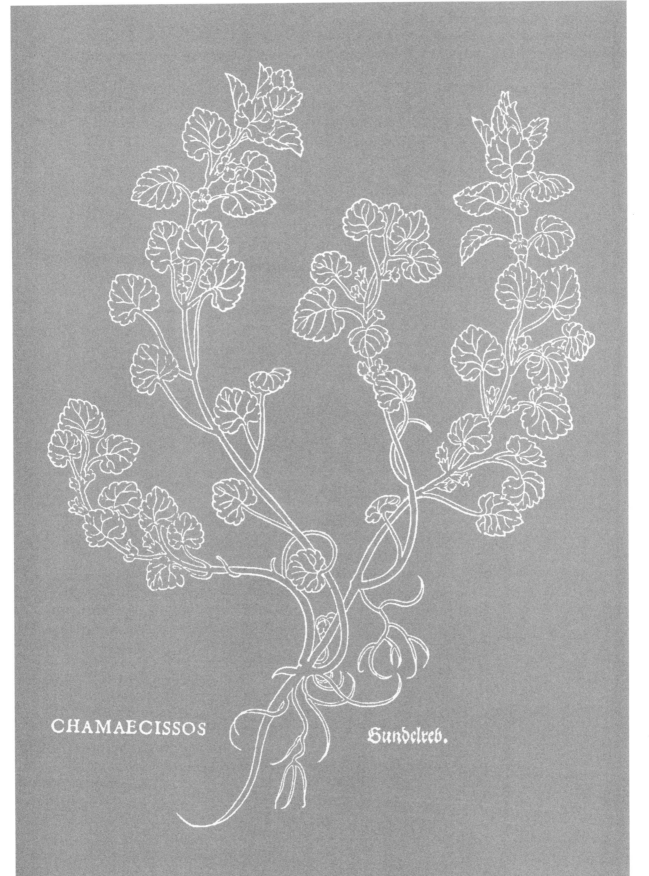

CHAMAECISSOS   Gundelreb.

The Four Element System of Traditional Greek Medicine (TGM)

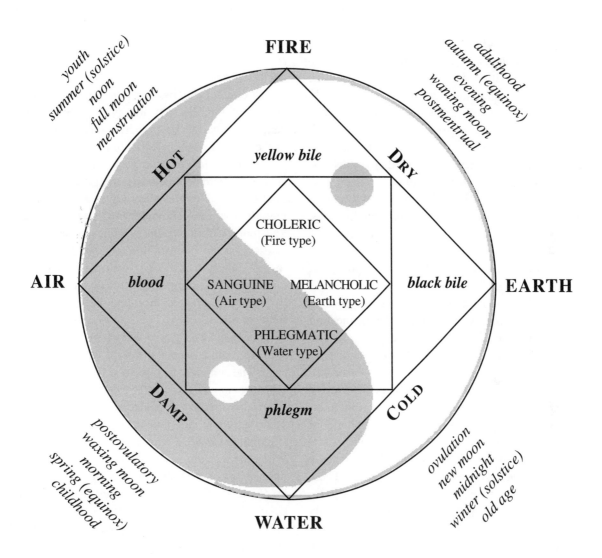

Key

From the outside to the inside:

- the four elements
- the four effective qualities
- the four fluids
- the four krases (temperaments or element types)

This diagram shows the basic system of correspondences used in traditional Greek medicine (TGM). Like the five element/phase system *(wu xing)* in Asia, this system is a fundamental Western cultural emblem linking the universe (the macrocosm) with the individual (the microcosm). This fourfold system of fully articulated correspondences was much refined by alchemist doctors during the Arabian/Persian phase of Greek medicine (the Tibb Unani phase). It then lived on in Europe as the basic medical paradigm right up to the late eighteenth century, when it was displaced by French clinical medicine and experimental science (including bacteriology and cell pathology). During this final European phase of Greek medicine, this system was common knowledge not only among doctors, wise woman healers, etc., but through farmer's almanacs and other popular publications, among people in general. Its applications included physical and psychological therapy, preventive health care, nutrition, lifestyle considerations, and so on.

The Greek system of correspondences consists of the four elements *(tessara stoicheia)*, the four effective qualities *(tessares dynameis)*, the four fluids *(tessares chumoi)*, and the four krases or temperaments *(tessares kraseis)*. Like many other cultural emblems of this kind, such as the Native American Medicine Wheel, this system includes the four spatial directions and the four phases of time-cycles, such as the four human life phases, the four seasons, the four times of day, the four moon phases and the basic menstrual cycle phases. These four archetypal phases progress clockwise.

The elements, qualities and fluids not only correspond to each other harmonically, but they also engender each other, like the *sheng* cycle of the Chinese five elements. The elements Water and Earth produce the effective quality *cold;* the elements Earth and Fire create the quality *dry,* and so on. In turn, the qualities *damp* and *cold* produce the fluid Phlegm; the qualities *dryness* and *cold* produce the fluid Black bile, and so on. As a result, Phlegm is the fluid that in an individual corresponds to the element Water, while Black bile is the fluid corresponding to the element Earth, and so on. Someone with a predominance of Phlegm and the qualities *damp* and *cold* is then said to have a phlegmatic krasis (temperament or constitution); in other words, that person is a Water type.

Likewise, it was understood from this chart that the elements control or oppose one another. Fire and Water control each other, as do Air and Earth. Along the same lines, the qualities *hot* and *cold,* and *dry* and *damp* also control each other. An excess of the fluid Yellow bile would also keep the fluid Phlegm under control. Combinations of elements, qualities and fluids also act antagonistically. *Hot* and *damp* control the qualities *dry* and *cold,* for instance.

In Greek medicine this four element system is applied to vitalistic physiology (body energetics), pathology, pharmacology, herbal therapy, nutritional therapy, lifestyle modifications and so on, in a preventive and curative way. The emphasis is always to regulate a person's energies with respect to the natural cycles, including day/night, full moon/new moon, summer/winter, youth/old age. The four element system is employed as much to assess a person's constitution and condition as it is to chart herbal and other treatment strategies, hygyenic considerations, lifestyle modifications (including geographic ones) and dietary guidelines, for example.

The word krasis is a better term than temperament to denote a person's state of energetic balance. The individual krasis is a particular mixture *(idios krasis)* of the effective qualities and fluids. When this mixture is balanced and well-regulated according to an individual true nature *(physis)*, this is called a *eukrasia* (literally, a "good mixture"). When the mixture is quantitatively or qualitatively imbalanced, a dyskrasia results (literally, a "poor mixture"). (GALEN also called a dyskrasia a *kakochumia.*) For example, an excess of yellow bile fluid and the qualities dry and hot in a person is considered a yellow bile dyskrasia—as is yellow bile that deteriorates in quality (i.e., becomes toxic) through cooking *(pepsis)*.

However, there is a deeper constitutional level to be considered when we determine the balance of qualities and fluids in an individual. If an excess of yellow bile is inherently part of an individual's normal make-up or constitution *(katastasis)*, then this is not considered a *dyskrasia*, but a *eukrasia*. Each krasis can therefore represent either a *eukrasia* or a *dyskrasia*, depending on the ground of the individual constitution in which it is found.

Synthesis of the Alchemical/Shamanistic
Greek and Chinese Element Systems

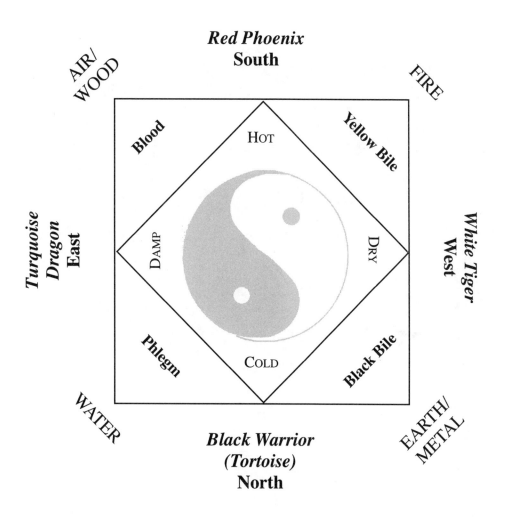

Key

On the outside: **the macrocosm / the universe**
- the four Chinese spiritual entities and their associated direction
- the four elements (Greek/Chinese)

This chart represents a combination of the original Greek and Chinese element systems, which were alchemical or shamanistic in nature.

The Greek element system itself is a synthesis of the Greek schools and the Persian/Arab alchemical schools of medical philosophy (S. MAHDIHASSAN 1973, *Theories and Philosophies of Medicine*).

The Chinese element system is based on ancient shamanistic, i.e., Daoist and alchemical cosmogony, and includes the spiritual entities of the four direc-

On the inside: **the microcosm / the individual**
- the four fluids
- the four effective qualities

tions *(se ling)* and their later rationalized versions, the elements *(xing)*. Note how the four spiritual entities and their colors resonate with the four qualities and fluids.

Although in medicine the Greek and Chinese element emblems serve the same needs, each has its own emphasis and differs somewhat in its scope and application. This is because they arise from different paradigms (see Chapter 1).

The Four Chinese Spiritual Entitites of the Four Directions

The Four Element Medicine Wheel

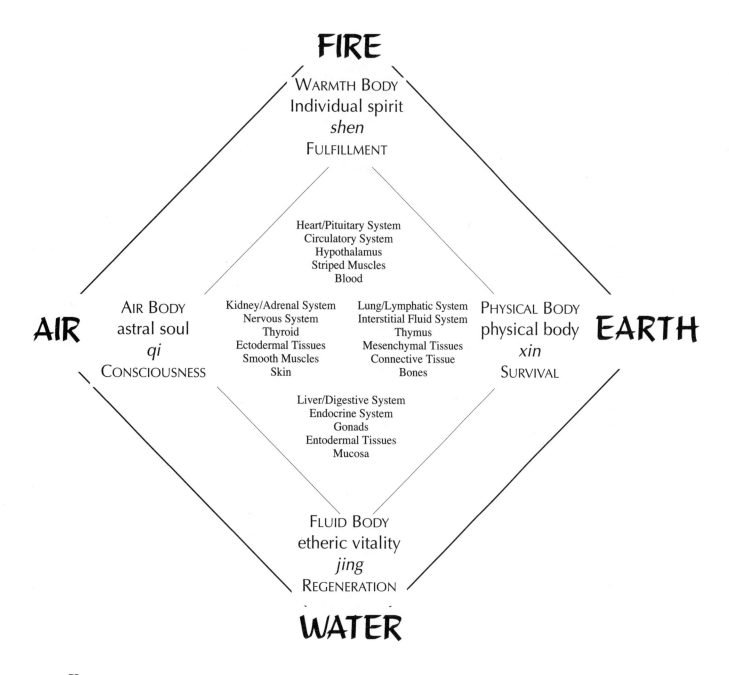

Key

On the outside
- the four elements
- the four bodies
- the four bodies in Chinese medicine
- the four purposes

(see page 92 for discussion of these correspondences)

On the inside
- the four cardinal organ systems
- the four essential body systems
- the four essential endocrine glands
- the four embryonic tissues
- other associated tissues

Appendix D

The Four Krases (Temperaments) and the Eight Biotypes

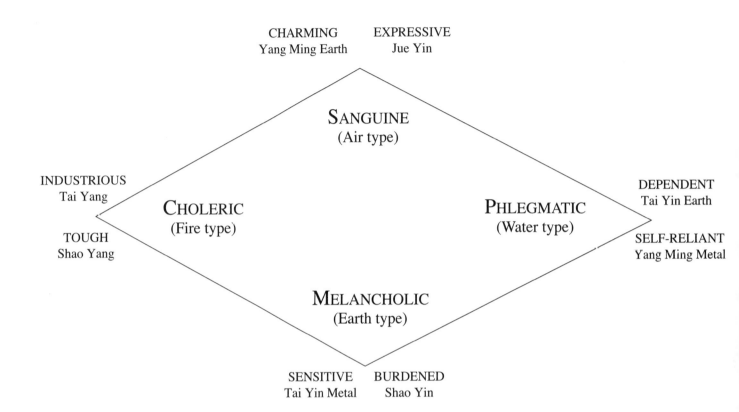

CHARMING
Yang Ming Earth

EXPRESSIVE
Jue Yin

SANGUINE
(Air type)

INDUSTRIOUS
Tai Yang

DEPENDENT
Tai Yin Earth

CHOLERIC
(Fire type)

PHLEGMATIC
(Water type)

TOUGH
Shao Yang

SELF-RELIANT
Yang Ming Metal

MELANCHOLIC
(Earth type)

SENSITIVE
Tai Yin Metal

BURDENED
Shao Yin

Key
From the outside to the inside
- Hakomi therapy names (RON KURTZ)
- Chinese names (YVES REQUENA)
- Greek four krases
See also p. 92

The Three Constitutions

Biliary/Mixed Iris
Phosphoric
Carbonitrogenoid
Ectomorph

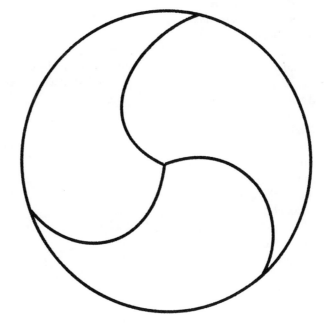

Lymphatic/Blue Iris
Carbonic
Hydrogenoid
Endomorph

Hematogenic/Brown Iris
Sulphuric
Oxygenoid
Mesomorph

Key

From the top to the bottom
- modern iridology (JOSEPH DECK 1984)
- modern homeopathy (R. STAHL 1957; HENRI BERNARD 1962; ROLAND ZISSU 1964)
- historical homeopathy (VON GRAUVOGL 1866)
- body typography (SHELDON 1954)

See also p. 92

Appendix F

Common Name Cross Index

Common Name	Botanical Name
Abscess root	*Plemonium reptans*
Abutua	*Cissampelos pareira*
Acacia	*Acacia* spp.
Acacia gum	*Acacia nilotica*
Aconite	*Aconitum napellus*
Aconite, Chinese	*Aconitum chinense*
Aconite, Sichuan	*Aconitum carmichaeli*
Adder's tongue	*Erythronium americanum*
Adonis	*Adonis vernalis*
Aduki bean	*Phaseolus calcaratus*
Agar-agar	*Gelidium* spp.
Agave	*Agave* spp.
Agrimony	*Agrimonia eupatoria*
Alder	*Alnus* spp.
Alder buckthorn	*Rhamnus frangula*
Alfalfa	*Medicago sativa*
Alkanet	*Alkanna tinctoria*
Allspice	*Pimento officinalis*
Almond	*Amygdalus communis* or *Prunus amygdalus*
Aloe	*Aloe* spp.
Alstonia	*Alstonia scholaris*
Alstonia (bark)	*Alstonia constricta*
Alum root	*Heuchera* spp.
Amaranth	*Amaranthus* spp.
Ambrette	*Hibiscus abelmoschus*
American centaury	*Sabbatia angularis*
American columbo	*Frasera canadensis*
American dwarf elder	*Aralia hispida*
American ginseng	*Panax quinquefolium*
American mistletoe	*Phoradendron flavescens*
American pennyroyal	*Hedeoma pulegioides*
American wormseed	*Chenopodium anthelminticum*
Anatto	*Bixa orellana*
Angelica, archangel	*Angelica archangelica*
Angelica, hairy	*Angelica pubescens*
Angelica, white	*Angelica dahurica*
Angelica tree	*Aralia spinosa*
Angostura	*Cusparia angostura*
Aniseed	*Pimpinella anisum*
Aphanes	*Aphanes arvensis*
Apple	*Pirus malus*
Apricot	*Prunus armeniaca*
Araroba	*Andira araroba*
Arborvitae	*Thuja occidentalis*
Arnica	*Arnica montana*
Arrowhead	*Sagittaria sagittifolia*
Artichoke	*Cynara scolymus*

Common Name	Botanical Name
Asafoetida	*Ferula assa-foetida*
Ash	*Fraxinus excelsior*
Ashphodel	*Asphodelus ramosus*
Ashwagandha	*Withania somnifera*
Asian ginseng	*Panax ginseng*
Asparagus	*Asparagus officinalis*
Asparagus, shiny	*Asparagus cochinensis*
Aspen	*Populus tremula*
Aster	*Aster tartaricus*
Astragalus	*Astragalus membranaceus*
Atractylodes, black	*Atractylodes ovata*
Atractylodes, white	*Atractylodes macrocephala*
Avens	*Geum rivale* and spp.
Bacopa	*Bacopa monnieri*
Bael fruit	*Aegle marmelos*
Balm of Gilead	*Populus balsamifera*
Balmony	*Chelone glabra*
Balsam fir	*Abies balsamifera*
Baneberry	*Actea arguta*
Barberry	*Berberis vulgaris*
Barley	*Hordeum distichon*
Basil	*Ocymum basilicum*
Bay laurel	*Laurus nobilis*
Bayberry	*Myrica cerifera*
Bearberry	*Arctostaphylos uva-ursi*
Bearded darnel	*Lolium temulentum*
Bear's breech	*Acanthus mollis*
Bearsfoot	*Polymnia uvedalia*
Beech	*Fagus sylvatica*
Beetroot	*Beta vulgaris*
Beleric myrobalan	*Terminalia belerica*
Belladonna	*Atropa belladonna*
Benzoin	*Styrax benzoin*
Bergamot	*Citrus aurantium* ssp. *bergamia*
Betel	*Piper betel*
Bethroot	*Trillium pendulum*
Betony	*Pedicularis* spp.
Bilberry	*Vaccinium myrtillus*
Biota	*Biota orientalis*
Birch	*Betula* spp.
Bird's foot trefoil	*Lotus corniculatus*
Birthroot	*Trillium pendulum*
Birthwort	*Aristolochia clematitis*
Biscuit root	*Lomatium dissectum*
Bistort	*Polygonum bistorta*
Bitter milkwort	*Polygala amara*
Bitter orange	*Citrus vulgaris*

Bitter root	*Apocynum androsaemifolium*
Bittersweet	*Solanum dulcamara*
Black alder	*Prinos verticillatus*
Black bamboo	*Phyllostachys nigra*
Black bryony	*Tamus communis*
Black cohosh	*Cimicifuga racemosa*
Black elder	*Sambucus nigra*
Blackhaw	*Viburnum prunifolium*
Black hellebore	*Helleborus niger*
Black horehound	*Ballota foetida*
Black mustard	*Sinapis niger*
Black nightshade	*Solanum nigrum*
Black pepper	*Piper nigrum*
Black poplar	*Populus nigra*
Black radish	*Raphanus sativus niger*
Black spruce	*Picea mariana*
Black walnut	*Juglans nigra*
Black willow	*Salix nigra*
Blackberry	*Rubus villosus*
Blackcurrant	*Ribes nigrum*
Blackthorn	*Prunus spinosa*
Bladder senna	*Colutea arborescens*
Bladderwrack	*Fucus vesiculosus*
Blazing star	*Chamaelirium luteum*
Bletilla	*Bletilla striata*
Blessed thistle	*Carduus benedictus*
Bloodroot	*Sanguinaria canadensis*
Blue cohosh	*Caulophyllum thalictroides*
Blue cypress	*Callitris intratropica*
Blue flag	*Iris versicolor/germanica*
Blue mallow	*Malva sylvestris*
Blue tansy	*Tanacetum annuum*
Blue vervain	*Verbena hastata*
Bluebell bulb	*Scilla nutans*
Blumea camphor	*Blumea balsamifera*
Bogbean	*Menyanthes trifoliata*
Boldo	*Peumus boldus*
Boneset	*Eupatorium perfoliatum*
Borage	*Borago officinalis*
Boronia	*Boronia megastigma*
Borneo camphor	*Dryobalanops aromatica*
Box	*Buxus sempervirens*
Brakefern	*Polypodium vulgare*
Brooklime	*Veronica beccabunga*
Broom	*Cytisus scoparius*
Brucea	*Brucea javanica*
Bryony	*Bryonia dioica*
Buchu	*Barosma betulina*
Buckthorn brake	*Osmunda regalis*
Buckwheat	*Fagopyrum esculentum*
Buddleia	*Buddleia officinalis*
Bugle	*Ajuga reptans*
Bugleweed	*Lycopus virginicus*
Bugloss	*Anchusa officinalis*
Bulbous buttercup	*Ranunculus bulbosus*

Bupleurum	*Bupleurum chinense*
Bur marigold	*Bidens tripartita*
Burdock	*Arctium lappa*
Burnet saxifrage	*Pimpinella saxifraga*
Burning bush	*Euonymus occidentalis*
Bush clover	*Lespedaza capitata*
Butcher's broom	*Ruscus aculeatus*
Butterbur	*Petasites officinalis*
Butternut	*Juglans cinerea*
Button snake root	*Eryngium aquaticum*
Cajeput	*Melaleuca cajeputii*
Calabar bean	*Physostigma venenosum*
Calamint	*Calaminta officinalis*
Calamus	*Acorus calamus*
California bay	*Umbellaria californica*
California laurel	*Umbellularia californica*
California poppy	*Eschscholtzia californica*
Caltrop	*Tribulus terrestris*
Calumba	*Jateorhiza palmata*
Camomile, German	*Matricaria recutita*
Camomile, Moroccan	*Ormenis mixta/multicola*
Camomile, Roman	*Anthemis nobilis*
Camomile, wild	*Matricaria matricarioides*
Camphor	*Cinnamomum camphora*
Canada fleabane	*Erigeron canadensis*
Canchalagua	*Erythraea douglasii/ muhlenbergii*
Cantaloupe	*Cucumis melo*
Caraway	*Carum carvi*
Cardamom	*Elettaria cardamomum*
Carob	*Ceratonia siliqua*
Carolina pink	*Phlox carolina*
Cascara sagrada	*Rhamnus purshiana*
Cassia cinnamon	*Cinamomum cassia*
Cassia tora	*Cassia tora*
Castor oil plant	*Ricinus communis*
Catnip	*Nepeta cataria*
Catsfoot	*Antennaria dioica*
Catuaba	*Juniperus brasiliensis*
Cayenne	*Capsicum annuum*
Cedarwood, Atlas	*Cedrus atlantica*
Cedarwood, Himalaya	*Cedrus deodara*
Cedarwood, Virginia	*Juniperus virginiana*
Celandine	*Chelidonum maius*
Celery	*Apium graveolens*
Celosia	*Celosia cristata*
Centaury	*Erythraea centaurium*
Chá de bugre	*Cordia salicifolia*
Chaparral	*Larrea divaricata*
Chapeu de couro	*Echinodorus macrophyllum*
Chastetree berry	*Vitex agnus castus*
Cherry	*Prunus cerasus*
Cherry laurel	*Prunus laurocerasus*
Chervil	*Anthriscus cerefolium*

Chickweed	*Stellaria media*	Cowhage	*Macuna pruriens*
Chicory	*Cichorium intybus*	Cowslip	*Primula veris*
Chirata	*Swertia chirata*	Cramp bark	*Viburnum opulus*
Chives	*Allium schoenoprasum*	Cranesbill	*Geranium maculatum*
Chrysanthemum	*Chrysanthemum* spp.	Cronewort	*Artemisia vulgaris*
Cimicifuga	*Cimicifuga foetida*	Croton	*Croton tiglium*
Cineraria	*Cineraria maritima*	Cubeb	*Piper cubeba*
Cinnamon, cassia	*Cinamomum cassia*	Cuckoopint	*Arum maculatum*
Cinnamon, Ceylon	*Cinamomum zeylanicum/verum*	Culver's root	*Leptandra virginica*
		Cumin	*Cuminum cyminum*
Cinnamon, Vietnam	*Cinnamomum loureirii*	Cup plant	*Silphium perfoliatum*
Cinquefoil	*Potentilla reptans*	Curare	*Strychnos castelnaei*
Citronella, Ceylon	*Cymbopogon nardus*	Cyclamen	*Cyclamen europaeum*
Citronella, India	*Cymbopogon citratus*	Cypress	*Cupressus sempervirens*
Clary sage	*Salvia sclarea*		
Cleavers	*Galium aparine*	Daisy	*Bellis perennis*
Clematis	*Clematis* spp.	Dalmatia pellitory	*Chrysanthemum cinerariifolium*
Cliffrose	*Cowania mexicana*	Dame's rocket	*Hesperis matronalis*
Clove	*Eugenia caryophyllata*	Damiana	*Turnera duffusa*
Club moss	*Lycopodium clavatum*	Dandelion	*Taraxacum officinale*
Cocaine	*Erythroxylon coca*	Date	*Phoenix dactylifera*
Cocillana bark	*Guarea rusbyi*	Deer's tongue	*Liatris odorantissima*
Cocklebur	*Xanthium spinosum*	Demerara pinkroot	*Spigelia anthelmia*
Cocoa	*Theobroma cacao*	Devil's claw	*Harpagophytum procumbens*
Coffee	*Coffea arabica*	Devil's club	*Oplopanax horridum*
Coleus	*Coleus forskohlii*	Dill	*Anethum graveolens*
Colic root	*Liatris spicata*	Dioscorea	*Dioscorea sativa*
Colocynth	*Citrullus colocynthis*	Dittany	*Cunila origanoides*
Coltsfoot	*Tussilago farfara*	Dodder	*Cuscuta* spp.
Columbine	*Aqilegia vulgaris*	Dog rose	*Rosa canina*
Combretum	*Combretum raimbaultii*	Dog's mercury	*Mercurialis perennis*
Comfrey	*Symphitum officinale*	Dogbane	*Apocynum cannabinum*
Common reed	*Phragmites communis*	Dogwood	*Cornus* spp.
Condalia	*Condalia lycioides* and spp.	Dong quai	*Angelica sinensis*
Condurango	*Gonolobus condurango*	Douglas fir	*Pseudotsuga manziesii*
Coneflower	*Rudbeckia laciniata*	Dwarf elder	*Sambucus ebulus*
Contrayerba	*Kallstroemia* spp.	Dyer's broom	*Genista tinctoria*
Coolwort	*Tiarella cordifolia*		
Copaiba	*Copaiba langsdorfii*	Echinacea	*Echinacea* spp.
Coral root	*Corallorhiza maculata*	Elecampane	*Inula helenium*
Coriander	*Coriandrum sativum*	Eleuthero	*Eleutherococcus senticosus*
Corkwood tree	*Duboisia myoporoides*	Elm	*Ulmus campestris*
Corn poppy	*Papaver rhoeas*	Endive	*Cichorium endiva*
Cornflower	*Centaurea cyanus*	Ephedra	*Ephedra vulgaris*
Cornsalad	*Valerianella olitoria*	Eucalyptus	*Eucalyptus* spp.
Cornsilk	*Zea mays*	Eucommia	*Eucommia ulmoides*
Corydalis	*Corydalis aurea*	European columbo	*Chasmanthera palmata*
Costmary	*Chrysanthemum balsamita*	European wintergreen	*Pyrola rotundifolia*
Cotá	*Thelesperma* spp.	Evening primrose	*Oenothera hookeri* or *biennis*
Coto	*Nectandra* spp	Evodia	*Evodia rutecarpa*
Cotton	*Gossypum* spp.	Eyebright	*Euphrasia rostkoviana*
Couch grass	*Triticum repens*		
Cow parsley	*Anthriscus sylvestris*	False Solomon's seal	*Smilacina racemosa*
Cow parsnip	*Heracleum lanatum*	Feather geranium	*Chenopodium botrys*
Cowberry	*Vaccinium vitis idaea*	Fennel	*Foeniculum vulgare*

Fennel flower	*Nigella sativa*
Fenugreek	*Trigonella foenum-graecum*
Feverfew	*Chrysanthemum parthenium*
Feverflower	*Dichroa febrifuga*
Field eryngo	*Eryngium campestre*
Field mint	*Mentha arvensis*
Field scabious	*Scabiosa arvensis*
Fig	*Ficus carica*
Figwort, black	*Scrophularia ningpoensis*
Figwort, knotty	*Scrophularia nodosa*
Figwort, water	*Scrophularia aquatica*
Fir	*Abies* spp.
Fireweed	*Erechtites hieracifolia*
Five-finger grass	*Potentilla canadensis*
Flax	*Linum usitatissimum*
Fleawort	*Pulicaria dysenterica*
Flower pollen	*Pollen*
Flowery knotweed	*Polygonum multiflorum*
Foraha	*Calophyllum inophyllum*
Forest pine	*Pinus sylvestris*
Forget-me-not	*Myosotis palustris*
Forsythia	*Forsythia suspensa*
Foxglove	*Digitalis purpurea*
Frankincense	*Boswellia* spp.
Fringe tree	*Chionanthus virginicus*
Fritillaria	*Fritillaria cirrhosa* and spp.
Frostwort	*Helianthemum canadense*
Fumitory	*Fumaria officinalis*
Galangal	*Alpinia galanga*
Galbanum	*Ferula galbaniflua*
Gamboge	*Garcinia hanburyii*
Gardenia	*Gardenia florida*
Garlic	*Allium sativum*
Gentian, large-leaf	*Gentiana macrophylla*
Gentian, scabrous	*Gentiana scabra*
Gentian, yellow	*Gentiana lutea*
Geranium	*Pelargonium graveolens*
Germander speedwell	*Veronica chamaedrys*
Ginger	*Zingiber officinalis*
Gingergrass	*Cymbopogon martinii* var. *sofia*
Ginkgo	*Ginkgo biloba*
Glasswort	*Salicornia herbacea*
Goat's rue	*Galega officinalis*
Goatshead	*Tribulus*
Golden ragwort	*Senecio aureus*
Goldenrod	*Solidago virgaurea* and spp.
Goldenseal	*Hydrastis canadensis*
Goldthread	*Coptis trifolia*
Gooseberry	*Ribes grossularia*
Gotu kola	*Hydrocotyle asiatica*
Goutweed	*Aegopodium podagraria*
Grand fir	*Abies grandis*
Grapefruit	*Citrus parasisii*
Grapevine	*Vitis vinifera*

Gravel root	*Eupatorium purpureum*
Great burnet	*Sanguisorba officinalis*
Great plantain	*Plantago maior*
Green bean	*Phaseolus vulgaris*
Green gentian	*Swertia radiata*
Green hellebore	*Veratrum viride*
Greenbrier	*Smilax rotundifolia*
Ground ivy	*Glechoma hederacea*
Groundsel	*Senecio vulgaris*
Guaiacum	*Guaiacum officinale*
Guaraná	*Paullinia cupara*
Guggul	*Commiphora mukul*
Gum ammoniac	*Dorema ammoniacum*
Gumweed	*Grindelia robusta*
Haircap moss	*Polytrichum juniperinum*
Haronga	*Haronga madagascariensis*
Hartstongue fern	*Scolopendrium vulgare*
Hawthorn	*Crataegus oxyacantha*
Hazel	*Corylus avellana*
Hazelwort	*Asarum europaeum*
Healall	*Prunella vulgaris*
Heartleaf	*Parnassia palustris*
Heartsease	*Viola tricolor*
Heather	*Calluna vulgaris*
Hedge bindweed	*Convolvulus sepium*
Hedge garlic	*Alliaria officinalis*
Hedge hyssop	*Gratiola officinalis*
Hedge mustard	*Sisymbrium officinalis*
Hedychium	*Hedychium acuminatum*
Helonias	*Chamaelirium luteum*
Hemlock, spotted	*Conium maculatum*
Hemlock, water	*Cicuta virosa*
Hemlock fir	*Tsuga canadensis*
Hemlock spruce	*Abies canadensis*
Hemlock water dropwort	*Oenanthe crocata*
Hemp agrimony	*Eupatorium cannabinum*
Hemp nettle	*Galeopsis ochroleuca*
Henbane (black)	*Hyoscyamus niger*
Henna	*Lawsonia alba*
Herb paris	*Paris quadrifolia*
Herb patience	*Rumex alpinus*
Herb robert	*Geranium robertianum*
Hibiscus	*Hibiscus sabdariffa*
Hog's fennel	*Peucedanum palustre*
Holly	*Ilex aquifolium* and spp.
Hollyhock	*Althaea rosea*
Holy thistle	*Carduus benedictus*
Honeysuckle	*Lonicera caprifolium* and spp.
Hops	*Humulus lupulus*
Horehound, black	*Ballota foetida*
Horehound, white	*Marrubium vulgare*
Horsechestnut	*Aesculus hippocastanum*
Horsemint	*Monarda punctata*
Horsenettle	*Solanum carolinensis*

Horseradish	*Cochlearia armoracia*	Ladies' slipper	*Cypripedium pubescens*
Horsetail, field	*Equisetum arvense*	Lance-leaf plantain	*Plantago lanceolata*
Horsetail, greater	*Equisetum hyemale*	Lapacho	*Tabebuia avellanedae*
Hound's tongue	*Cynoglossum officinale*	Larch	*Larix decidua*
Houseleek	*Sempervivum tectorum*	Larkspur	*Delphinium* spp.
Hydrangea	*Hydrangea arborescens*	Laurel	*Laurus nobilis*
Hyssop	*Hyssopus officinalis*	Lavender	*Lavandula angustifolia*
Hysteronica	*Hysteronica baylahuen*	Lavender, dentate	*Lavandula dentata*
		Lavender, fern-leaf	*Lavandula multifida*
Iceland moss	*Cetraria islandica*	Lavender, spike	*Lavandula latifolia*
Ignatia nut	*Strychnos ignatii*	Lavender, Spanish	*Lavandula stoechas*
Immortelle	*Helychrysum angustifolium*	Lavandin	*Lavandula x intermedia*
Indian hemp	*Cannabis sativa*	Leadwort	*Plumbago europoea*
Indian physic	*Gillenia trifoliata*	Leek	*Allium porrum*
Indian pipe	*Monotropa hypopytis /uniflora*	Lemon	*Citrus limonum*
Indian sarsaparilla	*Hemidesmus indicus*	Lemon balm	*Melissa officinalis*
Indian spikenard	*Nardostachys jatamansi*	Lemon verbena	*Andropogon citratus, Lippia citr.*
Indigo	*Indigo pulverata*	Lemongrass	*Cymbopogon flexuosus/citratus*
Inmortal	*Asclepias asperula*	Levant wormseed	*Artemisia cina*
Inula	*Inula graveolens*	Licorice	*Glycirrhiza glabra*
Ipecac	*Cephaelis ipecacuanha*	Life root	*Senecio aureus*
Irish moss	*Chondrus crispus*	Lilac	*Syringa vulgaris*
Ivy, common	*Hedera helix*	Lily of the valley	*Convallaria maialis*
		Lime	*Citrus aurantifolia*
Jaborandi	*Pilocarpus* spp.	Linden	*Tilia cordata*
Jack in the pulpit	*Arisaema triphyllum*	Litchi	*Litchi sinensis*
Jalap	*Ipomoea jalapa*	Little germander	*Teucrium chamaedrys*
Jamaica dogwood	*Piscidia erythrina*	Liverwort	*Hepatica triloba*
Jamaica sarsaparilla	*Smilax officinalis*	Lobelia	*Lobelia inflata*
Jambul	*Syzygium jambolanum*	Logwood	*Haematoxylon campechianum*
Jasmine	*Jasminum officinale*	Loosestrife	*Lythrum salicaria*
Jatobá	*Hymenaea courbarii*	Lotus	*Nelumbo nucifera*
Jewelweed	*Impatiens biflora*	Lovage, Asian	*Ligusticum sinense*
Jimsonweed	*Datura stramonium*	Lovage, garden	*Ligusticum levisticum*
Jojoba	*Simmondia chinensis*	Lovage, Sichuan	*Ligusticum walichii*
Jujube	*Zizyphus vulgaris*	Lungwort	*Pulmonaria officinalis*
Juniper	*Juniperus communis*	Lungwort lichen	*Sticta pulmonaria*
Jurubeba	*Solanum paniculatum*	Lupin	*Lupinus* spp
		Lysimachia	*Lysimachia* spp.
Kamala	*Mallotus philipinensis*		
Kava-kava	*Piper methysticum*	Madder	*Rubia tinctorum*
Kelp	*Laminaria* spp.	Madonna lily	*Lilium candidum*
Khella	*Ammi visnaga*	Magnolia (bark)	*Magnolia officinalis* and spp.
Kidney vetch	*Anthyllis vulneraria*	Magnolia (bud)	*Magnolia liliflora* and spp.
Kidneywort	*Cotyledon umbilics*	Maidenhair fern	*Adiantum pedantum*
Kino	*Pterocarpus* spp.	Male fern	*Aspidium filix-mas.*
Knapweed	*Centaurea scabiosa*	Mandrake	*Atropa mandragora*
Knotgrass	*Polygonum aviculare*	Manila elemi	*Canarium commune*
Kola nut	*Kola vera*	Manzanita	*Arctostaphylos manzanita*
Kousso	*Hagenia abyssinica*	Maravilla	*Mirabilis multiflorum*
Kudzu	*Pueraria lobata*	Marigold (garden)	*Tagetes glandulifera*
		Marigold (pot)	*Calendula officinalis*
Labrador tea	*Ledum latifolium*	Marjoram	*Origanum maiorana*
Lady's bedstraw	*Galium verum*	Marquosa bark	*Melia azadirachta*
Lady's mantle	*Alchemilla vulgaris*	Marsh mallow	*Althaea officinalis*

Marsh marigold	*Caltha palustris*	Oak	*Quercus* spp.
Marsh tea	*Ledum palustre*	Oat	*Avena sativa*
Marsh violet	*Pinguicula vulgaris*	Ocotillo	*Fouquieria splendens*
Marsh woundwort	*Stachys palustris*	Old man's beard	*Usnea barbata*
Massoia	*Cryptocarya massoia*	Oleander	*Nerium oleander*
Masterwort	*Imperatoria ostruthium*	Olive	*Olea europaea*
Mastix	*Pistacia lentiscus*	Onion	*Allium cepa*
Matarique	*Cacalia decomposita*	Opopanax	*Opopanax chironium*
Maté	*Ilex paraguaiensis*	Orange, bitter	*Citrus aurantium* ssp. *aurant.*
Matico	*Piper angustifolium*	Orange, sweet	*Citrus aurantium* var. *dulcis*
Mayapple	*Podophyllum peltatum*	Oregano	*Origanum vulgare*
Mayweed	*Anthemis cotula*	Oregon grape	*Mahonia repens*
Meadow saffron	*Colchicum autumnale*	Oriental sweet gum	*Liquidamber orientalis*
Meadowsweet	*Filipendula ulmaria*	Orris	*Iris florentina*
Medlar	*Mespilus germanica*	Oshá	*Ligusticum porteri*
Melilot	*Melilotus officinalis*	Oxeye daisy	*Chrysanthemum leucanthemum*
Melissa	*Melissa officinalis*		
Mercury	*Mercurialis annua*	Palmarosa	*Cymbopogon martinii*
Mesquite	*Prosopolis julifera*	Papaya	*Carica papaya*
Mezereon	*Daphne mezereum*	Para cress	*Spilanthes oleracea*
Microalgae	*Aphanizaomenon flos-aquae*	Pareira	*Chondodendron tomentosum*
	or *Chlorella* spp. or *Spirulina* spp.	Parsley	*Petroselinum crispum*
Milk thistle	*Carduus marianus*	Parsley piert	*Alchemilla arvensis*
Milkweed	*Asclepias speciosa*	Partridgeberry	*Mitchella repens*
Milkwort	*Polygala vulgaris*	Pasque flower	*Anemone pulsatilla* or *patens*
Mimosa	*Acacia dealbata*	Passionflower	*Passiflora incarnata*
Mint, corn/field	*Mentha arvensis*	Patchouli	*Pogostemon patchouli /cablin*
Mint, pepper	*Mentha* x *piperita*	Pau d'arco	*Tabebuia avellanedae*
Mint, spear	*Mentha spicata/viridis*	Peach	*Amygdalus persica*
Mistletoe, American	*Phoradendron flavescens*	Pear	*Pirus communis*
Mistletoe, Asian	*Loranthus parasiticus/yadoriki*	Pellitory	*Anacyclus pyrethrum*
Mistletoe, European	*Viscum album*	Pellitory of the wall	*Parietaria officinalis*
Moneywort	*Lysimachia nummularia*	Pennyroyal, American	*Hedeoma pulegioides*
Morning glory	*Convulvulus duartinus*	Pennyroyal, European	*Mentha pulegium*
Mother of thyme	*Thymus serpyllum*	Peony, garden	*Paeonia officinalis*
Motherwort	*Leonorus cardiaca*	Peony, red	*Paeonia obovata* and spp.
Mountain laurel	*Kalmia latifolia*	Peony, white	*Paeonia lactiflora*
Mousear hawkweed	*Hieracium pilosella*	Peppermint	*Mentha piperita*
Mugwort	*Artemisia vulgaris*	Perilla	*Perilla acuta* or *frutescens*
Muira puama	*Liriosma ovata*	Periwinkle	*Vinca minor*
Mulberry, black	*Morus nigra*	Peru balsam	*Balsamum peruvianum* or
Mulberry, white	*Morus alba*		*Myroxylom pareirae*
Mullein	*Verbascum thapsus*	Peruvian bark	*Cinchona calisaya/succiruba/*
Mustard, black	*Sinapis niger*		*officinalis*
Mustard, white	*Sinapis alba*	Phyllanthus	*Phyllanthus amarus*
Myrrh	*Commiphora molmol*	Pichi	*Fabiana imbricata*
Myrtle	*Myrtus communis*	Picrorhiza	*Picrorhiza kurooa*
		Pilewort	*Ranunculus ficaria*
Naked broomrape	*Orobanche uniflora*	Pillbearing spurge	*Euphorbia pilulifera*
Nasturtium	*Tropaeolum maius*	Pine	*Pinus* spp.
Neroli	*Citrus vulgaris*	Pineapple weed	*Matricaria matricarioides*
Nettle	*Urtica dioica*	Pinellia	*Pinellia ternata*
Niaouli	*Melaleuca quinquenervia*	Pinkroot	*Spigelia marylandica*
Nutmeg	*Myristica fragrans*	Pipsissewa	*Chimaphila umbellata*
		Pitcher plant	*Sarracenia purpurea*

Plantain, round-leaf	*Plantago maior*	Red sage	*Salvia colorata*
Plantain, lance-leaf	*Plantago lanceolata*	Rehmannia	*Rehmannia glutinosa*
Pleurisy root	*Asclepias tuberosa*	Restharrow	*Ononis spinosa*
Plum	*Prunus domestica*	Rhatany	*Krameria triandra*
Poison hemlock	*Conium maculatum* or	Rhineberry	*Rhamnus catharticus*
	Cicuta virosa	Rhodiola	*Rhodiola rosea*
Poison ivy	*Toxicodendron radicans*	Rhododendron	*Rhododendron anthopogon*
Poison oak	*Toxicodendron diversilobum*	Rhubarb	*Rheum palmatum*
Poke root	*Phytolacca decandra*	Ribwort plantain	*Plantago lanceolata*
Pomegranate	*Punica granatum*	Rock rose	*Cistus ladaniferus*
Pond lily, European		Rock tripe	*Umbilicaria* spp.
white	*Nymphaea alba*	Rocket	*Eruca sativa*
Pond lily, white	*Nymphaea alba*	Roman camomile	*Anthemis nobilis*
Pond lily, yellow	*Nymphaea lutea*	Rose, Cherokee	*Rosa laevigata*
		Rose, cabbage/May	*Rosa centifolia*
Poppy, corn	*Papaver rhoeas*	Rose, damask	*Rosa damascena*
Poppy, opium	*Papaver somniferum*	Rose, dog/brier	*Rosa canina*
Potentilla	*Potentilla erecta*	Rosebay willow herb	*Epilobium angustifolium*
Poria	*Poria cocos*	Rose geranium	*Pelargonium* x *asperum*
Prickly ash	*Zanthoxylum americanum*	Rosemary	*Rosmarinus officinalis*
Prickly pear	*Opuntia* spp.	Rosewood	*Aniba roseodora*
Primrose	*Primula officinalis*	Round-leaf plantain	*Plantago maior*
Privet	*Ligustrum vulgare* and spp.	Rowan	*Sorbus aucuparia*
Prodigiosa	*Brickellia grandiflora*	Rue	*Ruta graveolens*
Psyllium	*Plantago psyllium*	Rupturewort	*Herniaria glabra*
Pumpkin	*Cucurbita pepo*	Rye ergot	*Claviceps purpurea*
Purging cassia	*Cassia fistula*		
Purging flax	*Linum cartharticum*	Sabine	*Juniperus sabina*
Purple coneflower	*Echinacea purpurea/*	Safflower	*Carthamus tinctorius*
	angustifolia/pallida	Saffron	*Crocus sativus*
Purple deadnettle	*Lamium purpureum*	Sagapenum	*Ferula persica*
Purple orchid	*Orchis mascula*	Sage, cinnabar	*Salvia miltiorrhiza*
Purple sumac	*Rhus glabra*	Sage, clary	*Salvia sclarea*
Purslane	*Portulaca oleracea*	Sage (garden)	*Salvia officinalis*
		Sagebrush	*Artemisia tridentata* and spp.
Quassia	*Quassia amara*	Salsify	*Tragopogon porrifolius*
Quebracho	*Aspidosperma quebracho*	Samphire	*Crithmum maritimum*
Queen Anne's lace	*Daucus carota*	Sand sedge	*Carex arenaria*
Queen's root	*Stillingia sylvatica*	Sandalwood	*Santalum album*
Quince	*Cydonia oblonga*	Sandspurry	*Arenaria rubra*
		Sanicle	*Sanicula europaea*
Ragweed	*Ambrosia artemisiifolia*	Santolina	*Santolina chamoecyparisus*
Ragwort	*Senecio* spp.	Sappanwood	*Caesalpinia sappan*
Raspberry	*Rubus idaeus*	Sarsaparilla, hairy	*Aralia hispida*
Ratany	*Krameria* spp.	Sarsaparilla, Jamaica	*Smilax officinalis*
Rattlesnake plantain	*Goodyera repens*	Sarsaparilla, wild	*Aralia nudicaulis* or
Rauvolfia	*Rauvolfia serpentina*		*Smilax glauca*
Ravensara	*Ravensara aromatica*	Sassafras	*Sassafras officinalis*
Red clover	*Trifolium pratense*	Saussurea	*Saussurea lappa*
Red currant	*Ribes rubrum*	Savory, garden	*Satureia hortensis*
Red dock	*Rumex aquaticus*	Savory, winter	*Satureia montana*
Red elder	*Sambucus racemosa*	Savine	*Sabina cacumina*
Red peony	*Paeonia obovata*	Saw palmetto	*Serenoa serrulata*
Red root	*Ceanothus* spp.	Saxifrage	*Saxifraga granulata*
Red rose	*Rosa gallica*	Scabious	*Scabiosa succisa*

Scammony	*Convulvulus scammonia*	Stinking gladwyn	*Iris foetidissima*
Scarlet pimpernel	*Anagallis arvensis*	Stinking goosefoot	*Chenopodium olidum*
Schisandra	*Schisandra chinensis*	Stonecrop	*Sedum acre*
Schizonepeta	*Schizonepeta tenuifolia*	Stoneroot	*Collinsonia canadensis*
Scopolia	*Scopolia carniolica*	Stoneseed	*Lithospermum ruderale*
Scurvygrass	*Cochlearia officinalis*	Storksbill	*Erodium cicutarium*
Sea buckthorn	*Hippophaë rhamnoides*	Strawberry	*Fragaria vesca*
Sea holly	*Eryngium maritimum*	Strophantus	*Strophantus kombe/gratus*
Sea pink	*Armeria*	Styrax	*Liquidamber orientalis*
Sea wormwood	*Artemisia maritima*	Suma	*Pfaffia paniculata*
Selfheal	*Prunella vulgaris*	Sumac	*Rhus glabra*
Seneca snakeroot	*Polygala senega*	Sumbul	*Ferula sumbul*
Senna	*Cassia angustifolia*	Summer savory	*Satureia hortensis*
Senna, wild	*Cassia marylandica*	Sundew	*Drosera rotundifolia*
Sesame	*Sesamum indicum*	Sunflower	*Helianthus annuus*
Shatavari	*Asparagus racemosus*	Sweet chestnut	*Castanea vesca*
Shavegrass	*Equisetum arvense*	Sweet cicely	*Myrrhis odorata*
Sheep's sorrel	*Rumex acetosella*	Sweet flag	*Acorus calamus*
Shepherd's purse	*Capsella bursa-pastoris*	Sweet orange	*Citrus aurantium* var. *dulcis*
Sicklepod	*Cassia obtusifolia*	Sweet sumac	*Rhus aromatica*
Silver birch	*Betula alba*	Sweet yellow clover	*Melilotus officinalis*
Silver fir	*Abies alba*	Syrian rue	*Peganum harmala*
Silver thistle	*Carlina acaulis*		
Silverweed	*Potentilla anserina*	Tamarind	*Tamarindus indicum*
Simaruba	*Simaruba amara*	Tangerine	*Citrus reticulata*
Simaruba bark	*Picramnia antidesma*	Tansy	*Tanacetum vulgare*
Skullcap	*Scutellaria lateriflora*	Tansy mustard	*Descurainae sophia*
Skunk cabbage	*Symplocarpus foetidus*	Tarragon	*Artemisia dracunculus*
Slippery elm	*Ulmus fulva*	Tayuyá	*Trianosperma fiffifolia*
Smartweed	*Polygonum punctatum*	Tea	*Camelia sinensis*
Soapwort	*Saponaria officinalis*	Tea tree	*Melaleuca linariifolia*
Solomon's seal	*Polygonatum multiflorum*	Teasel	*Dipsacus sylvestris*
Sophora	*Sophora flavescens*	Texas snakeroot	*Aristolochia reticulata*
Sorrel, sheep's	*Rumex acetosella*	Thuja	*Thuja occidentalis*
Sorrel, wood	*Oxalis acetosella*	Thunder ball	*Mylitta lapidescens*
Sour wood	*Oxydendrum arboreum*	Thyme	*Thymus vulgaris*
Southernwood	*Artemisia abrotanum*	Thyme, Spanish	*Thymus mastichina*
Sow thistle	*Sonchus* spp.	Thyme, wild	*Thymus serpyllum*
Spanish lavender	*Lavandula stoechas*	Tiger lily	*Lilium tigrium*
Spanish thyme	*Thymus mastichina*	Toadflax	*Linaria vulgaris*
Spearmint	*Mentha viridis* or *spicata*	Tobacco	*Nicotiana tabcum*
Speedwell	*Veronica officinalis*	Tolu balsam	*Myrospermum toluiferum*
Spike lavender	*Lavandula latifolia*	Tormentil	*Potentilla erecta*
Spikenard	*Aralia racemosa*	Trailing arbutus	*Epigaea repens*
Spindle tree	*Euonymus europoeus*	Treacle mustard	*Erysimum* spp.
Spruce	*Picea excelsa* and spp.	Tree of heaven	*Ailanthus glandulosa*
Spurge	*Euphorbia helioscopia*	Tree peony	*Paeonia suffruticosa*
Squaw vine	*Mitchella repens*	Turkey corn	*Corydalis formosa*
Squills	*Scilla maritima*	Turmeric	*Curcuma longa*
Squirting cucumber	*Ecbalium elaterium*	Turpeth	*Ipomoea turpethum*
St. John's wort	*Hypericum perfoliatum*	Twinleaf	*Jeffersonia diphylla*
Star anise	*Illicium anisatum*		
Stargrass	*Aletris farinosa*	Uña de gato	*Uncaria guianensis/tomentosa*
Stavesacre	*Delphinium staphisagria*	Upright meadow crowfoot	*Ranunculus acris*
Stevia	*Rebaudiana bertoni*	Uva ursi	*Arctostaphylos uva-ursi*

Valerian	*Valeriana officinalis*	Wild ginger	*Asarum canadense*
Vervain, blue	*Verbena hastate*	Wild indigo	*Baptisia tinctoria*
Vervain, European	*Verbena officinalis*	Wild lettuce	*Lactuca virosa*
Vetiver	*Vetiveria zizanoides*	Wild meadow sage	*Salvia lyrata*
Viola	*Viola yedoensis*	Wild oregano	*Monarda menthaefolia*
Violet	*Viola odorata*	Wild sarsaparilla	*Aralia nudicaulis*
Viper's bugloss	*Echium vulgare*	Wild senna	*Globularia alypum* or
Virgin's bower	*Clematis virginiana*		*Cassia marylandica*
Virginia creeper	*Vitis hederacea*	Wild wormseed	*Chenopodium ambrosioides*
Virginia snakeroot	*Aristolochia serpentaria*	Wild yam	*Dioscorea villosa*
Virginia stonecrop	*Penthorum sedoides*	Willow, white	*Salix alba*
Vomit nut	*Nux vomica*	Winter cherry	*Physalis alkelengi*
Wafer ash	*Ptelea trifoliata*	Winter cress	*Barbarea vulgaris*
Wahoo	*Euonymus atropurpureus*	Winter savory	*Satureia montana*
Wake robin	*Arum triphyllum*	Wintergreen	*Gaultheria procumbens*
Wallflower	*Cheiranthus cheiri*	Witch hazel	*Hamamelis virginiana*
Walnut	*Juglans regia*	Witch's broom	*Usnea barbata*
Water bugle	*Lycopus europaeus*	Wonder apple	*Momordica balsamina*
Water dropwort	*Oenanthe phellandrium*	Wood anemone	*Anemone nemorosa*
Water figwort	*Scrophularia aquatica*	Wood betony	*Betonica officinalis*
Water germander	*Teucrium scordium*	Wood sage germander	*Teucrium scorodonia*
Water hemlock	*Cicuta virosa*	Wood sorrel	*Oxalis acetosella*
Water mint	*Mentha aquatica*	Woodruff	*Asperula odorata*
Water pepper	*Polygonum hydropiper*	Wormwood	*Artemisia absinthium*
Water plantain	*Alisma plantago*		
Watercress	*Nasturtium officinale*	Ylang ylang	*Cananga odorata*
White agaric	*Polyporus officinalis*	Yarrow	*Achillea millefolium*
White ash	*Fraxinus americana*	Yellow dock	*Rumex crispus*
White bryony	*Bryonia alba*	Yellow flag	*Iris pseudacorus*
White cohosh	*Actea alba*	Yellow goatsbeard	*Tragopogon pratensis*
White deadnettle	*Lamium album*	Yellow jessamine	*Gelsemium sempervirens*
White hellebore	*Veratrum album*	Yellow parilla	*Menispermum canadense*
White henbane	*Hyoscyamus alba*	Yerba buena	*Micromeria chamissonis*
White horehound	*Marrubium vulgare*	Yerba de la flecha	*Sapium salicifolium*
White mustard	*Sinapis alba*	Yerba de la negrita	*Sphaeralcea coccinea* or
White pond lily	*Nymphaea odorata*		*cuspidata*
White poplar	*Populus candicans*	Yerba mansa	*Anemopsis californica*
White willow	*Salix alba*	Yerba santa	*Eriodyction* spp.
Wikstroemia	*Wikstroemia indica*	Yew	*Taxus baccata*
Wild angelica	*Angelica sylvestris*	Yohimbe	*Coryanthe yohimbe*
Wild bergamot	*Monarda fistulosa*	Yucca	*Yucca* spp
Wild carrot	*Daucus carota*		
Wild cherry	*Prunus serotina*	Zedoary	*Curcuma zedoaria*
Wild daffodil	*Narcissus pseudonarcissus*	Zdravetz	*Geranium macrorhizum*
Wild geranium	*Geranium maculatum*		

Botanical Name Cross Index

Botanical Name	Common Name	Botanical Name	Common Name
Abies alba	Silver fir	*Alstonia constricta*	Alstonia bark
Abies balsamea	Balsam fir	*Alstonia scholaris*	Alstonia
Abies canadensis	Hemlock spruce	*Althaea officinalis*	Marsh mallow
Abies excelsa/pectinata	Fir	*Althaea rosea*	Hollyhock
Abies grandis	Grand fir	*Amaranthus* spp.	Amaranth
Abies sibirica	Siberian fir	*Ambrosia artemisiifolia*	Ragweed
Abutilon theophrasti	Abutilon	*Ammi visnaga*	Khella
Acacia dealbata	Mimosa	*Amomum tsaoko*	Amomum tsaoko
Acacia nilotica	Acacia gum	*Amygdalus communis*	Almond
Acacia spp.	Acacia	*Amygdalus persica*	Peach
Acanthopanax senticosus	Acanthopanax	*Anacyclus pyrethrum*	Pellitory
Acanthus mollis	Bear's breech	*Anagallis arvensis*	Scarlet pimpernel
Achillea millefolium	Yarrow	*Anchusa officinalis*	Bugloss
Achyranthes bidentata	Ox-knee root	*Andira araroba*	Araroba
Acorus calamus	Calamus	*Andrographis paniculata*	Heart-thread lotus
Aconitum carmichaeli	Aconite	*Andropogon citratus*	Lemon verbena
Aconitum chinense	Aconite	*Anemarrhena aspheloides*	Know-mother
Aconitum napellus	Aconite	*Anemone nemorosa*	Wood anemone
Actea alba	White cohosh	*Anemone pulsatilla/patens*	Pasqueflower
Actea arguta	Baneberry	*Anemopsis californica*	Yerba mansa
Adiantum pedantum	Maidenhair fern	*Anethum graveolens*	Dill
Adonis vernalis	Adonis	*Angelica archangelica*	Angelica
Aegle marmelos	Bael fruit	*Angelica dahurica*	Angelica dahurica
Aegopodium podagraria	Goutweed	*Angelica pubescens*	Angelica pubescens
Aesculus hippocastanum	Horsechestnut	*Angelica sinensis*	Dong quai
Agastache rugosa	Rugose giant hyssop	*Angelica sylvestris*	Wild angelica
Agave spp.	Agave	*Aniba roseodora*	Rosewood
Agrimonia eupatoria	Agrimony	*Antennaria dioica*	Catsfoot
Ailanthus glandulosa	Tree of heaven	*Anthemis cotula*	Mayweed
Ajuga reptans	Bugle	*Anthemis nobilis*	Roman camomile
Akebia quinata	Akebia	*Anthriscus cerefolium*	Chervil
Albizzia julibrissin	Mimosa	*Anthriscus sylvestris*	Cow parsley
Alchemilla arvensis	Parsley piert	*Anthyllis vulneraria*	Kidney vetch
Alchemilla vulgaris	Lady's mantle	*Aphanes arvensis*	Aphanes
Aletris farinosa	Stargrass	*Aphanizaomenon flos-aquae*	Microalgae
Alisma orientalis	Alisma	*Apium graveolens*	Celery
Alisma plantago	Water plantain	*Apocynum androsaemifolium*	Bitter root
Alkanna tinctoria	Alkanet	*Apocynum cannabinum*	Dogbane
Alliaria officinalis	Hedge garlic	*Aquilaria agallocha*	Aloeswood
Allium cepa	Onion	*Aqilegia vulgaris*	Columbine
Allium porrum	Leek	*Aralia hispida*	American dwarf elder
Allium sativum	Garlic	*Aralia nudicaulis*	Wild sarsaparilla
Allium schoenoprasum	Chives	*Aralia spinosa*	Angelica tree
Alnus spp.	Alder	*Aralia racemosa*	Spikenard
Aloe spp.	Aloe gel or resin	*Arctium lappa*	Burdock
Alpinia galanga	Galangal	*Arctostaphylos manzanita*	Manzanita
Alpinia katsumadai	Katsumada's galangal	*Arctostaphylos uva-ursi*	Uva ursi, Bearberry
Alpinia oxyphylla	Sharp-leaf galangal		

Areca catechu	Areca	*Berberis vulgaris*	Barberry
Arenaria rubra	Sandspurry	*Beta vulgaris*	Beetroot
Arisaema consanguineum	Dragon arum	*Betonica officinalis*	Wood betony
Arisaema triphyllum	Jack in the pulpit	*Betula* spp.	Birch
Aristolochia clematitis	Birthwort	*Bidens tripartita*	Bur marigold
Aristolochia reticulata	Texas snakeroot	*Biota orientalis*	Oriental arborvitae
Aristolochia serpentaria	Virginia snakeroot	*Bixa orellana*	Anatto
Aristolochia westlandii	Green birthwort	*Bletilla*	Amethyst orchid
Arnica montana	Arnica	*Blumea balsamifera*	Blumea camphor
Artemisia abrotanum	Southernwood	*Boldea fragrans*	Boldo
Artemisia absinthium	Wormwood	*Bombyx mori*	{Bombyx mori}
Artemisia annua	Annual wormwood	*Borago officinalis*	Borage
Artemisia apiacea	Celery wormwood	*Borneolum*	Borneo camphor
Artemisia argyi	Asian mugwort	*Boronia megastigma*	Boronia
Artemisia capillaris	Downy wormwood	*Boswellia carterii*	Frankincense
Artemisia cina	Levant wormseed	*Brickellia grandiflora*	Prodigiosa
Artemisia dracunculus	Tarragon	*Brucea javanica*	Brucea
Artemisia maritima	Sea wormwood	*Bryonia alba*	White bryony
Artemisia tridentata and spp.	Sagebrush	*Bryonia dioica*	Bryony
Artemisia vulgaris	Mugwort	*Buddleia officinalis*	Buddleia
Arum maculatum	Cuckoopint	*Bupleurum chinense*	Asian buplever
Arum triphyllum	Wake robin	*Buxus sempervirens*	Box
Asarum canadense	Wild ginger		
Asarum europaeum	Hazelwort	*Cacalia decomposita*	Matarique
Asarum sieboldii	Wild ginger	*Caesalpinia sappan*	Sappanwood
Asclepias asperula	Inmortal	*Calaminta officinalis* and spp.	Calamint
Asclepias speciosa	Milkweed	*Calendula officinalis*	Marigold (Pot)
Asclepias tuberosa	Pleurisy root	*Callitris intratropica*	Blue cypress
Asparagus cochinensis	Shiny asparagus	*Calluna vulgaris*	Heather
Asparagus officinalis	Asparagus	*Calophyllum inophyllum*	Tamanu, Foraha
Asparagus recemosus	Shatavari	*Caltha palustris*	Marsh marigold
Asperula odorata	Woodruff	*Camelia sinensis*	Tea
Aspidium filix-mas.	Male fern	*Camptotheca acuminata*	Camptotheca
Asphodelus ramosus	Ashphodel	*Cananga odorata*	Ylang ylang
Aspidosperma quebracho	Quebracho	*Canarium commune*	Manila elemi
Aster tataricus	Tartary aster	*Cannabis sativa*	Indian hemp
Astragalus membranaceus	Membraneous milkvetch	*Capsella bursa-pastoris*	Shepherd's purse
Atractylodes macrocephala	White atractylodes	*Capsicum annuum*	Cayenne
Atractylodes ovata	Black atractylodes	*Carduus benedictus*	Holy thistle
Atropa belladonna	Belladonna	*Carduus marianus*	Milk thistle
Atropa mandragora	Mandrake	*Carex arenaria*	Sand sedge
Avena sativa	Oats	*Carica papaya*	Papaya
		Carlina acaulis	Silver thistle
Bacopa monnieri	Bacopa	*Carthamus tinctorius*	Safflower
Balsamum peruvianum	Peruvian balsam	*Carum carvi*	Caraway
Baphicacanthus cusia	Baphicacanthus	*Caryophullus aromaticus*	Clove
Baptisia tinctoria	Wild indigo	*Cassia angustifolia*	Senna
Barbarea vulgaris	Winter cress	*Cassia fistula*	Purging cassia
Barosma betulina	Buchu	*Cassia marilandica*	Wild senna
Ballota foetida	Black horehound	*Cassia tora*	Cassia tora
Belamcanda chinensis	Leopard flower	*Castanea vesca*	Sweet chestnut
Belladonna	Atropa belladonna	*Caulophyllum thalictroides*	Blue cohosh
Bellis perennis	Daisy	*Ceanothus* spp.	Red root
Benincasa hispida	Waxgourd	*Cedrus atlantica*	Atlas cedarwood
		Cedrus deodora	Himalaya cedarwood

Celosia cristata	Celosia
Centaurea cyanus	Cornflower
Centaurea scabiosa	Knapweed
Cephaelis ipecacuanha	Ipecac
Cephalotaxus fortunei	Cephalotaxus
Cerasus vulgaris	Cherry
Ceratonia siliqua	Carob
Cereus grandiflorus	Cereus
Cetraria islandica	Iceland moss
Chamaelirium luteum	Helonias
Chasmanthera palmata	European columbo
Cheiranthus cheiri	Wallflower
Chelidonum maius	Celandine
Chelone glabra	Balmony
Chenopodium ambrosioides	Wild wormseed
Chenopodium anthelminticum	American wormseed
Chenopodium botrys	Feather geranium
Chenopodium olidum	Stinking goosefoot
Chionanthus virginicus	Fringe tree
Chimaphila umbellata	Pipsissewa
Chlorella spp.	Microalgae
Chondodendron tomentosum	Pareira
Chondrus crispus	Irish moss
Chrysanthemum balsamita	Costmary
Chrysanthemum cinerariifolium	Dalmatia pellitory
Chrysanthemum indicum	Wild chrysanthemum
Chrysanthemum leucanthemum	Ox-eye daisy
Chrysanthemum morifolium	Florist's chrysanthemum
Cibotium baromites	Dogspine
Cichorium endiva	Endive
Cichorium intybus	Chicory
Cicuta virosa	Water hemlock
Cimicifuga foetida	Rising hemp
Cimicifuga racemosa	Black cohosh
Cinchona calisaya or *succiruba* or *officinalis*	Peruvian bark
Cineraria maritima	Cineraria
Cinnamomum camphora	Camphor
Cinnamomum cassia	Cassia cinnamon
Cinnamomum loureirii	Vietnam cinnamon
Cinnamomum zeylanicum	Ceylon cinnamon
Cirsium japonicum	Japanese thistle
Cissampelos pareira	Abutua
Cistanches salsa	Fleshy broomrape
Cistus ladaniferus	Rock rose
Citrullus colocynthis	Colocynth
Citrus aurantifolia	Lime
Citrus aurantium ssp. *aurantium*	Bitter orange
Citrus aurantium ssp. *bergamia*	*Bergamot*
Citrus aurantium var. *dulcis*	Sweet orange
Citrus limonum	Lemon
Citrus paradisii	Grapefruit
Citrus reticulata	Tangerine, Mandarine
Citrus vulgaris	Bitter orange, Neroli
Claviceps purpurea	Rye ergot
Clematis spp.	Clematis
Clematis virginiana	Virgin's bower
Cochlearia armoracia	Horseradish
Cochlearia officinalis	Scurvygrass
Codonopsis pilosula	Downy bellflower
Coffea arabica	Coffee
Coix lachryma jobi	Job's tears
Colchicum autumnale	Meadow saffron
Collinsonia canadensis	Stoneroot
Colutea arborescens	Bladder senna
Coleus forskohlii	Coleus
Combretum raimbaultii	Combretum
Commiphora mukul	Guggul
Commiphora myrrha	Myrrh
Condalia lycioides and spp.	Condalia
Conium maculatum	Spotted/Poison hemlock
Convallaria maialis	Lily of the valley
Convulvulus duartinus	Morning glory
Convulvulus scammonia	Scammony
Convolvulus sepium	Hedge bindweed
Copaiba langsdorfii	Copaiba
Coptis trifolia	Goldthread
Coptis chinensis	Coptis
Corallorhiza maculata	Coral root
Cordia salicifolia	Cha de bugre
Cordyceps spp.	Caterpillar mushroom
Coriandrum sativum	Coriander
Cornus spp.	Dogwood
Coryanthe yohimbe	Yohimbe
Corydalis aurea and spp.	Asian corydalis
Corydalis formosa	Turkey corn
Corylus avellana	Hazel
Cotyledon umbilics	Kidneywort
Cowania mexicana	Cliffrose
Crataegus oxyacantha	Hawthorn
Crithmum maritimum	Samphire
Crocus sativus	Saffron
Crotalaria sessiliflora	Crotalaria
Croton tiglium	Croton seed
Cryptocarya massoia	Massoia
Cucumis melo	Cantaloupe
Cucurbita pepo	Pumpkin
Cuminum cyminum	Cumin
Cunila origanoides	Dittany
Cupressus sempervirens	Cypress
Curcuma longa	Turmeric
Curcuma zedoaria	Zedoary
Cuscuta spp.	Dodder
Cusparia angostura	Angostura

Cyclamen europaeum	Cyclamen	*Epilobium angustifolium*	Rose bay-willow herb
Cydonia oblonga	Quince	*Epimedium brevicornum*	Horny goat weed
Cymbopogon citratus	Citronella	*Equisetum arvense*	Horsetail
Cymbopogon flexuosus	Lemongrass	*Erechtites hieracifolia*	Fireweed
Cymbopogon martinii`	Palmarosa	*Erica cinerea*	Heather
Cymbopogon martinii		*Erigeron canadensis*	Canada fleabane
var. *sofia*	Gingergrass	*Eriobotria japonica*	Eriobotria
Cymbopogon nardus	Ceylon citronella	*Eriodyction* spp.	Yerba santa
Cynanchum paniculatum	Prime white	*Erodium cicutarium*	Storksbill
Cynara scolymus	Artichoke	*Eruca sativa*	Rocket
Cynoglossum officinale	Hound's tongue	*Eryngium aquaticum*	Button snake root
Cyperus rotundus	Sedge	*Eryngium campestre*	Field eryngo
Cypripedium pubescens	Lady's slipper	*Eryngium maritimum*	Sea holly
Cytisus scoparius	Broom	*Eryobotria japonica*	Eryobotria
		Erysimum spp.	Treacle mustard
Daphne mezereum	Mezereon	*Erythraea centaurium*	Centaury
Datura stramonium	Jimsonweed	*Erythraea douglasii*	
Daucus carota	Wild carrot	or *muhlenbergii*	Canchalagua
Delphinium spp.	Larkspur	*Erythrina indica*	Erythrina
Delphinium staphisagria	Stavesacre	*Erythronium americanum*	Adder's tongue
Dendrobium	Stonebushel	*Erythroxylon coca*	Cocaine
Descurainae sophia	Tansy mustard	*Eucalyptus* spp.	Eucalyptus
Desmodium pulchellum	Desmodium	*Eucommia ulmoides*	Eucommia
Dichroa febrifuga	Feverflower	*Eugenia caryophyllata*	Clove
Dictamnus albus	Burning bush	*Euonymus atropurpureus*	Wahoo
Dictamnus dusycarpus	Dittany	*Euonymus europoeus*	Spindle tree
Digitalis purpurea	Foxglove	*Euonymus occidentalis*	Burning bush
Dioscorea hypoglauca	Long yam	*Eupatorium cannabinum*	Hemp agrimony
Dioscorea sativa	Mountain yam	*Eupatorium perfoliatum*	Boneset
Dioscorea villosa	Wild yam	*Eupatorium purpureum*	Gravel root
Diplotaxis tenuifolia	Rocket	*Euphorbia helioscopia*	Spurge
Dipsacus sylvestris	Teasel	*Euphorbia pilulifera*	Pillbearing spurge
Dolichos lablab	Hyacinth bean	*Euphrasia rostkoviana*	Eyebright
Dorema ammoniacum	Gum ammoniac	*Euryale ferox*	Foxnut
Dorstenia contrayerva	Contrayerba	*Evodia rutecarpa*	Evodia
Drosera rotundifolia	Sundew		
Dryobalanops aromatica	Borneo camphor	*Fabiana imbricata*	Pichi
Dryopteris crassirhizoma	Shield fern	*Fagus sylvatica*	Beech
Dryopteris filix mas.	Male fern	*Fagopyrum esculentum*	Buckwheat
Duboisia myoporoides	Corkwood tree	*Ferula assa-foetida*	Asafoetida
		Ferula galbaniflua	Galbanum
Ecbalium elaterium	Squirting cucumber	*Ferula persica*	Sagapenum
Echinacea angustifolia	Narrow-leaf purple	*Ferula sumbul*	Sumbul
	coneflower	*Ficus carica*	Fig
Echinacea pallida	Pale purple coneflower	*Filipendula ulmaria*	Meadowsweet
Echinacea pupurea	Purple coneflower	*Foeniculum vulgare*	Fennel
Echinodorus macrophyllum	Chapeu de couro	*Forsythia suspensa*	Forsythia
Echium vulgare	Viper's bugloss	*Fouqueira splendens*	Ocotillo
Eclipta prostata	Field lotus	*Fragaria vesca*	Strawberry
Elettaria cardamomum	Cardamom	*Frasera canadensis*	American columbo
Eleutherococcus sentiosus	Eleuthero	*Fraxinus americana*	White ash
Eschscholtzia californica	California poppy	*Fraxinus excelsior*	Ash
Ephedra vulgaris	Ephedra	*Fritillaria* spp.	Fritillary
Epigaea repens	Trailing arbutus	*Fucus vesiculosus*	Bladderwrack, Kelp

876

Fumaria officinalis	Fumitory	*Hesperis matronalis*	Dame's rocket
		Heuchera spp.	Alum root
Galega officinalis	Goat's rue	*Hibiscus abelmoschus*	Ambrette
Galeopsis ochroleuca	Hemp nettle	*Hibiscus sabdariffa*	Hibiscus
Galium aparine	Cleavers	*Hieracium pilosella*	Mousear hawkweed
Galium verum	Lady's bedstraw	*Hippophaë rhamnoides*	Sea buckthorn
Garcinia hanburyii	Gamboge	*Hordeum distichon*	Barley
Gardenia florida	Gardenia	*Humulus lupulus*	Hops
Gastrodia elata	Celestial hemp	*Hydrangea arborescens*	Hydrangea
Gaultheria procumbens	Wintergreen	*Hydrastis canadensis*	Goldenseal
Gelidium spp.	Agar-agar	*Hydrocotyle asiatica*	Gotu kola
Gelsemium sempervirens	Yellow jessamine	*Hymenaea courbarii*	Jatobá
Genista tinctoria	Dyer's broom	*Hyoscyamus niger*	Henbane (black)
Gentiana lutea	Yellow gentian	*Hyoscyamus alba*	White henbane
Gentiana macrophylla	Large-leaf gentian	*Hypericum perfoliatum*	St. John's wort
Gentiana scabra	Scabrous gentian	*Hyssopus officinalis*	Hyssop
Geranium macrorrhizum	Zdravetz	*Hysteronica baylahuen*	Hysteronica
Geranium maculatum	Cranesbill		
Geranium robertianum	Herb robert	*Ilex paraguaiensis*	Maté
Geum spp.	Avens	*Ilex* spp.	Holly
Gillenia trifoliata	Indian physic	*Illicium anisatum*	Star anise
Gingiber officinalis	Ginger	*Imperatoria ostruthium*	Masterwort
Ginkgo biloba	Ginkgo	*Impatiens biflora*	Jewelweed
Glechoma hederacea	Ground ivy	*Indigo pulverata*	Indigo
Glehnia littoralis	Northern sandroot	*Inula brittanica*	Japanese elecampane
Globularia alypum	Wild senna	*Inula graveolens*	Fragrant inula
Glycirrhiza glabra	Licorice	*Inula helenium*	Elecampane
Gonolobus condurango	Condurango	*Iphigenia indica*	Iphigenia
Goodyera repens	Rattlesnake plantain	*Ipomoea jalapa*	Jalap
Gossypum spp.	Cotton	*Ipomoea turpethum*	Turpeth
Gratiola officinalis	Hedge hyssop	*Iris florentina*	Orris
Grifola umbellata	Grifola	*Iris foetidissima*	Stinking gladwyn
Grindelia robusta	Gumweed	*Iris pseudoracorus*	Yellow flag
Guaiacum officinale	Guaiacum	*Iris versicolor/germanica*	Blue flag
Guarea rusbyi	Cocillana bark	*Isatis tinctoria*	Woad
Haematoxylon		*Jasminum officinale*	Jasmine
campechianum	Logwood	*Jateorhiza palmata*	Calumba
Hagenia abyssinica	Kousso	*Jeffersonia diphylla*	Twinleaf
Hamamelis virginiana	Witch hazel	*Juglans cinerea*	Butternut
Haronga madagascariensis	Haronga	*Juglans nigra*	Black walnut
Harpagophytum procumbens	Devil's claw	*Juglans regia*	Walnut
Hedeoma pulegioides	American pennyroyal	*Juncus dicipiens*	Bulrush
Hedera helix	Ivy	*Juniperus brasiliensis*	Catuaba
Hedychium acuminatum	Hedychium	*Juniperus communis*	Juniper
Hedyotis diffusa	Snaketongue grass	*Juniperus virginiana*	Virginia cedarwood
Helianthemum canadense	Frostwort	*Juniperus sabina*	Sabine
Helianthus annuus	Sunflower		
Helichrysum spp.	Immortelle	*Kallstroemia* spp.	Contrayerba
Helleborus niger	Black hellebore	*Kalmia latifolia*	Mountain laurel
Hemidesmus indicus	Indian sarsaparilla	*Knoxia corymbosa*	Knoxia
Hepatica triloba	Liverwort	*Kochia*	Belvedere cypress
Heracleum lanatum	Cow parsnip	*Kola vera*	Kola
Hernandia voyronii	Hernandia	*Krameria* spp.	Ratany
Herniaria glabra	Rupturewort		

877

Lachnantes tinctoria	Lachnantes	*Lysimachia nummularia*	
Lactuca virosa	Wild lettuce	and spp.	Moneywort
Lamium album	White deadnettle	*Lythrum salicaria*	Loosestrife
Lamium purpureum	Purple deadnettle		
Larix europaea	Larch	*Macuna pruriens*	Cowhage
Larrea divaricata	Chaparral	*Magnolia liliflora* and spp.	Magnolia (bud)
Larix decidua	Larch	*Magnolia officinalis* and spp.	Magnolia (bark)
Laurus nobilis	Bay laurel	*Mahonia repens*	Oregon grape root
Lavandula angustifolia	Lavender	*Mallotus philipinensis*	Kamala
Lavandula dentata	Dentate lavender	*Malva sylvestris*	Blue mallow
Lavandula latifolia	Spike lavender	*Marrubium vulgare*	White horehound
Lavandula multifida	Fern-leaf lavender	*Matricaria recutita*	German camomile
Lavandula stoechas	Spanish lavender	*Matricaria matricarioides*	Pineapple weed
Lavandula x *intermedia*	Lavandin	*Medicago sativa*	Alfalfa
Lawsonia alba	Henna	*Melaleuca alternifolia*	Tea tree
Ledum latifolium	Labrador tea	*Melaleuca cajeputii*	Cajeput
Ledum groenlandicum	Labrador tea	*Melaleuca quinquenervia*	Niaouli
Ledum palustre	Marsh tea	*Melia azadirachta*	Marquosa bark
Leonorus cardiaca	Motherwort	*Melilotus officinalis*	Melilot
Leptandra virginica	Culver's root	*Melissa officinalis*	Melissa
Lespedaza capitata	Bush clover	*Menispermum canadense*	Yellow parilla
Liatris odorantissima	Deer's tongue	*Mentha aquatica*	Water mint
Liatris punctata	Gayfeather	*Mentha arvensis*	Field mint
Liatris spicata	Colic root	*Mentha* x *piperita*	Peppermint
Ligusticum levisticum	Garden lovage	*Mentha pulegium*	Pennyroyal
Ligusticum porteri	Oshá	*Mentha viridis /spicata*	Spearmint
Ligusticum sinense	Chinese lovage	*Menyanthes trifoliata*	Bogbean
Ligusticum walichii	Sichuan lovage	*Mercurialis annua*	Mercury
Ligustrum vulgare	Privet	*Mercurialis perennis*	Dog's mercury
Liquidamber orientalis	Storax	*Mespilus germanica*	Medlar
Lilium candidum	Madonna lily	*Micromeria chamissonis*	Yerba buena
Lilium tigrium	Tiger lily	*Milettia reticulata*	Milettia
Linaria vulgaris	Toadflax	*Mirabilis multiflorum*	Maravilla
Lindera strychnifolia	Lindera	*Mitchella repens*	Partridgeberry
Linum cartharticum	Purging flax	*Momordica balsamina*	Wonder apple
Linum usitatissimum	Flax	*Monarda fistulosa*	Wild bergamot
Lippia citriodora	Lemon verbena	*Monarda menthaefolia*	Wild oregano
Liriosma ovata	Muira puama	*Monarda punctata*	Horsemint
Litchi sinensis	Litchi	*Monotropa hypopytis/*	
Lithospermum ruderale	Stoneseed	*uniflora*	Indian pipe
Litsea cubeba	Cubeb	*Morinda officinalis*	Morinda
Lobelia inflata	Lobelia	*Morus alba*	White mulberry
Lolium temulentum	Bearded darnel	*Morus nigra*	Black mulberry
Lomatium dissectum	Biscuit root	*Mylitta lapidescens*	Thunder ball
Lonicera japonica and spp.	Honeysuckle (Japanese)	*Myosotis palustris*	Forget me not
Lopatherum gracilum	Lopatherum	*Myrica cerifera*	Bayberry
Lopophora williamsii	Jimsonweed	*Myristica fragrans*	Nutmeg
Loranthus parasiticus	Loranthus	*Myrospermum toluiferum*	Tolu balsam
Lotus corniculatus	Bird's foot trefoil	*Myroxylon pareirae*	Peru balsam
Lupinus spp	Lupin	*Myrrhis odorata*	Sweet cicely
Lycium chinense	Wolfberry	*Myrtus communis*	Myrtle
Lycopodium clavatum	Club moss		
Lycopus europaeus	Water bugle	*Narcissus pseudonarcissus*	Wild daffodil
Lycopus virginicus	Bugleweed	*Nardostachys jatamansi*	Indian spikenard
Lygodium japonicum	Japanese climbing fern	*Nasturtium officinale*	Watercress

Nectandra spp.	Coto bark	*Peucedanus graveolens*	Dill
Nelumbo nucifera	Lotus	*Peumus boldus*	Boldo
Nepeta cataria	Catnip	*Pfaffia paniculata*	Suma
Nerium oleander	Oleander	*Phaseolus calcaratus*	Aduki bean
Nicotiana tabcum	Tobacco	*Phaseolus vulgaris*	Green bean
Nigella sativa	Fennel flower	*Phellodendron amurense*	Siberian cork tree
Notopterigium incisum	Notopterigium	*Phlox carolina*	Carolina pink
Nux vomica	Vomit nut	*Phoenix dactylifera*	Date
Nymphaea alba	European white pond lily	*Phoradendron flavescens*	American mistletoe
Nymphaea lutea	Yellow pond lily	*Phragmites communis*	Common reed
Nymphaea odorata	White pond lily	*Phyllanthus amarus*	Phyllanthus
Ocymum basilicum	Basil	*Phyllostachys nigra*	Black bamboo
Oenanthe crocata	Hemlock water dropwort	*Physalis alkelengi*	Winter cherry
Oenanthe phellandrium	Water dropwort	*Physostigma venenosum*	Calabar bean
Oenothera hookeri/biennis	Evening primrose	*Phytolacca decandra*	Poke root
Olea europaea	Olive	*Picea* spp.	Spruce
Ononis spinosa	Restharrow	*Picea mariana*	Black spruce
Ophiopogonis japonicus	Dwarf lilyturf	*Picraena excelsa*	Quassia
Oplopanax horridum	Devil's club	*Picramnia antidesma*	Simaruba
Opopanax chironium	Opopanax	*Picrorhiza kurooa*	Picrorhiza
Opuntia spp.	Prickly pear	*Pilocarpus* spp.	Jaborandi
Orchis mascula	Purple orchid	*Pimento officinalis*	Allspice
Origanum compactum	Oregano compactum	*Pimpinella anisum*	Aniseed
Origanum maiorana	Marjoram	*Pimpinella saxifraga*	Burnet saxifrage
Origanum vulgare	Oregano	*Pinellia ternata*	Pinellia
Ormenis mixta/multicola	Moroccan camomile	*Pinguicula vulgaris*	Marsh violet
Orobanche uniflora	Naked broomrape	*Pinus pinaster*	Sea pine
Orthosiphon stamineus	Orthosiphon	*Pinus* spp.	Pine
Osmunda regalis	Buckthorn brake	*Pinus sylvestris*	Forest pine
Oxalis acetosella	Wood sorrel	*Piper angustifolium*	Matico
Oxydendrum arboreum	Sour wood	*Piper betel*	Betel leaf
		Piper cubeba	Cubeb
Paeonia lactiflora	White peony	*Piper methysticum*	Kava kava
Paeonia obovata/lactiflora	Red peony	*Piper nigrum*	Black pepper
Paeonia suffruticosa	Tree peony	*Pirus communis*	Pear
Panax ginseng	Asian ginseng	*Pirus malus*	Apple
Panax pseudoginseng	Pseudoginseng	*Piscidia erythrina*	Jamaica dogwood
Panax quinquefolium	American ginseng	*Pistacia lentiscus*	Mastix
Papaver rhoeas	Corn poppy	*Plantago lanceolata*	Lance-leaf plantain
Papaver somniferum	Poppy	*Plantago maior*	Round-leaf plantain
Parietaria officinalis	Pellitory of the wall	*Plantago psyllium*	Psyllium
Paris quadrifolia	Herb paris	*Platycodon grandiflorum*	Ballonflower
Parnassia palustris	Heartleaf	*Plemonium reptans*	Abscess root
Passiflora incarnata	Passion flower	*Plumbago europoea*	Leadwort
Paullinia cupara	Guaraná	*Podophyllum peltatum*	Mayapple
Pedicularis spp.	Betony	*Pogostemon cablin*	Patchouli
Peganum harmala	Syrian rue	*Pollen*	Flower pollen
Pelargonium graveolens	Geranium	*Polygala amara*	Bitter milkwort
Pelargonium x asperum	Rose geranium	*Polygala senega*	Seneca snakeroot
Penthorum sedoides	Virginia stonecrop	*Polygala tenuifolia*	Thin-leaf milkwort
Perilla acuta/frutescens	Perilla	*Polygala vulgaris*	European milkwort
Petasites officinalis	Butterbur	*Polygonatum multiflorum*	Solomon's seal
Petroselinum crispum	Parsley	*Polygonatum sibiricum*	Siberian Solomon's seal
Peucedanum arenarium	Asian masterwort	*Polygonum aviculare*	Knotgrass
Peucedanum palustre	Hog's fennel	*Polygonum bistorta*	Bistort

Polygonum cuspidatum	Japanese knotweed	*Raphanus sativus niger*	Black radish
Polygonum hydropiper	Water pepper	*Rauvolfia serpentina*	Rauwolfia
Polygonum multiflorum	Flowery knotweed	*Ravensara aromatica*	Ravensara
Polygonum persicaria	Lady's thumb	*Rebaudiana bertoni*	Stevia
Polygonum punctatum	Water smartweed	*Rehmannia glutinosa*	Rehmannia
Polymnia uvedalia	Bearsfoot	*Rhamnus catharticus*	Rhineberry
Polypodium vulgare	Brakefern	*Rhamnus frangula*	Alder buckthorn
Polyporus officinalis	White agaric	*Rhamnus purshiana*	Cascara sagrada
Polytrichum juniperinum	Haircap moss	*Rheum palmatum*	Rhubarb
Populus balsamifera	Balsam poplar	*Rhodiola rosea*	Rhodiola
Populus candicans	White poplar	*Rhododendron anthopogon*	Rhododendron
Populus nigra	Black poplar	*Rhus aromatica*	Sweet sumac
Populus tremula	Aspen	*Rhus glabra*	Sumac
Poria cocos	Poria	*Rhus toxicodendron*	Poison ivy
Portulaca oleracea	Purslane	*Ribes grossularia*	Gooseberry
Potentilla anserina	Silverweed	*Ribes nigrum*	Blackcurrant
Potentilla canadensis	Five-finger grass	*Ribes rubrum*	Red currant
Potentilla erecta	Tormentil	*Ricinus communis*	Castor oil plant
Potentilla reptans	Cinquefoil	*Rosa canina*	Dog rose
Primula officinalis	Primrose	*Rosa centifolia*	Cabbage/May rose
Primula veris	Cowslip	*Rosa damascena*	Damask rose
Prinos verticillatus	Black alder	*Rosmarinus officinalis*	Rosemary
Prosopis julifera/pubescens	Mesquite	*Rubia tinctorum* and spp.	Madder
Prunella vulgaris	Selfheal	*Rubus idaeus*	Raspberry
Prunus amygdalus	Almond	*Rubus villosus*	Blackberry
Prunus armeniaca	Apricot	*Rudbeckia laciniata*	Coneflower
Prunus cerasus	Cherry	*Rumex acetosa*	Sorrel, wood
Prunus domestica	Plum	*Rumex acetosella*	Sheep's sorrel
Prunus laurocerasus	Cherry laurel	*Rumex alpinus*	Herb patience
Prunus persica	Peach	*Rumex aquaticus*	Red dock
Prunus serotina	Wild cherry	*Rumex crispus*	Yellow dock
Prunus spinosa	Blackthorn	*Ruscus aculeatus*	Butcher's broom
Pseudostellaria heterophylla	Prince ginseng	*Ruta graveolens*	Rue
Pseudotsuga manziesii	Douglas fir		
Psoralea corylifolia	Scurf pea	*Sabadilla officinarum*	Sabadilla
Ptelea trifoliata	Wafer ash	*Sabbatia angularis*	American centaury
Pterocarpus spp	Kino	*Sabina cacumina*	Savine
Pueraria lobata	Kudzu	*Sagittaria sagittifolia*	Arrowhead
Pulicaria dysenterica	Fleawort	*Salicornia herbacea*	Glasswort
Pulmonaria officinalis	Lungwort	*Salix alba*	White willow
Pulsatilla chinensis	Pulsatilla	*Salix nigra*	Black willow
Punica granatum	Pomegranate	*Salvia colorata*	Red sage
Pyrola rotundifolia	European wintergreen	*Salvia divinorum*	Diviner's sage
Pyrrosia lingua	Felt fern	*Salvia officinalis*	Sage (Garden)
Pyrus communis	Pear	*Salvia lyrata*	Wild meadow sage
		Salvia miltiorrhiza	Cinnabar sage
Quassia amara	Quassia	*Salvia sclarea*	Clary sage
Quercus spp.	Oak bark	*Sambucus ebulus*	Dwarf elder
Quisqualis indica	Rangoon creeper	*Sambucus nigra*	Black elder
		Sambucus racemosa	Red elder
Rabdosia rubescens	Rabdosia	*Sanguinaria canadensis*	Bloodroot
Ranunculus acris	Upright meadow crowfoot	*Sanguisorba officinalis*	Great burnet
		Sanicula europaea	Sanicle
Ranunculus bulbosus	Bulbous buttercup	*Santalum album*	Sandalwood
Ranunculus ficaria	Pilewort	*Santolina chamaecyparisus*	Santolina

Sapium salicifolium	Yerba de la flecha
Saponaria officinalis	Soapwort
Sarcandra glabra	Smooth sarcandra
Sargassum fusiforme	Sargassum
Sarracenia purpurea	Pitcher plant
Sassafras officinalis	Sassafras
Satureia hortensis	Summer/Garden savory
Satureia montana	Winter/Mountain savory
Saussurea lappa	Wood aromatic
Saxifraga granulata	Saxifrage
Scabiosa arvensis	Field scabious
Scabiosa succisa	Scabious
Schisandra chinensis	Schisandra
Schizonepeta tenuifolia	Japanese catnip
Scilla maritima	Squills
Scilla nutans	Bluebell bulb
Scolopendrium vulgare	Hartstongue fern
Scopolia carniolica	Scopolia
Scrophularia nodosa	Figwort
Scrophularia aquatica	Water figwort
Scrophularia ningpoensis	Black figwort
Scutellaria baicalensis	Baikal skullcap
Scutellaria barbata	Barbed skullcap
Scutellaria lateriflora	Skullcap
Sedum acre	Stonecrop
Sempervivum tectorum	Houseleek
Senecio aureus	Golden ragwort/groundsel
Senecio spp.	Ragwort, groundsel
Serenoa serrulata	Saw palmetto
Sesamum indicum	Sesame
Siegesbeckia orientalis	Siegesbeckia
Siler divaricatum	Wind protector
Silphium perfoliatum	Cup plant
Simaruba amara	Simaruba
Simmondia chinensis	Jojoba
Sinapis alba	White mustard
Sinapis niger	Black mustard
Sisymbrium officinalis	Hedge mustard
Sisymbrium sophia	Tansy mustard
Symplocarpus foetidus	Skunk cabbage
Smilacina racemosa	False solomon's seal
Smilax officinalis	Jamaica sarsaparilla
Solanum carolinensis	Horsenettle
Solanum dulcamara	Bittersweet
Solanum nigrum	Black nightshade
Solanum paniculatum	Jurubeba
Solidago virgaurea	Goldenrod
Sonchus spp.	Sow thistle
Sorbus aucuparia	Rowan tree
Sophora flavescens	Yellow pagoda tree
Sphaeralcea coccinea/ cuspidata	Yerba de la negrita
Spigelia anthelmia	Demerara pinkroot
Spigelia marylandica	Pinkroot
Spilanthes oleracea	Para cress

Spirodela polyrrhiza	Spirodela
Stachys palustris	Marsh woundwort
Stellaria dichotoma	Stellaria
Stellaria media	Chickweed
Stemona japonica	Stemona
Stephania tetrandra	Stephania
Sterculia lychnophora	Sterculia
Sticta pulmonaria	Lungwort lichen
Stillingia sylvatica	Queen's root
Strophantus kombe/gratus	Strophanthus
Strychnos castelnaei	Curare
Strychnos ignatii	Ignatia
Strychnos nux vomica	Nux vomica
Styrax benzoin	Benzoin
Swertia chirata	Chirata
Swertia radiata	Green gentian
Symphitum officinale	Comfrey
Symplocarpus foetidus	Skunk cabbage
Syringa vulgaris	Lilac
Syzygium jambolanum	Jambul
Tabebuia avellanedae	Pau d'arco, Lapacho
Tagetes glandulifera	Garden/African marigold
Tamarindus indicum	Tamarind
Tamus communis	Black bryony
Tanacetum annuum	Moroccan blue camomile
Tanacetum balsamita	Costmary
Tanacetum parthenium	Feverfew
Tanacetum vulgare	Tansy
Taraxacum officinale	Dandelion
Taxus baccata	Yew
Terminalia belerica	Myrobalan (beleric)
Terminalia chebula	Myrobalan (chebulic)
Tetrapanax papyrifera	Tetrapanax
Teucrium chamaedrys	Little germander
Teucrium scordium	Water germander
Teucrium scorodonia	Wood sage germander
Thelesperma spp.	Cotá
Theobroma cacao	Cocoa
Thlaspus arvense	Thlaspus
Thuja occidentalis	Arborvitae
Thymus mastichina	Spanish thyme
Thymus serpyllum	Wild thyme, Mother of thyme
Thymus vulgaris	Thyme
Tiarella cordifolia	Coolwort
Tilia cordata	Linden
Torreya grandis	Japanese torreya
Toxicodendron diversilobum	Poison oak (Western)
Toxicodendron radicans	Poison ivy
Tragopogon porrifolius	Salsify
Tragopogon pratensis	Yellow goatsbeard
Trianosperma fiffifolia	Tayuyá
Tribulus terrestris	Caltrop
Tricosanthes kirilowii	Snakegourd

Trifolium pratense	Red clover	*Veronica beccabunga*	Brooklime
Trigonella foenum-graecum	Fenugreek	*Veronica chamaedrys*	Germander speedwell
Trillium pendulum	Birthroot	*Veronica officinalis*	Speedwell
Triticum repens	Couch grass	*Vetiveria zizanoides*	Vetiver
Tropaeolum maius	Nasturtium	*Viburnum opulus*	Cramp bark
Tsuga canadensis	Hemlock fir	*Viburnum prunifolium*	Black haw
Turnera diffusa	Damiana	*Vinca major*	Periwinkle, greater
Tussilago farfara	Coltsfoot	*Vinca minor*	Periwinkle, lesser
Typha spp.	Cattail	*Viola odorata*	Violet
		Viola tricolor	Heartsease
Ulmus campestris	Elm	*Viola yedoensis*	Viola
Ulmus fulva	Slippery elm	*Viscum album*	Mistletoe
Umbellaria californica	California bay	*Vitex agnus castus*	Chaste tree
Umbellularia californica	California laurel	*Vitis hederacea*	Virginia creeper
Umbilicaria spp.	Rock tripe	*Vitis vinifera*	Grapevine
Uncaria guianensis/t omentosa	Uña de gato		
Urtica dioica	Nettle	*Wikstroemia indica*	Wikstroemia
Usnea barbata	Witch's broom, Beard lichen	*Withania somnifera*	Ashwagandha
Valeriana officinalis	Valerian	*Xanthium strumarium* and spp.	Cocklebur
Valerianella olitoria	Cornsalad		
Vaccinium myrtillus	Bilberry	*Yucca* spp	Yucca
Vaccinium vitis idaea	Cowberry		
Veratrum album	White hellebore	*Zanthoxylum americanum*	Prickly ash
Veratrum viride	Green hellebore	*Zea mays*	Cornsilk
Verbascum thapsus	Mullein	*Zingiber officinalis*	Ginger
Verbena hastata	Blue vervain	*Zizyphus spinosa*	Sour jujube
Verbena officinalis	Vervain, European	*Zizyphus vulgaris*	Jujube

Pharmaceutical Name Cross Index

Pharmaceutical Name	Common Name	Pharmaceutical Name	Common Name
Bulbus Alii	Garlic bulb	*Flos Humuli*	Hops flower
Bulbus Scillae	Squills bulb	*Flos Jasmini*	Jasmine flower
		Flos Lavandulae	Lavender flower
Cacumen Cupressi	Cypress tip	*Flos Malvae*	Blue mallow flower
Cacumen Thujae		*Flos Matricariae*	German camomile flower
occidentalis	Arborvitae tip	*Flos Primulae*	Cowslip flower
Caulis et flos Cerei	Cactus stem and flower	*Flos Rosae*	Rose flower
Caulis Solani		*Flos Salicis*	Willow catkin
dulcamarae	Bittersweet stalk	*Flos Sambuci*	Elder flower
Cortex Betulae	Birch bark	*Flos Tanaceti*	Tansy flower
Cortex Cinnamomi		*Flos Tiliae*	Linden flower
cassiae	Cassia cinnamon bark	*Flos Trifolii*	Red clover flower
Cortex Cinnamomi		*Flos Tussilaginis*	Coltsfoot flower
zeylandici	Ceylon cinnamon bark	*Flos Verbasci*	Mullein flower
Cortex fructi Juglandis	Walnut fruit rind	*Folium Aloidis*	Aloe leaf
Cortex Myricae	Bayberry bark	*Folium Angelicae*	Angelica leaf
Cortex Populi	Poplar bark	*Folium Arctostaphyli*	Bearberry leaf
Cortex Pruni	Wild cherry bark	*Folium Barosmae*	Buchu leaf
Cortex Salicis	Willow bark	*Folium Betulae*	Birch leaf
Cortex Sambuci	Elder bark	*Folium Boraginis*	Borage leaf
Cortex Ulmi	Slippery elm bark	*Folium Convallariae*	Lily of the valley leaf
Cortex Xanthoxyli	Prickly ash bark	*Folium Cynarae*	Artichoke leaf
Cortex radicis Berberis	Barbery root bark	*Folium Eryodyctionis*	Yerba santa leaf
Cortex radicis Ceanothi	Red root bark	*Folium Eucalypti*	Eucalyptus leaf
Cortex radicis		*Folium Hydrocotylis*	Gotu kola leaf
Chionanthi	Fringe tree root bark	*Folium Juglandis*	Walnut leaf
Cortex radicis Rhudis	Sumac root bark	*Folium Lactucae*	Wild lettuce leaf
Cortex radicis Sambuci		*Folium Larreae*	Chaparral leaf
ebuli	Red elder root bark	*Folium Malvae*	Blue mallow leaf
Cortex radicis sassafrae	Sassafras root bark	*Folium Melaleucae*	
Cortex radicis Viburni		*leucadendris*	Cajeput leaf
prunifolii	Black haw root bark	*Folium Melaleucae*	
Cortex rami Aesculi	Horsechestnut branch	*linariifoliae*	Tea tree leaf
bark		*Folium Melissae*	Melissa leaf
Cortex ramuli Rhamni		*Folium Menthae piperitae*	Peppermint leaf
frangulae	Alder buckthorn branch	*Folium Menthae viridae*	Spearmint leaf
bark		*Folium Menyanthis*	Bogbean leaf
Cortex ramuli Rhamni		*Folium Mitchellae*	Squaw vine leaf
purshianae	Cascara sagrada branch	*Folium Oxalis*	Wood sorrel leaf
bark		*Folium Plantaginis*	Ribwort plantain leaf
Cortex ramuli Viburni		*Folium Pini*	Pine needle
opuli	Cramp bark branch bark	*Folium Rosmarini*	Rosemary leaf
		Folium Rubi fruticosi	Blackberry leaf
Flos Anthemis	Roman camomile flower	*Folium Rubi idaei*	Raspberry leaf
Flos Arnicae	Arnica flower	*Folium Salviae*	Sage leaf
Flos Calendulae	Marigold flower	*Folium Sennae*	Senna leaf
Flos Crataegi	Hawthorn flower	*Folium Taraxaci*	Dandelion leaf
Flos Grindeliae	Gumweed flower	*Folium Tussilaginis*	Coltsfoot leaf

Folium Urticae	Nettle leaf	*Herba Lamii cum radix*	White deadnettle herb/root
Folium Verbasci	Mullein leaf	*Herba Leonori*	Motherwort herb
Folium Vaccinii	Bilberry leaf	*Herba Lobeliae*	Lobelia herb
Folium Vitis	Grapevine leaf	*Herba Lycopi*	Bugleweed herb
Folliculum Sennae	Senna pod	*Herba Lysimachiae*	Yellow loosestrife herb
Fructus Angelicae	Angelica seed	*Herba Lythri*	Purple loosestrife herb
Fructus Apii	Celery seed	*Herba Marrubii*	White horehound herb
Fructus Arctii	Burdock seed	*Herba Medicaginis*	Alfalfa herb
Fructus Capsici	Cayenne fruit	*Herba Meliloti*	Melilot herb
Fructus Cardui benedicti	Holy thistle seed	*Herba Mentha pulegii*	Pennyroyal herb
Fructus Cardui mariani	Milk thistle seed	*Herba Nasturtii*	Watercress herb
Fructus Crataegi	Hawthorn berry	*Herba Nepetae*	Catnip herb
Fructus Cupressi	Cypress nut	*Herba Ocimi*	Basil herb
Fructus Dauci	Wild carrot seed	*Herba Origani majoranae*	Marjoram herb
Fructus Foeniculi	Fennel seed	*Herba Origani vulgare*	Oregano herb
Fructus Juniperi	Juniper berry	*Herba Passiflorae*	Passionflower herb
Fructus Lobeliae	Lobelia seed	*Herba Pelargonii*	Geranium herb
Fructus Petroselini	Parsley seed	*Herba Portulaccae*	Purslane herb
Fructus Piperus	Black peppercorn	*Herba Pulicariae*	Fleawort herb
Fructus Rhamni		*Herba Rutae*	Rue herb
cathartici	Rhineberry	*Herba Saniculae*	Sanicle herb
Fructus Sambuci	Elder berry	*Herba Satureiae*	Savory herb
Fructus Serenoae	Saw palmetto berry	*Herba Scrophulariae*	Figwort herb
Fructus Tamarindi	Tamarind fruit	*Herba Scutellariae*	Skullcap herb
Fructus Urticae	Nettle seed	*Herba Senecionis*	Ragweed herb
Fructus Vaccinii	Bilberry fruit	*Herba Solidaginis*	Goldenrod herb
Fructus Viticis	Chaste tree berry	*Herba Spiraeae*	Meadowsweet herb
Fructus Zizyphi	Jujube berry	*Herba Stellariae*	Chickweed herb
		Herba Tanaceti	Tansy herb
Gemma Betulae	Birch bud	*Herba Thymi*	Thyme herb
Gemma Populi	Poplar bud	*Herba Turnerae*	Damiana herb
Granum floris pollinis	Flower pollen	*Herba Verbenae*	Vervain herb
		Herba Veronicae	Speedwell herb
Herba Achilleae	Yarrow herb	*Herba Visci*	Mistletoe herb
Herba Agriomniae	Agrimony herb	*Herba Violae odoratae*	Violet herb
Herba Alchemillae	Lady's mantle herb	*HerbaViolae tricoloris*	Heartsease herb
Herba Artemisiaeabsinthii	Wormwood herb	*Herba et fructus Avenae*	Oat straw and grain
Herba Artemisiae vulgaris	Mugwort herb		
Herba Betonicae	Wood betony herb	*Lamina Tritici aestivi*	Wheatgrass
Herba Capsellae	Shepherd's purse herb	*Lignum Camphorae*	Camphor wood
Herba Cardui benedicti	Holy thistle herb	*Lignum Santali*	Sandalwood
Herba Centaurii mini	Centaury herb	*Liquamen Aloidis*	Aloe gel
Herba Chelidonii	Celandine herb		
Herba Convallariae	Lily of the valley herb	*Pericarpium Citri*	
Herba Droserae	Sundew herb	*aurantium*	Bitter orange rind
Herba Elsholtziae	California poppy herb	*Pericarpium Citri*	
Herba Equiseti	Horsetail herb	*limonum*	Lemon rind
Herba Erigerontis	Canada fleabane herb	*Planta tota microalgae*	Microalgae (whole plant)
Herba Eupatorii	Boneset herb		
Herba Euphrasiae	Eyebright herb	*Radix Althaeae*	Marsh mallow root
Herba Fumariae	Fumitory herb	*Radix Angelicae*	
Herba Galii aparinis	Cleavers herb	*archangelicae*	Angelica root
Herba Hedeomae	American pennyroyal hb.	*Radix Apii*	Celery root
Herba Hyperici	St. John's wort herb	*Radix Arctii*	Burdock root
Herba Hyssopi	Hyssop herb		

Radix Asclepiadis asperulae	Inmortal root
Radix Asclepiadis tuberosae	Pleurisy root
Radix Aristolochiae clematitis	Birthwort root
Radix Aristolochiae reticulatae	Texas snakeroot
Radix Aristolochiae serpentariae	Virginia snakeroot
Radix Baptisiae	Wild indigo root
Radix Cardui benedicti	Holy thistle root
Radix Caulophylli	Blue cohosh root
Radix Chelidonii	Celandine root
Radix Cichorii	Chicory root
Radix Cochleariae	Horseradish root
Radix Dauci	Wild carrot root
Radix Echinaceae	Echinacea root
Radix Eupatorii purpureae	Gravel root
Radix Gentianae	Gentian root
Radix Geranii maculati	Cranesbill root
Radix Geranii robertiani	Herb robert root
Radix Glycirrhizae	Licorice root
Radix Leptandrae	Culver's root
Radix Ligustici levistici	Lovage root
Radix Ligustici porterii	Oshá root
Radix Lobeliae	Lobelia root
Radix Panacis quinquefolii	American ginseng root
Radix Petasitis	Butterbur root
Radix Petroselini	Parsley root
Radix Phytolaccae	Poke root
Radix Rumicis	Yellow dock root
Radix Sambuci Ebuli	Dwarf elder root
Radix Scabiosae	Scabious root
Radix Smilacis	Jamaica sarsaparilla root
Radix Stillingiae	Queen's root
Radix Symphiti	Comfrey root
Radix Symplocarpi	Skunk cabbage root

Radix Taraxaci	Dandelion root
Radix Trillii	Birthroot
Radix Urticae	Nettle root
Radix Violae odoratae	Violet root
Ramulus Solani dulcamarae	Bittersweet twig
Resina Commiphorae	Myrrh resin
Resina Olibani	Frankincense resin
Rhizoma Acori	Calamus rhizome
Rhizoma Asari canadense	Wild ginger rhizome
Rhizoma Asari europaei	Hazelwort rhizome
Rhizoma Asparagi	Asparagus rhizome
Rhizoma Chamaelirii	Helonias rhizome
Rhizoma Cimicifugae	Black cohosh rhizome
Rhizoma Cypripedii	Lady's slipper rhizome
Rhizoma Dioscoreae	Wild Yam rhizome
Rhizoma Gingiberis	Ginger rhizome
Rhizoma Hydrangeae	Hydrangea rhizome
Rhizoma Hydrastis	Goldenseal rhizome
Rhizoma Inulae	Elecampane rhizome
Rhizoma Iridis	Blue flag rhizome
Rhizoma Piperis methystici	Kava kava rhizome
Rhizoma Podophylli	Mayapple rhizome
Rhizoma Potentillae	Tormentil rhizome
Rhizoma Rhei	Rhubarb rhizome
Rhizoma Sanguinariae	Bloodroot rhizome
Rhizoma Tritici	Couch grass rhizome
Semen Aesculi	Horsechestnut seed
Spica Prunellae	Selfheal spike
Stylus Zeae	Cornsilk style
Thallus Cetrariae	Iceland moss thallus
Thallus Chondri	Irish moss thallus
Thallus Fuci	Bladderwrack thallus
Thallus Laminariae	Kelp thallus
Thallus Stictae	Lungwort thallus
Thallus Umbilicariae	Rock tripe thallus
Thallus Usneae	Beard lichen thallus

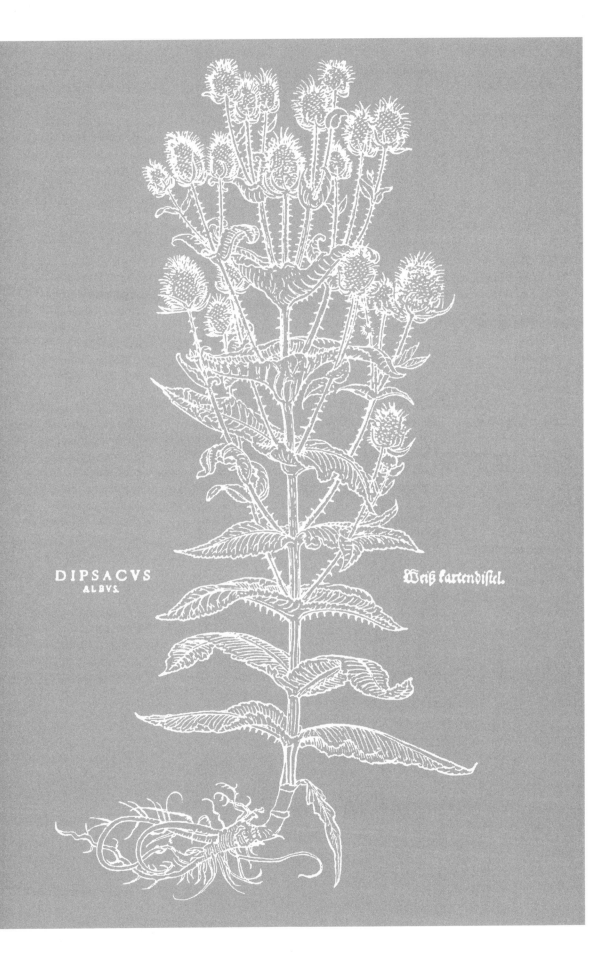

DIPSACVS
ALBVS.

Weiß kartendistel.

Important: Before using the Repertory for the first time, please read this short introduction to better understand:
• The concept of differential diagnosis as it relates to the layout of the Materia Medica
• The available options among herbal preparations (see also Chapter 8)
• The considerations attached to the use of medium-strength and strong category remedies (see also Ch. 5)
• The general context of herbal treatment among other treatment modalities

This Repertory is intended only as a quick reference list. Its use should be complemented by referring to the Materia Medica in this text, which comprehensively classifies remedy indications by both Western disease and symptoms, and Chinese syndromes. For best long-term therapeutic results it is usually neccessary to treat the systemic condition as well as provide immediate symptom relief. This is why it is considered important in traditional Oriental and Greek medicine to address the underlying syndrome of a manifested condition. Different syndromes can give rise to the same symptom. This Repertory presents the possible choices of remedies for a manifested condition, or symptom, only. Once you become familiar with the underlying syndromes, you can also look them up directly by using the General Index.

For best results, you may want to choose the particular remedy that also treats the underlying syndrome causing a cough, for example. However, you may not know the associated syndrome until you start exploring possible remedy options. The Repertory lists the most important remedies for a specific symptom. The design of this book will help you explore the different syndromes that can contribute to a single symptom. For instance, the cough may be related to the syndromes lung phlegm-cold, lung phlegm-heat or lung Qi constraint. By paying attention to the type of cough and any other symptoms you may notice, you can use the remedy descriptions within the text to help you differentiate one among the possible syndromes that are causing the cough. This is what a differential diagnosis is all about.

All remedies listed in the repertory should primarily be taken internally through oral preparations such as a decoction, an infusion or a tincture. However, the same remedies may, and in many disorders often should, also be used in the form of topical applications such as a swab, compress, gargle, vaginal sponge, etc. Remember, topical treatment applications often prove more effective when given in conjunction with an internal preparation. For best results in treating a particular condition, you must choose the most appropriate preparation(s). For example, in the case of a cough from bronchitis, you can apply a topical application of a compress, plaster or essential oil liniment in addition to internal use. When treating a tissue injury, for instance, internal use of *vulnerary, analgesic, sedative,* etc. remedies is usually necessary in addition to topical application of a swab, compress and the like.

Included in the Repertory are herbal remedies that belong to the medium-strength and strong therapeutic category. Those in the strong category are marked by an asterisk. Please read the section on page 78 to familiarize yourself with this important concept. Medium-strength and strong remedies entail certain considerations in their use, notably concerning their dosage, pharmacological and therapeutic cautions, and contraindications. This is another major reason to initially consult each remedy in the Materia Medica before using it. In particular, remedies in the strong category are fairly toxic, and in their crude, unprepared state are difficult to use by anyone untrained. In any case, they are more difficult to find in the crude herb trade. For all these reasons, they are better used in homeopathic preparation form in low potencies up to 12x. For example, Belladonna* in the Repertory means that this remedy belongs to the strong category and is best used in homeopathic form such as Belladonna 3x, 6x or 12x.

Another consideration when working with this Repertory is that many conditions listed here require therapeutic measures other than herbal treatment alone. The fact that herbal remedies are suggested for these problems, and especially for many complex, difficult conditions, should not lead us to assume that herbal remedies alone should or even can be used in treatment. This repertory of herbal and essential oil remedies simply represents possibilities for use in certain conditions. *It is not a specific therapeutic guide and in no way replaces professional diagnosis and treatment, herbal or otherwise.* As one of many forms of natural healing, herbal medicine usually works best when combined with other modalities that work in conjunction with the individual's vital force (Qi), such as nutrition, aromatherapy, acu-puncture, massage, craniosacral osteopathy, hydrotherapy, meditation, Qi Gong and other forms of energy work.

A few format details:

• Chinese herbal remedies are given by their compound clinical name, e.g., Ligusticum Chuan Xiong. The first word is the botanical genus, and the other words are the Chinese name. We have avoided use of the English names of Chinese herbs because they are so little known in the West. For in-depth information on any Chinese remedy, consult the author's source-book, *Jade Remedies: A Chinese Herbal Reference for the West.*

• **Remedies in *italics* may, and often for best results should, be used in essential oil form.**

• Mineral remedies are given in square brackets as follows: [Talcum Hua Shi].

• Animal remedies are given in curly brackets as follows: {Propolis}.

Abdominal distension, acute (same remedies as Indigestion)
> **chronic**: Barberry, Chaparral, Coptis Huang Lian, Dandelion, Goldenseal, Horsechestnut, Lady's mantle *Lemon,* Madder, Marigold, Ocotillo, Red root, *Rose,* Sanicle, Stoneroot, Wood sorrel, Yellow dock
> **cramp/pain** (see Intestinal colic)

Abscess (same remedies as Boil)

Acidosis (see Metabolic acidosis)

Acne (see also Food allergy, Hormonal disorders, Liver congestion, Toxicosis, microbial): Birch, Bittersweet, Blackcurrant seed (oil), Borage seed oil, Burdock, Chaparral, Dandelion, Echinacea, Evening primrose oil, Figwort, Jamaica sarsaparilla, Goldenrod, Marigold, Microalgae, Nettle, Poke, Scabious, Soapwort, Walnut, Watercress, Yellow dock
> (topically): *Bergamot, Cedarwood, Geranium,* Horseradish, *Juniper, Laurel, Lemon, Niaouli, Palmarosa, Patchouli,* Red grapevine, *Tea tree,* Witch hazel

ADD, ADHD (see Attention deficit [hyperactivity] disorder)

Adenitis (see Lymphadenitis)

Adhesion (see Scar tissue)

Adrenal cortex disorders (see Astma, Debility, Edema, Hypoglycemia, Immune deficiency, PMS, Urinary, etc.)
> **deficiency** (see *adrenocortical stimulants,* p. 782)

Aging, premature: Artichoke, Asparagus, Astragalus Huang Qi, Barley grass, Coconut oil, Cornsilk, Flower pollen, Garlic, Ginseng (all types), Microalgae, Oat, Polygonum He Shou Wu, Red clover, Reishi, Schisandra Wu Wei Zi, *Rosemary, Sage,* Wheatgrass

Agitation (same remedies as Nervous tension)

AIDS (see Autoimmune disorder, Diarrhea, Fatigue, Immune deficiency, Infection, viral, Weight loss, and other symptoms)

Albuminuria (see also Urination): Birch, Blue cohosh, Broom, Canada fleabane, Cherry stalk, Cornsilk, Couchgrass, Dioscorea Bi Xie, Echinacea, Fringe tree, Goldenrod, Helonias, Horsetail, *Juniper,* Knotgrass, Madder, Mistletoe, Motherwort, Mousear, Pipsissewa, Poke root, Sea holly

Alcoholism (see also Cerebral insufficiency, Free radical burden, Liver congestion): Bladderwrack, Eyebright, Garlic, Kelp, Microalgae, Nettle, Oat, Watercress, Wheatgrass

Alkalosis (see Metabolic alkalosis)

Allergy (immediate/type I; see also Adrenal cortex deficiency, Food allergies, Intestinal dysbiosis, Liver congestion, Nervous tension, Neuroendocrine deficiency, Toxicosis [all types]): ***antiallergics:*** Asarum Xi Xin, Blackcurrant oil, *Blue tansy,* Bogbean, Borage seed oil, Bupleurum, Burdock *(skin),* Cocklebur, Coleus, Echinacea *(skin),* Elderflower, Ephedra Ma Huang, Evening primrose oil, Eyebright, Figwort, Flower pollen, Garlic, *German camomile,* Goldenrod, Gumweed, Heartsease *(skin),* Licorice, Ligustrum Nu Zhen Zi, Lungwort lichen, Melissa, Mullein, Nettle *(skin),* Plantain *(skin),* Schisandra Wu Wei Zi, Scutellaria Huang Qin, *Rose, Tarragon,* Witch hazel, Xanthium Cang Er Zi, Yerba santa

Alopecia (see Hair loss)

Alzheimer's disease (see Cerebral insufficiency, Mineral depletion, Senility, premature, Toxicosis, heavy metal)

Amenorrhea (see Menstruation, absent)

Amnesia (see Memory loss)

Anaphylaxis (see Allergy)

Anemia (see also Appetite loss, Cerebral insufficiency, Malabsorption syndrome): ***nutritives, trace-mineral rich herbs***: Alfalfa, Angelica Dang Gui, Artichoke, Asparagus, Beet, Bladderwrack, Burdock, Chickweed, Chicory, Codonopsis Dang Shen, Comfrey, Dandelion, Dong quai, Flower pollen, Horsetail, Iceland moss, Irish moss, Jamaica sarsaparilla, Kelp, Lemon, Maca, Microalgae, Nettle, Oat, Parsley, {Placenta}, Red clover, Suma, Walnut, Watercress, Wheatgrass, Yellow dock

Angina laryngea (see Laryngitis)

Angina pectoris (same remedies as Coronary disease)

Angioedema (see Allergy, Skin)

Ankylosing spondylitis (see Autoimmune disorder, Inflammation, symptoms)

Anorexia (same remedies as Appetite loss; see also Anemia, Nausea, Weight loss))

Anosmia: *Basil*

Anuria (see Urinary obstruction)

Anxiety states (see also Food allergy): ***nervous sedatives, anxiolytics:*** Arnica, *Bergamot,* Biota Bai Zi Ren, Black cohosh, Black horehound, Bugleweed, California poppy, *Camomile* (all types), Cereus, *Clary sage,* Cowslip flower, Damiana, Gumweed, Hops, Jamaica dogwood, Kava, *Lavender,* Linden, *Mandarin, Marjoram, Melissa,* Mistletoe, *Neroli,* Pasqueflower, Passionflower, *Rose,* Skullcap, Scrophularia Xuan Shen, St. John's wort, Valerian, White horehound, White pond lily, *Ylang ylang,* Zizyphus Suan Zao Ren

Aphonia (see Voice loss)

Aphtha (see Ulcer, Thrush)

Apoplexy (see Stroke)

Appetite loss: ***bitter digestive stimulants/restoratives:*** Agrimony, Alder buckthorn, Artichoke, Barberry, *Bergamot,* Birth-root, Blessed thistle, Blue vervain, Bogbean, Boneset, Bugleweed, Calamus, Calumba, Cascara sagrada, Chaparral, Chicory, Condurango, Culver's root, Damiana, Dandelion, Elecampane, Fringe tree, Fumitory, Gentian, Helonias, Hops, Inmortal, Lobelia, Motherwort, Oregon grape, Pipsissewa, Pleurisy root, Poplar, *Sage,* Scabious, Selfheal, Speedwell, Stoneroot, Tansy, *Thyme,* Tormentil, Vervain, White horehound, Willow, Wormwood, Yarrow, Yerba mansa, Yerba santa

Arrhythmia, cardiac (see also Food allergy): Aconitum Fu zi, Adonis, Arnica, Black horehound, Bugleweed, *Camphor,* Cereus, Foxglove, Hedge bindweed, Lily of the valley, *Marjoram, Melissa,* Valerian, White horehound, Yellow jessamine*

Arterial occlusive disorder (see Circulation, insufficient arterial/capillary, associated condition, symptoms)

Arteriosclerosis (see also Free radical burden): Arnica, Artichoke, Asparagus, Birch, Blackcurrant oil, Blessed thistle, Borage seed oil, Celandine, Celery, Cornsilk, Couchgrass, Dandelion, Elder, Evening primrose oil, Flaxseed oil, Fumitory, Garlic, Ginkgo leaf, Hawthorn, Heartsease, Horsetail, *Juniper,* Kelp, Lady's mantle, Lecithin, *Lemon,* Lily of the valley, Linden, Microalgae, Mistletoe, Nettle, Passionflower, *Rosemary,* Rue, *Sage,* Shepherd's purse, Walnut, Watercress, Wood sorrel

Arthritis, acute rheumatoid (see also Autoimmune disorder, Food allergy, Infection bacterial): ***anti-inflammatories, analgesics:*** Camomile (all types), *Camphor,* Celery, *Citronella,* Clematis Wei Ling Xian, Devil's claw, Gentiana Qin Qian Cao, Figwort, Guaiacum, *Lemon,* Meadowsweet, *Ravintsara,* Stephania Han Fang Ji, Tripterygium Lei Gong Teng, White bryony, Wild yam, Willow

chronic rheumatoid (see also Autoimmune disorder, Connective tissue degeneration, Food allergy, Infection, viral, Toxicosis, metabolic): Acanthopanax Wu Jia Pi, Alfalfa, Apple cider vinegar, Artichoke, Asparagus, Birch, Bittersweet, Bladderwrack, Blue cohosh, Blue flag, Blue violet, Borage seed oil, Burdock, Celery,

Chicory, Cistus, Comfrey, Cowslip root, Dandelion, Devil's claw, Eucommia Du Zhong, Evening primrose oil, Figwort, Flower pollen, Garlic, Guaiacum, Heather, Heartsease, *Helichrysum*, Horsetail, Ivy leaf, Jamaica sarsaparilla, *Juniper*, Kelp, *Laurel, Lemon,* liquid trace minerals, Meadowsweet, Microalgae, Nettle, *Niaouli*, Pipsissewa, Poke root, Red clover, Sassafras, Siegesbeckia Xi Xian Cao, Watercress, Willow, Wood betony, Wild yam, *Winter savory,* Yellow dock, Yerba mansa

    osteo- (see Arthritis, Chronic rheumatoid, Connective tissue degeneration, Toxicosis, metabolic)

Arthrosis (see Arthritis)

Ascites (same remedies as Edema)

Asthenia (same remedies as Fatigue)

Asthma (see also Adrenal deficiency, Allergy, Bronchitis, Fatigue, Food allergies, Free radical burden, Infection, bacterial/viral, Inflammation, Stress): ***bronchodilators:*** Adonis, Angelica, *Aniseed*, Arnica, Asafoetida, *Bergamot*, Birthroot, Bittersweet, Black cohosh, Blackhaw, Black horehound, Bloodroot, Blue cohosh, Bugleweed, Butterbur, *Cajeput, Camomile, Camphor,* Celandine, Celery, Coleus, Coltsfoot flower, Cramp bark, *Cypress*, Elderflower, Ephedra Ma Huang, *Fennel*, Flower pollen, Gumweed, Hazelwort, Hops, *Hyssop*, Inmortal, Kelp, *Lavender*, Lobelia, *Marjoram*, Melilot, *Melissa*, Mistletoe, Mullein, *Oregano*, Pasqueflower, Passionflower, Pennyroyal, Perilla Zi Su Zi, Pillbearing spurge, *Pine*, Pleurisy root, Prunus Xing Ren, Red clover, Red root, {Royal jelly}, Rue, *Sandalwood*, Sea holly, *Siberian fir,* Skunk cabbage, St. John's wort, Stoneroot, Sundew, Tansy, *Thyme*, Valerian, Sea holly, Vervain, Virginia snakeroot, White deadnettle, Wild cherry, Wild ginger, Wild indigo, Wood betony, Yerba santa

Atherosclerosis (same remedies as Hyperlipidemia; see also Autoimmune disorder, Blood pressure, high, Cerebral insufficiency, Coronary insufficiency, Hyperglycemia, Infection, bacterial)

Athlete's foot (see Infection, fungal, Toxicosis, microbial)

Attention deficit disorder (ADD) (see also Adrenal deficiency, Food allergy, intestinal, Hyper-/hypoglycemia, Intestinal dysbiosis, Malabsorption, Nervous tension, Toxicosis, chemical/heavy metal/ microbial): American ginseng, Eleuthero, Gotu kola, Ginkgo, *Grapefruit, Lemon, Lime,* Polygonum He Shou Wu, Schisandra Wu Wei Zi

Attention deficit hyperactivity disorder (ADHD) (see same conditions and remedies as ADD, as well as remedies for Nervous tension)

Autoimmune disease: *immune regulators/inhibitors:* Asian ginseng, Cistus, Elecampane, Ganoderma Ling Zhi, *Hyssop*, Indian sarsaparilla, Licorice, Oat, Poke (?), Reishi, *Sage*, Schisandra Wu Wei Zi, Tripterygium Lei Gong Teng, *Vetiver* (?)

Autonomic nervous dysregulation: *Angelica, Hyssop, Rosemary*

Backache, lower (see also Arthritis, Food allergy, Muscle spasm, Nervous tension): ***analgesics*** and others: Arnica, Barberry, Black cohosh, Cornsilk, Goldenrod, Hydrangea, *Juniper, Lavender, Marjoram,* Pennyroyal, Pipsissewa, Prickly ash, Uva ursi, Valerian, Yarrow

Bad breath (see Halitosis, Liver congestion)

Bedsore (see Wound, atonic)

Bedwetting (see Urinary incontinence)

Biliary colic/spasms (see Gallbladder colic)

Biliary insufficiency: *cholagogues, choleretics:* Artemisia Yin Chen Hao, Artichoke, Balmony, Birch, Black radish, Blessed thistle, Blue flag, Bogbean, Boldo, Butternut, Calumba, Canna Mei Ren Jiao, Cascara sagrada, Celandine, Chicory, Citrus Chen Pi, Citrus Qing Pi, Culver's root, Dandelion, Elecampane, Fieldmint, Fringe tree, Fumitory, Gardenia Zhi Zi, Horsechestnut, *Lemon*, Liverwort, Madder, Mayapple, Milk thistle, Mugwort, *Peppermint*, Prodigiosa, Rhubarb, *Rosemary*, Saussurea Yun Mu Xiang, Silver thistle, Turmeric, Wahoo, Wormwood

Bipolar affective disorder (see Manic depressive disorder)

Bladder (see Urination, Urinary)

Bleeding (see part or organ affected)

Blepharitis (see Eye infection)

Blood congestion (see Abdominal distension, chronic, Dysmenorrhea, congestive, Portal congestion)

Blood pressure, high (see Hypertension)

    low (see Hypotension)

Blood sugar (see Pancreas disorders)

Boils: Arnica, Beet, Birthwort, Bittersweet, Blue flag, Bogbean, Burdock, Calamus, *Camomile*, Centaury, Chaparral, Chickweed, Cleavers, Coltsfoot, Comfrey, *Cypress*, Dandelion, Echinacea, Elderflower, Figwort, Flower pollen, *Geranium*, Ground ivy, Hops, Jamaica sarsaparilla, Lady's mantle, *Lemon*, Licorice, Marshmallow, Meadowsweet, *Laurel, Lavender,* Melilot, Mullein, *Niaouli*, Onion, Passionflower, Pipsissewa, Poke root, Purslane, Plantain, *Rose*, Rue, Sanicle, Scabious, Selfheal, Soapwort, Solomon's seal, Taraxacum Pu Gong Ying, *Thyme*, Viola Zhi Hua Di Ding, Watercress, White deadnettle, Wild indigo, Wormwood, Yellow dock

Bone disorders: Calamus, Horsetail, Poke root, Queen's root, Walnut, Yarrow

Bone spurs (see remedies under Mineral depletion)

Breast engorgement: Blue violet, *Camomile, Camphor*, Chickweed, Coltsfoot, *Fennel*, Figwort, *Geranium*, Marigold, Plantain, Poke root, Red clover, Scabious, Skunk cabbage, Yarrow

  engorgement with milk: Bittersweet, Couchgrass, *Cumin, Fennel, Geranium*, Heartease, Parsley seed, *Peppermint*, St. John's wort

Breast milk, scanty: *galactagogues:* Alfalfa, Aniseed, Black cohosh, Blessed thistle, Blue cohosh, Blue mallow, Burdock, Caraway, Celery, Chasteberry, Dandelion, Dill, Elderflower, *Fennel*, Hawthorn, Iceland moss, Jasmine, Marshmallow, Mullein, Nettle, Oat, {Placenta}, Raspberry, Saw palmetto, Vervain, Watercress

  excessive: Aloe, *Clary sage,* Cranesbill, *Cypress,* Canada fleabane, *Geranium,* Parsley root, *Peppermint, Sage*

Breathing, difficult (see Asthma)

Bright's disease (see Nephritis, acute)

Bronchitis, acute (see also Infection, bacterial/viral, Inflammation): *cool expectorants:* Aconite*, Agrimony, *Bergamot*, Black horehound, Blue flag, *Camomile*, Coltsfoot, Comfrey, Costmary, Elderflower, *Eucalyptus*, Feverfew, Hazelwort, Horsechestnut, Houttuynia Yu Xing Cao, Lungwort lichen, Mullein, Peucedanum Qian Hu, Phyllostachis Zhu Ru, Pleurisy root, Plantain, Queen's root, Red root, Sanicle, Scabious, Skunk cabbage, Soapwort, Speedwell, Usnea, White bryony, White horehound, Wood betony

  chronic (see also Allergy): *expectorants:* Angelica, *Aniseed,* Asarum Xi Xin, Asparagus, *Basil,* Bayberry, *Bergamot*, Bittersweet, Blessed thistle, Bloodroot, Blue vervain, Bogbean, Butterbur, *Cajeput,* Calamus, Canada fleabane, Cardamom, Chasteberry, Common ivy, Coltsfoot, Cowslip root, Elderflower, Elecampane, *Eucalyptus, Fennel, Fir, Frankincense,* Hazelwort, Heartsease, *Helichrysum,* Horseradish, *Hyssop,* Inmortal, Ivy leaf, *Jasmine, Juniper, Marjoram,* Milk thistle, Motherwort, Mullein, *Myrrh, Myrtle,* Nettle, *Niaouli, Oregano,* Oshá, *Palmarosa,* Pau d'arco, Pennyroyal, *Peppermint,* Peucedanum Qian Hu, Pillbearing spurge, *Pine,* Pinellia Ban Xia, Poplar bud, *Ravintsara, Rosemary, Sandalwood,* Saw palmetto, Scabious, Seneca snakeroot, Solomon's seal, Speedwell, *Spruce,* St. John's wort, *Thyme, Turpentine,* Vervain, Violet, Watercress, White horehound, Wild ginger, Wood betony, Yerba mansa, Yerba santa

Bruise (see Contusion, Hematoma)

Burns (topically): *anti-inflammatory tissue healers:* Aloe gel/resin, Arnica, Bilberry, Bletilla Bai Ji, Borage, Cabbage, Chaparral, *Camomile*, Chickweed, Cleavers, Coptis Huang Lian, Coltsfoot, Comfrey, Couchgrass, Echinacea, *Eucalyptus, Fennel,* Figwot, Flaxseed oil, *Geranium,* Goldenrod, Great burnet, Horsechestnut, Iris, Ivy, Jamaica dogwood, Lady's mantle, *Lavender, Lemon,* Marigold, Marshmallow, Meadowsweet, Mullein, *Myrrh,* Nettle, Passionflower, *Peppermint,* Plantain, Poke root, Poplar bark/bud, Purslane, Red clover, *Roman camomile, Sandalwood,* Scabious, St. John's wort, Tormentil, Typha Pu Huang, Wheatgrass, White deadnettle, Wild lettuce, Witch hazel, Yarrow

Bursitis (see Food allergy, Inflammation, Pain)

Calculus (see Gallstone, Urinary stone)

Cancer (see Immune deficiency, Tumor)

Candidiasis (see Allergies, Biliary insufficiency, Cerebral insufficiency, Digestive enzyme deficiency, Discharge, Fatigue, Gastric hypoacidity, Hypoglycemia, Immune deficiency, Infection, fungal, Malabsorption, Toxicosis, microbial, Vaginitis, other symptoms)

Canker sore (see Stomatitis, aphthous)

Carbuncle (see Boil)

Carpal tunnel syndrome (see Inflammation, remedies under Neuralgia)

Cataract: Bilberry, Celandine, Lily of the valley, Plantain seed

Celiac disease (see Coeliac sprue)

Cellulite (see also Hyperlipidemia): Artichoke, Birch, Bittersweet, Bladderwrack, Blue flag, Chaparral, Chicory, Clematis, Dandelion, Flower pollen, Fumitory, Horsechestnut, Horsetail, *Juniper*, Kelp, *Lemon*, *Lemongrass*, Melilot, *Oregano*, Red grapevine, Squills, White horehound

Cerebral insufficiency: *cerebral restoratives:* Arnica, Ashwaghanda, Asian ginseng, *Basil*, Bacopa, Bilberry, Blackcurrant oil, *Black pepper*, Borage seed oil, Brahmi, Brewer's yeast, *Camphor*, Cardamom, Cereus, Coconut oil, Cowslip, Evening primrose oil, Damiana, Flaxseed oil, Flower pollen, *Frankincense*, Ginkgo leaf, Gotu kola, *Hyssop*, Lecithin, *Lemon*, Ladies' slipper, Lily of the valley, *Marjoram*, Melissa, Microalgae, Nettle, Pasqueflower, Polygonum He Shou Wu, Rhodiola, *Rosemary, Sage,* Schisandra Wu Wei Zi, Sesame seed, Skullcap, Suma, *Tea tree, Thyme,* Valerian, Vervain, Wood betony

   concussion: Aconitum Fu Zi, Acorus Shi Chang Pu, Arnica, *Basil*, {Bufo Chan Su}, Calabar bean, *Camphor,* Cayenne, Cowslip flower, Foxglove, Lily of the valley, Liquidambar Su He Xiang, Lobelia, *Myrrh, Neroli, Rosemary,* Rye ergot, *Sage*, Valerian

   congestion: *arterial cerebral decongestants:* Belladonna*, Cereus, Colocynth, Cowslip, Boneset, Gardenia Zhi Zi, Hedge bindweed, Hedge hyssop, Hellebore, Jalap, *Lavender*, Melilot, Mistletoe, Pennyroyal, Rye ergot, Scammony, Selfheal, White bryony, Yarrow, Yellow jessamine*

   contusion (same remedies as Cerebral concussion)

   hemorrhage: *hemostatics:* Bilberry, Black cohosh, Gardenia Zhi Zi, Ginkgo, Rye ergot

Cervical dysplasia (see Infection, viral, Pelvic congestion, Wart, genital)

Chancroid (see Infection, bacterial; topically see Ulcer, genital)

Chest oppression (precordial oppression): Adonis, Arnica, Cereus, Ginkg, Hawthorn, Ligusticum Chuan Xiong, Lily of the valley, Valerian

Chickenpox (see Fever, eruptive, Infection, viral, Wound, atonic)

Chilblain: *Cajeput*, Celey, Garlic, *Geranium*, Hawthorn, *Lemon*, Marigold, *Tea tree, Turpentine*, Watercress

Childbirth (see Labor)

Chlamydia (see Discharge, Infection, bacterial, Lymphatic congestion, Pelvic inflammatory disease, Ulcer, Urination)

Chlorosis (see Anemia)

Cholecystitis (see Gallbladder inflammation)

Cholera (see also Infection, bacterial): Bistort, Cajeput, Coptis Huang Lian, Cranesbill, *Geranium*, Hellebore, Lobelia, Prickly ash, Purple loosestrife, Scutellaria Huang Qin, Tormentil, Turpentine

   infantum: Aconite*, Bistort, *Cajeput*, Canada fleabane, *Cypress*, Echinacea, European columbo, *Geranium*, *Niaouli*, Oak, *Peppermint*, Plantain, Poplar, Purple loosestrife, Rhubarb, Slippery elm, Wild yam

Cholesterol, high blood (hypercholesterolemia) (see Hyperlipidemia)

Chorea: (see Seizure, Spasm)

Chronic fatigue syndrome (CFS) (see Adrenal cortex deficiency, Autoimmune disorder, Cerebral insufficiency, Fatigue, Infection, viral, Immune deficiency, Toxicosis, chemical/heavy metal)

Chronic obstructive lung disease (see Asthma, Cough, Infections, chronic, Nicotine addiction, associated condition, symptoms)

Circulation, insufficient arterial: *arterial stimulants:* Angelica, *Basil*, Bayberry, Bittersweet, *Black pepper,* Blue cohosh, *Cajeput, Camphor,* Cayenne, Celandine, Cinnamon (all types), Garlic, *Ginger*, Guaiacum, Hazelwort, Horseradish, *Hyssop, Juniper,* Lobelia, Milk thistle, *Myrrh*, Pasqueflower, Prickly ash, *Rosemary,* Sassafras, Virginia snakeroot, Wild ginger, *Winter savory,* Yarrow

   insufficient capillary: *capillary stimulants:* Bayberry, Bilberry, Calamus, Cayenne, Echinacea, Ginkgo, Hawthorn, *Hyssop, Lemon,* Ligusticum Chuan Xiong, Lily of the valley, Lobelia, Marigold, *Myrrh*, Pasqueflower, Prickly ash, *Rose, Sage,* Salvia Dan Shen, Selfheal, *Tea tree,* Turmeric, Typha Pu Huang

   insufficient cerebral: Arnica, Bilberry, *Camphor*, Cowslip, Ginkgo, Gotu kola, *Lemon*, Lily of the valley, Skullcap, Valerian

   insufficient coronary (see Coronary insufficiency)

   insufficient portal (see Portal congestion)

   insufficient venous: *venous restoratives:* Barberry, Bilberry, Broom, Butcher's broom, *Cedarwood, Cypress,*

Dandelion, *Geranium*, Goldenseal, Heartsease, Horsechestnut, *Lemon*, Marigold, Mayapple, Melilot, *Patchouli*, Red grapevine, Red root, *Rosemary, Sandalwood,* Shepherd's purse, Sophora Huai Hua, Stoneroot, Witch hazel, Yarrow

Cirrhosis (see Liver cirrhosis)

Coeliac sprue (see Digestive enzyme deficiency, Food allergy, Malabsorption, Mineral depletion, Weight loss)

Cold, common (see *diaphoretics,* Class 1, Infection, bacterial/viral, Rhinitis, Sinusitis)

Cold extremities (see Circulation, insufficient arterial)

Cold sore (same remedies as Herpes, genital)

Colic (see Intestinal colic)

Colitis, ulcerative (see Inflammatory bowel disease)

Coma (same remedies as Cerebral concussion, Cerebral insufficiency)

Concussion (see Cerebral concussion)

Condyloma (see Wart)

Congestive heart failure (see also Arrhythmia, Coronary deficiency, Edema, Hyperlipidemia, Hypertension, other conditions): *cardiac stimulants:* Aconitum Fu Zi, Arnica, {Bufo Chan Su}, Adonis, Broom, *Camphor*, Cereus, Coleus, Dogbane, Foxglove, Hawthorn, Lily of the valley, *Ravintsara,* Squills, Strophanthus, Thevetia Huang Hua Jia Zhu Tao

Conjunctivitis (see Eye infection)

Connective tissue deficiency/degeneration: Acanthopanax Wu Jia Pi, Bilberry, Dandelion, Eucommia Du Zhong, Gotu kola, Hawthorn, Horsetail, *Lemon*, Meadowsweet, Nettle, *Vetiver*

Constipation, acute: *stimulant laxatives:* Alder buckthorn, Aloe resin, Balmony, Blue flag, Butternut, Cascara sagrada, Culver's root, Elder bark, Fringe tree, Gentian, Golden ragwort, Rhubarb, Senna

chronic: *demulcent laxatives:* Apricot kernel, Butternut, Chickweed, Dandelion, Dendrobium Shi Hu, Figwort, [Glauber's salt], Kelp, [liquid trace minerals], [magnesium/sodium sulphate], Peach kernel, Plum kernel, Poplar bud, sea vegeta-bles, Walnut, Yellow dock

Contagious disease (see Infections, chronic)

Contusion: *anticontusion remedies:* Agrimony, Angelica, Arnica, Burdock, Cajeput, Calamus, *Camphor*, Cardamom, Celandine, Cinnamon, Cowslip, Drynaria Gu Sui Bu, *Fennel*, Figwort, Fumitory, *Geranium, Helichrysum*, Horseradish, *Hyssop, Lavender,* Lily of the valley, Oldenlandia Bai Hua She She Cao, *Melissa, Myrrh,* Panax San Qi, Parsley, Pennyroyal, Plantain, Rhubarb, *Ravintsara, Rose, Rosemary, Sage,* Sassafras, Selfheal, Solomon's seal, Stoneroot, St. John's wort, Tansy, *Tea tree, Thyme,* Vervain, Wikstroemia Liao Ge Wang, Wormwood, Yarrow, Yerba mansa

Convalescence (see Debility)

Convulsion (see Seizure)

Coronary insufficiency/disease: *coronary stimulants:* Aconite*, Arnica, Blackcurrant oil, Borage seed oil, Carthamus Huang Hua, Celandine, Celery, Cereus, Coleus, Evening primrose oil, Flaxseed oil, Garlic, Ginkgo, Hawthorn, Inmortal, Khella, Lecithin, Ligusticum Chuan Xiong, Lily of the valley, Lobelia, Mistletoe, Motherwort, Salvia Dan Shen, Valerian, Yellow jessamine*

Coryza (same remedies as Cold, common)

Cough, dry: *demulcent expectorants:* Asparagus Tian Men Dong), Coltsfoot leaf, Licorice, Iceland moss, Lungwort lichen, Marshmallow, Mullein, Ophiopogon Mai Men Dong, Plantain, Squills

full: Angelica, Blackcurrant, Bloodroot, Bittersweet, Boneset, Borage, Butterbur, Coltsfoot flower, Coral root, Cowslip, Elecampane, *Eucalyptus*, Ground ivy, *Hyssop, Laurel, Oregano, Pine,* Plantain, Queen's root, *Ravintsara*, Saw palmetto, Scabious, Speedwell, Violet, White horehound, White pond lily

uncontrollable/spasmodic: *antitussives:* Aster Zi Wan, Black cohosh, Black horehound, Celandine, Common ivy leaf, *Cypress*, Fritillaria Bei Mu, Gumweed, *Helichrysum, Hyssop,* Ivy, Jamaica dogwood, *Laurel,* Lobelia, Lungwort lichen, Mullein flower, Passionflower, Pillbearing spurge, Pleurisy root, Prunus Xing Ren, Queen's root, Red clover, Skunk cabbage, Stemona Bai Bu, Sundew, *Thyme,* Vervain, Wild cherry, Wild ginger, Wild lettuce, Yellow jessamine*

with bloody sputum: *demulcent* or *astringent antitussives:* Asparagus Tian Men Dong, Avens, Black horehound, Bugle, Chickweed, Comfrey, Irish moss, Foxglove, Goldenseal, Great burnet, Horsetail, Iceland moss, Ipecac, Knotgrass, Mistletoe, Mullein, Nettle, Oak bark, Plantain, Red grapevine, Rhodiola, Rye ergot, Shepherd's purse, Speedwell, Tormentil, Turpentine, White deadnettle, Willow, Witch hazel, Wood betony, Yarrow

Cramp, intestinal (see Intestinal colic)

  of limbs (see Seizure, Spasm)

  menstrual (see Menstruation, painful)

  muscle (see Muscle spasm)

Crohn's disease (see Inflammatory bowel disease, Autoimmune disease)

Croup (see Cough, uncontrollable, Fever, Infection, bacterial/viral, Laryngitis)

Cut (see Wound)

Cystitis (see Urinary infection)

Debility (same remedies as Fatigue; see also Anemia, Metabolic disorder, Malabsorption syndrome, Nervous debility)

Decubitus ulcer (see Bedsore)

Dehydration: *nutritive demulcents:* Anemarrhena Zhi Mu, Asparagus, Asparagus Tian Men Dong, Borage, Chickweed, Comfrey, Iceland moss, Irish moss, Lungwort lichen, Marshmallow, Ophiopogon Mai Men Dong, Slippery elm bark, Solomon's seal

Delirium, violent: *CNS sedatives:* Belladonna*, Black cohosh, Hellebore*, Jaborandi, Rye ergot, Stramonium*, Typhonium Bai Fu Zi, Woodruff, Yellow jessamine*

Demineralization (see Mineral depletion)

Depositions: *dissolvents:* Arborvitae, Bladderwrack, Kelp, Mistletoe, Poke

Depression, nervous (same remedies as Cerebral insufficiency, Nervous debility)

  affective/endogenous (same remedies as Liver congestion; see also Food allergy)

Dermatitis, allergic/atopic (see also Allergy, Skin inflammation/itching): Burdock, Echinacea, Heartsease, Plantain, Poke (?), Sophora Ku Shen

  neurogenic (see Nervous tension, Skin eruption)

  seborrheic (see Food allergy, Skin inflammation)

Development, children's slow (see also Metabolic disorder, *thyrotropic growth hormone,* p. 783): Bladderwrack, {Cervus Lu Rong}, Chicory, {Chinemys Gui Ban}, Eleuthero, Flower pollen, Horsetail, Kelp, Microalgae, Oat, Salvia Dan Shen, Walnut

Diabetes mellitus (see Dehydration, Fatigue, Hyperglycemia, other symptoms)

Diaper rash (see Infection, fungal, Skin rash)

Diarrhea (see also Food allergy, Gastroenteritis, Inflammatory bowel disease, other conditions): *astringent antidiarrheals:* Agrimony, Avens, Barberry, Bayberry, Bilberry, Birthroot, Bistort, Blackberry, Calumba, Canada fleabane, Cayenne, Cinnamon, Comfrey, Cranesbill, Culver's root, *Geranium,* Goldenrod, Great burnet, Jasmine, Knotgrass, Lady's mantle, Madder, Marshmallow, Meadowsweet, Lady's mantle, *Myrrh,* Nettle, *Niaouli,* Nutmeg, Oak bark, Pau d'arco, Plantain, Pleurisy root, Poplar, Raspberry, Red *Rose,* Rhubarb, *Sage, Sandalwood,* Sanicle, Shepherd's purse, Stoneroot, Sumac, Terminalia He Zi, Tormentil, Uva ursi, Walnut, White dead-nettle, White horehound, White pond lily, Wild cherry, Witch hazel, Yarrow

Digestive disorders (see Food allergies, Gastric, Gastritis, Gastroenteritis, Indigestion, Intestinal, Liver, Ulcer)

  enzyme deficiency: *enzymatic remedies:* Barley sprout, Bromelain, {Gallus Ji Nei Jing}, Haronga, Hawthorn berry, Massa fermentata Shen Qu, Papaya, Pancreatin, Pepsin, Pineapple, Rice sprout

Diphtheria (see also Croup, Fever, Infection, bacterial, Lymphatic congestion): Belladonna*, *Bergamot,* Cayenne, Echinacea, *Eucalyptus,* Goldenseal, *Juniper,* Lobelia, *Lemon,* Marshmallow, *Myrrh,* Poke root, *Tea tree, Thyme, Turpentine,* Witch hazel

Discharge, genital/urinary: Birthroot, Bittersweet, Blackberry, Blue cohosh, Buchu, Calamus, Cinnamon (all types), Cornus Shan Zhu Yu, Cranesbill, Damiana, Dioscorea Bi Xie, Dipsacus Xu Duan, Elecampane, *Geranium,* Goldenrod, Goldenseal, Golden ragwort, Gravel root, Great burnet, Helonias, Horseradish, *Juniper,* Kelp, *Lavender,* Loosestrife, Madder, *Marjoram, Myrrh,* Nettle, Partridgeberry, Pasqueflower, Poplar, Red root, *Sage, Sandalwood,* Sassafras, Scabious, Speedwell, St. John's wort, Stoneroot, Sumac, Tamarind, Tansy, *Thyme,* Tormentil, Turpentine, Walnut, White deadnettle, White pond lily, Yerba mansa

Dizziness (same remedies as Vertigo)

Drug addiction (see Liver toxicosis, Malabsorption, Nervous debility, Toxicosis, chemical, other symptoms)

Dysbiosis (see Intestinal dysbiosis)

Dysentery (see Diarrhea, Intestinal infection)

Dysmenorrhea, congestive (see also Menstruation): *uterine decongestants:* Barberry, Bilberry, Biota Ce Bai Ye, Blackhaw, Butcher's broom, *Cedarwood,* Cereus, *Cypress,* Golden ragwort, Goldenseal, Heartsease, Helonias, Horsechestnut, Lady's mantle, *Lemon,* Madder, Marigold, Mistletoe, Paeonia Chi Shao, Partridgeberry, Peony, Red grapevine, Red root, *Sandalwood,* Shepherd's purse, Soapwort, Stoneroot, Water pepper, White deadnettle, White peony, Witch hazel, Yellow dock, Yarrow

    spasmodic: *uterine spasmolytics:* Asafoetida, *Basil, Bergamot,* Black cohosh, Blackhaw, Blue cohosh, Bupleurum Chai Hu, Butterbur, *Camomile,* Cereus, *Chasteberry, Clary sage,* Coleus, Cow parsnip, Cowslip root, Cramp bark, Cyperus Xiang Fu, *Cypress,* Damiana, Dong quai, Golden ragwort, Hops, *Hyssop, Juniper, Laurel,* Ligusticum Chuan Xiong, Lovage, *Marjoram, Melissa,* Mistletoe, Motherwort, Oat, Paeonia Bai Shao, Paeonia Mu Dan Pi, Parsley seed, Pasqueflower, Paeonia Bai Shao, Pennyroyal, *Peppermint,* Pleurisy root, Prunus Tao Ren, Purple nutsedge, Rue, Saffron, *Sage,* Tansy, Tiger lily, Vervain, White peony, Wild ginger, Wild yam, Wood betony, Yarrow

Dyspepsia (see Indigestion)

Dysuria (see Urinary pain)

Ear infection (see also Allergy, Food allergy, Infection, bacterial/viral): *Camomile, Camphor,* Coptis Huang Lian, *Eucalyptus,* Eyebright, Goldenseal, Houttuynia Yu Xing Cao, Pasqueflower, Plantain, Selfheal, Scutellaria Huang Qin, Stoneroot, *Tea tree*

    inflammation (same as Ear infection)

    ringing: Black cohosh, Black horehound, Gastrodia Tian Ma, Hawthorn, Horsetail, *Hyssop, Melissa,* Mistletoe, Pasqueflower, Selfheal, Uncaria Gou teng, Wood betony, Yellow jessamine*

Earache: Aniseed, *Basil, Camomile* (all types), Elder, Eyebright, Fieldmint, Garlic, *Hyssop, Lavender,* Melilot, Mullein, Olive oil, *Peppermint,* Plantain, *Rosemary,* Wormwood, Violet, Yarrow

Eclampsia (see Albuminuria, Edema, Infection, High blood pressure, Seizure)

Eczema (see Skin eruption, Dermatitis, Allergy)

Edema (see also Food allergy): *draining diuretics:* Alisma Ze Xie, Artichoke, Asparagus, Birch, Bittersweet, Bladderwrack, Blessed thistle, Blue flag, Broom, Burdock, *Cedarwood,* Celandine, Celery, Cereus, Chasteberry, Chicory, Cleavers, Couchgrass, Dandelion, Elder bark/flower, *Fennel,* Figwort, Garlic, *Geranium,* Goldenrod, Gravel root, Horseradish, Imperata Bai Mao Gen, *Juniper,* Kelp, Lovage, Meadowsweet, Mugwort, Nettle, Parsley piert, Parsley seed, Partridgeberry, Pellitory of the wall, Polyporus Zhu Ling, Sassafras, Squills, Virginia snakeroot, Wahoo, Wild carrot, Wild ginger, Wormwood

Emaciation (see Weight loss)

Emission, nocturnal (see Discharge)

Emphysema (see Asthma, Cough)

Endocarditis (see Myocarditis)

Encephalitis (see Infection, viral, Nervous debility, symptoms)

Endometriosis (same remedies as Dysmenorrhea, congestive, Estrogen accumulation; see also Hemorrhage, Inflammation, Liver congestion, Nervous tension, Pain, Pelvic congestion, PMS, *progesterone stimulants,* p. 783)

Energy, low (see also associated condition): American ginseng, *Angelica,* Artichoke, Ashwagandha, Astragalus Huang Qi, *Basil, Black spruce,* Blessed thistle, Brewer's yeast, Bogbean, Calamus, *Camphor, Cinnamon, Clove, Cypress,* Damiana, Elecampane, *Fir,* Flower pollen, Gentian, *Geranium, Hyssop,* Kelp, Lecithin, Licorice, Microalgae, *Neroli, Niaouli,* Oat, *Palmarosa, Pine,* Poplar, Prickly ash, *Ravintsara, Rosemary, Sage,* Spruce, Suma, *Tea tree, Thyme,* Wheatgrass, *Winter savory,* Wormwood

Enteritis (see Intestinal)

Enterocolitis (see Diarrhea, Intestinal infection)

Enuresis (see Urinary incontinence)

Enzymes (see Digestive enzyme deficiency)

Epicondylitis (same remedies as Bursitis)

Epidemic (see Contagious disease)

Epigastric fullness/pain (see also Biliary insufficiency, Digestive enzyme deficiency): Artichoke, Barberry, Black radish, Blessed thistle, Blue flag, Butternut, Dandelion, Celandine, Centaury, Citrus Chen Pi,

Curcuma Yu Jin, Fumitory, Hops, *Peppermint, Rosemary,* Saussurea Yun Mu Xiang, *Spearmint,* Turmeric, Wormwood, Yarrow

Epilepsy (see Seizure)

Epistaxis (see Nosebleed)

Erysipelas (see Fever, Infection, bacterial, Skin inflammation)

Estrogen accumulation (see Intestinal dysbiosis, Liver congestion, *estrogen inhibitors, progesterone stimulants,* p. 783)

　deficiency (see *estrogen stimulants,* p. 783)

Eye infection/inflammation (topically; see also Allergy, Infection, bacterial/viral): ***anti-inflammatories:*** Bilberry, Blue violet, Buddleia Mi Meng Hua, Camomile, Celandine, Celosia Qing Xiang Zi, Chickweed, Chrysanthemum Ju Hua, Cornflower, Elderflower, Eyebright, Goldenseal, Lavender, Licorice, Marigold, Meadowsweet, Melilot, Melissa, Red grapevine, Rose, Plantain, Selfheal, Tansy, Tormentil, Walnut, Witch hazel, Yarrow

　irritation/tiredness (topically): Agrimony, Blue mallow, Cassia Jue Ming Zi, Chrysanthemum Ju Hua, Eyebright, *Fennel,* Hollyhock, Lettuce, Marigold, Rose, Selfheal

Eyesight (see Vision)

Failure to progress (see Labor, stalled)

Failure to thrive (see Children's development)

Fatigue (see also associated condition): American ginseng, *Angelica,* Artichoke, Ashwagandha, Astragalus Huang Qi, *Basil, Black spruce,* Blessed thistle, Brewer's yeast, Bogbean, Calamus, *Camphor, Cinnamon, Clove, Cypress,* Damiana, Elecampane, *Fir,* Flower pollen, Gentian, *Geranium, Hyssop,* Kelp, Lecithin, Licorice, Maca, Microalgae, *Neroli, Niaouli,* Oat, *Palmarosa, Pine,* Poplar, Prickly ash, *Ravintsara,* Rhodiola, *Rosemary, Sage,* Spruce, Suma, *Tea tree, Thyme,* Wheatgrass, *Winter savory,* Wormwood

Fatty liver (see Alcoholism, Hyperlipidemia, Weight gain, associated conditions, symptoms)

Fear (same remedies as Anxiety states)

Fever, acute/spiking: *antipyretics:* Artichoke, Belladonna*, Birch, Blue vervain, Boneset, Bupleurum, Centaury, Chicory, Dandelion, Elderflower, *Eucalyptus,* Gardenia Zhi Zi, Gentian, [Gypsum Shi Gao], *Lavender, Lemon, Lemongrass,* Linden, Meadowsweet, Melilot, Phragmites Lu Gen, Phyllostachys Zhu Ru, Purslane, Red grapevine, *Rose,* Scabious, *Spearmint,* Tamarind, Tansy, Usnea, Vervain, Willow, Yarrow, Yellow jessamine*

　eruptive: Bayberry, Bittersweet, Black cohosh, Blue violet, Borage, Burdock root/seed, Butterbur, Catnip, Cherry stalk, Cistus, Coltsfoot, Elderflower, *Eucalyptus, Hyssop, Lavender,* Lobelia, Meadowsweet, Pleurisy root, Sassafras, Scabious, Schizonepeta Jing Jie, Wild ginger, Woodruff

　intermittent: Artemisia Yin Chen Hao/Qing Hao, Balmony, *Bergamot,* Blessed thistle, Blue vervain, Boneset, Bupleurum, *Camphor,* Catnip, Cayenne, Celandine, Chaparral, Chicory, Culver's root, *Eucalyptus,* Feverfew, Fringe tree, Gentian, Hazelwort, Hops, *Hyssop,* Inmortal, Lungwort lichen, *Myrrh,* Pennyroyal, Sassafras, Tansy, Virginia snakeroot, Wahoo, Wild ginger, Wild indigo, Wormwood

　tidal (remittent): American ginseng, Anemarrhena Zhi Mu, Arnica, Borage, Bugleweed, Calamus, *Camomile, Camphor,* Celery, Chicory, Cleavers, Gravel root, Lungwort lichen, Mistletoe, Ophiopogon Mai Men Dong, Pipsissewa, Poplar, Sea holly, Valerian, Willow

Fibrocystic breasts (see also Edema, Estrogen accumulation, Liver congestion, Lymphatic congestion, *progesterone stimulants,* p. 783), Alfalfa, Bladderwrack, Burdock, Elecampane, Fritillaria Bei Mu, Kelp, Marigold, Mugwort, Pinellia Ban Xia, Poke, Polygonum He Shou Wu, Yarrow

Fibroids (see Uterine)

Fibromyalgia (FM) (see also Cerebral insufficiency, Fatigue, Hyperuricemia, Inflammation, Insomnia, Irritable bowel syndrome, Nervous tension, Neurasthenia, Numbness, Pain, other symptoms): Arnica, *Basil,* Bearsfoot, Birch, Bittersweet, Black cohosh, *Black pepper,* Blue cohosh, *Cajeput, Camomile* (all types), *Camphor,* Cayenne, Chaparral, *Citronella, Clary sage,* Clematis, Clove, Devil's claw, *Eucalyptus,* Feverfew, Hazelwort, Guaiacum, *Hyssop, Juniper, Lavender,* Lungwort lichen, *Marjoram,* Mugwort, *Niaouli,* Nutmeg, Oat, Pasqueflower, Prickly ash, *Ravintsara, Rosemary, Sage,* Sassafras, Siegesbeckia Xi Xian Cao, St. John's wort, *Thyme, Turpentine,* Twinleaf, Virginia snakeroot, Wild yam

Fibromyositis (see Fibromyalgia)

Fistula, anal: Arborvitae, Centaury, Condurango, Goldenseal, Horsetail, Oak leaf, Phellodendron Huang Bai, *Rosemary, Sage*, Thuja, Walnut, Yarrow

Flatulence (same remedies as Indigestion)

Flu (see Infection, viral, Infections, chronic)

Fluid retention (see Edema)

Food allergy (see Allergy, Diarrhea, Digestive enzyme deficiency, Gastric hypoacidity, Indigestion, Infection, fungal, Intestinal dysbiosis, Liver congestion, Malabsorption, Toxicosis, microbial)

  poisoning (see Poisoning, Vomiting)

  intolerance (same remedies as Digestive enzyme deficiency)

Fracture (see also remedies under Mineral depletion): ***bone tissue healers:*** Comfrey, Dandelion, Dipsacus Xu Duan, Drynaria Gu Sui Bu, Horsetail, Liquid trace minerals, Nettle, Oat, Panax San Qi, Parsley, {Royal jelly}, Wikstroemia Liao Ge Wang

Free radical burden: ***antioxidants:*** Aloe gel, Bilberry, Blackcurrant, Chaparral, Coconut oil, Eleuthero, *Ginger*, Ginkgo, Ginseng (all types), Hawthorn, Licorice, Ligustrum Nu Zhen Zi, Polygonum He Shou Wu, Reishi, *Rosemary, Sage,* Salvia Dan Shen, Scurvygrass, Selfheal, *Thyme,* Turmeric, vitamin C-rich plants, Wolfberry

Frigidity (same remedies as Impotence)

Frostbite (topically: see *astringents* under Diarrhea; internally: see Circulation, arterial/capillary)

Fungus (see Infection, fungal)

Furuncle (see Boil)

Gallbladder (see also Biliary)

Gallbladder colic (see also Food vallergies, Hepatitis, Jaundice): ***biliary spasmolytics:*** Agrimony, Artichoke, Butterbur, Celandine, Cornsilk, Dandelion, Fringe tree, Gardenia Zhi Zi, Fumitory, Lobelia, Lysimachia Jin Qian Cao, Meadowsweet, Nettle, *Peppermint, Roman Camomile,* Wild yam, Wood betony, Yarrow

  inflammation: ***biliary anti-inflammatories:*** Artichoke, Barberry, Black radish, Box, Celandine, Chicory, Cornsilk, Dandelion, *Eucalyptus,* Fringe tree, Gardenia Zhi Zi, Horsetail, Linden, Lysimachia Jin Qian Cao, Mayapple, Meadowsweet, Melissa, Milk thistle, Passionflower, *Peppermint, Pine,* Rhubarb, *Rosemary,* Scutellaria Huang Qin, Senna, Soapwort, *Thyme,* Valerian, Willow, Wood sorrel, Wormwood

Gallstone (see also Hyperlipidemia, Liver congestion): ***biliary antilithics:*** Alder buckthorn, Artichoke, Balmony, Barberry, Birch, Black radish, Cascara sagrada, Celandine, Centaury, Cornsilk, Couchgrass, Dandelion, Desmodium Guang Dong Jin Qian Cao, Flower pollen, Fringe tree, Grapefruit, Hemp agrimony, Horsetail, *Lemon,* Linden, Lobelia, Lysimachia Jin qian cao, Mayapple, Meadowsweet, Milk thistle, Nettle, *Niaouli,* Olive oil, Quassia, *Rosemary, Turpentine,* Vervain, Wild yam, Wood betony

Gangrene (see Circulation, insufficient capillary, Wound, atonic)

Gas (same remedies as Indigestion)

Gastric cancer (see also Tumor): ***antitumorals:*** Blue violet, Celandine, Codonopsis Dang Shen, Comfrey, Curdled milk, *Geranium,* Hops, Oldenlandia Bai Hua She She Cao, Tricosanthes Tian Hua Fen

  hemorrhage: ***hemostatics:*** Bistort, Bletilla Bai Ji, Cranesbill, Eyebright, Goldenseal, Horsetail, Knotgrass, Lady's mantle, Oak leaf, Plantain, Rye ergot, Sanicle, Shepherd's purse, Tormentil, Witch hazel, Yarrow

  hyperacidity: Alfalfa, Blue violet, Calamus, *Camomile,* Canada fleabane, Codonopsis Dang Shen, Cranesbill, Iceland moss, *Lemon,* Licorice, *Marjoram,* Meadowsweet, Passionflower, Poke root, Poria Fu Ling, Wheatgrass, Wild carrot, Wood sorrel

  hypoacidity: Alfalfa, Barberry, Blessed thistle, Bogbean, Calamus, Calumba, Centaury, Gentian, Iceland moss, *Juniper,* Prodigiosa, Suma, Watercress, White horehound, Wormwood

  ulcer (see also Food allergy, Infection, bacterial, Toxicosis, microbial): Aloe gel, Bistort, Bletilla Bai Ji, Blue violet, *Camomile* (all types), Codonopsis Dang Shen, Comfrey, Couchgrass, Cranesbill, Dendrobium Shi Hu, Flower pollen, *Geranium,* Hops, Iceland moss, Irish moss, *Juniper,* Lady's mantle, Licorice, Lungwort lichen, Marigold, Meadowsweet, Nettle, Oak bark, Oat, Poplar bud, {Royal jelly}, Slippery elm, Suma, Violet

Gastritis, acute: *gastric anti-inflammatories:* Acacia, Barberry, Blessed thistle, Blue flag, Butterbur, Calamus, *Camphor,* Centaury, Citrus Qing Pi, Fumitory, Iceland moss, *Lavender,* Licorice, Marshmallow, Meadowsweet, Melissa, Oregon grape, *Peppermint,* Rhubarb, *Rosemary,* Wheatgrass, Wormwood, Yarrow

Gastroenteritis, acute: *intestinal anti-inflammatories:* Agrimony, Arborvitae, Barberry, *Basil*, Bilberry, Birch, Bistort, Blackcurrant, Bupleurum, Butternut, Cajeput, Calamus, Canada fleabane, Costmary, Couchgrass, Cranesbill, *Geranium*, Goldenrod, Goldenseal, Horsetail, Iceland moss, Knotweed, Loosestrife, *Marjoram*, Marshmallow, Mullein, *Niaouli*, Oak bark, *Palmarosa*, Pau d'arco, *Peppermint, Ravintsara,* Saussurea Yun Mu Xiang, Senna, Tamarind, *Tea tree*, Tormentil, Uva ursi, Walnut, White bryony, White deadnettle, Willow, Yellow dock

    chronic: *intestinal stimulants:* Angelica, Bayberry, *Black pepper,* Blessed thistle, Calamus, Calumba, *Camphor*, Cardamom, *Cinnamon, Clove,* Culver's root, Garlic, Ginger, Horseradish, *Juniper*, Kava, *Myrrh, Niaouli,* Prickly ash, *Thyme*

Genitals (see Discharge, Dysmenorrhea, Impotence, Menstruation, Monilia, Sexual overstimulation, Uterine)

Giardiasis (see Infection, parasitic, Malabsorption syndrome, Nausea, Weight loss)

Gingivitis (see also Inflammation, Stomatitis, Toxicosis, heavy metal, remedies under Arthritis, chronic): *astringents:* Agrimony, Bilberry, Blackberry, Cattail pollen, Eyebright, *Geranium*, Goldenseal, Great burnet, Horsetail, Knotgrass, *Lemon*, Loosestrife, Microalgae, Mousear, *Myrrh*, Nettle, Poke root, Raspberry, Red grapevine, Red root, *Rose, Sage,* Sanicle, Shepherd's purse, Tormentil, Walnut, Wheatgrass, Witch hazel, Wood betony, Yarrow

Glaucoma: Bilberry, Cassia Jue Ming Zi, Celandine, Coleus, Eyebright, Pasqueflower

Glands, swollen (see Lymphatic congestion, Tonsillitis)

Gleet (same remedies as Discharge)

Glossitis (see Anemia, Infection, bacterial, Inflammation)

Glycogen storage disorder (see also Hypoglycemia, Immune deficiency, other conditions): Alfalfa, Artichoke, Codonopsis Dang Shen, Flower pollen, Lycium Gou Qi Zi, Microalgae, Nettle, Rehmannia Shu Di Huang, Watercress, Wheatgrass, Zizyphus Da Zao

Goiter: Bladderwrack, Blue flag, Canada fleabane, Figwort, Goldenseal, Kelp, Poke root, Strophanthus, Thuja, Watercress

Gonorrhea (see Discharge, Fever, Infection, bacterial, Urination, Vomiting)

Gout (same remedies as Arthritis, rheumatoid; see also Hyperuricemia, Toxicosis, metabolic)

Growth, children's insufficient (see Development, children's slow)

Gums (see Gingivitis, Periodontitis, Pyorrhea, Stomatitis)

Hair loss (also topically; see also Aging, premature, Testosterone deficiency): Aloe gel, Arnica, Birch, Bogbean, Burdock, Calamus, *Cedarwood* (all types), Centaury, *Clary sage, Cypress,* Eclipta Han Lian Cao, Horsetail, *Juniper*, liquid trace minerals, *Marjoram*, Nasturtium, Nettle, Parsley, *Rosemary, Sage, Spike lavender, Thyme*, Walnut, Watercress

Halitosis (see Indigestion, Liver congestion; gargles with remedies under Infection, bacterial)

Hayfever (see Allergy)

Headache (see also Allergies, Anemia, Anxiety, Blood pressure, high, Constipation, Estrogen deficiency, Fatigue, Fever, Food allergy, Hypoglycemia, Liver congestion, Migraine, Nervous tension, Sinusitis, Toxicosis [all types]): Birch, Bitter orange, Black cohosh, Blue flag, Blue violet, *Camomile* (all types), Catnip, Cowslip flower, *Eucalyptus*, Feverfew, Fieldmint, Garlic, Hops, Lady's mantle, *Lavender*, Ligusticum Chuan Xiong, Lungwort thallus, *Marjoram*, Meadowsweet, Melilot, Mistletoe, Oat, Pasqueflower, Passionflower, *Peppermint*, Prickly ash, *Rosemary*, Skullcap, St. John's wort, *Thyme*, Uncaria Gou Teng, Valerian, Vervain, White bryony, Willow, Wood betony, Wormwood

Heart disorders (see Angina pectoris, Arrhythmia, Congestive heart failure, Myocarditis, Palpitations, Tachycardia, Valvular disorder)

    weakness: *cardiac restoratives:* Aniseed, Arnica, Bloodroot, Broom, Bugleweed, Butterbur, *Camphor*, Cereus, Chickweed, *Cinnamon*, Coleus, Cowslip, Dogbane, Figwort, Foxglove, Garlic, Hawthorn, Inmortal, *Lemon*, Ligusticum Chuan Xiong, Lily of the valley, Marigold, *Melissa*, Motherwort, Oat, *Palmarosa*, Pink root, Prickly ash, *Rosemary*, Salvia Dan Shen, *Sandalwood*, Shepherd's purse, *Spearmint*, Squills, Tormentil, Wall-flower, Wild cherry, Valerian, White horehound

Heartburn (see Allergy, Gastric hyperacidity/ulcer)

Heat syndrome (see Cerebral congestion, Dehydration, Fever, Muscle spasm, Nausea)

Heavy metal poisoning (see Toxicosis, heavy metal)

Hematoma: Cleavers, Daisy, Dong quai, Fumitory, Garlic, *Helichrysum*, *Helichrysum*, Horsechestnut, Lady's bedstraw, *Lemon*, Ligusticum Chuan Xiong, Lily of the valley, *Lime*, Linden, Lomatium, Melilot, Red clover, Safflower, Salvia Dan shen, Soapwort, Squills, Turmeric, Yarrow

Hematuria (see Urinary bleeding)

Hemophilia: Biota Ce Bai Ye, Bletilla Bai Ji, Cattail pollen, Cranesbill, Dipsacus Xu Duan, Goldenseal, Great burnet, Horsetail, Knotgrass, Lady's mantle, Marigold, Nettle, Panax San Qi, Plantain, Rhubarb, Shepherd's purse

Hemoptysis (see Cough with bloody sputum)

Hemorrhage, internal: *hemostatics:* Agrimony, Bilberry, Blackberry, Cattail pollen, Eyebright, *Geranium*, Goldenseal, Great burnet, Horsetail, Knotgrass, *Lemon*, Loosestrife, Microalgae, Mousear, *Myrrh*, Nettle, Poke root, Raspberry, Red grapevine, Red root, *Rose*, *Sage*, Sanicle, Shepherd's purse, Tormentil, Walnut, Wheatgrass, Witch hazel, Wood betony, Yarrow

Hemorrhoids (also topically; see also Constipation, Portal congestion): *astringent decongestants:* Arborvitae, Barberry, Bilberry, Biota Ce Bai Ye, Bistort, Blackhaw, Blackberry, Butcher's broom, *Cedarwood*, Cramp bark, Cranesbill, *Cypress*, Figwort, *Geranium*, Goldenseal, Heartsease, Horsechestnut, Horsetail, Knotgrass, Madder, Mistletoe, Mullein, Oak, Ocotillo, Partridgeberry, *Patchouli*, Pellitory of the wall, Pilewort, Red grapevine, Red root, Rye ergot, *Sandalwood*, Sophora Huai Hua, Stonecrop, Stoneroot, Thuja, Tormentil, White deadnettle, Witch hazel, Yarrow

Hepatitis (see also Infection, viral, Liver congestion): *anti-inflammatory liver decongestants:* Aconite*, Artemisia Yin Chen Hao, Barberry, Bella-donna*, Bloodroot, Blue flag, *Camomile* (all types), Canna Mei Ren Jiao, Celandine, Chaparral, Chicory, Culver's root, Dandelion, Fringe tree, Gardenia Zhi Zi, Goldenseal, Lactobacillus bifidus, Licorice, Lysimachia Jin Qian Cao, Madder, Microalgae, Milk thistle, *Myrrh*, *Ravintsara*, {Royal jelly}, *Sage*, Schisandra Wu Wei Zi, White bryony, Wormwood, Yarrow

Herpes, genital (see also Conjunctivitis, Fever, Infection, viral, Lymphatic congestion, Ulcer, Urination): *antivirals:* Arborvitae, Burdock, *Cajeput, Camphor,* Chaparral, Coptis Huang Lian, Echinacea, Hemlock spruce, *Lavender, Lemon,* Marigold, Microalgae, *Myrrh, Niaouli,* Oat, Pau d'arco, {Propolis}, *Ravintsara, Sage,* St. John's wort, *Tea tree,* Thuja, *Thyme*

Herpes simplex (see Herpes, genital)

Herpes zoster (see Shingles)

Hiccups: *Aniseed,* Blackhaw, *Fennel, Marjoram*

Hives (see Allergy, Liver congestion, Skin)

Hoarseness (same remedies as Voice loss)

Hookworm (see Parasites, skin)

Hormonal disorders (see Acne, Cervical dysplasia, Dysmenorrhea, Fibrocystic breasts, Impotence, Infertility, Menopausal syndrome, Menstruation, Osteoporosis, PMS, Uterine fibroids)

Hot flashes (see also *estrogen/progesterone stimulants,* p. 783, Menoapusal syndrome): Boneset, *Geranium,* Hawthorn, *Marjoram,* Melilot, Melissa, Valerian

Hydrophobia (see Infection, Fever, Lymphatic congestion, Spasm)

Hyperactivity (see Attention deficit hyperactivity disorder)

Hyperchloremia: *hypochloremiant diuretics:* Alisma Ze Xie, Asparagus, Birch, Broom, Butcher's broom, Elder, Elecampane, *Fennel,* Meadowsweet, Onion, Parsley, Sea holly, Squills, Stoneseed, Strophanthus

Hyperglycemia: *hypoglycemiants:* Agrimony, Alfalfa, Artichoke, Asparagus, Bilberry, Blackberry, Blackcurrant, Blue cohosh, Bugleweed, Burdock, Celandine, Celery, Centaury, Chicory, Cranesbill, Dandelion, Devil's club, Elecampane, *Eucalyptus, Fennel,* Figwort, Garlic, *Geranium,* Goat's rue, Horseradish, *Juniper,* Knotgrass, *Lemon,* Lettuce, Lily of the valley, Microalgae, Mugwort, Nettle, Nutritional yeast, Oat, Olive, Onion, Periwinkle, Prodigiosa, Raspberry leaf, Rehmannia Shu Di Huang, *Rosemary, Sage,* Saw palmetto, Scrophularia Xuan Shen, Selfheal, Suma, *Thyme,* Tormentil, Vetivert, Walnut, Watercress, Wheat gluten, Winter-green, *Ylang ylang*

Hyperhydrosis (see Perspiration, excessive)

Hyperinsulinemia (see *adaptogens,* Class 7, *adrenocortical restoratives,* p. 782, Fatigue, *insulin stimulants,* p. 783, Liver toxicosis)

Hyperlipidemia: *antilipemics:* Alfalfa, Alisma Ze Xie, Artichoke, Bilberry, Birch, Blackcurrant oil, Boldo, Borage seed oil, Coconut oil, Chicory, Chickpea, Combretum, Dandelion, Evening primrose oil, Flaxseed oil, Fumitory, Ganoderma Ling Zhi, Gardenia Zhi Zi, Garlic, Goldenrod, Hawthorn, *Helichrysum,* *Lactobacillus acidophilus,* Lecithin, Lentil, Licorice, Linden, Lycium Gou Qi Zi, Mousear, Nutritional yeast, Olive oil, pectin-rich foods, Polygonum He Shou Wu, Reishi, Rhubarb, *Rosemary,* Shiitake, Suma, Tea, *Thyme,* Turmeric, Walnut meat

Hypersensitivity disorders (see Allergy, Autoimmune disease, Food allergies, Immune deficiency, chronic)

Hypertension (see also Arteriosclerosis, Hyperthyroid, Kidneys, Stress): *hypotensives:* Arnica, Barberry, Birch, Black cohosh, Blackcurrant leaf/oil, Blackhaw, Blue vervain, Borage seed oil, California poppy, *Camo-mile* (all types), Cassia Jue Ming Zi, Celandine, Chrysanthemum Ye Ju Hua, Coleus, Evening primrose oil, Flaxseed oil, Fumitory, Ganoderma Ling Zhi, Garlic, Hawthorn, Hellebore, *Hyssop,* Ivy, *Lavender, Lemon, Lemon* balm, Ligusticum Chuan Xiong, Linden, Lobelia, *Niaouli,* Olive leaf, Parsley, Passionflower, *Marjoram, Melissa,* Mistletoe, Motherwort, *Neroli,* Rauvolfia Luo Fu Mu, Red grapevine, Reishi, Rue, Selfheal, Shiitake, Skullcap, Shepherd's purse, Stoneseed, Violet, Wood betony, *Ylang ylang*

Hyperthyroid (see *thyroxine inhibitors,* p. 783)

Hyperuricemia: *uricosuric diuretics:* Apple, Artichoke, Ash, Birch, Blackcurrant, Blue cohosh, Brewer's yeast, Canada fleabane, Cherry fruit, Cornsilk, Cowslip root, Goldenrod, Gravel root, Hawthorn, Jamaica sarsaparilla, *Juniper,* Meadowsweet, Nettle, Onion, Poplar bark, Reed, Stoneseed, Uva ursi, Vervain, Yerba mansa

Hypocalcemia: {Amyda Bie Jia}, {Chinemys Gui Ban}, {Equus E Jiao}, [Haliotis Shi Jue Ming], Watercress

Hypochlorhydria (see Gastric hypoacidity)

Hypoglycemia (see also Adrenal cortex deficiency, Food allergy, Hypothyroid, Liver congestion, Malabsorption, Mineral depletion): *hyperglycemiants:* Artichoke, Citrus Chen Pi, Citrus Qing Pi, Dandelion, Devil's club, Flower pollen, Fritillaria Chuan Bei Mu, Garlic, Microalgae, Nettle, Nutritional yeast, Oat, Ophiopogon Mai Men Dong, Rehmannia Shu Di Huang, Suma, Wheatgrass

Hypotension: *hypertensives:* Aconitum Fu Zi, Adonis, Asian ginseng, Bayberry, Blessed thistle, Broom, Cereus, *Camphor,* Clove, Elecampane, Garlic, Flower pollen, *Hyssop, Lemon,* Lily of the valley, Milk thistle, Motherwort, *Ravintsara, Rosemary,* Shepherd's purse, *Sage, Thyme, Winter savory*

Hypothermia (see Circulation, insufficient arterial/capillary)

Hypothyroid (see *thyroxine stimulants,* p. 783, Liver congestion, symptoms)

Hysteria (see Delirium, Nervous tension)

Immune deficiency, chronic: *immune enhancers:* American/Asian ginseng, Astragalus Huang Qi, Brewer's yeast, *Black spruce,* Dandelion, Elecampane, Eleuthero, Flower pollen, *Frankincense,* Ganoderma Ling Zhi, Jamaica sarsaparilla, Licorice, Microalgae, Prickly ash, Reishi, Rhodiola, {Royal jelly}, *Sage,* Schisandra Wu Wei Zi, Shiitake, Spruce, Suma, *Vetiver*

Impetigo (see Infection, bacterial, Skin eruption)

Impotence: American/Asian ginseng, Asparagus, *Basil,* Blackcurrant oil, Bloodroot, Borage seed oil, Celery, Cinnamon, Clove, Curculigo Xian Mao, Damiana, Epimedium Yin Yang Huo, Evening primrose oil, Fenugreek, Flaxseed oil, Flower pollen, *Ginger,* Golden ragwort, Helonias, Jasmine, Maca, Morinda Ba Ji Tian, *Neroli, Niaouli,* Oat, *Pine,* {Placenta}, Poplar, *Rose,* Saw palmetto, Sea holly, *Spruce,* Suma, Sundew, White deadnettle, Wild carrot, Willow (all types), *Winter savory, Ylang ylang,* Yohimbe

Indigestion (see also Digestive enzyme deficiency, Epigastric fullness, Food allergy, Intestinal colic, Nausea): Angelica, Aniseed, Artichoke, *Basil, Bergamot,* Bitter orange, *Black pepper,* Blessed thistle, Calamus, *Camomile* (all types), *Camphor,* Caraway, Cardamom, Catnip, Celery seed, Citrus Chen Pi, Coriander, Cumin, Dill, Elecampane, *Fennel,* Fieldmint, Garlic, *Geranium, Ginger,* Horseradish, *Hyssop, Juniper, Lavender, Lemon,* Lovage, *Mandarin, Marjoram, Melissa,* Milk thistle, *Neroli,* Onion, *Oregano,* Parsley seed, Pennyroyal, *Peppermint, Pine,* Rhubarb, *Rosemary,* Rue, *Sage,* Sassafras, Saussurea Yun Mu Xiang, *Spearmint,* Star anise, *Thyme,* Watercress, White horehound, Wild carrot seed

Infection (see also Contagious disease, Fever, Food allergy, Immune deficiency, Infections, chronic/recurrent, Toxicosis, particular condition, disease or part involved):

bacterial: *antibacterials:* Barberry, Birthwort, Butterbur, *Cajeput, Camphor,* Chaparral, Chrysanthemum, Cinnamon, Clove, Coptis Huang Lian, Echinacea, *Eucalyptus,* Forsythia Lian Qiao, Garlic, *Ginger,* Goldenseal, Horseradish, *Juniper, Lavender, Lemon,* Lonicera Jin Yin Hua, *Manuka,* Marigold, Microalgae, *Myrrh, Myrtle, Niaouli, Oregano, Palmarosa,* Pasqueflower, Pau d'arco, *Pine,* {Propolis}, *Ravin-*

tsara, Rose, Spruce, Tea tree, Thyme, Usnea, Wild indigo, *Winter savory,* Wormwood

fungal: *antifungals:* Arborvitae, Boldo, Burdock, *Cajeput,* Celandine, *Cinnamon,* Coptis Huang Lian, Echinacea, Garlic, *Geranium,* Goldenseal, *Lactobacillus acidophilus/bifidus, Lavender,* Lemongrass, *Manuka,* Marigold, *Niaouli, Myrrh, Oregano, Palmarosa,* Pau d'arco, Phellodendron Huang Bai, {Propolis}, *Sage,* Scutellaria Huang Qin, *Spruce, Tea tree,* Thuja, *Thyme,* Usnea, Walnut, *Winter savory*

parasitic: *antiparasitics:* Agrimonia He Cao Ye, Xian He Cao, Aloe resin, Annual wormwood, Blue vervain, Boldo, Brucea Ya Dan Zi, Centaury, Cinnamon, Clove, Dichroa Chang Shan, Elecampane, *Fennel,* Garlic, Horseradish, *Hyssop,* Knotgrass, Male fern, Mugwort, Parsley seed, *Peppermint,* Pink root, Quisqualis Ya Dan Zi, Red squash seed, Rue, Soapwort, Spruce, Tansy, *Tea tree, Thyme,* Valerian, Vervain, Walnut, Watercress, Wormseed (European/ American), Wormwood

viral: *antivirals:* Arborvitae, *Basil, Blue cypress, Camphor,* Chaparral, *Cinnamon, Cistus, Clove,* Coptis Huang Lian, Echinacea, Elderberry, *Eucalyptus radiata,* Forsythia Lian Qiao, Garlic, Goldenseal, Isatis Ban Lan Gen, Isatis Da Qing Ye, *Laurel,* Ledebouriella Fang Feng, Lomatium, Lonicera Jin Yin Hua, *Manuka,* Marigold, Mayapple, Microalgae, *Melissa, Myrrh, Niaouli,* Olive leaf, *Oregano, Palmarosa,* Phyllanthus, {Propolis}, *Ravintsara, Sage,* Shiitake, St. John's wort, *Tea tree,* Thuja, *Thyme, Winter savory*

Infections, chronic/recurrent: *immunostimulants: Angelica,* Arnica, Astragalus Huang Qi, Birthwort, Butterbur, Calamus, *Camphor,* Chaparral, *Clove,* Dandelion, Echinacea, *Eucalyptus, Fennel,* Flower pollen, Forsythia Lian Qiao, *Frankincense,* Garlic, *Ginger,* Heartsease, Jamaica sarsaparilla, *Juniper, Lavender,* Licorice, *Lemon,* Lobelia, Lonicera Jin Yin Hua, Lungwort lichen, Marshmallow, Microalgae, *Myrrh, Neroli, Niaouli, Pine,* Rue, *Tea tree, Thyme,* Vervain, Wild indigo, *Winter savory,* Wormwood, Yerba mansa

Infertility (see also *gonadotropic, progesterone* and *estrogen stimulants, p. 783,* other conditions): Black cohosh, {Cervus Lu Rong}, Chastetree, Damiana, Epimedium Yin Yang Huo, Helonias, Maca, Milky oat, Polygonum He Shou Wu, *Rose, Sage,* Saw palmetto, Wild yam

Inflammation (see also part or disease involved, Infection, other conditions): *anti-inflammatories:* Aconite*, Akebia Mu Tong, *Basil,* Black cohosh, Bladderwrack, *Blue tansy,* Bilberry, Blue cohosh, Bogbean, Bupleurum, Butternut, *Camomile* (all types), Celery, Centaury, Chaparral, Chrysanthemum Ju Hua, Clematis Wei Ling Xian, *Clary sage,* Coptis Huang Lian, Echinacea, *Eucalyptus,* Evening primrose, Figwort, *Frankincense,* Gardenia Zhi Zi, Gentian, Gentiana Jin Qian Cao, *Geranium,* Goldenrod, Goldenseal, Hawthorn, Indigo, Japanese honeysuckle, Lady's mantle, *Lavender,* Licorice, *Lime,* Marigold, Meadowsweet, *Myrrh, Niaouli, Peppermint,* Pleurisy root, Queen's root, *Rose,* Saw palmetto, *Sage,* Scutellaria Huang Qin, St. John's wort, Tansy, *Turmeric,* Wheatgrass, White bryony, White poplar, Wild indigo, Wild yam, Willow, Witch hazel, Woad, Wormwood, Yellow jessamine*

Inflammatory bowel disease (IBD) (see Diarrhea, Fatigue, Inflammation, Intestinal pain, Mineral depletion, Toxicosis, microbial)

Injury (see Contusion, Hematoma, Wound)

Insect/animal bite (also topically): *detoxicants:* Angelica, Aniseed, Arnica, *Basil, Bergamot,* Bilberry, Blessed thistle, Blue vervain, Cajeput, Calamus, *Cinnamon,* Echinacea, *Fennel,* Garlic, *Juniper, Lavender, Lemon,* Licorice, Lily of the valley, Lobelia, Marigold, *Niaouli, Oregano,* Plantain, Purslane, Rue, Skullcap, St. John's wort, Pennyroyal, *Tea tree, Thyme,* Valerian, Vervain, Virginia snakeroot, *Winter savory,* Wormwood

repellent (topically): Annual wormwood, *Basil, Cedarwood, Citronella,* Clove, Dalmatia pellitory, *Eucalyptus, Geranium, Gingergrass, Lavender, Lemon,* Pennyroyal, *Peppermint,* Stemona Bai Bu, Tansy, Tripterygium Lei Gong Teng, Walnut leaf

Insomnia (see also Anxiety, Cerebral insufficiency, Depression, Food allergy, Indigestion, Nervous tension): *nervous sedatives:* American ginseng, Biota Bai Zi Ren, Black horehound, California poppy, *Clary sage,* Hops, *Camomile* (all types), Coleus, *Lavender, Marjoram, Melissa,* Melilot, Oat, Passionflower, Scrophularia Xuan Shen, Schisandra Wu Wei Zi, Skullcap, Valerian, Wild lettuce, Woodruff, Yellow jessamine*, Zizyphus Suan Zao Ren

Insulin resistance (see Hyperinsulinemia)

Intestines (see Constipation, Diarrhea, Digestive enzyme deficiency, Food allergy, Gastroenteritis, Intestinal, Inflammatory bowel disease, Irritable bowel syndrome, Malabsorption syndrome, Toxicosis, microbial)

Intestinal colic/pain: *intestinal relaxants/spasmolytics: Angelica, Aniseed, Basil, Bergamot,* Black cohosh,

Blackcurrant, Blackhaw, Black horehound, Bupleurum, *Camomile* (all types), Calamus, Calamint, Catnip, Celandine, Chastetree berry, Cinnamon, *Clary sage, Clove,* Coleus, Costmary, Cramp bark, Cumin, Cyperus Xiang Fu, *Geranium, Ginger,* Gumweed, Jamaica dogwood, Jamaica sarsaparilla, *Laurel, Lavender,* Licorice, *Lime,* Lindera Wu Yao, Lovage, Magnolia Hou Po, *Marjoram,* Melilot, *Melissa,* Motherwort, *Nutmeg,* Oshá, Parsley seed, Pennyroyal, *Peppermint,* Pleurisy root, Prickly ash, Rue, *Sage,* Silverweed, St. John's wort, Stoneroot, Tansy, Turpentine, Vervain, Virginia snakeroot, Wild carrot, Wild cherry, Wild ginger, Wild lettuce, Wild yam, Wormwood, Yellow jessamine*

dysbiosis (same remedies as Toxicosis, microbial; see also Indigestion)

hemorrhage: *hemostatics:* Avens, Bayberry, Bletilla Bai Ji, Bistort, Canada fleabane, Cirsium Da Ji, Cistus, Cranesbill, Goldenseal, Great burnet, Horsetail, Knotgrass, Mullein, Oak leaf, Plantain, Sanicle, Senna, Shepherd's purse, Sumac, Tormentil

infection (see Gastroenteritis)

mucus: *Angelica,* Atractylodes Cang Zhu, *Bergamot, Black pepper,* Blessed thistle, Calamus, Cardamom, Chastetree berry, Citrus Qing Pi, *Fennel,* Horseradish, *Juniper, Marjoram, Myrrh, Peppermint, Rosemary,* Saussurea Yun Mu Xiang, *Thyme,* Watercress

parasites (see Diarrhea, Infection, parasitic, Malabsorption, Weight loss)

Irritability (same remedies as Nervous tension)

Irritable bowel syndrome (IBS) (same remedies as Intestinal colic; see also Food allergy, Indigestion, Inflammation, Nausea, Spasm)

Itching (see Skin itching)

Jaundice (see Anemia, Gallbladder inflammation, Gallstone, Hepatitis, Liver cirrhosis/congestion, Tumor)

Kidneys (see Nephritis, Urinary)

Labor, difficult (see also Pain): *parturients:* American mistletoe, Angelica, Birthroot, Birthwort, Black cohosh, Blackhaw, Blue cohosh, *Clary sage,* Clove, Cramp bark, Garlic, Golden ragwort, Gravel root, Hazelwort, *Jasmine, Juniper,* Lady's mantle, *Lavender,* Ligusticum Chuan Xiong, Lobelia, Lovage, *Marjoram, Melissa,* Motherwort, Mugwort, *Myrrh, Oregano,* Oshá, *Sage,* Shepherd's purse, Uva ursi, Vervain, Virginia snakeroot, Wild ginger, Wood betony, *Ylang ylang,* Yellow jessamine*

stalled: *oxytocic parturients:* Achyranthes Niu Xi, Birthroot, Birthwort, Black cohosh, Blue cohosh, Blue flag, Broom, *Clary sage,* Goldenseal, *Lemon,* Ligusticum Chuan Xiong, Lobelia, Lovage, Madder, Mistletoe, Motherwort, Mugwort, *Myrrh,* Oshá, *Sage ,* Sundew, Tricosanthes Tian Hua Fen, Vervain

Lactation (see Breast milk)

Laryngitis (see also Allergy, Infection, bacterial/viral, Toxicosis, microbial/metabolic, Voice loss): Acacia, Aconite*, Agrimony, Barberry, Bayberry, Belamcanda She Gan, Benzoin, Blackberry, Blackcurrant, *Black pepper,* Bloodroot, Bogbean, Borage, Burdock seed, *Camphor,* Cayenne, *Clary sage,* Clove, Coltsfoot, Comfrey, Elderflower, *Eucalyptus,* Eyebright, Fieldmint, *Geranium,* Goldenrod, Goldenseal, Gumweed, *Hyssop,* Iceland moss, Ivy, Lady's mantle, *Lavender, Lemon,* Licorice, Loosestrife, Lungwort (lichen), Marshmallow, Melilot, Mullein, Pipsissewa, Plantain, Platycodon Jie Geng, Poke root, Poplar bud, Prickly ash, Purslane, Queen's root, *Rose, Sage,* Saw palmetto, Scabious, Slippery elm, Stoneroot, Sumac, *Tea tree, Thyme,* Tormentil, White horehound, Witch hazel

Learning disability (see Mineral depletion, Nutritional deficiency, Toxicosis, heavy metal)

Legs (see Edema, Ulcer, Veins)

Leucorrhea (see Discharge, Infection, fungal/parasitic, Skin itching)

Lice (see Parasites, skin)

Lichen planus (see Infection, viral, Skin eruption/itching)

Liver cirrhosis (see also Anemia, Edema, other symptoms): Artichoke, Birch, Blackcurrant oil, Borage seed oil, Cabbage, Cascara sagrada, Celandine, Cornsilk, Elder, Evening primrose oil, Flaxseed oil, Hedge bindweed, *Juniper,* Lactobacillus bifidus, Microalgae, Milkthistle, Mousear, Onion, Poke root, *Rosemary,* Schisandra, Squills, White bryony

congestion: *liver decongestants:* Artemisia Yin Chen Hao, Artichoke, Alder buckthorn, Balmony, Barberry, Birch, Blackcurrant, Black radish, Blessed thistle, Bloodroot, Blue flag, Bogbean, Boldo, Boneset, Box,

Butternut, *Carrot seed,* Cascara sagrada, Celandine, Celery, Centaury, Chaparral, Chicory, Culver's root, Dandelion, Elecampane, Figwort, Fringe tree, Fumitory, Gardenia Zhi Zi, Golden ragwort, Goldenseal, Horsechestnut, Inmortal, *Lemon,* Liverwort, Loosestrife, Madder, Marigold, Mayapple, Milk thistle, Mugwort, *Myrtle,* Oregon grape, Pasqueflower, Pennyroyal, Poke root, Queen's root, Red root, Rhubarb, *Rosemary,* Rue, Silver thistle, Soapwort, Speedwell, Squills, Tansy, Turmeric, Vervain, *Vetiver,* Wahoo, Watercress, White bryony, Wild indigo, Wormwood, Yellow dock

    toxicosis: *liver detoxicants:* Alfalfa, Artichoke, Astragalus Huang Qi, Atractylodes Bai Zhu, Boldo, Chicory, Dandelion, Flower pollen, Licorice, Lovage, Microalgae, Milk thistle, Nettle, Phyllanthus, Picrorhiza, Rehmannia Shu Di Huang, Reishi, Salvia Dan Shen, Schisandra Wu Wei Zi, *Turmeric,* Wolfberry

Liver enlargement: Citrus Qing Pi, Cucumis Tian Gua Di, Fringe tree, Mayapple, Red root, Wild indigo

Lumbago (see Backache, lower)

Lung disorders (see Asthma, Bronchitis, Emphysema, Pleurisy, Pneumonia, Silicosis, TB)

Lupus (SLE) (see Arthritis, acute, Autoimmune disorder, Infection, viral, Inflammation, Nephritis, Toxicosis, metabolic/ microbial, *progesterone stimulants,* p. 783)

Lyme disease (see Infection, bacterial, symptoms)

Lymphadenitis (see Lymphatic congestion)

Lymphangitis (same remedies as Tonsilitis)

Lymphatic congestion (see also Digestive enzyme deficiency, Food allergy, Intestinal dysbiosis): *lymphatic stimulants:* Angelica, Arborvitae, Bittersweet, Bladderwrack, Blue flag, Blue violet, Burdock, Chickweed, Cistus, Cleavers, Couchgrass, *Cypress,* Echinacea, Figwort, Forsythia Lian Qiao, Fritillaria Bei Mu, Fumitory, *Geranium,* Germander, Heartsease, Horseradish, Inmortal, Kelp, Knotgrass, *Laurel,* Lonicera Jin Yin Hua, Marigold, Melilot, Ocotillo, Pipsissewa, Plantain, Poke root, Queen's root, Red root, *Sandalwood,* Selfheal, Soapwort, Sundew, Thuja, Walnut, Watercress, Wild indigo, *Winter savory*

Malabsorption syndrome (see also Anemia, Fatigue, Food allergy, Weight loss): *anastative nutritives:* Alfalfa, American ginseng, Atractylodes Bai Zhu, Codonopsis Dang Shen, Flower pollen, Iceland moss, Jamaica sarsaparilla, *Lactobacillus acidophilus/bifidus,* Licorice, Microalgae, Nettle, *Palmarosa,* Parsley root, Red clover, Saw palmetto, Soapwort, Solomon's seal, Tormentil, Walnut, Watercress, Wheatgrass

Malaria: *antimalarials:* Annual wormwood, Baikal skullcap, Brucea Ya Dan Zi, *Camomile,* Culver's root, Dandelion, Dichroa Chang Shan, *Eucalyptus,* Gentian, *Myrrh,* Pennyroyal, Periwinkle, Peruvian bark, Sunflower flower, Wahoo, White horehound, *Winter savory,* Yellow Jessamine*

Malnutrition (see Malabsorption)

Mania (same remedies as Delirium, violent)

Manic depressive disorder (see Depression, affective/nervous, Cerebral insufficiency, Liver congestion, Mineral depletion, Nervous tension)

Mastitis (see Breast engorement, Fever, Infection, bacterial, Pain)

ME (see Chronic fatigue syndrome)

Measles (see Infection, Fever, eruptive, Wound, atonic)

Memory loss (see Cerebral insufficiency; see also Anxiety, Depression, Estrogen deficiency, Insomnia, Mineral depletion)

Ménière's syndrome (see Allergy, Cerebral insufficiency, Edema, Hypoglycemia, symptoms)

Meningitis (see also Fever, Headache, Infection, bacterial, Inflammation, Seizure, other symptoms): Arnica, Belladonna*, Calabar bean, *Camphor,* Croton oil, Cow parsnip, Echinacea, Isatis Da Qing Ye, Lobelia, *Lavender,* Poke root, Skullcap, St. John's wort, {Ursus Xiong Dan}, Valerian, White bryony, Wormwood, Yellow jessamine*

Menopausal syndrome (see also Atherosclerosis, Coronary insufficiency, Depression, Hot flashes, Insomnia, Memory loss, Mental fatigue, Osteoporosis, Skin itching, Sleep disorder, Urinary, Uterine bleeding, Vaginal dryness, Vaginitis, Veins, *estrogen/progesterone stimulants,* p. 783, other disorders/symptoms): Alfalfa, American ginseng, Anemrrhena Zhi Mu, Angelica, Birthroot, Black cohosh, Bugleweed, *Camomile* (all types), *Chasteberry, Clary sage,* Coconut oil, *Cypress,* Dong quai, Elecampane, Flower pollen, *Geranium,* Hawthorn, Helonias, Licorice, Motherwort, Nettle, Red clover, Rehmannia Shu Di Huang, *Rose,* Scrophularia Xuan Shen

Menorrhagia (see Menstruation, heavy, Uterine fibroid)

Menstruation, absent/delayed/scanty (see also *estrogen stimulants*, p. 783): ***uterine stimulants (emmenagogues) and restoratives:*** Aloe resin, American mistletoe, Angelica, Arborvitae, Artichoke, Birthroot, Bittersweet, Black cohosh, Blackhaw, Bloodroot, Blue cohosh, Burdock, Butterbur, Calamus, Celandine, Celery, Chastetree, *Cinnamon, Clary sage,* Costmary, Cotton root, Culver's root, Dong quai, Elecampane, *Fennel,* Figwort, *Geranium,* Golden ragwort, Hazelwort, Helonias, Horseradish, *Hyssop,* Inmortal, Ivy, *Jasmine, Juniper,* Ligusticum Chuan Xiong, Lovage, *Marjoram,* Motherwort, Mugwort, *Myrtle,* Nettle, Ocotillo, Parsley, Partridgeberry, Pennyroyal, *Peppermint,* Raspberry, *Rosemary,* Rue, *Sage,* Sassafras, Senna, Squills, Sundew, Tansy, *Thyme,* Vervain, *Vetiver,* White deadnettle, Wild carrot, Wild ginger, Wild lettuce, Wild yam, Wormwood

   heavy/flooding (see also Dysmenorrhea, congestive): ***uterine decongestants:*** Barberry, Bilberry, Birthroot, Blackhaw, Broom, Butcher's broom, Cinnamon, Cotton root, Cramp bark, Cranesbill, *Cypress,* Golden ragwort, Goldenseal, Greater periwinkle, Heartsease, Helonias, Horsechestnut, Lady's mantle, *Lemon,* Madder, Marigold, Melilot, Milk thistle, Mistletoe, Nettle, Oregon grape, Paeonia Chi Shao Yao, Partridgeberry, Plantain, Red grapevine, Red root, *Rose,* Rubia Qian Cao Gen, Rye ergot, Selfheal, Shepherd's purse, Stoneroot, White deadnettle, Witch hazel, Yellow dock, Yarrow

   irregular (see also *progesterone stimulants, p. 783*): Black cohosh, Blue cohosh, *Chastetree* berry, Damiana, Dong quai, Eleuthero, Lady's mantle, Oregon grape, *Rose,* Saw palmetto, White deadnettle, Yarrow

   painful (see Dysmenorrhea, congestive, spasmodic)

Mental fatigue (same remedies as Cerebral insufficiency)

Metabolic acidosis (see Dehydration, Diabetes, Metabolic disorder, Malabsorption syndrome, Vomiting)

   alkalosis (see Diarrhea, Metabolic disorder, Nervous tension, Tachycardia, Vomiting)

   disorder/deficiency (see also Glycogen storage disorder, Hypoglycemia): Bladderwrack, {Cervus Lu Rong}, Dandelion, Eleuthero, Flower pollen, Horsetail, Kelp, Microalgae, Nettle, Oat, {Placenta}, Rehmannia Shu Di Huang, Schisandra Wu Wei Zi, Watercress, Wolfberry

Metabolic syndrome (see component disorders, conditions and chief symptoms)

Migraine (see also Allergy, Anxiety, Constipation, Depression, Food allergy, Liver congestion, Toxicosis): Almond, Blackcurrant, *Basil,* Bogbean, Cabbage, *Camomile,* Cherry fruit, Cowslip flower, Feverfew, Ginkgo, Hops, *Lavender,* Ligusticum Chuan Xiong, Linden, *Marjoram,* Melilot, *Melissa, Neroli,* Onion, Pasqueflower, Peach fruit, *Peppermint, Rosemary,* Speedwell, Valerian, Vervain, Wild yam, *Winter savory,* Wood betony, Wormwood, Yellow jessamine*

Mineral depletion (see also Debility, Fatigue, Metabolic acidosis): ***mineral nutritives:*** Alfalfa, Bladderwrack, Celery, Chickweed, Comfrey, Dandelion, Flower pollen, Horsetail, Kelp, liquid trace minerals, Microalgae, Nettle, Oat, Parsley, Red clover, sea vegetables, Walnut, Watercress

Miscarriage, chronic: ***uterine restoratives:*** Birthroot, Blackhaw, Blue cohosh, Gravel root, Helonias, Lady's mantle, Lovage, Partridgeberry, {Placenta}, Raspberry, *Rose,* Sea holly, White deadnettle, Wild yam

   threatened: Artemisia Ai Ye, Blackhaw, Cramp bark, Dipsacus Xu Duan, Eucomia Du Zhong, Gravel root, Helonias, Lobelia, Partridgeberry, Raspberry, Scutellaria Huang Qin, Stoneroot, Vervain, Wild yam

Moniliasis (see Discharge, Infection, fungal)

Mononucleosis (see Fatigue, Fever, Infection, viral, Laryngitis, Lymphatic congestion, Spleen enlargement, other symptoms)

Morning sickness (see also remedies under Nausea): Blackhaw, Elecampane, Raspberry leaf, Wild yam

Motion sickness (same remedies as Nausea)

Mouth (see Candidiasis, Gingivitis, Glossitis, Periodontitis, Stomatitis, Ulcer)

MS (see Multiple sclerosis)

Mucous membrane (see Bronchitis, Croup, Discharge, Gastritis, Inflammation, Intestinal, Sinusitis, Ulcer)

Multiple sclerosis (MS) (see Autoimmune disorder, Depression, Infection, viral, Inflammation, Nervous debility, Stress, particular symptoms)

Mumps (see Infection, viral, particular symptoms)

Muscle spasm/cramp: ***striated-muscle relaxants:*** Black cohosh, Blackhaw, California poppy, *Camomile* (all types), Chastetree berry, Chickweed, Cramp bark, Jamaica dogwood, *Laurel, Lavender,* Lobelia, Magnolia Hou Po, *Marjoram,* Passionflower, Poplar bud, *Rosemary,* Siegesbeckia Xi Xian Cao, Stephania Han Fang Ji, St. John's wort, Valerian, Wild lettuce

   pain (same remedies as Fibromyalgia)

Muscular disorders (see Fibromyalgia, Muscle spasm, Muscular dystrophy, Paralysis)

Muscular dystrophy: Acanthopanax Wu Jia Pi, Comfrey, Eucomia Du Zhong, Horsetail, Nettle

Myalgic encephalitis (see Chronic fatigue syndrome)

Myocarditis (see Infection, bacterial/fungal/parasitic/viral, associated condition, symptoms)

Nausea: Aniseed, *Basil*, Blue flag, Cajeput, Calumba, Cornus Wu Zhu Yu, *Fennel*, Fieldmint, Fringe tree, *Ginger*, Iceland moss, Ipecac, Mayapple, *Melissa, Lavender, Peppermint, Pine,* Pinellia Ban Xia, Saussurea Yun Mu Xiang, *Spearmint*, Wood sorrel, Wormwood

Nephritis, acute (see also Albuminuria, Edema, Food allergy, Infection, Inflammation, Urinary): *anti-inflammatory diuretics:* Aconite*, Agrimony, Alisma Ze Xie, Arborvitae, Borage, Cranesbill, Comfrey, Figwort, Goldenrod, Gravel root, Helonias, Horsetail, Imperata Bai Mao Gen, Kelp, Lobelia Ban Bian Lian, Lovage, Marshmallow, Meadowsweet, Nettle, Oak bark, Pipsissewa, Sassafras, Squills, Thuja, Uva ursi, Wood sorrel, Wormwood, Yellow jessamine*

   chronic (see also Anuria, Edema, Hypertension, Urinary bleeding): *kidney-restorative diuretics:* Adonis, Alisma Ze Xie, Astragalus Huang Qi, Belladonna*, Blue cohosh, Borage, Buchu, Canada fleabane, Celery, Couchgrass, Dandelion, Elderflower/berry, Elecampane, Goldenrod, Gumweed, Horsetail, Hydrangea, Jaborandi, *Juniper*, Lily of the valley, Lovage, Meadowsweet, Mistletoe, Motherwort, *Myrrh*, Parsley, Pipsissewa, Plantain, {Royal jelly}, Squills, Tormentil, Yarrow

Nervous debility: *nervous restoratives* and *trophorestoratives:* American/Asian ginseng, Arnica, Bacopa, *Basil, Bergamot,* Bitter orange, Blue vervain, Brewer's yeast, *Camphor,* Cardamom, Cereus, *Clary sage,* Damiana, Eleuthero, Flower pollen, *Hyssop, Jasmine,* Lady's mantle, *Lemon,* Melissa, Microalgae, *Neroli,* Oat, *Palmarosa,* Pasqueflower, *Peppermint,* Polygonum He Shou Wu, Prickly ash, Rhodiola, *Rosemary,* {Royal jelly}, *Sage, Sandalwood,* Schisandra Wu Wei Zi, Sesame seed, Skullcap, *Spruce,* St. John's wort, Suma, *Tea tree, Thyme,* Valerian, Vervain, *Winter savory,* Wood betony

   depression (see Cerebral insufficiency, Nervous debility)

   tension (see also Anxiety, Food allergy): *nervous relaxants: Bergamot,* Biota Bai Zi Ren, Black cohosh, Black horehound, Brewer's yeast, California poppy, *Camomile* (all types), Catnip, *Clary sage,* Cowslip flower, *Geranium,* Hawthorn, Hops, Jasmine, Ladies' slipper, *Lavender,* Linden, *Mandarin, Marjoram,* Melilot, *Melissa, Myrtle, Neroli,* Passionflower, *Ravintsara, Rose,* Rue, *Sandalwood,* Scrophularia Xuan Shen, Skullcap, Tansy, Valerian, White pond lily, Wild lettuce, *Ylang ylang,* Yellow jessamine*, Zizyphus Suan Zao Ren

Nervous system disorders (see Autunomic nervous dysregulation, Cerebral, Chronic fatigue syndrome, Cramp, Hair loss, Insomnia, Meningitis, Nervous, Neuralgia, Neurasthenia, Neuritis, Neurocardiac syndrome, Neurogenic bladder, Parkinson's disease, Poliomyelitis, Seizure, Senility, Shingles, Spasm, Spinal disorder)

Nettle rash (see Hives)

Neuralgia, intercostal/sciatic: *nervous analgesics:* Aconite*, Arnica, Beet, Belladonne, Black cohosh, *Camomile* (all types), *Camphor,* Celery, Cereus, Clematis, Cowslip, *Eucalyptus,* Feverfew, Fieldmint, Hemlock spruce, Hops, Indian hemp, Ivy, Jamaica dogwood, Kava, Ladies' slipper, *Lavender,* Lobelia, *Marjoram,* Meadowsweet, Melilot, Oat, *Oregano,* Pasqueflower, *Peppermint,* Poke root, Poppy, Prickly ash, Rue, Siegesbeckia Xi Xian Cao, Skullcap, Stramonium*, St. John's wort, Tansy, Tribulus Bai Ji Li, *Turpentine,* Valerian, Vervain, Wild yam, Willow, *Winter savory,* Wood betony, Wormwood, Yellow jessamine*

   trigeminal/facial: *nervous analgesics:* Aconite*, *Camomile* (all types), Feverfew, *Geranium,* Hops, Jamaica dogwood, Kalmia, Meadowsweet, Pasqueflower, *Peppermint,* Skullcap, Stavesacre, Stramonium*, Typhonium Bai Fu Zi, Vervain, White bryony, Wild yam, Wintergreen, Wood betony, Yellow jessamine*

Neurasthenia (see Nervous debility)

Neuritis (see Neuralgia, remedies under Infection, Metabolic disorder, Nervous debility, Toxicosis, heavy metal)

Neurocardiac syndrome (see also Palpitations, Anxiety): *neurocardiac relaxants:* Arnica, Black cohosh, Blackhaw, Bugleweed, California poppy, Cereus, Corn poppy, Cramp bark, Hawthorn, Hops, *Marjoram, Melissa,* Mistletoe, Motherwort, Pasqueflower, Passionflower, Scrophularia Xuan Shen, *Ylang ylang,* Zizyphus Suan Zao Ren

Neuroendocrine deficiency (see *neuroendocrine restoratives,* p. 260)

Neurogenic bladder (see Urinary incontinence/obstruction, associated condition)

Neurovegetative dystonia (same remedies as Nervous tension)

Nicotine addiction (see Circulation, insufficient arterial/capillary, Cough, Liver toxicosis, Nervous debility/tension): Eyebright, Garlic, Kelp, Watercress

Night sweat (same remedies as Perspiration, excessive)

Nipples, cracked (topically): Aloe gel, Benzoin, Cabbage, *Cedarwood*, Comfrey, *Geranium*, Mallow, Marigold, olive oil, *Patchouli*, Plantain, Red clover, *Rose, Rosewood, Sandalwood, Vetiver,* Yarrow

Nonspecific genitourinary infection (see Discharge, Infection, bacterial/viral, other symptoms)

Nosebleed (see also Blood pressure, high, Dehydration): *hemostatics:* Canada fleabane, Cattail pollen, *Cypress, Geranium,* Goldenseal, Horsetail, Milk thistle, Mistletoe, Red grapevine, Shepherd's purse, *Turpentine,* Witch hazel, Wood betony, Yarrow

Numbness of extremities (see Arteriosclerosis, Circulation, insufficient)

Nutritional deficiency (see Anemia, Malabsorption syndrome)

Nymphomania (see Sexual overstimulation)

Obesity (see associated conditions, Weight gain)

Obsessive-compulsive disorder (same remedies as Anxiety state)

Oligomenorrhea (see Menstruation, scanty)

Oliguria (see Urinary obstruction/scantyness)

Ophthalmia (see Eye)

Osteoporosis (see Menstruation, absent, Connective tissue deficiency, Metabolic acidosis, Mineral depletion, *estrogen stimulants, progesterone stimulants,* p. 783)

Otitis media (see Ear)

Ovarian cysts (see also *progesterone stimulants,* p. 783): Blue flag, Burdock, Butcher's broom, Chastetree, Cleavers, Cotton root bark, *Cypress,* Dong quai, Lady's mantle, Marigold, Mistletoe, Ocotillo, Partridgeberry, Pipsissewa, Poke, Red root, Saw palmetto, Yellow dock

Ovarian pain (see also Dysmenorrhea, spasmodic, Pain, Polycystic ovarian syndrome): *uterine analgesics:* Black cohosh, Blackhaw, Bupleurum, Cramp bark, Melilot, Pasqueflower, White peony, Wild yam, Yellow pond lily

Ovaries (see Dysmenorrhea, Menstruation, Ovarian cysts, Ovarian pain, *estrogen stimulants,* p. 783)

Overweight (see Weight gain)

Ozena (see Rhinitis, Infection, viral)

Pain (see also organ or part affected): *analgesics:* Black cohosh, Blackcurrant oil, Borage seed oil, Bupleurum Chai Hu, *Camomile* (all types), Corydalis Yan Hu Suo, Evening primrose oil, Feverfew, Flaxseed oil, Henbane*, Hops, Jamaica dogwood, *Lavender, Marjoram,* Meadowsweet, *Melissa,* Mistletoe, Passionflower, Siegesbeckia Xi Xian Cao, Stephania Jin Bu Huan, White bryony, Wild lettuce, Willow, Yellow jessamine*

Palpitations: Adonis, *Aniseed,* Arnica, Black cohosh, Blackhaw, Black horehound, Bugleweed, Cereus, Cherry laurel, Cowslip flower, Elder bark, Gumweed, Heartsease, Indian *spikenard,* Inmortal, *Lavender,* Ligusticum Chuan Xiong, Linden, Lobelia, *Mandarin, Marjoram, Melissa,* Mistletoe, Motherwort, *Neroli,* Oat, *Palmarosa,* Pasqueflower, Passionflower, Polygonatum Yu Zhu, Skullcap, Squills, Stoneroot, White horehound, Wild cherry, Valerian, Yarrow, *Ylang ylang,* Zizyphus Suan Zao Ren

Pancreas disorders (see Diabetes, Digestive enzyme deficiency, Hyperglycemia, Hypoglycemia, Pancreatitis)

Pancreatitis (see Drug addiction, Hyperlipidemia, Infection, viral, Weight gain)

Papilloma (see Wart)

Paralysis: Arisaema Tian Nan Xing, Arnica, Cabbage, Cayenne, Chasteberry, Feverfew, Ginseng (all types), Heather, Lily of the valley, Lobelia, Nux vomica, Oat, Prickly ash, *Sage,* Scurvy grass, St. Ignatius bean, St. John's wort, Strychnos Zhi Ma Qian Zi, Typhonium Bai Fu Zi, Tansy, Vervain, Wood betony

Parasites, skin (also topically; see also Infection, fungal): Aloe gel, *Camphor,* Chaulmoogra seed, Cinnamon, Clove, Cnidium She Chuang Zi, Cranesbill, *Eucalyptus, Geranium,* Hibiscus Mu Jin Pi, *Juniper, Lavender, Lemon,* Parsley seed, *Patchouli, Pine,* Sophora Ku Shen, Stemona Bai Bu, *Thyme, Turpentine*
 intestinal (see Infection, parasitic)

Paresthesia (see Numbness)

Parkinson's disease (see Nervous debility, Seizure, Spasm)

Pediculosis (see Parasites, skin, Skin itching)

Pelvic congestion (see Dysmenorrhea, congestive)

Pelvic inflammatory disease (PID) (see also Discharge, Infection, bacterial, Inflammation): Bilberry, Black cohosh, *Blue tansy,* Bupleurum, *Camomile,* Coptis Huang Lian, *Cypress,* Goldenseal, Heartsease, Horsetail, Lady's mantle, *Lemon,* Marigold, Melilot, Oldenlandia Bai Hua She She Cao, Plantain, *Rose,* Witch hazel, Yellow dock

Pericarditis (see Myocarditis)

Periodontitis (same remedies as Gingivitis; see also Connective tissue degeneration, Infection)

Periods (see Dysmenorrhea, Menstruation)

Periostitis (see also Inflammation): Horsetail, Poke root, Queen's root

Peripheral arterial deficiency: Echinacea, Ginkgo, *Lavender,* Ligusticum Chuan Xiong, Lily of the valley, Linden, Lobelia, Marigold, Motherwort, Melissa, Pasqueflower, Salvia Dan Shen

Perspiration, excessive (see also Nervous tension, related condition): *anhydrotics:* Avens, Bittersweet, *Camphor,* Cornus Shan Zhu Yu, Cranesbill, *Cypress,* Elecampane, Ephedra Ma Huang Gen, *Eucalyptus,* Foxglove, *Geranium,* Goldenseal, Hops, Horsetail, *Hyssop,* Nettle, Oak leaf/bark, Onion, *Pine, Sage,* Schisandra Wu Wei Zi, Strawberry, Sumac, Walnut, Wood betony

  insufficient: *diaphoretics:* Bittersweet, *Camomile* (all types), Catnip, Elderflower, *Eucalyptus,* Fieldmint, Ginger, *Hyssop,* Inmortal, *Lavender,* Ligusticum Chuan Xiong, Lindenflower, *Peppermint, Spearmint,* Yarrow

Pharyngitis (same remedies as Laryngitis)

Phlebitis (see also Inflammation, Thrombosis): Belladonna*, Bilberry, Biota Ce Bai Ye, Black cohosh, *Cypress, Eucalyptus citriodora,* Goldenrod, Goldenseal, Heartsease, *Helichrysum,* Horsechestnut, *Lemon,* Marigold, Milkthistle, Red grapevine, *Rose,* Sophora Huai Hua, Willow, Witch hazel, Yarrow

Phobia (see Anxiety state)

Pinworm (see Parasites)

Pituitary disorders (see Development, children's slow, *thyrotropic growth hormone stimulants,* p. 783)

Pityriasis rosea (see Autoimmune disorder, Infection, viral, Inflammation, Skin eruption/itching)

Placenta, retained (see *stimulant parturients,* Class 16)

Pleurisy (pleuritis) (see also Asthma, Inflammation, specific disease/condition involved): Black cohosh, Black horehound, Hellebore*, Lobelia, Pleurisy root, Skunk cabbage, Spurge, White bryony, Yellow jessamine*

PMS (see also Anxiety, Edema, Fatigue, Headache, Menstruation, Nervous tension, other symptoms, estrogen/ *progesterone stimulants,* p. 783): *Angelica,* Angelica Dang Gui, Black cohosh, Blackcurrant oil, Blue cohosh, Borage seed oil, *Camomile* (all types), *Chasteberry, Clary sage,* Cyperus Xiang Fu, Damiana, Dong quai, Elecampane, Evening primrose oil, Flaxseed oil, *Geranium,* Helonias, Ligusticum Chuan Xiong, *Marjoram,* Mugwort, *Rose,* Saw palmetto, *Vetiver,* Wild yam root

Pneumonia (see Bronchitis, Fever, Infection, bacterial/fungal/viral)

Poison oak/ivy rash (see Skin inflammation)

Poisoning, food/herb (see also Infection, bacterial Toxicosis, microbial, Vomiting): Agastache Huo Xiang, Angelica, Areca Da Fu Pi, Arnica, *Black pepper,* Burdock, *Camphor,* Dolichos Bai Bian Dou, Echinacea, Elsholtzia Xiang Ru, *Fennel,* Garlic, *Geranium, Ginger,* Horseradish, Jamaica sarsaparilla, *Juniper, Lavender, Lemon,* Licorice, Lobelia, *Myrrh, Pine,* Raphanus Lai Fu Zi, *Tea tree,* Tormentil, Valerian, Virginia snakeroot, Wild indigo, Wormwood

  chemical (see Toxicosis, chemical)

  heavy metal (see Toxicosis, heavy metal)

Poliomyelitis (see Infection, viral, Inflammation, Paralysis): Arnica, *Clove,* Strychnos Zhi Ma Qian Zi

Polycystic ovarian syndrome (PCOS): (see Hyperinsulinemia, *progesteronics,* p. 783, *testosterone inhibitors,* p. 780, associated conditions and symptoms)

Polyps, nasal: Common ivy leaf

Portal congestion (see also Circulation, insufficient venous, Liver congestion, Pelvic congestion): *portal decongestants:* Barberry, Blackcurrant, Butternut, Chaparral, Coptis Huang Lian, Dandelion, Fringe tree, Gardenia Zhi Zi, Goldenseal, Horsechestnut, *Lemon,* Madder, Marigold, Ocotillo, Red root, Rhubarb,

Stoneroot, Wood sorrel, Yellow dock

Postpartum disorders (see Anxiety states, Appetite loss, Cerebral insufficiency, Depression, Fatigue, Insomnia, Nervous tension, Weight gain/loss, other conditions/symptoms)

Posttraumatic stress disorder (see Anxiety states, Cerebral insufficiency, Nervous tension, other symptoms)

PPD (see Postpartum disorders)

Premature ejaculation (see Discharge, Nervous tension, Sexual overstimulation)

Premenstrual syndrome (see PMS)

Prickly heat (see Dermatitis)

Progesterone deficiency/accumulation (see *progesterone stimulants/inhibitors,* p. 783)

Progressive systemic sclerosis (see Circulation, insufficienct arterial/capillary, Connective tissue deficiency, Intestinal dysbiosis, symptoms)

Prolapse, visceral (see also Connective tissue deficiency): Arborvitae, Bayberry, Bilberry, Birthroot, *Black pepper,* Burdock, Canada fleabane, Chaparral, Cimicifuga Sheng Ma, Golden ragwort, Helonias, Kava, Nettle, Oak bark, Raspberry leaf, Stoneroot, Sumac, Tiger lily, Tormentil, Thuja, Walnut, White pond lily, Witch hazel

Prostate congestion/enlargement/hyperplasia (see also Circulation, insufficient venous, Urinary): *prostate decongestants*: Arborvitae, Asparagus, Birth root, Blackcurrant, Buchu, Cereus, Cleavers, *Cypress,* Flower pollen, Garlic, Golden ragwort, Goldenrod, Goldenseal, Gravel root, Heather, Helonias, Horsechestnut, Hydrangea, Kava, Mistletoe, *Myrtle,* Nettle root, *Niaouli,* Ocotillo, Parsley seed, Partridgeberry, Pipsissewa, Poplar, Pumkin seed, Saw palmetto, Speedwell, Spruce, Stavesacre, Thuja, Uva ursi, Vaccaria Wang Bu Liu Xing, White pond lily, Wintergreen, Witch hazel

Prostatitis (see Prostate, congested, Inflammation, Infection, Urinary deposits)

Pruritus (see Skin itching)

vaginal: *Bergamot,* Bittersweet, *Blue tansy,* Chickweed, Gentiana Long Dan Cao, *Geranium, German Camomile,* Heartsease, Helonias, Kava, knotgrass, Lady's mantle, *Lavender,* Mullein, *Palmarosa, Rose, Rosewood,* Scabious, Sophora Ku Shen, Watercress

Psoriasis (see Autoimmune disorder, Free radical burden, Infection, Nervous tension, Skin eruption, Toxicosis, chemical/microbial)

Psychosis (see Nervous tension, Toxicosis, metabolic)

Purpura, allergic (see Allergy, Autoimmune disorder, Food allergy, Infection, bacterial, Toxicosis, associated condition, symptoms)

Pyelitis (see Nephritis)

Pyorrhea (see Stomatitis, Periodontitis)

Rabies (see Fever, Infection, viral, Lymphatic congestion, Spasm)

Radiation sickness (see Toxicosis, radiation)

Rashes (see Fever, eruptive, Skin eruption)

Raynaud's disease (see Circulation, insufficient arterial/capillary, Nervous tension, Spasm, *vasodilators,* associated condition, other symptoms)

Respiratory disorders (see Asthma, Bronchitis, Emphysema, Laryngitis, Pleurisy, Pneumonia, Silicosis, TB, Whooping cough)

Rheumatism (see Arthritis, Bursitis, Fibromyalgia)

Rheumatic fever (see Fever, Infection, bacterial, Inflammation, Pain)

Rhinitis (see also Allergy, Food allergy, Infection, Stress): *mucostatics:* Agrimony, Arborvitae, Bayberry, Bittersweet, Calamus, *Camphor,* Cowslip flower, Elderflower, Ephedra Ma Huang, Eyebright, Goldenrod, *Laurel, Lemon,* Lungwort lichen, Magnolia Xin Yi Hua, Mullein, *Niaouli,* Oat, Oshá, Pillbearing spurge, Plantain, *Ravintsara, Sage, Thyme, Turpentine,* Wild cherry, Xanthium Cang Er Zi, Yarrow, Yerba santa, Yerba mansa

Rickets (see Malabsorption, Metabolic disorder, Mineral depletion, particular symptoms)

Ringworm (also topically; see Infection, fungal)

Rosacea (see Acne, Food intolerance, Gastric hypoacidity)

Roundworm (see Parasites, skin)

Salmonellosis (Gastroenteritis, acute, Intestinal colic, Vomiting)

Satyriasis (see Sexual overstimulation)

Scabies (see Parasites, skin)

Scalp conditions (see Hair loss)

Scar tissue (topically): Arborvitae, Foraha oil, *Geranium, Patchouli,* Rose hip seed oil, *Spearmint,* Thuja

Scarlet fever (see Eruptive fever, Infection, bacterial, symptoms)

Schizophrenia (see Cerebral insufficiency, Depression, Fatigue, Nervous tension, Toxicosis, heavy metal)

Sciatica (see Neuralgia)

Scrofula (see Lymphatic congestion, Tuberculosis)

Scurvy (see also anemia, fatigue, Hemorrhage, Stomatitis): Acerola cherry, Aloe gel, Asparagus, Barley grass, Cabbage, Celery, Garlic, Hops, Horseradish, *Lemon,* Onion, Orange, Papaya, Pumpkin seed, Raspberry leaf, Rose hip, Scurvygrass, Shepherd's purse, Watercress, Wheatgrass, Yellow dock

Seizure (see also Arteriosclerosis, Food allergy, Hypoglycemia, Infection, Toxicosis, heavy metal): Adonis, Arisaema Tian Nan Xing, Asafoetida, *Basil,* Belladonna*, Black cohosh, Black nightshade, Box, Cereus, Coleus, Cowslip, *Clary sage,* Cramp bark, Duboisia, Feverfew, Gastrodia Tian Ma, Hellebore*, Hemlock* (all types), Henbane*, Hops, Jamaica dogwood, Ladies' slipper, *Lavender,* Lily of the valley, Linden, Lobelia, *Marjoram,* Mistletoe, Mugwort, Olive oil, Passionflower, Rue, Skunk cabbage, Stone-root, Stramonium*, Tansy, Uncaria Gou Teng, Valerian, Wormwood, Yellow jessamine*

Senility (premature) (see Anemia, Cerebral insufficiency, Free radical burden, Immune deficiency)

Septicemia (see also Boils, Fever, Infection): ***anti-infectives:*** Coptis Huang Lian, Echinacea, Goldenseal, Plantain, Scutellaria Huang Qin, Sophora Ku Shen, Wild indigo

Sexual overstimulation: Anemarrhena Zhi Mu, Bittersweet, *Camphor,* Chasteberry, Hops, *Marjoram, Myrrh, Oregano,* Phellodendron Huang Bai, Purslane, *Roman camomile, Sage,* Skullcap, Valerian, White pond lily, Wild lettuce, Willow (all types)

Shingles (also topically; see also Immune deficiency, Infection, viral, Nervous debility): Aconite*, *Basil, Camomile,* Clove, Hops, Lobelia, Motherwort, *Peppermint, Ravintsara,* Red clover, Rue, *Sage,* Skullcap, St. John's wort, Tansy, *Thyme,* Tribulus Bai Ji Li, Wood betony

Shock (same remedies as Coma, Heart failure, congestive)

Silicosis (see also Asthma, Bronchitis): Horsetail, Iceland moss, Nettle, Oshá

Sinusitis (see also Allergy, Cold, common, Food allergy, Stress): Angelica, Angelica Bai Zhi Asarum Xi Xin, *Basil,* Bayberry, Bloodroot, Cajeput, Calamus, *Camomile, Camphor, Cardamom,* Catnip, Clove, Elderflower, *Eucalyptus,* Eyebright, *Fir* (all types), *Hyssop, Laurel, Lavender,* Lungwort lichen, Magnolia Xin Yi Hua, *Myrtle, Niaouli, Peppermint, Pine,* Prickly ash, *Ravintsara, Rosemary,* Skunk cabbage, *Tea tree, Thyme, Turpentine,* Watercress, Wheatgrass, White horehound, Wild ginger, Wild indigo, Xanthium Cang Er Zi, Yerba mansa

Sjögren's syndrome (see Autoimmune disorder, Connective tissue deficiency, associated condition, symptoms)

Skin eruption (also topically; see also Allergy, Dermatitis, Food allergy, Hypochlorhydria, Liver congestion, Toxicosis, microbial/ metabolic, Stress): ***detoxicants:*** *Birch,* Bittersweet, Blackcurrant (oil), Black nightshade, Blue flag, Bogbean, Borage seed oil, Brewer's yeast, Burdock, Butterbur, Butternut, Celandine, Chaparral, Chicory, Cleavers, Coleus, Couchgrass, Dandelion, Echinacea, Elecampane, Evening primrose oil, Figwort, Flaxseed oil, Fumitory, *Geranium,* Goldenrod, Gotu kola, Guaiacum, Gumweed, Heartsease, Herb patience, Hops, Horseradish, Jamaica sarsaparilla, Juniper, Kelp, Knotgrass, *Lemon,* Lithospermum Zi Cao, Marigold, Microalgae, Mullein, Nettle, Oat, Oregon grape, *Palmarosa,* Pau d'arco, Pipsissewa, Plantain, Poke root, Queen's root, Red clover, {Royal jelly}, Rue, Sassafras, Scabious, Scurvy grass, Smilax Tu Fu Ling, Soapwort, Solanum Long Kui, Sophora Ku Shen, Speedwell, Walnut, Water-cress, Wheatgrass, White horehound, Wild yam, Yellow dock

inflammation (also topically; see also Allergy): ***anti-inflammatories:*** Aloe gel, Arnica, Barberry, Birch, Bilberry, Bittersweet, Blue flag, *Blue tansy,* Bogbean, Burdock, *Camomile* (all types), *Camphor,* Catnip, Chickweed, Echinacea, Fieldmint, Figwort, Goldenseal, Gotu kola, Gumweed, Heartsease, Hops, Jamaica sarsaparilla, *Lavender,* Licorice, Lobelia, Marigold, Marshmallow, Meadowsweet, Melilot, *Patchouli,* Plantain, Poplar bud, *Rose, Sandalwood,* Selfheal, Sophora Ku Shen, St. John's wort, Uva ursi, White pond lily, Willow

itching/pruritus (also topically; see also Eczema, Infection, Food allergy, Liver congestion, Metabolic alkalosis, Parasites): ***antipruritics:*** Blackcurrant oil, Borage oil, Burdock, *Camomile* (blue types), *Cedarwood*, Dictamnus Bai Xian Pi, Elecampane, Evening primrose oil, Fieldmint, *Geranium*, Heartsease, *Jasmine,* Knotgrass, *Lavender, Niaouli, Peppermint,* Queen's root, *Rosewood, Sandalwood,* Scabious, Soapwort, Sophora Ku Shen, Thuja, *Thyme,* Xanthium Cang Er Zi, Yarrow, Yellow jessamine*

Skin, chapped/cracked (same remedies as Skin inflammation)

Skincare, general (topically): Aloe gel, *Bergamot,* Calamus, *Cedarwood,* Celandine, Chickweed, *Cypress, Fennel, Geranium,* Hops, Horsechestnut, *Lavender,* Lovage, Nettle, *Niaouli, Palmarosa,* Plantain, Poplar bud, *Rose, Sandalwood,* Scabious, Walnut, Witch hazel

Sleep disorder (see Cerebral insufficiency, Insomnia)

Smoking addiction (see Nicotine addiction)

Snakebite (see also remedies under Infections, chronic): Arnica, Belamcanda She Gan, Birthwort, Black cohosh, Burdock, Chaparral, Cocculus Mu Fang Ji, Echinacea, Garlic, *Lavender,* Lobelia, Oldenlandia Bai Hua She She Cao, Pau d'arco, Plantain, Skullcap, Solanum Long Kui, *Tea tree,* Virginia/Texas snakeroot, Wikstroemia Liao Ge Wang, Wild indigo

Snoring: *Marjoram*

Sore (see Bedsore, Infection, fungal, Stomatitis, Wound)

Sore throat (see Laryngitis, Toxicosis)

Spasm: *spasmolytics:* Angelica, Arisaema Tian Nan Xing, Asafoetida, *Basil,* Black cohosh, Blackhaw, Calamint, *Camphor,* Catnip, *Camomile,* Cowslip, Gatsrodia Tian Ma, Hops, *Hyssop,* Jamaica dogwood, *Laurel, Lavender, Lime,* Linden, Lobelia, *Marjoram,* Melilot, *Melissa, Myrrh, Neroli,* Passion-flower, *Sage,* Skullcap, Stoneroot, Uncaria Gou Teng, Valerian, Wild yam, Willow, Yarrow, Yellow jessamine*

Sperm, insufficient/incompetent: Alfalfa, Aniseed, Asparagus, Celery, *Fennel,* Ginseng (all types), Iceland moss, Muira puama, Nettle, Oat, Polygonum He Shou Wu, Purslane, *Rose,* Saw Palmetto, Sesame seed

Spermatorrhea (see Discharge)

Spinal disorders: Horsetail, Poke root, Skullcap, St. John's wort, Valerian, Walnut

Spleen congestion: *spleen decongestants:* Asparagus, Barberry, Butternut, Chicory, Citrus Qing Pi, Couchgrass, Culver's root, Dandelion, *Fennel,* Fringe tree, Mayapple, Mullein, Nettle, Oak bark, Red root, Speedwell, Wormwood

　enlargement: Bogbean, Citrus Qing Pi, Cucumis Tian Gua Di, Fringe tree, Grindelia squarrosa, *Lavender,* Nettle, Red root, White deadnettle, Wormwood

Spleen disorders (see Allergy, Anemia, Edema, Infections, chronic, Spleen congestion)

Sprain, strain (see Contusion, Wound, acute)

Sting (see Bite)

Stomach (see Epigastric fullness, Gastric, Gastritis, Indigestion, Nausea)

Stomatitis, acute herpetic (see Fever, Infection, viral, and remedies under Gingivitis)

　aphthous (see Food allergy, Anxiety state, Fatigue, Fever)

Stone (see Gallstone, Urinary stone)

Strangury (see Urinary obstruction)

Strep throat (see Infection, bacterial, Lymphatic congestion, particular symptoms)

Stress (same remedies as Anxiety states, Nervous tension; see also particular symptoms)

Stretch marks (same remedies as Scar tissue)

Stroke (see Cerebral insufficiency, Circulation, insufficient capillary, Hemorrhage, Hyperlipidemia, Seizure, Thrombosis, associated condition, symptoms)

Stye (same remedies as Boil; topically see Eye infection)

Sunburn (see Burn)

Sunstroke (see Heat syndrome)

Sweating (see Perspiration)

Syphilis (see also Chancroid, Infection, bacterial/fungal, Lymphatic congestion): Arborvitae, Bittersweet, Box, Blue flag, Burdock, Celandine, Condurango, Echinacea, Guaiacum, Ivy, Jamaica sarsaparilla, Marigold, Mayapple, Plantain, Poke root, Queen's root, Red clover, Smilax Tu Fu Ling, Sophora Ku Shen, Thuja, Turkey corn, Usnea, Yellow dock

Tachycardia: *cardiac relaxants/regulators:* Aconite*, Adonis, Aniseed, Black cohosh, Bugleweed, Cereus, Hawthorn, Hellebore*, Indian spikenard, Ladies' slipper, *Lavender*, Lobelia, *Marjoram, Melissa,* Mistletoe, Passionflower, Polygala Yuan Zhi, Scrophularia Xuan Shen, Strophanthus, Valerian, Yellow jessamine, *Ylang ylang*

Tapeworm (see Intestinal parasites)

TB, lung (see Cough, Dehydration, Infection, bacterial/fungal, Fatigue, Weight loss)

Teething pain (same remedies as Nervous tension)

Tendinitis (same remedies as Bursitis)

Tennis elbow (same remedies as Bursitis)

Testosterone deficiency (see *androgen/testosterone stimulants,* p. 780)

Threadworms (see Intestinal parasites)

Throat (see Laryngitis, Voice loss)

Thrombophlebitis (see Phlebitis)

Thrombosis (see Hematoma)

Thrush (see Infection, fungal)

Thymus deficiency (see Allergy, Asthma, Immune deficiency, Infections, chronic)

Thyroid disorders (see *thyroid stimulants/inhibitors,* p. 783; see also Cerebral insufficiency, Circulation, Depression, mental, Goiter, Hyperlipidemia, Hyperthyroid, Hypoglycemia, Hypothyroid, Menstruation, Muscular disorders, Weight gain)

Tinea versicolor (see Infection, fungal)

Tinnitus (see Ear)

TMJ (same remedies as Nervous tension)

Tonsillitis (see Infection, bacterial/viral, Infection, chronic, Inflammation, Lymphatic congestion, particular symptoms)

Toothache (topical swab): *Camphor,* Cayenne, *Clove, Fir, Hyssop, Juniper, Peppermint, Pine,* Prickly ash, *Rosemary,* Sassafras, *Spruce, Thyme*

(internally): Angelica Bai Zhi, Asarum Xi Xin, *Juniper, Laurel,* Pasqueflower, Prickly ash, Virginia snakeroot

Toxicosis (for all types see also Free radical burden, Immune deficiency, Liver toxicosis): *detoxicants/ depuratives:*

heavy metal (see also remedies under Cerebral insufficiency, Nervous deficiency, other conditions/ symptoms): Bladderwrack, Chaparral, Charcoal, fermented foods, Flower pollen, Garlic, Ground ivy, Jamaica sarsaparilla, *Juniper,* Kelp, Lecithin, Microalgae, Miso, Nettle, Nutritional yeast, pectin-rich foods, Red clover, seaweeds, Selfheal, Smilax Tu Fu Ling, Wheatgrass, Wood sorrel

chemical (see also remedies under Cerebral insufficiency, Nervous deficiency, Impotence, Sperm, insufficient/incompetent, Toxicosis, microbial and other conditions/symptoms): Alfalfa, Artichoke, Buckwheat, Chaparral, Charcoal, Dandelion, Eclipta Han Lian Cao, Eleuthero, fermented foods, Flower pollen, Ginseng (all types), Gotu kola, Gumweed, Kelp, Lecithin, Licorice, Ligustrum Nu Zhen Zi, Micro-algae, Milk thistle seed/leaf/flower, Millet, Miso, Nutritional yeast, Oat, Polygonum He Shou Wu, *Sage,* Salvia Dan Shen, seaweeds, Sesame seed, Skullcap, St. John's wort, Turmeric

metabolic (see also remedies under Arthritis): Acanthopanax Wu Jia Pi, Alfalfa, Asparagus, Birch, Blackcurrant, Blue cohosh, Broom, Burdock, Cascara sagrada, Celery, Chaparral, Clubmoss, Dandelion, Figwort, Flower pollen, Fumitory, Garlic, Germander, Heartsease, Horsetail, Hydrangea, Jamaica sarsaparilla, *Juniper,* Knotgrass, Meadowsweet, Microalgae, Nettle, Papaya, Parsley, Pipsissewa, Poke root, Red clover, Selfheal, Soapwort, Walnut leaf, Water pepper, White horehound, Yellow dock

microbial: Aloe resin, Areca Bing Lang / Da Fu Pi, Atractylodes Cang Zhu, Bloodroot, Butternut, Calamus, Chaparral, Cinnamon, Clove, Echinacea, *Eucalyptus,* fermented foods, Garlic, Goldenseal, Horseradish, *Hyssop, Juniper, Lactobacillus acidophilus/bifidus,* Miso, *Myrrh, Palmarosa,* Pasqueflower, {Propolis}, Raphanus Lai Fu Zi, *Ravintsara,* Rue, Sassafras, Scurvy grass, Sophora Ku Shen, *Spruce, Tea tree, Thyme,* Watercress, Wheatgrass, *Winter savory*

radiation (see also remedies under Infections, chronic, Toxicosis, chemical): Alfalfa, Aloe gel, Asian ginseng, Beet, Bladderwrack, Buckwheat, {Bufo Chan Su}, Charcoal, chlorophyll plants, Eleuthero, fermented foods, Flower pollen, Ganoderma Ling Zhi, Garlic, Goldenrod, Kelp, *Lavender,* Lecithin, Ligusticum Chuan Xiong, Liquid trace minerals, Microalgae, Millet, Miso, *Niaouli,* Olive oil, Peanut oil, pectin-rich foods, Rehmannia Shu Di Huang, Reishi, seaweeds, Sophora Ku Shen, St. John's wort, Tea (black, green), *Tea tree*

Travel sickness (same remedies as Nausea)

Tremor (see Seizure, Spasm)

Trichomoniasis (see Discharge, Infection, parasitic, Menstruation, Urination)

Tuberculosis, lung (see TB, lung)

Tumors (see also Immune deficiency): ***antitumorals:*** Alfalfa, Aloe resin, Arborvitae, Bittersweet, Bladder-wrack, Bloodroot, Blue flag, Blue violet, Burdock, *Camomile*, Celandine, Chaparral, Chickweed, Cleavers, Clove, Coconut oil, Echinacea, Figwort, Flower pollen, Garlic, *Geranium,* Goldenseal, Green tea, Hearts-ease, Horsetail, Kelp, *Lemon,* Licorice, Lily of the valley, Maitake, Marigold, Mayapple, Microalgae, Mistletoe, Nettle, Ocotillo, Oldenlandia Bai Hua She She Cao, Periwinkle, Pipsissewa, Poke root, {Propolis}, Queen's root, Red clover, Rhodiola, Rhubarb, Salvia Dan Shen, Scutellaria Ban Zhi Lian, Shiitake, Soapwort, Solanum Bai Ying, Sophora Ku Shen, Sophora Shan Dou Gen, Suma, Tansy, Thuja, *Turmeric,* Violet, Walnut, Water pepper, Wheatgrass, Wormwood, Yellow dock

Typhoid fever (see Fever, Headache, Infection, Intestinal colic)

Typhus (see Fatigue, Fever, Infection, bacterial/viral, Infections, chronic)

Ulcer, mouth/throat/genital/corneal (topically; see also associated condition): ***tissue-healing astringents:*** Agrimony, Arborvitae, Bilberry, Bistort, Blackberry, Bletilla Bai Ji, Cattail pollen, Cistus, Eyebright, *Geranium*, Goldenseal, Great burnet, Horsetail, Knotgrass, Lemon, Licorice, Lithospermum Zi Cao, Loosestrife, Marigold, Marshmallow, Microalgae, Mousear, *Myrrh,* Nettle, Oak, Pau d'arco, Plantain, Poke root, Pond lily, Raspberry, Red grapevine, Red root, *Rose, Sage,* Sanicle, Selfheal, Sumac, *Tea tree,* Thuja, Tormentil, Usnea, Walnut, Wheatgrass, Wild indigo, Willow, Witch hazel, Wood sorrel, Yarrow, Yellow dock, Yerba mansa

duodenal/peptic (see Gastric ulcer)

skin/leg/varicose (see Varicose veins, Wound, atonic)

Ulcerative colitis (see Inflammatory bowel disease)

Underweight (see Weight loss)

Iric acid diathesis (see Hyperuricemia)

Urinary bleeding: ***urinary hemostatics:*** Agrimony, Birthroot, Blackberry, Broom, Comfrey, Couchgrass, Cranesbill, *Cypress, Geranium*, Golden ragwort, Goldenseal, Great burnet, Heather, Hedge hyssop, Helonias, Horsetail, Ipecac, *Juniper*, Knotgrass, Lungwort, Lygodium Hai Jin Sha Teng, Madder, Marigold, Milk thistle, Mullein, Nettle, Oak bark, Plantain, Pyrrosia Shi Wei, *Sage,* Shepherd's purse, Strawberry leaf/root, Sumac, Turpentine, Uva ursi, Vervain, Wintergreen, Witch hazel, Yarrow

deposits (sand, gravel, stones): ***urinary dissolvants, antilithics:*** Agrimony, Artichoke, Ash, Asparagus, Bilberry, Birch, Blackcurrant, Burdock, Butcher's broom, Calamus, Celery, Chaparral, Cherry stalk, Chicory, Cleavers, Cornsilk, Couchgrass, Cowslip root, Dandelion, Desmodium Guang Dong Jin Qian Cao, Eyebright, Flower pollen, Fringe tree, Garlic, *Geranium,* Goldenrod, Gravel root, Hawthorn, Heartsease, Heather, Hops, Horsetail, Hydrangea, *Hyssop,* Jamaica sarsaparilla, *Juniper,* Khella, Knotgrass, *Lemon,* Lysimachia Jin Qian Cao, Madder, Meadowsweet, Microalgae, Mugwort, Nettle, Parsley, Parsley piert, Pellitory of the wall, Pipsissewa, Restharrow, Sassafras, Speedwell, St. John's wort, Strawberry, Tormentil, *Turpentine,* Uva ursi, Valerian, Vervain, Watercress, White oak, Wild carrot, Yellow dock

discharge (see Discharge)

incontinence: ***antienuretics:*** Agrimony, Arborvitae, Asparagus, Black horehound, Buchu, Celery, Chaparral, Cornsilk, Cornus Shan Zhu Yu, Cowslip, Cranesbill, Cuscuta Tu Si Zi, *Cypress,* Damiana, Dioscorea Bi Xie, Euryale Qian Shi, *Fennel,* Gravel root, Heartsease, Helonias, Horsetail, *Juniper,* Kava, Madder, Meadowsweet, Nettle, Nux vomica, Parsley root, Pipsissewa, Poplar, Sea holly, Silver birch, Sumac, Tormentil, Uva ursi, White deadnettle, Wild carrot

infection (see also Infection, bacterial/viral, Food allergy): ***urinary antiseptics:*** Agrimony, Akebia Bai Mu Tong, Alisma Ze Xie, Arborvitae, Bilberry, Bladderwrack, Blue flag, Buchu, Canada fleabane, Celery, Chickweed, Cleavers, Clove, Comfrey, Cornsilk, Couchgrass, Damiana, Dianthus Qu Mai, Elderflower, *Eucalyptus,* Goldenrod, Gravel root, Heather, Horsetail, Hydrangea, *Juniper,* Kava, Kelp, Knotgrass,

Lady's mantle, Meadowsweet, Melilot, Mugwort, Mullein, Nettle, *Niaouli*, Ocotillo, *Palma-rosa*, Parsley piert, Pau d'arco, Pichi, Pipsissewa, Purslane, Pyrrosia Shi Wei, Plantain leaf/seed, Red clover, Red grapevine, *Sandalwood*, Slippery elm, Speedwell, [Talcum Hua Shi], *Tea tree, Thyme,* Thuja, Uva ursi, Willow, Yerba santa

> **irritation**: *urinary demulcents:* Alisma Ze Xie, Angelica, Blue mallow, Buchu, Canada fleabane, Cereus, Cleavers, Comfrey, Cornsilk, Couchgrass, *Cypress*, Damiana, *Fennel*, Flower pollen, Golden ragwort, Gravel root, Heartsease, Hops, Horsetail, *Juniper,* Kava, Licorice, Lysimachia Jin Qian Cao, *Marjoram,* Marshmallow, Melissa, Mullein, Parsley seed, Pipsissewa, Poplar, Raspberry leaf, Red clover, Saw palmetto, Sea holly, Soapwort, St. John's wort, Stoneroot, Strawberry, Trailing arbutus, Watercress, Wild carrot, Wood betony, Yarrow, Yellow dock

> **obstruction/scantiness/strangury**: Agrimony, Alisma Ze Xie, Artichoke, Asparagus, Birch, Borage, Broom, Butcher's broom, Butterbur, Canada fleabane, Celery, Coix Yi Yi Ren, Cornsilk, Couchgrass, Dandelion, Elder, *Fennel, Geranium,* Goldenrod, Gravel root, *Juniper*, Heather, Horseradish, Horsetail, Hydrangea, Imperata Bai Mao Gen, Knotgrass, Lovage, Meadowsweet, Nettle, Onion, Partridgeberry, Pipsissewa, Raspberry, Restharrow, Sea holly, Speedwell, Uva ursi, Wild carrot, Yarrow

> **pain**: Alisma Ze Xie, Coleus, Cornsilk, Couchgrass, Cramp bark, *Fennel, Geranium,* Gravel root, Heartsease, Horseradish, Horsetail, Hydrangea, Imperata Bai Mao Gen, Kava, Malva Dong Kui Zi, Marjoram, Marshmallow, Melissa, Nettle, Parsley piert, Parsley seed, Partridgeberry, Pellitory of the wall, Pichi, Pipsissewa, Poplar, *Sage,* Saw palmetto, Sea holly, St. John's wort, Tetrapanax Tong cao, Wild carrot, Yarrow

Urinary disorders (see Albuminuria, Diabetes, Edema, Nephritis)

Urticaria (see Hives)

Uterine bleeding: *uterine hemostatics:* Artemisia Ai Ye, Bayberry, Bilberry, Birthroot, Blackhaw, Blackberry, Broom, Canada fleabane, Cereus, Cotton root, Cramp bark, *Cypress*, Dogbane, *Geranium,* Golden ragwort, Goldenseal, Great burnet, Helonias, Horsetail, Ipecac, Lady's mantle, Madder, Mistletoe, Nettle, Paeonia Chi Shao Yao, Periwinkle, {Placenta}, Poppy, Purple loosestrife, Red grapevine, Red root, Rehmannia Sheng Di Huang, Rose, Rosehip, Rye ergot, *Sage,* Selfheal, Shepherd's purse, Sophora Huai Hua, Speedwell, Tormentil, Typha Pu Huang, Walnut, Witch hazel, Wood sorrel, Yarrow

> **dystocia** (see Labor)

> **fibroids** (see also Estrogen accumulation, Hypoglycemia, Pelvic congestion, Progesterone deficiency): Blue flag, Chaparral, Chastetree, Cotton root bark, Goldenseal, Ivy, Knotgrass, Marigold, Mistletoe, Ocotillo, Paeonia Mu Dan Pi, Pipsissewa, Poke root, Salvia Dan Shen, Shepherd's purse, Sparganium San Leng, Walnut leaf/hull, Water pepper, Yellow dock

> **pain** (see Dysmenorrhea, Ovulation pain)

> **prolapse** (see Prolapse, visceral)

> **subinvolution**: Arborvitae, Ash, Barberry, Bearsfoot, Birthroot, Black cohosh, Corn ergot, Cotton root bark, Golden ragwort, Goldenseal, Helonias, Madder, Motherwort, Paeonia Chi Shao Yao, Paeonia Mu Dan Pi, Pasqueflower, Red root, Rye ergot, Salvia Dan Shen, Witch hazel

Vaginal discharge (see Discharge)

> **dryness** (see also *progesterone stimulants,* p. 783): Angelica Dang Gui, Birthroot, Blackhaw, Butcher's broom, *Chasteberry,* Dong quai, Elecampane, *Fennel, Geranium,* Helonias, Jamaica sarsaparilla, Lady's mantle, Mugwort, *Rose, Vetiver,* Wild yam, Yarrow

Vaginitis (see Discharge, Infection, bacterial/fungal/parasitic, Skin itching)

Valvular disorder (see also associated condition, symptoms): Aconite*, Artichoke, Birch, Black cohosh, Bugleweed, Cereus, Colocynth, Cowslip flower, Hawthorn, Hedge hyssop, Hellebore*, *Juniper*, Lily of the valley, Mousear, *Niaouli,* Poke rooot, *Sage,* Squills, Scammony, Spigelia, Stoneseed, Strophanthus, White bryony, Yellow jessamine*

Varicose veins (see also Circulation, insufficient venous): *venous restoratives:* Alfalfa, Barberry, Bilberry, Biota Ce Bai Ye, *Blue tansy,* Broom, Butcher's broom, *Cedarwood, Clary sage, Cypress,* Garlic, *Geranium,* Goldenseal, Hazel leaf, Heartsease, Horsechestnut, Knotgrass, Lady's mantle, *Lemon,* Linden, Marigold, Melilot, Milk thistle, Mistletoe, *Niaouli,* Oat, *Patchouli,* Pau d'arco, Red grapevine, Red root, *Rose, Rosemary,* Rue, *Sandalwood,* Shepherd's purse, Soapwort, Sophora Huai Hua, Stoneroot, *Tea tree,*

Water pepper, White deadnettle, Witch hazel, Yarrow

Vasculitis (see Autoimmune disorder, Circulation, insufficient capillary, Inflammation, symptoms)

Venereal infection (see Discharge, Infection, specific disease)

Venous insufficiency, chronic (see Circulation, insufficient venous, Edema, Ulcer, leg, Varicose veins)

Verruca (see Wart)

Vertigo (see Anemia, Blood pressure, high/low, Cerebral insufficiency, Coma, Middle ear infection, Nervous tension)

Vision impairment: Aniseed, Asparagus, Bilberry, *Black pepper,* Blessed thistle, Calamus, Cassia Jue Ming Zi, Chaparral, Chicory, Cuscuta Tu Si Zi, Eyebright, *Fennel,* Hawthorn, *Hyssop,* Ligustrum Nu Zhen Zi, Microalgae, Pasqueflower, Plantain seed, Purple loosestrife, *Rosemary,* Rue, Valerian, Vervain, Wood betony, Wormwood

Voice loss: Agrimony, Arnica, Burdock seed, Cayenne, Celery, *Fennel,* Flower pollen, Jasmine, Licorice, *Oregano,* Parsley seed, Platycodon Jie Geng, Raspberry leaf, *Rose, Sage,* Saw palmetto, Squills, Stoneroot, Sundew, *Thyme,* Treacle mustard, Wild carrot seed, *Winter savory*

Vomiting (see Nausea)

Wart, common, and genital/venereal (also topically; see also Infection, viral): Arborvitae, Bloodroot, *Blue cypress,* Celandine sap, Chaparral, Isatis Ban Lan Gen, Mayapple, *Myrtle, Niaouli,* Papaya, Sundew, *Tea tree,* Thuja, Wild lettuce

Water retention (see Edema)

Weakness (see Debility, Fatigue)

Weaning (see Breast milk, excessive)

Weight gain: *metabolic* **and** *liver stimulants:* Artichoke, Birch, Bittersweet, Blackcurrant, Bladderwrack, Blue flag, Chaparral, Chickweed, Coconut oil, Dandelion, Flower pollen, Fumitory, Hawthorn, Hazel catkin, Horsechestnut, Horsetail, Kelp, Lindera Wu Yao, liquid trace minerals, Meadowsweet, Melilot, Microalgae, Nutritional yeast, Poke root, Red grapevine, Scurvy grass, Squills, Tea (gree/red/black), White horehound, Winter cherry

  loss (see also Debility, Fatigue, Malabsorption): *metabolic restoratives:* Alfalfa, Astragalus Huang Qi, Fenugreek, Flower pollen, Jamaica sarsaparilla, Microalgae, Oat, {Placenta}, {Royal jelly}, Saw palmetto, Strawberry fruit

Wheezing (see Asthma)

Whooping cough (see Cough, uncontrollable, Infection, bacterial)

Wind (same remedies as Indigestion)

Worms (see Diarrhea, Infection, parasitic, Weight loss)

Wound (see also Contusion, Hematoma): *vulneraries,* incl. *tissue healers, antiseptics:*

  acute (internally and topically): Agrimony, Blackberry, *Blue tansy,* Bromelain, Burdock, *German Camomile,* Cayenne, Celandine, Cleavers, Cowslip root, Cranesbill, *Cypress,* Drynaria Gu Sui Bu, Figwort, *Frankincense,* Fringe tree, Goldenrod, *Lavender,* Lily of the valley, Linden, Loosestrife, Melilot, Oak bark, Panax San Qi, Parsley seed, Pau d'arco, Pennyroyal, Pipsissewa, Plantain, *Rosemary,* Sanicle, Scabious, Selfheal, Shepherd's purse, Solomon's seal, *Thyme,* Tormentil, White deadnettle, Wikstroemia Liao Ge Wang, Yarrow

  atonic/gangrenous (internally and topically): Agrimony, Aloe gel, Arborvitae, Astragalus, Benzoin, Blackberry, Blessed thistle, Bletilla Bai Ji, Butterbur, Cabbage, *Camphor,* Centaury, Chaparral, Cistus, Clay, Coltsfoot, Comfrey, Cranesbill, Echinacea, Figwort, Garlic, *Geranium,* Goldenrod, Goldenseal, Ground ivy, Gumweed, Hazel leaf, Horsetail, Ivy, Lady's mantle, *Lemon,* Lily, Loosestrife, Marigold, Melilot, Microalgae, *Myrrh,* Oldenlandia Bai Hua She She Cao, Pasqueflower, Passionflower, Pau d'arco, Pipsissewa, Plantain, Polygonum Hu Zhang, Poke root, Prickly ash, Red clover, *Rose, Sage,* Salvia Dan Shen, Sanicle, Scarlet pimpernel, Soapwort, St. John's wort, Tansy, *Tea tree,* Thuja, *Thyme,* Tormentil, Usnea, Walnut, White pond lily, Wild indigo, Willow, Witch hazel, Yarrow, Yellow dock, Yerba mansa

  infected (internally and topically): Andrographis Chuan Xin Lian, Burdock, *Camphor,* Chaparral, Echinacea, *Eucalyptus, Hyssop,* Lady's mantle, *Lavender, Lemon, Myrrh, Niaouli,* Oldenlandia Bai Hua She She Cao, *Palmarosa,* Pau d'arco, *Sage, Tea tree, Thyme,* Usnea, White horehound

Yeast infection (see Discharge, Infection, fungal, Skin itching, associated disease, symptoms)

Selected Herbal Medicine Resources

North America

Dragon River Herbals
www.dragonriverherbals.com
800 813-2118 *tel*
505 583-2348 *tel*
505 583-2339 *fax*

Founded in 1983, Dragon River offers a full range of high-quality plant tinctures and formulas for the health-care professional. This company has always pioneered hard-to-find organic and ethically wildcrafted herbal products, especially those prepared from Southwestern herbs.

Pacific Botanicals
www.pacificbotanicals.com
541 479-7777 *tel*
541 479-7780 *fax*

Founded in 1979, Pacific Botanicals is the most experienced and diversified medicinal herb farm in North America. Their line includes over 175 medicinal herbs and spices in whole, cut or powder forms.

Western Botanical Medicine
www.westernbotanicalmedicine.com
707 986-9506 *tel*
707 986-7221 *fax*

Western Botanical Medicine offers certified organic tinctures to practitioners and the public alike, available as single herbs and pre-blended formulae. Owned by NIMH-licensed Medical Herbalists who use these tinctures in their clinical practice, Western Botanical Medicine is committed to the highest standards of therapeutic efficacy.

S.L. Aromatherapy
www.snowlotus.org
800 682-8827 *tel*
707 577-8219 *fax*

This company specializes in genuine essential oils and formulas for therapeutic use. The oils are carefully sourced from organic and ethically wildcrafted plant sources worldwide. They offer bulk quantities as well as small dispensing sizes.

United Kingdom

The Organic Herb Trading Co.
www.organicherbtrading.com
1823 401-205 *tel*
1823 401-001 *fax*

This company imports and distributes a diverse range of organically certified herbal materials in raw or liquid form. Some are grown at the organic farm on which they are based. Products include fresh and dried herbs and spices, tinctures, juices and liquid extracts.

Index

For the full index of symptoms and disorders, please consult the Repertory (p. 889).